The Haitians

A book in the series Latin America in Translation / en Traducción / em Tradução

This book was sponsored by the Consortium in Latin American and Caribbean Studies at the University of North Carolina at Chapel Hill and Duke University.

The Haitians

A Decolonial History

JEAN CASIMIR

Translated by LAURENT DUBOIS

With a Foreword by WALTER D. MIGNOLO

The University of North Carolina Press
Chapel Hill

Translation of the books in the series Latin America in Translation /
en Traducción / em Tradução, a collaboration between the Consortium in
Latin American and Caribbean Studies at the University of North Carolina
at Chapel Hill and Duke University and the university presses of the
University of North Carolina and Duke, is supported by a grant from the
Andrew W. Mellon Foundation.

Set in Adobe Text Pro by Westchester Publishing Services
Manufactured in the United States of America

The University of North Carolina Press has been a member of the
Green Press Initiative since 2003.

Library of Congress Cataloging-in-Publication Data
Names: Casimir, Jean, author. | Dubois, Laurent, 1971– translator. |
  Mignolo, Walter, writer of foreword.
Title: The Haitians : a decolonial history / Jean Casimir ; translated by
  Laurent Dubois ; with a foreword by Walter D. Mignolo.
Other titles: Latin America in translation/en traducción/em tradução.
  Description: Chapel Hill : University of North Carolina Press, 2020. |
  Series: Latin America in translation/en traducción/em tradução |
  Includes bibliographical references and index.
Identifiers: LCCN 2020022322 | ISBN 9781469651545 (cloth : alk. paper) |
  ISBN 9781469660486 (paperback : alk. paper) | ISBN 9781469660493 (ebook)
Subjects: LCSH: Sovereignty. | Haiti—Politics and government. |
  Haiti—History. | Haiti—Colonization—History.
Classification: LCC F1921 .C267 2020 | DDC 972.94—dc23
LC record available at https://lccn.loc.gov/2020022322

Cover illustration: Laurent Casimir (Haitian, 1928–1990), *Crowded Market*
(1972, oil on Masonite, 36" x 48"), Milwaukee Art Museum, gift of Richard and
Erna Flagg, M1991.117. Photograph by Larry Sanders, used by permission of the
Milwaukee Art Museum.

Photographer credit: Larry Sanders

Contents

Foreword

Thinking Decoloniality beyond One Nation–One State

WALTER D. MIGNOLO

I

In her celebrated TED talk, "The Danger of a Single Story," Chimamanda Ngozi Adichie makes a powerful political statement, a politics that no doubt touches the core of the well-crafted discourses of scholarship, journalism, state, banks, and corporations. She asserts that individuals' single stories are dangerous not only because the storyteller (whether scholar, journalist, banker, or officer of the state) acts on the assumption of the truth, without any parentheses, of what the story conveys (what the storyteller "says"), but also because the storyteller assumes that there is only one place to start the story.

Adichie captured this second aspect of storytelling (whether scientific, scholarly, journalistic, literary, political, economic) when she underscored that stories truly depend on where you start. She gave a couple of examples, and I will paraphrase one: if you start from asserting the failure of state building in Africa, you may very well end up justifying colonialism. If you start from the fact that state building in Africa truly comprised a colony of European imperialisms (a map of Africa in 1900, a decade and a half after the Berlin Conference, reveals that there is not one single corner of the continent that was not under the control and management of European countries), then you may very well end up apprehending and understanding the lies that justified and continue to justify colonialism. That is, you may very well end up disparaging and critiquing the lies of modernity (such as conversion to Christianity, progress, the "civilizing mission," and development).

This is precisely what Jean Casimir's argument in this book, as well as in his previous publications, intends to do: to expose the limits (and the dangers sometimes) of extant stories and interpretations of Hispaniola, Saint Domingue, and finally Haiti (three different names that erased, from the early arrival of Spanish ships, the name that the Taínos had for their territory— Ayiti). The analytic story that Casimir offers to us as "*la merveilleuse* invention of Haiti" is precisely that: the renaming and territorial reconfiguration of a trajectory that started with the Spanish genocides of the Taínos; followed by the French appropriation of a sector of the islands the Spaniards called

Hispaniola and the French called Saint-Domingue; and after 1804 (after a revolution that lasted from 1791 to 1804), the revolutionaries' adoption of the name Haiti to honor the memories of the indigenous inhabitants of the island, before indigenous people from Europe invaded and exterminated them.

The question is who are the Haitian revolutionaries, what shall we understand by the term *Haitian Revolution*? The answer to this question would depend on where you start from. Would you start from the well-known heroes of the revolution Jean-Jacques Dessalines, Toussaint Louverture, and Henry Christophe, who confronted France's management of the island but without questioning the nation-state form that they wanted to create, or from the first president of Haiti, after the assassination of Dessalines, Alexandre Pétion and his conciliatory politics with the French government? Well, it so happened that Casimir starts from neither of those points: he starts from the "power and beauty of the sovereign people." Beyond the official stories we are used to and which are identified by proper names (the proper names I mentioned), there are the silences of the past—in the happy formulation of Michel-Rolph Trouillot, *la beaute du peuple souverain*. Here precisely is where Casimir starts:

> If readers ask what I have learned from writing this book that I now offer to them, my answer is that above all, in how I live my personal life, I no longer see my ancestors as former slaves. I don't even think of them as a dominated class. Their misery is only the most superficial aspect of their reality. It is the reality that colonialists prefer to emphasize, along with those among them who oppose the cruelty of some colonists but don't ultimately reject colonization itself. Having finished this book, I have come to realize that my ancestors, as individuals and as a group, never stopped resisting slavery and domination. I am the child of a collective of fighters, not of the vanquished. *I have chosen to venerate them, to honor these captives reduced to slavery, and those emancipated in thanks for their military service to colonialism. I do so despite their errors and their occasional failures.* (chapter 1; emphasis added)

The statement is crucial to understand Casimir's argument both in what he says and in his saying, in what he enunciates and in the enunciations he builds, which I emphasized in italics in the previous sentences. The statement is crucial also because Casimir plays the game of scholarship (his archive is solid, his sociological training and practices of historiographical sociology through the years has been impeccable) but at the same time, he disobeys it. And herein is the force of his argument: the moment that he uses scholarship to advance the cause of the "sovereign people" instead of using the "sovereign people" to advance scholarship. Casimir, as is clear in the statement and through the argument, let himself be guided by his emotions ("I am the child of a collective of fighters, not of the vanquished") exposed in his reasoning. It depends on where you start from: if you start from the heroes and maintain the silence of the "sovereign people," you remain within the colonial politics of knowledge. If you shift the geography of reasoning and let it be guided by your emotions, you engage in the growing processes nowadays of decolonial politics of knowing, sensing, and believing.

II

"Captives reduced to slavery"—another crucial distinction that reinforces Casimir's putting up from his *locus enunciationi*, which is normatively silenced in any of the existing disciplines: disciplines promote objectivity and direct your attention to the said while veiling the act of saying. Consequently, Casimir proposes "a decolonial reading" of the invention, formation, and transformation of "the Haitian people" since 1804, but one grounded in the experiences and shared memories, mainly orally transmitted (no archives for historians here), of the daily praxis of living in re-existence, building the communal in spite of state politics, in any of their variety from 1804 to today. How could "the people" have gained and maintained its sovereignty? Two distinctive praxes of living emerge from Casimir's argument. One is explicit and explained in detail in chapter 7: the question of language. While French language remained the official language of the state of Haiti, Creole remained the language of the "sovereign people." Throughout the period of the French monarchic state before 1789 as well as the succeeding bourgeois French successions of republics and empires, "the sovereign people," though captive and physically enslaved, never surrendered and therefore were never captive or enslaved in the sphere of language.

As Casimir states, "All behavior implies knowledge" (chapter 8). What we, all of us human beings, know is the outcome not so much of what we see or read, but of what we do (by will or force) and share in storytelling and conversations from the moment we come into this world, in whatever region and moment one is born. For those who were born in Africa, in any of the existing kingdoms, languages, and systems of belief (religions), and were captured, transported, and enslaved in New World plantations, their doing was marked by the experience of being hunted, of being transported, and being enslaved. For their descendants, it was the experience in the New World as captive and enslaved, until the revolution started in 1791 at Bwa Kayiman. All of that built a memory alien to French schooling before the revolution and French-style schooling after the revolution: French language and Christianity remained alien to "the sovereign people" for whom the Creole language and Vodou spirituality became the glue of the communal re-existence.

I would highlight spirituality and language, without of course forgetting labor and the biological praxis of living necessary to provide labor of any kind (living labor, forced labor, or waged labor). I am highlighting language and spirituality because it is difficult to engage in conversation and tell stories about labor by doing labor, unless that labor is the labor of engaging in conversations about labor and engaging in communal spirituality to propel and maintain the communal via the knowledge and culture "the sovereign people" creates, innovates, and enjoys. Casimir doesn't elaborate much on joy and love, but I heard him talking about it. And frankly, one cannot understand the survival of "the sovereign people" without mentioning the joy and love derived from language (Creole) and spirituality (Vodou), which made possible not only their survival but also their re-existence in love, which means here care, respect, and affection. Care, in the moral sense, means fundamental elements of relationality and complementarity in life, where humans are but a small portion of the universe's living energies. Respect implies relations of complementarity (relationality) toward human beings and for living energies and organisms on the planet. It means respect for elders, who are the philosophers and the guides for re-existence and communal life. These are the ancestors Casimir identifies as his own. Casimir operates from the knowledge of his ancestors, addressing an audience schooled in disciplinary formations. In this sense, Casimir is shifting the geography of emotions and reasoning.

III

Chapter 9 is titled "An Independent State without a Sovereign People." The foundational idea of the modern European nation-state, the form of governance of the European ethno-class (Sylvia Wynter), the bourgeoisie, was precisely this: to each state corresponds one nation. This is the secular nation-state that in Europe displaced the monarchic state and its religious support (Christianity, either Catholic or Protestant). In the colonies, it has always been, and continued to be, something else. To start with, the European bourgeoisie that created the nation-state after the Glorious Revolution in England and the French Revolution was indigenous to Europe.

> *Indigenous (adj.)*
> "born or originating in a particular place," 1640s, from Late Latin *indigenus* "born in a country, native," from Latin *indigena* "sprung from the land, native," as a noun, "a native," literally "in-born," or "born in (a place)," from Old Latin *indu* (prep.) "in, within" + *gignere* (perfective *genui*) "to beget, produce," from PIE root *gene- "give birth, beget," with derivatives referring to procreation and familial and tribal groups.[1]

In Haiti (and in all former colonies) there were no bourgeoisie, whether the population building the state was indigenous (like in India after 1947 or Algeria after 1962) or native (in the biological sense of Creole: being born in a country from immigrant parents):

Creole (people)

Spanish Criollo, French Créole, originally, any person of European (mostly French or Spanish) or African descent born in the West Indies or parts of French or Spanish America (and thus naturalized in those regions rather than in the parents' home country). The term has since been used with various meanings, often conflicting or varying from region to region.[2]

Instead of bourgeoisie, in the nation-state building after independence in former colonies what we have are either indigenous elites (generally in Africa and Asia) or native/Creole elites in the Americas and the Caribbean. The indigenous population in the Americas and Caribbean ("Indians" because of Columbus's mistake) were either exterminated or marginalized and pushed outside the public sphere. In Haiti, the nation-state was founded mainly by foreigners from Africa (Jean-Jacques Dessalines and Henry Christophe) and by natives/Creoles from African parents (like Toussaint Louverture) and from wealthy French fathers and free mulatta mothers (Alexandre Pétion). Plantation owners in the former colonies did not equate with the European bourgeoisie that emerged from the wealth extracted from the colonies and the incipient (at the turn of the nineteenth century) Industrial Revolution.

In that historical frame of political, economic, and cultural dependency from France, the rebellion that started in Bwa Kayiman in 1791 engendered the revolution and two trajectories after 1804. One was the trajectory of building the state, including internal disputes between the North (Toussaint, Christophe) and the South (Pétion), and since then, between the political parties that formed the modern/colonial nation-state. The other trajectory was the emergence of the "sovereign people," which is not, as it should be per the definition of the nation-state, a constitutive sphere of the independent state of Haiti. The state is a legal and administrative institution, while the nation is the ethnic and cultural dimension of the state. In the colonies, it is hardly the case that the nation or nations match the state, as was the case in Europe (France, Germany, England, Italy) when the modern nation-state emerged.

The soul of the "sovereign people" is not constituted by the law of the state and the administration of culture dependent on French language, education, and political and economic theories; instead, it is constituted by the experience and memories of the slave trade, captivity and enslavement, forced labor and dehumanization. If knowledge is grounded in what we do rather than in what we see or read, then the Creole language and Vodou spirituality are the glue of the "sovereign people," as Casimir narrates and argues in this book. Near the end of chapter 9 Casimir writes:

> The Haitian peasantry—and those of the entire Caribbean—constituted themselves in opposition to the processes of integration and assimilation to the commodity-producing plantation. Their culture was and remains a response to slavery, a form of self-defense responding to the abuses inflicted by modern, colonial society. *From the moment the captives took control of their gardens and provision grounds and demanded more free days in the wake of the general insurrection, the counter-plantation system and the institutions through which it was articulated were put into place. These included gender relations, family, the* lakou, *indivisible collective property, Vodou temples, rural markets, garden-towns, leisure, crafts, the arts. They were reproduced within and thanks to the local language the counter-plantation system appropriated. Taken together, all of these became specific tools for the class struggles of the Haitian peasantry.* All the attempted attacks from the modern/colonial world represented by the oligarchs of the country shattered against these ramparts. Those who imagined they could fight on another terrain were not conscious of the importance of class. They could not comprehend the collection of structured institutions that make the Haitian a Haitian. (emphasis added)

IV

Readers less familiar with Vodou and the history of African diaspora in Haiti may know the meaning of *lakou*. It is a crucial concept to understanding the foundation of "the sovereign people" and the line that separates the *lakou* from the state geographical administration (state territory). The *lakou* names the confluence of land (meaning complementarity of life and earth, not a piece of private property) that implies the extended family (not the Christian/bourgeois family and its private property) and spirituality (rather than institutional religion, which is a necessary component of even Western secular states). To these components should be added the *peristil*, or shrine (the equivalent of church, mosque, or synagogue) where the sacred mapou tree links (as in many nonmodern cosmologies) the *poteau mitan* (the center, the woman-mother), the spiritual world, and the earth (land). The *lakou* is inextricable from Haitian praxis of living, the Creole language, and Vodou spirituality; hence, it is the soul of "*le peuple souverain.* Casimir closes chapter 9 with the following words: "The words of Aunt Tansia recorded by

Mimerose Beaubrun in *Nan dòmi* (2010, 200) define the local community as the cradle of national sovereignty: 'The lakou, aunt Tansia told me, is a well-defined geographical space. But the civil authorities have no authority over this space.'"

Lakou is equivalent to *ayllu* among the Aymara- and Quechua-speaking and spiritual communals, and equivalent to Greek *oykos* and Nahuatl *altepetl*—all of them, and many more in in Asia and Africa. There is, for example, Ibn Khaldun *assabihya*, which runs parallel in Arabic civilization to Islamic *ummah*. And of course Chinese (or Mandarin) *tianxia* (all under heaven). All these are not premodern, they are nonmodern; they have never gone away in spite of the veil that Western concepts placed on them and the premodern temporality to which modern temporality relegated them. There is no premodernity: modernity and nation-state are Western equivalents that had the institutional, linguistic, political, epistemic, and economic privilege to make us believe that all these nonmodern practices were premodern, and once modernity arrived they all became fossilized in the past, where they remain in the imaginary historical museum of world traditions.

This fiction was enacted by coloniality of knowledge hidden under the promises of Western modernity. One assumption of Western epistemology consists in positing that "knowledge" needs no qualifier. That is why it is not common to say "modernity of knowledge." The grammar of modern European vernacular languages, which are imperial and the language of modern epistemology, prevents "knowledge" from being modified by "modernity," turning modernity into an adjective: modernity of knowledge. But that is precisely what the grammar of decoloniality requires—to see both sides of knowledge: modernity of knowledge and coloniality of knowledge.

What is a decolonial reading? First, by disassociation, it is not a sociological, historical, anthropological, political reading. That is, it is a reading that delinks from existing options. Therefore, the decolonial is an option, but an option that is and it is not disciplinary: it is an option that starts from the personal, subjective relations with Casimir's ancestors and then uses sociology, history, anthropology, political theory, and economics instead of using disciplinary formations. Coloniality of knowledge highlighted either the positive (economic gains) or negative (slave trade) of the French colony Saint-Domingue. When it comes to the revolution, coloniality of knowledge silenced the Haitian people to highlight the independence, the heroes of the independence, and the role of France in this new configuration. Coloniality of knowledge—or what is the same, accounts based on principles of social sciences and humanities of Western modernity—tells half of the story. Casimir starts from an elsewhere, from the half of the story that was silenced: the formation of the Haitian nation despite the Haitian state. This shift, this disobedience, this drive toward independent thought, is a fundamental step to decolonial freedom.[3]

> I define the Haitian Revolution as the destruction of a slave system through the creation of a national community. Women played a fundamental role in the foundation of this new community, which was based on a family structure embedded within a broader social environment created precisely to ensure that this structure could flourish (Casimir 2009, 185). This is the most beautiful Haitian creation: the simultaneous invention of a nation, of the conditions for its social and economic existence, and of the institutions that could guarantee its survival. The reflections I offer here are meant to open the way for what I dare hope will be the contribution of the emerging generation of thinkers: the codification of our way of re-existing, despite the infinite turpitudes imposed on us by the modern West from 1492 to the present day (Mignolo and Gómez 2015). In this book I show how we were able to re-exist by reconstructing our sovereignty and the institutions that supported it, and by prioritizing them over our relationships with the outside world.

Decolonial reading means reading how modernity/coloniality is at work generating images of the world (reality) that prevent us from seeing what is in front of us; in many interpretations, there is a curtain that prevents us from seeing what is behind it. It is common to think, for example, that *slave* is a word that names an entity, that creates an ontology of the entity that fits the meaning of the word. A human being named *slave* vanishes as a human being, absorbed by the meaning of the world. To delink from that illusion is one of the tasks of decolonial reading, of exposing the ontological fiction of Western modernity's vocabulary in all its modern vernacular languages. That is why Casimir insists on distinguishing *captive* from *slave*.

In this sense, the decolonial option was already part of the sphere of the imperial state, but it remained unthinkable within or from this sphere. The state thought with its own concepts, and its own blindness. Given that the decolonial option could not be avoided as one of the targets of its activity, the empire constantly took measures aimed at preventing any counterthinking from expressing itself and creating an alternative consciousness—that is, from institutionalizing a locus of enunciation outside of the control of the public administration, a location of power that could defy it.

The entity named *slave* is constitutive in the formation of Haiti's modern/colonial state but at the same time unthinkable from the perspective in which the sphere of the state is conceived, imagined, and enacted. What is unthinkable from the assumptions and storytelling of Western modernity is what

Michel-Rolph Trouillot underscored: the Haitian Revolution is a nonevent because slaves are unthinkable as revolutionary actors. To make the unthinkable thinkable, to bring silences into the conversation, a noncolonial locus of enunciation is necessary. Casimir finds the decolonial option necessary at the moment in which the connection with his ancestors (the fighters) and the beauty of "the sovereign people" calls for a narrative that could no longer be rendered through the channels of disciplinary formations. This is a moment in which the silences of modernity can no longer be kept hostage, when bringing them to the surface and to the present is not only a question of the politics and ethics of scholarship in getting the record straight, but above all about pursuing the necessary and unavoidable option of disclosing the naturalization of repression, dehumanization as the basic technology of racism. This means revaluing what modernity devalues, and celebrating the praxis of living that the imaginary of modernity has taught us to see as an impediment to progress and development.

Given today's obvious failure of the nation-state form of governance. The implications of Casimir's argument extends beyond the history of Haiti and helps us understand, through the political creativity and communal ethics of "the Haitian people," the trajectories of all the *pueblos originarios* in the Americas, from southern Chile and Argentina to Canada. What neither the monarchic state and the viceroyalty nor the republics (nation-states) created after independence from Spain and Portugal in South America and from England (the United States) and France (Canada) in North America were ever able to colonize was the communal will, the original languages, the wisdom of the elders. Today, the vocabulary of re-existence, of re-emergence, and of re-existence is the common and crucial vocabulary in their praxis of living, in spite of and confronting the state. In a general sense of decoloniality, it is the decolonial consciousness that guides their/our will to epistemic, political, ethical, and economic liberation despite, again, the state. The Zapatistas in southern Mexico have been also the most visible communal praxis of re-existence.

But that is not all. The financial crisis in Argentina (2001) imprinted a tragic mark on the middle class. It was a colonial wound, but not a racist and sexist wound. It had a psychological effect on people, losing what they had taken for granted: that they were citizens and the state would take care of them (Lewkowicz 2012).[4] All of a sudden came the realization, which today is expanding, that the state (any state, not just Argentina) cares less and less for its citizens. The modern nation-state created in Europe toward the end of the eighteenth and during the nineteenth century, the nation-state that consolidated the secular bourgeoisie over the monarchic state and the church, the nation-state that expanded to the colonies and became the key institution to regulate political coloniality, that state is today losing its mask. The mask is torn away in the European Union by immigrants and refugees; in the United States by immigrants and by the financial and corporate sector taking over the state; and in the former colonies (cf. North Africa and the Middle East) because, as Chimamanda Ngozi Adichie reminds us, the state was an imposition of European governance on entire continents.

There is more than meets the eye in Jean Casimir's powerful argument. It is on the one hand an anatomy of the formation, transformation, and limitations of the Haitian state and of the emergence, in spite of the state, of the sovereign people. On the other hand, and indirectly, it is a window through which the reader can began to see, in the distance, that (to paraphrase Coetze's feliticious title) the "barbarians" are coming to hunt the "civilization" that named them "barbarians."

Preface and Acknowledgments

This study is destined for those who wish to listen to the Haitian people in order to understand what they are saying. Their speech is barely audible, because the modern world imprisons it within the dominant culture and its writing of the past, trying to make us believe it doesn't even exist.

The Haitian people are not voiceless, even if they express their will to live in private. Western modernity—that world that speaks and writes loudly— has its goals, and it doesn't need to listen to the Haitians. The researcher who does wish to listen to them has to navigate through a series of roadblocks— the histories constructed with concepts this modernity has derived on the basis of its supposed right to conquest. Its cross and sword allow it to be deaf and blind in its relationship to the contemporaries it claims to have conquered. But it has to continue to conquer them every day. Plugging its ears and closing its eyes, Western modernity feels satisfied with its assumption that it holds them prisoners to the past.

Those who wish to lead the Haitian nation by following well-worn paths will not find the propositions I make here particularly useful. I don't bear any good news. And I accept, as my point of departure, that for the Haitian population itself, whatever I might say is so obvious that it seems ridiculous to have to say it. This book is besieged by the noise of modernity, and my incomplete mastery of the thoughts and feelings of this world that has shaped me doesn't allow me to stop its interference. But I have worked hard to return to the well of the history of the Haitians with care and veneration, and without apology.

Suffering, rage, blood, and the experience of pitiless extermination—that is the language of the survivors of the slave system. Those who try to usurp their representation have managed to make themselves heard, and their voices have gotten more and more deafening as time has gone on. I examine this discourse in order to discover the defiance it seeks to suffocate. I visualize the victory of my people, beyond the splendors of a Pearl of the Antilles that only the dust of an oligarchy claim to see.

I am only beginning to learn the lessons passed on from those who birthed me. I try to do so by consulting the archives that document the chains of their enslavement. My study is, a priori, unfinished, because the thought from which I have emerged, and which invents me, can serve only as a background.

We have only begun testing out the tools necessary to filter out the din that covers over the voices from the past, or prevents us from seeing through the fog that obscures the scenes of yesterday. So my book is an invitation to research, and its only goal is to establish the scope of the thinking that guided my ancestors and guides my compatriots.

The modern state in Saint-Domingue, and in Haiti, deliberately cuts me off from my wellspring. By exercising its sovereignty, in pursuit of its goals, it has built seemingly impregnable fortifications, made up of institutions and public services that are supposedly universally accessible. In the process, it has defined slavery, and what it wants me to remember about it. I cannot comprehend the amplitude of the captivity of my ancestors, or of my own captivity, if I remain within the knowledge and laws built by empire as it has arranged its hegemony over what it defines as the universe. I cannot seek out what interests me without questioning the sovereignty and legitimacy of imperial power, the way those who gave birth to me did.

At the beginning of the twenty-first century, the Haitian population confronts major difficulties in trying to occupy the little world in which they live to their satisfaction. It has always been this way. This population's supposed poverty, and the low levels of what the Western world calls education, are not the cause of this. The greatest successes it has accomplished—liberation from slavery, and independence—didn't depend on this education, or on the values and principles of the Western world. According to this world's standards, it comprised at the time—and still comprises—the poorest and most abject human group in the universe. But despite this rather unflattering assessment, in the past and in the present, the circumstances imposed on the Haitian people have never overcome their will to live and to continue to struggle against the winds and the tides in order to defend their choices.

This book targets the Haitian nineteenth century, from its origin in 1791—with the general insurrection in the northern plain—to its endpoint with the beginning of the United States occupation in 1915. It draws attention to the autonomy of popular forces in the midst of a colonial world that was in the process of universalizing itself. And it points to the path taken by these popular forces as the primary wellspring of national history.

Though the scholarly community will be the primary judge of this study's merits, I do hope to reach a broader audience with it. But there remains a limited group of readers for it in Haiti. This creates certain constraints, the result of the formations, and deformations, caused by the limited means the colonial and Haitian public administrations have invested in the training of the intermediary classes. The traditional penury of institutions of higher education corresponds with the increased patronage of metropoles and international organizations that think they compensate for the lack of local production of knowledge. The self-assurance of their interventions seems to indicate that knowledge of the local context is less and less necessary for the completion of the goals of global modernization.

What I want to propose to whatever readership is left, made up of a small group of students and professionals, is a way of filling in certain gaps in our knowledge of Haiti's past. My goal is to offer my readers another way of seeing our history, and more specifically the origins, location, and endurance of what remains of our sovereignty.

To reach this goal, I start by using the concepts the sovereign people used, the most important of which is that *tout moun se moun*—"every person is a person," which translates more accurately as "all people are of equal value." The corollary of this is the foundational principle of sovereignty—namely, that a sovereign people is one that is responsible only to itself. This is expressed in Creole as *pèp souvren granmoun tèt li*, or "the sovereign people are the parents of their own minds." As I have sought to join with this thinking, friends from the academic community have helped me out. They are, in fact, the real authors of this study. I am infinitely grateful to them, but since I have had the audacity to filter their opinions and advice, I bear sole responsibility for all that doesn't do justice to their contributions. My point of departure has been the current state of social science among the literate in our country, and not that of present-day social science more broadly.

Haiti experienced the deepest revolution of the eighteenth century. Its history is traditionally written as the sequel to that of Saint-Domingue, which itself had extended that of Hispaniola, with a focus on the victories and blunders of colonialism. The names *Hispaniola* and *Saint-Domingue* are just labels stuck on by modern Europe. A history of the Haitians (or Ayitiens)—that is to say, of those who live in this territory (Vastey [1814] 2013, 74), and have no choice but to live there—starts by recognizing the secondary character of this official periodization. It traces out the path taken by the population itself. It avoids getting lost in the inescapable labyrinth of factors of external origin.

The population made choices in order to exist and reproduce. The researcher can't avoid making choices too, and for the same reasons. My reflections explore the wellsprings of our behaviors. They are not determined by colonial empire. Despite its supposed total power, we are not its creations. Those creations are, in fact, the very obstacles surpassed by our imagination.

I have searched for the sovereign people by following the path originally identified in my book *La cultura oprimida* (1981). The first formulation of my argument was shaped by dependency theory, whose leading thinkers I spent time with in the 1960s. Soon afterwards, during a conference of the Central

American Sociological Association, I became friends with the Puerto Rican sociologist Angel (Chuco) Quintero Rivera. We dialogued intensely until the beginning of the 1990s. My conversations with Angel Quintero helped me confirm the nuances I brought to dependency theory. I specified the dimensions and characteristics of the fracture between the two foundational components of our society: a multiplicity of ethnicities, on the one hand, and a European metropole on the other. I argued that we cannot seek out Haiti's specificity in its dependency on France. Instead, it is to be found in its response to France, in its oppressed culture and its counter-plantation system.

Angel Quintero was the first person to echo this proposition, whose corollary conceptualizes the Caribbean peasantry through its confrontation with the artificial yoke of the export commodity-producing plantation, rather than seeing this group as an evolution or an involution of the capitalist slave system. His critiques brought me, in the present study, to show how the establishment of Haitian private life worked in opposition to government policies and much of the state structure of the nineteenth century. I am even drawn to the idea of analyzing this private life as the arms depot of class struggle throughout the Caribbean, and as the natural space for the development of these struggles.

Laënnec Hurbon's signal *Le barbare imaginaire* (1987) encouraged me to pursue this perspective. When I returned from exile in 1988, I sought to better define this problematic in my article "Tout moun granmoun" in *Chemins Critiques*.

The support I then got from Gérard Barthélemy in his *Le pays en dehors* (1989) was particularly precious. Barthélemy was the first in Haiti—and, for a long time, the only one anywhere—to use and deepen my propositions on the oppressed culture and the counter-plantation system. I am deeply indebted to him for that. He combined fieldwork with inveterate bibliomania, and went further than me in terms of anthropological analysis. While I considered the state to be the key concept to explore, he focused on the *bossale* (the African-born captive)—and his transformation—as the key social actor.

I was educated during the development and unfolding of the 1946 revolution in Haiti. My generation was hypnotized by the state, by its management and reform. In 2005, the historian Michel Hector and the anthropologist Laënnec Hurbon organized a conference on the genesis of the state in Haiti, with the support of the UNESCO project *La Route de l'esclave*. All the Haitian social scientists were there. As the debates unfolded, I came to feel that we lacked a definition of the state, as a total institution, that fit our circumstances. That set me on this search that, since then, has absorbed all my attention.

As I moved forward, I became convinced that when use the definitions inherited from the colonial nations, we always end up replicating their governing formulas. We adopt the goals of the colonial state and its public administration, which are too limited to correct the disequilibrium implanted among us. To the great despair of my historian friends, I have spent ten years abusing their patience, asking them all kinds of questions about all kinds of aspects of the past that I am ignorant about.

Michel Hector and I contributed an article to UNESCO's *General History of the Caribbean* (2011) that we had previously published in Haiti under the title "Le long 19e siècle haïtien" (2003). Our endless discussions, all too often provoked by my hasty and insufficiently nuanced conclusions or the gaps in my knowledge, took place under an almond tree in his courtyard, where we could raise our voices and roar with laughter without bothering the neighbors too much.

On Sunday afternoons, a small group of social science specialists who leaned on historiography got in the habit of gathering at Hector's house. At the center of this coterie were Hector and his historian colleague Claude Moïse, animating a dialogue between the political scientists Cary Hector and Sabine Manigat, the anthropologist Laënnec Hurbon, the writer Yanick Lahens, the teachers Denise Hector and Adeline Chancy, and the philosopher Bérard Cénatus, with Luc Smarth and me representing sociology. These colleagues were all survivors of exile. And we made it our duty to "rearrange the world," and always remembered to leave some question open for the next gathering.

Due to a lack of interest rather than a lack of resources, the Haitian public administration doesn't support scholarly work, and especially not historical research. This deliberate policy forces groups like ours to protect their informal meetings like a haven. Those who gathered religiously under the almond tree are not responsible for the errors contained in this book, but I owe to them the majority of the judicious propositions it includes. It is in this sense a collective work.

And, thanks to the recommendation of the now departed and much missed Cary Hector, this group offered commentary and critique on the work on two occasions. The first meeting took place at the Société Haïtienne d'Histoire, de Géographie et de Géologie, whose president was then Pierre Buteau. Among the participants were Laurent Dubois (who, along with Cary Hector, had suggested having such a discussion), the writer Évelyne Trouillot, the publisher and sociologist Frantz Voltaire, and the publisher Anaïse Chavenet.

The second gathering brought together the Conspirators of the Almond Tree, as Cary Hector liked to call us.

In the same way, I also want to acknowledge the contributions of a network of friends who live in the United States, whose intellectual work and preoccupations help clarify the Haitian situation. Fortuitously, I became friends with the historian Laurent Dubois, an American of Belgian background, whom I mentioned above. And I am happy to recall how this connection came to be, because it gives me the chance to pay homage to a brother, reader, and assiduous critic and advisor, the former prime minister Smarck Michel, now passed on, who accompanied me as I wrote this book. He had received Dubois's *Avengers of the New World: The Story of the Haitian Revolution* (2004) as a gift. Fascinated by the book, he asked me to read it. During our conversations, he offered to find the funds to pay for a translation into French, since he considered it a fundamental work that the Haitian public needed to have access to. I wrote to Dubois, whom I had met during one of the meetings of the Association of Caribbean Historians, and learned that the book had already been translated into French and that there would be no problem publishing it in Haiti. So it was that my friendship with Smarck Michel connected me with Laurent Dubois, and from there I became part of a web made up of historians, philosophers, anthropologists, and literary critics who have influenced my thinking decisively.

It all began, in fact, in 2004. At a conference at the Institut des Hautes Études de l'Amérique Latine et l'Union Latine, I talked about my perpetual topic in a presentation titled "Le planteur avait une esclave, ma grand-mère était une captive: Peuplement et latinité en Haïti." The Puerto Rican sociologist Ramón Grosfoguel was in the audience, and he asked me point-blank why I wasn't using the concept of coloniality. I confessed I had never heard the term. He invited me to a conference he was organizing at the University of California at Berkeley and, thanks to him, I reconnected with the Peruvian sociologist Anibal Quijano and his thought. The Argentine thinker Walter Mignolo was one of the other presenters at this conference. I also owe to Grosfoguel the gift of Mignolo's book *Local Histories/Colonial Designs: Coloniality, Subaltern Knowledges, and Border Thinking* (1999), which immediately initiated me into decolonial thinking.

Following this first meeting, Walter Mignolo invited me to continue our dialogue at Duke University in North Carolina, where he directed the Center for Global Studies and the Humanities. He introduced me to the Colombian scholar Arturo Escobar. During a meeting, one colleague asked me why I didn't mention Frantz Fanon in my presentation. I had to admit the charge; I had spent my entire professional life in his shadow, and in *La cultura oprimida* I had not cited him once.

It was only in working on this book, a dozen years later, that I realized how much the urban dwellers of Saint-Domingue and Haiti are the twins of Martinicans and Guadeloupeans, with the difference that they are a tiny minority, which isn't the case in their sister societies of the Eastern Caribbean. In my work, I privilege those who conquered their liberty with weapons in hand, rather than the Creoles who didn't fight for it, or who fought for a *white liberty*, or a *white justice*, to paraphrase Fanon. In the United States, he writes, "the Negro battles and is battled" (Fanon [1952] 1986, 172). He could easily have added that in Haiti, he has battled and emerged victorious from the battle.

Without having realized it, I had drawn from Fanon another framework for observing the Haitian population. The master thinker is categorical: "To speak a language is to take on a world, a culture" (Fanon [1952] 1986, 25). We won the war of 1791 to 1804. So why should we speak French? Why should we embrace that world and its culture? We had, in fact, already taken on our national language, Creole, as a marker of identity even before independence. Dessalines testifies to that.[1] How can we reclaim another set of working hypotheses so that we can hear ourselves talking more clearly?

The Center for Global Studies and the Humanities offered me the opportunity to participate in its project "Shifting the Geo-graphy and Bio-graphy of Knowledge," and an opening beyond the Latin American and Caribbean region. In 2008, it published its third web dossier of the year, titled *Thinking Haiti, Thinking Jean Casimir*. The articles presented therein made up the core of my book *Haïti et ses élites: L'interminable dialogue de sourds* (2009), the first version of my conceptualization of Haitian popular sovereignty.

Soon afterward, at the beginning of 2010, I was supported by the Mellon Foundation for a semester in residence as an invited professor at the Duke University Center for Latin American and Caribbean Studies. I was able to take advantage of this thanks to a leave granted by my home institution, the Faculté des Sciences Humaines of the Université d'État d'Haïti, and I am grateful for the support. This residency opened up more doors into contemporary research on Haiti's history, which to the shame of Haitian governments, takes place largely outside the country. During this semester I learned about the literary analyses of Professor Deborah Jenson and her reflections on the political thought of Toussaint Louverture and Jean-Jacques Dessalines.

Having started down this path, fortune smiled on me, and Walter Mignolo invited me to the summer school he organizes with Mexican scholar Rolando Vázquez-Melken, supported by the Center for Global Studies and the Humanities and University College Roosevelt at the University of Utrecht. At this yearly gathering in Middelburg, in the Netherlands, I became friends with philosophers including Maria Lugones, from Argentina, and Ovidiu Tichindeleanu, from Romania, as well as with the organizers of the event. The curator and artist Alanna Lockward, from the Dominican Republic, the choreographers and actors Fabian Barba from Peru, Jeannette Ehlers from Denmark, Patricia Kaersenhout from Holland, and other participants in decolonial thinking who participated in the summer school also inspired me. As I observed the productions of this multidisciplinary network, particularly that of Rolando Vázquez-Melken, I discovered that I was probably searching for a path that my compatriots had in fact already been patiently surveying for two centuries. Before 1804, they had certainly not expected the public administration to pull them out of the misery it had deliberately buried them in. Why would they have changed their opinion after independence?

The teachers of the Middelburg summer school became my mentors in decolonial studies. As I dug into my local history, I drew on the richness of their reflections. It wasn't always easy, given the difficulty of comparing a multiplicity of different circumstances and angles of observation, so different from my little Caribbean chapel and my preoccupations as a sociologist of local history. More than once, I betrayed their thinking and methods. But at the very least, I must recognize my debt to them.

Given how little institutional support there is for scientific research in Haiti, it is worth emphasizing the generosity of the librarian Patrick Tardieu, always ready to point me toward texts published by Haitian authors of the period and help me get access to them.

Since I have never had the opportunity to live in a monolingual, Francophone country, and have spent my entire life wandering among Creolophones, Hispanophones, Lusophones, and Anglophones, my mastery of the French language leaves something to be desired. So I cannot end these acknowledgments without thanking Anaïse Chavenet of Communication Plus, who corrected this book. I know she did everything possible to ensure a bit of readability in my wanderings far off beaten paths. So I thank her on behalf of my readers as well.

To all these friends and to those who I couldn't cite by name: thank you.

I sincerely thank the students of the Faculté des Sciences Humaines of the Université d'État d'Haïti, the first to suffer through my incursions into the unknown, as I invited them to work relentlessly to discover the beauty of the journey taken by our sovereign people.

Translator's Note

LAURENT DUBOIS

How can we rethink our understanding of the history of the world from the perspective of Haiti? That is the question and the challenge posed by Jean Casimir in this remarkable book, the culmination of decades of thought by one of the Caribbean's most important contemporary thinkers. Trained as a sociologist and anthropologist in Mexico, Casimir has combined teaching and research with work for the United Nations, and served as the ambassador of Haiti to the United States from 1991 to 1996. Since the 1980s, his works written in Spanish, French, and Haitian Creole have deeply influenced currents of decolonial theorization. But very little of his work has been translated into English until now.

Jean Casimir's *The Haitians: A Decolonial History* offers a reconceptualization of the history of his country. It is, as he notes, not a history of Haiti as much as it is a history of Haitians, of their political imagination and uncompromising culture of sovereignty. The book navigates from the arrival of Columbus in the late fifteenth century, through the period of colonization and the struggle for independence that culminated in 1804, and then analyzes the nineteenth century through the beginnings of the U.S. occupation in 1915. Not strictly chronologically arranged, the work moves among historical periods in order to offer a conceptual remapping of the very categories through which to understand the history of sovereignty in Haiti. It puts forth a series of reinterpretations of major issues in Haitian history, including the particular implications of Haiti's African majority among the enslaved; the history and centrality of the Kreyòl language; the particular courses of the regimes of Christophe and Pétion; the importance of movements rooted in rural society, such as those of Goman and Acaau; and the ultimate impact of the U.S. occupation of Haiti within the broader course of the country's history.

Casimir's book is also a critical retheorization of the very nature of slavery, colonialism, and sovereignty. It offers readers a way of rethinking the history of slavery from the perspective of the enslaved, and the history of the constitution of the modern world from the perspective of those whose perspectives have been systematically marginalized and silenced through the colonial process itself. As such, it is vital reading for those interested in understanding the institution of slavery from the space of the captives who were caught within it but never acknowledged its legitimacy. It is vital reading for those seeking to rethink political history from outside of Europe in order to develop new paradigms. And it is more broadly a methodological treatise, offering a way forward for new forms of cultural and social analysis.

In pursuing this goal, Casimir's work is itself a kind of work of translation. It takes familiar terms—*slave* and *captive*, *state* and *government*, *sovereignty* and *autonomy*—but rewrites them from the perspective of Haiti's history. He draws on and deploys a range of concepts and terms drawn from Haitian culture as well, such as the idea of the *malheureux*, a person who experiences misfortune and suffering. As the translator of Casimir's work of conceptual translation, I have sought to transmit the energy and movement of his prose. This has meant seeking to maintain the sharpness, humor, and poetry with which he makes his arguments. In some cases, I have drawn on more vernacular terminology from other parts of the Caribbean, for instance in my translation of *malheureux* as "sufferers," a term with resonances in Rastafari practice and reggae music that condenses many of the same meanings because it is rooted in a parallel historical experience.

The conceptual core of this book is drawn from Casimir's earlier work *La cultura oprimida* (1981), in which he coined the term *counter-plantation* to describe the culture of the Haitian majority in the rural areas of the country. It is from the perspective of this culture, in its *longue-durée* development and rooting in the country's landscape, that he seeks here to rewrite our very categories of thought. This counter-plantation system expressed a totally different vision of what life should be, and how it should be structured, than that held by those who controlled the administrative structures in Haiti. But it was the counter-plantation institutions that in fact controlled most of Haitian space and made its ongoing autonomy—and the flourishing of new ways of life—possible. It would be a misnomer, therefore, to describe this system as an alternative. It was, in fact, the dominant reality, though one that was in conflict with—and denied by—the structures of authority that controlled the state as administration. This administration, Casimir therefore argues, was never a true state as an expression of sovereignty. Instead, actual sovereignty resided among the majority of the Haitian people and in their institutions.

In writing from a counter-plantation perspective, Casimir seeks to decenter the French language from within. What he means when he uses certain words is not necessarily what most readers will first imagine. Much of the book, in fact, cycles around the constant parrying with, and redefinition of, terms whose dominant mode of usage is saturated by a Eurocentric understanding of political history, one in which European models are always understood to be the reference and unimpeachable model.

This is clear in Casimir's use of the term *state*. There are two conflicting definitions of this word, as he shows. One defines the state as a system of institutionalized conviviality that orders the public life of a particular society. It allows for a living together of different parts of society. While there are of course tensions, conflicts, and repression that accompany the state's action, it nevertheless—in this definition—does oversee, produce, and reproduce an integrated system of living together within a particular society, based on long-term historical processes that can be identified. In this definition, the state is an expression and condensation of the sovereignty of a particular people.

But the word *state* can also be used to define something narrower—that is, the administrative machinery that governs in a particular society. That state also has a certain solidity. It can be defined in some sense as what remains when a particular government falls, including a range of forms of public administration that are institutionalized and anchored enough that they can stay in place across different regimes.

What happens when we try and define these terms not by imposing them on Haiti from elsewhere, but by thinking them from within Haiti? Casimir argues, first, that there was never a state in the first sense in Saint-Domingue/Haiti. A colonial administration can never be a state, for it always governs from outside, for outside, and cannot acknowledge or relate to any form of sovereignty in the territory it controls. It is the extension, and imposition, of a state from elsewhere into a conquered territory. And, as Casimir shows, in Haiti this form of colonial public administration was not expelled or transformed when the country became independent. Instead, the national administration in Haiti—what we might call the state in Haiti (i.e., the administrative machinery put in place after independence)—maintained the original problem of a state that was attempting to impose an external vision rather than being created out of internal sovereignty.

One of Casimir's major goals in this book is to explain the reasons for this through an analysis of long-term ideological and structural continuities that moved across major political transformations. The outward-focused nature of the public administration in Haiti, which remained anchored in the forms of thought of the original colonial administration, also created an intellectual tradition in which colonial categories continued to dominate conceptual analysis of the country by its own thinkers. This has meant that the reigning intellectual paradigms for interpreting Haiti have had tremendous difficulty apprehending Haitian reality.

Throughout the work, Casimir points out many different examples of this. He emphasizes that one major area of continuity: the maintenance of the idea of the right of conquest between different periods in Haiti's history. The claim to the right of conquest was the basis for colonialism, and it is the reason why a colonial administration can never truly be a state that expresses sovereignty. But, he argues, the Indigenous Army that defeated the French and won

Haitian independence didn't fundamentally refuse the original right of conquest of the colonial power. Instead, it appropriated this right. The new nation's leaders considered that having defeated the original conquerors, they became the owners of the land—its new conquerors. And they thought about how the land should be used by following the colonial models, focusing on maintaining plantation agriculture. As such, they were and always remained at odds with the dominant counter-plantation system built by those who had been captives of the system, and had refused and continued to refuse any form of enslavement.

But the rulers of the country have, as Casimir shows, largely failed to impose this repurposed colonial vision on the majority of the population. The result is that they could never create a robust state that expressed and institutionalized their own vision. And they refused to acknowledge and develop a state form that would be based on the existing sovereignty of the Haitian people, one that would actually express the majority's political and social vision. This situation, Casimir argues, continues to this day, creating an ongoing political impasse that must be conceptualized and confronted from a better understanding of Haiti's history.

Casimir grounds his critique of the dominant political and intellectual currents in Haiti in the counter-plantation system created by the majority of the population over the course of the country's history. He attempts to craft a different way of thinking by cultivating this set of counterhistories, and seeks to imagine and reconstruct how colonial projects looked and sounded to those who were brought to Saint-Domingue as captives and then succeeded in creating truly independent spaces for themselves. He shows clearly that the colonial vision, while it always survived, never really triumphed or actually controlled the ways of thinking of the majority. Instead, they developed their own forms of sovereignty anchored in forms of solidarity and community. These were rooted and institutionalized within a set of robust, long-term institutions. These didn't formally constitute an alternative state, and yet they addressed most of the core needs that a state could in principle address and shape: economic life, including agricultural production and markets, family structure and gender relations, education, spiritual and cultural life, and spatial and geographical organization and movement.

Haiti's future, Casimir suggests, can be built only out of the perspectives and projects embodied within the country's counter-plantation sovereignty. He celebrates the "beauty and power of the sovereign people," ultimately offering us a glimpse of what alternatives are possible, of the conceptualize foundations for such reimaginings that are ever-present within Haiti's history, if only we can learn to see them.

Since I first met Jean Casimir in the early 2000s, he has been a profound intellectual influence on me, and he has become a close friend. In the spring of 2010, just after the earthquake in Haiti, we taught a class together on the history of the country at Duke University, where he was hosted by the Center for Latin American and Caribbean Studies as a Mellon Visiting Professor. He has taken me and other colleagues on remarkable journeys to different parts of Haiti over the years, always accompanied by spiraling conversation, song, and endless good humor and insight. Having the opportunity to translate this work has been a tremendous honor for me. During the process, I have been in constant conversation with Jean as I have sought to translate his words, concepts, and perspectives for an Anglophone readership. Jean carefully reviewed the translation on two occasions, and so what is offered here is the result of this collaboration over this new form for his work.

I am lucky to have as my colleague at Duke University Walter Mignolo, who has been in dialogue with Casimir over many decades. Walter and I had collaborated several years ago on a dossier of Casimir's work published at Worlds and Knowledges Otherwise, through the Duke Center for Global Studies and the Humanities, and have often talked about the need for a much broader readership to engage with Casimir's work. It was Walter's determination, and the intellectual and financial support he provided for this translation, that has made this happen. Elaine Maisner at University of North Carolina Press immediately grasped the importance of the work and has been a tremendous advocate and support, as well as a great editor. She also came up with an ideal translation for the title. Marlene Daut read the proposal as well as the final translation for the press, and offered invaluable comments on the final version. I am grateful to them, and to all those at UNC Press who have contributed in different ways to the editing and production of the work. And Kaiama L. Glover, an accomplished translator of several Haitian novels, offered her insights and support as I worked on the translation along with comments on an earlier draft of this translator's note. Through these many hands the work has passed, so that it now can be in yours.

The Haitians

Chapter 1

Introduction

Perspective

If we don't sit
on the same hill
we won't see
the same plain

—Frankétienne, *Voix Marassas*, 1998

Current theories on the emergence of the modern state rarely take note of the fact that this institution was born and consolidated thanks to the absorption of the almost immeasurable wealth extracted from the American colonies (Quijano 2000).[1] The Europeans who discovered the continent believed that they had a right to its riches. And today, dominant theories see still no reason to recognize that the Americas have made any significant contribution to European modernity. As Sylvia Wynter reminds us, the sixteenth-century Scottish theologian John Mair declared that the very nature of the conquered—those he called savages and pagans—justified the right of the conquerors to seize lands that belonged to no one: terra nullius (Wynter 2003, 283, 291). The conquerors also saw these people as having no history.

My main interest is not how and why the political forces of Hispaniola, Saint-Domingue, and Haiti besieged Haitians, whether indigenous peoples, African ethnicities kidnapped by slave traders, or the agricultural laborers of the nineteenth century. Though I analyze the implantation of the modern state and engage with questions explored in European thought, I look at this thought from outside rather than following its gaze. Europeans, a majority in their homelands, study their history and their states without much taking into account the considerable contributions of those majorities that, since 1492, they have exploited without restraint. Yet, whatever the qualitative importance we might concede to them, Europeans are a tiny minority among us. They do not significantly influence the daily social relations or the private lives of our population. Studies of European modernity have been carried out for five centuries without considering the significant contribution of the colonies. I invite readers to place Haitians at the center of their thinking and to recognize the role of external influences without getting distracted by their logic and the norms derived from that logic. The focus here is on the logic and norms of behavior of Haitians themselves.

The actions of the colonial empires were an accident of history. They set in motion choices on the part of the colonized populations that were founded on their own collection of knowledges, practices, and aptitudes. Within the colonial context, the popular majority found a way to express itself, one way or another. They embarked on their own journey, even when this journey led to collective suicide or gradual extermination. The Haitians of yesterday, and of today, are the architects of their own history. That history was not produced by those who came from overseas—the *moun vini*, those who arrived from elsewhere. Haitians think for themselves and by themselves.

Since the imperial state—that state that possesses colonies—was born in Europe and did not emerge within the Haitian context, I refer to the "state in Haiti," which is not to be confused with "the Haitian state." My goal is not to describe how the formation of overseas colonies sought to shape Haitian reality in order to contribute to the happiness and well-being of Europeans. Instead, I show how local society stubbornly preserved its specificity and therefore its sovereignty. I start from the premise that the people are by definition sovereign and do not need any help in expressing and asserting their own principles.

The republican state was not born in and through empire, but outside and against it. Following Fustel de Coulanges, we can say that power flows less from the point of a lance or a gun than from the work of human beings and of juridical and political institutions (Kriegel 1998, 68–70). In Haiti, real power— and therefore, stability over the long term—depends on the work of human beings carried out within local institutions. In contrast, in the spheres of government power and its administration, there are only crises, unpredictable changes, and constant fluidity: kingdoms, republics, empires, constitutions upon constitutions, coup d'états, elections, and so on. Meanwhile, without batting an eyelid and with little fuss, rural institutions and the civil society have combined to create national life and ensured its peaceful continuity.

The modern state that governed the colony from 1492 to 1791 was not interested in the well-being of the Haitian population. It was only after the gathering at Bois Caïman, three centuries after Christopher Columbus's remarkable discovery, that this well-being became a focus. That changed the course of history. The revolt that began in 1791 led to the consolidation of a social movement that ultimately created a nation. Unsurprisingly, that nation turned its back on the modern colonial state, or else simply ignored it. The French, the local privileged classes, and the international community worked hard and used every means at their disposal to stop the Haitian population from taking command of what we can consider an essential human pursuit—

that of seeking a better life. The result was an institutionalized disjuncture. On the one hand was the trajectory of a nation seeking a better life, defined on its own terms; on the other were public authorities seeking to prevent the population from gaining access to the resources necessary to fulfill their aspirations for well-being. The authorities considered the aspirations of the population irrelevant.

If readers ask what I have learned from writing this book that I now offer to them, my answer is that above all, in how I live my personal life, I no longer see my ancestors as former slaves.[2] I don't even think of them as a dominated class. Their misery is only the most superficial aspect of their reality. It is the reality that colonialists prefer to emphasize, along with those among them who oppose the cruelty of some colonists but don't ultimately reject colonization itself. Having finished this book, I have come to realize that my ancestors, as individuals and as a group, never stopped resisting slavery and domination. I am the child of a collective of fighters, not of the vanquished. I have chosen to venerate them, to honor these captives reduced to slavery and those emancipated as a reward for their service to colonialism. I do so despite their errors and their occasional failures. As María Lugones has written, "If we think of people who are oppressed and not consumed or exhausted by oppression, but also as resisting or sabotaging a system aimed at molding, reducing, violating, or erasing them, then we also see at least two realities: one of them has the logic of resistance and transformation; the other has the logic of oppression. But, indeed, these two logics multiply and encounter each other over and over in many guises. I want to consider them here in the two moments of resistance and oppression" (Lugones 2003,12).

Until the U.S. occupation in 1915, the majority of Haitians were part of a mass of workers that the slave trade had deposited on the island. But through my research I have found that they always refused the forms of social reproduction demanded of them by the triangular trade and the international commerce that substituted for it later on. They avoided it as much as possible and refused dependence on the market and the way it used the human labor it required. The working class escaped the precarity created by the squalid slave trade by institutionalizing the conditions necessary for their own natural reproduction and well-being. They did so firmly, and on their own. They built their own economic and social system, leaving behind the hell of the plantation slavery forced on them by colonial modernity. They protected themselves and survived, overcoming their oppression by developing a form of sovereignty that enabled them to challenge colonial modernity. Before 1791, they never allowed slavery to appropriate their bodies and their spirits. After 1804, they refused attempts to re-enslave them. From the moment in August 1791 when they took the emblematic oath at Bois Caïman, they began to create their own modernity. Their struggle drew sustenance from the memories of even the most miniscule victories. They always maintained their willpower, and they never gave in. By following this path, they constantly nourished the power of their communities to surpass their unthinkable present. They cherished even the most modest gains they obtained.

I define the Haitian Revolution as the destruction of a slave system through the creation of a national community. Women played a fundamental role in the foundation of this new community, which was based on a family structure embedded within a broader social environment created precisely to ensure this structure could flourish (Casimir 2009, 185). This is the most beautiful Haitian creation: the simultaneous invention of a nation, of the conditions for its social and economic existence, and of the institutions that could guarantee its survival. The reflections I offer here are meant to open the way for what I dare hope will be the contribution of the emerging generation of thinkers: the codification of our way of re-existing, despite the infinite turpitudes imposed on us by the modern West from 1492 to the present day (Mignolo and Gómez 2015). In this book, I show how we were able to re-exist by reconstructing our sovereignty and the institutions that supported it, and by prioritizing them over our relationships with the outside world.

Toward a History of Haitians

In 1492, Christopher Columbus took possession of a continent whose riches surpassed his imagination. He arrived on the island of Ayiti, armed with his cross and his sword, and decided to call it Hispaniola. To build this Little Spain, he annihilated the indigenous people and destroyed a way of life 7,500 years old (Moscoso 2003, 293). So when, two centuries later, French pirates supported by the corsairs of King Louis XIV took over the western side of the island, they had to repopulate it. This small territory became Saint-Domingue.

Father Jean-Baptiste Labat was one of the first European historians of the Caribbean. Throughout his work, he describes the attitude of the French nobility as they implanted themselves in the New World, and the casualness with which they used what they perceived to be their right to conquest: "Monsieur the Comte de Cerillac was informed of the great profits that the property-owning Lords of the islands made every day, and wanted to take part. But since there were no more islands to conquer from the Caribs, he thought it would be easier to buy one that was already inhabited. His gaze fell on Grenada, which was already owned by Monsieur du Parquet" (1742, 5:164).

Two calamities—the appropriation of the resources of Saint-Domingue and its repopulation through the slave trade—shaped the modern history of Haitians. Starting in 1697, France governed this territory, where it amassed isolated individuals, without history, tradition, or knowledge of the place in which they found themselves.

The French seized the property of others, as well as the laboring populations, even as they trumpeted the sanctity of private property. France saw the history of their transatlantic possessions as simply a tropical unfolding of their own society. They determined the present and future of this new geography. They abolished its past. The space belonged completely to them. The French transformed the savages they found there, and those they controlled in the colonial space, into primitives, assigning themselves the duty to civilize these savages and bring them into a contemporary, and civilized, way of life. By appropriating the history, and the time, of these conquered populations, they instated themselves as the prototype their victims had to copy. Those lives that unfolded in a non-European past became superfluous and perishable (Mignolo 2015, 280). Their only vocation lay in supporting the metropolitan future. In this space of barbarism, the right to conquest went hand in hand with that of eradicating the memory of peaceful populations. It was they, rather than their exterminators, who were presented as savages. The only reason for these unfortunates to exist was so that they could be useful to their murderers (Vázquez 2011, 4). Outside of this contribution, their past and their traditions, their spirituality and their emotions, their knowledge and their memories, were all emptied of meaning. Nothing of what the indigenous people or the captives possessed was given any value, other than their energy as laborers.

France possessed the capital and the labor force, which it believed it could administer as it wished. Through its inexhaustible discourse of self-adulation, echoed by its intermediaries in the colony, France congratulated itself for the reality it had created through its successful use of force, from which it derived its presumed monopoly over knowledge itself. Yet, what it conceived of as an inevitable form of control over what it saw masked the vitality and functioning of a multiplicity of other realities. France was largely unable to understand these realities, or at least disdained and underestimated them.

The Haitians of the contemporary world were born in these circumstances, in which a conquering France constructed a project that did not correspond to the way of life of the people it conquered or reduced to slavery. As soon as they disembarked, these captives began to build a new world, at the antipodes of France and the French.

If I seek to understand the state that implanted itself on the territory from 1697 to 1915, it is not because I want to determine how Spain conceded a portion of territory, which did actually not belong to it, to France, or how it came to be that France and Europe attained such dominance in the history of Ay-iti (or of humanity). I am not interested either in explaining whether one or another imperial army could have won during the English and Spanish invasions of Saint-Domingue during the 1790s. Even the civil wars that followed during the nineteenth century and the vagaries of governments during this period do not retain my attention. The fact that force is used to gain power does not determine people's way of life.

My quest is to understand how Haitians have been able to exist, subsist, and live in the midst of political structures that completely exclude them from participation. The goal of the colonial administration was to force the new social actors it created in the colonial context to cohabit with one another, one way or another. I sketch the contours of the society that organized itself in response. To attain its objectives, the colonial administration proclaimed regulations it declared would secure the submission of those reduced to slavery. I argue that, in response, the vanquished developed their own vision of the world through a process of negotiation with those who dominated them. The state bureaucracies did take note of the projects of the captives. But they deliberately misrepresented them in order to eliminate the alternative possibilities they represented, or else sought to render them invisible. I am interested in uncovering these alternative possibilities, produced by the oppressed in an effort to recuperate their power to make their own decisions, to grant themselves autonomy and control over their lives. The forms of resistance the oppressed set in motion enabled their survival and re-existence (Mignolo 2014). The policies of the government powers, in contrast, aimed to convert the oppressed into perishable and disposable merchandise, to produce them with the express intention of consuming them as inputs into the commercial system.

From my point of view, the relationship between the dominators and the dominated creates a single, stable system of power relations. This system, strictly speaking, is what constitutes the modern colonial state. The administrative machinery of this state, under the direction of its legislative, judicial, and executive powers, seeks to render invisible and irrational the institutions of resistance created by the oppressed. In order to do this, those in charge of the colonial structure of control and governance seek to monopolize the label "state" and eradicate the popular forces that defy their official policies. But the social reality is actually constituted through these two contradictory processes. It transmits the visions of both the conquerors and those who resist conquest. The challenge for the researcher is to extract the vision of the vanquished from historical circumstances in which the vanquishers worked constantly to silence and destroy the elaboration of even the most basic means of expression on the part of the colonized.[3]

To discover the origins of the Haitian nation, I must go beyond the concept of the state as a simple administrative structure of control and management. Instead, I see within this state the imbrication of conflicting political wills, each of which seeks to establish a model of living that is incompatible with the other. In my conception of the state, what is more important than the administrative structure and forms of governance are the norms of the system of social relations that this political-administrative machine seeks to control. These norms are what guarantee an infinite reproduction of the system, and of the obstacles to its management.

The imperial perspective sees what has to be managed and the administrative structure through which it is to be managed as a unified totality. In metropolitan society, the rulers and subjects generally are seen as part of one, single nation. The world of the conquered, in contrast, includes at least two nations. My goal in this study is to avoid posing the question of the construction of the nation-state in the terms set by the imperial West (modern, racist, and colonial). Instead, I center my attention on the response to colonialism as it was articulated through the development of a new form of sovereignty, one founded on the people's refusal to be vanquished by brute force. I do not believe there is a form of nation-state that is, or could be, suited to the interests of the conquered. I am simply interested in understanding how a new state was constituted, and in analyzing its particular characteristics generated by the cohabitation of the popular will and the will of the oligarchy. Each of these groups was as imperturbable as the other in the autonomous expression of their need to live and sustain themselves.

In Haiti, from colonial times on, the authorities have sought to perpetuate the intervention of foreign powers, who were driven by the goal of creating a unipolar world. These powers embedded themselves in the conquered territory without consideration for ancient civilizations, in the case of the indigenous peoples, or of the majority community of individuals brought together, for the first time in their lives, by the slave trade and the whips of the colonial plantation.

My analysis of the process that led to the formation of the state in Haiti emphasizes the fact that the sovereign people understood that the misery of slavery was a deliberate product of the modern colonial state. They clearly had no reason to expect that the authors of their misery would invent the means to end the damnation to which they had been condemned. That damnation, they understand, was the basis for the political power of the state, founded as it was on brute force. The indigenous peoples responded to the genocide perpetrated by the Spanish conquerors by making use of a range of institutions and means of defense, including collective suicide. Incapable of protecting themselves from the irrational violence of the invaders, they chose to fight to the point of extinction. The human merchandise that flooded into the island through the slave trade behaved in a similar way. The difference between them and the indigenous peoples was that the French were not in a position to massacre their enslaved victims. At the same time, however, the French refused to see these individuals as anything other than merchandise. They did everything they could to constrain and defeat the sovereign people as it was being born. But through their resistance to slavery, the enslaved walked their own path, creating a history that led them to found a society in parallel to the supposedly dominant one that sought to control them.

The Haitian administrative structure did its best to maintain colonial policy. It didn't really change the way the victims of the slave trade were treated, and didn't offer them a way of expressing and fulfilling their potential. But my main focus here is less on that fact than on the choices made by these victims, on their decision to live free or die. My goal is to describe the logic and consequences of this choice.

The Slave Trade

The past of the *bossales*—the African-born enslaved who were the majority in Saint-Domingue—is usually overlooked. But when we look at their history, we suddenly see the beauty and successes of these American nations of African origin. Their victory was to plant, germinate, and cultivate a tolerable existence in the midst of the hell in which the Europeans had imprisoned them. The removal of young people, stolen from myriad ancestral villages, is easily described. The key is to feel a modicum of interest in and solidarity with these martyrs, immolated in the modern plantations of colonial America. In seeking to design a life with at least a tiny bit of autonomy, they ended up inventing the nations of Afro-America.

There is ongoing debate about how many human lives were destroyed by the slave trade. It was at least ten million people. Whatever the numbers, however, the repugnant and barbaric character of the traffic is clear (Vastey [1814] 2013). The trade wasn't a form of commerce; it was a form of social violence (Rodney 1972, 144). It was raw and unbridled, a crime against humanity (as French politician Christiane Taubira would call it). By producing and reproducing the enslavement of blacks (Meillassoux 1986), it contributed to the transformation of human life into the main form of merchandise in the modern European economy, and to the institutionalization of the superfluous and futile character of human life (Mignolo 2006) within the history of humanity inaugurated by capitalism.

The traded African was a "naked migrant" (Glissant 1997, 112). The trade invented an absolute individual, forced to start life again in an unprecedented and unpredictable solitude, lost in the void, with no interlocutors, no institutional and emotional referents, and no one to turn to. The slave traders turned them into nothing more than talking plows, reducing them to the status of an atom in a society with little meaning. They were not born into slavery, and they did not live as slaves. They were enslaved through intense torture, through revolting abuse and forms of humiliation that are a disgrace to humanity.

Why is it that, despite the claim of their importance made by Vastey in 1814, Haitian historiography and social thought has ignored the *bossales*? Their introduction onto the plantations was not a rare event. They were not an insignificant minority, an oddity in daily life. Almost the entire population of Haiti—more than 90 percent—descends directly from them. How can we explain the blindness on the part of all chroniclers, both French and Haitian, who conceive of the history of the country as starting with slaves, rather than with captives? Once they were captured, the captives had to be converted into slaves, and this transformation was not instantaneous. In Saint-Domingue, the text of the Code Noir was turned into flesh and blood only through the deliberate policies of the French colonial empire and its henchmen.

The trade placed two characters in conflict. On the one side was a being stripped of all recourse, and on the other a person exercising total power over this unfortunate. This kind of power is not limited by any kind of supervision. No justification or accounting has to be offered to anyone. For the captive individual, the master is a source of life and survival. For the master, the captive is nothing but perishable merchandise, a laborer to immolate. The two encounter one another in the midst of an artificial society whose principles and norms are structured to satisfy the needs of the colonial metropole. These needs are external to both sides of the master-slave couple.

The all-powerful masters granted themselves a monopoly over knowledge. This explains, to a great extent, why they granted a certain individuality to the captives, and why the rhythm of their work depended on changing situations and imperial policies. The result was that the laborers reduced to slavery negotiated their survival within limits fixed by the volatile interests of the motherland, which worried far less about their life expectancy than about their contribution to agro-industrial production. Since the reproduction of the workers took place through the slave trade, there was little possibility of any kind of autonomy in the relationship between property owners and captives. All local social relations were shaped by their primary goal, the satisfaction of the objectives of metropolitan France. These were always prioritized over the objectives of the actors in the colonial context itself.

As a result, and by definition, the people in captivity could not master the knowledge necessary for smooth functioning of the context into which they were placed. That knowledge was based on practices shaped in places far beyond their horizon and field of activity. Their life and their survival were defined by an isolated apprenticeship into the rules of the plantation system. They had to offer blind obedience to injunctions that, in the final analysis, came from an inaccessible elsewhere. The relative severity or benevolence of these instructions, and their presumed appropriateness, was not derived from the needs of the enslaved, or their performance as laborers, or even their negotiations with those among their executioners with whom they worked most closely.

The potential conflicts between slave owners and imperial authorities amplified the vulnerability and the powerlessness of the captive individuals. In this midst of a system set up in this way, these unfortunates could not pursue anything constant, cumulative, or self-propelled that would offer any improvement in their well-being. The slave system constructed their poverty—or more precisely, denuded them—by operationalizing their powerlessness. It articulated a social order in which their existence was justified only through their absolute availability to the will of masters close and far. The masters, in turn, lived as prisoners of the vagaries of French society and the itinerary of the broader colonial empire.

In sum, the colonial workers fabricated from the prisoners offered by the slave trade were forced to creolize (acculturate) themselves in order to survive. This immersion in a dominant system that institutionalized their absence of rights, however, did not guarantee their survival. Their existence as slaves remained a favor granted by their owners. In order to create this worker, the state worked relentlessly to convert this collection of young people it had kidnapped into individuals who were absolutely poor, vulnerable, and powerless, denuded of any possibility of exercising their own will or of producing knowledge useful for their own lives. This class of laborers was caught in a system that made it impossible for them to negotiate any improvement in their standard of living. That system itself was subordinated, and polarized, within a broader imperial system whose motivations and ways of functioning existed far beyond the daily experiences of the enslaved. In the end, this Caribbean laboring class, which essentially comprised the totality of the population, had only one option: to manipulate and sabotage the dominant system, without ever accepting its premises as their own. These premises, they understood, produced results that they could not control.

The carefully molded policies of empire had as their goal to produce the poverty and powerlessness of the colonial worker. They could never be the point of departure for a journey toward a new life. The agricultural laborer who understood the parameters of the slave society, whether this understanding served the interests of the planters and their supporters or worked against these interests, could not translate this into upward social mobility. The pursuit of the objectives of the slave society, which lined up with those of the metropole, always reinforced the chain of structural dependency and created an insurmountable rampart that protected the plantation society. Living within this enclosure, colonial laborers could subsist only by closing their eyes at the innumerable deaths provoked by these unnatural institutions and armoring themselves in the face of the traumas imposed by a victorious slavery and the amnesias it created.

The Leaders of the Public Colonial Order

The Republic of Haiti is a very small country, but it is sixty-four times larger than Barbados, the first and one of the most perfect plantation societies in the region. If you add the territory of the Dominican Republic, the island of Haiti is 175 times larger than Barbados. Establishing plantation slavery in Barbados required controlling and mastering the geography in which the captive laborers moved.

In his classic work *Black Rebellion in Barbados: The Struggle against Slavery, 1627–1838*, the historian Hilary Beckles distinguishes two models of plantation society. The first, the typical model, includes total plantation societies, including Barbados, Martinique, Guadeloupe, Antigua, and Saint Kitts. The second, which he calls open plantation societies, included Suriname and Saint-Domingue during the seventeenth and eighteenth centuries. As for the plantation societies established during or after the Industrial Revolution and after the implantation of colonialism in Africa, they have different features and involve a particular set of complexities that are not helpful for my analysis here.

Beckles describes the structuring of the society of Barbados in this way: "From an early stage, Blacks in Barbados found themselves enslaved under a powerful military regime, and within a physical environment which offered little assistance for armed struggle" (1984, 121). Beckles's analysis draws on this observation to identify and relate various characteristics of this particular slave society, including the relatively small size of these agro-industrial enterprises, their large number and proximity to one another, the characteristics of a settler colony in which the first colonists came with their nuclear families, the absence of rotation in land tenure and slave ownership, the small number of emancipated slaves and free people of color, the significance of a process of creolization that was almost complete starting at the end of the seventeenth century, and the role of Christian churches in addressing the spiritual needs of the captives. Through this work, then, we see that Barbados had a kind of relatively autonomous apartheid system, in contrast to exploitation colonies where the labor force was reproduced almost entirely through the slave trade.

This detour through the characteristics of the plantation society of Barbados allows us to emphasize the central role that local history plays in understanding the formation of Caribbean societies and nations. Geographer Georges Anglade (1982) emphasizes that, in contrast, the plantation society of Saint-Domingue was quite fragmented. It was an open plantation society, with a great diversity of social structures.

I would argue that in Saint-Domingue there were in fact multiple societies. In the North society was close to the Barbados model, while in the South social formation was closer to Jamaica and Brazil, where the success of free people of color as planters tended to attenuate the effects of racial stratification (Fick 1990; Garrigus 2006). The multiplication of maroon communities, the *doko* and *maniels*, in the center and the eastern part of the island, parallels the situation of Jamaica with its village societies, the northeast of Brazil with its *quilombos*, and Suriname with its bush societies. In other words, local histories detail a variety of relations between planters and captives that we need to take stock of in order to understand how the *bossales* constructed a human life in the hell of the colonies of the Caribbean.

Hilary Beckles explains the stability of the plantation society of Barbados by emphasizing the severity of the garrison system that the United Kingdom imposed as structure of development. Historians Dubois and Garrigus, however, point out that before the conflicts of 1790, the planters of Saint-Domingue bragged that they possessed the most stable and peaceful slave regime of the region. The colony had experienced only relatively small insurrections that did not have a tremendous influence: Padrejean's revolt in 1679, and those led by Plymouth in 1730, Polydor in 1734, and Pompée in 1747. That said, we need to attentively consider Makandal's revolt, which lasted eighteen years before the *maréchaussée*, the colonial police force, captured him in 1758 (M. Hector forthcoming).

In Jamaica, in contrast, there were eight major revolts during the late seventeenth and the eighteen centuries (Dubois and Garrigus 2006, 17). They left a deep mark on colonial history and geography. Even in the case of Makandal in Saint-Domingue, it is possible that those eighteen years of revolt were nothing but the product of the imagination of the colonists. They may have panicked as they discovered the autonomy, effectiveness, and rootedness of a system of knowledge among the captives, based around the making of objects called *makandals* or *wangas*, which they used in confronting their oppression and seeking forms of healing (Mobley 2015, 287).

At first, daily life in these parts of the French colonial empire was organized by pirates, buccaneers, Huguenots and other heretics, and Jews. It was a mostly male population. These marginal individuals fleeing metropolitan society still shared in a fraction of the total power of the West. The empire appropriated their search for a decent and free life, and sometimes celebrated them as pioneers who cleared the land. In order to encourage them to settle in recently acquired territories, colonial authorities offered them the opportunity to acquire women on the market. These were generally miserable prisoners or prostitutes recruited from the dregs of society. They were, in other words, white slaves.

During the same period, captives from the Atlantic coasts of Africa, imbued with the values and customs of the societies of West and Central Africa, began to flood into the same space. In the years just before and at the beginning of the establishment of the plantation system in Saint-Domingue, some of the first colonists, including some nobles, established households with their domestic slaves rather than marrying indigent white women of doubtful morals and rough manners (Raimond 1791a, 2). So it was that alongside the plantation society was born a group of free people of color who never had to be emancipated. With the sudden and dazzling economic development of the colony, this group of free people of color grew wealthy. As leaders of the emancipated slaves, both *métis* and free blacks, they became central to the maintenance of the order of slavery through the roles they played in the *maréchaussée* (police) and the militias.

The reproduction of slavery depended on the activity of the slave trade, which guaranteed the constant production of *bossales*. Yet, as Julien Raimond noted perceptively, the production and reproduction of the captive as a slave depended on the work of free people of color and emancipated slaves.[4] The colonists of Saint-Domingue bragged about possessing the most stable colony of the region despite the fact that the geographical environment was not conducive to the development of a total slave society and the limited military aid offered by a the French kingdom busy fighting different wars in Europe. As a result, the success of the Pearl of the Antilles came to depend on the free people of color and free blacks, who were—as they themselves admitted—pillars of the colonial order.

The modern, imperial, and capitalist West, then, deliberately created the poverty of captives reduced to slavery. It did so thanks to the services of free people of color and emancipated slaves, an intermediary class (a middle class!) that we can count among the few privileged members of the slave society. This class was born and lived by consuming the instructions and knowledge of the colonial administration, which made their existence as a group possible. They did not produce their own knowledge. Instead, they transmitted it.

Sometimes, people mistakenly confuse following instructions with being educated. The privilege of this group flowed from the manipulation of orders received from elsewhere, not those they came up with themselves.

This group, out of which the oligarchs of Haiti would emerge, was part of a pyramid of tyrants, at the summit of which were the *grand blancs* and the *petits blancs*. They took charge of subjugating the captives and putting in place the measures needed to contain them in their role as enslaved workers—that is, as perishable merchandise. By bullying them and assuring their circulation in the labor market, this class of intermediaries helped give birth to the colonial black person, conceived of as a sum of lacunae, a social void, introduced into the marketplace in complete nakedness and isolation (Casimir 2004b, 40). Since the bulk of the captives reduced to slavery arrived within the decade before the 1791 insurrection, these two segments of the colonial population shared only a very brief period together in the common experience of life in the plantation system. Their reciprocal enmity was born as much of their divergent political interests and behaviors as from the differences in the traditions and practices that were part of their respective collective memories.

There is no reason to expect that the agricultural laborers, with or without their chains, would entrust their will to create a better life to a few urban residents who were the servants of the modern, imperial, and colonial West and the avowed and impenitent authors of their suffering. The laboring class responded to the repressive structure of the plantation system with a principled opposition against the system of domination and those who made it function. The historiography has taken note of the dissimilarity of their visions of life in postindependence society, but it appears not to realize that the descendants of the *bossales* made up the overwhelming majority, who would have found no valid reason to follow in the footsteps of the urban Creoles, any more than this tiny minority could imagine making themselves the students of the *bossales*. The two groups began their independent life with their backs turned to one another.

Coloniality, or the Continuation of the Public Colonial Order

This study of the sovereignty of the Haitian people is inspired by the ideas developed by Guillermo Bonfil Batalla starting in the 1980s, and extends the use I made of them in *Pa bliye 1804: Souviens toi de 1804* (2004).[5] In the first chapter of that book I argue: "The 'Indians' and the 'Blacks' (of America) inhabited only the universe of the colonists. They cannot be found anywhere else. . . . The only place where the color of the skin indicates the function of social actors is within colonialist projects" (Casimir 2004b, 50). Interpretations that privilege race (and color) in their analysis of Saint-Domingue erase the very ethnicities that plantation accounting took note of, in its own way, at the moment when captives were acquired. In so doing, they incorporate the colonial perspective that enabled the transformation of these individuals into homogenized colonial laborers. Such interpretations implant, in our social reality, an error equivalent to that of Christopher Columbus, who discovered India in America. As a result, following the great discoverers of the world, these interpretations erase from the history of humanity the variety of life experiences (memory, knowledge, language, emotions, institutions) that existed before, during, and after enslavement. The Code Noir stops being an object of study and is converted into a tool for interpreting observed facts. Our social behavior is explained according to the meanings given to our skin color by our executioners, rather than through reference to what we have learned from our own knowledge, our daily experiences, and the way we live these experiences. We end up no longer being the primary motors of our actions, and are seen instead as acting from within the parameters defined by our abductors.

The planters, making use of their imperial prerogatives, eliminated the African nations from the functioning of local society and created the opposition between black and white. In the process, they created two foundational aggregates that had no history outside of the colonial gesture. A ladder of shades of skin, going from black to white, erased all the itineraries that any member of the subsets that resulted from their crossings might construct for themselves. The descendants of Africans lost any space in which they could reproduce their particular traits. Local history—their efforts, as blacks, to seize their future with their own hands—was deprived of any distinct content. This reinforced the viability of the chromatic ladder, which deepened their absence.

In contrast, a decolonial reading that chooses to look at the behaviors the imprisoned themselves put in motion seeks to unearth the contradictory course of the modern colonial public order. The adults brought into captivity reacted to new circumstances on the basis of a past they could not leave behind and, in this way, sculpted a new character that exceeded the imagination of the Western colonial project. They did so by protecting themselves, as much as possible, from its premises and developments.

The fact is that in Saint-Domingue or in rural Haiti in the nineteenth century, the transformation of African ethnicities into colonial blacks didn't materialize. At the moment of rupture with empire, at least two-thirds of the captives had been born in Africa. The colonial blacks were only among the Creoles, and essentially within the small urban areas. This absence of colonized blacks requires us to make a distinction between the history of Haiti—

that is, the official history diffused by the Haitian state—and the history of Haitians—that is, that which Haitians live in their daily lives, through the most modest of gestures. The story told by the first group, the blacks of the towns, the colonized blacks, does not include those in rural areas as legitimate partners, but rather as backwards masses that have to be civilized, Christianized, and modernized. That sentiment is not shared by those it characterizes, who are the overwhelming majority.

The weakness of the process of creolization, along with conflicts that remained unresolved because of the failure of an externally focused society and economy, continued into the nineteenth century. The political entity shaped by the outcome of the War of Independence was urged to demonstrate, with as much emphasis as possible, that it belonged to the modern world—that is, the space occupied by the independent nations of the time, all of which were European, imperialist, and racist. Otherwise, Haiti risked exposing itself to their collective aggression.

The crucial role of the racialization of social relations in maintaining the links between the colony and its metropole, and the implications this had for the relaunching of the plantation economy, shaped the first proclamation of independence, issued less that fifteen days after the victory at Vertières, on November 29, 1803. The explicit condemnation of color prejudice on the part of the signatories of the declaration—Dessalines, Christophe, and Clervaux—was addressed to the white property owners, without ever mentioning the principal victims of racial discrimination: "Property-owners of Saint-Domingue, who are wandering in foreign lands, in proclaiming our independence we are not outlawing you from returning and taking back your property. Such an unjust idea is far from our thoughts" (Manigat 2001, 418). Still, as if in response to the cataclysm underway at the time, eight days later the Declaration of Haitian Independence, issued on January 1, 1804, announced to the generals of the Armée indigène the intention of Dessalines to permanently guarantee a stable government for Haitians. It then issued a challenge to foreign powers by informing them of the general's resolution to make the country independent.

In his proclamation to the people of Haiti, pronounced on the same occasion, Dessalines addressed himself to what he called the *indigènes*, or indigenous population, and unequivocally affirmed his determination to forever guarantee the empire of liberty in "the country where we were born." He contradicted the proclamation of November 29 by denouncing the "ghost of liberty" that France offered, and emphasized the recovery of liberty by the population. In so doing he alluded to the liberty that the *bossales* enjoyed in Africa, and in order to be even clearer, his proclamation warned those who might try and take this liberty once again. The general-in-chief embraced the entire population, and particularly the *bossales*, and invited the people to choose extermination—that is, collective suicide—rather than leaving an example of cowardliness for generations to come. That is the motto, "Liberty or Death," inscribed on his red and black flag.

The nineteenth century was at a crossroads of two political orientations: the Pétion-led approach of so-called republican governments and the Dessalines-inspired approach of January 1804 that was put into practice in peasant society. The line of thought of Dessalines undoes the sociogenic (Fanon 1952, 32) approach that served as the foundation for the Declaration of Independence of November 29, 1803 and eliminates the colonial black from the history of Haiti. On the other hand, the narrative chosen by Pétion is constructed on the basis of the colonial black and entrusts the future of the country to the Creoles.

Notwithstanding the Constitution of 1805, the concept of the black person in Saint-Domingue and in Haiti (the colonial black) hides two unnameable things. First, it helps camouflage the intersection between the interests of property owners, whether free blacks or free people of color. Toussaint, a planter and slave owner, sees himself as the champion of these unfortunates because he is black like they are. This conceit is rarely discussed in national historiography. His struggle for their emancipation—which he often calls their liberty—serves as a lever for him to promote the interests of his class, as is made clear by his agricultural regulations, whose draconian severity is also never discussed.

Julien Raimond, meanwhile, pursued the same objective for the group of slave-owning planters under his command by underlining the role played by emancipated slaves in the maintenance of public order. The thought of this influential capitalist, which is of a diamondlike clarity, disappeared from Haiti's intellectual history nearly as soon as he completed his polemic with Moreau de St. Méry, the paladin of the Club Massiac. The difference between the black planter Toussaint and the planter of color Raimond, if it exists at all, disappears when it comes to the treatment of the *cultivateurs*, the ex-slave agricultural laborers. In this same direction, and still under the racist sociogenic logic contained in the Declaration of independence of November 29, 1803, the free people of color were absorbed into the group of emancipated slaves, as Moreau de Saint-Méry had hoped.

The fact that skin color is used as a marker of social status makes it easier to avoid naming the ethnic conflicts between property owners and workers. As a result, they are presented as being part of a temporal continuum, rather than as contemporaries. The differences in geographical origin, by this logic, explain the distance between African savagery and European civilization. These are transposed onto another scale, and seem to localize behaviors within a particular time period. They are seen as stretching from traditional and archaic to modern and contemporary. The result is that we lose sight of their actual contemporaneity and all that results from it (Vázquez-Melken 2014). The two-thirds of the colonial population who are *bossales* are seen as demonstrating behaviors that are part of a past era, typical of a childish mentality. For their own good, they have to be put in the care of generous planters, transformed into affectionate family patriarchs. What explains the disordered reactions of the *bossale* is not the deviant behavior of the slave traders and their bosses, but rather the stubborn localization of the *bossales* in an expired moment in history where savagery dominated.

The workers are seen as black and savage, and their feelings and motivations as being part of a past time. This allows the planters, all Creole or French, to fight with one another without upending the plantation society. Their quarrels, all very modern, play out in a civilizational space in which Europe, particularly France, is enthroned. The unfolding conflicts between whites, free people of color, and blacks do not put in question the right of the metropole to appropriate the resources of the territory or of the captives, and then to grant them to the privileged groups it choses, or the right of the planters to imprison within the walls of the plantation laborers who have been declared free. The result is a minimum of understanding between parties, in which the only loser remains the black agricultural laborers, enslaved or indentured, beneficiaries of a bizarre liberty that grants them no rights. Deprived of all resources, these blacks have no choice but to bow before a union that accepts the pre-eminence of the racist West.

Ardouin presents with candor the awkward predicament that results from replacing the ethnic dimension with a racial one. It is not because it is black that the majority of the population is excluded in order to project the social order, but rather because it is barbarous, to borrow Laënnec Hurbon's terminology (1987):

Pinchinat . . . Montbrun and . . . Marc Borno had to come rapidly to an agreement, a regrettable one perhaps, but whose energy could and would throw all the African sorcerers into a stupor, submitting them to the ascendancy of their intelligence. It was in the interest of these masses to have capable leaders. The three of them decided Halaou had to die for this reason, not because of a hatred for those blacks. That sentiment never entered their hearts, that day or later when Toussaint Louverture, Dessalines and Christophe, who had become the leaders of the government, also eliminated African sorcerers like Halaou, seeing them as threats to public tranquility who were capable, through their fetishism, of undermining the civilization of the masses. In 1803 Dessalines acted for the same reasons when he killed Lamour Dérance who, through African fetishism, was creating major obstacles for him during the War of Independence (Ardouin 1853, 2:361).

The argument here is that Halaou and Lamour Dérance should have civilized themselves before protesting against slavery or against the ghost of liberty offered to them by the heroes of independence in the name of France. Toussaint, Pinchinat, Montbrun, Borno, Dessalines, and Christophe all were shaped by their era, of course. But recognizing that is not enough. We have to remember that they were not just a part of the repressive era of the colony. Rather, they chose to participate in a modern, racist, and Eurocentric project. That project did not, however, govern the behavior of the majority of the earth's population. And it certainly did not govern the behavior of the majority of African captives in Saint-Domingue, who Ardouin felt paid far too much attention to their African sorcerers.

It is also worth asking the question in reverse, which no doubt would be of interest to the majority of the population: what did Halaou, Lamour Dérance, and the other leaders of the insurgent bands think of the self-proclaimed leaders of the War of Independence? For, certainly, the opinion of this overwhelming majority had implications for the future of the country!

By accepting the perception that Haiti was the first black republic, the oligarchs thought they were standing up to racism, that they were showing that they were equal to the white race, not its inferiors. But the sense of racial pride among Haitians of the intermediary classes did not refer to interethnic relations within the country. For the intermediary group, the life of the worker reduced to slavery was simply the antechamber of the civilized world. The great Haitian intellectuals of the nineteenth century, staunch defenders of the black race, were both problack and Africanophobic (Hoffman 1990). They dreamed of regenerating the black race by using the very principles and tools the West used to degrade them.

The question of culture—that is, of the elaboration of a project for life on the basis of concrete experiences—was absent from the reflections of the writers and thinkers of the nineteenth century. They were proud of the fact that they were excellent consumers of education, knowledge, and erudition, and unable to imagine that out of an escape from slave exploitation there might emerge a civilization of resistance and institutions that could save the nation. In the nineteenth century, Haiti saw itself as a kind of lighthouse for the black race, because among so many savages, their sons and daughters were less savage than the others because they were closer to the West. Rosalvo Bobo, an unimpeachable nationalist, expressed this directly: "Our little habitat is an insult to the New World, being the only one . . . that still offers a refuge for Africa, that is to say, for crime, wallowing in shadows, and barbarism" (quoted in Hoffman 1990, 40).

The racial consciousness and pride of the Haitian oligarchs of the nineteenth century were built on a disdain for Africa. In order to protect the social order offered by the Christian, racist West, they took on the project of rendering local culture invisible. Progress was understood as the washing away of this insult to the New World, or at least as an effort to lock the forms of thought of the sovereign people within the (visible and invisible) dungeons of their memory.

Decoloniality, or the Permanence of the Response

Starting from this repugnance for local culture manifested by the oligarchs from the seventeenth through the nineteenth centuries, I think through popular sovereignty and how it operated despite the attacks coming from increasingly powerless government authorities. Following the goals of modern Europe, the slave trade buried aggregates of individuals without attachments in an unspeakable desolation in Saint-Domingue, inviting them to suicide and infanticide. The reflections that follow seek to understand the routes and methods used by these sufferers to reactivate their will to live and invent a mode of existence that would enable their production and reproduction as human beings.

A plantation society could not exist without the slave trade. Other than suicide, the desocialized, decivilized, and depersonalized captives (Meillassoux 1998, 99) that were dumped into it had only one form of autonomous action at their disposal. They had to weave together social relations and create groups to protect and help one another. No human being exists outside a community. The captive population had to create new communities, overcoming the many obstacles placed in their way by the Code Noir and those who applied it.

The organization of these communal groups and the re-establishment of social links depended on a set of parallel preconditions. The prisoners had no choice but to learn the rules of the plantation order. But in order to protect and help one another on their own terms during this apprenticeship process, they had to come to know one another. They were comrades in misfortune, and they taught one another about the particularities of the different ethnic groups they came from. Building on their experiences with one another and their relationship with the system imposed on them, together they established a series of norms that guided the shaping of the new links between them. These norms were aimed at supporting their interests, in terms of both personal survival and the productive structuring of the group of sufferers. The knowledge accumulated through these relationships with one another—the symbols, markers, concepts, and strategies derived from common experiences—were conserved in their own language, which served to tighten their reciprocal links and to identify them and distinguish them from those who exploited them.

The community of captives appropriated the Kreyòl language and reconstructed it. They transformed Creole into its own project, one that transmitted the group's memory and culture. The language recuperated and conserved the keys to acceptable behavior. It identified the paths to success, along with the punishments that awaited those who deviated from the emerging social norms. The new system of knowledge and values redefined each individual as a member of a community they had participated in inventing. The community offered them forms of support and recourse that were codified in the institutions it reproduced. These norms, values, and principles of action were developed autonomously, free from the influence of any authority that was not part of this group of equals.

Assembling the empirical data we need to confirm these observation means reading the actions and gestures of the dominant system against the grain. Why, we can ask, did the plantation system outlaw gatherings of those it considered to be slaves? In the slaver's conception of the world, after all, slaves were livestock, talking plows, with no minds of their own. Why, then, couldn't they pray to their own gods, given that it is a waste of time to address oneself to fetishes and idols that aren't listening anyway? If they were so powerless and incapable, why couldn't they be allowed move around freely and create their own spaces for thinking through their actions and behavior? Why did the plantation system consider any expression of their free will a form of defiance so dangerous it had to be destroyed relentlessly in order to guarantee the normal functioning of agro-industry? What, precisely, was it that these savages could do so effectively that it threatened a form of power that considered itself boundless? In fact, beyond the regulations of the dominant system and the punishments they were threatened with, the captives were building another reality. And it threatened the colonists so much that they wanted to dismantle it at all costs (Casimir 1973, 31).

The plantation society limited the exercise of freedom by the captives by isolating them from one another. It also prevented them from reconstructing social relationships on their own terms. The local context of different colonies shaped the development and expression of popular sovereignty. During the end of the eighteenth century and the beginning of the nineteenth, Haitian society was never fully creolized through acculturation and cultural mixing. France was never able to inoculate this society with the feeling that the Christian West was all-powerful. On the contrary, by the time that the majority of Haitians had been born in America rather than Africa, and that the sentiments associated with this could shape their life experience, they were already far into the process of savoring their victory over modern colonialism, despite the fact that their guides, the African sorcerers, had been assassinated. The image of an all-powerful West was not constitutive of their culture of sovereignty. Only the class of the emancipated slaves, the intermediaries created by the colonial regime over the course of the eighteenth century, had absorbed this Eurocentric perspective.

The fragility of the captive population in Saint-Domingue explains the absence of significant revolts and insurrections before the end of the eighteenth century. And the fragility of the state administration after 1804 helps us understand how a system of knowledge that never stumbled in its search for new solutions aimed at assuring control over daily life was established and took root. Only the oligarchs and the intermediary classes in the urban areas suffered from the endemic bovarism of the colonized, because they were the only ones truly shaped by the colonial empire. They were the only ones who had been truly colonized.

Conclusion: A Decolonial Reading

The state of Haiti was born into a world that considered its very existence inconceivable and undesirable. When we study this state on the basis of imperial theories about the construction of modern states (nation building), we are evaluating it according to a goal it could never reach, and assuming it could have controlled processes that were in fact absent from its colonial beginnings. Above all, we imagine that the Haitian state could and should have acted the same way the colonial government did. But the modern, racist, capitalist, and Christian world could never accept the Haitian state. The surrounding nations never invited Haiti to be part of this exclusively Western club. And the more the Haitian administration knocked at its door and managed to accelerate efforts at rapprochement, the more Haiti found itself subjugated and humiliated.

The oligarchs who controlled nineteenth-century Haiti were well aware that the modern colonial world was watching. So they cultivated the idea that it was their good fortune to have emerged from the Pearl of the Antilles and its slave system. As a result, they remained fixated on the maintenance and ultimate reconstruction of the colonial social relations that had created them and continued to shape the image they had of themselves. This made it unthinkable, undesirable, and unacceptable for them to imagine any kind of future for popular sovereignty. The truth was, however, that they were surrounded on all sides by a rural mass that they could not penetrate. In fact, with the meager means at their disposal, they could not influence it all. On the contrary, without being willing to admit it, they allowed themselves to be absorbed by the autonomy of the countryside. They ended up moving beyond simple coexistence with the rural population, and instead peaceably participated in the forms of life it organized. They got used to the idea that the administrative structure of the state, their fiefdom, would maintain the colonial heritage. They accepted that it would be organized to focus on securing their own survival and reproduction, without influencing the ways of life of the national majority.

I am not at all interested in the Western state and its objectives, or in the transformations within its administrative machinery that took place once it implanted itself among the Haitians. I am not interested in explaining how and why Europe arrived in our world. What interests me is how we received the West, or rather how we avoided receiving it by creating our own world and negotiating with it on the basis of our own positions. I prefer to maintain the advantage I gain by freeing myself from the foundational norms and values of colonial empire. In order to survive, I have to understand the functioning of the administrative structures Europe implanted among us in order to civilize us. I have to understand the values that undergirded this enterprise. But those efforts are part of Europe's history, a history situated outside of my realm of action, one that I have almost no way of influencing. I, instead, take consciousness of the path taken by the heroes of independence, without trying to determine whether the option they chose was necessary, desirable, or viable.

My position of strength comes from observing the outside world through Haitian eyes. When I do the opposite, I place myself in a position of inferiority by accepting the definitions put in place by the gaze of another, one who thinks they are my master. My task is to find out how Haitians created themselves and how they received Europe. In doing so, I enrich my life as a Haitian and, as a result, I can share that richness with all of humanity. It is not my job to decide whether we have done well or badly, if we have failed or succeeded. I simply want to be able to look at myself, as I am, with my own eyes. "The point of view of the oppressed develops from what is inside, and moves toward the outside. It is the inversion of the paths of oppression. It has always been this way" (Casimir 1981, 265).

It is obvious that the community of rural people in the nineteenth century didn't see the state in which they lived as a form of savagery, or a fall backwards into an earlier period in history. They situated themselves in the present, facing the modern world. Once we have understood this community's logic, there is no reason to assume that it would ever have evolved toward the replication of the structure of a modern state that abhorred its very existence, to the point that it considered them unsuited to exist as contemporary, civilized beings. And there is no reason to dream that the modern state would ever provide this community with what it needed to reproduce itself according to its own wishes, as every sovereign people must do.

As long as historiography imprisons itself in the paradigms of European modernity, it validates the idea that the colonized are savages. In making this choice, it takes on the parameters that undergird these paradigms—namely, the idea that Europeans have a right to conquer lands and colonize their inhabitants, along with the racism that accompanies the abuses. It grants the state of savagery a historical legality, and destroys its contemporaneity with modernity (Quijano 2007; Mignolo 2011; Vázquez-Melken 2014).

The unfolding of the history of Haitians diverges significantly from the itineraries followed by the French, which is why it remains indispensible to stay as close as possible to the local history created by the sovereign people. The preeminence of external relations in shaping local evolution and relationships within the country is the legacy of modern times. But it leads researchers to treat national life using rags (*pèpè*) cast off from the international marketplace of ideas.

Historical sociology is not a way of reading a specific history on the basis of accepted sociological theories. It is not about applying these theories to the specific historiography of the colonized country. The unit of analysis in all sociology remains the social relation, the link between groups and their members situated in a specific place and time. Every country has its specific history, and historiography endlessly captures it and discovers new specificities. Historical sociology consists in developing a theory of the evolution of the inhabitants of a country, building on a historiography located within a particular time. Questions and answers formulated on both sides create a reciprocally enriching relationship between Historical Sociology and the writing of history.

Unless we postulate that there is a possible, or even necessary, evolution from the colonial state to a colonialist and imperial state, I cannot see how we can study the Haitian people according to a matrix developed to explain the development of the French people. If I follow this path, I should not be surprised when I run up against an enigma that I have created for myself: the impossibility of explaining why the political system of Haiti is not structured like that of France. I would waste my time trying to discover some kind of tour de force that might have enabled those elements placed in the colony by the French state to emulate, or even compete with, their mother country, without being able to depend on some other Pearl of the Antilles to help them along as Saint-Domingue had done for France. Such a path, in any case, would push Haitians to become more French and less Haitian every day. "The liberty [I offer you] is bringing you from nothingness into existence. Show yourself worthy of this liberty. Forever reject indolence and banditry; have the courage to wish to be a people, and soon you will be the equals of the European nations" (Sonthonax, in Ardouin 1853, 2:244).

The goal of our existence was to be determined by the history of Europe. A few intermediaries who rallied to the side of the dying colony celebrated this half-baked liberty granted during the days of the civil commissioner Sonthonax. But the sovereign people did something else with it. They used it to destroy the colony. For them, Sonthonax's decree was a trampoline used in a leap toward a liberty without borders.

To ask myself whether the sovereign people turned their back on other, more viable, options is no more reasonable than trying to figure out whether the recognized heroes of independence could have chosen a different path. We must simply acknowledge that the nation that was in the process of emerging moved in the opposite direction of that chosen by those who declared themselves its leaders and took over the reins of government. In this decolonial reading of the history of Haitians, I examine the state that organized the nation's political life in relation to the efforts carried out by the sovereign people, from 1697 to 1915, to take control of the circumstances in which they had to live. My goal is to understand the articulation between these two opposed tendencies, and the way that over the course of the nineteenth century they established of a form of living together. It is the interlacing of the agendas that oriented these two tendencies during this period that in fact constituted what I call the state in Haiti.

Chapter 2

Resisting the Production of Sufferers

Introduction: The Sufferers

In Haiti, those who live precarious lives define themselves as sufferers. There is no explanation for their presence among the needy, and it is understood that they will escape this modest condition only thanks to a stroke of luck as unpredictable as the misfortunes that precipitated them into it. They show no sign of resignation or fatalism, but rather of a consciousness of the condition in which they find themselves and in the midst of which they have to construct the best life possible. Any person worthy of respect remains imperturbable in the midst of this distress, which must be conquered daily. The best example of this attitude was the movement led by Jean-Jacques Acaau, who at the head of the Army of Sufferers fought for rights that were violated and disregarded.

The losses experienced by the captives before 1804 and the misery of the cultivators (field-workers) who inherited their misfortune were initially caused by the French state—modern, imperial, racist. Subsequently, the poverty of the majority can be blamed on the oversight of the oligarchs who took control of the administration and tried, without success, to follow the path shown to them by the former colonial power. The international environment in which these oligarchs developed did not make their pursuit of this social project any easier. Although they claimed to belong to the modern world, they lived at the margins of the concert of nations. This added to their difficulties as they faced the cultivators, who gained more room to maneuver as a result of their country's international marginalization. What followed French colonialism was a century of the independence of the Haitian people, which the silence of the oligarchs prevents us from fully celebrating.

In the pages that follow, I bring together the paths of reflection of theorists of the coloniality of power, notably Anibal Quijano and Walter Mignolo, with that of Louis Sala-Molins, who has analyzed the Code Noir (1987) and argue that its legacy makes clear that there is an obvious requirement for a process of reparation for the harm inflicted (2014). In so doing, I consolidate the method I developed in my first book, *La culture opprimée* (1981). I observe Saint-Domingue and Haiti from the beach, alongside the indigenous peoples who were fascinated by the spectacle of the caravels emerging from the ocean, and I defy the perspective of those who, from the bridges of the caravels, trained their telescopes on the island (Casimir 2004b, 11). In the same way, I contrast the sufferings of the *bossales* exhibited in the stalls of the slave market with the snickers and the arrogance of those who bought these agricultural laborers. "Social science has no real point other than to discover how the dominated will recuperate their history" (Casimir 1981, 255). By allying myself with the victims, with the help of local history, my goal is to try and capsize—for those who are interested in joining me—the traditional way our nation's society has been conceived. My goal is to reinstall the conquered in their role as agents of their own destiny. Over the course of the Haitian nineteenth century, I show, the slaves whom Louis XIV dreamed of discovering in Saint-Domingue (Sala-Molins 1987, 7) recovered from the terror of the plantation society by taking their lives into their own hands.

Louis XIV and the Slaves

The Underside of the Code Noir

In the seventeenth century, a small number of French settlers arrived on the island of Tortuga and then the west coast of Ayiti, which had been baptized *Hispaniola* by the Spanish conquerors. They were marginal people: pirates, filibusters and other journeyers on the sea. Later came Huguenots fleeing religious persecution and discrimination. In 1697, with the Treaty of Ryswick, Spain ceded its sovereignty over the territory to the French state, which after some hesitation began to develop plantations to produce commodities for export goods. The colony took its place among the domains of a state that already had a half-century of experience governing the slave colonies of Guadeloupe and Martinique.

The state made land grants of various sizes, depending on wealth and rank, to the French inhabitants who settled its new acquisition. It guaranteed them the right to property over this land and their other possessions. Among these other possessions were *slaves*.[1] In 1685, Louis XIV explained that "the promptness of our attempts to assist" the French subjects in the colonies in fulfilling their "needs" had led him to issue the Code Noir "to regulate the status and conditions of our slaves" in the "American islands." He used royal institutions to offer his subjects what was necessary for their well-being, including laws and regulations that assured their ability to fully exploit the slaves they possessed. In doing so, he distinguished between two fundamental categories of people in the colony: his subjects and foreigners reduced to slavery (Sala-Molins 1987, 90, 100).

Contemporary scholarship must grapple with the enduring effects of these decisions made by the sovereign will of the Sun King. Louis XIV's 1685 Code Noir codified the normative structure of the colony as it was projected by the authorities who were its principal architects. The code defined the fundamental social categories and their supposedly permanent relationships. It pronounced what social system was to be put in place, presenting itself as the mother of the legal constitution of the French slave colonies. The subsequent laws and regulations that shaped the life of these structures were made to fit the logic of this code, which consecrated imperial will as the source of all legitimacy.

To the extent that the metropole was able to impose this structure constitutive of colonial society, the relationships that flowed from it in time became habitual and served as the basis for social expectations. Little by little, the founding social architecture implanted by the empire went beyond the normal course of things—that is, what people expected—and transformed itself into what people had to expect, or simply what was understood as having to be (Heller 1961, 202). A cluster of common expectations emerged, creating the rhythm of daily life for the conquerors and the conquered. In this way, the imperial state laid the foundations of the very memory of the society it developed.

This original arrangement determined the routines of subjects, and it gradually acquired an immutable character, freed from the consent or dissent of individuals. They obeyed the stipulated norms and orientations, because *they seemed self-evident.* This transformation of the normative into the normal took place without difficulty for the natural subjects of the king, since it satisfied their primary and immediate interests. The adopted subjects, freed or emancipated slaves who served as intermediaries between the French settlers and the class of agricultural workers, also adopted these rules, which converted them from victims of the system into the executioners of their companions in misfortune.

It was a different story for the captives who had to be converted into slaves. Their subjection was carried out through continual coercion, and their status as merchandise was internalized through a process that grew increasingly complex and unpredictable as the rhythm of their arrival and rotation among masters accelerated over the course of the eighteenth century. The severity of the coercion necessary to obtain their work explains why their death rates were so high. The only way to renew and grow the workforce was to constantly import more slaves to replace the victims of the brutalities that accompanied creolization.

The relationships between the social categories invented by the Code Noir became the armature of the slave society. Institutions were created to protect, renew, and consolidate these legal dispositions and the interests of those they protected. The knowledge and management of the rules of daily life guided the behavior of the freed slaves and the Creole or creolized captives. Their survival depended on learning and either conforming to or dexterously manipulating the rules imposed on them.

The metropolitan architects of colonial society considered the asymmetry between property owners and slaves, between whites and blacks, to be natural. They simply enunciated it. Over time, the adaption of the emigrants from the metropole to the new system took place smoothly because they shared the institutionalized ideology and racist principles. But it was not always this way. In fact, this represented a conquest of the modern state itself, then in the process of consolidating its control over the world.

It may not be surprising that the writings of Ottabah Cugoano, an author of African origin who was consigned to slavery and then emancipated—*Thoughts and Sentiments on the Evil and Wicked Traffic of the Slavery and Commerce of the Human Species* (1787)—have largely been overlooked. But it is more striking that those of Las Casas and Albornoz, who were well-known monks during the sixteenth century, have been as well. Albornoz asked how it was possible to be a Christian and to justify the slave trade of blacks as a form of salvation for souls, without investing oneself the way the apostles did in evangelizing them in their African homelands? At the dawn of modern times, these theologians spoke of the natural liberty of blacks (Sala-Molins 1987, 70).

Later, a century before Cugoano, two Capuchin monks, Franciso José de Jaca and Épiphane de Moirans, lobbied in Spain and Rome against the slave trade in the Caribbean.[2] On March 20, 1686, the "Decree of the Holy Office on Several Doubts That Have Been Submitted by the Sacred Congregation of the Propagation of the Faith" agreed with them:

> In consequence, all those who, in whatever way, cause the death of slaves and who participate in the unjust slavery of the blacks, are commanded to provide restitution. Therefore kings, traders, whether Spanish or French, merchants, buyers and sellers of blacks, all those who transport them, the captains of ships and all those who effectively participate in this commerce, whether they are masters or buyers in the Indies or in Europe, re-sellers, and all those who buy or retain, in any of the forms enumerated, are all obligated to grant the blacks their liberty and the price of their work and reparation for the suffering and damages they have endured. (Sala-Molins 2014, 92)

As early as the seventeenth century, Moirans prepared a response to Tocqueville's famous phrase, which was so useful to slavers: "If blacks have a right to become free, it is incontestable that the colonists have the right not to be ruined by the liberty of the blacks." The Capuchin retorted:

> First of all, liberty is of an order superior to all other goods in the world. So it must be defended even at the cost of the loss of all the Indies, of every Spain, every France: better to enter naked into heaven than to descend rich into hell. Secondly: Blood is the price of the labor of black slaves. Europeans have therefore grown rich on their blood. They must provide restitution, even if it costs them all their possessions. Thirdly: Europeans have gotten rich through iniquity, trespasses, and the oppression of blacks. So, badly. They are therefore obligated to lose everything through restitution, under pain of eternal damnation, and in accord with the principles of justice: "No one must enrich themselves by causing harm or prejudice to another" (Boniface Octave, Book VI). So, if they arrived naked in the Indies, they must come back to Spain naked. (Sala-Molins 2014, 101)

The king of Spain and the Council of the Indies decided, however, that "there is no reason to doubt either the need for these slaves for the maintenance of the kingdoms of the Indies, or the fact that the public interest is best served by conserving this system without any innovation" (Sala-Molins 2014, 115). The imperial state acted with determination and put a battery of institutions into place that were meant to convince the colonists and the emancipated slaves to close their eyes to the crimes being committed daily.

But the vast majority of the population reduced to slavery were not dupes. That was especially true because they had other cultural horizons based on their prior experiences. We face a core methodological choice: As observers, do we situate ourselves on the side of the minority of conquerors? Or do we take the side of those who were attacked and colonized? One can approach the history of Saint-Domingue and Haiti the way Louis XIV, Versailles, and their Code Noir did, without asking any questions about the sudden presence of these foreigners consigned to slavery (Sala-Molins 1987, 7). But it is also reasonable to conclude that there was no way the captives were going to spontaneously discover and then accept the legitimacy of the suffering inflicted on them by colonialism. The slaves had to be trained. They did not erupt from the earth like mushrooms. They were not born of a history without history. I have explored the history of the societies from which they came, and of the routes and actions that led to their presence so far from the lands where they were born. In the process, I have gathered the tools necessary to better understand the logic of their behavior and the social particularities of the plantation societies, both of which were concealed by the colonial authorities, the planters, and their panegyrists. I can't avoid making a choice between my people and the colonists.

In this way, I have come to understand the importance of the baggage—of ideas, and feelings—that accompanied the captives into the Golgotha France sent them into. Although the king of France did not recognize this aptitude on their part, most of those caught up in the French slave trade he supported were adults who were able to think and act for themselves. Empire trivialized their history and sought to erase it, even in their own eyes, so that the core of their behavior as *bossales* has come to seem illogical and aberrant. They were, certainly, foreigners when they disembarked in Saint-Domingue. The intent of the authorities and the laws in place was to keep them in that state forever. The goal of the structures of oppression was to exhaust them through mistreatment in order to extract from them a profession of a desire to reduce the distance that separated them from the new world of the plantation. The goal was for them to integrate themselves into the social relations that enabled the functioning of the plantation. These policies of human resource development were not inscribed on untouched wax tablets. They incited significant resistance. That is why we observers can see the constant conflicts between the planters and the descendants of the agricultural laborers reduced to slavery.

The imperial state determined what was to be remembered. The slaves deserved no consideration on the part of the colonial authorities and the subjects of the king. As a result, the data gathered by current historiography offers us too little information on their characteristics. The king, his subjects, and their scribes had no interest in the ordeal the captives went through as they struggled to preserve a basic minimum of human life and mental health.

To be useful to the colonist, the slave had to be a captive who had lost all memory of any life before their transformation into merchandise. The master gained power by accelerating the degradation of the slave's cultural memory and erasing its contours. It is, therefore, impossible to sketch out even a vague tableau of who the captive was on the basis of a literal reading of the documents of the epoch. In order to conserve the few privileges they enjoyed, meanwhile, the strata of emancipated slaves closest to the enslaved masses had to push aside the memory of the ancestors, on their maternal side, and refuse to allow that memory to guide their behavior and practices.

Starting from this observation, I seek to define for those of us living in the present day who the captive in chains during the period of slavery really was. I seek to explain the despicable norms promulgated by the authorities. I move beyond the inevitable absences in the official documents by postulating the existence of a power that slavery had to dominate at all costs, whose stubbornness justified the aggressiveness of the colonial administration. This inexhaustible energy had to be muzzled. What animated the victims of illegitimate colonial power was the quest for autonomy, sovereignty, and the appropriation of one's own responsibilities. What they sought was empowerment. It is their power that explains the promulgation of the Code Noir and the abusive regulations derived from it. The underside of this vile text that sought to strip the slaves naked, to make them ugly, reveals all the beauty and potential of the captives.

The Persistence of the Vocabulary of the Slavers

There is no analytical justification in seeking to explain the history of Haitians on the basis of the concepts brought to the island by the slave traders. The categories *white, emancipated, mulatto, black*, and *slave* were key tools of the slave trade and the slave system. From the beginning they signaled what the captives—the future Haitians—were not. But they also pointed to what their enemies wanted to make sure they would never be. They were names for the very things the captives courageously resisted being. They were the product of a process of sociogenesis that our research must unapologetically seek to overturn. I take it as truth that the tools of thought inherited from the slave system can only perpetuate slavery.

In defining the nature of the state in Haiti, my goal is not to point out the evolution or transformation of the French colonial state into a state that was— in principle—national, modern, and independent, like all the similar entities of the period. That would mean basing my reflections on something that I in fact have to prove first. I also don't want to simply offer a description of the transformation of a colonial state built on slavery into an administrative structure whose vocation was to protect the interests of a nation that did not necessarily exist. For if I did that, I would exit the terrain of empirical observation and turn myself into the spokesperson for those oligarchs who wish to impose their nation building on reality.

The plantation economy disappeared from Saint-Domingue nearly a century before it did from the other islands of the region. In observing the behavior of the workers reduced to slavery and of the *cultivateurs* or *inhabitants* that succeeded them, I show that life in Haiti was built on an economic model that is less celebrated but just as real as that of the commodity-producing plantation (Casimir 1981).[3] Indeed, it is historically more resilient. Nevertheless, the leaders of the country have persistently reproduced the modes of perception that were so useful to the slave traders, the very authors of the invisibility that has made it so difficult to see the contributions of the captives to their own survival. These leaders have always claimed that they knew what was good for the unfortunate people, better than the population knew themselves. In their opinion, the rural population's pursuit of a society centered on itself, and governed by itself, has been the cause of their poverty. They have held on to this opinion despite all the proof to the contrary offered by the comparison between this new Haitian life and the life experienced in colonial times, or that of the enslaved in neighboring colonies. This consistent contradiction between the orientation of the near totality of the population and the ideology of the governing authorities produces the impression of a disjointed political system, incapable of mastering the national situation or of orienting it in any particular direction.

In Europe, the modern state was organized during the same period when the world economy was being constructed. In the colony, in contrast, a power structure that was already established and structured in Europe created the local society and built its economy. The state as it existed in France was introduced through the intermediary of the colonial administration. It was as an already constituted entity whose irruption into the new context needed to be managed. It did not conceive of itself as a creation or an arrangement of local political forces working to accommodate one another in an international environment. The modern Eurocentric state that existed in Haiti after 1804 continued this pattern, and saw itself as penetrating into milieu it considered vulnerable and archaic. The modern state had to implant itself in Haiti, a place that was dependent on Europe and had to remain subject to it, because it was backwards and traditional. The splendors of Versailles and the ports of France were never seen as being linked directly to the crucifixion of their Pearl of the Antilles. Instead, they were held up as destinations to travel toward on the path to the production of material wealth and well-being.

The inhabitants of this third of an island had the knowledge and ability necessary to oppose this continuation of colonialism. They refused the reimplantation of the very mercantilist capitalism that had subjected them during the sixteenth and seventeenth centuries. The key, then, is not to study how a modern colonial state might implant itself in an archaic milieu, but rather to ask how these captives developed their alternative to colonial power. Given that the modern state put them in chains with the goal of consuming every last bit of their laboring energy, it makes little sense to assume that they based their struggle to liberate themselves and break their chains on the deceptive promises of the very institutions they were fighting. To carry out their struggle within imperial political structures would have been a last resort, a last plank of wood floating in the water that they might reach for only after admitting their project had shipwrecked. What seems clear is that, instead, their immediate objective was to create their own modern state, and not to reproduce the colonial and imperial, Eurocentric, and racist state that had existed before.

Only those who, consciously or unconsciously, look at Haiti from the decks of the caravels, or else believe that they can, and even must, place themselves at the helm of an administration built on colonial tradition, will use the same categories as the slave traders to observe Haitian society. Those who disembarked from the boats into the Gehenna of the plantation had two options. They could, like the inhabitants of Haiti in the nineteenth century, resist to the point of shattering their chains. Or they could accept certain abusive constraints they could not escape in the hopes that, at some point barely visible on the horizon, they would attain a quality of life superior to what they could construct with the meager resources at their disposal. This latter path toward a different kind of modern state was ultimately followed in some of the total plantation societies of the Caribbean, with different conditions than that of Saint-Domingue.

The captives came from many different African regions. In their memories, they carried fragmented knowledges from across the Atlantic, their experiences of this crossing and, above all, a consciousness gained from their local history. Thanks to all this, they knew their personhood was not circumscribed by the ignominy invented by the slave traders and their modern colonial state. They used the materials they had gathered over the course of their captivity in colonial territory to construct and organize themselves during the nineteenth century. As I will show, they wove together the weft of their social relations in the midst of the hell of the colonial plantation. Slavery was never able to constrain them so fully that they traveled only within the structures of oppression. As was the case everywhere else in the Caribbean, the memory that guided their behavior over the course of the nineteenth century was comprised of, above all, their own knowledge and experience. They built on the techniques they had used to move beyond the daily oppression they experienced. They used the intangible assets that they had invented, and that only they possessed. But the specific path taken by the Haitians within the archipelagos of the Caribbean is the result of the fact that the structural crises that upended the French metropole at the end of the eighteenth century provoked a cataclysm in the colonial plantations of Saint-Domingue from which they never recovered.

To the extent that "the end of political power is to assure and guarantee the private property of individuals" (2003, 64), a properly Haitian political society would have as its function to protect and develop the knowledge, the experience, and the consciousness that had made it possible to overcome slavery. These were the essential and exclusive property of those who had disembarked as captives in Saint-Domingue. The modern state administration that emerged after 1789, in the form of the French colonial state or the colonial version passed on to the Haitian oligarchs, was incapable of fulfilling this function.

The behaviors of the captives and their descendants were born of a specific memory and can be observed, alongside the destruction of the plantation system. From this I deduce that the captives exercised a political power of the same nature as that of the modern state. There were two different watersheds, sustained by two different rivers of memory, in Haiti: that of the oligarchic governing authorities and that of the captive laboring classes and their descendants. The majority of the population never involved themselves directly in formal politics. But they practiced a form of escape by disobeying the Code Noir and the principles derived from it. The existence was constituted out of epistemological refusal. The researcher who seeks to inhabit the borderland between these worlds in conflict (Mignolo 2015, 59) must begin by recognizing the difference between these two watersheds and their memories, between the worlds of the oligarchs and the agro-industrial workers. The recognition of this difference is the researcher's compass.

A Haitian state would defend the property of Haitians. But, above all, it would defend the specific properties of Haitian being: the people's memory, their identity, the knowledge drawn from their daily experience. To instead accept that Haitian life would be managed through a nominal nationalization of the structures of oppression put in place by colonialism means simply installing oneself at the helm of the slave ship, taking the place of those who previously protected the colonists. The conditions under which the state emerged in Haiti guaranteed that such an approach could not be realized without a tenacious opposition on the part of the insurgent population. They understood that this project sought to deprive them, at all costs, of their civil and political rights. It is not surprising that the misrecognized power exercised by the people refused the projects of the authorities who sought to eradicate the civil and political rights tied to their sovereignty. Seen from the outside, this state or governmental administration sometimes seems strong because it is despotic, but at other times weak because it its powerless.

That said, I cannot think about the state in Haiti, or the Haitian state, without taking into consideration the impact of French colonization. My reflections begin with the Haitian nation's rupture with France. Rather than summarizing the supposedly historical facts that preceded this date or shaped the period of separation, or the presumed steps in the passage from one political environment to another, I seek to conceptualize this rupture. My objective is to analyze the continuities from the eighteenth through the nineteenth century in the obstinate pursuit of the annihilation of the civil and political rights of the population, and how the sovereign people ingeniously managed to exercise their rights despite the barriers constructed by the authorities during and after their liberation from slavery.

In the seventeenth century, the French imperial state possessed Saint-Domingue and leased it to mercantilist, commercial companies in order to assure its peopling and administration. The Royal Company of Saint-Domingue was granted all the prerogatives of sovereignty (Barbé-Marbois 1796, 38). In addition, the archetypal property owner, the *grand blanc*, was usually an nobleman. In 1788, with clouds gathering in the colonial empire's sky, a group of wealthy planters emphasized this in a letter to the king: "Your entire court is Creole, sire; the links of blood have permanently united your nobility *with Saint-Domingue*" (Garran 1797, 1:47; emphasis in the original).

The state created both property owners and slaves. In 1804, nothing changed. The relationships between the landowners and cultivators remained the same. Born out of a victorious army, the new government appropriated the rights or privileges of the French state, validated the property rights that had previously been granted, and seized all the land that was not owned before independence. It enthroned lords of war and gave them control over domains it distributed at will. Simultaneously, the authorities eliminated the free access to land on the part of the nation's residents ("cultivators and citizens attached to the land"), and issued agricultural regulations or rural police codes that allowed them to distribute the landless laborers among various plantations. Since the complete destitution of the landless wasn't enough to convince them to hire themselves out a plantation wage laborers, the authorities combined the hoarding of land with draconian laws punishing what they called *vagabondage*.

From the beginning of European control over the territory, the monopoly over land and the monopoly over labor were inseparable. Over time, the first of these monopolies gained some nuance through the distribution of land to a clientele of favorites. The second gained nuance, similarly, though a bit of liberty tolerated among laborers fixed on a plantation. Nevertheless, the control over land and the control over labor were indissolubly linked.

In fact, the relationship between the monopoly over land and the status of the labor force was the major stumbling block for the social forces put in motion through the general insurrection of 1791. In the wake of independence, there was an attempt to reconstruct this relationship, and the assassination of Emperor Dessalines was a corollary to the earlier death of General Moïse. These two events are rarely compared, for the role of General Pétion in the conspiracy that took Dessalines's life incites enough passion to obscure the entire panorama. But the parallel is worth its weight in gold if, in appreciating the two tragic events, we take note of the different behavior of the masses:

the assassination of the father of the nation provoked a deafening silence, in contrast to the execution of General Moïse.

Conceiving of the slave, the former slave, or the newly emancipated as a social actor requires endowing emptiness with political agency. It means refusing to codify, and think from the perspective of, the logic of the behaviors that defied the authorities and their projects. Toussaint Louverture maintained the colonial approach to using labor, with only small modifications, and defended the metropole's right to conquest. The ascension of Napoléon Bonaparte interrupted the steps Toussaint was taking to construct his sphere of influence, just at the moment when he was completing his mastery of local political forces. Since he did not have to directly confront the retraction of the decree of general emancipation, he sought to negotiate the struggle for general liberty and the struggle for independence without having to make an unequivocal and transparent choice (Wilder 2009b, 34). During this same conjuncture, Moreau de Saint-Méry and the wealthy planters were moving in the direction of supporting some form of independence. But they did so precisely with the goal of containing the impact of general liberty. They had tight links to the slave-trading companies. Toussaint even alluded to taking advantage of the dangerous recourse of the importation of workers in his 1801 Constitution.

The models of the state envisioned by Toussaint as well as the wealthy planters he worked with were tied to a modern Eurocentric vision of the world. This led to the institutionalization of a gap between the planters and the agricultural workers, whether they were called *slaves*, *Africans*, or *cultivators*. The colonial state constructed itself in opposition to the right of the collectivities in formation to flourish with and through their differences. It sought instead to recruit each of its members to participate as individuals in the world economy. The nation-state that succeeded the colonial state also opposed the rights of collectivities, the rights of people, and the rights of ethnicities. The concept of the sovereign people was as foreign to it as it had been to the colonial state. The state, in its administrative structures, remained the affirmation of the rights of property that it dared consider sacred even though it was in fact dealing with pirates' loot.

The governmental powers in Haiti imposed themselves thanks to the prerogatives—rather than rights—conferred on them by the victory of the Indigenous Army over the French expeditionary army. For both these military forces, the right to property did not depend on that property having been acquired legitimately. The power of the state flowed from an appropriation of society's wealth, justified by the control of police power and the capture of state institutions. As in all states governed by the law of the sword, the ascendancy to power of the superior officers in the army took place without the consent of their subordinates.

In 1804, the Haitian nation didn't quite exist. A struggle over the acquisition of civil and political rights unfolded before and after this date. But which social groups carried these demands for rights? Like the nation itself, support for this cause was not born overnight. It was organized in the heart of the hell of the plantation itself. The processes put in place by the authorities have prevented us from seeing this initial process of germination for what it was.

To my knowledge, Vastey is the only public official, except for Dessalines, and the only historian of the nineteenth century to link the life of the slaves of Saint-Domingue to that of the Africans. In fact, he made the connection to Africa the starting point for his reflections ([1814] 2013). I can make out this preoccupation between the lines of the agricultural regulations of the Christophe's kingdom. But the civilizing mission the oligarchy of the North granted itself tended to superimpose itself over the popular will, and obscure it. In the South, Pétion and Boyer, alongside their historians Madiou and Ardouin, declared themselves opponents of slavery but never really escaped the conceptual company of the slave traders.

At the moment of independence, there were three social forces on the island, oriented toward three distinct and dissimilar futures. The administrative machinery of the state of Haiti was controlled by an alliance between two of these forces, whose political and economic interests largely overlapped (Moïse 2009, 34). With the exception of the period of civil war that followed the assassination of Dessalines, this alliance governed during the entire period under observation here. This third force, the decapitated power of the armies of maroons and Africans, hid in the background. I will analyze it later on. The key thing to remember now is that it monopolized and managed economic production without ever needing to seize control of the state.

The local oligarchs of the nineteenth century shared with the leaders of the French Revolution a conception of the role that should be occupied by the majority of the colonial population. They saw them as occupying the depths of society, contained within an empire in which the political hegemony of the sovereign people of the metropole was being assured, hand in hand with the exclusion of the newly emancipated of the colonies. Racism reigned, and mastered even the most radical sectors. The Society of the Friends of the Blacks couldn't envision the "sudden granting of rights to blacks who carried not a single drop of European blood in their veins" (Sala-Molins 1987, 263). Condorcet advocated for a moratorium of at least seventy years before blacks were given "control over their own happiness and authority of their family" (Sala-Molins 1987, 272). On the other end of the spectrum, the racism of Napoléon Bonaparte and the coterie of planters who surrounded him enabled the formulation of a project to exterminate the population. This left the local forces loyal to France with no option other than secession. These circumstances forced the oligarchs to unite against the metropole, and the independence of Haiti went against the current of the designs of the modern nation-states of the nineteenth century. Above all, it defied the intransigent racism of the Christian West.

But the visible leaders of Haitian independence didn't imagine a structure for governance distinct from that of the metropole. They did everything they could to reproduce the modern, secular, imperial, and Eurocentric state. They imposed a few nuances based on the fact that they believed in the equality of the races. But these were overshadowed by a consensus surrounding the superiority of Western civilization. The result was that those who carried exotic forms of thinking and acting—and who happened to largely belong to the black race—became the internal targets of the civilizing mission that the West imagined itself to be undertaking.

The first step in defining the state as it was constituted in 1804 is to examine the relationships between the local oligarchs and the outside world. The state privileged the power of the state. It embodied the institutionalization of an act of secession that was carried out because of relatively minor differences between the local oligarchs and the metropolitan oligarchs. The few reforms proposed by the authorities in 1804 did not change the power *within* the state—the relationship between the authorities and the population, between property owners and cultivators. The control of the Westernized over the barbarians was preserved! The philosophy that justified the presence of slave traders on the beaches of Haiti was still there, largely unchanged.

Just as I would not expect the slave-trading imperial state of the eighteenth century to provide happiness to the slaves of the Pearl of the Antilles, I cannot imagine that a Haitian state administration conceived in this way would demonstrate any principled concern for the cultivators. As it began its journey, the government created in 1804 saw the world the way the slave traders did. It spoke their language. That vision and vocabulary had been hegemonic among the intermediary classes long before independence. The generals of the Indigenous Army who had arrived with the Leclerc expedition took measures to make this vision permanent. Those who were part of Toussaint's government had considered a few correctives aimed at repairing some of the harm suffered by the former captives. But the expeditious elimination of Henry Christophe's lieutenants suggests that this group was a small minority. The two-decades–long interlude represented by Christophe's regime did not significantly change the behavior of the oligarchs who reigned during the nineteenth century. No one thought, as Jaca and Moirans did in the seventeenth century (Sala-Molins 2014), about the need for reparations for the abuses and humiliations suffered by the captives consigned to slavery.

The Journey from Liberty to Slavery

Among the first Haitian historians, the fundamental and unique contribution of Vastey was to establish that it is impossible to understand our history without anchoring it in the trajectories of the African societies of origin and the journey from this source of life, happiness, and comfort into the Gehenna of the plantation. In doing so, Vastey also established his own particular locus of enunciation, an avowal the scholars who followed him over the course of the nineteenth century preferred to carefully avoid. Following the latter example, the majority of urban Haitians ask themselves few questions about their ancestors and, when they do, think only of the European ancestor who—probably by accident or debauchery—initiated their lineage. The fact is that the heroes of Haitian independence have been selected strictly from among the emancipated or Creole ancestors, in a society made up of a majority of *bossales*. The observation made by Jean Price-Mars in the preface to *Ainsi parla l'Oncle* is still relevant today: "As for [the term] 'African,' it is the most humiliating insult that can be addressed to a Haitian" ([1928] 1954, ii). The thinker was referring to the Haitians of the towns. In the memory of the Haitians of the countryside—almost the entire population during the period under study—that is not the case. Africa is called *Guinée*, the paradise to which you will return after a life of tribulations. In this study, when I speak of African traditions, I will use a word that Madiou (1847, 5:107) dates back to the colonial period, referring to *Guinean* traditions.

In the eighteenth century, the Africans that slave ships deposited in Saint-Domingue came to be called *bossales*. In the Romance languages this term was extremely negative, a synonym for *savages* and *barbarians*. But we need to envision the experience of captivity from the perspective of the contingents of victims who crossed from Africa to the Americas. Doing so invites us to revisit the question of how Africa was lived in Haiti during the nineteenth century. Vastey argued that, in a general sense, Africa was less civilized than the West. But he was concerned with how to provide some remedy for the sufferings of the unfortunate survivors of the triangular trade and the Middle Passage. For him, the defining legacy of the French colonists was the indignities and suffering they had inflicted on these survivors.

The writings of Vastey did not convey an elite vocation to the nation, or a stratum within it, that commanded it to help the black race emerge from the shadows. Colombel, his sworn enemy and personal secretary to President Alexandre Pétion, declared at the inauguration of the national high school,

"Haitians, you represent the hope of two-thirds of the known world. . . . You deserve the beautiful name of Regenerators of Africa" (Ardouin 1858, 8:291). The speech was given in 1817, three years after the publication of Vastey's *Système colonial dévoilé*.

Our first historian never suggests, the way that Hannibal Price did near the end of the nineteenth century, that it was in Haiti that "the black man made himself man" (Hoffman 1990, 21). The Haitian intellectual elite granted itself a civilizing mission based on the assumed savagery of Africans and the idea that France was a benevolent benefactor who had pulled them out of it. Vastey opposed Colombel, and differs from most intellectuals of the nineteenth century, on the matter of this supposed generosity of France and its civilizing mission. The difference is rooted in conflicting perceptions of the black people who disembarked in Haiti. The secretary of the kingdom in the North described the Haitians at the cusp of their implantation in the Americas in sharply different terms than the perspective offered at the beginning the twentieth century by Anténor Firmin, one of the greatest minds our nation has ever produced: "The blacks transported to Saint-Domingue had no disposition to immediately evolve toward superior social forms. Not only did they not have the psychological disposition to do so, but in the depths of their being there were often ancestral inclinations that pulled them toward an unfortunate regression" (Firmin 1905, cited in Hoffman 1990, 38). Firmin was describing the black people who inhabited and haunted the universe of the Haitian oligarchs. This characterization enabled the self-proclaimed elite to absolve and forgive the tortures and humiliations their people had suffered. They refused to bear witness to this historical suffering, the way Vastey did. The oligarchs incorporated modern racism into their thinking, convincing themselves that during slavery the minority they continued to represent had been civilized by France, so that they could become the example of the ideal that their fellow Haitians could eventually attain. The tortures, physical suffering, humiliations, and gratuitous abuses experienced by their ancestors were seen as the price they had paid to gain this privilege. The elite was therefore exempted from any need for compassion in the face of the cries of pain and tears of the multitude of sufferers from which they had emerged. They could empty their minds of the memories of all maternal affection and fixate only on the prestige and the power of the paternal male lineage.

In 1789, there were around 400 free people of color who had been born of a father and mother who were both free. These were sometimes called *ingénus* (Sala Molins 2003, 262). Another 20,000 free people of color followed them down the ladder of racial stratification. These 20,000 had a mother or father who was a slave, or had themselves been born into captivity. They interacted every day with the 400,000 slaves. Still, somehow France managed to extract the experience of the conversion from slavery to a life of the emancipated from the memory of the intellectual elite! What differentiated the vision of Vastey from that of Firmin, to cite only two of our greatest intellectuals, was a different way of seeing the Code Noir in which the king of France, the owner of the colony, had declared that the human lives of our ancestors were insignificant.

The reader should not conclude that everyone thought and acted this way at the time. Vastey was one exception, as early as 1814. The Africans themselves obviously didn't think their lives were useless. And they were the majority. The Tupis, Mayas, Aymaras, Iroquois, and other Amerindians, the Chinese, the Indians, the Indonesians, and other Asian peoples, also were not convinced that human life was insignificant. Europeans were and remain the minority in the human race. And we cannot entrench ourselves in the patterns of thought this minority claims is for our own good, despite the fact that they seem all-powerful. This thinking has, after all, not been good for us in Saint-Domingue, or in Haiti, or in Africa. The formatting through which the Haitian oligarchs accepted the Code Noir, without having to admit that they were doing so, is an impressive achievement of French social engineering!

The Code Noir had two different faces. It was, as Vastey noted from the first lines of his work, the cornerstone of the colonial edifice. Within it there exists a *black* who was not seen as emerging from a history without history, but rather from the history of France: "They dropped the black slave on the docks straightaway, at the edge of the ports of Saint-Domingue. Where did he come from? Who brought him there? Why was he a slave? The Code Noir said nothing about any of this" (Sala-Molins 1987, 7). Vastey, the first Haitian historian, refused all the assumptions of this willful blindness, explaining his approach in his *Réflexions sur une lettre de Mazarès*: "I start by defending the cause of the Africans, my ancestors, before discussing the rights of Haytians, my compatriots" (Vastey 1816, 81).

If we begin from the principle that the Code Noir created *slaves*, just as it created *affranchis*, *whites*, and *blacks*, but don't ask any questions about whether it had the right to do so, we are unable to see what Sala-Molins points out—that this is the most monstrous juridical text produced in modern times (2003, viii). The text "succeeded in an incredible performance through which the French monarchy created a law that excluded black slaves from the right to the state of law, defining them solely and uniquely through their lack of juridical existence" (2003, 24).

The king of France divided the inhabitants of the colony into two categories: his subjects and their slaves. The latter were not people in the kingdom that deliberately produced their destitution. They could not own anything that did not belong to their masters (Art. 28). Their body, their time, their spouse, their offspring, their ability to move about in the geography of the colony . . . everything they were or could be was considered the property of their master. They were stamped with an indelible social and juridical inferiority passed on to their descendants. They gained a juridical existence only when they disobeyed. The offences they committed were punished with physical abuse, torture, mutilations, and of course arbitrary killing (Sala-Molins 1987, 72). France invented and systematically reproduced the slave and could not conceive that its creature might liberate itself by disregarding France's supposed right to property, and the dominance of the culture that produced the horror it called the slave.

In this insane world, the 1789 revolution found a positive dimension to the Code Noir, seeing it as necessary for the good functioning of the colony and the security of the colonists. In 1792, the members of the Society of the Friends of the Blacks celebrated the fact that the Code Noir granted the same rights to the mixed-race castes as it did to the white colonists:

> If we do not assure "the political status of the free people of color,"
> we will "expose the white colonists to the insurrections of the slaves,
> because they are only held back by the free people of color; that would
> lead to the destruction of the colonies and the annihilation of French
> commerce." . . . "The Rights of Man . . . are the foundation for the
> French Constitution" but we fear the idea of making the whites vulner-
> able to the insurrection of the Blacks. Here, then, the utility of the *Code
> Noir* is clear: it serves to "whiten" the free people of color and submit the
> Blacks, not for eternity, but for an undefined period. (Bonnemain 1792,
> cited by Sala-Molins 1987, 266)

Sala-Molins chooses to read the history of the Code Noir from the perspective of the enslaved (1987, ix) and compares it to the insights of fifteenth-century Spanish philosophers and the juridical and philosophical principles operating in Europe during the period when it was produced. In his writings, much earlier, Julien Raimond confirmed the role the free people of color played in support of slavery. As for Vastey, he seems to have been inspired by Bonnemain's critiques of slavery, which were published a year before the ratification of the decree of General Emancipation, in writing his *Essai sur les causes de la Révolution et les guerres civiles en Hayti* (1819).

In order to study the functioning of the state in Saint-Domingue and Haiti from the perspective of social majority, I ask a series of questions that I will return to throughout this analysis: What did the hundreds of thousands of captives who disembarked on the docks of the colony think of the Code Noir and the collection of regulations that controlled their behavior? What did they make of the authorities who decreed these regulations and administered the society on the basis of these norms? How did they conceive of liberty in the midst of this kind of society, where they constituted a mass of people considered superfluous, destined to be immolated for the well-being of unknown others? What general ideas did they have about the way authorities governed, and about politics, as they observed the spectacle presented to them by the colonial state? And what intellectual gymnastics would they have had to go through in order to evaluate their journey from their way of life in Africa to that of the Saint-Domingue plantation as a form of progress?

The Inheritor of Louis XIV

Willingly or unwillingly, the emancipated slave silenced the sufferings that had transformed him from captive into slave, and cultivated the memory of the privileges conceded to him by the master. In exchange for these privileges, he became the fulcrum of the slave system. The government that succeeded the colonial administration in 1804 represented a continuation: it did not aim to assure the well-being of the descendants of slaves, but rather that of the descendants of masters. Those descendants and those who replaced them struggled to preserve the way of life that existed before the French Revolution. Their vision of the state was one in which the newly emancipated or cultivators were meant to remain in a position as close as possible to that forced on them by the Code Noir.

Having purged the chiefs of the *bossale* bands, the leaders of the emancipated slaves seized control of the vacant properties. It might seem logical that land concessions were made according to officer's ranks, in relation to their contribution to the eviction of the French and the conquest of the territory. But the "advantages and privileges" beyond "those that flow naturally from the consideration of and in recompense for services rendered to liberty and independence" (1805 Constitution, Art. 3, in Janvier 1886, 31), were not perceived in the same way within all spheres of society. Madiou himself (1847, 6:455) observed that the inhabitants of the mountains and the plains had a much greater right to "consideration of and recompense for services rendered to liberty and independence" than did the urban officers in the army. If Madiou's evaluation is correct, Article 3 of the 1805 Constitution cannot explain or justify the scramble for the land left vacant by the departure of the metropolitan colonists. The dispossession and systematic destitution of the former captives was the result of racism, Eurocentrism, and the egoism characteristic of the intermediary classes of the colonial society. It is important to remember that the country had a maximum of 300,000 to 400,000 inhabitants, that there was plenty of agricultural land, and that the descendants of the cultivators had a certain amount of political power. So this explanation is not sufficient, and we'll have to return to the question.

The glaring inequalities in the formal distribution of the most important resource of the conquered territory—land—laid the unequal and polluted foundations for the social project to come. Independence did not modify, and did not even claim to modify, the country's internal structure. It did not introduce new norms of social justice. The end of slavery, which was a condition for the recruitment of warring forces, didn't upend the class hierarchy. Colonial society was simply decapitated, and the highest-ranking members of the Indigenous Army replaced the wealthy white planters and the colonial administration. The right to decree laws and apply them was granted based on a role in the victory over the French metropole, and not on the consensus of the insurgents or a consideration of their demands. From the moment Toussaint issued his regulations on plantation work, a first draft of a system of militarized agriculture, the cultivator was seen as a kind of soldier. The state created in 1804 made this conception its own. In other words, the government system did not possess a political class. It granted itself the right over life and death in order to defend what the military leaders called the fatherland.

The will to power of the Indigenous Army that defeated Leclerc's expeditionary forces served as the axis for the construction of the state after 1804. The leaders of the wars of independence defeated the French by making use of the natural right to use force in defense of the existence of the members of a nation, and of their right to exercise their free will and self-determination. Other natural rights—to security and life, to property, to well-being and happiness—were all eclipsed by the natural right to self-defense in the face of a threat of extermination. Afterwards, positive law did not immediately reflect the rights of individuals, but rather translated the right of the state and the fatherland to its own self-defense. Justice, based on the rights of man, became secondary, and administrative decisions became unassailable. The reason of state was not founded on any principle or superior authority.

The seizure of power by the Indigenous Army meant that the descendants of the *bossales*, the Africans, retained their status as foreigners and were excluded from the structures of power. The Code Civil did not address private life. Those who governed, along with the legal structures they created, took no interest in the *lakou, plaçage*, relationships between husbands and wives, hierarchies based on age, rights to succession, indivisible collective property, the *combites*, relations of reciprocity, rural markets, religious traditions, and all the institutions that managed interpersonal relations. To the extent that they paid attention to them at all, it was to decry and attack them, sensing danger in the way they seemed to tolerate or promote forms of local autonomy in opposition to the central executive power. All the institutions of rural Haiti were essentially invisible in the picture of sovereignty created by the military conquest of the colony carried out through the War of Independence. The productive citizen (the inhabitant), the male citizen who headed a household (*le placé*), the commercial citizen (*la madan sara*), the working citizen (the farmer or livestock breeder, the fisherman, the artisan) were nowhere to be found in the postindependence legal codes. They had to be transformed in order to push them into the law, so they could be married, hired, educated, and educated through one form or another of colonization.

The oligarchs expressed their colonial mentality as they developed a project to structure Haiti's society on the basis of a model contested by the majority of the population. A few families obtained a substantial patrimony from the Indigenous Army, in eternal thanks for some dubious service offered by an ancestor during the wars of independence. Other families proclaimed themselves the legal inheritors of metropolitan colonists and worked to get these claims recognized. Brandishing their property titles and demanding respect for the lineage that connected them to the metropolitan colonists, these families paraded their filiation with the beneficiaries of the generosity of King Louis XIV (of the French state). From their perspective, the rupture with the metropole should have no impact on the rights of property claimed by the French sovereign.

After Dessalines's assassination, France's original right to Saint-Domingue remained the foundation for the approach taken to land ownership. The Haitian oligarchs seized power, claiming a lineage with France, one which the French administration itself didn't recognize, and which the Club Massiac contested virulently. They shrouded this claim in legitimacy. Despite their knowledge of these objections, these oligarchs founded their social preeminence on the idea that they belonged, at least culturally, to the world of the Sun King.

The French Revolution, the general insurrection of the enslaved, and the conflicts that devastated the country over the course of nearly two decades seemingly had no significant impact on the mentality of the colonial and Haitian oligarchs. The bipolar social structure (property owners vs. cultivators), along with the justifications for this structure, were transposed into Haitian society, despite the fact that the collective of captives had been fighting against this structure for years.

The two sections of the Haitian oligarchy shared the perceptions of the conquering state—despotic, modern, secular, imperial, and Eurocentric—that had implanted colonialism in the country.[4] In Saint-Domingue and then in Haiti, the governing authorities and the administrative machinery of the state did not base their management of the country's resources on a mandate received from subjects or citizens tied together in any kind of collectivity. Like the colonial government, these new authorities did not perceive the existence of a collectivity of citizens. They appropriated the country's resources and the right to manage them without developing a corresponding political project. From the perspective of the agro-industrial laborers, there was no significant change in the form of state administration. They were still surrounded by a colonial model. They were able to impose some modifications, but these were not reflected formally in positive law. Still, the laborers used their own ideas, building on the struggle between classes in the colony, to resist and push back against the machinery of the government, wresting control over the management of the economy from it.

The independence of Haiti was not the result of an incompatibility between the economic interests of colonial France and those of the generals of the Indigenous Army. There were fewer differences between them regarding the organization of labor than is often thought. The divergences that did exist had to do with issues of practical expediency and opportunism, and were not expressions of principled positions. The generals of the Indigenous Army generally opposed the use of physical abuse to discipline the agricultural laborers, though there were numerous exceptions. The historian Vertus Saint-Louis shares an observation attributed to Dessalines to the effect that black people were lazy and would only work under physical constraint (Saint-Louis 2006, 159). But generally speaking, both before and after 1804, the oligarchs agreed on the necessity of keeping the cultivators prisoners on the plantations, constraining their movement and the possibility of their acquisition of land as much as possible.

Both before and after 1804, the oligarchs and urban sectors remained ardent promoters of the plantation system. Given that they defined themselves as defenders of the plantation and of large-scale landownership, it is not surprising that alongside the authorities the urban dwellers established themselves comfortably as inheritors of a colonialism that they had little to complain about. Made up of free people of color and free blacks from the urban sectors, the oligarchs set themselves up in opposition to the laboring classes. In the process, they carried colonial despotism into independent Haiti.

The antislavery position of officers surrounding Toussaint do not make of him a paladin of natural right or the rights of nations, even though the philosopher Nick Nesbitt remains convinced that, for the sector led by the governor-general, the right to liberty was more important than the prerogatives of the right to private property (Nesbitt 2008, 161). It remains to be proven that rather than simply being a weapon in the political conflict, this posture in favor of general liberty was based on a defense of natural rights, as Toussaint Louverture himself affirmed. On the one hand, he rejected the self-management of the agro-industrial enterprises proposed by Polvérel, which I will return to in chapter 7. The commissioner, in 1793, "wished to organize society in such a way that the unequal distribution of resources undermined Liberty and Equality as little as possible, and didn't lead to anarchy or the dissolution of the political body" (Debien 1949, 305). On the other hand, Toussaint considered it undeniable that the success of "large-scale agriculture was the best guarantee for the liberty of the blacks" (Lacroix 1819, 1:324). As a result, the liberty of the blacks remained in the vice grip of the colonial matrix of power—that is, in the monopoly over property and its corollaries: the control of political authority, of the economy, of knowledge and subjectivity itself (Mignolo 2015, 46).

Toussaint Louverture's social project was based on the existence of a laboring class made up of the dispossessed. During the revolution, the American colonists avoided like the plague any expression of abolitionist sympathies. The core characteristics of the structures of authority taken over by the new leaders in 1804 remained. They followed the example of the colonial state, creating a structure situated outside the local political community, or more specifically, an existence that refused to acknowledge the existence of such a political community within the territory they governed. From its beginnings, the Haitian state structure was limited to the army (Madiou 1847, 3:154). Article 4 of the Constitution of 1805 declared that "the armed forces fundamentally obey, and no armed group can deliberate." The Haitian Revolution, then, institutionalized itself without the kind of political body (Bellegarde-Smith 1985, 180) that is the prerequisite for any form of lived citizenship.

In these circumstances, the only kind of citizenship that could bud was ceremonial. It was experienced only as an analogy. The regulations, constraints, rights, and privileges that governed social relations were not derived from the local condition of individuals in the nation. The political and economic history of the spheres of Haitian leadership began locked within a modern, colonial vision, belonging to the epoch of primitive capital accumulation. But the militancy of the laboring classes successfully contested the monopolization of land, which therefore lost its function as capital. This property instead served as loot, captured in war, awaiting the foreign capital that could make it flourish. In the interregnum, it served as political leverage in the attempted ongoing subjection of the cultivators, without any plan for local capital accumulation.

Independence institutionalized the common denominator among the oligarchic forces who oversaw the secession of 1804—that is, their commitment to surviving in the face of the threat of the project of extermination

Napoléon asked his expeditionary army to carry out. The need for the defense of the territory from foreign invasion was used to legitimize and protect the monopoly of the army and the servants of the state over landed property. The deeper changes in the social order, before or after 1804, were not the result of the initiatives of the oligarchs of landed property or those of the military bureaucracy.

The victory of the Indigenous Army over the French made them a conquering army and not a revolutionary army. They seized the power of the colonial state, appropriating what Louis XIV had created at the end of the seventeenth century, complete with its foundational political structure and despotic administration. Given the circumstances of the French defeat, the structures of authority emerged weakened by the struggles for independence. It was easy to see that the tools of domination were increasingly powerless in the face of the profound reconstruction of socioeconomic structures that was underway. Popular participation in social conflicts, including the movements led by Goman and Acaau, only deepened the fracture between the oligarchs and the masses.

The authorities could not maintain a professional army over the long term. And the national executive branch wasn't able to deploy the means of coercion of the colonial state, and therefore could not overcome the barely concealed resistance of subordinates. Those in power watched, powerless, as their own soldiers left the garrisons and established themselves as autonomous cultivators or inhabitants. Incapable of controlling the economy of the country, they persisted in preserving an unmodified version of Louis XIV's vision of the population, even though this perspective no longer had any meaning for the peasantry.

Despite its inability to manage national life, the conquering state retained its status as the origin of the collectivity, the midwife of the nation, simply because it managed to keep foreign colonial armies at bay. It also unintentionally facilitated the melding together of the ethnic groups that composed the population. The gap separating the privileged from the masses was the result of a lack of reciprocal economic relationships, deepened by a reciprocal refusal to try and create such relationships. The colony of Saint-Domingue and the administration of the state of 1804 were imperial organizations through which the lords of war dictated laws and granted themselves the right over the life and death of their subjects. The difference is that in the second case, the lords of war preserved their political prestige without being able to sustain it through the deployment of local troops. They watched, unable to do anything else, as their army transformed itself into a collective of inhabitants and the old sugar colony became a new kind of settler society. The result was the emergence of an antislavery, antiracist, anticolonialist, and antiplantation state (M. Hector 2006a, 7) that wore, like a hat, a Eurocentric, proslavery, racist, colonialist, and proplantation government.

Intermediaries and Cultivators

In Haiti, we are taught in school to perceive power relations—visible and codified political relationships—using the same notions that were used by France to set up the colony of Saint-Domingue. These notions, older than the colony itself, are a kind of condensed version of the history of France and the factors that shaped that history. If I don't question this, I accept French history as my own and marry the objectives pursued by this mother country. I define myself, for better or worse, as a French person of the tropics, a "Haitian despite myself"—as Vastey described Pétion (1819, 136).

It is certainly true that a small number of Haitians came from France. But the vast majority of the population came from Africa. School doesn't teach us how to see the world the way they did. And so we lose the perspective of the vast majority of our ancestors. It does not teach us how to distinguish our world from that of the former colonial power, or to even recognize our respective borders. As a result, this education pushes me to perceive myself, as well as my ancestors, as wax tablets into which France pressed its indelible stamp, deeper and deeper each day. The further I get from my ancestors, the more I dilute myself into French culture and civilization. My schooling destines me to be absolutely anyone other than who my ancestors were.

Yet the French arrived quite late in my family home, and they didn't come in through the front door. Those who entered came from the disinherited sectors of metropolitan society. If I think of myself as the descendent of *bossales*, coupled with some sailor or peasant fleeing the vicissitudes of their European village, and I examine Saint-Domingue and Haitians from this perspective, my history and that of my people take on a very different light. I begin from the understanding that I inhabit a double border: that which divides the world of my ancestors from that of metropolitan France, and that which divides the world of the disinherited of Africa and Europe from that of colonial modernity. By recuperating the disinherited of Europe and using them for its own ends, Europe co-opted many of my ancestors. That is why I will pay attention only to the encounter between the African and European worlds in Saint-Domingue and Haiti.

The Memory of the Conversion into Merchandise

Once I distance myself from the vision of Louis XIV and the European nobility and refuse to content myself with imagining that I just suddenly appeared on the coasts of the Americas as nothing but the kind of chattel they called *bossales*, I can reconstruct my origins and the circumstances of my birth. On this basis, I can understand the difference between my social group and the tiny minority of oligarchs France left behind as it withdrew from the colony.

In order to scale the wall of silence by which the West in general and the Code Noir in particular trivialized the process that brought slaves to the plantations, I must retrace the broad outlines of our journey from the villages of the coast or the interior of Africa to the concentration camps of America. I base this reconstruction on the reflections of Claude Meillassoux (1986), supplemented by the admirable and more recent studies of historians, notably John K. Thornton (1993), Terry Rey (1998), and Christina Mobley (2015). Their work demonstrates the range and complexity of the African societies that were the source for the agricultural workers carried to the colony by the slave trade, and it offers us a way to gain a more diverse understanding of the behavior of the captives in the hell of Saint-Domingue.

The human merchandise that disembarked into the slave market of the colony had difficulty imposing themselves as significant social actors. To understand their experience, we need to examine the variety of contexts that served as the backdrops for their experiences, the interpersonal relationships they developed with one another, and the other determinants of the behaviors they developed within the plantation system. Unfortunately, the accounts written by their enslavers and executioners are not particularly useful for gaining this understanding. But I see nothing to indicate that this mass of workers resisting their enslavement ever doubted their humanity or dignity, despite the fact that they lived in unimaginable circumstances.

The misdeeds of this racist, slaving modernity contrast strikingly with the responses of the victims of these abuses. Despite their vulnerability, they defied the course of a history that still refuses to take note of their achievements. By following the captives from Africa to Saint-Domingue, on their journey through the structures that worked to enslave them to their successful conquest of liberty, I gain insight into the routes and means they used to reconstruct themselves, to re-exist, and, by re-existing, to invent a new society. Following this itinerary leads us to the question of how to understand their form of sovereignty, which I consider in the final three chapters.

From this point of departure, I describe the feats of these wretched of the earth, their will and the power to act, as well as the beauty and excellence of the result they obtained, with great effort and with the few resources they were able to gather. Some may consider their achievements shockingly modest. But I show the sophistication of the process through which a new life emerged, one built outside the dictates of the imperial powers, as well as the many possibilities created by the oppressed in the midst of terrible circumstances of exploitation and wars of extermination.

In order to situate the memory of the crossing of the Atlantic and the arrival of the *bossales* within the history of Haiti, it makes sense to start by clarifying exactly how and why my ancestors' odyssey has been erased from my own. The colonial working class gained consciousness of its own situation by articulating a response to three aspects that defined the behavior of the French: first, the colonist's need to produce and reproduce captives; second, their project of converting captives into slaves in order to reproduce their slavery and captivity; and finally, the need to annul their natural reproduction in order to intensify and maximize their exploitation. This final exigency led inevitably to a botched process of acculturation. The need to produce and reproduce the Pearl of the Antilles as quickly as possible required an intensification of the slave trade and the destruction of the processes of institutionalization that might have served to support natural reproduction among the population. This in turn meant the acceleration of the process of the absorption of the new arrivals and their required conversion into slaves. Community, family, and women themselves represented potential obstacles to the development of the modern economy within a plantation system in full expansion, because they obstructed the disaggregation of labor and reduced the fragility and vulnerability necessary for the smooth functioning of the labor market.

The shining wealth of the Pearl of the Antilles did not protect the majority of the population from living through the horrors of the slave trade and slavery and its impact on daily life. The development of this human traffic depended on a disdain for human life on the part of those who managed the system, a disdain that surpasses all understanding. But the idea that the victims of this traffic and their descendants might erase their unspeakable suffering from their collective memory is even more extraordinary. How are we to explain that the emancipated slaves who were my ancestors, walled within the small towns and villages of the colony, were able to exclude this horrifying tableau from their memory and establish such a distance between themselves and the captives consigned to slavery who were their own ancestors? How did this pain evaporate from the feelings and thought of the intermediary classes of the colony?

In his 1814 *Le système colonial dévoilé*, Vastey asked his compatriots to pay attention to the martyrdom of their ancestors. Referring to the young people the slave traders forced to journey across the Atlantic, he wrote: "Try and imagine the deplorable situation of five to six hundred unfortunates in this state, laden with chains, kidnapped by means of violence, deceit, theft, and a thousand other equally shameful methods. Consumed with grief, their hearts filled with bitterness and despair, never more will they see the land that gave them birth, never again will they see their kinsfolk, their friends. All the bonds that could attach them to life are broken, destroyed forever" (trans. Bongie 2014, 94–95). The people the colonial empires sought to reduce into slavery were captured in village societies that for centuries had been organized autonomously to satisfy their way of life. Merchant slavery used military tools or pillaging bands from aristocratic slaving societies to regularly raid peaceful, self-sufficient settlements. From there, the captured villagers were sold to slave traders who lived off the distribution of captives to the slave societies on the other side of the Atlantic. It was these societies that turned them into slaves.

The desocialized captives lost their links to a network of kinship relations that in their lives in Africa had welcomed and protected them, stimulated them to success, and consoled them in their sufferings. Removed from all frames of reference, the captives were deprived of all connections with a civil society that might provide recourse in case of difficulties or of conflicts and fights with their peers. They found themselves completely at the mercy of their owners, whether they were raiders, slave traders, or planters. They were living on borrowed time, absolute strangers, a consciousness with no frame of reference, a will with no capacity to act concretely.

If we follow Vastey, we can imagine young people in the flush of youth, sequestered by these bandits, walking with chains on their feet, hundred and hundreds of kilometers to the island of Gorée, to Ouidah, Cape Verde, Cabinda, Luanda, or other slave-trading ports; humiliated, dying of hunger and thirst; discovering new landscapes, unknown populations, strange languages; witnessing the murder of one of their companions each day of the journey; terrorized and constantly experiencing their extreme vulnerability and fragility; without recourse, without family, all alone! Let us imagine them discovering the ocean for the first time, pulled up onto unknown ships, piled like sardines in the holds, bathed, fed, taken out into the sun, locked away according to a rhythm determined by those who had stolen them! Let us imagine this long journey on this river without banks, the disembarkation in Saint-Domingue or some other nightmarish island, their distribution to the displays of the slave markets, where they were touched and humiliated by sellers and buyers! Let us imagine them being branded, like oxen! Let us imagine all the effort it took to try and understand the reasons for all this unthinkable and unending humiliations! It is not that difficult to have some idea of the suffering, sadness, sense of revolt, and infinite degradation experienced by these young people who, a few months earlier, were cavorting with gazelles in the African savannah. I don't know how forgetting gets invented, but I believe that those who survived this apocalypse must, one way or another, have communicated their sense of confusion and dismay and passed on the feeling of these unbelievable tribulations to their offspring.

The facts are there: some witnesses of African descent such as Moreau de Saint-Méry and Julien Raimond do not express this pain, while Vastey, their contemporary of the same stock, describes it poignantly in his famous work *Le système colonial dévoilé* (1814). The three authors I've mentioned are all of mixed ancestry, but their specific individual trajectories can probably help illuminate why each expressed their experiences as they did. But beyond the vision each of them had, beyond their distinct actions and personal choices, they circulated within social groups that were built, one way or another, out of this material of remembrance. The social groups they were a part of could not avoid building their thinking on the basis of these traumatic experiences. Still, we need to understand how collective memory was split apart in its treatment of the same empirical reality.

The captive integrated herself into colonial society by becoming a slave, joining the social class that the economy was built on. She was the raw material for this modern form of social engineering, the sociogenesis of the colonial black person. To the extent that she succeeded in withdrawing from this transformation into a slave, she loosened the vice of colonization and colonialism by conserving and developing the very specificities that made her an individual who had to be painstakingly re-engineered into a docile servant. This transformation, and her resistance to it, were concomitant processes, each one as important as the other.

> In the slave societies of the Americas, therefore, the captives were born and reproduce themselves far away from the environment in which they were originally put in chains, in the midst of commercial relations rather than at the breast of women and families that accompany humans from the moment of their conception to their birth and adult life. It follows that captive women lost their attributes as women and were subjected to a radical de-feminization. Their function in the reproduction of human beings and the collection of institutions that normally surround and regulated this production and reproduction of social life were held in check. Caught between women slaves stripped of their sex and distant mothers stripped of their children. (Depestre, cited by Meillassoux 1986, 303)

To the extent that the natural reproduction of the population rooted itself in the colonized territory, there developed an opposition at the heart of the plantation system between private and community life on the one hand and life as a laborer on the other. This seemingly was the goal of the architects of this artificial society. Through the statutes of the Code Noir, the colonial administration pursued the well-being of the subjects of the king through the consumption and devouring of the captive workers (Hurbon 1987, 214). It didn't take long for the captives to learn that a colonist could mutilate or kill them at leisure, just to send a message to their peers. Similarly, Napoléon Bonaparte could order General Richepanse to massacre the insurgents of Guadeloupe and General Leclerc to exterminate the population of Saint-Domingue in order to assure the stability of the French colonial empire.

The captive had to learn how to survive under this sword of Damocles, how to survive as disposable merchandise, as something that could easily be sacrificed (Mignolo 2015, 226), destined only to sustain the greater well-being of the French and the French state. The basis for his life as a human, and his natural reproduction, were in conflict with what he must do to survive as a slave. The latter took place in the midst of the public sphere, while his private life delimited a community he built for himself. France needed him only as a laborer, and worked hard to convert him into a zombie (Hurbon 1987, 296).

If, unlike the captives themselves, I erase the arrival of the merchandise-laborers in Saint-Domingue from my interpretation, and disregard their individual histories, I will construct their trajectory in an entirely different way. Moreau de Saint-Méry celebrated the exploits of his motherland, of how it enslaved people and brought happiness to the colonists. He emphasized the generosity with which they granted emancipation to the slaves. For him, the worker was by definition a slave. It is important to uncover the quality of the social technology that the French state put into place to justify the slave trade. But more crucial for me is to understand the genesis, in the mind of the emancipated among the colonized, of this feeling of pride and admiration in the face of the magnanimous behavior of the planter!

> The first observation inspired by the existence of this class (the emancipated), writes De Saint-Méry, is that it was in *France* that laws were made for the maintenance of the servitude of Africans in America; . . . it was *France* that sought to appropriate the products of the commerce of the slave trade, which the colonies themselves were banned from doing directly; the gains from this exclusive privilege went to France. The colonists owed to themselves alone the idea of emancipating slaves, of this happy pact that restored the rights of humanity to a slave, giving the master a way of doing what was right, of expressing a feeling of generosity that profited the slave and added to the political strength of the colonies. (Ardouin 1853, 1:75; emphasis in the original)

It is certainly not surprising that Julien Raimond and Vastey rebelled against such an absurd expression of gratitude. But the most important thing is to remember that the contradictions between these individual choices were part of a set of experiences common to all the groups present in the colony. Executioners and assistant executioners, victims and terrorized witnesses, those who acquiesced, rebelled, or remained indifferent, all lived in the same world, though they interpreted and codified it according to their own personal choices. Whether they wanted it to be or not, this shared world became the substratum that created a tenacious and deep cohesion underlying the divergences that developed.

What interpolates the researcher is the question of what propelled these divergences. How was it that different social groups were able to either exclude or include the collective memory of these violent traumas? That may be the unknown variable in the construction of a national society like ours, born of circumstances that made impossible the development of a harmonious conviviality between all who comprised it. The production of forgetting among the oligarchs, started by De Saint-Méry and the Haitians in spite of themselves, led in one direction. The reactivation of the painful memories that propelled Vastey and his companions in struggle, not to mention the immense majority of the population, moved in the opposite direction, toward the institutionalization and structuring of our specific social relations, which held and still hold the key to the organizing how we live together.

The Citizens of the Nineteenth Century

The slave traders systematically constructed the vulnerability of our ancestors. In this book, I describe the path they took to defend themselves. The true scale of their opposition to the slave system became clear as day when they organized the 1791 general insurrection in the Northern Plain. The goal of this movement was to appropriate their being, and therefore their bodies and their thoughts. It contested the racialization of social relations that was the foundation for their transformation into slaves. By fighting for the gradual reduction, and ultimate elimination, of the physical violence used against them, the captive workers attacked the central tool used to extract labor from them: torture. At the same time, they contested the commodification of their being and their labor, as well as their reproduction through the slave trade.

No modern system can obtain the commodification of the labor force without dispossessing them of all their means of existence other than their physical labor. In the regime of plantation slavery, torture fulfilled the function usually served by the salary (Casimir 2001, 91). When corporal violence, whether real or virtual, was removed as a possibility, the plantation lost its available labor force. In economies where the planters and the state were able to conserve a monopoly over the means of subsistence, they negotiated the hiring of workers, at varying intensities, based on their capacity to starve the population they had rendered destitute. An embryonic form of salary gradually replaced torture. But the laborers had room to maneuver to the extent that they could thwart the precarity imposed on them. They could therefore reduce their total dependence on being hired into the capitalist system by optimizing their own use of the very resources that maintained this system.

The conflict between the *grands blancs* and the property owners of color, along with the general insurrection of 1791, created a crisis for the plantation and large-scale agriculture in Saint-Domingue. From the beginning, the main preoccupation of the workers facing the accelerating dismantling of the organizational structure of the plantations was to produce the food necessary for their daily subsistence (Debien 1974, 360; Dubois 2004b, 186). The traditional historiography focuses on the conflicts between the wealthy property owners and administrators, and offers little information on the needs of the vast majority of the invisible people who had to furnish themselves with daily nourishment. But this need created a concomitant one: that of constructing institutions that could guarantee the production of food, and more broadly their own reproduction as human beings.

The army and the colonial authorities conceived of the agricultural laborers liberated by the decree of 1793 as *nouveaux libres*—newly freed. While the machinery of domination formulated its agricultural policy on the basis of such illusions, these so-called newly freed acted on the basis of ideas of liberty formed in the midst of the African villages where they had received their earliest education, and on the basis of experiences and knowledge accumulated on the plantation. As the revolutionary crisis accelerated, these ideas of liberty became more and more operational. These people had not been initiated into the idea of liberty as defined by the environment of the modern, colonial, capitalist plantation. Under the noses of the colonial authorities, they built institutions meant to guarantee their daily life and natural reproduction, within completely autonomous new communities. They overthrew the processes of individuation carried out by the slave trade, which were the very foundation for the creation of the capitalist society.

The terms of the conflict didn't change after 1804. The government authorities and the property owners squabbled over the appropriation or distribution of the land that remained vacant, while the newly freed focused on the immediate needs of their communities in formation. They obtained small concessions from the established authorities, or else carried out their own steady dismemberment of the domains where property owners sought to hold them as prisoners. They did so by occupying the land in ways that didn't alarm the owners or provoke a hostile reaction from them.

The political militancy of the former captives in the conquest of national independence made it impossible to reinstitute a regime of forced labor, despite the purges carried out against their leaders. Such a regime would have had to have the material and ideological resources necessary to separate out a privileged stratus of commanders, militia members, and police from among the subjected masses, as had been done in colonial times. That was not possible, and the agricultural regulations and police codes promulgated one after another throughout the entire nineteenth century could never be applied. As a result, the authorities in power made the control of private property the center of their management of the political system. In this sense, they maintained the colonial tradition. But they couldn't control the economic system.

In the wake of the French Revolution, starting in 1793 but especially after 1804, the governing institutions could no longer create sufferers by converting people into slaves or pseudo-slaves (cultivators!). They could not influence the communities who now had the means to situate themselves outside the liberal capitalist system by reinforcing the solidarity between their members based on relationships of reciprocity. The authorities permitted themselves to consider these communities marginal, even though the universe they created actually gained greater economic and social power than anything the authorities offered.[5]

The only thing the authorities could do, then, was to manipulate the political sphere but without the support of the majority of the population. Since you can't organize a republican environment without citizens, the authorities imported the concept of "active citizens" established by the civil commissioners of the French Republic into their October 12, 1792, proclamation: "All free men who are twenty-five years old, property owners, or lacking property who have lived in the colony for two years, and paying any kind of tax, will be considered active and eligible citizens" (*Débats* 1795 94).

In France, both passive and active citizens were born from the collective of the king's subjects. They were all part of one nation. In Saint-Domingue, subjects of the king had been brought together with foreigners reduced to slavery. Transforming the latter into citizens-by-decree did not create the kind of historical relationships that united the French subjects of the king, who in any case had transformed their political regime into a republic. The definition of the active citizen in Pétion's letter to Marion, which I discuss below, highlights the role of the *formerly freed* (those who were free before the decree of abolition) in governmental policy. But, as I have already mentioned, this group was not able to constitute itself as a political body.

The definition of active citizens institutionalized a latent state of war between the government, comprised of the army and allied with the property owners, and the dispossessed population. Starting in 1793, agricultural workers took all necessary measures to create and reproduce their communities by inventing forms of access to and use of the land that avoided a confrontation with property owners. In this way they constructed their internal sovereignty and separated it from the social mechanisms and prejudices inherited from the Code Noir. The government, however, was not founded on popular sovereignty. When the population did solicit government intervention, they never expressed a willingness to modify their own communal structure. And the myopia of the ruling oligarchs made it difficult to codify any form of popular participation in political life that did not rupture the duality of the system.

The New Relationship of Social Forces

The intermediary classes of Saint-Domingue were made up of people of African descent born of *free* parents and of *freed* black and mulatto slaves. They established their status, way of life, and interests on the basis of the distinctions made by the Code Noir between those who were free and those who were not. As they carried out their daily tasks, these intermediaries did not question the racialization of human relations they were tasked with enforcing. They received instructions and concepts from France that were meant to manage the artificial society that had been invented. Using these tools of knowledge, the intermediaries carried out a process of social engineering that sought to transform the captive into slave. They worked as overseers, militia members, police, low-level administrators, and artisans. They forced the slaves to work, chased after deserters and fugitives, fought the brigands and armed bands, pillaged and destroyed the *doko*, executed the sorcerers and burned their temples and their fetishes, and carried out punishments, mutilating and torturing delinquents.[6] It was by doing so that these intermediaries earned their belonging to the world of the free.

The Baron de Vastey contested the distinction between *free* and *slave*. In his opinion, "the so-called free may not have had specific masters, but the white public was their master" ([1814] 2013, 14). He nevertheless conceded that the customs, habits, traditions, knowledge, and spiritual practices of the captives deserved to be extirpated because they were part of a civilization inferior to that of the West.

Vastey helps us see that the one group that never had to be liberated was the white colonists. No one could confuse them with the freed slaves. They were the ones who decided who was a *slave*, a *deserter*, a *fugitive*, a *brigand*, a member of an *armed band*, a *sorcerer*. They decided what counted as a superstition. They determined what punishment the delinquents deserved. And in both the colony and the former colony, the liberty and equality of individuals—whether freed or captive—evolved within the prison of colonial, modern thought. The limits imposed by the colonial matrix (Quijano 2008, 181) restrained liberty, even for a thinker like Vastey. It was impossible to emancipate oneself from the control by the white public if one conceded the superiority of the latter's civilization.

In other words, the preponderance of the white public in public life forced the intermediary classes or the emancipated slaves to participate in (1) the centering of all power within the colonial state, to the exclusion of all other institutions; (2) the task of controlling labor and production on the slave plantation; (3) the choice of using the slave trade for the reproduction of the labor force, rather than natural reproduction; and (4) the enthroning of race as the basis of all socially significant classification. Racial identities were institutionalized within the context of this matrix, which determined the conditions of material and spiritual life. They legitimated colonial exploitation and violence and subordinated all other potential sources of subjectivity. The social order based on the sacred character of private property was unchangeable, and those who were foreigners to this structure of power—the slaves and the intermediaries—were not free to act or to think on their own terms.

The result was an unbridgeable gap between the colonists, the emancipated slaves, and the captives reduced to slavery. There was no logical way these three broad categories of colonial society could share the same concepts of liberty and equality. There were so many social fractures in the colony: conflicts between wealthy whites and the poor whites and mulattoes, the interminable polemics between Moreau de Saint-Méry and Julien Raimond, and the profound hatred the *bossales* felt toward the black Creoles. Inequality and subordination were indispensible to the very definitions of *white* and *black*, which were foundational concepts for the practice of colonialism and coloniality.

In his justification for the killing of the chiefs of the bands, cited in the first chapter, Ardouin emphasized this rupture. He candidly noted that Pinchinat, Montbrun, and Bruno, who were all mulattoes, conspired to assassinate Halaou, a *bossale*, not because of a hatred of blacks, but because of the sorcerers who accompanied him, the disturbance they caused to public tranquility, and the obstacles their fetishism posed to the process of civilizing the masses. Ardouin supported his argument by pointing out the several black generals—Toussaint, Dessalines, and Christophe—who were authors of similar crimes carried out for exactly the same reasons. His reasoning concretely establishes that race and ethnicity belonged to distinct realities. Race emerged from a modern, colonial process of sociogenesis, one in which individuals are seen as being born naked. Ethnicity is the fruit of the evolution of communities. Extirpating the African nations or ethnicities from our social future was a way of firmly locking these societies within the coloniality of knowledge and power.

Ardouin didn't have a problem with the fact that Halaou and the other chiefs of the bands opposed the harshness of slavery. But he refused them the right to do so in the company of their sorcerers. What he wanted was for their protests against slavery to take the appropriate form, preferably issued in Parisian French rather than in their African languages or the local Kreyòl language. They should, he suggested, have attacked the way they were being treated as slaves without questioning the process that made them slaves in the first place. It is in this latter dimension, where the slave is produced, that acceptable forms of behavior, language, and thought are established. The logic of the colony could not be changed, and the discussion must not move beyond its confines. The modern world was made up, on the one side, of whites, blacks, and people of mixed ancestry, all civilized, and on the other, of savages and barbarians. The latter groups entered into social existence only by civilizing themselves as demanded by the Code Noir. Halaou and his sorcerers, on the other hand, changed the terms of the conversation (Mignolo 2009, 4). That was as unacceptable for Ardouin as it was for the generals whose accounts he shared.

Unfortunately for the strata of the oligarchy in command from 1791 to 1804, the captive population had the opportunity to break their chains. In the process, they realized that they were subsisting without the support or the recognition of the authorities on the plantations and without the comprehension of the colonial powers. More and more, they came to control their own work and what they produced. They ended the slave trade as a form of production of workers, and eliminated the need to organize patriarchal families or to subordinate themselves to the colonial state. Above all, they were able to display their own forms of identity without any restriction. Starting with the Bois Caïman ceremony, their actions were based on their own feelings and experiences, and on the increasing visibility of their equality with the supposedly dominant society.

The emancipated slaves used the tools of perception offered to them by the colonists so that they could fulfill their function as privileged auxiliaries for slavery. So they dealt with only a tiny piece of reality, that which was visible to the colonists. But those colonists had no idea that there was an entire universe stretching out beyond the world of the plantation, inaccessible to them. But the border inhabited by the emancipated slave was itself a fluid space that colonialism could reduce or amplify depending on whether the situation was one of peace or of crisis. The choices offered to the social actors who managed the links between the colony and the metropole varied according to the acuteness of the crisis. They expanded under Toussaint's rule and were whittled down to the point of disappearance when Leclerc arrived to carry out Napoléon's instructions. The intermediaries therefore carefully juggled the dominant groups and the captives, because their own state was precarious and their extermination remained possible, if not probable. Their challenge was to figure what sovereignty meant on the border they inhabited between cultures.

Correction of the Myopia of the Oligarchs

With independence and the drastic reduction of French influence, there was a polarization of possibilities and a debate over the fluidity of various choices. The initial reaction of the agricultural workers, who were traditionally excluded from public life, was to consolidate the institutions through which they had organized their private lives on the plantations. Over the course of fourteen years of war, they had built communities in which they pursued their well-being with increasing autonomy. Gabriel Debien has underlined the importance of this tendency and its impact on the demographic growth of the population. The population's successful control over resources was also expressed and defended through larger movements such as those of Goman and the construction of the *Gran Doko*, and later that led by Acaau.

During the three and a half decades of the governments of Pétion and Boyer, the behavior of the highest spheres of the intermediary class toward the cultivators was characterized by the same staggering flippancy and lack of respect shown by the colonial authorities. General Gérin affirmed publicly that the son of a peasant, even before the law, was not the equal of his own son (Ardouin 1856, 5:9). Boyer made it known that he saw Goman not as a revolutionary but as a maroon who spent most of his life in the woods (Magloire 1909, 49).

The traditional historiography eliminated Goman, as they did the maroon leaders of the North and the West before him, and as a result it overlooks his impact on the broader social system. But we can credit him with having laid the foundations for a form of peasant autonomy that did not have to defend itself in its relationship with the urban world. It was the movement led by Acaau, the first of its size in the history of independent Haiti, tied together with the bourgeois liberal reaction of Rivière-Hérard, a member of the southern oligarchy, that brought the era of Pétion and Boyer to an end. While it remained centrally a peasant movement, it emerged in a tight relationship with the broader social transformations of the era.

Goman's movement was characterized by the withdrawal of the peasantry. Acaau's, in contrast, inhabited the border between the cultivators and the urban population. This enabled it to measure up to the political system. If we go beyond the personality of their spokesman and focus on the precedents and premises of the second of these two insurrections, we can see important continuities between the two. This enables us to look from below at the power structures of the era. Organizers from Goman's movement made their presence felt in Grande Anse. Furthermore, a series of movements on the part of marginalized people in the urban areas, in Port-au-Prince, Léogâne, Les Cayes, and Torbeck, contributed to political effervescence and the contestation of the political regime (Hector 2006a, 164).

In 1844, Acaau called himself the Chief of the Demands of His Co-citizens and marched at the head of the Army of Sufferers, which was also called the Army of Equality (Manigat 2001, 2: 27). His movement defied the established authorities. His speeches awakened the rural population, who followed him and marched to conquer their rights. They sowed panic among the oligarchs who, without absorbing the principles of the insurrection, were forced to tolerate its leader. From the perspective of the oligarchy, his incorporation into the government institutionalized a dichotomous, hierarchical social order in which the superposition of two worlds became the fundamental characteristic of Haitian society (Manigat 2001 2: 2). The uprisings of Goman and Acaau set the tone for the social and political structure of the country.

In order to fully understand Manigat's observation on the structure of the state in Haiti, it is important to connect it to a key discovery by Michel Hector (2006a, 123). He emphasizes that Goman's uprising—and, I would add, that of Acaau—developed in the South of Haiti, far from the zones where the plantations had been rebuilt, in the North and the West. Hector, along with Carolyn Fick, adds that this central involvement of armed agricultural laborers in these cases didn't lead to the brutal purge of their leaders, as it did in the two other departments. I deduce from this that the duality of society was not essentially a response to the plantation economy and its monopoly over land, or to the enslavement of captives. It was the expression of a positive orientation: the affirmation on the part of the sovereign people that they wished to live in complete independence from the projects and goals of both the colonial oligarchs and those who followed them in the nineteenth century, no matter what those projects were.

The description of the movement by Manigat highlights three important aspects. First, the panicked oligarchs unreservedly expressed their disdain and hatred of the cultivators. In 1846, the newspaper *La Réforme* declared they wished that the these "ferocious bands" would be finished once and for all. Louis-Joseph Janvier described Acaau as "an unschooled genius." Firmin emphasized that Acaau's arrest at Aquin was "fortunate." He added that between 1843 and 1846, the popular masses showed clearly they were not equipped to take on political responsibilities. Pauléus Sannon noted that "Acaau gave himself up to a kind of eccentric sovereignty, a clownish tragi-comedy, provoking both laughter and tears." In his opinion, he was "nothing but a rude, burlesque counterpart to Rivière-Hérard" (Sannon 1905, 133, 135). Finally, Dantès Bellegarde referred to an "infestation of *piquettiste* bands" (Manigat 2001, 2:28).

Reports targeted Acaau personally. They couldn't move beyond how the leader looked. His appearance irritated them profoundly:

> A straw hat full of holes, a torn tailored jacket, pants, pistols attached to his belt, sandals. The same newspaper offered other elements to the portrait: "He is always extremely wary. He is dark, badly dressed in a tunic and an old straw hat. He wears spurs on his bare feet, and marches surrounded by two hundred loyal, or seemingly loyal, men. He affects a kind of devotion full of contemplation and mysticism." But it is the portrait of Acaau by Céligny Ardouin that is the most revealing: "The little Lieutenant Acaau, devalued, unknown to society, wearing a police uniform without epaulettes, shoeless, but who had made himself the leader of a party that marched rapidly toward inciting a social upheaval through its attacks against people and property." (Manigat 2001 2:68).

Dressed in these manifestly rebellious clothes, Acaau wasn't asking for his integration, or that of the masses, into the dominant society. His demand for autonomy was terrifying. He realized that only the exercise of political authority could enable the rural population to protect its rights. He therefore asked for a measure of control over government administration and forced the central power to deal with him. His revolt was essentially a protest against taxes, and it sought the creation of equilibrium in the relationship between the cities and the rural areas and a mechanism to oversee the weight of different forms of taxation (Manigat 2001 2:64).

In this chapter titled "Resisting the Production of Sufferers" it is important to recall that in fact, the oligarchs did recognize the challenge posed by the trajectories of Goman and Acaau. As was the case before 1804, they could not tolerate the idea that the rural population could walk its own path in complete sovereignty. Resentful, they invented the concept of a governance by stand-in. They believed this reflected the reality that the leaders of peasant origin who followed Acaau were asking only for autonomy in rural life, and did not seek to influence all the aspects of the life of the nation.

During the second half of the nineteenth century, there were profound changes in the international community's relationship to Haiti. These incited a hardening of Haitian policy, which President Sylvain Salnave attempted to correct. The impact that the physical appearance and bearing of Salnave had on the members of the urban upper class, as well as on journalists and historians, may explain why the similarity between Acaau and Salnave has rarely attracted the attention of thinkers. Sylvain Salnave presented himself as the antithesis of the Chief of the Demands of His Co-citizens. Born in the former capital of the colony, he was classically elegant, a mulatto with very light skin, descendant of a soldier of the Indigenous Army who had received a small property that had allowed him to prosper. According to Gaillard, Salnave was part of the petite bourgeoisie of Le Cap and surrounded himself with the most authentic bourgeois of the city. His father was a merchant and coffee speculator and his mother was illiterate (Gaillard 2003, 15).

Like Acaau, Salnave inhabited the border between the urban and rural worlds. But that border was not the same as it had been twenty years earlier. He inaugurated the arrival of the urban masses into political militancy (Adam 1982, 31) and a tighter alliance with the dispossessed rural population. He introduced two new actors into the political scene: women and young people (77). Though he was urban and Francophone, he used Kreyòl in his speeches, leaving to his minister Demesvar Délorme the task of scolding the Church and the international community in the imperial language (149). In his role as president, he actually went further than Acaau, brandishing the autonomy of the rural world and the rights of the majority as a political banner in what he considered a vital struggle for the defense of national sovereignty.

From the time of Dessalines to Soulouque, the foreigner had been considered the enemy: the international community, though certainly courted, was kept at a distance from politics, while the Church was simply subjected to the state (Adam 1982, 167). Geffrard entered history as the first head of state to open the country to foreign influence. Under his rule, as Janvier put it, the international community became a state above the state (Adam 1982, 65). Salnave's movement ratcheted this up a notch: it directly confronted imperialism and fought to the last cartridge against it.

The commotion he caused in Haitian politics can confuse the issue. Roger Gaillard emphasizes this fact in the title of his book, *Le Cacaoïsme bourgeois contre Salnave* (Bourgeois cacoism against Salnave). In other words, Salnave was not a Caco. On the political chessboard, the bourgeois Cacos represented an alliance between the large property owners and the cultivators, one that has not been sufficiently explored. After the U.S. occupation, this relationship between the large property owners, the allies of the political regimes, and their supposed rural clientele was redirected to more radical ends through the movement of Charlemagne Péralte.

It makes little sense to postulate that the Cacos of the North were part of a political clientele, while asserting that the Piquets were an autonomous movement. In all cases, from Goman to Salnave, all the peasant uprisings opposed the central administration. Salnave's administration was not the same as Boyer's, but it was still at the center of the nation. Administrative autonomy remained the common denominator of peasant struggles and their antidote to the myopia of the oligarchs.

Salnave's execution, applauded by both branches of the oligarchy, inaugurated a historical period that lasted until the U.S. occupation. It was a time when governments found it necessary to take the interests of the popular classes into account, even as they avoided institutionalizing their direct participation in the political system. Manigat adroitly alludes to this orientation by quoting Léon Audain. "At times, nevertheless, he [the peasant] collectively, and angrily, reacted to an order or a measure that struck against him, and stood up, machete in hand, to defend his interests. The authorities, realizing that they had gone too far, didn't follow their natural propensity toward repression, which would have led to the hatching of new Acaaus. Instead, they discreetly retreated, in order to avoid riots and a broader contestation of the continuation of the system" (Manigat 2001, 2:91).

Conclusion: The Power of the State in the Nineteenth Century

Europe incorporated the Caribbean forcibly into its history; it even refers to the islands as the *Spanish, English, French*, and *Dutch* Caribbean. The difficulty on this side of the ocean consists in delimiting the extent to which this European history is part of our own. The control and management of the government in Haiti was a copy of the despotic French colonial state. But ultimately, the people survived by doing without it. My goal is to understand how they managed to do so.

Local populations are rarely invited, as significant actors, into the quarrels worked out along the avenues of institutional power. The case of Saint-Domingue created an accidental exception. The exacerbation of the fratricidal struggles provoked in Europe by the French Revolution created a conjuncture that offered the sufferers of the colony an opportunity to intervene as arbiters in the conflicts between the slaveholders. As a result, the itinerary they were pursuing subtly became more visible.

This victory was inconceivable within the understandings of the Western powers. This success and its repercussions in the Atlantic World have haloed its leaders as the *black Jacobins*, with such fame that they are seen as the architects of the revolutionary process. The popular participation that was the foundation for this victory has been pushed into the background, or else became the object of the most fantastical interpretations, promoted in fact by the descendants of these presumed architects. The state project that sought to carry on French colonialism took satisfaction, initially, in disdain for the laboring class, and reproduced this in their legal system.

In France, however, the state—even when it was personified in the absolute power of kings—had institutional limits: a juridical system that condensed the entire history of the country surrounded the government. The evolution of these institutions led to the institutionalization of popular sovereignty. The public administration in Haiti, on the other hand, was born of the history of Saint-Domingue and the structuring of the social forces that emerged from it. It preserved the colonial administration of Saint-Domingue, and not the public administration of France.

The distorted vision of the public administration eluded the question of the origin of the Haitian nation and its nationals. Haitians were blacks belonging to a same history without history. The Haitian oligarchs reproduced the haughty view of the Code Noir and expressed the greatest disdain for the country's laborers. How is it possible to imagine that they would place their fate in the hands of this sovereign people, these unfortunates, these sans-culottes, following the sacred formula of the French Revolution? In Haiti, they called the people who made up nearly the entire population *maroons, vagabonds, marauders, fools.* The most famous sons of the country—Gérin, Janvier, Firmin, Bobo, Bellegarde—regularly trumpeted the disdain they felt at living alongside this population . . . and from the heights of their enlightenment they endeavored to create a political project of modernization and civilization. Two centuries later, they still haven't been able to put it into practice, and even less to impose it, or even to adapt it in any way to the reality of the country.

The administrators of the colonial state and of independent Haiti operated as if there was no civil society, or just a semblance of civil society that included only the tiny minority of conquerors and intermediaries. But there was an abyss between their vision and the rest of the country. There was no actual possibility for modernizing and reproducing Saint-Domingue in the world of the Haitian nineteenth century. The Pearl of the Antilles was part of French Haiti and not of the history of Haitians. To them, it was dead—forever.

Both the colonial and independent administrations operated *on* a nation in the process of becoming, or the nation that was already constituted. They never operated *within* the nation, and even less *with* the nation. This distinction goes back two hundred years, and makes clear that it makes no sense to use the model of the French nation-state to interpret the former colony of Saint-Domingue or independent Haiti. Just as Louis XIV didn't worry about the origins of the slaves piling up in the colonies, the oligarchs who appropriated the victory of 1804 took no note of the particularities of the populations they governed and who they wished to force into service. They were so blind to them that they weren't even capable of understanding why it was impossible for them to obtain the same results as those achieved by the colonial administration.

Meanwhile, the captives reduced to slavery and their descendants responded to the colonial desire to destroy them by creating institutions that translated their social project into reality. The deported individuals could not avoid creating and maintaining social connections. The laboring class chose to re-exist (Mignolo 2014). They never confined themselves to their executioners' projects.

So it was that soon after the declaration of independence, the governors of Haiti, orphaned of the support of the great European empires, found themselves increasingly incapable of commanding the formerly conquered population. Their resistant power remained inconceivable and invisible to those in power. The cultivators, meanwhile, simply ignored the prejudices that served as the premise for the claims of those in power. The communication between oligarchs and those they called the people became more and more difficult. The power *of* the state—as a unit facing the entities of an international community in the era of imperialism—did not absorb the power *in* the state, and was unable to respond to the demands of the popular majority.

The masses had changed in nature, and they took a new direction. They didn't follow the strategy of the communities led by maroon generals. Instead, the populations of the nineteenth century gradually reformulated the role of the political authorities in their daily life by influencing the practices of the local leaders who were closer to them than to the central state, operating between urban and rural society. The country experienced thirty-five years (Hector and Casimir 2004) of political stability at the national level, built upon the peaceful evolution of the rural zones. The population enjoyed a well-being rooted in the production of food in the *bourgs-jardins* (Manigat 2001; Anglade 1982), the small settlements with provision grounds and gardens, throughout the country.

By the end of the nineteenth century, the systematic policy of creating sufferers that had been carried out by the state since the time of the Code Noir had been softened. The oligarchs balked at the idea of identifying themselves to the nation they observed, and complained about the modus vivendi that was imposed on them, despite its remarkable success. They painted a portrait of a Haiti that was Catholic and Francophone, the "eldest daughter of Africa," the most European of the daughters of the barbarous continent. But their talk was directed at the international community or the tiny sectors of the urban intermediaries. They had to wait until 1915 to return to their role as colonial intermediaries who, with help from outside, monopolized the state administration without being able to modify its structure. For their part, the popular masses remained proud to serve the laws, or *lwa*, of Guinée.

Chapter 3

Colonial Thought

Introduction: The State and Property

The French colonies were the property of the Crown, which controlled their administration and government. It distributed land—real estate—to those close to the king, most often the younger children of noble or wealthy families (Gauthier 2007, 333). These subjects developed plantations and profited from them thanks to a labor force reduced to slavery, purchased through the large-scale commerce sustained by French ports. By promulgating the Code Noir, the Crown legislated the lives of its subjects and their slaves—of those who were free, and the foreigners who served them.

The Crown also decreed that the emancipation of a slave would be considered an act of naturalization into French society. This created a group of Creoles of enslaved ancestry who lived alongside the beneficiaries of landed property and their enslaved workers. These Creoles also had rights to royal concessions. The Crown envisioned embryonic settlement structure developing in this exploitation colony: a Creole society. But there was the potential that this new Creole society would generate resentment toward the many absentee property owners who remained in France, whose norms and values were shaped by a different context and set of projects. This possibility was a particular danger among the Creole property owners who were descended from a mix of metropolitan colonists and the enslaved: the group known as *free people of color*. In fact, however, the economic and cultural ties between this group and the metropole generally remained stronger than their ties to the colonial population (King 2001, 272).

At the end of the eighteenth century, the French Revolution challenged the absolutism of royal power. In the colony, the sovereign people of the French nation took over the role formerly occupied by the royal administration. But respect for private property remained the compass guiding the reason of state, and the changing colonial administration focused on managing that property. Malouet, a former deputy in the Constituent Assembly, described the war that began between colonists and revolutionaries as being "not a question either of the system or of political interests," but rather of "property defending itself against banditry, by invoking a protective power"—that of England (Malouet 1797, 8). He was suggesting that the foundation for the colony's social framework was France's right of conquest and the right to property that flowed from it. From his perspective, the question of how property should be managed was the only political matter truly open for discussion. Barnave, one of the great voices of the Constituent Assembly, offered a precise articulation of the metropolitan vision of the question: "Principles are for the free people of color, as I've always told you. There is only one reason of state" (Gauthier 2007, 309). Barnave saw the political power of the free people of color as a major obstacle to the system he sought to install. He argued that legal values should not be the basis for the functioning of colonial society. Imperial arbitrariness was sufficient.

But reality wasn't that simple. It wasn't created by the pure will of empire. The revolutionary transformation of the political structure, and the questioning of royal power, exacerbated conflicts with rival powers in Europe. The administration and management of private property was placed under the control of the emerging reason of state. But that didn't prevent some groups from placing themselves under the banners of the enemy. The slave colonies could not defend themselves, because they weren't able to convert enough of the labor force into soldiers or sailors (Gauthier 2007, 147). French colonists were torn between patriotism and the attractions of treason, which gave them access to a power that could protect their particular interests as slave holders better than the French metropole. The treason of many French planters, who turned to England in order to preserve slavery, created an opening for the enslaved. They embarked on an unexpected journey, governed by another set of values whose impact should not be underestimated.

In the overseas colonies, it was impossible to replace the authority of the king with the authority of the sovereign people. The Declaration of the Rights of Man and Citizen was inoperable there. The colonies needed specific laws, approved by the metropolitan legislative assembly. In the midst of the debates over these laws, the actors in colonial society began to express their own social and political projects.

These projects, whether assimilationist or secessionist, maintained their colonialist and proslavery nature. Malouet argued that colonial conquest had laid the foundation for the centrality of the right to property, and many agreed with him. In their discussion of how to treat the slaves, they garnered the support of the Abbé Grégoire, the Société des Citoyens de Couleur (Society of the Citizens of Color), and the Société de Amis des Noirs (Society of the Friends of the Blacks). No one in France was thinking in terms of the immediate abolition of slavery. No one in England was either. European states universally accepted the Christian West's right to conquest, the right to property over the islands and over the slaves.

The only divergences surrounding question of how to manage private property had to do with the question of what role should be played by the small number of property owners who were descendants of slaves, and especially those who were born of free parents. The embryonic structure of settlement envisioned by the Code Noir had created this problem, which ultimately led the Jacobins and the Society of the Friends of the Blacks into a direct attack on the slave trade (Gauthier 2007, 130ff.). They sketched out a project of general emancipation that would be carried out over the long term, one conceptualized around the question of how to ensure the gradual assimilation of foreigners from Africa.

> It was therefore not yet time to ask for liberty; all that was asked was to stop constantly slitting the throats, each year, of thousands of blacks, in order to produce hundreds of captives. . . . These arguments were meant to contribute to understanding on the part of the colonists that they had a new interest: to substitute the development of laborers on site in the colonies to the African slave trade. . . . Eliminating the slave trade would mean changing the form of reproduction of slave labor, abandoning the system of replacing *bossales* by new *bossales* and instead launching a general development of slave labor on site, which would replace these *bossales* with Creole slaves. At the end of all these changes, the Creole slave would be able to change their condition by buying their freedom and becoming a "free" worker, and a consumer according to the European economic model. (Gauthier 2007, 123–125)

The conflicts of the end of the eighteenth century were unable to deal fully with the key issue: the need for local reproduction of labor in the colony. But there was another problem that modern colonial thought had not predicted or prepared for: the managerial autonomy of the institutions that emerged from the local reproduction of labor and which, at the deepest level, explains the Haitian nineteenth century, as I will show. The state administration that emerged after 1804 dreamed of a colonial society under the control of a minority of property owners, served by destitute free people who had no other option than to sell their labor under conditions determined by their former masters. The Western state—modern, colonial, capitalist, and racist—cannot survive without creating sufferers, without creating and then appropriating *animals who creep along on the earth* (Gen. 1:28).

Slaves and Colonists of Color

In my earlier work, I analyzed the characteristics of the Haitian population— its ethnic origins and its historical process of formation—and emphasized the creation of new forms of knowledge and institutions by the groups who resisted colonial oppression. There were always many more of them than there were oligarchs, and they never followed the latter's models in developing their way of life, their vision of the world, or the weapons they used in their struggles.

I concluded that the culture of Haiti's dominant classes was similar to the Creole culture characteristic of the knowledge systems of Latin America. I used the term *oppressed culture* to describe the practices and thinking of the exploited classes. They were imprisoned and surrounded by a dominant Creole culture governed by the modes of thinking and acting that at the time were seeking to organize the world on a global scale (Casimir 1981). But the way the term *Creole* is used in the Latin American context can be confusing when applied to the Caribbean, and I should have opted for a different term, for instance *local French culture*. The harm is done. But I want to clarify that my use of the term *Creole culture* did not refer to the culture of monolingual Creole speakers, whose culture was that of the oppressed.

The local French culture of the oligarchic classes of Haiti—like those of their Spanish, English, and Dutch counterparts in Latin America and the Caribbean—was born through processes of creolization and acculturation. The difference is that the Creole cultures of Latin America were built starting in 1492, while those of the Caribbean are much more recent, and therefore less autonomous and closer to their European mother cultures.

The European mother culture organized the colony of Saint-Domingue on the basis of the norms, values, and institutions put in place by the Code Noir. Its appointed managers were the modern, colonial state and the white colonists. Building mainly on the work of Jean Fouchard, I have already described the process they used to convert their captives into slaves. The Baron de Vastey, a witness to the enslavement of the unfortunate Africans, left us a poignant description of the functioning of this social engineering responsible for transforming free beings into submissive slaves. He denounced the behavior of France and the French colonists and asked, stunned: "Is there anywhere in this world or any other a race of executioners destined to torture human beings? Are the ex-colonists, here on earth, what the demons are in hell?" (1819, 92).

Once the Code Noir was issued, the question of whether the people of color belonged to French colonial society was no longer a subject of discussion. They were perceived and perceived themselves as an integral part of this world. Since the society as a whole was deeply stratified, the question that emerged was whether they were considered equal to other subjects of the king or, later, other citizens of the republic. In fact, in the midst of the revolution, in 1790, they were sometimes seen as being more important than the white citizens for the successful functioning of the system.

> The men of color are the true inhabitants, the natives of Saint-Domingue. They are the only ones who are truly devoted to the colony. They root themselves there for their entire lives, while almost all of the whites are passing through, appearing for a moment in this climate in order to amass, as quickly as possible, enormous fortunes, which they then dissipate in the midst of pleasure and vice. The men of color are infinitely useful property owners: they are the ones who clear the land, who cultivate the unproductive areas of the soil: it is their properties that are the most divided up, the best maintained. The whites took over all the fertile areas, they have vast domains, where they force production in order to rush toward their pleasures. We can see that the men of color possess a quarter of the plantations. They are also the ones who carry out the policing of slaves in the colony. (Pétion 1790, 30)

Julien Raimond, a contemporary of Vastey, described the efforts of the colonists of color to gain access to the same privileges enjoyed by the white colonists. In his 1791 publications, he trumpeted to all who would listen: the key role the colonists of color and the emancipated played in the preservation and protection of the French colonial empire and the slavery that was its foundation. Vincent Ogé, in a speech to the Club Massiac, expressed his fear of the black hordes, and André Rigaud expressed the same sentiments in his *Mémoires*. In their plea in favor of the free people of color, these authors never whispered a word about the conditions of the blacks held in captivity:

> Before the French people broke the heavy chains that despotism had forged, before they recovered the rights that tyranny had destroyed, the men of color and free blacks of Saint-Domingue suffered under the weight of oppression and a vile prejudice that the time and the law of the strongest had consecrated. Most of them were property owners, and wealthy, contributing to all public spending, always the first to take up arms when the enemy threatened the French territory. . . . They barely enjoyed the status of human beings, were subjected to disdain, and vegetated in the midst of disgrace and humiliation. (Rigaud 1797, 3)

The American colonists, like the European colonists, did not consider the enslaved part of the French population. In 1791, the men of color argued that the foundation for their status and their social power was their assimilation with the white colonists. Their interests were, they insisted, linked to those of the colonial empire. They emphasized their historical role in the conservation of the exploitative structure of slavery.

In revolutionary France, the Third Estate redefined its role within the political structure and the governance of society. These changes generated a general outcry among the other colonial empires, whose military forces threatened French sovereignty over its colonial possessions, including Saint-Domingue. In the midst of these transformations, various groups in the colonies along with metropolitan philosophers began to debate the future of the colonial workforce, and what it should be called. In the short term, however, they agreed on what the status and function of this workforce should be.

At the time, the only major concentrations of laborers were on the colonial plantations. Circumstances forced the French administration to make this unchained workforce into a group of citizens, or almost-citizens, who were not completely free, and only partially paid for their labor. But the authors of the period couldn't settle on one term to describe this mass of workers essential to the survival of the empire.

In the wake of the revolutionary explosions of the period, the oligarchs took their place in the political life of a now independent country. They were strengthened by the departure of the metropolitan colonists, and monopolized the public discourse. As they solidified their power, they unhesitatingly erased the traces of the methods they had used to gain their position at the top of the social hierarchy. The only thing they publicly recalled about the history of their actions during the height of the Pearl of the Antilles was their success as promoters of the colonial order. They didn't specifically mention the methods they had used to perfect this order, particularly the services they rendered to the police forces and militia units that secured the exploitation of the slaves.

Studying the state in Haiti requires observing the emergence of social forces and the evolution of the relations among them. The very oligarchs who had sustained the colonial world were, to a large extent, those who took charge of the future of the new state during the nineteenth century. This meant that, from the beginning, they stood in opposition to the formerly enslaved laboring masses. Having been given the responsibility of assuring the smooth functioning of Saint-Domingue, they now carried the architecture of the colony into independent Haiti. "The interests of the free men of color are tightly linked to the re-establishment of the colony. Like us, they own slaves and plantations. Like the whites, they have to put all their efforts into making them thrive. And having no other home or mother country than this land, they can find their own peace and quiet only through its perfect tranquility. Consider their current existence in the midst of a number of men ten times larger than them, whose ferocity they already experienced under the reign of Toussaint" (Laujon n.d., 237).

Colonists of Color and Emancipated Slaves

The project of colonial society depended on the exercise of the right of conquest. But it was applied in two different ways: the approach taken by Julien Raimond, Vincent Ogé, and Jean-Baptiste Chavannes, versus that offered by Moreau de Saint-Méry and the Club Massiac. The first group was made up of Creoles. They were capitalist entrepreneurs who lived in the colonial society, mostly property owners. They were descended from enslaved people, though with various degrees of proximity. They focused on the embryo of the structure of settlement in the colony and the question of how it should be managed. The second group emphasized the interests of property owners who were generally absent, and privileged the acquisition of material profits in the shortest time possible. Their model clearly exposed the traditional project of the plantation colony.

The larger institutions shaping the social order codified the distance separating the masters who lived in the colony from their manual laborers. The people of color and emancipated slaves modulated their relationships with the laborers still reduced to slavery according to the privileges they each enjoyed in colonial society. Among free people, the emancipated blacks were at the bottom of the social ladder. Their vision of the public order was nuanced by the shades of Toussaint Louverture's politics. He used skin color as a political weapon against lighter-skinned opponents. The people of color were more intransigent in maintaining the distance separating themselves from the slaves. They protected themselves by turning as much as possible to the metropole to support their power and pretensions to superiority. Their defense of the established order rarely included requests for its softening. They rarely expressed any antagonism toward the determinants of colonialism itself.

During the years of the French Revolution, Julian Raimond imposed himself in the successive Parisian legislative assemblies as the most influential and famous among the colonists of color. He was an illustrious defender of the only embryo of a national bourgeoisie Haiti has ever known. The traditional historiography of Saint-Domingue, however, has always privileged Moreau de Saint-Méry as a source for information on the social structures of the colony. This neglect of the writings of Raimond is unfortunate, since his contributions to the legislative assembly's deliberations created a notable corpus of work illuminating the texture of colonial society. He also had a significant impact on the relationship between France and its overseas territories, as well as on the efforts to save an empire in crisis. He was admitted to the Société des Citoyens de Couleur and regularly frequented the Société des Amis des Noirs. His 1793 book *Réflexions sur les véritables causes des troubles et des désastres de nos colonies, notamment sur ceux de Saint-Domingue; avec les moyens à employer pour préserver cette colonie de la ruine totale; adressées à la Convention Nationale* (Reflections on the true causes of the troubles and disasters of our colonies; notably on those of Saint-Domingue; with the means to use to preserve this colony from total ruin; addressed to the National Convention) is worth citing in particular. He considered himself French.

It is important to examine the influence Raimond's efforts had on the conservation of the empire. But my analysis also focuses on what we learn from his writings about his position toward the metropolitan power, and about the characteristics of the group of colonists of color whose interests he defended so fiercely. The many written traces he left through his interventions and struggles expose the traits and mentality of his numerous correspondents, the ways they imbricated themselves within Saint-Domingue's society and the French colonial empire, and the omissions that this form of imbrication required of them. My project is to use these traces to reconstruct the principles, norms, and values of this interest group and illuminate its relationship to the core social classes of Saint-Domingue. These reflections enable me to describe and analyze the trajectory this group proposed for the society of which they considered themselves to be the elite. In the process, I will make clear the reasons why it naturally granted itself this role, before even lifting a pinky finger to earn a right to it.

Julien Raimond's thought was characterized by a disdain for African people, which situates him at the heart of the racism of the modern period. Compared to the slaves, he insinuated, people of color were deeply vulnerable. The injustices they experienced could be repaired only by granting them the same privileges as European colonists.[1] He sought the support of the metropolitan authorities to rectify a series of shocking abuses:

> If the slave was able to surmount all these difficulties, once freed he
> still remained under the dependence of all the whites of the colony, a
> dependency that was a hundred times worse than the slavery he had just
> escaped. As a slave, only his master had rights over him, and was his
> defender against any who wanted to do him harm. Freed, it was as if
> he was the property of all the whites; any one of them had the right to
> humiliate and attack him, in his person and his property. If he dared
> resist oppression through the only means that were left, he faced torture
> put in place by a sanguinary law. For that law, far from protecting him as

it did other members of society, had on the contrary accumulated every sort of rigor against him. (Raimond 1793, 23).

Julien Raimond anchored his activism in an intransigent defense of the right to private property. This included the property of the one-third of the slaves of the colony owned by free people of color. The possession of this important workforce was connected to the control of a portion of the land in the colonial territory. He was willing to envision negotiations surrounding the ownership of slaves only to the extent that this had no impact on the prerogatives of plantation ownership. The lobby that he represented divided the colonial population into two groups: those who had access to property and those who did not. There were free people and nonfree people. The former were subjects of the king or citizens of the republic. The latter were foreigners.

Like the antiabolitionist planters, Julien Raimond was convinced that thanks to its right to conquest, the colonial state was the source for the right to property. The defense of this right, furthermore, should be based on a defense of sovereignty. He defined the active citizen of Saint-Domingue as a property owner who paid his taxes and commanded a minimum number of slaves. Having established that, he argued that there was no justification for any kind of discrimination that limited the prerogatives of those who fulfilled these attributes. All free men acted in the same relationship to the state, and the colonists of color, like all property owners, were free and paid taxes (1791a, vii, 44).

The free population was itself divided into two groups: the white colonists, who were essentially the aristocrats and nobles of the colonies, and the colonists of color (1791a, 48). It was therefore impossible to confuse the cause of the *people of color* (property owners) with that of the *slaves* (merchandise that was owned; 1791a, 1). The implication of Raimond's thinking here is that while the right to property granted by the state to one or another of its subjects or citizens was considered an attribute of the free person, in the colonial context, freedom as such was something granted by the state, and like property itself, could be conceived of only within this broader order. The citizen was free, but the status of the free person as an active or passive citizen depended on whether they were a property owner or not. And this status was always granted by the sovereign. It should be clear how difficult it was to reverse this equation in order to transform the captives reduced to slavery into a sovereign people.

Not all free people gained access to the status of active citizens in the same way. Among them, Julien Raimond differentiated the free people par excellence, "whites who have always been free" (1793, 27). They were subjects of the king and later, citizens of the republic. Next came free people who were born of people who were also free, whom he might have called *freed people* to distinguish them from the free people par excellence. At the bottom of the ladder, struggling, were the *emancipated*, those who had been born *slaves* but obtained their freedom by one of the routes authorized by the sovereign state. The complete term to describe them was the composite of the noun *slave* and the adjective *emancipated*. Where did these beings born outside the confines of freedom come from? And why were they born into this state of inferiority? Everyone—if by everyone we mean the tiny minority of European origin—seemed to know. But the colonists of color avoided confronting this question, since doing so would lead to questioning the right of conquest itself.

Blacks were, indisputibly, at the bottom of the stratification among nonwhites. This status was based on the formal linkage between the right to private property, participation as a citizen, and racial belonging. Julien Raimond informed his readers that there was a fundamental difference between what he called the mulatto and a person of color of mixed blood. The first, according to him, was the product of a white man and a black woman, while the person of color or mixed blood was the product of mulattoes among themselves or of mulattoes and whites, and of their various offspring. It is worth noting that, after he laid out these differences in 1791, he sometimes confused the terms to the point that he included free blacks in the category of men of color.

Taking this caveat into account, however, we can see that the person of color was generally born free of free parents who were legitimately married. According to Raimond, only 200 among the group had themselves not been emancipated in their lifetimes. There were no more than 1,500 free blacks among the people of color, 1,000 of them born free.[2] As he realized, the fears of the colonial administration and white colonists about the free people of color were not the result of the size of the population, which was tiny in relation to the total population. What was alarming was its rate of growth in comparison to that of the white population. The growing visibility of people of color, particularly noticeable in the Southern Province, could be seen even in an isolated area like Mirebalais. In the towns of the North and West, the presence of a group of artisans made up of free blacks helped to obscure this contrast.

In the midst of the revolutionary commotion, the people of color claimed to be struggling for the rights they had enjoyed thirty years before the French Revolution (1791a, 14). They were fighting for the maintenance of the status quo. But they were the ones who spread ideals of this revolution in Saint-Domingue, and with lightning speed they followed a path that had a significant impact on the revolution of the slaves. For Raimond, however, it was not the people of color who were truly responsible for the uprising of the slaves. He blamed the whites, both the planters and the poor whites, who, he argued, imprudently fought against one another and spoke too freely in front of their slaves (1791a 31, 38).

In his debates with Moreau de Saint-Méry, the lobbyist never hid his racism. He insisted that the people of color were the only ones who had been capable of containing the slaves (1791b, ii). The slaves' "cause," he wrote, was "separated" from that of the free people of color in the way that "light is separated from darkness" (1791b, 2). His class, he insisted, remained the only boulevard that could guarantee the security of the colony. Raimond bluntly described Moreau de Saint-Méry as a liar and criticized his diatribe against Ogé. He demanded that the French public recognize that the mulattoes were the axis of the prosperity of the colony (1791b, 39, 59, 68).

As the deputy of the citizens of color, Raimond advocated three objectives: assuring the conservation of the colony for the metropole, avoiding an interruption in agricultural production caused by slave uprisings, and putting an end to the conflicts in the colony. These objectives, he argued, could be realized only through the recognition of the civil and political rights of the people of color (1792, ii). Their citizenship was essential to the preservation of the colony and the maintenance of slavery and the colonial order. The men of color were truly committed to the flourishing of the colonial system of slavery, but that system kept placing obstacles in their way, irrationally depriving itself of this necessary and unavoidable source of support.

Raimond argued that the white colonists were being particularly reckless in their insistence on relentlessly persecuting the men of color and refusing support from the only force capable of containing the slaves. The men of color, he noted, had no interest in encouraging an uprising among the slaves, since they owned a third of them (1793, 31, 34, 38). To assert the contrary was a vile calumny. Without them, it would be impossible to repress the revolts and to re-establish order to save the colony (1792, 38–39). Given that the people of color were always first to contribute to order and stability, their total assimilation would guarantee against all subversion among them. They would gain nothing from insurrection or revolution, and obtain everything they sought through the abolition of prejudice (1792, 47).

In his 1793 letter to the deputies of the National Convention, Raimond once again emphasized that the demands of the people of color had no connection whatsoever to the possible emancipation of the slaves. The attachment of the people of color to the revolution and to France was their lifeline. Any project of independence was ridiculous (1793, 19). The racialization of human relations (1793, 12) remained essential for society, which is why the distinctions among nonfree people (the *slaves*), the *emancipated slaves*, and the *people of color* born of free fathers and mothers remained vital.

Raimond signed his 1793 *Réflexions*, cited above, as a "colonist of Saint-Domingue," and in it he referred to *our* colonies. Since these were slave colonies, he also could have spoken of *our* slaves, or *our* people-without-rights. But given the dangers to French sovereignty over the colonies in general, and Saint-Domingue in particular, that resulted from the 1789 revolution, he did admit there could be some interest in having the slaves participate in some of the benefits of the revolution, just to make sure they weren't seduced by its enemies (1793, 5). The improvement he sought in the situation of the slaves was a function of the protection they could offer French sovereignty, an imperative justified by reasons of state.

The people reduced to slavery, he argued, had no rights of their own. They had to accept their fate, and could access liberty only by obeying the laws prescribed by the Code Noir. The idea of their sudden emancipation and spontaneous access to rights was crazy and unthinkable (1793, 13, 18). Raimond refused to question this conclusion, but he also understood the urgency of improving the situation of the slaves. His compromise was to propose that they should be given the possibility of buying their freedom in installments. That way, they could gradually gain liberty without undermining the sacred character of private property. Unsurprisingly, he saw the slaves as childlike and wrote that they might be happier than French peasants (1793, 27). For him, these people—whose potential had been entirely annihilated by the French—could improve their situation only by making a sustained contribution to the well-being of their abusers.

Given his religious veneration of the right of conquest, it makes sense that Raimond called on the king or the state to defend the interests of the colonists of color. The rights of this segment of colonial society, like the liberty to which the slaves might gain access, emanated from the sovereignty of the state. It was essential to obey its laws: "Obey the decree of the Corps législatif in order to be reintegrated into your rights, you who own at least a third of the lands of the colony and a quarter of the slaves. Our class, which represents at least half of the free people, is indispensable to the maintenance of slavery" (1791a, 2, 13).

Raimond urged the colonists of color to surpass the whites in their patriotism and moral virtue (1791a, 13). Martinique, he wrote, owed its tranquility to the fact that the men of color were the armed auxiliaries of the white planters in maintaining slavery. He proposed that six million livres be donated as proof of their group's belonging to the French nation (1791a, 2). He concluded the pamphlet he addressed to Moreau de Saint-Méry with the following phrase: "Here are the great advantages that France will find in the decree that makes the people of color what they are, and what it is inconceivable to deny them: MEN and FRENCH" (1791b, 68; emphasis in original).

In Raimond's description of colonial society, color prejudice had appeared late and gotten worse over time. It developed during the period when the local society autonomously institutionalized the organization of stable Creole families. These were based on models that did not correspond to the metropolitan practices and expectations, and that protected the interests of the local community.

In the earliest days of the colony, the Code Noir required an unmarried master who had children with a female slave to free the woman and marry her. In this way, some of the earliest colonists linked themselves to women and shared households with them. Raimond argued that they preferred marrying them to the poor white women who were imported to the colonies but were considered to be lacking in virtue. Since land was relatively accessible in the early history of the colony, the children born of these unions established themselves. They took advantage of the privileges they were granted as subjects of the king, who followed an assimilationist policy. Since there was a lack of educational institutions in Saint-Domingue, many of these children were sent to school in France. To the great displeasure of the poorer European immigrants, the *little whites*, they implanted the forms of conviviality characteristic of the mother country in the colony. Color prejudice did not yet reign among the wealthier classes in the colony.

Despite conflicts in Europe—the War of the League of Augsburg (1688–1697) and the War of Spanish Secession (1701–1713)—the pace of immigration across the Atlantic didn't rise to a level sufficient to change the habits of the most privileged residents. But a few decades later, the War of Austrian Secession (1743–1748) and especially the Seven Years' War (1756–1763) had an entirely different impact on colonial society. By then, the wealthiest among the mixed-race classes were solidly established, and their proportion among the free population was growing steadily. Many of the young metropolitan arrivals seeking fortune couldn't gain a foothold in the colony. Their negative predispositions toward the people of color deepened, encouraged by the return of young white Creoles who were now wealthier and better educated. According to Julien Raimond, the jealousy provoked by the people of color among the whites of modest means turned into hatred.

The irritation of the new arrivals and of racists like Moreau de Saint-Méry reached a fever pitch because the people of color refused to feel they owed anything to the white colonists, and showed no gratitude or respect toward them. The fact that the laws and punishments put in place to guarantee deference on the part of people of color toward whites constantly had to be reissued and reiterated shows that, ultimately, it was impossible to force the internalization of this attitude. The feeling among the people of color was that they had not gained their status as a result of any kind of process of emancipation that required an expression of gratitude. It was bad faith to confuse them with the freed slaves or the emancipated, and in so doing to paint them as beneficiaries of the largesse of the enslaving colonizers.

The political and economic successes of the people of color distinguished them from the broader population and imposed and institutionalized new values and norms defining the Creole family as one with no debt to lordly generosity. Their behavior was a clear form of defiance to the pretensions of the whites, both wealthy and poor. The illusion that the origins of their group lay in rape and other sexual abuses, Raimond claimed, was connected to the idea that their social and economic success was the result of the overflowing generosity of a few owners of slaves. This vision sustained the many forms of discrimination that prevented them from reaching the highest echelons of society. These policies were put in place by the royal power itself, despite its assimilationist policies. People of color were, for example, outlawed from participating in the creation of municipalities; occupying any role in the judiciary; carrying weapons; practicing medicine, surgery, or midwifery; or taking up clerical roles. In addition, they were banned from wearing certain clothes and jewelry, excluded from dances, and outlawed from using European names.

It is definitely true that, despite their attachment to their mother country of France, the demographic growth and socioeconomic success of the people of color threatened to substantially alter the model of an exploitation colony dreamed of by metropolitan authorities. The true target of the forms of segregation put in place by the administration was the particular structure that family had taken on in Saint-Domingue, and its autonomous development. Metropolitan expatriates carried out a systematic persecution of the forms of private life adapted to colonial circumstances, and rejected the shared behavioral norms defined locally and based on principles of dignity and conviviality.

It is worth emphasizing the ways in which discrimination against women and their families, even nuclear families, punished men who were subjects or active citizens.[3] As early as 1703, Louis XIV pared back the rights of women of color by refusing to admit men married to *mulâtresses* into the nobility. Starting in 1733, any man married to a *négresse* or *mulâtresse* was outlawed from occupying a public position or office in the colony. And in 1771, a new requirement was put into place forcing any colonist requesting the granting of a noble title to undergo research into their ancestry: "In the beginning, the research into the ancestry of spouses was aimed at protecting the purity of the French nobility. Then, in the 1770s, color prejudice began to be used explicitly as the cement of the colonial slave society, to maintain the slaves in a state of inferiority and divide the emancipated and mixed-bloods. Progressively, the placement outside the law of women of mixed blood extended to men of mixed blood. They found themselves outlawed from exercising military or judicial roles, which were sought-after positions that offered power and notoriety" (Gauthier 2007, 57).

Color prejudice and discrimination against mixed-bloods aimed to slow down or reverse the rooting of the colonial population and their reproduction through the multiplication of families. The regulations against mixed marriages and the banning of those involved in these marriages, and their children, from leadership roles and liberal professions guaranteed the primacy of the metropole and the subordination of the colonized. An entire political, bureaucratic, and commercial armature was consolidated on the basis of the destruction of Creole families. Their loyalty toward the shared motherland didn't matter.

Racial discrimination and color prejudice attacked the construction of a civil society that responded to the inescapable need for reproduction and private life by creating a sustainable form of colonial life. The modern, colonial state inserted itself into the management of the intimate lives of citizens in an effort to destroy the embryos of an autonomous, sovereign way of life. By closing the doors to the major avenues of social promotion in public life, the state circumscribed the private life of people of color with increasingly narrow and modest limits.

Julien Raimond's reflections illuminate the particularities of the colonial class structure. But they also suggest that these particularities were the result of the construction of a way of life that clearly depended on the metropole and the system of slavery but also sought to manage the emerging context with a certain level of independence. After the French defeat in the Seven Years' War, colonial society was increasingly restructured around the concept of race. Colonists demanded that the metropole put an end to the military regime, and they allied themselves with colonial administrators to underline the importance of the culture and political community that connected whites to one another. Then, starting in 1780, the French colony expelled the mixed-bloods from white society, becoming more like the United States and less like the societies of Brazil and Jamaica. Families that in Brazil or Jamaica would have been considered *white*, with no affinity whatsoever with their *slaves*, now faced social exclusion (Garrigus 2006, 7).

The central role played by women of color in the establishment of the norms and values of the foundational local institutions incited jealousy among white women. The modest means of existence of the majority of the latter, combined with the doubts articulated about the virtues they brought to family life, justified the notorious and extensive list of policies of discrimination against people of color and the whites who married them. What drove these attacks against women and Creole families was the desire on the part of poor whites, who often worked as their employees even as they became new recruits to the group of white colonists, to get access to their property. As the French Revolution began, the aristocrats and wealthy planters of the colony, besieged in the metropole by the emergence of the sovereign people, saw control over the political system as an urgent goal. They sought an autonomy that would accommodate an increasingly sharp segregation as a guarantee for the continued forms of exploitation that were the basis of their wealth.

Despite his credentials as a committed racist, meanwhile, Julien Raimond was also a pragmatist. He chose to seek out the support of the dominated classes, though with the prudence required by the pitfalls of the moment. Contemporary Haitian thinkers have not dwelled on the links between Julien Raimond's insistence on the Frenchness of his sector of colonial society and his subsequent choice of Haitian nationality. Vastey described Pétion as being a "Haitian despite himself," having chosen this allegiance only to avoid death at the hands of his compatriots at the time of the Leclerc expedition (1819, 146). I dub this part of the population the *French Haitians* (Casimir 2010, 69).

For the higher classes, the American colonists, Saint-Domingue was born from the French right of conquest, and therefore insurrections could lead only to its total destruction. From their perspective, the colony had to stay within the orbit of the French metropole one way or another. Dubois (2004b, 226) notes this orientation on the part of Toussaint, and a recent study by Gary Wilder has traced its continuing presence from Toussaint to Victor Schoelcher and on to Aimé Césaire (Wilder 2005). Their political stance differed from that of the absentee planters, who sought autonomy as a way of protecting slavery and the racialization of human relationships. Without taking this distinction into account, it is difficult to comprehend the logic of the struggle of the colonists of color and Julien Raimond in particular. It is easy to get caught up in the study of their conflicts and alliances with the revolutionary forces of the captives, and their opposition to those who frequented the Club Massiac. In the midst of this interpretive imbroglio, the autonomy gained through the departure of the French and the elements used to explain the evolution of nineteenth-century Haiti become limited to a narrow reading of the quarrel between blacks and mulattoes and the inexplicable weakness of the bureaucratic organization of the state. The common denominator that linked the two branches of the oligarchy in their struggle against the former captives—their interest as possessing classes—becomes invisible.

We cannot ignore the fact that Julien Raimond formulated his vision of the colony while defending the interests of a tiny minority made up of a few hundred people. Nevertheless, this group is qualitatively important not only because of the pace of its growth but especially because it was the vector for the implantation of capitalism in the territory. Julien Raimond's argument was rooted in the defense of private property, and therefore in the defense of the primitive accumulation of capital, without regard for the moral values violated in the process. Raimond was part of colonial modernity, and instrumental reason was his only compass.

The social model offered by Raimond consisted in ending the forms of racial discrimination put in place after the Seven Years' War and centering colonial stratification on the wealth of citizens and their access to property. The order he proposed was one in which the free people of color would guarantee, as they always had, the control over the *bossales* and their subjection in the slave system. As Gauthier (2007, 123–125) explains, the hope was that gradually the local breeding of slaves would make the slave trade unnecessary. Raimond traveled to Paris with the express purpose of making sure the legislative assemblies in Paris were aware of this possible solution to the crises in the colonies. His efforts were successfully translated into the strategy of the Brissotins, who recognized that the people of color were the best defense against the rebellion of the slaves, and accordingly passed the decree of April 4, 1792 (Dubois and Garrigus 2006, 26).

In his article titled "Vincent Ogé Jeune (1757–91): Social Class and Free Colored Mobilization on the Eve of the Haitian Revolution" (2011), John Garrigus offers precious information that completes our understanding of the questions explored by Julien Raimond. The historian documents the activities of Vincent Ogé, who was in Paris at the same time as Raimond, but for other reasons: he had to deal with financial problems that were on the verge of causing the bankruptcy of his businesses. Ten years younger than Raimond, he was one of the richest merchants in Saint-Domingue and essentially a courtier. In the midst of the dangers that revolutionary events posed to social life in the colony, he offered himself as an intermediary between the wealthy planters of the Club Massiac and the colonial population, promising that his skillful approach would slow down the process of change. The key to his strategy was the consolidation of the union of all the property owners through the creation of an assembly of Americans that would bring together the Creoles and the rich residents of the colony. The absentee planters, the poor whites, and the freed slaves of little means would be excluded from this assembly. The government of the colony would essentially be in the hands of the property owners who lived there. Unsurprisingly, the Club Massiac, packed with absentee plantation owners, ignored the proposal.

Searching for a group to whom he could offer his services, Ogé approached the Société des Citoyens de Couleur, made up of artisans and servants who made very modest salaries. This aspect of his adventure unveils to us another zone of colonial life. Ogé adopted the claims of the *Cahiers de doléances* (Registers of grievances) of the Society of Citizens of Color, which declared that all Creoles were brothers and that racial discrimination should not be allowed in the colony. Raimond registered with the group soon after Ogé in July 1789. Both of them were received at the Société des Amis des Noirs a few months later, in November 1789.

On his return to Saint-Domingue, Ogé joined forces with Chavannes, who like him was a quadroon and coffee planter. Chavannes had served in the militia and fought at the Battle of Savannah during the American Revolution. Much less wealthy than Ogé, he identified with the free people of color who were of similar condition to him, rather than with the two hundred born of free parents. The demands of Chavannes and his peers were not founded on property and the management of significant material possessions, but rather on the vital services they had rendered to the maintenance of public order in the militia. They were not at all interested in the idea proposed by their brethren in Paris of an alliance between all Creoles without distinction of color.

Garrigus argues that the extent of the rebellion carried out by Ogé and Chavannes, and the conflict between them and troops sent from Le Cap to meet them at Grande Rivière du Nord, has been exaggerated. In the face of the opposition to their demands on the part of the colonial authorities, their movement disbanded rapidly. Ogé and Chavannes took refuge in Spanish Santo Domingo and were arrested and extradited back to the French authorities, while their followers retreated to the neighboring mountains.

The revolt of Ogé and Chavannes, Garrigus argues, had less of an impact on colonial society than their rapid execution without trial. They were tortured in the plaza in front of the cathedral of Le Cap, their heads sliced open and impaled. Shocked by these abominations, the urban mass of the free people of color and the free blacks, used to carrying out the tasks of the police and militia, rose up (Garrigus 2011, 61). In the wake of the actions of Ogé and Chavannes, this group of *métis* and free blacks, well trained through military and police activity, entered into the political arena. They decided to begin arming the captives and confront the colonial authorities.

Six months after the February 1791 execution of Ogé and Chavannes, the call to general insurrection was issued at Bois Caïman. Raimond's partisans entered the fray, brandishing their favorite weapon—their control over landed property. The popular urban sector of *métis* and free blacks, however, were armed with the services they had previously rendered to the colonial order in carrying out the subjection of the captives and their transformation into slaves. Both groups shared the same loyalty to France, on the one side because they were property owners and colonists and on the other because they were the guarantors of public order. They therefore shared the same racism and disdain for the rights of the near totality of the local population. Nevertheless, there was a difference between them. The partisans of Raimond, generally property owners and industrialists, aligned themselves with the thinking of the Société des Amis des Noirs and the Jacobins of the French Revolution. The urban popular sector, meanwhile, according to historians Thomas Madiou and Beaubrun Ardouin, aligned themselves with the projects of the Club Massiac and Moreau de Saint-Méry, determined enemies of Julien Raimond.

This divergence between the American colonists, busy managing their plantations, and the *emancipated* in the strict sense of the term, who were dedicated to urban activities, is of fundamental importance. The composition and functioning of the latter sector, made up almost entirely of former slaves and free blacks, meant that they were not connected to colonial thought in the same way as the wealthy whites and the American colonists. They did, however, represent the nerve center of colonial society: the mechanisms of management that had been created by the right claimed by France to conquer and possess a territory on the other side of the Atlantic, as well as its inhabitants. As we know, the American colonists were dedicated essentially to the production of agricultural export commodities. The free blacks, while they didn't shy away from economic activities, owed their status to the management of colonial society as a whole. The behavior of the American colonists, with the exceptions we have presented, followed the path created by the wealthy planters. They were, after all, to a large extent their heirs (King 2001, 209). The behavior of the free blacks, on the other hand, was the expression of their movement up a social ladder imposed by the metropole, armed with only the resources they had struggled to create for themselves.

These titled servants and mediators specialized in the maintenance of public order. The collusion between their interests and those of the colonists—whether European or American—is easy to miss, given the modesty of their lives and the instability of the conditions under which they worked and lived. The focus on the discrimination they suffered draws our attention away from the misdeeds of the order itself, and from the devotion with which this group worked in service of the established order. And the situation is even more complicated because as *anciens libres*—that is, the *formerly emancipated*, those who were freed before the revolutionary emancipation of 1793—these intermediaries sought to dress themselves up in revolutionary costume with the aim of validating their opportunistic political orientation and converting their loyalty to France into a form of altruistic service supposedly aimed at promoting the interests of the traditional, backward masses.

When we read Haitian history from the perspective of the metropole, the efforts at social ascension on the part of the free blacks seem more important than the class conflicts they were involved in.[4] It is logical to assume that in order to gain freedom from their masters, slaves had to prove their loyalty to the slave system. It is therefore not surprising that all the emancipated were required to be part of the militia or the police forces (King 2001, 247)—the forces of repression. A military career and pursuit of maroons was one available way to escape the conditions of servitude put in place by colonialism. The exploits carried out by these soldiers contributed to the expansion of the French colonial empire (notably in the case of the famous expedition to Savannah), and they became integrated into the dominant society as part of the colonial military elite. They didn't, however, free themselves from the control of the masters and mentors.

In order to function well, the colony depended on loyal and relatively well-paid police forces. Their salaries, the bonuses they received for capturing maroons or fugitives, the bribes, their participation in overseas military expeditions, all came together to allow them to detach themselves from the masses of the slaves. The elite among the free blacks was made up of the non-commissioned officers in the forces of public order and the members of the militia, while the artisans and salaried servants gathered together in a less privileged group. In the colonial system, the liberty of the former slaves was inextricably linked to their core task—that is, the security and support of the whites. To accede to the rank of the emancipated meant, unavoidably, to always behave as a freed slave.

The self-proclaimed leaders of the War of Independence emerged from this group of professional servants. It is not surprising that they took pride in the fact that they were completing and perfecting the task of colonization and colonialism that had produced them. This social strata created the bureaucracy of the nineteenth century. They were the guardians of an order that they had not produced and that they did not seek to change. In the midst of the broader conversation over social change and revolution, this group stood out for their admitted powerlessness and foundational, existential opportunism. The American colonists, meanwhile, like the other planters of the colony, rushed to leave it behind as soon as the general insurrection and the demands for the rights of the workers made the functioning of a modern, capitalist, and colonial economy impossible. It was the emancipated of Saint-Domingue who made it over the hurdle of 1804, still armed with the colonial thought of modern times.

Moreau de Saint-Méry and the Club Massiac

French royal authority envisioned an embryonic structure of settlement in the colony, and its primary objective was the edification of an exploitation colony built on slavery for the pure profit of the metropole. It was undergirded by a normative project aimed at converting territory into a mercantilist site for the primitive accumulation of capital. When we center this project in our thinking, we tend to overlook the significant social groups who were in a position to resist this project's development. The pamphlets and memoirs written by Moreau de Saint-Méry to the Constituent Assembly created a tableau in which all human beings were enlisted in the service of the conquerors of the territory. His work lays out the justifications for their exploitation.

From the perspective of the colonial ideology, the population of Saint-Domingue was divided into three social classes: the whites; the emancipated slaves, generally of mixed blood; and the slaves themselves, who were blacks. The empire had the responsibility of strengthening the class of whites, the conquerors and masters of the colony. The official ideology of Pétion's republic adopted this tripartite, racist conception of the social structure and got into the habit of not distinguishing between the mixed-bloods and the people of color who were born free. As a result, this thought didn't take stock of the existence of the embryo of a local bourgeoisie as a socially distinct group.

The author of the *Description topographique, physique, civile, politique et histoire de la partie française de l'Ile de Saint-Domingue* popularized a racial ladder constructed out of permutations and combinations of two primary races, black and white, as if it was universally used in the colony. Vastey, who lived in the midst of these observed phenomena, refused to distinguish between the nonfree and the free, because the white public was the master of the latter ([1814] 2013, 14). In this he drew on the arguments of his predecessor, Julien Raimond (1793, 23). The thinkers of Pétion's republic privileged Moreau de Saint-Méry's perspective over that of the two victims of colonial racism, whose work they must have been familiar with. The Haitian educational system has integrated an idea of colonial society taken from Moreau de Saint-Méry, and not from the observation of these two compatriots.

Saint-Méry is known as a mixed-race colonist who lived as a white person by hiding his *métissage* (Gauthier 2007, 237). Beaubrun Ardouin cites a November 1790 note from Brissot proving that Haitian intellectuals were aware of the racist currents in their preferred historiographical reference and of his arrogance toward his fellow people of color: "Brissot, in a letter addressed to Barnave in November 1790, wrote: 'There are deputies from the islands in the National Assembly (MM. Moreau de Saint-Méry and Cocherel, for instance), who are impossible to distinguish from mulattoes. I have been assured that in the colonial assemblies, in some of the most distinguished positions, there are true mixed-bloods who have succeeded in disguising their origins. Can you believe that these brothers of mulattoes are their most ardent and arrogant enemies?'" (Ardouin 1853, 1:80). Moreau de Saint-Méry advocated for a model of colonial society where the capital of white property owners would profit from the labor of black slaves, controlled by freed slaves of mixed race who were subordinated to the whites so that there was no perspective whatsoever of equality between these three castes. He wrote this in black and white: "It is unacceptable for citizens of color to have equal rights" (Gauthier 2007, 262). At first, the Declaration of the Rights of Man and Citizen concerned neither the free people of color nor the free blacks. In a more general sense, it had no intention of significantly modifying the situation in the colonies (Gauthier 2007, 91).

For this colonist and public official, there could be no juridical mediation of the relationships between masters and slaves. He was an apologist for the right to use and abuse private property. For him, power in a slave colony derived, without restrictions, from the right of conquest. "So, in 'slave colonies,' the masters must be the exclusive source of power over the slaves and the emancipated. The existence of any power superior to the masters would undermine the respect and fear that cement these relationships. . . . Master-slave relations have no law, only the power of the former over the latter, that is a relationship of direct force" (Gauthier 2007, 271). The Constituent Assembly had a choice. They could decide to preserve the colonies and decide that the Declaration of the Rights of Man and Citizen was an obstacle to their development. Or they could abandon them to their independence (Gauthier 2007, 274). Writing under the pseudonym "Anonymous," Moreau de Saint-Méry recognized that color prejudice was the hidden spring within the colonial machine. Barnave, serving on the powerful Comité des colonies (Committee on the colonies) in the Constituent Assembly, took up his arguments and passed legislation that preserved the full enjoyment of liberty only for colonists of the white race, the only true new men of the territory. "So the political and legal project was to construct the ignorance of the slaves and free people of color in the colonies by transforming it into a prejudice, in order to maintain them in a state where they did not understand that they belonged to human kind, that they were born free and had the rights to remain free" (Gauthier 2007, 327).

This vision of colonial life shaped the propositions of the Assembly of Saint Marc and especially the more explicit decree that the Assembly of the South issued on May 9, 1790, in reference to the colonists of color: "You should avoid making demands that are incompatible with the state of subordination in which you must remain and preserve toward the whites, and the respectful deference that you owe them. Do not have the pride or the delirium to believe that you can ever WALK IN EQUALITY WITH YOUR PATRONS, YOUR BENEFACTORS, YOUR FORMER MASTERS, AND TO PARTICIPATE IN ALL THE PUBLIC OFFICES AND RIGHTS" (Gauthier 2007, 192; emphasis in the original). Moreau de Saint-Méry was a founding member of the Club Massiac, where the wealthy absentee planters, generally aristocrats, met with the network of merchants from the slave trading ports to make sure that the French Revolution didn't impact colonial life (Liébart 2008). The club played on the generalized opposition to the authoritarianism of the Crown to gain acceptance in assemblies in which they didn't have a formal right to participation. Some of its representatives even pronounced the Tennis Court Oath. In addition to preventing any kind of slave uprising, the goal of this lobby was to prevent the Parisian assemblies from intervening in the affairs of Saint-Domingue and strengthening the government on the island. Die-hard physiocrats, they opposed the monopoly system and as a result, ended up in conflict with the merchants of the port towns.

Raimond thought that the club's real goal was independence for the colony. The club was opposed to having the Assembly discuss the problems of the colony, and it also took measures to prevent the ideas circulating in France from crossing the Atlantic. The club did everything it could to make sure that the colonial political structures were consolidated under the control of the white planters. The internal conflicts in the group worsened with the arrival of the planters known as *léopardins*, who were accused by Saint-Domingue governor Pernier of treason, while the loyalist planters of the Northern Province traveled to counteract their influence and support the executive power. These conflicts became meaningless once the general insurrection of 1791 began, making whatever consequences could have resulted from them irrelevant.

Moreau de Saint-Méry and the Club Massiac, in contrast to the dispositions of the Code Noir, sought to lead the Constituent Assembly in a direction opposite from that of the assimilationist policies of the royalty, and to push society to a more radical project. Theirs was essentially a project of segregation, which from the beginning rejected the idea of equality of rights for all citizens and contributed to moving the Assembly in a counterrevolutionary direction.

Following Florence Gauthier, I will add that Moreau de Saint-Méry left another sad legacy in Haitian society, through the mediation of the historians of Pétion's republic. His work obscured the interpretation of social relations before and after 1804 by pointing it in the direction of the color question. This maneuver obfuscates the much more serious damage caused by the monopolization of private property and the tacit acceptance of the right of conquest on the part of the colonizers and their direct descendants. Moreau de Saint-Méry fiercely defended the position of the French colonial empire.

Too often historiography has allowed itself to get stuck in the trap set up by Moreau: this is the case of the population statistics cited for the population of Saint-Domingue in the second half of the eighteenth century, which invariably present the three types of status that the monarchy wanted to have recognized: the whites, seen as the only true colonists, the emancipated, and the slaves. . . . But these percentages, themselves fictive . . . reflect a political project that was not legally recognized at the time, and was unique to its theoretician Moreau de Saint-Méry. Under the cover of supposedly objective statistics there is in fact a remarkable ideological machine. The theoreticians of color prejudice imagined a new legal order made up of three types of status: the free, those who were emancipated but were divided by nuances of color, and the slaves. This new legal order corresponded to a new colonial policy that was to be put into place while a new Creole society evolved. (Gauthier 2007, 334)

The Haitian inheritors of French colonialism might have built on the ideological positions and values—themselves quite timorous—that inspired Julien Raimond, the Society of Citizens of Color, and the Society of the Friends of the Blacks, which at least struggled in favor of the sovereign people in the metropole. Instead, they chose to base their thinking on the counterrevolutionary dealings of the Club Massiac and Moreau de Saint-Méry. Once secession had been carried out, the oligarchs in power took care not to reproduce subversive republican ideas, which were also put into the archive in France itself, with the exception of the four years of the Second Republic. The perspectives of Moreau de Saint-Méry and the Club Massiac can be explained and are well known, along with those of Julien Raimond. But those of Madiou and Ardouin are much less understood. The fact is that these thinkers led Haitian historiography astray by (blithely!) accommodating to the hegemony of urban, racist, colonial thought and not integrating the more plausible perspective described by Raimond, a member of what today we would call the national or local bourgeoisie.

The oligarchs of Saint-Domingue and of Haiti didn't create—and could not create—a republic that embraced all the inhabitants of the territory. In contrast to the metropole they idolized, at no moment did they consider creating a sovereign people that would be the repository of all national power. Instead, they worked hard to slow down the revolutionary process of the restructuring of the political system, and hung on to the ways of life from before 1789, which had been built on deep disdain for the laboring classes who were ethnically different from them.

A Modern, Colonial Reading of Independence

The thought of the administration of the state in Haiti—particularly that of Pétion's republic—was based on this second source, the blindest of the two currents of colonial thought. Moreau de Saint-Méry and Barnave considered that the whites remained the source of all authority, to the exclusion of other groups or social classes in society. The free people of color born of free parents—not even one-hundredth of the population—were convinced that as landed property owners and taxpayers they contributed to the power of the state and its political strength. The tenth of the population made up of those responsible for the maintenance of the slavery, mulattoes and free blacks, announced that they deserved to share the inherent rights of citizenship, from which the huge majority of slaves—foreigners to the formal structure of power and, by definition, the cause of potential trouble—were excluded. The castes and interest groups responsible for the public colonial order acted with the sentiment that they comprised the base of the administration and were a key part of the presence of the French colonial empire in Saint-Domingue. So they thought that the upheavals provoked by the revolutionary transformations in France, and the resulting changes in the relationship between imperial powers, would not have an impact on the slaves, inferior beings subjected to their will, and they got to work making sure that would remain the case. This group holds the keys to the written archives of the nation.

Of course, contrary to these dreams of exploitation, imperial rivalries and metropolitan crises in fact upended the situation in the colony. The series of unexpected events that followed opened up a space for the emergence of deep tendencies that had, until then, remained unseen. In order to save its right to conquest over the territory, challenged by England and Spain, France was forced to renegotiate the position of the classes and interest groups in Saint-Domingue. The mass of slaves was called on to activate its potential as a political force. The conservation of the overseas possessions and especially the Pearl of the Antilles was too important to be undermined by the quarrels between property owners. In calling on the newly freed, the metropole itself assisted in overturning the social order, in defiance of its upper classes. Its effort to redress the situation failed.

The emancipated of the urban police, those responsible for the maintenance of the colonial order, had absorbed the idea of the importance French sovereignty of the country's crown jewel. This led them to limit the Haitian Revolution to their own victory over the Napoleonic troops, carried out in the name of Western civilization, and certainly not in the name of the African traditions carried by the majority of the population. The secessionist army put in place with the defeat of the French expeditionary forces was a purely administrative collective—a military government. It considered itself a *state* (1807 Constitution, Art. 6). But the sovereignty of this new state, whatever the theories of Pétion's *republic*, could not root itself, in its relationships with the entities outside its own social group, outside of this political entity. This foundational sham, just eleven years after the French Revolution, consisted in anchoring national sovereignty in the relations between the state and the international community. It made it possible to elude the challenging question of popular sovereignty and, surreptitiously, to make it nothing more than a by-product of a so-called national sovereignty.

Those who supported the struggles of the broader population introduced political nuances into this social evolution as they consolidated their own interests. But this did not shape the problematic surrounding national sovereignty, which through the maneuver I've described was placed entirely in the hands of the armed forces. The Armée indigène, led by the colonial police forces, took on the task of nation building, establishing itself as the architect of the nation. Even the local bourgeoisie, whose interests were linked to the markets of the Atlantic ports of France, compromised and privileged the development of a military bureaucracy that eclipsed any consideration of the specific characteristics of the internal social groups, or of the basis for the relationships between them.

By privileging the threats of independence issued by the colonial powers, this way of thinking transposed the premises of colonialism into the structuring of Haitian society. All the political orientations of the new state recalled from the crises that had led to 1804 were the struggles carried out by the Armée indigène. They minimized the role played by the armed bands of maroons and the laboring population as a whole. In this context, the transfer of ownership over the territory from the mother country was so important that, despite the consciousness of their victory over the French expeditionary army, these former guarantors of the colonial order took the initiative to offer the imperial power a fabulous sum of money to compensate it for the loss of this property. By offering this indemnity, they also sought to immunize themselves against any influence on the part of the popular forces within the country or any new class of landowners.

Even more important, the offer of the indemnity to the former colonists was calculated based on the value of their land before the Revolution of 1789, as if the popular struggles that had taken place from 1791 to 1804 were nothing but an unfortunate parenthesis. The sovereignty of the state created in 1804 was negotiated based on the real estate market as it had been defined during the period of primitive accumulation, without any connection to the trajectory (and even less, the awakening) of the Haitian people.

Sonthonax, the civil commissioner of the metropolitan government, had gotten it completely wrong when he declared the blacks to be the "true sans-culottes, and the only ones capable of defending the country" (Dubois 2003, 294). From the perspective of Pétion's republic, Haitian independence did not flow from the Declaration of the Rights of Man and Citizen. Its national sovereignty was limited to seizing a territory and then legalizing that seizure by paying a high price.

The orientation of the working classes of slave origin, of course, were given no importance, since the only *active citizens* were the small number of property owners whose ownership was consecrated by this military administrative state. The governments took care not to distribute land to the mass of *passive citizens* and took the necessary measures to prevent them from acquiring them by their own means.

The workers themselves were ignored by Moreau de Saint-Méry, Julien Raimond, Vincent Ogé, Jean-Baptiste Chavannes, and all the imperial powers of the day. They had to trace their own path, perhaps spontaneously, as they navigated their impossible transformation into agricultural laborers—that is, into tools of a European future, or a future for the inheritors of the Europeans. As slaves and foreigners, and eventually newly freed and potential indentured servants, they were not concerned with the conquest of the territory. They remained tools of labor, their inferiority maintained. Along with power, the political administration born in 1804 carried on the vision of the wealthy whites of the Club Massiac: "Property is one of the principal conditions of the existence of society, and legitimate and unthreatened property is the condition for its happiness" (Barbé-Marbois 1826, 18).

But the fact that the state and the colonial and postcolonial oligarchs wished to believe that the workers were politically invisible, and constructed their discourse on the basis of this phantasm, doesn't justify studying the history of the country on the basis of these fantasies. On the contrary, we need to understand that it was the behavior of the laboring classes reduced to slavery, even if they were not part of the visible power structure, that both built the colonial political system and dug its grave. The *slaves*—so-called—were at once the reason for the existence of the modern, colonial state established in Saint-Domingue and its executioner. It was inconceivable that they would not be a part of it, and just as inconceivable that the definition of the state would not include them, despite the claims of Pétion's 1807 Constitution.

The key is to come to understand, despite the rhetoric of the Code Noir and the laws of the period, the ways in which the captives reduced to slavery participated in the colonial state. By landing in America, the state that was being constructed—modern, colonial, Eurocentric, and racist—took the measures necessary to produce the political invisibility of the first nations and those of African origin who resisted. It conceived of itself as a form of unified sovereign domination within conquered territory. It even tended to confuse itself with the administrative, governmental structures that managed its monopoly over violence. On the basis of this belief in its supreme power, it developed political discourses that rhymed with those of the Age of Enlightenment.

It should be easy to see that this conception could not be shared by the unsubdued, the insurgents, the dissidents who resisted imperial power. The civilizing mission that drove that power represented their devastation, and that of their world. The victims brutalized by conquest were, from the beginning, confronted with the necessity of protecting themselves from the desolation the colonizers sowed wherever they went.

The ruse of modernity's discourse was that it presupposed the social inexistence of these martyrs, but could operate only through constructing that inexistence. For the modern state to give birth to its colony, it had to annihilate their resistance, which meant it necessarily had to deal with their presence and their oppositional behavior. The content of the measures taken necessarily trace out the sufferers' opposition through what they outlaw. Whatever the illusions of the modern, colonial state and its administrators, the victims were an integral part of the structure of power, and they determined its content through their existence and their resistance.

Concretely speaking, the captive could not think of liberty from inside the export-oriented plantation system unless all exits were closed off. They could not conceive of the offer of general emancipation that France ended up making as an offer of liberty, given the locus of enunciation from which it came. For there to be an insurrection and especially a revolution—that is, for the captives to manage their own modernization (Nesbitt 2008)—they had to be mentally free, even in the midst of the concentration camp, even with chains around their ankles. The captive's freedom of thought, the reality and practice of that freedom, are what provoked and motivated the speeches defending the ownership of slaves in front of the metropolitan assemblies. If the captives had not behaved as if they were free, the masters and their representatives would not have had to demand that they submit. and even less, to force them to do so.

The captive's freedom could not be captured. It was used to justify the repressive measures that the colonial state had to take in order to respond to the groundswell that emerged from the enslaved society. The administrators of the state spoke of liberty because they recognized that the captivity of the labor force—or more precisely, the need to make this captivity effective—was what defined the borders of slavery. This distinction between captivity and enslavement was a watershed, one that emerged and was expressed because it constituted the space of the slave plantation. Otherwise, no one would have noticed. Nevertheless, it was constituted outside the discourse of the plantation, even as it used its victims and their response and resistance as the backdrop for the enunciation of its word.

In this sense, the decolonial option was already part of the sphere of the imperial state, but it remained unthinkable within or from this sphere. The state thought with its own concepts, and its own blindness. Given that the decolonial option could not be avoided as one of the targets of its activity, the empire constantly took measures aimed at preventing any counterthinking from expressing itself and creating an alternative consciousness—that is, from institutionalizing a locus of enunciation outside of the control of the public administration, a location of power that could defy it.

The discourse of the state, its norms and behaviors, attested to the political presence of the oppressed, whose invisibility it constantly had to renew. The content of the modern, colonial state's sphere emerged from its perception (one that, certainly, was repressed!) of the alterity of the philosophy, forms, avenues of expression, and methods of resistance of the oppressed. Starting in 1492, this challenge always escaped the universalist pretensions of the modern, colonial state. Those who choose to study the emergence of a conscious political force among the victims of colonialism, struggling to defend their liberty, make this challenge the object of their research.

My concern here is not to explore why, at the end of the eighteenth century, the stormy conversation among French property owners, both white and of color, didn't lead to an agreement. As interesting as it is, that question can be posed only within the realm of imperial domination. That quarrel, however, created a broad space for political maneuvering. Unable to depend on a united front among the regime's privileged classes, the colonial authorities found themselves condemned to watch, powerless, as a working class in the midst of its own transformations into a peasantry took control of the economy starting in 1791, and especially after 1804. This was the reverse of the absorption of peasant communities into Western, capitalist industry.

With the departure of the colonists, both white and of color, the production of material life passed into the hands of the agricultural laborers, their families, and their communities. The plantation disappeared as the foundational institution in the economic landscape. The basis of structural dependence was swept away. The prior invisibility of the workers reduced to slavery, and of their conditions of existence, produced a blindness among those who took over the positions of the oligarchy. Work itself, and its autonomous potential, became invisible. The oligarchy perceived the forms of existence that flourished outside the capitalism of the commodity-producing plantations as simply the expression of varieties of laziness, idleness, and vagabondage. They repeated the unrealizable dreams of large-scale agriculture, which governed the political discourse of the nineteenth century, with exhausting monotony. Meanwhile, without fanfare, the majority of the population appropriated the sociopolitical space through communal solidarity. Tiptoeing forward, the overwhelming majority of cultivators refused the government's attempt to convert them into marginal people. Instead, they transformed themselves into the inhabitants of the rural territory.

Conclusion: A Decolonial Itinerary

The reflections that follow represent an effort to understand how this new actor emerged, and how it armed itself to defend the communities that the conquerors and their collaborators wished to reduce to nothingness. I want to discern how and why, despite its all-powerful nature, the imperial state failed to fully possess the colonial workers or to imprison them in material conditions that would have forced them to bend to the injunctions of the capitalism that was in the midst of its own development at the time. I want to identify the circumstances in which the Haitian people invented themselves.

If, as I have written, "social science has no justification other than discovering how the dominated can recuperate their history" (Casimir 1981, 255), then there are some choices to be made in the way we study the history of Haitians (or any colonized people). I can study it from the bridge of the *Santa María*, standing alongside Christopher Columbus, and I'll discover Hispaniola. I can also chose to stand in Ayiti alongside the indigenous peoples Columbus baptized as *Indians* (Casimir 2004b) before exterminating them. In choosing the latter option I take note of the fact that, as they disembarked from the slave ships, the *bossales* indigenized themselves in complete solitude, on the beaches, so that they would become Haitians. From this perspective, what I see on the island are Taínos and not *Indians*, a variety of African nations and not *blacks*, captives and not *slaves*.

We were born from our ancestors' response to a triple crime: the abusive appropriation of the lands of America by the European states, the ignominy of the massacre of the original nations, and the criminal slave trade. There are, among us, some who were born in the hold of the *Santa María*, or who have climbed onto that ship: the *emancipated slaves*. Among them, some consider that reality unavoidable! Others think that what can be seen from that caravel does not exhaust reality. On the beach are those who are not *being discovered*, but who are in the process of *discovering*.

Before the arrival of the European caravel on the shores of the island of Haiti, there were no *Indians* in America, and even less so were there *blacks* (Bonfil Batalla 1981). There was no America. Nor was there a Latin America

(Mignolo 2005). America, the *Indians*, and the *blacks*—these are expediencies of the European discourse. In response, we invented Haitians, Jamaicans, Barbadians, and so on.

Colonial thought, in both its progressive and conservative forms, uses all the means at its disposal to oppose our comprehension of our own power, of the possibilities for our empowerment. It is our responsibility to describe, with more precision, the circumstances under which we were born here in America, and how we succeeded in transforming the merchandise of the slave ship into a powerful political actor.

The influence of colonialism in Haiti is profound. But it is largely limited to the social class that monopolizes the official forms of expression. Colonial thought presupposes another way of thinking that contradicts it. But it never allows it to be seen. When colonialism is effective, this other way of thinking is made invisible. The colonial gaze, however, is not the only significant perspective.

The majority of the colonial population was made up of captives reduced to slavery who, for this very reason, served as the justification and the target of colonial thought. But we cannot push aside the question of what was in their minds, of what means of expression they used and what institutions they built to sustain themselves. This study seeks to contribute to the visibility of this counterthought, which in Haiti has never tired of expressing itself in its own language.

There is another, and less obvious, question that is rarely brought up in studies of Saint-Domingue and the genesis of the state in Haiti. The total power of the colonizers was constructed to face off against the universe of the struggling oppressed. But the daily management of the institutions and instruments of oppression was hard work. And the privileged, busy reaping the profits of their power, preferred to delegate it to subalterns. They invented a specific social category to carry out this relatively thankless work: the *emancipated slaves*. As long as the social order was maintained according to the principles emitted by the metropole, the emancipated remained a group of loyal intermediaries in the pay of the dominant system. But once official policy ordered them deported or massacred, this sector was forced to detach itself and find a way to survive on its own. That is how they became Haitian in order not to perish (Vastey 1819, 136). And that is how the governing classes were born, in unexpected and unfortunate circumstances. The emancipated were molded within and by the very French colonial thought that justified their killing and deportation. The urgency with which they separated from France was not at all linked to the ultimate necessity of conceiving of a form of government endowed with its own thought and its social project. The sector of the emancipated, or the *formerly freed*, as they were called, carried the colonial matrix of power forward. They were the ones who were responsible for the maintenance of capitalist domination over the population. They governed the country with the conceptual tools they received from colonialism.

The freed could not rid themselves of these tools, which were the foundation for their existence. They received them as a subordinated group, a disdained minority. Their survival depended on the dexterity with which they appropriated and used these conceptual tools for the maintenance of public order. As an intermediary group, they did not possess, nor could they invent, a form of social thought different from that of their masters. They rebelled, then, within the limits of the vision projected by their masters, demanding of the latter that they follow their initial principles. In the face of the realpolitik of empire, they had no other option. The instructions issued to Leclerc by Napoléon Bonaparte make that clear. As intermediaries, they were prisoners of metropolitan thought and could not liberate themselves from it.

Chapter 4

Slaves or Peasants

Introduction: A Society without a Peasantry

The classic histories of Hispaniola, Saint-Domingue, and Haiti narrate the adventures of those who conquered these territories and their populations. They give voice to the protagonists of these conquests, foregrounding these builders of states, who hoped to transform the colonies into nation-states miming the formal structures of power then being put into place in Western Europe. Their discourse, and its logic, justifies the massacre of the indigenous peoples, the enslavement of hundreds of thousands of captives imprisoned in Africa, and later the exploitation and persecution of the cultivators. This logic also demands that its victims remain silent. It describes the order imposed by Europeans on the peaceful inhabitants of the island of Haiti. And it declares that there is no need to know or understand these inhabitants.

The reverse of this logic—the history of the Haitians themselves, rather than just the history of Hispaniola, Saint-Domingue, or Haiti—was not registered in the official archives of the time. In fact, these archives represented the codification of the approach that assailed and sought to eradicate certain behaviors among the Haitians. They document the desire to repress what was seen as subversive to the order the Spanish, the French, and later the Haitian oligarchs sought to implant at any cost. In order to build their New World, the colonists needed to invent colonial social actors: the indigenous people and the captives imported from Africa to replace them. They conceived of these actors as being empty of any useful content—or more precisely, as beings to be emptied of all meaningful content. The indigenous people and the enslaved were seen as lacking in all virtue, destined to allow themselves to be shaped by their self-proclaimed owners. Their destiny was meant to be the perfection of a form of submission that was to be even more complete than that suffered by the most exploited sectors in Europe: the serfs and peasants who were products of millennia of bullying.

Colonial history is just a minor chapter in the broader history of the European oligarchy. They deprived the slaves of their history in order to imprison them in a form of nothingness, forcing them to be devoted entirely to the service of the West. But the Haitian oligarchs who succeeded them in 1804 had to invent their own history. They had to endow themselves with a reason to exist. It had to be different from the reasons used by their European creators, but still allow them to remain as part of their creators' world, and its future. Whatever ideas these oligarchs had about those they called the *newly freed*, they couldn't construct their history without conceding to this group at least some place within it. They couldn't exist as a distinct entity without them. They had to carry that burden, whether they liked it or not. This made it impossible for them to dissolve themselves, in body and soul, into the West. But it also justified their existence. So they had to name that burden and invent a turning-to-nothingness specific to Haiti's history. The local oligarchs dreamed desperately of an independent Haiti without an independent population.

When it came to the treatment of the population, there was no significant difference between this dream and that of the eighteenth-century capitalists of Saint-Domingue. The two groups of property owners, European and American, worked together to replace the term *slave*, which had become politically unacceptable in revolutionary France. But they didn't change the character's role. In collaboration with metropolitan philosophes, they scrutinized the vocabulary of the imperial language and sought out a new designation for this category that had to change in appearance while conserving all its content. During the pivotal period before 1804, they rebaptized the colonial worker, the *slave*, as a *cultivator*. In so doing, they marked out the territory where they hoped to contain the agricultural workers in the nineteenth century.

The emancipated worker in the colony was not, and could not be, a peasant. The newly freed remained essentially a landless agricultural laborer. During the nineteenth century the word *peasant* retained precisely the meaning it had previously held in Saint-Domingue. The French peasant cultivated the earth, but was not a *cultivator* according to the definition developed for this term in the colony and in the Republic of Haiti. The Haitian *cultivator* was not a *peasant* according to the laws of the country. He remained a former *slave* who could own a few things, in contradistinction to Article 28 of the Code Noir, but who had to remain miserable and always available as a laborer.

The Workforce of the Peasants and the Slaves

This was an era marked by both transformations in the status of metropolitan workers and discussions about the abolition of slavery. So it is not surprising that comparisons were made between the disinherited on opposite sides of the Atlantic. Antiabolitionists posited that the Caribbean slaves were happier than European peasants, and abolitionists were convinced the opposite was true. From all they observed, each group selected what was necessary to justify what they considered unavoidable forms of subjugation.

Many colonists, it is believed, were of peasant background. Returning from a journey to Saint-Domingue, one representative of the French nation claimed a link between the two classes. He recalled a joke that had circulated among the European settlers during the early period of colonization in the Caribbean, which called for a migration of nobles to Saint Christopher, bourgeois to Guadeloupe, soldiers to Martinique, and peasants to Grenada (Delaporte 1775, 102). During their lives, many colonists had directly experienced some part of the endemic turmoil suffered by the peasants of the regions from which they had come (Hilliard d'Auberteuil 1777, 141).

In a January 27, 1733, declaration, the king enumerated the groups he placed at the bottom of the social ladder: "vagabonds, outlaws, artisans, tradespeople, prisoners, sailors, peasants and others of this quality who are not of the rank of those who we allow and accept to carry weapons" (Chambon 1783, 521). The slaves of the kingdom joined this group to complete the universe of the abandoned. Indeed, to some, peasants were *slaves* (Wimpffen 1797, 172).

In their comparisons between the two categories of workers, abolitionists and antiabolitionists referred indiscriminately to *slaves* and *blacks* as a homogenous group of laborers. They described the peasants outside the Atlantic context, in contrast, as having diverse characteristics that varied from one place to another. Voyagers observed them in Asia, America, France, Poland, Prussia, Russia, Turkey, Syria, and so on (Descourtilz 1795, 106). The comparative differences between the diverse nations or tribes of blacks, meanwhile, escaped them. The racialization of social relations created a basic principle in defining labor relations. Certain workers had specialized skills, but that didn't increase their prestige among the slaves. Servants who were useful to the objectives of the plantation system remained powerless individuals. Only the gaze of the master differentiated them.

Despite the disdain with which they were treated, or perhaps because of this disdain, this disinherited population remained the main workforce available during the period. They were, inevitably, a key subject of discussions on political economy and the future of society. During the second half of the eighteenth century, structural changes led to new kinds of reflection. Once the members of the Third Estate insisted on the centrality of popular sovereignty in the construction of the political structure, the question of the abolition of slavery became part of the discussion. The many comparisons between peasants and slaves were attempts to define the components of the population and the sovereign people in order to formulate, or reformulate, their rights and ultimately the roles they could or should play within the political system. The key goal was to find a way to exclude the liberated slaves from the new order.

The Abbé Sibire argued that the servitude or slavery of domestics, peasants, and blacks was the only remaining source of labor that could be freely manipulated by owners of land and other forms of capital (1789, 3). This labor force had certain characteristics, which M. de Tussac underlined aptly. He wrote that even if you offered the children of peasants and day laborers the same education as the children of the wealthy destined to occupy high-level government positions, you still wouldn't have solved the problem of the need for labor. "People the earth with scholars, and it will remain sterile" (Tussac 1810, 71). It was therefore necessary to keep these ignoramuses ignorant. In other words, humanity—Western humanity, that is—flourished thanks to the existence of the dispossessed. When there were no longer enough of them, the West went and procured more along its periphery, by plundering the African continent. The only way to subjugate them was to deprive them of all resources and, above all, of all knowledge. "It was necessary to subjugate this multitude of people without property (the blacks) to a handful of Europeans" (Gouy 1792, 9). To this end, it made sense to slander the dispossessed and transform them into imaginary barbarians (Hurbon 1987).

European authors did not see any characters in Haiti that reminded them at all of European peasants. Strictly speaking, there is no rural population within a flourishing plantation society, and certainly no peasants. The agricultural workers in Saint-Domingue lived garrisoned in barracks or the workshops of agro-industrial factories. They were no more rural residents than the prisoners in a penal colony or a concentration camp located in the countryside. "Traveling around the towns and countryside of Saint-Domingue, we never saw a people, or any kind of human beings that could be compared to our peasants in Europe" (Raynal 1785, 37). In Jamaica, however, villages of independent producers in what was known as the "free village system" were subject to special legislation, and tolerated on the margins of the colonial system.[1]

The Appropriation of the Land

Descourtilz concluded that it was impossible for the *blacks*, by which he meant the *slaves*, to become peasants: in order to establish "the regime that reigns in France, you would have to proscribe all the masters, for their rights were an insurmountable and invincible obstacle to this project" (1795, 306). It would be necessary, he went on, to follow the example of Robespierre and eliminate "all the rich and successful men," as Polvérel and Sonthonax attempted to do. The state would have to kill the masters, that part of humanity that counted, in order to transform the slaves into peasants.

The master's right to property would clearly be violated. The planter Malouet upped the ante: Why should the blacks be emancipated, our properties alienated? Why should we share our land with them? Everything the colonists owned had been acquired perfectly legally. Indeed, "What possible reason is there to emancipate them? Would the nation become stronger if they became property owners? Doesn't every society have as its only object the common strength and happiness? It cannot be forced to work toward the growth of another society" (1788, 52). The *slave*, and more generally the *black*, Malouet reminded his readers, was a foreigner who had not been conquered. So his lands were not stolen. How could their mass absorption into French society be conceived?

The occupation of Saint-Domingue was perfectly fair in those times of generalized piracy (among Europeans). In his *Essai sur l'administration de St. Domingue*, Guillaume T. de Raynal lamented that it had been necessary to "turn the terrible right of the strongest into law" (1785, 13). The right to property and the right to conquest were inseparable. It makes more sense to call them the "right to appropriation." The empire seized the lands in the territory, distributed them to whomever it wished, and reserved for itself the right to decide under what conditions the beneficiaries could alienate their supposed property. So it was that in the colony and long after independence, public authorities granted themselves the right to decide who could buy land, in what quantities, and for what reasons.

The conquering state distributed the land. But it never ceded its right to decide, without consulting the population, what the economic characteristics of the country would be. The agricultural regulations and rural codes make this clear. The defense of large-scale property, in Saint-Domingue as in Haiti, was based on France's right to seize the island and, subsequently, the right on the part of the victorious Indigenous Army of 1804 to take over this loot and distribute it among the people who mattered.

In contrast to the lands of France, the territory of the colony was part of the king's domains. He granted the right to enjoy this territory to privileged subjects who became colonists or planters (Blancpain 2003, 28). Early on, this distribution was carried out through the intermediary of the large mercantilist companies. Land tenure in Saint-Domingue therefore differed profoundly from what prevailed in the metropole. In France, land historically belonged to the feudal lords, who over the centuries had conceded limited portions of it to serfs. They, in turn, converted themselves into peasants who labored in the fields in exchange for some kind of compensation. In the seventeenth and eighteenth centuries, facing pressures including that of emerging capitalism, the descendants of serfs and peasants who didn't have land, or not enough of it, sold their labor as day laborers.

The right of the king (or the state) to conquer a territory and imprison captives in foreign lands had been recognized. So it is easy to see that even the limited social and geographical mobility of peasants didn't transfer to the colonial context of large-scale plantations focused on export commodities. The peasants of France or Prussia could become soldiers (Delacroix 1771, 112), and in Turkey or Syria they could get so wealthy that they were sometimes confused with lords (Pagès 1782, 262, 387, 389). Their movements from one place to another often facilitated their upward social mobility. But this kind of mobility would have interfered with the production cycle of colonial agricultural exploitation. Barbé-Marbois explained why: land-owning blacks would abandon their masters, establish themselves with their families on their own land, and have even more rights and greater ability to rebel against injustice than the French peasants (1796, 200).

Barbé-Marbois built on this attack on the idea of giving slaves the right to property—something that in any case was outlawed by the Code Noir—to conclude that the colonial worker shouldn't and couldn't have a family. It is true that it would have taken a lot of imagination to institutionalize a European-style, patriarchal family headed by a man dispossessed of all property, with no access to any means of subsistence.

In the end, the emancipation of the slaves represented an attack on the rights of citizens. While the French peasant at least had a modest right to private property, the slave couldn't possess anything. To the extent that they had some access to property, the peasant could claim a minimum of power to make their own decisions. The emancipation of the slave could not lead to such consequences. The freed slave could not participate in civic life as a citizen unless they unconditionally accepted the right to conquest and its corollary, the right of the strongest. To defend their interests in even the most basic sense would mean attacking the monopoly of private property, or working around it, and negotiating with those who were stronger.

Labor Relations

The comparisons between peasants and slaves did not take into consideration the potential existence of a slave or a peasant who rebelled against their condition. To speak of a *rebel slave* was a contradiction in terms. It meant trying to give substance to the nothingness engendered by the system in place. The rebel cannot be a slave, because the rebel is not subjugated by their master. To be compared to a peasant, a particular character has to be subjugated. The peasant owes their condition to divine providence, while the slave is the product of the will of a master protected by the machinery of the state.

During the colonial period, the comparison between slaves and peasants was linked not so much with their relationship to masters or feudal lords as with their means of subsistence. Many argued that in this regard, slaves enjoyed serious advantages over peasants and were happier than they were. The idea that the slaves were materially better off than peasants, and therefore had fewer worries than them, was a way of challenging readers familiar with their treatment on the plantation.

Antiabolitionists argued that slaves were lucky because "the interest of the master fulfilled the functions of Providence" (Dubuisson 1780, 43). Unlike a peasant, a slave could confidently depend on the master to assure he was taken care of well enough to serve until the end of his days. In exchange for his boundless dependence and subordination, he was protected by the self-interest of his owner. The powerful shield constituted by the egoism of the master, who would accept no infringement that was not profitable to him, made it possible for the devoted servant to look unworriedly toward the future. The slave was part of the master's family, his chains protected him from any lack of food and shelter, and his life unfolded in insouciance, without accidents or surprises. Lemonnier-Delafosse, lieutenant-colonel in Leclerc's expeditionary army, expressed it candidly: "Yes, I say it with all the sincerity of my soul, having studied the question, it is a hundred times better to be a black cultivator than a white cultivator" (1846, 78). The poor peasant, meanwhile, was at the mercy of the vagaries of the seasons.

This argument depended on the depiction of the slave as a child, free from preoccupations, secure in the midst of family, their happiness born of indifference about the days to come. "From the time of childhood, the *nègre* is, like your little peasants, in the bosom of family, submitted to a paternal authority, but better cared for and fed than the poor villagers" (Würtz 1822, 116). The use of the model of childhood was particularly suggestive because in Europe it was the head of the peasant family who oversaw agricultural labor, though without the sophistication in methods required for the intensive production of plantation commodities.

Understood as children and stripped of all freedom of choice and all rights, the slaves could be commanded at will. The master might well treat his horses better than his slaves, as the author of *Le More-Lack* noted (Lecointe-Marsillac 1789, 77), but that didn't alter this perception. According to Tussac, after all, "To the shame of humanity, the peasant tries to save money when it comes to buying medicines for his wife or children, but spares no expense when it comes to healing his cow" (1810, 72, 73).

The slaves also had no interest in losing their subordinate status and in fact had no wish to do so, since they were more pampered by their fate than the peasant. The independence and autonomy of the peasant, which defined them as a social category, was the main cause of their suffering. Subject to their lord, facing a consistent lack of resources they had to surmount, they had to trace out their own path and overcome the anxieties of solitude. As long as their master was "human" (Raynal 1785, 13; Hilliard d'Auberteuil 1776, 135), however, the slave's spirit was at peace. The peasant's submission was the result of several millennia of oppression. The captive's submission was obtained by a kind of novitiate where, through a few years of "seasoning," the worker was prepared for the deep work called *creolization*. This creolization taught them the rules surrounding social relations within the plantation system.

The Submission of the Slave and of the Peasant

One of the writers who approach the subject, De Gastine (1819, 264), remarks that since the time of ancient Rome, slaves have been dominated by patricians, "and since then, throughout Europe, serfs or peasants" have been submitted "to their lords." For the authors of the eighteenth century, in short, the peasant no longer has to be subjugated. They are subjugated by definition, their status transmitted from father and mother to son and daughter in the midst of a culture shared by all levels of metropolitan society. That culture teaches them to have faith in divine providence.

The peasant, then, is docile by nature, while the slave is so only because of a legal decision and the trituration of their masters. The master has to be able to constrain, manufacture, and construct the slave. He has to be able to complete the conquest. In late eighteenth-century Saint-Domingue, the slave was a juridical fiction, a being-that-must-be, an ideal accessible only if the root of the lack of submission was conquered.[2] Seen from this angle, the process of creolization becomes a functional necessity for the system rather than being optional, or simply a potential outcome.

The captive controls the world alien to him through the will of his master, who has to conquer that world in order to accede to the status of the owner of a servant. He certainly legally owns the captive, but in daily life he is always in the process of taking possession, and seeking to occupy what he appropriates. The master is confronted with the captive's will to exist. But he is not able to identify the self-propelled source of that will, and even less capable of destroying it.

It is inevitable that the master doesn't know what the captive wants, or could want. That is not only because, in his arrogance, he disdains the captive; it is also because the captive nourishes his own will beyond the gaze of the master. To paraphrase Gouy, "the multitude of people without property" that the state puts at the disposal of a handful of Europeans, and that have to be subjugated, by this very fact possess a property of their own that cannot be captured, the source of their happiness. For the European peasant, the descendant of a line of dispossessed generations going back millennia, this autonomous spring of knowledge has dried up. Among the captives, slavery has to destroy it and to deliberately transform those who carry such knowledge into ignorant people—otherwise, "the land will remain sterile"! (Tussac 1810, 71). It is, however, impossible for the master to accept what drives the captive—his contradictory will—as a source, and certainly not as a valid source, of accumulated knowledge.

It therefore is imperative to consecrate the role of brute force in the functioning of the social system that has been put in place. The black person is a *slave*, and the slave is *black*. His creation and his exploitation belong to the realm of social relations and not that of natural law. Once the right to appropriate a conquered territory has been secured, along with the submission of the slave that conquest has made it possible to manufacture, it follows logically that the slave will be happy as long as he accepts his condition the way the peasant does. But the master is a human in flesh and bone, with egotistical interests that are more effective than the distant benevolence of divine providence. The slave does not have to think about tomorrow, unlike the peasant, powerless in front of nature's elements. From the point of view of the masters given to him by divine kindness, his happiness is greater than that of the peasants of France, abandoned as they are to the will of the eternal, without any mediation. It makes sense to believe that, as long as he behaves as a slave, his happiness derives from the promise of daily bread, a promise hidden within the inescapable labor relationship.

Subjugated since time immemorial to feudal lords, the peasants had to provide for the well-being of their family, and deal with nature's caprices, on their own and without assistance. Providence was their only support, and their worries could be appeased only sporadically, to return more acutely with each passing season. The misery of the peasants and the uncertainty of their existence required them to constantly live by their wits in order to survive. Some decided to flee from this condition in order to find work as day laborers. Since their degradation was endemic, the writings of the period often confused workers and the independent laborers of the agricultural sector, such that in more than one case the concept of peasant designated the rural population in a general sense. Contrary to the slaves and despite their destitution, the peasants experienced horizontal social mobility, and sometimes even upward mobility. Some moved into other occupations or were recruited as soldiers or sailors, and others lived comfortably and were well educated. Slavery spared the subjugated blacks from ever experiencing such adventures!

But among both peasants and blacks, the source for any ultimate change in status was the same: a will to live despite terrible circumstances. The difference came from the fact that this will was anesthetized among the traditional peasantry, which explains their submission. In the colony, that will had to be annihilated through the implementation of a full-fledged project of social engineering whose goal was to make the captive blacks taste—even despite themselves!—the joy of being subjugated!

The Dead End of a Captive Labor Force

The plantation was the first concentration of laborers in modern times. It was an innovation within the global world economy. "An inhabitant is not a bourgeois, a plantation is neither a farm or a fiefdom, and *Nègres* are not peasants" (Raynal 1785, 171). The unit of production of the plantation differs from that of peasant agriculture in terms of both its organization and its productivity. "In the sugar islands, it is necessary to have a large number of arms that can be commanded at will" (Malouet 1788, 39–41).

While a plantation was not organized like a farm, however, it had a similar private character. External authorities, particularly the legal system, were not meant to penetrate into it under any pretext (Garran 1797, 320). The management of a plantation was organized around a discourse of "soft, fraternal harmony, like that connecting a father to his children" (Barbé-Marbois 1796, 198). In "a decree to guarantee the *perpetuity of slavery* in the colony . . . the colonial assembly . . . in virtue of the constitutional law of 28 September 1791, recognizes and declares . . . that *the slave is the property of the master, and that no authority can infringe on this property*" (Ardouin 1853, 1:361; emphases in the original). The father, the planter, and the king all enjoyed an absolute authority over the universe confided to their benevolence and solicitude.

After the 1789 Revolution, the Third Estate could go as far as to think about the rights of peasants. They were French, and the units of production in their care produced merchandise essential to the metropole's socioeconomic life. But it was impossible to think about the rights of slaves or of a revolution they might launch. They participated in the social structure only through the intermediary of their owners. As slaves, they had no legal existence of their own (Sala-Molins 1987, 24). As such, they didn't truly contribute to economic life, and their contribution to the goods sold on the Sunday market was not understood as a right, only tolerated. The slaves could not own anything that wasn't actually owned by their masters (Code Noir, Art. 28).

If the slaves were able to enjoy the right to participate in social life, the plantation as a unit of production would be subdivided into as many family parcels as there were male slaves. Each of these family units would produce what they needed for their own needs, without privileging the objects of metropolitan commerce. The 1789 revolution was compatible with the economic structure of the society that produced it, and the peasant had a place within it, even if it was a modest one. But the liberty and equality extolled by the French Revolution could not be exported to an exploitation colony, as was demonstrated by the unfortunate experience of Guadeloupe after Delgrès (Dubois 2004a, 411), the atrocities of Leclerc's expeditionary forces, and the evolution of the British and French Caribbean during the nineteenth and twentieth centuries. Even a project as sophisticated as that presented by Polvérel on February 28, 1794, required a form of despotic power. This would have been even more the case for any reconstruction of the slave plantation.

The demands and propositions for liberty and equality implied an attack against private property, which was considered sacred when it came to land as well as to captive individuals. Property in land and in slaves were indissolubly linked together by a single principle: the right of the strongest. If you monopolize ownership of land, the workers will have to submit to the conditions imposed on them by the property owners: slavery, indentured labor, domestic labor. And the emancipated, the free, who participated in the 1804 revolution could, at best, share the ideas of the French abolitionists who preached progressive emancipation. Free access to land, even if it started timidly with small parcels, destroyed any possibility of reactivating the production of commodities on the plantations. After its own general emancipation, the British Empire launched a massive immigration of workers from South Asia in which laborers were indentured on a fixed contract. This injection of laborers who were unfamiliar with the plantation system made it possible to counteract the insurmountable obstacle posed locally by access to small plots of land on the part of former slaves. It also made it more complicated for laborers to negotiate with employers because of the addition of new ethnic conflicts.

Confronted with extreme penury, the peasant moved toward salaried labor in a market context where he was able to place his labor at the disposition of the person offering the highest salary. The evolution of the slave, on the other hand, led to the impasse in which only the providence of a master eliminated penury. In other words, the European peasant, educated into submission to feudal lords, offered a portion of his labor for day labor as soon as misery found him. The conjunction between this offer and an ultimate demand for it created the labor market. But while the use of labor in European agriculture could move toward salaried labor, any such transformation was impossible in the economy of the colonial plantation, because when a slave was acquired, so was their agency and their will. The possibility that they might offer the available energy of their labor and negotiate a price for it vanishes because their will has no legal effect (Sala-Molins 2003, 77) and the master does not have to respect it. The slave's education and experience, furthermore, will not orient them toward the search for a solution negotiated with the very person who has taken all measures to assure their filial subjugation!

After 1793, the project and the itinerary conceived for the foreign captives before the French Revolution could no longer be pursued. That was the case not only because of the need for military support from the captives in defense of the French territory, but also because the philosophy of these African foreigners could not accept the approach that the tradition of millennia of subjugation made possible among European peasants. Having become citizens circumstantially, the foreigners imprisoned in their workplaces still conceived of their jailers as enemies. They could not do otherwise. To consider them equals with whom the value of labor could be negotiated would have required a much longer life experience together. After 1804, with the French expelled, it was even less likely that the newly freed would happily accept negotiating over labor with landowners who had emerged through an unconvincing logic. The sudden equality of these former slaves did not create a common denominator that could be the foundation for work contracts written up and executed in good faith. As far as the former slaves were concerned, the colonial social structure had to collapse.

Polvérel already understood, in 1794, that it was impossible to convert the slave into a salaried worker (Brutus 1968, 1:525). So he was forced to create a kind of social actor that imagined itself as something new, the *cultivator*. The historiography and legal scholarship of the country make the Haitian cultivator a fully formed figure who was to replace the peasant, just as the colonial thought of the eighteenth century wished to create plantations that would produce commodities. Throughout this study, I will show how the figure of the peasant ended up imposing itself despite the efforts of the oligarchies and the public authorities to deny that people who were part of this category even existed within the country.

An Intentional Blindness

To capture the perspective of the captives converted into slaves, it is important to recall that capitalism established itself simultaneously in the European economies and the peripheral economies of the Americas (Quijano 2000). In the European context, this way of life began by dismantling the communal connections among the rural population. On the plantations of the Caribbean, the process went in the opposite direction. Thanks to the slave trade, capitalism invented individuals devoid of social links and took the necessary measures to prevent the emergence of communal relations that could unite them in networks of solidarity. In response, new communities, nations, and peoples autogenerated themselves by contesting the injunctions of the capitalist system. These new formations survived by endowing themselves with the means that could sustain their contestation and limit their total absorption into the empire's proletariat.

The new way of life was focused on the disaggregation of primary human groups, the pulverization of their links of solidarity, and their reproduction through the market in slaves. Since the slaves were more useful to capitalist development than peasant producers, they were described as happier than them. The very fact that there was a debate on this topic exposes the fundamental weakness of the common arguments on the part of metropolitan thinkers about the uselessness of the family unit for the reproduction of agricultural laborers, given that they were simultaneously legitimizing the slave trade through which the economic system provided itself with a raw labor force with no familial attachments. The very fact of feeling pity about the fates of the slaves or the peasants underlined the inhuman character of the treatment inflicted on these individuals, who were observed without any deeper reflection about their personalities, their deracination, and their hellish solitude in the context of this capitalist enterprise. Within it, the human being was considered waste that could easily be discarded, a kind of coating that dirtied the purity of the workforce, of the energy capital consumed.

Peasants were anxious because they were prisoners of family-run businesses that were based on solidarity and respectful of ancestral traditions and customs, but also fragile because they were being besieged by market forces. Contemporary authors noted the particular characteristics of their businesses, including the fact that their harvests were sold on the market only after family needs were taken care of, which limited the expansion of the system of production, condemned them to a mediocrity and stunted their growth. And their productivity, obtained through a limited division of labor, grew slowly because it was essentially geared toward satisfying the autonomy of the peasant family. The proletarian, on the other hand, had been pulled out of the shackles that imprisoned the individual and hindered economic expansion. His role was primarily to fulfill his potential as a salaried worker and an indispensible contributor to the blossoming of the market, and only secondarily to participate in the satisfaction of his family's needs. The restrictions on peasant life in Europe led to some social and geographical mobility that enabled the displaced to penetrate into the subaltern groups in the cities.

Understood in this way, the peasant embodied a model that was not suited to the agricultural workers of Saint-Domingue. The *peasant* was referred to in the colonial environment only as an expression of the desire to see the emergence of an intermediary group between the wealthy planters and the slaves, similar to the rich peasants in France. The idea was that the presence of such a strata of small planters would reduce the distance between the enslaved plantation worker and the dominant classes (Raynal 1785, 89) and would help soften the extreme inequalities in the society.

This line of reasoning was developed by French authors examining the conditions of life in the Antilles during the end of the eighteenth century. But it did not change during the period that followed. The ideal of liberty and equality promoted at the beginning of the French Revolution barely influenced contemporary thinkers in their approach to the agricultural worker, for it was impossible for them to question the right to conquest and the right to property. The antiabolitionists insisted that it would be unjust to deprive masters of their slaves without due compensation (Dard 1821, 36).

In the mid-nineteenth century, meanwhile, the abolitionists argued that the metropolitan population of the Antilles was made up of "outlaws, rebel sailors, ignorant peasants and vagabonds," the castoffs of the disarticulation of rural European communities. They could not, accordingly, claim any nobility in their origin compared to the blacks and the free people of color (Linstant 1841, 24). They even argued that the blacks and European workers behaved in exactly the same way when it came to labor, which undermined any justification for the forms of discrimination that were in place (Hormoys 1862, 11). As Barbé-Marbois pointed out, however, his leveling of inequalities from below never grappled with the question of human reproduction within the family unit. These reflections remained trapped within a conception of the labor market that involved only human beings with no attachments.

Victor Schoelcher underlined the role of the imperial state in the systematic manufacturing of misery in the Caribbean. It was incumbent on political authorities, he argued, to improve the standard of living of the population there, especially given the institutionalized powerlessness of the workforce. He concluded his description of the fate of laborers in these terms: "Such is the condition of the workers of the Antilles, who some dare claim are happier than the peasants of Europe! Nothing effective is being done to ease their condition, and it almost seems as if nothing can be done, to judge from the actions of those in charge of the colonies at the Ministry of the Navy" (Schoelcher 1847, 423).

The Haitian thinkers of the first half of the nineteenth century strictly followed the conclusions of metropolitan analysts and didn't take stock of a specific group of social actors in Haiti distinct from the agricultural laborers who might remind them, even from a distance, of the European peasant. Fixated on the need to relaunch the plantation, they also couldn't envision the emergence of such a peasant group. The Baron de Vastey, to whom Haiti owes the first description of the struggles of the slaves of Saint-Domingue, didn't notice any peasants in the kingdom in the North. In all his treatises, he mentions peasants only in the Vendée. In his subsequent observations of national life, Madiou never spoke of peasants in his voluminous work, except for—again—the heroic peasants of the Vendée (1847, 2:301) and a proposition he made to the Haitian government to encourage the immigration of German peasants in 1825 (1847, 4:422).[3] Ardouin was similarly reticent on the subject. He recalled that Hilliard d'Auberteuil considered "the laboring *nègre* . . . happier than the peasant who works as a day laborer" (1853, 1:50) and shared a statement by General Gérin, who when seeking the presidency in Pétion's republic declared in front of his officers that "the son of a peasant is not my son's equal, not even in the eyes of the law" (1853, 6:9). Ardouin was more insightful than his contemporaries in that he at least referred to the migration from the countryside to the towns in Haiti and noted that the peasants in France did the same. But in his entire history of Haiti, he never referred to the Haitian cultivator by using the term *peasant* (1853, 9:247). In other words, while the category was certainly part of the social classification used by the authors, they didn't observe its salience within Haiti itself.

The result was that when the peripheral capitalism of Saint-Domingue entered into crisis after 1789 and communities began to gradually reorganize themselves, the dominant system didn't take note of the importance and scope of the emergence of their communally focused agricultural production. The goal of this production was to satisfy the needs of people who had been emancipated but remained imprisoned on the plantations. They were neglected and disdained by the political order, but represented 90 percent of the total population. The political system and its thinkers did everything they could to slow down the growth of any kind of autonomous life that would threaten the eventual redevelopment of an export economy. Both colonial policy and that of the independent administration sought to keep laborers in a condition of extreme vulnerability in order to guarantee the ultimate reactivation of the plantation system.

Given that the peasant was present everywhere in French literature of the eighteenth and nineteenth centuries, the figure's absence from nineteenth-century Haitian legislation and official historiography suggests an interested silence and even a deliberate choice. After 1804 the oligarchs and the state administration in Haiti, lacking the necessary financial resources and technical knowledge to pursue their project, grew increasingly violent in the tone in their descriptions of communal institutions. By the end of the nineteenth century they had reached the levels of a medieval inquisition. Still today, the term *peasant* is not used in the legal literature or the rural codes in Haiti.[4] The public administration has not yet imagined a place for peasants in the sociopolitical structure of the country, and as such, cannot incorporate them.

The Formation of Two Memories

Carolyn Fick (1990, 161) and John Garrigus (2006, 171) both offer details about the growing economic power of the colonists of color during the 1780s, as well as the tight family relationships they maintained with the Jewish merchants of the French port towns, particularly Bordeaux, and with Curaçao and Jamaica. They also offer a portrait of the people of color around Cap Français, Port-au-Prince, Croix-des-Bouquets, and Mirebalais. Garrigus emphasizes the fact that in the middle of the general insurrection of 1793, Julien Raimond and his associates actually increased their investments, a measure of their great confidence in the future of the colony.

In the wake of the fracturing of the dominant class, accentuated by Napoléon Bonaparte, the interface between the colonists and the available laborers that had previously been imposed by the public administration was shattered irreparably. As the political instability that ultimately led to the defeat of Leclerc's expeditionary army increased, the economic empire of the colonists of color diminished. Descourtilz (1795, 254, 315) opined that Sonthonax was interested in encouraging their emigration, and Pamphile de Lacroix suggested something similar. He referred to the "political difficulties and cruel wars that afflicted Saint-Domingue and chased away the majority of the property owners, and often even interrupted the transmission of inheritance" (Lacroix 1819, 397).

In other words, during the period identified by Descourtilz, from the administration of Sonthonax to the proclamation of independence, the public administration could not assure the forced labor of workers, who had to be redeployed for the defense of national sovereignty. Once the chains of the captives had been broken, agro-industrial capital fled. The people of color who celebrated Haitian independence on January 1, 1804, were mostly modest artisans of urban origin or former members of the police and the militia. During the Haitian nineteenth century there were no noted industrial entrepreneurs in the country. The American colonists disappeared, along with the prestigious label they had taken on during the French Revolution.

Under these conditions, local power holders no longer had access to people with the knowledge and capital necessary for the rebuilding and management of agro-industrial businesses. At the same time, during the nineteenth century, the power of the intermediary group over the labor force diminished. The social structure that was built was incomplete, in the sense that it didn't have a local dominant class, at least not one that fit the meaning of the term as the capitalist West understands it (Casimir 1984).

Obviously, the Creoles of the now independent territory avoided publicly brandishing their status as French people, which they had once so proudly declared. On January 1, 1804, in the "Proclamation du Général en Chef" (Proclamation of the general-in-chief), Dessalines declared that no white colonist would ever set foot in Haiti as a property owner. In 1814, Vastey, the ideologue of Christophe's kingdom, fulminated against the colonists but without ever noting that a few decades earlier the people of color among them had insisted on the need to join the white colonists in their rank, privileges, and rights. Clearly, Madiou and Ardouin, high-ranking notables of the Haitian Republic, would have been the last to emphasize this aspect of the struggle for civil and political rights on the part of the emancipated. The historiography is not chatty when it comes to the relationship between the ineffable American colonists and their slaves. In 1794 the planter Felix Carteau, having returned to France, offered an insight that could help the research of those who place color prejudice at the center of the history of Haiti: "These *Nègres* either died or dragged themselves along in weakness, denuded: in short, there were no slaves as unfortunate as those owned by free people of color, or any property owners as uncomfortable as they were" (1802, 266).

The American colonists left the colony at the moment of independence. The new oligarchies, made up of a majority of formerly freed slaves, suffered from a brief loss of memory, or perhaps the need to invent a new identity for themselves, which distanced them a bit from the "French name that still shadows our lands," that Dessalines described in his proclamation. Second-order bureaucrats during the colonial period, they now substituted themselves for the local capitalist bourgeoisie. In the police forces or the militia, they took responsibility for disciplining the masses of black workers and filled the role of bounty hunters in the struggle against marronage. In exercising these functions as zealous civil servants, they must have sharpened their disdain for manual laborers along with their sense of the distance that separated them from those unfortunates, which Julien Raimond (1791a, 2) described as the distance "separating light from darkness."

In independent Haiti, the pretension on the part of these intermediaries that they were above the emerging social classes did not come from the relationships maintained in economic production. The opposition between the reigning oligarchs and the agricultural workers no longer reflected a lived experience of the management of property and of a larger number of subordinates, and even less of carrying out this management while moving and manipulating imposing means of production. The supposed superiority of the oligarchs derived from an imaginary continuum moving from their culture and civilization to the savagery of the backward, ignorant masses. This civilizational ladder was not justified by any form of spiritual or material production that the supposedly backward masses might take note of. It was expressed exclusively through the memory of the primary role of fulfilling tasks ordered by the colonial administration, along with the prestige the outside world granted to the mastery and use of the imperial language. There was, as I have noted, absolutely no chance that the so-called ignorant masses would be impressed in any way by these achievements, or that they would modify their behavior because of this illusory transcendence.

The civilizing mission that served to justify the exploitation of slaves took refuge in the dreams of a governmental administration whose managers were no longer responding to the demands of a bourgeoisie of wealthy planters. The tasks of these managers were reduced to simply cultivating and maintaining the distance that traditionally separated them from the descendants of the *bossales*, while they waited for the re-establishment of the plantation economy. In the meantime, they lived off what they could drain from the production surplus the peasantry had set aside to exchange for manufactured goods. In the midst of this process, there was no longer any reason to cross linguistic barriers or expand the scope of the imperial language, which in daily life served to separate the reigning oligarchs from the rest of the population. Creole monolingualism, meanwhile, was the basis for productive activity and local distribution, and in time it connected all sectors of society, except perhaps the tiny minority who circulated in the highest spheres of the public administration or in foreign commerce.

Having lost the oligarchy of colonists who dominated Saint-Domingue, Haiti found itself overseen by two tiny oligarchies born of the wars of independence. One of them had emerged from the militia and the police forces and was not familiar with the management of agricultural enterprises. They limited their agricultural policy to encouraging a kind of tenant farming that destroyed large-scale export agriculture. Their official policy of rebuilding the plantations and producing export commodities was really just a form of grandstanding whose monotonous repetition was proof of the fact that they were incapable of realizing their declared objective. The second branch of oligarchs emerged from the position of the agricultural inspectors instituted by Toussaint Louverture's regime. They had managed forced labor on the sequestered plantations of royalist *émigrés*, and so had some experience in agricultural management. Their vision molded the agrarian policy of Christophe's kingdom in the North. Their remarkable success, however, lasted only two decades. After his fall, this small group of agricultural inspectors didn't have the capacities necessary to maintain or relaunch that project.

The tattered remnants of the oligarchies of Saint-Domingue that subsisted in Haiti did their best to convince the colonial empire that they were participating in the same history through which Europe had transformed the black masses into slaves (Fanon 1952, 117). They embraced the project of the French metropole, their mother country, and held firm to the itinerary it had traced for them. As they followed this path, their rhetoric of remembrance around the actions that led to independence and the signal victory over the Napoleonic troops accommodated the most reactionary aspects of the Old Regime. This rhetoric skirted the core inheritance of 1789 and, except during the interlude of Christophe's regime, never asked the question of how to assure the well-being of a population. Instead, the focus was on preserving the availability of this population for the expansion of so-called modern business.

Moreau de Saint-Méry, as I have already mentioned, was part of the Club Massiac, the den of the most committed antiabolitionists in France (Gauthier 2007). Nevertheless, he has a near-hegemonic role in our national historiography, fed through Thomas Madiou and Beaubrun Ardouin. From his first writings on the need to grant the wealthy planters of the overseas territories the right to determine people's status, he enthroned the color question as the central power driving Haitian history. Toussaint shared his opinions on the question of colonial autonomy and the importance of color.

It is therefore appropriate to read Madiou's and Ardouin's accounts in order to evaluate the collection of facts they present or, more precisely, to offer an inventory of what they left out. They were preeminent members of the traditional oligarchy during the nineteenth century and, following the approach laid out by Moreau de Saint-Méry, they passed on the selection criteria for observable phenomena. Without having to express it directly and be condemned for having a politically unacceptable perspective, they nevertheless eliminated sovereignty from the political system and gave themselves the task of convincing the urban sectors that the exclusion of nearly all citizens from all decisions was for the greater good of the nation, believing this exclusion would enable its (impossible) transformation into a European entity.

At the very dawn of our life as an independent country, however, Vastey— in his *Le système colonial dévoilé*—denounced the ways our historical writings tend to undermine the national project: "Most of the historians who wrote about the colonies were white, and even colonists. They went into the tiniest details about production, climate, the rural economy, but they always made sure not to unveil the crimes of their accomplices" (1814, 38).

The political thought of the traditional oligarchy revived the vision the old regime had used to manage colonial reality, make sure it did not evolve autonomously and outside its control, and prevent it from becoming similar to the metropolitan way of life and form of governance. The thinking of Moreau de Saint-Méry and the Club Massiac installed itself comfortably in the memory of the Haitian oligarchs and their official vision. The nobles of the Club Massiac had insisted colonial Saint-Domingue, even if it had some autonomy, should not undo its subordination to France. It was to remain captive to the French public. After independence, the Haitian oligarchs maintained this vision.

The comparisons between slaves and peasants that we find in the literature of the second half of the eighteenth century served as a reservoir of ideas for the Haitian oligarchs as they mapped out an itinerary for those they proposed to oppress in order to assure their own dependency on the metropole. The historian Vertus Saint-Louis (2006) has described the confusion among the governing classes in Saint-Domingue in the wake of general emancipation as they sought to name the former slaves, those foreigners who according to the French Revolution had suddenly become equal citizens before the law. The historian Laurent Dubois exposes this dilemma in Guadeloupe by choosing as the title of one of his works a flagrant contradiction: *A Colony of Citizens* (2004). Whether in Saint-Domingue or Guadeloupe, to transform formerly enslaved foreigners into citizens was to attempt the impossible, even more so because they were the overwhelming majority of the population.

Starting with Robespierre's famous speech opposing the use of the term *slave* in the National Assembly, the problem of finding a single definition for the agricultural worker proved impossible to resolve. This figure, an ex nihilo creation of the law of the strongest, ceased to exist once the supposedly superior power that engendered it was successfully defied. On the other hand, the freed slaves identified themselves first as Africans, or more exactly in the local vocabulary, as people who obeyed the laws (or *lwa*) of Guinée.

The use of the term *African* could lead to confusion, since it could potentially encompass all the blacks, even those who were free, emancipated *bossales*. The word *cultivator* gained common use. But French peasants were also cultivators. The comparison of the fate of the slave with that of the peasant or the European agricultural laborer produced an abundant but inconclusive literature, because the social thought of the French Revolution and those who opposed it were referring to experiences that didn't fit with the events unfolding in the colony. Starting in 1793, the French and Haitian oligarchs peopled their wild fantasies with cultivators, the doubles of their slaves, who would come to the rescue of the plantations and the export economy. But a careful analysis of the structural differences between the two modes of production that confronted one another—the newborn counter-plantation economy and the capitalist plantation in agony—makes clear that there was no chance for rapprochement between two conceptions and forms of management of two different kinds of labor: the cultivator/slave, or indentured laborer, on the one hand, and the cultivator/inhabitant, or independent producer, on the other.

In Saint-Domingue, nearly all of the laboring population inherited from the Old Regime had just arrived from Africa or were descended from recent arrivals. The challenge in the new society was how to accommodate these foreigners, a majority who had suddenly been nationalized, within the necessarily autonomous interrelations woven together by daily life. It was also necessary to make sure that the republicanism that might be useful in the metropolitan society didn't seduce the majority of these foreigners, who might decide that they wanted to navigate the threatened ship, or sail it on an unfamiliar path. The colonial oligarchs had to manage the so-called slaves whose status was modified by a metropolitan revolution that had no connection to colonial economic and social life.

The planters—whether they were white or free people of color—were French. A decree of the National Assembly conferred this nationality on the former slaves of Saint-Domingue. But this decision was the expression of the arrogance of those who wished to remain their owners. And the decree could not inject a citizen's behavior into the new recruits, or a desire on their part to participate in France's particular institutions, just as baptism didn't make the captives sold by the slave traders into Christians. And by seeking to function with newly anointed citizens, the republic was courting danger. Moreau de Saint-Méry and Toussaint Louverture considered it wise to have autonomous colonial assemblies legislate this new political status rather than allowing the metropole to do so.

For their part, the enslaved population had broken their chains through a series of epic struggles. They invented a home for themselves, despite a total lack of material resources, in the process defying the state administration and the wealthy property owners who were convinced they possessed the territory. The official thinkers of the new public administration never dwelled on the complexities of this process, which was deeply confusing to them. The population at times hesitated as they traced out their path, seeking to fill the absence of norms and the lack of models for social relations. All day long, they had to find ways to slip away from the oligarch's uncontrolled exercise of the law of the strongest. There was no clear path laid out for collective behavior outside the specific spaces where they had implanted themselves. And there was no refuge, and nowhere to turn to for assistance. There were so many questions provoked by the absence of landmarks in this universe of the unknown.

The architects of the modern administration were not preoccupied by the obstacles the deported and their descendants had to overcome in order to inhabit this land which had been constructed to consume them alive, to *eat* them. Instead, they interpreted the population's actions as a form of ignorance, an incapacity to apprehend the rationality of capitalism and the racism that underlies it. All of the efforts taken by these autonomous communities to establish themselves, and to create a space where the personal sovereignty of the victims of the slave trade could flourish, were vilified and attacked as antisocial.

It makes sense that the metropolitan French, observing the destruction of what they considered their colonial property—their land, their slaves— raised their voices to complain and demand compensation. The French state had misled them, and owed them reparation. The Haitian oligarchs of the early nineteenth century were also victims of the loss of property acquired under the same conditions (Casimir 2009, 205). But unlike the metropolitan colonists, these supposed property owners were rejected by their protectors and had no authorities to whom to address their claims and complaints. To repair the wrongs they felt they had suffered, they either had to emigrate to the metropole or resolve the problem themselves by taking power, by taking the law into their own hands. The police forces, the militia members, the artisans, and the urban population as a whole all carried their particular memory of prerevolutionary times as they looked toward the future. As they moved up the rungs into the oligarchy, these classes who lacked any experience in the management of agro-industrial activity were not in a position to satisfy their own daily needs. As a consequence, they didn't have the resources to develop norms to orient the practice of sovereignty.

The international community, busy during most of the nineteenth century with other imperial adventures, abandoned the Haitian authorities—its born servants—to themselves. The community relationships of agricultural workers developed without restrictions or major interference and ended up gaining the upper hand in the organization of the nation's society. The oligarchs came out of this process even more weakened in their relationship with imperial capitalism. The Haitians of the rural areas and the provinces appropriated the country for themselves, ignoring the self-proclaimed leaders of the territory and their constant slander.

The agricultural regulations and rural codes promulgated during this period make clear that the postindependence space of Haiti was no longer populated by planters and inhabitants, in the colonial sense of the term. The legislation described property owners and farmers and, facing them, *cultivators* or agricultural laborers. The basic objective remained the reconstruction of a plantation economy aimed at the production of commodities for export, but the legislators could no longer refer to the planters or *inhabitants* of the eighteenth century, who had disappeared during the revolutionary turmoil.

The 1804 revolution may not fit the definition usually given to the term *revolution*. It was not propelled by a bourgeois sector being held back from self-fulfillment by an abusive metropole, as was the case in the United States of America, or by an aristocracy and a clergy, as was the case in France. It was certainly not carried out by an agricultural proletariat seeking to improve their status and material conditions within an export agriculture oriented toward the satisfaction of the needs of the international market. The transition from the eighteenth to the nineteenth century in Haiti was carried out without any bourgeoisie at all, beyond the control of the urban sectors and without a working class organized around leaders who could articulate their demands. The 1804 revolution can be explained only by observing how the masses of workers—who, in the beginning, were ethnically fragmented and geographically dispersed—developed their perception of themselves and of the classes who were supposedly leading them, structured community institutions, and invested themselves in the satisfaction of their own needs, all the while consolidating the vessel that gathered this experience as well as the spirituality derived from it, their exclusive language: Creole.

The fake bourgeois and urban groups who threw themselves onto the structures of formal political power made sure to anchor their apparent preeminence in a discourse that masked their powerlessness in the face of imperial power. They had the monopoly over the written word and the traditional archives. But the fictive character of this local preeminence was on full display in the failure of their attempts to exert power, in the incompetence and the uselessness of the public administration in the face of the autonomy of the masses of agricultural workers and peasants, who focused on the pursuit of the material necessities for daily life.

As they took control of the conditions of their existence on the island, the masses developed their own perspective on what society should be. They established themselves in the Haitian countryside—a space they created—thanks to communal institutions impervious to urban influence. The rupture that took place at the end of the eighteenth and the beginning of the nineteenth century strengthened the weapons they had at their disposal, enabling them to root themselves in the territory and inhabit it in full sovereignty despite the wishes and projects of the state administration. Confronting its powerlessness, this administration modified its traditional function. Unable to maintain the forms of individuation imposed by capitalist slavery during the eighteenth century, it instead planned for the disaggregation of the new rural communities by maintaining the idea that they had to be civilized, and blocking their access to natural resources. To cap it all off, this administration, dependent on a very thin layer of French-speaking Haitians, could not carry out this civilizing mission themselves and had to ask for help from the

Breton clergy, the Conservatoire de Paris (Brutus 1948, 625), and other foreign institutions.

The state in Haiti is the articulation between these two disjointed forms of memory. It is defined by the coexistence of these two memories, and the impossibility of one among them to erase the other through any kind of sustained daily practice. Forced to live together, these memories ultimately had to converge around a single system of norms and values shared by all within and for the management of a shared existence. But the administrative machinery of the state reproduced itself by cultivating a hierarchical separation, following the wishes of the international community.

From Slaves to Day Laborers

Saint-Domingue was the creation of the French state, and it evolved within its political structure. It was built on territory it conquered, with captives it held prisoner, in a public order that it conceptualized. At the end of the eighteenth century this social project, which believed it could exist without consent, entered into crisis. This was not so much the outcome of an internal process of contradictions and conflicts as the result of attacks against its sovereignty on the part of rival empires. To get out of a difficult situation, France temporarily granted a bit of its political power to subordinate interest groups. Then, facing the difficulty of taking back the concessions it had made to these temporary allies, it sought to liquidate them. Facing certain death or deportation, these allies responded by choosing secession. The political dimensions of the process that led to the independence of Haiti were developed outside the life of the colony itself.

The heroes of this unexpected independence considered the economic structure built around agro-industrial production for export to be the normal environment of the country. Their discourse on political restructuring aimed to rebuild this structure without introducing any substantial changes to the relationship between capital and labor. The titled leaders of the gesture of independence bluntly expressed the ideas they had about the laboring classes. Seeking to satisfy their own interests, they returned, with a few differences that shouldn't be exaggerated, to the logic that presided over the inequalities that preceded the French Revolution.

The transformation of Saint-Domingue into an entity called Haiti was not a reflection of an evolution in social relations based on changes in modes of production or material life. The colony and its daughter, the Haitian administrative state, were artificial, modern political entities whose leaders didn't have to respect millennia of traditions or evolve according to their normative orientations. With the collapse of French colonization and the departure of the metropolitan and American colonists, a formal political power that considered itself sovereign and of the same nature as that of the colonialists fell into the hands of the Francophile intermediary classes. They had no experience of administrative control and were armed with insurmountable prejudices toward the masses of African origin, who substantially outnumbered them.

The agricultural laborers, left with little room to maneuver in the midst of an economy in crisis, constructed the institutions they needed to survive and re-exist. They showed a notable indifference to the traditions, culture, and history of France, a country they barely knew. As the colonial situation decayed, the power of the agricultural laborers grew more robust and radical. It sealed the retreat of local capital by successfully conquering popular sovereignty in the areas of the production of knowledge and of identity, the oversight of economic production and the relationship to natural resources, and the management of gender relations and reproduction within the population.

There were two vectors at this turning point in the history of Haitians. On the one hand was the dynamic of the local working classes, and on the other, the orientation of the metropole and its positioning in the midst of the international community. This latter vector guided the intermediaries who were responsible for the colonial social and political order. The implications of the reformulation of metropolitan social relations, magnified by the general insurrection set in motion by the conspiracy at Bois Caïman and the attacks of rival colonial powers, required a deep renegotiation of the roles and functions of the foreigners reduced to slavery. The social actors produced by colonial modernity never considered a questioning of social hierarchies, and never put forth a viable path for an escape from the crisis. They were incapable of seeing the extent to which, as their position on the international stage declined rapidly, they lost their ascendancy over the agricultural workers. Facing this loss of influence, the workers of the plantation system—the so-called slaves—imposed their own vision of modernity.

Ultimately, in 1804, the intermediaries between the imperial state and the mass of laborers seized the reigns of public administration, hoping to learn from there how to manage economic production. The conceptualization of the factors of production we find in their discourse comes from the Old Regime in its pre-1789 version. They maintained the vocabulary of the planters, the producers of export commodities, who could conceive of peasant production for the market only as being subsidiary to the needs of external trade. But it was the local production of provisions that defined the way of life of the peasant.

There was a rupture between metropolitan thought and that of the working class, but not between metropolitan thought and that of the allies of the colonial economy. What was said and thought by the French of Saint-Domingue, colonists and emancipated slaves alike, emerged from a conversation that unfolded in the mother society between philosophes, writers of encyclopedias, politicians, wealthy merchants, intellectuals, and activists in favor of empire. The public authorities of the Haitian nineteenth century, trained outside of any necessity for consensual management of society, sought to implement a form of labor based on the roles defined by the eighteenth-century colonial order. They planned to live within the plantation environment they had come out of, and which had given them their social power. But the economic model they wished to save no longer fit with the regional realities of the nineteenth century, and especially not with the transformations underway in independent Haiti.

When the concepts referring to the use of labor in France were applied to the colony, they overlooked the specificity and urgency of the local situation and privileged the production of goods for an external market, disregarding the popular will. But the concepts and language of the oligarchs of Saint-Domingue and Haiti differed in significant ways from that of the mother country. They reflected daily reality as the oligarchs wanted to see it, or else expressed what they wanted to transform that reality into, rather than the reality as it was evolving on its own. Not surprisingly, the conceptual tools of the much larger majority of agricultural laborers in full insurrection were articulated in a language distinct from that used by the oligarchs overseeing the visible public order. These tools reflected a different set of aspirations and models for living. The order the oligarchs were seeking to impose got caught up in its own normative formulations, while daily life pursued its own course, free from the intervention of authorities busy managing inexistent or moribund economic institutions.

The agricultural laborers were in the process of transforming themselves into peasants. But the law refused to grant them any kind of sovereignty over their own persons, or to accept the public effects of their will. For the metropolitan and colonial oligarchs, as for those of the Haitian nineteenth century, the slaves and their free descendants could never convert themselves into individuals responsible for themselves. They couldn't take charge of their own families, or structure their own institutions or community. The values and norms that governed these families, institutions, and communities could not be the basis for the codification of positive law. Within the social project born of the colony, the Haitian peasants could not be Mexican *rancheros*, Cuban *guajiros*, Brazilian *sitiantes*, or even less, U.S.-style *farmers*. They remained cultivators—essentially, employees of the large plantations—day laborers, *peons*.

It is easy to see why the concept of popular sovereignty that anchored the political transformations in France was resisted by the oligarchs of Saint-

Domingue and Haiti. Even the major transformations in economic and so-cial structures around them couldn't convince them to modify their way of thinking about how labor should be managed, or about the meaning of popu-lar will. If it had been up to the oligarchs of the imperial state, whether in the colony or the independent country, popular will would never have flourished on Haitian soil.

The Undesirable Peasant

The privileged groups in emerging Haiti stayed within the confines of pro-slavery and racist metropolitan thought. They expressed themselves through the conceptual tools they had inherited from the imperial power. They had no desire to flirt with the local sovereign people. These oligarchs were the products of mercantilist slavery, or military service to French sovereignty, and of the way the 1789 revolution had approached Saint-Domingue. But when it came to the way they saw Haitian sovereignty, they had no ideological affin-ity with the movement of 1789. They did use the same vocabulary in their po-litical discourse. But sticking too close to the lexicon of the late eighteenth century when we listen to the Haitian oligarchs leads to errors of interpreta-tion, and to analytic and political confusion. It overlooks the difference between the dominant metropolitan culture and the local dominant cul-ture. The latter was focused on applying the civilizing mission of the former. But it didn't have the means it needed at its disposal to put that civilizing mission into practice.

Eighteenth- and nineteenth-century writings relating to Saint-Domingue and Haiti, and seeking to contribute to their governance, generally used the lens of colonial metropolitan thought to represent local reality. As a result, they got lost in half-baked analogies and remained indifferent to the concrete reality, which they tried to put into boxes by using normative definitions of social facts. Everything unfolded as if it was vital for Haiti to follow the same path as France, and its social groups would transform themselves into met-ropolitan analogs. The slaves of Saint-Domingue would, in a few years, be-come agricultural workers, a rural proletariat not too far removed from slavery. Planters and property owners would become bourgeois capitalists. The middle class, as was the case everywhere else (that is, in Europe), would become the pivot for a fluid social organization where elites would peacefully renew themselves through social capillarity.

What the oligarchs—those intermediary classes misidentified as middle classes—didn't understand was that Haiti had its own self-generated reality. This reality had no subordinate relationship to France. It had no need or vocation to become something France hadn't been able to turn it into. The nation born in 1804 was an actor in the international community, like any other. It negotiated its own path, like all other nations did, despite the ups and downs in its fortunes.

The Haitian oligarchs dreamed of modeling themselves on the tastes of Western civilization. They never worried about the well-being of the majority of the population, and avoided confronting certain questions, even when they were actually unavoidable. What human groups did they think made up the country? And how did they plan to make French institutions function in Haiti?

Haitian social thought stubbornly continues to overlook the political strength of the social category of laborers. If the workers in the most advanced capitalist enterprises of the eighteenth century tumbled down toward sharecropping and found a way to become a traditional peasantry hostile to all participation in the labor market (Casimir 2007, 84), this was not the result of the actions of the property owners of the period. They had no choice. "Pétion, seeing that [the cultivators] had imagined all kinds of ways to escape from the property owners or the leasers of state property . . . advised or suggested to these property owners or leasers to split what was produced in half with the cultivators, after a deduction made for the expenditures necessary for the exploitation of the entire plantation; he led by example by doing this on the properties he was renting. That is how the system known as *de moitié* [of half] in the country, which is none other than what is known in Europe as *métayage*, was born" (Ardouin 1853, 7:37).

There was, however, a fundamental difference between *métayage* (a version of sharecropping) in Europe and in Haiti. In 1814, Sismonde de Sismondi celebrated the advantages of this form of labor relations by underlining that "it was under these conditions that slavery was abolished on its own throughout the Mediterranean and Europe" (Sismondi 1814, 52). The gradual abolition of slavery followed the implantation of *métayage*. In France and Italy, serfs and lords shared the same expectations and social objectives, elaborated over the course of millennia of living together. They jointly created the same idea about the outlets for productive labor. They could speak together, and move from one type of labor relation to another.

In Haiti, there was rupture and revolution: the *métayage* suddenly followed the abolition of slavery, rather than the other way around. Abolition in Europe, in any case, had taken place very gradually. It is impossible to explain to a captive who has just met his European jailer that it is legitimate, logical, or normal that he be owned and branded like an animal. It is impossible to make him understand that property and things and people can go together to satisfy the needs of another society, situated across the ocean. In the course of his own struggle for liberation it is impossible for him to distinguish between his right to take control over his own body, of his being, and his right to gain access to the goods indispensable for the maintenance of this self.

In the wake of the temporary European defeat in Haiti, the required refusal of slavery on the part of the local oligarchs led to the invention of citizens attached to a particular plot of land. When it came to the labor force, however, this process culminated in the impossibility for the reigning oligarchs to formalize their family businesses within the legal and mental framework inherited from the former metropole. These oligarchs had only themselves to blame for this, because of the way they monopolized control over the land but were incapable of gauging the power of the laboring class.

In the journey of a complex capitalist adventure like that of a plantation system aimed at producing export commodities, the movement into *métayage* on the part of a labor force that had been reduced to slavery—its own victory over slavery—cannot be seen as a step backwards. To accuse the rural Haitian population of traditionalism and archaism for the choice they made in the nineteenth century is to argue that the captives who were crippled on the slave plantations behaved in a way that was more modern than the maroon deserters who turned their backs on these prisons. It is to spit on those who experienced the torments of slavery, to disparage their suffering, their tears, and the blood they spilled in their efforts to reorient the terms of social negotiation. The transformation of the newly freed into a landless peasant, or one owning a tiny plot of land, condemned to a doubled form of precariousness, was not produced spontaneously as a normal outcome of some process, or of just letting things happen. It was conquered through the highest form of struggle. To choose dignified precariousness, instead of—and in the face of—a false comfort within humiliation and shame, was the expression of knowledge gained from experiencing irrational exploitation conjoined with constant harassment.

Conclusion: The Economic Uselessness of Large-Scale Property

The public authorities who issued the laws governing the rural life of the population were unable to absorb the peasantry as a meaningful social category. They were incapable of managing peasant autonomy because they were unable to negotiate their own independence from foreign control and international trade. They were, in any case, more at ease in this outside world than in the company of the Haitian majority.

The oligarchs of the country might have taken a different approach. Instead of exhausting themselves trying to stamp out the informal practices of peasantry, or engineering an escape from an apparently obvious poverty that stretches from 1804 to the present, they might have cast a critical eye on what the modern world describes as the periods of abundance and profitability in the history of Saint-Domingue and Haiti. The wealth of the Pearl of the Antilles before 1791, the rebuilding of the plantation economy by Toussaint Louverture and its expansion in Christophe's kingdom, all deserve to be evaluated with serious reservations given the cruelty that undergirded them. But the common denominator between all three cases of development remains the intensive use of landed property. Neither the wealthy planters of Saint-Domingue nor Toussaint Louverture and Henry Christophe were familiar with the idleness of landed property.

The colonial administration did face the problem of absentee ownership, but this was not the core of the issue. All three administrations used various techniques to enforce the demands of the capitalist system, including the payment of debts and the payment of rent to the state for some of its domains. They didn't allow land to be left idle. The pressure applied by the markets that had invested funds in the exploitation of commodity-producing plantations, along the rigors of the forced labor put in place by administrations thirsty for money and weapons, made sure of that. But the oligarchs deluded themselves about their control over the country. Once they had come to possess its only true material wealth, the land, they demonstrated either a notable incompetence in the management of the national economy or a remarkable lack of imagination.

"The very large number of propertyless *nègres* can only live on the land of the whites: we must therefore force the blacks to live there, and to accept a moderate type of labor which, all over the world, is the duty of civilized people" (Viénot-Vaublanc 1797, 3). This sentence, from a report to the Corps législatif on the organization of the colony, highlights the lack of vision on the part of the oligarchs during the revolutionary period. The property owners of the nineteenth century, similarly, were unable to lucidly evaluate their actual political power and, like Polvérel, to offer a compromise solution. They lacked the required technical knowledge and economic understanding that was essential for the management of plantations. And they didn't realize—or refused to realize—that they also lacked the means to constrain the population and force them to hand themselves over to the plantation labor. They did not realize that they could not reproduce the economic model of the previous century. It was the laziness, carelessness, and lack of imagination of the oligarchs that held back the economic development of the country, not the ignorance of the cultivators.

The labor force was, however, able to stand up to the oligarchs and preserve their freedom over their work. This raises a much more difficult question. The powerlessness of the large-scale landowners of the nineteenth century, and their incapacity to rebuild large-scale agriculture, allowed the workers to make use of rural property on their own terms. The response on the part of the labor force to the hoarding of landed property seems largely to have been to institutionalize indivisible family property on tiny plots of land. The effectiveness of this institution led the oligarchy's thinkers to burden it with all kinds of negative qualifiers: they claimed indivisible family property was archaic, traditional, contrary to the modern world, and informal. The cultivator's response to the oligarch's exercise of the right to use and abuse property that was acquired unfairly was the sophisticated management of the precariousness in which they lived. The labor force was able to thwart the abusive use of landed property by pulling out of the labor market, which existed only thanks to the monopolization of the land. But we have to wonder: why didn't the workers invade the noncultivated properties, especially since they made up both the army and the police forces?

The panorama gets even more confusing if we add to it Michel Hector's observation, cited above (2006a, 123), that the peasant revolutions of the first half of the nineteenth century took place in the regions where the oligarchs were not seeking to rebuild the commodity-producing plantation, and where the monopolization of the large domains was not excessive (M. Hector 1998). Furthermore, in the second half of the century, the peasants in the plantation zones supported the *le cacoïsme bourgeois contre Salnave*, to quote the title of Roger Gaillard's 2003 book. They supported the owners of large plots of land and urban dwellers, while the peasants of the South joined the popular movements.

There are two possible explanations. The first emphasizes the deep cultural differences between the laboring masses and the oligarchs as a way of understanding the specifics of class struggle in Haiti. The Haitian *métayers* and peasants do not seem to have the same conception of private property as their analogs in Europe. The Haitian population was excluded from any participation in the decision making by the formal structures of the state. While that population successfully incited the collapse of the plantation system, it did so without carrying out any invasion of noncultivated land. The logical conclusion is that their political approach to landed property was guided by values different from those of the modern West. They were not driven by the anxious desire to accumulate all the natural riches within reach. Instead, they were guided by other values, contrary to those of the imperial knowledge system and its management of power. They created a culture in which the right to conquest—the conjoined right to seize the rights of others and the riches of nature—had no place, or at least didn't play a central role.

There is, however, an alternative explanation possible. From the eighteenth century on, the population had a clear understanding of the fact that the Haitian oligarchs were trapped in a larger system, one that their very local and fragile political power did not allow them to defy with impunity. This understanding shaped the population's actions.

Perhaps, ultimately, we can combine these two hypotheses. The Haitian population didn't pursue the excessive exploitation of nature because they considered themselves to be an integral part of it. And, at the same time, they understood that invading the properties of the Westernized oligarchs might cause a gathering of foreign forces to flood into the territory with their lethal weapons. From the beginning of the struggles for liberation, they would have understood lucidly and correctly that imperialism was watching over the right to property of the oligarchs, derived as it was from its right to conquest.

In either case, the remarkable quality of life of the Haitian population during the nineteenth century indicates that they were using a different concept of the relationship between human beings and nature. This population lived on the basis of its memories of Amerindian and African agricultural work, its knowledge of the local landscape and context, and its innovative organization of the territory that combined *bourgs-jardins*—settlements organized around productive gardens—and rural markets. The remarkable quality of life can be explained by the quality and level of the education offered by the oppressed culture. Whatever deficiencies this system had can largely be attributed to the wastefulness caused by the economically useless monopoly over private property on the part of the idle owners of large plots, inheritors of the European conquest.

The shortages experienced by nineteenth-century Haitians were also due, to a lesser extent, to the incapacity of the peasantry to develop its way of life in order to take care of an increasingly large population surrounded by a hostile world. The republic experienced a prosperous nineteenth century, and its absentee and parasitical oligarchs had nothing to do with that. At the end of the century, the quality of life in the countryside began to go downhill, and this provoked the beginnings of an exodus. In this context, it is hard to explain why the rural population continued to tolerate the existence of large tracts of fallow land possessed in principle by the state or idle absentee owners.

The colonial empire and the state administration in Haiti that succeeded it considered that the laws that created landed property could never be questioned. These laws were, after all, the foundation for colonialism. The authorities of independent Haiti maintained this blindness, situating and defining political power as a form of colonial power. The agricultural worker, therefore, managed his relationship to his own plot of land through customary law. Everyone knows that in Haiti, the sharecropper tends to keep everything they produce, satisfying the supposed property owner with only symbolic gifts, and would steadfastly refuse to ever leave the parcel of land where they probably saw their own children born and buried their umbilical cords!

The problem of the distribution and use of land was, like the original seizing of the territory by France, a political question. It was the expression of a violent relationship. In a territory that was once a colony focused on exploitation, the right of conquest that was the foundation for the monopolization of land and the denuding of the sufferers had to be questioned. By the end of the nineteenth century, the characteristics of the oligarchic classes had not substantially changed. But the sufferers in the population could no longer find ways to work around the privileges that flowed from the rights the oligarchs claimed. That was because by that time, imperial capitalism had once again fixed Haiti in its sights. The exactions characteristic of the colonial period began again, and the mechanisms for the appropriation of land were reinforced. Pillage was justified through the reactivation of traditional definitions of the agricultural worker. The goal of disaggregating rural communities was pursued in part by resituating education in the parish schools, a policy that can be compared to the antisuperstition campaigns of the end of the century. The struggle of the oligarchs and the foreign consulates against President Salnave included a search for ways to quash rural autonomy. The U.S. occupation of 1915 carried out this project successfully through the destruction of any open resistance to the political order that might have mobilized the rural population.

Chapter 5

The Pursuit of Impossible Segregation

Introduction: Beyond the Coloniality of Power

Everything in Haiti was transformed at the beginning of the nineteenth century. All the dimensions of social life changed: there was a new country, a new nation being born. There were negotiations over the creation of a form of governance adapted to totally new circumstances. As the situation unfolded, this was all articulated within a conflict between, on the one hand, the orientations of the mass of laborers in revolt against the conditions of existence the oligarchs sought to impose on them, and on the other hand, the chimerical goals the oligarchs pursued within an imperial universe based on wild racism and Eurocentrism. Usually, the victors in these kinds of upheavals are the ones who tell the story afterwards. That wasn't the case in Haiti. Those who mastered the imperial language were the ones who provided the reports, and they only half-admitted their own defeat. We have to clear a path through what they wrote in order to get an idea of the breadth of the process of change that affected the majority of the population.

The Haitian Revolution, when understood as a victory of slaves over French armies, reflects the surprise of the international community in the face of an unthinkable event (Trouillot 1995). When conceived of this way, the event resulted in more commotion overseas than it did in the lives of the local population. And for good reason! For Haitians, a victory of *slaves* is an oxymoron, one that transmits a Eurocentrism infused with a light whiff of racism. When did the victors destroy their status as slaves—during or after the rebellion? If we are talking about a *slave revolution*, then the cultivators of the Rural Codes are perhaps rightfully in their place during the nineteenth century! The history presented in this chapter, however, shows that they defied the prescriptions of the law with remarkable success. The revolution of 1791 to 1804 didn't take place along the famous Slave Route that UNESCO has designated in Africa, because the slave traders—despite their arrogant pretensions—didn't have the power to define who was a *slave*, either before or after 1804. The African mothers who cried for the loss of their daughters and sons had not given birth to *slaves*.

Social science can allow itself to be seduced by the surprise of the international community and focus on the fallout from these events we produced in overseas contexts, where they were considered unexpected and unwanted. But the potential of the events that unfolded from 1791 to 1804 is much more powerful and significant in our local daily life than in that of modern Western societies, which are solidly built on the racialization of human relations and endowed with institutional mechanisms adequate for the recuperation of the transformations issuing forth from an island lost in the Atlantic Ocean.[1]

First of all, whatever the West and the Westernized among us might think, slavery didn't have the impact on Haitian society with which it is often credited. The vast majority of the ancestors who set in motion and lived through the revolutionary period had arrived directly from Africa and had been familiar with merchant slavery (Meillassoux 1998, 235) only for two or three decades at most. There is no proof that they interiorized the idea of black inferiority lauded by the plantation society. Their colonial experience, instead, was more of resistance to oppression than of the servile submissiveness of chained servants.

That was not the case for the minority of *freed* slaves—less than one-tenth of the population—usually Creoles who had never lived in a society without merchant slavery and who rushed to take advantage of the successes of the Haitian Revolution. The furniture of their memory was made up of the facts and daily gestures of life in the plantation system. They and their families were able to overcome, to an appreciable degree, the bitterness of colonial life. The indirect information they received about non-Western forms of life probably didn't shape their imagination, since these didn't have the scope or present the seductions of the Western epic. These Creoles and their thinkers didn't pay attention to the reorganization of the grass roots of Haitian society, if they noticed it at all. Given the conditions under which independence was gained, the oligarchs who appropriated the revolution were more interested in preserving the status quo than promoting the emerging social forces, which they preferred not to see. They invested more energy in pursuing and shoring up their integration into the West than in understanding and appreciating the exploits of the oppressed colonial class. For this reason, their references to local social life are partial and distorted.

The Haitian oligarchs considered themselves formerly freed, and the idea they developed of the workers of the agro-industrial sector was revealed in their treatment of the slaves who rebelled, the fugitives and the deserters known as *maroons*. The maroon was the antithesis of both the slave and the captive. The French perceived maroons as untamed, savage animals; that is where the name came from. In the middle of the revolution, Toussaint Louverture described them as "vagabonds" and "lazy," and during the nineteenth century the rural police codes converted them into a special type of criminal: the *outlaw*.

The treatment of the *unknown maroon* is typical of the sallies the oligarchs and intermediary classes carried out in their attempts to surreptitiously return to the pre-1789 situation. The *unknown maroon* is the hollow ghost who can be venerated without difficulty because the maroons in flesh and blood—Sans-Souci, Petit Noël Prieur, Jacques Tellier, Cagnel, Jasmin, Mavougou, Vamalheureux, Labruni, Kakapoul—are considered too embarrassing. Imagine having to trade the name of Rue Monseigner Guilloux for that of Halaou, Romaine la Prophétesse, or Kakapoul![2]

The well-known conflict over color, that fundamentally colonial struggle between the black and mulatto military leaders—Toussaint, Dessalines, and Christophe on one side and Rigaud, Pétion, and Boyer on the other—covers up the more fundamental issue of the fact that it was impossible to receive and incorporate the rebel workers, who remained more understood than unknown. For the great generals of the Indigenous Army, the union of blacks and mulattoes always remained an ideal to be pursued. But they considered the possibility of reconciliation between the various leaders of insurgent groups and any form of alliance with the *bossales* to be an unthinkable step backwards. To them, attachment to the metropole and its concepts represented the advance of civilization. Keeping company with and endorsing African savagery (Saint-Louis 2000, 92) meant its retreat.

The fact that Haitian urban society pushed aside Kakapoul and his companions is more significant to understanding the country's history than class conflicts with a European aroma. Urban Haitians never imperiled the rebuilding of the plantation, while the leaders of insurgent groups did because their power represented the expression of the core philosophy of the society's ethnic, African-born majority (Mignolo 2005, 17). Their action and presence superseded the types of class conflicts that would have been meaningful within a Eurocentric framework. The ethnic problematic changed the terms of the conversation and required a choice between popular sovereignty and structural dependence, and between modernity/coloniality and decolonality. The goal of the oligarchs of Haiti and their intellectual elites was to use their black skin to better polish their white masks. As inheritors of the ideas of the Club Massiac, and long deeply dependent on the executive powers of the metropole, the local oligarchs were incapable of imagining any kind of equality with laborers. They blamed the fact that their policies never obtained any palpable or cumulative result on the endemic collapse of government administrations. But above all, their failure exposed their incapacity to think through the political power of the sovereign people, or their stubborn refusal to do so.

Polverel's February 27, 1794, Règlements de police sur la culture et les cultivateurs (Police regulations on agriculture and the cultivators; Debien 1949, 402) enables us to see the distance between the vision of this Jacobin civil commissioner and that of the Creole leaders—the formerly freed!—who presided over the destiny of the state in Haiti. They used their leadership role to do everything they could to imprison the nation in a Eurocentric straight-jacket, inspired by the capitalist slave system. But they didn't have the means to do what they wished. The civil commissioner, on the other hand, without moving away from the requirements of his position, placed the formerly freed and the newly freed in a set of social relations defined by equality. In the path he imagined, *bossales* and Creoles would connect with one another through forms of daily practice that in the long term would lead to the elaboration of a common vision of a new plantation society. That was the theory, and the hope. The self-management he envisioned was brushed aside by the Creoles, Toussaint first among them, who were in the process of gaining access to the superior levels of the society. But, with the exception of Christophe's agricultural system, the classic versions of agro-industry they sought to build on all failed miserably after 1791. Only those wearing blinders could believe that the plantation system could realistically be rebuilt.

In this chapter and the two that follow, I will describe how the oligarchs of the country insisted on trying to relaunch the traditional plantation focused on the production of export commodities. And I will explore how their governments built a wall separating them from the peasant classes. The segregation they worked hard to institutionalize left the working population with only one choice: that of exercising its sovereignty in isolation. These efforts to barricade them were a way of protecting the urban classes from the shame they felt at the constitutive Africanness of Haiti's agricultural workers. They translated the broader ideological currents of the period, during which the capitalist societies and economies were relocating their interests from the small spaces of the Caribbean to the vast reaches of the planet. During this phase of imperialist development, Western economies produced and consumed a large variety of manufactured goods and primary materials, and their new colonies supported major migratory movements. The extension of the colonial empires was accompanied by a deepening of their racism, which terrorized Haitian thinkers even more. There was no chance that in this context Haiti and the Caribbean would be heard, or be considered part of the concert of nations. There was no space for them to be granted any kind of dignity by the broader Western world. Whether they liked it or not, the Haitian oligarchs were on the margins. They swam against the current and fought European scientific racism. But in doing so, they still used the models of imperial culture and the languages they transmitted as the only recognizable proof of humanity.

But an intense development of the counter-plantation system and its way of life compensated for Haiti's isolation from capitalist investment and production. The governing classes were unaware of this development, or preferred to be unaware of it, because it was driven by a non-Western philosophy of the world. The last three chapters of this book explore the power that the supposedly subordinated classes accumulated by resolving their daily problems for themselves, in complete autonomy. Here, I offer observations on the ways in which the Westernized classes, who had no means of containing the development of the counter-plantation society, sought to survive on the margins of the thinking that fuelled the true sovereignty of the popular classes.

A "Republican" Reform of the Plantation

After the May 13, 1791, decree of the Constituent Assembly (Saint-Louis 2006, 149), the colonists began replacing those they called *slaves*, and treated as such, with persons of a new category, the *cultivator*. The inconvenient modification was forced on them by revolutionary France and had no connection with local history. A few months later, in August 1791, however, the working classes of the North started a general insurrection. This culminated in 1793 in the elimination of their status as *slaves* and of their traditional role within Saint-Domingue's society. The civil commissioners were forced to consent to general abolition and negotiate a new form of treatment of the agricultural laborers, given the unavoidable need to use them—even if only temporarily—throughout the territory for military objectives more urgent than the production of commodities for export. The agricultural laborers–turned-soldiers played a central role in preserving the sovereignty of the French state over the colonial territory.

General emancipation was the result of the loss of the monopoly of violence by the colonial armies. The colonial administration was at the center of the storm, and with its emancipation decree of August 1793 it declared the foreign-born majority of the country to be French citizens. In 1794 and again in 1798, the general-in-chief of the colonial troops, Laveaux, described them as citizens (Saint-Louis 2006). Sonthonax and Polvérel used the same language.

To conceive of the cultivators as citizens of the republic required changes that Polvérel partially gathered together in his Règlements de police sur la culture et les cultivateurs (Debien 1949, 402). There were now two camps facing each other. On one side was the labor force liberating itself from its chains through its own actions. On the other side was an oligarchy of landowners who were ready to betray their mother country. The civil commissioner produced a model that provided for equality between property owners and cultivators in terms of their rights to citizenship. It also insisted on the need for the cultivators to constitute a deliberative body that would give them the means to defend themselves against the potential privileges of the property owners.

In developing his argument that Haitian peasant society is "almost post-capitalist," Gérard Barthélémy took note of Polvérel's project. The commissioner was working within the context of the colonial republic, but he seems to have been thinking of the potential role to be played by the sovereign people in the society's future. The colony, however, actually had no sovereign people. It was part of the private domain of the French state. But it was precisely because the state remained the ultimately property owner that Polvérel could imagine surpassing the exclusion and denuding of the cultivator. In his system, the individual property owner would lose some of his prerogatives and become simply a bondholder and creditor (Blancpain 2003, 67) with no more rights than the cultivators.

Polvérel drafted a system in which capital and labor could negotiate with one another without encroaching on the monopoly of violence held by the administration, or the right of the sovereign to justify actions by evoking the reason of state. He promoted a system for self-management that sought to preserve the functioning of the economic activities useful for the metropole. In his system, the metropole's needs maintained a certain precedence in determining the needs and orientations of the workers and the property owners.

All the workers were free and enjoyed the rights of French citizens. They did, however, have to submit to one condition: continuing to work on the plantations. These were to be run by an administrative council made up of a manager and *conducteurs* (drivers), previously known as *commandeurs* (overseers). But these were to be elected through the universal suffrage of the cultivators. The laborers, therefore, were promoted to the level of valuable interlocutors who could be integrated into the colonial society.

The thinking of the civil commissioner remained close to the philosophy of the Code Noir on one essential point. The cultivators remained emancipated slaves—that is, slaves that the state consented to liberate. Their history prior to their captivity still retained no real value. They were forced to behave according to the principles and norms dictated by French society. In this sense, Polvérel's proposal was based on the right of conquest over the island and the role of the despotic state as its uncontested owner. He understood, however, that under conditions of liberty and equality, the state could no longer continue to enjoy the benefits produced by *its* Pearl of the Antilles without imposing some form of self-management on plantation production. The planters therefore had to accept a role as subalterns. The external power of the metropolitan state would orient economic activity and arbitrate social negotiation.

What did the *bossales* think of Polvérel's plan? There certainly was not unanimity among them. The evolution of the dialogue between capital and labor surely involved conflicts. Polvérel was acting as a conscientious colonial functionary, seeking out a viable option that could work within the revolutionary legal context. But his thinking makes clear that in the midst of the inescapable conjuncture of general emancipation, metropolitan sovereignty over the colony could be protected only through a good faith alliance with the labor force. His proposal was based on a negotiation between capital and labor that both Toussaint and Napoléon rejected, opting instead for an authoritarian and despotic solution—using authority to establish the rules of the game, following the model that had been in place before 1789.

That Polvérel did his best to defend metropolitan interests seems normal. The important point here is not about the viability or naïveté (Blancpain 2003, 63) of his thought, but rather its anchoring in the premises of the French Revolution.[3] He sought to translate the equality of all citizens, property owners, and cultivators into reality.

Except for Dessalines, the heroes of independence—at least those who are recognized as such—did not engage with the project of establishing equality among the citizens of the republic. They remained locked in a Eurocentric posture, and positioned themselves against any parity between Creoles and *bossales*. This posture didn't necessarily imply the superiority of white race over the black race. But it didn't reject it clearly either. It conceded unequivocally that there was an uncontestable excellence in white civilization that made it superior to black civilizations. The inequality in access to land between the property owners, who were presumed to be creolized, and the cultivators, understood in principle as being ignorant and savage, slipped from blatant racism into what the intermediary classes euphemistically called "color prejudice." The empire of the colonialists over the oppressed classes, who they characterized as living in a "state of banditry, shaped by violence and maintained by force" (Kriegel 2003, 229) was therefore preserved intact. The republic—colonial, and without its sovereign people—was ready to embark on a slow and interminable journey, like a donkey trying to reach a carrot.

That was the basis for Toussaint's drastic opposition to all popular participation, which was taken up by the Haitian government regimes of Christophe and Pétion. This policy postulated that the liberty of the blacks could be guaranteed only by the prosperity of export agriculture. It asked the working classes to entrust the use of their labor and the nation's riches to representatives chosen from among the property owners, under the watch of the public administration. Polvérel's proposal still operated within a Eurocentric schema. But, in contrast to the other approaches, it invited the working class to entrust themselves to the wisdom of a central public administration while negotiating their own participation in agro-industrial production with the property owners directly.

It is easy to understand why the despotism of Toussaint's regime provoked an alarming increase in the number of maroons (Lepkowski 1969, 80), and why vagabondage increased under the national administrations. The constant efforts on their part to control this social menace make clear how widespread it was. Polvérel's model sought to enlist the popular interest in a project that would serve the interest of the oligarchs and, through them, that of the metropole. Toussaint and the Haitian oligarchs underestimated the power of the cultivators and wanted them to commit their hopes to the know-how of their representatives of color. In a population made up of a majority of new arrivals and their immediate descendants, the typically colonial concept of the *black*, used as a synonym for the colonial worker, was obviously not going to be completely accepted. Toussaint and the national oligarchs were well aware that the whip was the main common denominator that the dominant system offered the Hausas, Kongos, Nagos, and Ibos in a situation of oppression.

As the crisis slowly gave way to a new equilibrium, the distinction between active citizens (the property owners) and cultivators surfaced again. And while the indigenous generals adopted measures aiming to re-establish the colonial order, thanks to the military genius of Toussaint Louverture, the former slaves, now called *Africans* or *cultivators*, took up their place at the bottom of the social ladder, once again. Haitian officialdom was unanimous on this point. For Toussaint and Rigaud, the *nègre* understood nothing about freedom, while for Dessalines, he was a lazy person who would work only when threatened with the stick (Saint-Louis 2006, 59). As Saint-Louis argues, the term *African* "designated the cultivator, proclaimed free but excluded from equality before the law, principally by the indigenous leaders" (2006, 152, 166).

Facing the wall of prejudices shared by the planters and their allies in the military and police, the working class forged a response that transformed Haitian history and became its foundation. Their strength came from the fact that, despite all the racial discrimination present at the turn of the eighteenth century, their help was essential for the re-establishment of the social order. The central role they played in the conflicts between property owners, and in protecting the French state's sovereignty over the colony, destroyed the plantation system of Saint-Domingue. The resulting impact on the political and economic structure of the country explains the Haitian nineteenth century.

What to the oligarchs seemed a temporary and merely formal emancipation, decree in response to imminent danger, was interpreted totally differently among the oppressed. The popular masses inscribed a self-sufficient civil society into the life of the nation. It was distinct from the plantation society. They didn't find it necessary to affirm their presence in the formal political scene. Plantation society was characterized by its inability to survive without national and international political support. The working masses, on the other hand, institutionalized their ways of being, which satisfied their needs, without using the political processes imposed by the dominant society. This new way of life budded, and flourished, after 1793.

In the wake of Napoléon's victories in Europe, the French colonial police returned to its prerevolutionary orientation. From 1790 to 1804, the military dimension took precedence in social struggle. But this happened within a broader context of a transformation in civil life that is too often overlooked because it developed outside the realm of Eurocentric orientations. As the conflicts deepened, the cultivators were enlisted in the army through military mobilizations ordered by different factions fighting one another. Production for export disintegrated, and never recovered. During the period before independence a new kind of agricultural laborer was born—known as *l'abitan* in Kreyòl. The term had many resonances, and could be translated as *settler*, though the more literal translation is *inhabitant*. They provided for the daily needs of the population. Without moving from the plantations where they lived, they ceased being cultivators. The Haitian peasantry, and the counter-plantation system, had hatched.

Anyone living on a plantation at the end of the colonial period had to feed themselves from day to day. The crisis undermined the export of commodities. But it didn't stop all agricultural production—far from it. Instead, it enabled the institutionalization of an alternative to large-scale agriculture. Communal institutions renewed themselves and multiplied throughout the entire territory (Debien 1974, 360). The need for property owners to integrate the cultivators into armed conflicts made it impossible to institute the industrial discipline that characterized plantation work, and stimulated the development of the cultivation of provisions. The classic forms of the circulation of products to and from the agro-industrial enterprises were also transformed. The organization of daily life within and around the plantations began to look like the approaches invented in the *doko*, populated by those the European slave owners and the Creoles called *fugitives* or *deserters*. The counter-plantation system evolved in a crescendo over the fourteen years of the war of national liberation. It generalized itself throughout the Haitian countryside.

Through these years of intense military activity, the population consolidated the solutions it found to the problems of daily life and reproduction. The maroons lived in *doko* organized in structured settlement units. The cul-

tivators requisitioned on the plantations, while remaining linked to the colonial production model, transformed themselves into soldiers of fortune
temporarily liberated from the customary tasks of the dominant plantation
system. Economic and social life was in ebullition.

The change in the mode of production and of reproduction of the working class had repercussions for its participation in the political system. Starting during this period, the laborers expressed their rights with more and more
self-assurance: in the South, with Goman's rebellion from 1807 to 1819, then
Acaau's in 1843, and later across the nation with the uprising of Sylvain
Salnave from 1867 to 1869. And it was the Caco cultivators who were the
only ones who steadfastly, and with weapons in hand, opposed the U.S.
occupation.

Marronage: A Defiant Response to Forced Labor

The maroons or vagabonds, the sworn enemy of colonialism and slavery, radically resisted the social relations defined by the proponents of European
civilization. They wisely chose not to bend to the life conditions imposed by
foreign authorities. They became the people to track down, either to force
them to bend to the will of the public authorities or to extirpate them from
the countryside and society in general (Law No. 24, Sur la Police des Campagnes, *Bulletin des lois* 1862, 54). They were constantly persecuted and
threatened with punishments because they were generally considered to be
the principal transmitters of the *African system*, particularly the system of reciprocity that tied together those who particpated in it. For the authorities
and the oligarchs, there was to be no one facing the property owners or
leasers of land except the cultivators of the plantations: the newly freed.
Marronage denied slavery. Vagabondage constituted itself as the opposite of
captivity, as it was defined by the agricultural regulations and rural police
codes through the second half of the nineteenth century: "Article 1: Any individual living in the countryside must be a property owner, producer, leaser
of property, or sharecropper. Otherwise they will be arrested . . . and judged
as a vagabond, unless they can prove that they are living in the rural section
and carry out some rural work that is sufficient to provide for their family"
(Law No. 4, Sur la Police des Campagnes, 1862, 54).

The public authorities considered that those without land should, whether
they wanted to or not, hire themselves out for life. They also wanted to prevent them from managing their precarious existence in such a way as to avoid
the imposition of the martial labor discipline demanded of the slave and the
indentured servant. They considered that if they managed to survive without hiring themselves out as laborers, they must be living off thievery. They

were criminals, or at least potential criminals. But rural society absorbed this population, one way or another, into structures that the minority couldn't perceive. Far from penalizing them for their behavior, this society seemed to defy the city and its rules around work. Only repressive policing seemed to limit the number of maroons, which otherwise grew uncontrollably. The authors of Geffrard's Rural Code, again, admitted that "in a country like ours, where public wealth is based on the productions of the soil, to protect agriculture is to protect everyone's wealth. Even if this has to be done to the detriment of certain principles of individual liberty" (Saint-Amand 1872, 53).

Modern Europe linked access to land to individual liberty. In Saint-Domingue and in Haiti this connection was not made in the same way. Access to liberty, and the exercise of this right, was not linked to landownership for the oppressed. The two basic social classes in these societies distinguished themselves from one another on the basis of whether they privileged the possession of land as the sine qua non condition of liberty or considered the possession of material goods to be an independent variable unrelated to the exercise of one's right to personal liberty. The leadership classes considered landownership to be a favor granted by the imperial state, which also oversaw the social order and defined the limits or extent of the liberty that was to be given to any particular individual. For them, liberty itself was a favor that could be granted to those who deserved it because they put themselves in the service of the property granted by the supreme powers.

But for those who accepted individual liberty as a natural right that all human beings benefitted from, the ownership of an immense property or a few hectares of land was secondary and could have no effect on the inherent liberty of the person who used that land. Therefore, especially if there were food shortages, the environment needed to be managed in such a way as to make it possible to enjoy that liberty to the fullest extent possible. The fact that certain individuals controlled property had no impact on the freedom to use oneself, one's own being, the only guaranteed possession a person could have. Property over one's own body and one's own thoughts and the management of one's own will were more than a right—they defined a person, and were essential to them. Property, far from being a condition of liberty, was reduced to the role of a simple tool through which the free will of a subject was exercised. "The right to property, maintained Robespierre, can prejudice neither the security, nor the freedom, nor the existence, nor the property of our fellow men. All possessions and traffic that violate this principle are illicit and immoral" (cited in Nesbitt 2008, 161).

It is of course possible to devise footbridges between the two conceptions of the world. But in Saint-Domingue, and later in Haiti, autonomous social life was built on a fundamental incompatibility between the capitalist, Eurocentric plantation social order based on state monopoly of land versus the exercise of individual liberty conceived as the very essence of a person, as their natural right.

For the oligarchs, given the untouchable majesty of the conquering state, possession of material goods and especially land constituted the central value at the basis of social organization. The indestructible relationship between the monopoly of the right to property (the right of conquest) and the enslavement of the labor force was captured by the ineffable Malouet: "Look at Victor Hugues in Guadeloupe: can't he make the *nègres* work? They are no longer punished as slaves. They are shot as free men, and they obey with much more exactitude" (1797, 28).

For the oppressed majority, on the other hand, the axis of life was a non-negotiable liberty redefined and validated by their peers. This meant that the traditional justifications for the right of conquest were seen as unacceptable infringements on the dignity of human beings, and of community. Every avenue, every interstice offering even the tiniest bit of autonomy in life became a space of defiance to the illegitimate state monopoly over spiritual and material resources.

From the point of view of the oligarchs and the state administration, the behavior of the maroon/vagabond was irrational. They could not comprehend how a maroon/vagabond could build a life if they didn't own anything. I want to make sure to emphasize that this does not mean that the maroon or the vagabond necessarily contented themselves with precarity. They just preferred it to the humiliating life offered to them by the system (Barnet 1968). From their perspective, it was the behavior of the public authorities that made no sense, because those authorities granted themselves the right to create inequalities among human beings without taking into consideration their individual achievements.

We can never sufficiently emphasize Article 28 of the Code Noir, which codified the situation of the population of agricultural laborers reduced to slavery. This was the starting point of the integration of the worker into the society and economy of Saint-Domingue, and of their participation in Haitian society and economy:

> We declare that slaves cannot own anything that is not owned by their
> masters, and everything that comes to them through their own work,
> or through gifts from other people, or in any other way, no matter the
> conditions, is considered completely the property of their masters. The
> children of slaves, their mothers and fathers, their relatives and all others
> can never claim property through successions, contracts between living
> people, or because of death. We declare any such dispositions null and

void, along with all promises and obligations they have made, because they were made by people who are incapable of arranging and making contracts for themselves.

Madiou expressed doubts about the effectiveness of this standard, asking whether "the African, even though a slave, ever completely stopped being free" (1847, 1:v). But the key is to understand that the laws and thought of the public authorities in Haiti were the result of the application of this foundational colonial principle in the Code Noir. That modern state and those who serve it refused the right to property to the totality of the population. And on the basis of this deprivation, they concluded that they couldn't exercise their right to liberty: "The cultivation of the land, all production, all forms of labor, and the entire social order depend on the maintenance of these properties" (1806 Constitution, Art. 22).

The difference between the colonial administration and that of Haiti was that the latter was far less effective than the former in the application of this principle. The Haitian oligarchs were incomparably more powerless in their monopoly over violence, which was more virtual than real. The constitutional authorities could not explain how "people who are incapable of arranging and making contracts for themselves" could survive autonomously. And they could not tolerate that they did so in contempt of the decrees they were issuing. The state found their attitude all the more irritating in the face of its attempts to govern because the destitute seemed to be deliberately choosing to act like criminals, when it was perfectly possible to follow the law. Even worse, the threat of punishments, even when they were applied, didn't seem to discourage them. The destitute—that is, those from whom the public administration had deliberately taken all property and even the right to acquire any—were by definition in constant contravention of the social order, even before they did anything. And they didn't seem worried about it at all.

Marronage and vagababondage defied the criminalization of workers, the house arrest to which they were condemned by the simple fact of being declared slaves or descendants of slaves by some authority that, from their perspective, was illegitimate. Their behavior defied the right these authorities had to constrain their movements. They preferred living like sociable beings are supposed to, not on the basis of their control over the outside world but rather out of their simple will to exist as they pleased.

At the time, Sonthonax and Polvérel, Jacobins freshly disembarked from France, immediately indicated the centrality of the relationship between a person's social status and their right to move. Blancpain reports that on the day after general emancipation, May 4, 1794, they annulled an order by Faubert, the commander of the Central district, requiring cultivators to get permission if they wanted to leave the plantation. The two commissioners, in response, justified their decision by laying out its motivations: "Considering . . . that to require one man's permission for another may to have the right to walk around is to annul the liberty that is a gift from nature; that to require the permission of a renter or a manager is to subordinate the cultivator to the authority of the renter or the manager, which is directly contrary to the October 31, 1791, proclamation and the February 28th regulation which established that the overseer-manager could not exercise any authority of the cultivators . . . considering that an eight-day detention imposed on a man for walking around suggests that the exercise of natural liberty is a crime." (Blancpain 2003, 70).

The decision of the commissioners reaffirmed the individual's right to legal security and the appropriation of his or her own life. In this way, it regulated the equality of all in concordance with the French Revolution and its republicanism. The political structure that was to flow from the primacy of law would be the pillar of the public administration, and would lead to the establishment of an order built on political rights, at the antipodes of the prerogatives of a despotic state. The central issue would not be to determine whether the state needed large-scale plantation agriculture or not, but rather whether it had the right to appropriate the lives of the cultivators, to force them to sign labor contracts, to constrain their movements. The question would have been whether it could do any of this in conditions of liberty and equality.

There is a choice that has to be made between natural rights and instrumental reason. When, for reasons we don't need to get into here, the imperial state declared the liberty of those who had been deprived of it by slavery, and granted them the status of French citizens, the reflex of its first agents was to avoid placing barriers around the freedom of movement of these new citizens. Sonthonax and Polvérel expressed an unassailable natural right. The Eurocentrism of the commissioners, however, made it impossible for them to imagine that once the cultivators had acquired this freedom based on natural rights France had decreed, they might not pursue a path that followed the norms and principles of the Christian, capitalist, and racist West.

The traditional governing bodies in the colony quickly moved away from this choice of equality among citizens to instead center themselves on abstract equality and liberty and the implications of making them the basis for political life. They instituted the reason of state at the center of the exercise of power—"the prosperity of agriculture will guarantee the liberty of the blacks" (Toussaint Louverture, in Lacroix 1819, 1:324)—and the political class and rights were both irrevocably eliminated. In order to protect general liberty (for whom?), the individual freedom to appropriate oneself was no longer recognized! It became the privilege of the totality of citizens and of none of them in particular. This contradiction between the rights of man and citizen and the freedom of the colonial agricultural worker could not be resolved within the modern/colonial Haitian state, unless it took up the Règlements de Police sur la Culture et les Cultivateurs (Clarkson 1835, 10; Debien 1949, 160).

A few months after the declaration of Sonthonax and Polvérel, Toussaint Louverture issued a set of draconian agricultural regulations as part of his effort to rebuild the commodity-producing plantation system. In laying out his motivations, he almost candidly expressed his vision that the destitute, the barefoot, should be criminalized on principle. The solution he was offering regarding the relationship between liberty of movement and the specific status of given social actors, he argued, was a necessary response to a series of abuses, "considering that since the revolution *cultivateurs* and *cultivatrices* who were too young to do agricultural work in the past now do not wish to do this work because, they say, they are free, and spend their days doing nothing but running about and wandering" (Moïse 2001, 92).

Toussaint didn't feel the need to explain exactly by what means these young people who had not yet done agricultural labor had become cultivators. It is difficult to know how one could be a cultivator without ever having cultivated anything, unless it is simply because one is black and poor. For, as Ardouin confirms, "Every time the decrees said cultivators, it was understood that meant blacks" (Ardouin 1853, 4:360). Denying the link between forced hiring on the plantations and the constitutive racism of modernity becomes a quite difficult task. And allying oneself with a Eurocentrism that is not modified by the Declaration of the Rights of Man and Citizen is a way of enthroning color prejudice as the axis of class relations, to be negotiated within a Western conception of the world. If they wished to negotiate, the newly freed were to present their demands for the acquisition of civil or political rights to the authorities. This would be done within the context created by the right to conquest, and therefore the appropriation of all the land in the country by the state.

Article 3 of Toussaint's agricultural regulations stipulated that all people had to demonstrate a "useful state," defined as the fact of paying, or being able to pay, a contribution to the republic. Under these conditions, vagabonds, those who didn't work, the poor, the beggars, and the destitute all occupied the same, single social category invented by the all-powerful, despotic state when it put them into chains, gave them no land, and deprived them of any means to get land. This group comprised only blacks, and very likely *bossales* blacks.

For the oligarchs under the guidance of Toussaint, agricultural labor was required, and the similarity between the maroon and the vagabond was obvious. Since the obligation to perform agricultural labor under the orders of a third person never received the consent of the supposed laborer, the administration had to put together a battery of measures and a repressive apparatus charged with chasing down and calling to order those people who were not invited to share in the state's possession of the territory (Vandal 1992, 72). At least during the period under study, the authorities of Saint-Domingue and Haiti would accept no modification to this basic relationship.

As a result, before exploring the treatment of the cultivators, it would be useful to sketch the profile projected by the country's governments onto the thousands of anonymous people who, without beating drums or blowing trumpets, took the place of the maroons. Unsurprisingly, they were almost certainly more numerous than the members of all the oligarchic sectors put together. These outlaws and vagabonds did not work in the way the authorities wanted them to. If they defied the punishments imposed by the police, it is either because there was plenty of work outside the projected plantation system or because they systematically refused the conditions of labor that were being offered. Short of accepting that these poor devils had no idea what made them happy, we have to concede that these vagabonds lived or survived as best they could outside the system that took itself as dominant, or that this system, despite all its boasting, could not absorb them.

In any case, the oligarchs and urban classes unanimously supported the idea that these vagabonds and outlaws deserved to be sanctioned. And they paid little attention to the fact that landed property, having been monopolized for generations, was now lying idle. Even as the public administration and the urban sectors criminalized and pursued the people they declared idle, by which they meant those they had decided were destined to work the land, they took no note of the idleness of the land given to privileged families as a reward for supposed services rendered to the nation.

Classes and Ethnicities in Conflict

Taken together, the accounts that circulate about the creation of the Haitian flag—the transformation from the French tricolor to the national bicolor—give us a clear idea of national identity as the urban classes like to define it. They do their best to hide the specific characteristics of the vast majority of the manual laborers under their skin color. In the colony, the metropolitan tricolor signified the union of the whites, the blacks, and the reds (those of mixed ancestry). In Haiti, the bicolor symbolized a soldering in which whites no longer have a place. For centuries in the modern West, the racialization of humankind had defined the relationships with colonized nations in a world where only Western culture and civilization counted as such. In republican Saint-Domingue, the tricolor and bicolor were attempts to mask the variety of ethnicities that colonization was unable to convert into black. The union symbolized by bringing together these colors was just as illusory in France as it was among the uniformed insurgents.

As I have already mentioned, soon after emancipation, the Jacobin Polvérel revoked Faubert's ordinance outlawing cultivators from leaving the plantation without permission. In this measure, we can see the strong imprint of the French Revolution and its insistence on the liberty and equality of all citizens. But in endorsing this decision, the commissioner perhaps did not realize that the multitude of the maroons crisscrossing the countryside were only superficially black. Their conversion from the ethnicities to which they belonged into a subset of the black race had not been completed during the years they had spent in chains. That is why, as Madiou and Ardouin noted, it was necessary to assassinate "their leaders who fought in the regalia of their tribes" (Madiou 1847, 12:322; Ardouin 1853, 2:361).

As a corollary to this, the inapplicability of Polvérel's decrees and their revocation even under his own leadership, which was also a problem faced by the rural codes that followed, seemed to establish that the *metropolitan citizen* and the *colonial citizen* were not of the same nature. The dominant system's need for segregation hid the specific breach between the social classes of Saint-Domingue, and delimited the border between modernity and coloniality. The modern/colonial world was incapable of managing a variety of knowledge systems. So we cannot invent an equivalency between the state in one context and the state in another, given that these institutions are based on citizens of a different nature.

At the time, the plantation produced commodities for export on the basis of the work of a majority of foreigners, held in captivity and deprived of all rights. The Jacobin commissioner proposed a solution that did not fit with the customs and habits of the property-owning citizens, equipped to deal with blacks and not tribal groups. The agricultural regulations emitted by Toussaint attempted to re-establish order on the basis of forced labor that made the cultivator an undifferentiated soldier in the agricultural industry. His decision rejected any expression of ideas on the part of the agricultural workers with regard to the tasks that were demanded of them. This step backwards institutionalized inequality between citizens and imposed silence on the majority of them. The changes in Saint-Domingue, then, paralleled those being explored in the United States, where the republic cohabited happily with slavery—that is, the extreme exploitation of the voiceless. Toussaint's approach locked freedom up within a founding inequality that was maintained in all the rural police codes of the nineteenth century. From this point of view, Haiti, an unnatural daughter of the French Revolution, took the measures necessary for the creation of a second slavery. It may have been less violent than that which preceded it, but it was as close as possible to a complete segregation, given the emergence and increased effectiveness of the oppressed culture.

Polvérel's approach respected the sovereignty of the French state over the territory. But its search for equality between citizens and the way it opened the way to popular sovereignty operationalized the possibility of a social dialogue that was unacceptable in an organized climate of racial and ethnic hierarchy. The political solutions that were viable for the people of color and the emancipated slaves could not be derived from an ethic based on popular sovereignty. These sectors of the population did not identify themselves with the majority made up of the *bossales*.

Toussaint Louverture and Napoléon Bonaparte negotiated over autonomist approaches that tended to differentiate the metropolitan state from the colonial administration. But these could not accept any participation on the part of the laborers. Polvérel's approach, on the other hand, assumed the centralization of metropolitan power and the absence of any breach between it and the colony. Interethnic relations, however, were invisible in all three cases. They didn't take into consideration any divergences in ways of life or conceptions of the world, beyond the nuances tolerated by the modern colonial world. The terms of the conversation were the same. It unfolded within a Eurocentric context, though one that was negotiable.

Saint-Domingue received most of its laboring population not long before the French Revolution. This population was made up of twenty-four different ethnicities. So the distance between the king's subjects and the foreigners reduced to slavery remained essentially the same at the end of the seventeenth century and the end of the eighteenth century. The mostly Creole and urban intermediary classes, as a result, condemned what they saw as expressions of savagery among the agricultural laborers. The displays of the sorcerer's emblems of superstition among these bands of maroons, as well as their gathering into tribal groups, provoked a nausea among the emancipated slaves that was far greater than that incited by slavery itself, and even the violence that accompanied it. From their perspective, the spectacle of the barbarous behavior of the oppressed had motivated, and even justified, the rigors of enslavement. Worse, they reflected badly on the intermediaries by maintaining a doubt among the French authorities about whether they were sufficiently civilized and cultured.

Julien Raimond exhibited this repulsion and condemnation of the *bossales* in the pamphlet he wrote in support of the demands of the *gens de couleur* for access to the civil and political rights granted them by the Code Noir. Vincent Ogé was even more trenchant in his speech to the Club Massiac.

Jean-Pierre Boyer expressed the same opinion when he declared that Goman was not a revolutionary but rather a maroon who had spent half of his life in the woods (Magloire 1909, 49).[4]

In Saint-Domingue and Haiti, the problematic of equality contained in the Declaration of the Rights of Man and Citizen referred to the parity among citizens, not between them and the foreign slaves or the cultivators who succeeded them. For the loyal servants of colonialism and those privileged by it, the idea of equality among citizens promoted by Polvérel's project was entirely out of the question. It placed the savage *bossales* on the same level as Westernized people, for whom it was inconceivable to contest that they were "MEN AND FRENCH" (Raimond 1791, 68; emphasis in the original).

The Code Noir simultaneously institutionalized slavery and the racialization of human relations. It rationalized the functioning of an artificial society where class exploitation and the exploitation of an inferior race were one and the same. Nevertheless, in the case before us, the majority of the labor force didn't behave as they were expected to in the midst of the racial entity that was supposed to absorb them. They didn't struggle as *blacks*, but rather as a composite of Kongos, Ibos, Aradas, and so on. This disaggregation into ethnic groups created a clear problem for the pursuit of *national* independence, the goal of the Creoles who pursued their struggle within the modern and colonial definitions of whites, blacks, and mulattoes.

In *Pa bliye 1804*, I argued that the Indians of North America and the blacks lived within the universe of the colonists (2004b, 51). Precisely because they were the product of a colonial sociogenesis, it is important to pay attention both to the raw materials that served to fabricate them and to the process of completion of this fabrication. The captives, the raw material, were not useful until they were converted into *slaves*—that is, *blacks*. The worst of it was that these captives did not allow this to be done to them easily. In principle, the will of the slave was to have no public effect (Sala-Molins 2003, 74). According to Bossuet, the slave was not a person within the state. Victor Schoelcher noted that under Napoléon, they were not included in the *état civil* (Sala-Molins 2003, 147). Yet, by imposing an effect on the public through their will to live (Dussel 2006), the captives shattered the crystal palace of the French colonialists.

The agricultural laborers themselves didn't see themselves as *slaves*. They didn't rebel as *slaves*. They didn't free themselves as *slaves*. Work, riches, and rebellion were all the achievements of the captive. Modernity claims to be the future of those it imprisons in its coloniality. It is the future of the *slave*, and captivity is the nursery where this *slave* is cultivated. At first just physical, captivity also became mental for the emancipated or freed slave (Vastey [1814] 2013, 74). Within the confines of the modern colonial project, Western society sought to inculcate its values in all the colonial laborers. It did so for the simple reason that, among these laborers, there were other, competing values in operation (Santos 2009). In scorning this alterity, the colonist dug his own grave.

Even establishment historians concur that these new arrivals didn't identify themselves according to their skin color or race, but by their tribal or ethnic affiliation. The problem of equality among individuals in diverse human groups was not raised, at least not in the way the French understood it. Equality was a founding value of the ethnic group. Reduced to slavery, the members of the nation or ethnic group brandished their equality with similar groups as the lever for its own uplift. They measured themselves up to the French, whether Creoles or metropolitans, in the name of this parity. That was why they displayed their superstitions during their struggles, as marks of distinction that separated them from other groups they were contending with.

The intermediary classes were distributed along the color ladder that organized the colony, and they couldn't even recognize the legitimacy of ethnic categories. The *bossales*, the historiography shows, similarly were horrified by the values that united the diverse Creoles as a group and with the metropolitans. Disdain and repugnance went both ways. Vastey describes the violence used to force the captives to work, adding that it is conceivable that the victims ended up identifying themselves with the authors of these methods. The years of civil war, furthermore, occurred not long after the arrival of the majority of the agricultural laborers. They were offered the possibility of either joining the hostilities or contributing to the consolidation of the social connections that united those who had to provide for themselves on plantations in crisis. And since the workers' contestation emerged victorious from the confrontation with the authorities of the slave regime, there was no chance at all that the ethnic groups struggling against the colonial system had any desire to get closer to the Creoles, or felt even a tiny bit inferior.

The expression of reciprocal disgust between the two social classes of the formerly freed and the cultivators regarding other's norms, values, and expressions of solidarity illustrates an opposition on the level of interethnic relations that went much deeper than class contradictions. During the wars of independence the struggle between classes didn't operate through a battle between the divergent interests of the bourgeois and the proletariat, of capital and labor, of rich and poor. It focused particularly on the defense of contrasting modes of life and society. The struggle between the Indigenous Army and Leclerc's expeditionary forces was negotiable, which is proven by the fact that it took so long for them to separate into two military entities. The same can be said of the negotiations over the recognition of independence a few decades later. The struggle that opposed the liberation of the emerging nation from the attempts to subjugate it to the complex of colonial modernity was much more immediate, and went far deeper. It is also, to a large extent, ongoing. It started in 1791, and in it we can see the values of boundless liberty and equality the deported had enjoyed in distant Africa, which they carried with them to the plantations and among the maroons of Saint-Domingue. These concepts of liberty and equality were founded on personal, communal, and class sovereignty. They demanded a different conversation—which took in the totality of the coloniality power (Quijano 2000; Mignolo 2005).

As a result, the impact of two extraordinary events—the American Revolution and the French Revolution—on the transformation of Haiti into a modern nation-state remained superficial when it comes to the centrality of the distinctive aspects of the nation itself. The eighteenth-century European revolutions were part of the modern and colonial world in expansion and, at best, inspired only the tiny minority of the Creole population. They influenced only formal political organization, and not the real power relations that undergirded daily life. While they were clearly qualitatively important, the emancipated Creoles were only one-tenth of the total population, about 30,000 out of 400,000 to 500,000. The political game proposed by these freed slaves was ultimately built around rules based on either a despotic and liberal kind of philosophy or one derived from the Jacobin, republican, and egalitarian project. It would have been a titanic project to penetrate, in record time—that is, before independence—the mentality of the mass of the workers who were fully engaged in their self-propelled process of liberation.

During this period, the *gens de couleur* and freed slaves drew on the Code Noir to contest the discriminations that had resurfaced in the wake of the Seven Years' War (Dubois and Garrigus 2006). Their demands connected better, in fact, with the Code Noir than with the Declaration of the Rights of Man and Citizen. Demands for popular sovereignty emanating from the philosophy of the Enlightenment were certainly part of the French history. There is no doubt that their adoption and transfer to the colony depended on a foundational Eurocentrism and visceral dependence on the metropole and its particular history. These principles were developed during a revolutionary period that was specific to the metropole, and they incorporated a set of traditional oppositions between classes that remained contained within a certain conception of society and of the world. Class conflicts within one national grouping were very different than what was at work in a colonial reality based on the racialization of human relations, where the majority of the colonized did not accept this racialization. It was, furthermore, rejected immediately by the last of the deported—two-thirds of the entire group—who had arrived on the island. In such conditions, popular sovereignty could not cross the Atlantic.

The two social classes of Saint-Domingue, the colonists and the cultivators, therefore were not in conflict only for economic reasons. The need to recognize the right of particular people to use their own bodies as they wished and to pursue their own needs was rooted in the memory of distinct social experiences linked to the specific place, within colonial society, of the formerly freed or the enslaved cultivators. That society was an artificial assemblage of social forces. It barely took on the synchronization of the visions of the world carried by the diverse groups that comprised it, and that process was not achieved during the period of French colonial rule.

As a solution to the separation of the two branches of the formerly freed, the mulattoes and the blacks, the ideal of the sacred union of the blacks and mulattoes replaced the ethnic fracture between the Creoles and the *bossales* and muddled the perception of this rupture in Haitian society's vision of itself. The pretexts offered by the generals of the Indigenous Army for their purges of the chiefs of the bands consecrated the definitive victory of the Eurocentrism that presided over the birth of the new public administration. The need to eliminate the differences between blacks and mulattoes—two creations of colonial sociogenesis—was an attempt to deny the urgency of surpassing material conditions. It forged the memory that presided over the institutionalization of the ways of life that were distinct from Western principles. The memory of the recognized revolutionary groups gave birth to the Haitian public administration. The sacred union of the blacks and the mulattoes sought to eliminate the autonomy of the working class and to obscure its extreme exploitation. Its simultaneous aim was to obfuscate the centrality of the large-scale property owners, which, in its generosity, the supposedly national public administration had increased beyond what was inherited from the colonial period.

The amalgamation of the black and mulatto free citizens erased the distinction between active citizens (property owners who were almost all Creoles) and passive citizens (the cultivators who were almost all *bossales* agricultural laborers). Among the property-owning active citizens, furthermore, there were on the one hand the free people of color and the mulattoes and on the other the formerly free blacks, and they were traditionally opposed to one another because of the discrimination that was part of color prejudice. While the intermediaries conquered their well-being and prestige by assuring the application of the colonial system's regulations, the workers used their knowledge of the system to define their paths and means of survival. They both used the local dominant culture, but put their knowledge of it to diametrically opposed uses.

For the former captives who did not limit their universe to a Western world to which they did not have access, the demand for liberty and equality was nonnegotiable. They considered themselves to have full rights, even more than the formerly freed of Saint-Domingue, and didn't imprison their knowledge and their self-respect within colonial principles. As they successfully imposed themselves on the French and the local oligarchies, they validated their rejection of the postulates of a colonialism in retreat and re-enforced their anchoring in the traditions issued from their knowledge and mastery of the milieu in which they lived.

The colonial state and the international community, on the other hand, took it upon themselves to maintain and protect the intermediary classes, the right hand of the planter oligarchies. The intensification of racial discrimination in the wake of the Seven Years' War, and later the Napoleonic threat of deportation or extermination, fully exposed the limits of this collaboration. These developments forced them to firmly depend on the masses of the insurgent workers, once they had assassinated the leaders of this ethnically diverse assemblage. Thanks to this purge, the Eurocentric and racist premises that validated the right of conquest and colonialism carried the day during the official conclusion of the war.

Once the wars of independence were over, the military oligarchies sought to impose a project of living together around the reconstruction of the commodity-producing plantation, by depending on the sovereignty of the state's public administration, as in the good old days of the French colony— that is, the period before 1789. They failed. Their attempts were undone by the exercise of popular sovereignty on the part of the working classes who were in the process of establishing themselves in peasant communities. "Since independence, we have seen develop among us a generation split into two classes both called to take power, marching side by side, under the influence of conflicting ideas, with nothing in common but their love of national independence. One of them, the inhabitants of the towns, composed of blacks and men of color, have received knowledge given to them from the first instincts of European civilization. The other, made up almost entirely of black laborers, grew up under the imprint of African customs long practiced, and still practiced today, in our countryside" (Madiou 1847, 2:176).

The fiction that the public administration and the state were identical (1807 Constitution, Art. 6) sustained the monopoly over social leadership inherited from eighteenth-century colonialism. In this context, the gap between a racist, colonialist, and Eurocentric administration and the isolated local space that was inventing an escape from oppression made it impossible to negotiate juridical control over power relations (Kriegel 2002, 85). The management of these two contradictory orientations in the wake of 1804—of this arranged marriage between the working class and the oligarchies of a colonial nature—explains the nascent political system. The oligarchies buttressed themselves on the state formation that had given birth to them and protected them as they sought to deepen their subordinate position on the international chessboard. Their function and that of the intermediary urban sectors was to block the road for the working classes, the core and majority of the sovereignty people. For them, the only choice—other than suicide—was to struggle for the equality necessary for the creation of a liberty without borders. Through this confrontation, the Eurocentric, racist, despotic, and proslavery public administration was absorbed into an independent state that was antiracist, antiplantation, and antislavery.

The security of the two poles in this political arrangement depended crucially on a relationship between the metropole (or multiple metropoles) and the colony (or the former colony). Liberty and equality, meanwhile, referred to the relationships between local social groups in the production of daily life. The landowners, essentially inspired by a colonial and Eurocentric perspective, considered the security of the state in the midst of the international community to be an advantage that above all, helped them to keep at a distance those these supposed property owners called the *newly freed*.

This study seeks to diagnose the bipolar nature of daily life during the nineteenth century and its management by Haitians. The pact of independence concluded by the blacks and the mulattoes was a way of sidestepping an investment in favor of the self-managed republican plantation or the counter-plantation. The oligarchies rejected both of these solutions as too radical. Instead, they chose to dream of a return to the pre-1789 slave plantation. This solution required the extreme exploitation of the labor force. But the local and international resources at their disposal reduced their project to a policy of segregating the entire rural population, with no repercussions on what colonial modernity calls "development." The ideal of a union between blacks and mulattoes had the virtue of transforming the frightening lack of equilibrium between rural and urban worlds into a kind of virtual parity between two entities of the same importance, each of them useful for political maneuvering, but without any significance for the production of material and spiritual life. In the meantime, the counter-plantation exhausted itself without civil services, without the production of higher forms of knowledge, with no opening onto the international economy and no way of managing variation in rates of exchange. In the midst of the strength of its internal cohesion, the peasantry marched forward with no compass, inventing its own national sovereign entity, that of the Haitians.

The Impossible Return of the Plantation

The Battle of Crête-à-Pierrot was one of the most important battles in the Haitian wars of independence. The fort is located in the Artibonite Plain, and during the fighting Toussaint Louverture's general staff there were besieged by the influential members of the staff of General Leclerc, the commander of Napoléon's expeditionary forces. The absentee planters in France hadn't enlisted in the expeditionary army fighting with Leclerc to take back control of Saint-Domingue. And the rich colonists in Saint-Domingue didn't join in the siege of Crête-à-Pierrot to force Toussaint and his partisans to submit to metropolitan policies. The armies fighting there were two different groups of intermediaries. The working classes who expressed their discontent through the armies of maroons were not present at this military joust, either.

With the independence of Haiti and the assassination of Dessalines on October 17, 1806, those who besieged the fort at Crête-à-Pierrot installed themselves in the South with Pétion and Gérin, while those who were besieged in the fort gathered around Christophe in the kingdom in the North. The country was governed, on one side and the other, by the intermediary strata who were put in charge of applying a policy that corresponded to the interests of those who commanded them. Yet, we can ask whether these two groups of commanders, though they fought each other, were in fact any different from each other. In fact, the conflict unfolded between two factions of the same group: the freed slaves. Both factions claimed to speak in the name of national sovereignty. But we cannot identify their governments and administrations as the state, as they would have wished, unless we exclude two central social groups who were apparently absent from the melee—the French colonists and the cultivators. Whenever we confuse the state with the public administration, and try to define good management as something produced by groups of autonomous technocrats, we return to this absence.

The War of Independence was carried out in the name of certain central actors, against certain others. When they are excluded, it becomes difficult to accurately comprehend the state in Haiti. Nineteenth-century historiography doesn't speak of the aristocratic absentee planters such as those who founded the Club Massiac—Louis Marthe de Gouy d'Arsy, Malouet, and Larchevesque-Thibaud—or the American colonists such as Julien Raimond and his self-made fellow colonists of Sephardic Jewish background, including Michel Depas-Medine, the Pierre family, and David Casamajor (Fick 1990; Geggus 2002). More recent studies, meanwhile, ignore the dominated classes, following the legislation of the time by interpreting them as if they were essentially a group of passive citizens. Following the leaders of the period, these studies assume that the governed were an amorphous and ignorant group, and take as a fact that those who controlled the public administration constituted the state. Despite the feats of the so-called cultivators, from Goman to the Cacos, popular participation in political life was not integrated into the state structure. It didn't correspond with the forms of activity defined by the Western world, the author of the segregation between those who owned property and those who didn't. This popular participation, furthermore, sidestepped the traps of the idea of the right of conquest and of the right to private property that supposedly flowed from it.

In this chapter, I show how the intermediary classes—the formerly freed slaves—who claimed to dominate the society of the nation were incapable of carrying out their project of exploitation. They were unable to subordinate the means of production to the projects of the powerful metropoles, or orient it toward the satisfaction of the current demands of the international market. My conclusion is that they were, therefore, not a dominant class, for such classes by definition succeed in carrying out their social projects (Casimir 1984, 171). By the same logic, those groups that called themselves the *middle classes* were not situated in the middle of the social hierarchy, or in the middle of a global hierarchy, for that matter. What they were was a pivotal class positioned between the country's property owners—on both the national and international levels—and the much larger majority, the masses of cultivators and potential agricultural workers. When we observe the forms of life and the aspirations of this supposedly middle sector, we see immediately that they were not situated equidistant from the masses and the metropolitan world. They identified with the international property owners and were much closer to them than to the workers. They were not part of any middle.

Within the intermediary class so constituted, the intellectual elites worked to mask the Eurocentrism that guided the behavior of the oligarchs and urban society in general, including the heroes of independence. Their job was to produce an interpretation of the relationship between property owners and cultivators that enabled the state to function. Racist segregation, disguised by the appearance of color prejudice that soiled the distribution of land inherited from the colonial empire, was sifted through the tune of an ardently desired union between blacks and mulattoes, or more precisely, between black property owners and mulatto property owners. This sacred union dissimulated the unconditional acceptance of the empire's right to conquest, a right that could be justified only by the conviction that the property owners were incontestably superior to the dispossessed (John Mair, c. 1550, in Wynter 2003, 283). This acceptance closed the door on any negotiation with the dispossessed, whose only choice was to develop and put into practice a model of life in a parallel world, despite the necessary fragility of the construction.

From the Code Noir of Louis XIV to the Code Rural of Geffrard, the agricultural worker was supposed to have access to only marginal resources. This guaranteed their availability for the tasks required on the so-called modern plantations. They had to be taken care of, one way or another. And since the dominant system considered them to be minors, the old tune that from the time of the old regime placed their fate in the hands of their provident master was constantly repeated. We find it in the Code Noir (Art. 54), in Christophe's agricultural regulations (Art. 1), in Pétion's police regulations (Art. 14), in Boyer's Rural Code (Art. 61). It is worth underlining that the agricultural regulations of Toussaint and of Geffrard didn't include it.

The masters or property owners, then, appropriated the cultivators as their property. Following the example of the Code Noir, they never considered the question of their origin or their fate (Sala-Molins 1987), and even less, their dignity as human beings. In 1794, a proclamation by Rigaud noted sarcastically: "It has been a year since the Africans gained the priceless blessing of liberty. . . . Since all invitations that have been made to them in support of their own interests have fallen on deaf ears, the majority of them persist in refusing to work. We therefore find ourselves forced to turn to measures of authority, and, we might say, to force their well-being on them despite themselves" (Ordinance of September 25, 1794, in Saint-Louis 2006, 154).

In her work *État de droit ou empire?* (State of law or empire?), Blandine Kriegel defines this kind of relationship as one binding a person to his lord (Kriegel 2002, 93). But the relationship between a feudal lord and a serf wasn't racialized. Neither was that of the bourgeois and the proletarian (González Casanova 1969, 196). That is why the English and French Revolutions were possible: they were carried out in within a nation or ethnic group united by a single, cohesive set of traditions, values, and norms.[5] In Saint-Domingue, however, the relationships between the cultivator and the landowner were racialized from the beginning, and this made it impossible to apply the principles of equality that undergirded the English and French Revolutions in this context. The relationships that were woven after 1804 certainly confirmed the end of typical slavery, but they turned the cultivator into an indentured laborer for life, fundamentally inferior to the intermediary classes. If today's urban population seeks to blur the memory of these new indentured laborers, or even to erase it, in an attempt to turn them into classic peasants, that amnesia is not the result of the omissions of the oligarchs, but rather of the inflexible behavior of the oppressed classes.

The public administration, and more generally the urban residents, imagined replacing the planter of the colonial period with new property owners or leasers of land. Along with the cultivator, these groups constituted the social categories at the basis of the social order of the nineteenth century.

The public authorities pretended not to take note of the ethnic origins of either the cultivator or the property owner. This omission made the state administration in Haiti a counterpart to the European states, still the leading operators of the slave trade, and seats of limitless imperial power. But this omission couldn't alter reality and couldn't convert the Haitian state into a homologue or copy of the Western imperial state.

In France, the properties of the modern state existed alongside those of individuals. Initially, these were feudal sovereigns or lords whose traditional roles as property owners were inherited from old traditions. The prerogatives and limits of private property were negotiated, over many centuries, among equals. In contrast, in the colony, the power exercised by the state engendered private property and particularly land ownership. As I mentioned in chapter 4, the modern state was never the owner of France or of the largest part of its land, whereas all of Saint-Domingue was its domain starting in 1674 (Blancpain 2003, 28). The king's subjects, furthermore, benefitted from his largesse, though once they became citizens of the colony, the state could still brandish its all-powerful reason of state to disregard the rights conceded to them.

Landownership in the Haiti of the oligarchs was an inheritance from French colonization. In Haiti, as in Saint-Domingue, the state invented landowners, whether large or small.[6] The absence of a definition of the landowner in Haiti's rural codes meant that the appropriation of property flowed from the rights of conquest of the metropole, which were acquired through the victory of November 1803 and validated through the purchase of the territory at the time of the signature of the recognition of independence in 1825. The absence of a definition placed the property owners in the ambiguous and vulnerable situation of being indebted because they had received free favors from a superior authority, rather than being title holders with inalienable rights. They were in no position to defend themselves from the reason of state, especially given that it derived from changes at the international level, where the right of conquest had been established. Whatever power the property owner seemed to have was always at the mercy of the public authorities that fused together sovereignty and suzerainty. They had no recourse, not even the majesty of law. As for the cultivators, their precarious condition left them subjected as much to the property owners as to the authorities. Haitian intellectuals, close as they were to the international community, never questioned the right to conquest. This created a rather uncomfortable situation with regard to their treatment of the behavior of the rural masses.

We know that the number of maroons grew substantially during Toussaint's government, and that before the victory of the Indigenous Army, the heroes of independence, Dessalines in particular, carried out killings of maroons with an intensity that surprised even Leclerc. Madiou and Ardouin both made shameless attempts to justify this purge of revolutionary leaders. But already during Toussaint's rule, the agricultural regulations and rural codes were obsessed with the fight against vagabondage and idleness. After the defeat of the maroons, the vagabonds and lawless people became the bane of the agricultural economy. We need to understand their mode and means of living, to ask how they were able to so successfully defy the norms issued by successive governments, in order to explain why this endemic problem of vagabondage subsisted.

If we assume that the captives contested the right of France to kidnap them or have them kidnapped in Africa and, subsequently, the right to reduce them to slavery, then by the same token we should admit that they must have also doubted France's right to appropriate the lands of Saint-Domingue. In its reflections on the distribution of land, social science easily confuses the fact of the appropriation of land with a supposed, and possibly natural, right to property on the part of the king or the French state. This right could be imposed on the captives, but it would not have been logical to seek their assent to this right. Dispossessed of everything, they were forced to become slaves. But the facts show that they didn't accept being slaves, and also didn't accept their total destitution and their total lack of any kind of landownership.

The colonists' right to property over the persons of the captives was just a corollary to the monopoly the state granted itself over the territory. In 1681, the Capuchins Francisco José de Jaca and Éphiphane de Moirans spoke before the Sacred Congregation of the Propagation of Faith at the Vatican and argued that it was necessary not only to grant liberty to the blacks but also to offer them reparation for the tortures they had suffered, even at the cost of all the Indies, or of Spain and France (Sala-Molins 2014, 101–102). Implicitly, Robespierre—cited earlier—also questioned the right of conquest by referring to its illicit and immoral character, noting that it harmed the lives of other human beings. From the first days of independence, Dessalines, too, denounced it. It is logical to suppose that a near majority of the population, in opposing slavery, also rejected the monopoly of landed property, since a total absence of means of subsistence locked them in absolute dependence on the property owners. The Haitian constitutions, however, assume that private property is the foundation for the social order. Given such profound divergences about the very basis of the social order, it became materially impossible to agree about the basis of the social order.

Pétion's Agrarian Policy

Pétion was born in 1770, twenty years before the general insurrection. He knew Saint-Domingue at its apogee as a Eurocentric, racist slave society, and could testify to the splendor of the Pearl of the Antilles. Like Polvérel and Toussaint, he did not produce a code for rural policing, but rather a regulation or law that was much simpler and refined in its structure. On April 20, 1807, a year after having taken power, he ratified Law No. 111, Concerning the Policing of the Plantations, the Reciprocal Obligations of Property Owners and Renters, and of Cultivators, which he placed before the Senate.

The first goal laid out by Pétion in the proposal was to "assure that the cultivators will have access both to the fruit of their labor and to all the advantages they can receive on the plantations." The reader will notice that it was decided for the cultivators that they would live on the plantations. The law distinguished between two groups: the property owner/renter and the cultivator. The legislator did not need to define the invisible actor behind the indefinite pronoun *we* who was issuing the regulations, the creator of the distinction between the groups. The cultivators were in effect foreign servants whose state—whose fate—was to work the land. *Cultivators* and *property owners* were social categories that were transmitted from the colony to the independent society without modification. Pétion's Haiti was nothing more than a self-governing Saint-Domingue. The ideological orientation of his administration was to try and make sure that 1804 didn't turn into a revolution. National independence was perceived as a change in the administrative regime. For the international community, this simple transformation was already extraordinary, if not monstrous: an unthinkable slave revolution.

Pétion and the Senate realized that the flourishing of agriculture and the well-being of the cultivators were not necessarily going to be linked, and that the wealth of the country was far from incompatible with the denuding of its labor force. They took note of the need to reduce the misery inherent in the status of cultivator. They proposed to work toward the development of agriculture and to assure the cultivators access to the fruits of their labor as well as to the advantages that *we* can procure for them on the plantations. The law therefore recognized the precarity in which the population lived, which was indispensible for the development of large-scale agriculture, but it made no reference to any kind of obligation to repair the abuses this population had suffered or any kind of settling of accounts with this undefined power that could procure it certain advantages.

The legislator reaffirmed the separation between property owner and cultivator, the foundation for public order both before and after independence. It is interesting to note that in its elaboration there was no reference to either colonists or settlers (in the sense of those who managed a plantation), only to property owners and their relationship to the land itself, and not specifically to agricultural labor. Following a critique—of very Louverturian flavor—of the workers who were abandoning themselves to laziness, nonchalance, and vagabondage, he declared his intention to protect the model cultivator who had acquired "any quantity of land, by virtue of legal title." This land would be "maintained in his property as long as, within a year and one day, he has established coffee trees, cotton, or other commodities on it" (Art. 1).

The cultivator who owned any "quantity of land," however, was not a property owner like the others. Pétion and the senators seemed to have perceived the difference that separated them from the privileged without having to express it. Three years after 1804, the agricultural laborer was no longer one who could not own anything that wasn't owned by their master, as the Code Noir had established. He could even acquire "any quantity of land, by virtue of legal title." But to use this land he required the authorization of the state, and he could receive this authorization only if he produced commodities for export. The *normal* or *ordinary* property owner was not constrained by such stipulations. Like the state itself, he could leave his lands uncultivated without risking the loss of his right to property. But the right to possess was not an attribute of the cultivator, but rather an accident, an anomaly that seemed to have to be validated by the production of commodities, even if the land was acquired "by virtue of legal title." The worker could not own land only in order to satisfy his own demands for consumption, and those of his family. The transition was from a laborer deprived of all rights and all resources, as laid out in the Code Noir, to a free cultivator whose existence could be justified only by the production of certain merchandise, determined by the government. In addition to finding himself imprisoned on the plantations, he was locked up in the circuit of production for an international market, his own needs becoming secondary. The zeal of the government to satisfy external commerce lines up with John Stuart Mill's (1871, 243) view of what a plantation colony in the West Indies should be, which I will return to in chapter 6.

Pétion's agricultural regulations start with the obligations of the cultivator, explaining to them how they can conserve the property they have legally acquired (Art. 1), prohibiting them from acquiring properties of less than ten *carreaux* (Art. 2), giving them access to one-quarter of plantation revenues (Art. 4), and requiring them to hire themselves out to a plantation.

In his Instructions No. 369 and 377 to Generals Marion and Beauvais, respectively dispatched to Les Cayes and Jérémie in January and March 1814, the general-president offers a devastating description of the treatment of the cultivators in those areas. The instructions exposed his approach to the latent conflict of interest between the cultivator and property owner. He suggested to General Marion that he facilitate access to small properties as long as this didn't disturb the principal plantations (Recueil 1886, Document No. 369). He offered General Beauvais a detailed table of the relationships between cultivators and landowners. There was no policy of rectification, just an abundance of fine words and encouraging visits. There was no suggestion of any kind of reparation to accompany the realization of the fact that they "have always been treated with rigor, and more or less injustice." The president asked his envoy to explain to the cultivators "that they are free . . . that they can go work wherever they wish . . . as long as they work. He wishes to require those who owe them to pay them, and opines that these acts of justice, equity, and humanity will necessary bring the cultivators back to feelings of moderation and confidence." The president believed that "assaults" should disappear on the plantations, and that "free people should not be whipped" (Recueil 1886, Document No. 245).

So Pétion landed on a precise description of the newly freed (Casimir [1991] 2007 81), having admitted that what characterized their conduct was distrust and latent dissatisfaction. An 1816 law (Receuil 1886, Document No. 457) deplored their generalized employment in the private service of officers, as if they were domestics. His government protested these excesses, without ever comprehending the inherent injustice of the division between the cultivator and property owner. His irritation as a father-with-a-good-heart sprang from the fact that the cultivators were mistreated. He did not note that the wealthy mistreated them because they were stripped of all material resources. The parameters of justice and equity were situated within the terms of a foundational inequality that defined the two social categories.

During the same period, Malouet, the minister of the marine and the colonies under Louis XVIII, argued that Saint-Domingue could exist only on the basis of slavery. Given that the slaves had risen up, he suggested that "we buy the work and services, rather than the person, of the African" (Vastey 1814b, 23). Pétion had no objection to this kind of reform of the system he had known his entire life. But in contrast to Malouet, who expressed a vision of an economy where the labor force was used to produce merchandise in enterprises managed unilaterally by the choices of capital, Pétion proposed an economic regime that was not founded on the operations of capitalist managers. He envisioned a system operating with tenant farmers in the service of an aristocratic, parasitic way of life. He wasn't thinking in terms of the mode of production. While Malouet referred to a system of agricultural enterprises, Pétion limited himself to thinking about land tenure, without dealing with the problematics of its exploitation and the process that led to the production of export commodities.

On the one hand, Pétion's regime managed, distributed, or rented out large properties to its accomplices. On the other hand, it dribbled out tiny parcels of land to a few cultivators, who quickly turned them into the equivalent of provision grounds. He assigned the management of the constellation of tenant farmers who were primarily responsible for agricultural production to the property owners, making it a part of their internal organization of their plantations. It might be possible to argue that the republican general began a "distributive agrarian reform" that was pioneering in Latin America (Manigat 2007, 70), as long as we recognize the property owners' right to the lands they seized and the Crown's power to grant them that right. It remains to be proven that the cultivators shared this sentiment, or necessarily had to.

It is more difficult, however, to credit Pétion with the intention of wishing to "lay the material foundations for liberal democracy" and "implant it within reality by providing it with economic roots" (Manigat 2007, 100). Pétion's agrarian policy reflected his protection of property rather than any vague desire to consolidate the society's economic roots. He never regulated the production by sharecroppers. He concentrated on the plantation, though he contributed to its destruction by promoting the development of sharecropping.

In fact, his regime was not based on any policy of agricultural development. Opening the way for sharecropping couldn't be the basis for the management, or saving, of agriculture. The distribution of parcels of land with no visible or viable economic objectives, along with attendant labor, couldn't stand in for agrarian reform. The large-scale plantation couldn't be relaunched without capital or managers. Neither the sharecropping promoted by the government nor the circulation of the commodities that were ultimately produced through it were ever the focus of principled reflection or systematization that could support their management and think through what was needed to support them. Pétion's government, hounded by a latent rebellion on the part of the mass of the agricultural workers, wasn't strong enough to eradicate the discontent of the rural population. The regime rained down laws against vagabondage. In the South, starting in 1807, the rebellion of Goman demonstrated that one possible compromise was a more intensive production of food, accompanied by export commodities that didn't require sophisticated preparation, such as coffee, cotton, and logwood, in the context of a reform in the labor regime. In seeking to protect the main plantation, the public administration retreated and neglected commodities such as sugar and indigo, whose financial and technical demands outstripped the capacities of both the administration and private enterprise after 1804.

The promotion of sharecropping and its implantation during the nineteenth century couldn't cover up the political power of the popular masses or the way they imposed themselves on government policies. Under pressure from the masses, Pétion diffused this form of land use and in the process, destroyed the unity of decision over the processes of any form of complex agro-industrial production. The sharecropping arrangements managed by the cultivators escaped the landowners and the public authorities. The colonial plantation ceased being a unit of production and was transformed into a simple geographical reference, or else an aggregation of independent agricultural enterprises focused on the reproduction of the peasant family and, secondarily, on the production of export commodities. The "economic roots of democracy" (Manigat 1962) contradicted the declared policy of relaunching the commodity-producing plantation.

The truth is that Pétion's policy reflected the flight of the capitalist planters and of the knowledge and know-how that accompanied that emigration. Manigat underlines this judiciously: "Many of the formerly emancipated had their doubts about the viability of national independence. They didn't really believe in the national future, or else were not partisans of the creation of a black nation-state. In any case, they did not feel solidarity with the blacks of Haiti. . . . We forget too often that it wasn't only white colonists who voluntarily and definitively left Saint-Domingue between 1791 and 1806. Between 1803 and 1806, we saw some among the formerly emancipated sell their property and flee abroad" (Manigat 2001, 1: 311).

The likes of Julien Raimond and Vincent Ogé disappeared. So did a host of entrepreneurs of color of Sephardic origin, including Michel Depas-Medine, Michel Lopez Depas, Pierre and David Casamajor, the García Depas, Jacques Thomas Ploy, Jeanne Henriette Lauzenguez, Delauney, and others, whose businesses required tight relations with Europe and the rest of the Caribbean (Garrigus 2006, 171). The barons of agro-industry left Haiti, and Pétion couldn't relaunch the commodity-producing plantation without their collaboration. The fact that Moreau de Saint-Méry's accounts of the social structure of Saint-Domingue are at the basis of so much analysis of nineteenth-century Haiti explains why it so often misses the point. The classic historiography retains a simplified tripartite scheme where the free people of color inappropriately fused themselves into the strata of the freed slaves: the capitalist entrepreneurs amalgamated with their employees thanks to the shared color of their skin. After independence, these same employees thought they could replace the cream of the economic elite of Saint-Domingue despite their total lack of capital, know-how, and the means to penetrate the world of international finance.

In fact, the timid distribution of land that Pétion is credited with can best be interpreted as an awkward maneuver aimed at saving the urban intermediary class and helping them gain control over the country's land. Sharecropping resolved this problem. But the question of how to finance the government and the system of production destroyed by the wars of independence, as well as how to distribute the commodities that were produced to the international market, outstripped his administration. The difference between his foreign policy and that of Christophe with regard to the former metropole can be easily explained in this way.

Christophe's Agrarian Policy

The success of the agrarian policy of the kingdom in the North was negated by the victory of the troops from the West, soon after the king's suicide. The ideology that animated Christophe's reforms is particularly interesting because, while it recognized the legacies of colonialism, and despite the limitations of the international environment of the period, his policies were shaped by a clear taking of sides in favor of the agricultural laborer and a deliberate effort to repair and correct the harms done to the population.

Christophe's Law concerning Culture began by laying out the reciprocal obligations of property owners, renters, and agricultural laborers. The first chapter of this first part was titled "The Duties of the Property Owners and Renters toward the Agriculturalists." As if to offer a counterpoint to the proposals of Pétion and later, Boyer, Christophe underlined that it was in the interest of the landowners and renters to act as good family fathers toward the agriculturalists (Art. 1). Article 2 laid out the procedures that could be followed to register complaints against them. Following these injunctions came three articles dealing with the protection of the sick and infirm as well as the health care that is to be offered to the agricultural laborers.

The second chapter dealt with the obligations of the laborers. It is important to note, first of all, that only rarely did the law refer to them as *cultivators*. In fact, the Code Henry almost never used this concept, opting instead for *agriculteur*, or *agriculturalist*. The chapter on their obligations dealt with idleness, vagabondage, prostitution, and begging. Work schedules and religious practices were also codified. Of particular interest is the role of property owners and renters as well as civil and military authorities in policing the good management of provision grounds.

The second title deals with large-scale agriculture and the third with provision grounds. It is this last title, along with the taking of sides in favor of the agriculturalist, that makes the law unique. Neither Pétion, Boyer, nor Geffrard demonstrated a similar interest in furnishing provisions. As a legislator, Christophe spent a great deal of time on the food sovereignty of the population. He referred, in order of importance, to the provision grounds that were to supply the king, the agriculturalists, and the property owners and renters. Furthermore, he included instructions for the cultivation of precious trees, such as banana trees, breadfruit trees, mango trees, and royal palms.

And he concluded by insisting on striking a necessary balance between the cultivation of commodities for export and for local consumption (provisions, grain, and fruit trees).

The emphasis on food sovereignty demonstrated by the kingdom was part of the defense of territory. The Citadelle Laferrière, the only inland fortification in the Caribbean, was part of the same strategy of an anticolonial combat, founded on the maintenance of provision grounds and the capacity of popular resistance to repel possible imperialist aggression. While the plantations and the production of export commodities provided the resources necessary for acquiring manufactured goods from abroad, the participation of the population in the hills in national defense depended on well-furnished depots of consumer goods and the protection of agriculture for local consumption. This contrasted with the scorched-earth policy applied to the cities and plains into which expeditionary armies might penetrate.

The support in favor of the agriculturalists probably helps to explain the success of large-scale agriculture in Christophe's regime, even if it is difficult to evaluate precisely the extent of its contribution. The experience that had been gained by agricultural inspectors who had been serving this function since the time of Toussaint's government must have played a role, too, in the reconstruction of the plantation system. It is therefore important to credit the royal administration with two extremely important factors: its intolerance with regard to idle and uncultivated land and its total monopoly over police power, which enabled it to enforce and maintain the form of militarized agricultural labor that had been put in place by Toussaint.

The crumbling of this foundational structure after the death of the king helps to explain the rapid collapse of the plantation system he had rebuilt during his regime. Nevertheless, there is room for some doubt, for those who managed this expanding economy would not have let themselves be so easily vanquished by this kind of political adversity. Without claiming to resolve this difficulty, I can offer four angles of interpretation and explanation. The two administrations of Pétion and Christophe both confronted the problem of repressing vagabondage. The means that Christophe had at his disposal in the North, the cradle of the Indigenous Army, were different from those available in the South, where maroon insurgent armies had played a more important role in the anticolonial struggle. Second, the republic in the South didn't have access to sufficient outlets for its export commodities. It maintained commercial relationships with the United States, but neither Pétion or Boyer developed the kind of intensive exchange with England or Germany that characterized the kingdom in the North (C. Hector 2012).

Third, everything suggests that Christophe's administration was conscious of the fragility of the class in power, tackling at once the political and economic interface of the nation-state with the outside world and the interface of this set of relationships with the daily life of those within the nation. The king invented from whole cloth a nobility of seventy aristocrats, chosen from all social classes, to whom he assigned this vital role. Fourth, to support the activities of this potential elite, the royal government stood out for its pursuit of international co-operation in the realms of scientific development and the promotion of public education, which had the potential to fill the gaps left by the emigration of the technicians of agro-industry and to systematically prepare the education of new generations of leaders.

After the regime of the South took power, external commercial relations were mostly oriented toward the United States and France. Technical knowledge and administrative management were no longer energized with a dynamic system of scientific development and advanced education, and the flow of capital and external aid dried up until Geffrard's presidency. Boyer seemed unable to recruit new groups of relatively dispossessed young people, seeking social mobility and access to prestigious positions, into the oligarchy that was comfortably installed at the top of the society.

The urgent need to reduce the impact of these factors likely pushed the republican government to accelerate the negotiations aiming to gain recognition for independence from France, as well as encouraging the promulgation of the Rural Code of 1826. Unfortunately, while Charles X recognized independence in 1825, starting in 1829 his kingdom began picking a fight with the Algerian authorities and in 1830 began its colonialist adventures in Africa. The Haitian agricultural economy and its potential commodities were no longer of any particular interest to the former metropole. Under such conditions, Boyer's Rural Code, to the extent that it was applied, couldn't open up an era of economic expansion. The Haitian nineteenth century participated in the general sluggishness of the Caribbean economy during the period that, in more than one island, opened the way for the development of a relatively flourishing peasantry.

Boyer and the Marginalization of the Cultivators

The Boyer regime, armed with a nominal monopoly over police forces, built the normative and administrative architecture that governed the country during the nineteenth century (Moïse 2009, 83). It can be read as the rationalization of the isolation and powerlessness of the public administration and the codification of its ineffectiveness.

The president and his collaborators, it is true, affirmed that they wished to rebuild intensive agriculture aimed at the production of export commodities, or large-scale agriculture. Taken together, the articles of the 1826 Rural

Code developed corollaries of Toussaint's October 12, 1800, Règlement de Culture (Petit-Frère, Vandal, and Werleigh 1992). The goal was to create not a rural society but rather an aggregation of concentration camps that allowed no participation on the part of the population, and particularly the labor force, in the management of the social, economic, and political environments. Boyer dreamed of recreating that fragmented space of the eighteenth century (Anglade 1982). Meanwhile, without him, the regionalized structure that was characteristic of the nineteenth century was being built all around him. The public authorities no longer had a centralized repressive force at their disposal, the way that the colonial metropole or the kingdom in the North did. So there was essentially no application of these regulations. Under Boyer, the militarized agriculture that had been at the root of the success of Toussaint and Christophe was extinguished forever.

Jean Vandal notes that the 1826 Rural Code "remains . . . a legislative achievement of eminently national inspiration, maybe the only one of the period of truly national inspiration" (Vandal 1992, 73). But we should perhaps say instead that it was of *local* or even *colonial* inspiration, since the legislation did not imply any assent on the part of the nation. Elaborated less than a year after France had accepted Pétion's proposition of paying an indemnity in exchange for the landed property of the former colonists (Inginac 1843, 29), the Rural Code was meant to help pay this debt that also willed itself to be national. It condensed the relationships that the apprentice colonists wanted to impose on the entire population in order to guarantee and reinforce their social preeminence.

For Vandal, while the Civil Code is the expression of common law, the Rural Code is a law of exception that was applicable only to the cultivators, an exception that, in other words, applied to almost the entire population. The apartheid system was put in place from the beginning: the Code Civil protected the "urban residents, the high-level officers of the Indigenous Army, those who owned major businesses, those who held high office and had access to property and means of production," while the Rural Code governed the activities of more than 90 percent of the population (Vandal 1992, 71). The analysis that follows lays out how the legislator conceived of the foundational components of the society.

For the Rural Code, the basis of all prosperity was agriculture. This activity was protected and encouraged by the state (Art. 1), which decreed that all citizens who were required to sustain the administration had to cultivate the soil, unless they offered other indispensible services (Art. 3). The legislator was interested less in the happiness or well-being of the citizens than in that of the state, as it was defined in Pétion's 1807 Constitution (Art. 6)—that is, as the government. The source of national sovereignty was reversed. The state/government was the sovereign, rather than the people, who owe obedience to this sovereignty (or more precisely, suzerainty!)

The cultivator is attached to the land. As with the Civil Code, Vandal raises a question about the relationship between the Rural Code and the Penal Code. Through its Articles 227-1 and 227-2, the latter instituted the crime of vagabondage. But it didn't define it. Article 174 of the Rural Code, however, partly took this on, describing as "vagabonds all people who are not the property owners or renters of rural property they are attached to, or those who have not agreed to a contract with a property owner or main renter." Such people were also described as "idle" (Art. 181) or "outlaws" (Art. 182).

Article 3 defined these citizens who worked in agriculture by what they lacked; they were persons who could not justify their means of existence because they were descended from "a slave incapable of owning anything that did not belong to his master." There was no discussion of their aptitudes, even less of their knowledge. The state or public administration had no responsibility to take care of them, even if it depended on them for its prosperity (Art. 1). It was their responsibility to make themselves useful by placing themselves in the service of the state/government. Vandal notes that usually it is up to the state to furnish citizens with prospects for working and to create the conditions for them to do so. He adds: "All things considered, the Penal Code offered the beneficiaries of the Civil Code a system of protection for their patrimony, since except for infractions against the security of the state and the established order, it largely identified infractions against land and property. It is notably among the ranks of the peasantry that the clientele of the Penal Code would be recruited" (Vandal 1992, 72).

The Rural Code's second article outlawed the distraction of citizens working in agriculture from their professional activities. In its third article, it defined those workers and in its fourth it fixed them in the countryside. As in the Code Noir, the legislator never asked the question of where the citizens working in agriculture came from, or of how or why this profession was attributed to them. There was also no definition of their opposites—that is, the property owner or the main renter—just as Louis XIV had not taken pains to say who his subjects were, or why.[7]

The "citizens working in an agricultural profession, attached to cultivation" could not leave the countryside to go live in the cities or towns without authorizations from a magistrate in the location where they lived as well as one in their destination. They also needed approval from the military authorities. Article 5 also banned their children from heading to the cities or towns in order to educate themselves or learn a profession, unless these same authorities gave them permission. Citizens who did not follow these rules were considered vagabonds (Art. 4) or outlaws (Art. 182) and put in prison until they were hired by a property owner or renter (Art. 175), and therefore imprisoned themselves on a plantation. It is easy to see that the Rural Code of 1823 and all the nineteenth-century legislation it inspired didn't perceive the peasant at all. We have seen that this form of thought was, throughout time, well established in the French Antilles. As Eric Williams (1970, 401) reports, in the sphere under British control, in 1865 the governor of Jamaica informed the Royal Commission that the blacks of the Caribbean could not be treated like the peasantry of Europe.

The labor of the citizens attached to the land was not linked to their own prosperity or well-being but that of the prosperity of agriculture and the well-being of the state. They couldn't be recruited for military service, except in cases of imminent danger (Art. 6). The principle route of social mobility was therefore cut off. As was the case in Toussaint's agricultural regulations, they were linked to the plantations the way a soldier was to the army, with that difference that in their battles, success was never rewarded with a promotion. The Rural Code called them "citizen of agricultural profession" or "citizen attached to the land." The term *citizen* was probably used in order to remind the state institutions of their filiation to the French Revolution, for in daily reality this newly manufactured citizen maintained no relationship with public life and even less with politics. On the contrary, this mob was forbidden from entering the town, from coming into the city, as was the case in the time of the colony.

In truth, once the importance of the citizen for the life of Boyer's republic was mentioned, the Rural Code never alluded to their existence, and in fact used this term on only one other occasion—to refer to notables who employed cultivators (Art. 165). All the dispossessed—all the sufferers—were by definition cultivators, independent of their aptitudes, choices, or preferences. There was no opportunity offered to opt for a different role, and they could not shake off the one assigned to them from the time of the colony. Their poverty, the result of the actions of the state/government that was the successor and double of the colonial public administration, produced a great supply of labor. To assure the prosperity of the country, the state offered it the poor, the people without property. Louis Marthe de Gouy d'Arsy (1792, 9), whom I cited in the previous chapter, could not have expressed it better when he described the slaves and peasants of the eighteenth century.

While the activities of the cultivators made them into persons of agricultural profession, one might assume that the property owners, their opposite, fulfilled some kind of professional function. But that was not the case. They were the source and origin of the state administration, and didn't have to justify the status granted them thanks to the conquest of the island and the slave trade.

Everyone had to work in agriculture, except for a few exceptions specified in Article 34. The law authorized those in active duty in the military and others employed by the state to hire themselves out to a plantation, as long as their obligations were compatible with their public duties (Art. 75). Article 57 stipulated that children between nine and sixteen years old, as well as the elderly and the infirm, should work the land to the best of their abilities. The legislator seemed to expect an excess of laborers, ready to hire themselves out (Art. 75 and 76), and full employment that recalled the times of slavery. It is curious that he accommodated the hiring of soldiers, suggesting that the regime didn't envision having a garrisoned military. It is unclear how they dreamed of attaching citizens to the land.

The objective of full employment that animated the code leaves us to wonder whether it envisioned that the citizens attached to the land would have any kind of private life or leisure, since they were meant to take care of their gardens during "their hours or days of rest" (Art. 38 and 58). It is worth noting that the state regulated the use of their free time as much as possible. During workdays, the cultivators could not leave work in order to "abandon themselves to dances and festivals either during the day or at night." For, as Article 190 specified, Saturdays, Sundays, and holidays were at their disposal. They could leave only at the end of the week (Art. 71), except in "extraordinary cases" where they were also working on Saturday, as Article 183 specified.

Mandatory employment could lead to contracts that varied from two to nine years or three to nine years, depending on whether the work was being done in secondary crops or manufacturing, or in the cultivation of export commodities (Art. 46 and 47). The labor of the worker was paid in kind and not with money, with the cultivator receiving either half or a quarter of what he produced, or as a subrenter (Art. 54, 55, 56, and 57). Since movement outside the plantation could take place only on certain days, within a limited perimeter, and in very specific circumstances, the code made it possible for the property owner or main renter, or the overseer, to sell on behalf of the cultivators the portions of the harvest that were their due.

When we link Article 48, on the lengths of contracts, with Article 57, which allowed for the hiring of children between the ages of nine and eleven, as well as the elderly and infirm, then it becomes clear that when he hired himself out to a planter, the cultivator was also hiring out his wife and children. In fact, since he could not travel without the written permission of the property owner or main renter, it was essentially required that he marry on the plantation or at least in the rural section.

Since he could not move around without the permission of his employer, and even then, only within a limited radius, it was also impossible for him to sign a new contract with someone else, except by some kind of miracle of providence. The two- to nine-year contract essentially became a lifetime contract . . . to "guarantee their interests." The citizen of agricultural profession was not only attached to the land, he was condemned to perpetual house arrest. And just as the regime prevented him from joining the military, it also closed off access to landed property. In their own profession, cultivators were outlawed from taking initiative as a collective, by buying or renting the plantation where they worked, or a portion of it, as a group (Art. 27).

They were not free to build houses where they wished to live. Instead, they had to live in the same place as the other cultivators within the agricultural complex (Art. 31). The place where they lived and worked was meant to be self-sufficient, producing all necessary food (Art. 36). There was no provision for, and certainly no promotion of, the access to the rural market and the circulation of merchandise that was necessary to sustain peasant life. In fact, the code outlawed both wholesale and retail trade in the countryside (Art. 7) and insisted that it was prohibited to buy or sell export commodities there as well (Art. 43 and 114).

The maintenance of public roads, furthermore, depended on the plantations in proportion to the number of people who worked there (Art. 194). It was the duty of the cultivators to participate, in turn and without pay, to do this work (Art. 191). The maintenance and repair of the dikes, basins, and distribution canals that provided the water necessary for the inhabitants also depended on their gracious contribution of labor (Art. 40). Neither the worker or the property owner or main renter could avoid the obligation of maintaining the infrastructure without risking serious fines or imprisonment (Art. 196, 197, 198, and 202).

The state tied up the citizens attached to the land by forcing them to sign their contracts in front of notaries. These were set contracts, and they had no opportunity to negotiate the terms of either the duration of the contract, their work hours or the payment for their work (Law No. 3, Art. 45ff.). Since the citizens could neither read nor write and didn't speak French, only the word of the property owner, renter, or notary could save them from vagabondage. Without this word, they lost their place in society and became antisocial and criminals. They had a choice between poverty and perpetual submission or a fugitive life as an outlaw, which came to about the same in terms of their well-being. That is what makes the document unique, as the historian Roger Petit-Frère notes: "For the first time the dominant classes, through a set of synthetic laws, unambiguously expressed their conception of the state of power, of the state, of society. . . . Through the Rural Code work, production, the life of the peasant, all was regulated as if in a garrison" (Petit-Frère 1992, 63).

The Property Owner. The Rural Code detailed the instructions offered to the property owners or renters, as well as the sanctions they would suffer if they violated them. In addition to their duties toward the cultivators, for the conservation and maintenance of their property they had to mark the boundaries of their concession (Art. 15), take care of its crops (Art. 37), hire a manager who would replace them if they were absent (Art. 155, 156, and 157), maintain the dikes, water distribution basins, and canals (Art. 40), furnish workers for the repair of roads (Art. 195 and 197), authorize the sale of plantation commodities (Art. 42, 44, 51–54, and 63) and facilitate inspection by military authorities (Art. 148).

In order to make the situation of the cultivator as close as possible to that of the slave, Boyer's Rural Code had to convert the property owners into planters, inhabitants, and colonists. In contrast to the colonial administration, Boyer had an extremely difficult time cultivating or getting others to cultivate the land. In fact, property owners were never bothered if they didn't take care of what they owned. The economic punishment that would have struck the negligent property owner during colonial times was replaced by police measures. In the eighteenth century, a property owners could not have allowed themselves this luxury; the laws of the market would have punished their insouciance. During the Haitian nineteenth century, in contrast, they could count on the public authorities to protect them from the market. This forces us to ask: what exactly was the economic system of the nineteenth-century state/government?

Article 15, the first of Law No. 2, General Administration of the Various Agricultural Establishments, referred to concessions made by the state either as national properties or as partial donations. It then formulated the instructions for those granted these concessions. Government agents or functionaries were to take charge of making sure the Rural Code was respected in the organization and management of these domains.

In a word, the Code Rural—like the Code Noir—was constructed to furnish cheap labor to property owners. It contained the measures necessary to annul any attempts at negotiation on the part of the agricultural laborers. The property owner, in contrast, was a personality already established at the summit of the society, and the demonstration of his superior status had consequences that were all the more disastrous because his property delimited the border that separated him, as an active citizen, from the majority excluded from the political system. The manna that fell from heaven permitted the property-owners to create a republic of rentiers that held no attraction for labor or risks taken on by the captains of industry. As I will show, the incontestable preeminence of a type of property owner that the law could not define had the virtue of reinforcing the relative autonomy of the administrative machinery inherited from the colony, and of its behavior as a suzerain. By allowing property owners to convert the large plantations of the eighteenth century into their treasure, the society promoted by Boyer locked up its economic system. The productivity of the counter-plantation grew more and more autonomous, and the rent drawn from it by the property owners through sharecropping or contributions to the state's coffers was consumed by idle property owners functioning as active citizens.

In short, the Haitian political regime institutionalized a division of society into two distinct castes: all-powerful property owners and pariah cultivators. In addition, the Rural Code included a provision reiterating the obligation that cultivators had to submit to and respect their employers, under threat of imprisonment (Art. 69, 75, 188, and 189). Therefore, the plantation owner became untouchable and haloed with impunity in their relationships with the agricultural laborers. In the minds of the oligarchs, the citizens attached to culture remained newly freed (Casimir [1991] 2007, 81), the equivalents, at best, of the indentured laborers of the seventeenth century or those from Southeast Asia imported a few years later to the colonial empires of Britain, Holland, and France.

The situation of the Haitian newly freed was worse than that of the indentured laborers of the seventeenth or nineteenth century in two critical ways. On the one hand, their contracts were virtually unlimited. But they also had no way to remedy their poverty. After a period of hard labor, the thirty-six-month indentured laborers in the early Caribbean benefited from a piece of land on which to establish themselves. That was not the case for the Haitian cultivator. Boyer's republic therefore codified the contours of a second slavery, three decades after general emancipation.

Boyer's Rural Code never really left the drawers of his desk. But the fact that it wasn't applied doesn't diminish the importance of the idea of a second slavery for my reflection here. What I am seeking to do is to identify the characteristics of the state in Haiti. Like all observers, I take note of the fact that the country did not experience a second slavery. But I also recognize that that is not for lack of effort on the part of Boyer or the oligarchs he represented. Their intentions are clearly sculpted in the law. The failure of their agrarian policy, then, reveals the power of the peasantry and the scope of its participation in the structuring of the state in Haiti. What we need to conceptualize and codify is this form of participation in the political structure of the country.

There is no need to dwell on what is obvious—that is, that Haiti didn't experience a second slavery despite the intentions of the governments. What we need to do is emphasize the victory of the sovereign people and, inversely, the defeat of those who held power and of their political administration. We cannot ever reproach the public authorities for the fact that they didn't serve the Haitian peasantry or the counter-plantation system. It is in their very nature not to do so, given their class composition. But their power is not the only power. And the government is not the state, despite its pretentions.

In fact, the despotism of Boyer's Rural Code was operationalized during the U.S. occupation of 1915, after the military defeat of the peasantry. Nevertheless, despite the fact that U.S. imperialism took control over the public power, neither it nor the international community that served it was ever able to transform the world of the peasants. They contented themselves with strangling it and completed this task very slowly, though surely, as we must recognize.

Segregation Revisited

Geffrard's Code Rural offers nothing new that is worth taking note of in the context of this discussion. But an interesting annotated version of it that has circulated thanks to M. J. Saint-Amand, a lawyer and deputy in the legislature who was also the chief of cabinet of the president of the republic. This member of parliament, a lawyer by profession, laid out the values relating to agricultural workers that guided both executive and legislative power in its approach. His version exposed the legal snags inherited from prior legislators and the corrections that in some cases were introduced to resolve them. It also expressed the justifications made for the violations of rights that the new rural code sanctioned. In the process, it exposed the intentions of the government.

The candor with which the presidential advisor took stock of the violations of rights sanctioned by the Rural Codes of Boyer and Geffrard, and the justifications offered for these violations, brings us back to Louis Sala-Molins's reflection on the Code Noir. It was, he notes, a law that carried out the "incredible performance" of enabling the French monarchy to "*found within law the absence of a right to the state of law on the part of the black slaves, whose juridical inexistence constituted their only, unique, legal definition*" (Sala-Molins 2003, 24; emphasis in the original).

The preamble to Geffrard's Rural Code laid out the relationship between national prosperity and agriculture (meaning agricultural production focused on export commodities), along with the pillars on which the latter was built: respect for property, encouragement for labor, and the repression of vagabondage. It invited its readers to recall that the state—by which they meant the government—created both property owners and workers.

In the preamble of the text, M. Saint-Amand confessed frankly that the law was a reaction to the population's response to the inapplicable and clumsy instructions of Boyer's Rural Police Code. The resistance of the laboring masses required the elaboration of a new law. In the process, Saint-Amand took note, without admitting it, of the political power that had enabled the targeted population to impose its own orientations on political leaders. As he explained: "The Rural Code of 1826 was written under the empire of the ideas of the period; many of its chapters, especially those relating to the contracts and agreements between property owners, renters, and cultivators, were inspired by a too-violent desire to regulate everything, and were stained by arbitrariness and partiality. They all too openly wounded the principles of individual liberty and that of private transactions. This code . . . confronted partial attacks from the moment it was issued, and then a resistance that was almost unanimous and systematic, so that without being abrogated it fell into disuse" (Saint-Amand 1872, v).

This member of the Chamber of Deputies exposed how the failure of Boyer's code had pushed the juridical authorities under President Geffrard to take measures to adapt legislation to the needs and habits of the population. Before submitting a new proposal for a Rural Code to the president to be transmitted to the legislature, the secretary of state of the interior and of agriculture put it through a deeply illustrative double test. It was to be evaluated by those who would be asked to apply it, who, thanks to their "experience with agricultural labor and a daily residence in the midst of the rural population, had learned to know their habits and needs." (Saint-Amand 1872, v) These experienced evaluators were chosen from among the military bureaucracy, the commanders of arrondissements and communes, and communal councils. Then, the secretary of state asked a consultative commission formed from a selection of large-scale property owners from the arrondissement of Port-au-Prince to examine the draft code. The presidential advisor made clear, without meaning to, that the law was to be executed not by the citizens whose consent was of no interest, but rather by government functionaries. Its injunctions referred to the cultivators but were not addressed to them. It is easy to understand why the cultivators of Boyer's time couldn't discuss the terms of their work contracts.

The law, then, was produced by the oligarchs and employees of the state who "knew the habits and needs of the rural population," but who of course had never held the tools of agricultural labor in their hands. In its attempt to police the rural population, the law was situated within the same tradition of thought that inspired the large land grants to large property owners and the concomitant attempt to guarantee a supply of rural workers through regulations aimed at forcing the newly freed to remain within the plantation system. In the wake of the unsuccessful Boyerist attempt to supply indentured workers to the regime's favorites, the public administration sought to force those they called *vagabonds* and *outlaws* to accept certain labor conditions by trying to limit their access to their means of subsistence.

In his commentary on Article 27 relating to the renting of rural property and to the agreements between property owners and main renters, sharecroppers, cultivators, or laborers, the author raised the stakes further. He described the aptitude of the latter to flatly refuse government injunctions, along with the extreme injustices of the dispositions of the previous code: "This regulation (Law No. 3 of the 1826 Code) violated common law and placed those in contracts under a kind of legal tutelage. It clearly had advantages, but in practice it quickly created serious inconveniences and created many difficulties. This situation meant that the majority of people, whose rights and interests were attacked rather than protected, had no scruples in openly violating the law when it couldn't be eluded" (Saint-Amand 1872, 12).

Although he recognized these violations of common law, Saint-Amand justified the retraction of the law on the basis of its negative impact rather than because of a need to correct abuses of power on the part of the executive and legislative branches. Geffrard's code was therefore opportunistic. It set aside the famous synallagmatic codes and left the property owners and laborers to negotiate their relationships through agreements they made freely with one another. It put its confidence in the apparatus of juridical repression to force those in need to come to agreements with the property owners. Once again, the decisions of the executive had to do with more than just law. The labor market was replaced with legal mechanisms of coercion.

Saint-Amand, though a member of the Chamber of Deputies, seemed more worried about the interests of the executive than of the majority population. He emphasized Chapter 6, "On the Maintenance of Order in the Countryside and the Repression of Vagabondage," as one of the most important advantages of the code. Severe repression of this crime, he argued, assured order in the countryside and more labor for the property owners. He argued that in the new Rural Police Code a stricter application of laws regarding private property—that is, of the monopoly over land—would force the landless to submit to existing labor conditions. The new code's Article 113 took up dispositions similar to those of the earlier codes.

The chief of cabinet of the president of the republic cited Article 403 of the Penal Code to lay out his argument that "those who do not have a domicile or means of subsistence, and who do not regularly exercise a trade or profession, are vagabonds or outlaws." He added that Article 97 of the Code of Criminal Instruction limited the liberty of those imprisoned for vagabondage even after they were released. Henceforth, once they had completed their sentence—which consisted in doing forced labor for the commune—these vagabonds were to remain under the surveillance of the police until they found a job to justify their means of existence. In his commentary, the author noted that the punishment was neither injurious nof afflictive, because it was a means of moralization. Vagabondage was something done by those who were part of a sui generis category of criminals—either immoral or amoral, we don't know which.

Saint-Amand made sure to emphasize that the Rural Code criminalized disobedience or an insult on the part of the cultivator toward a plantation owner (Art. 108–109). These were considered attacks on the public order. The lawyer did his best to explain how this disposition, "though contrary to rights, is necessary as a preventative measure to avoid disorder in the countryside":

> We cannot avoid recognizing here, with regard to the dispositions of Article 109 and those laid out in the following articles, that the prescriptions of this code as a whole had as their central preoccupation on the part of legislators above all to protect agriculture, field labor, and order, even to the detriment of certain principles of individual liberty. . . . Should we blame our legislators for having allowed themselves to be controlled by this preoccupation? Obviously not. In a country like ours, where public wealth depends on the products of the soil, this is the way of protecting everyone's wealth. (Saint-Amand 1872, 53)

It seemed obvious to him that the "everyone" he was talking about didn't actually include the majority of the population. Once again, what was at stake was the maintenance of an artificial, despotic social order. The agricultural worker was expected to accept it without complaint. Instrumental reason rather than rights served as the foundation for the law and the behavior of the despotic state. It was also the basis for the harmonization of the points of view of the legislative and judicial powers.

Everything unfolded the way it did during slavery, when public order could only be achieved to the detriment of individual liberty. On August 21, 1685, the Council of the Indies and the king of Spain rejected a request for equality and reparations made by the Capuchins Jaca and Moirans on behalf of the slaves, in terms the Geffrard government could have easily used to their advantage:

> The introduction of blacks to the Indies . . . serves the public utility. . . . Those people were born to serve, as it is said, and so in their case it is not appropriate to speak about several dispositions taken against the rights of people, as it is done for other populations. . . . And the conditions of blacks is so low that we must be able to set aside the question of rights in order to consider their slavery legitimate, without any other

consideration. . . . There is therefore no reason to doubt either the need for these slaves for the maintenance of the realms of the Indies, or the fact that the public interest is served by conserving this institution without any innovations. (Sala-Molins 2014, 112–115)

The cultivators were guilty, by definition, of the crime of wishing to move freely, to follow their own moral principles, to disobey the property owners and even insult them. They were guilty of conceiving of their own form of public order. The acknowledged necessity of taking preventative measures against disorder in the countryside attests to the fact that the oligarchs were conscious of the incompatibility of the two systems of thought within Haitian society. It was this recognition that justified the need to violate the principles of individual liberty in order to protect public order. And that was the even case during Geffrard's regime, the most liberal of the nineteenth century.

Conclusion: A Sorrowful Cohabitation

The plantation society was an artificial system put together with disarticulated masses of captives, converted into slaves and maintained in isolation from one another. Its goal was to make the captives as vulnerable as possible in order to optimize their exploitation. This system was constructed without the consent of the people or groups that composed it. It was the pure product of a despotic imperial will. But in order to build it and keep it running, its architects needed help from intermediaries: the freed slaves to whom they assigned the maintenance of public order. This type of society was not derived from pre-existing ways of life or forms of production. Its evolution unendingly repeated the authoritarian model imposed from outside. It entered into crisis only as a result of political fissures caused by functional difficulties in the triangular trade system (metropole—source of captives—colony) and the monopoly system on which it depended.

In the preceding chapter, I discussed how the political crisis provoked by the French Revolution surprised those in Saint-Domingue. This crisis accelerated two concurrent social experiences: that of the captives resisting their conversion into slaves and that of the freed slaves seeking to maintain the colonial order in order to profit from the few advantages they gained from it.

At the end of the eighteenth century, the French colonial empire overestimated its control over international politics and economy. This facilitated the secession of its marquee colony, which began its independent life with two separate but connected memories, born of two contradictory experiences. The cohabitation of social groups of very different sizes, with unequal power, was articulated by a single state entity. But the oligarchs were incapable of formalizing this articulation successfully, because the defining thinking of these oligarchs was born of colonial despotism. It was built specifically on the principle of negating the importance of the variety of resources that were available to sustain the lives of the majority of the population. The emancipated slaves carried a particular memory, and a culture they had shaped under the patronage of the empire, into the trajectory they followed after independence.

The leaders and spokesmen of the country, born and educated in colonialism, did not perceive that there was truly a difference between the individuals and citizens of Saint-Domingue and those of independent Haiti. Their objective was to make sure that the political and social structures born of the rupture with the metropole actually reproduced as much as possible the power relations and stratifications that pre-existed the French Revolution. The end of colonization was meant to be only a changing of the guards. The oligarchy of expatriates who had maintained public order before was replaced by a bicephalous oligarchy made up of blacks and mulattoes, of Creoles who considered themselves superior, by definition, to the masses of the newly freed.

The two groups of what colonial thought defined as the *formerly freed* placed themselves at the top of the administrative machinery of the state. They didn't promulgate laws that could rationalize or universalize the daily practices of a sovereign population. On the contrary, they remained irredeemably devoted to the need to reproduce the social model projected by the French colonial empire: a plantation society.

The rural police codes put forth a plan for social relations, and particularly labor relations, that translated the need for the state administration to anchor itself in a kind of despotism similar to that exercised by the mother country that had been expelled. They sought to encourage negotiations aiming to re-establish the links that had been temporarily damaged by France's refusal to recognize the civil and political rights granted to the emancipated by the 1685 Code Noir. The *formerly freed*, as they called themselves during the transition period, did not pay attention to the needs, ideals, and rights of workers. Their juridical framework channeled their behavior toward strengthening the power of the landowning oligarchies. Those oligarchs, strangers to material production, gradually transformed themselves into a parasitical rentier class, overseers of a constellation of tenant farmers. These new relationships didn't create any shared formula for living together. There was no way to gradually overcome the barriers that deliberately segregated the workforce through the monopolization of land.

During the period under analysis, the despotic administration didn't have the scope or strength that could have enabled it to override the labor force's veto of its agrarian policy. In addition to lacking an effective monopoly over the public administration, it didn't have the financial tools, the technology, or the management skills to carry out its policy of rebuilding the commodity-producing plantation. As long as the major economic stakes for the great colonial empires were situated outside the Caribbean region, the administration still enjoyed a certain room to maneuver in the realm of international relations. But as soon as the United States decided to infiltrate continental geopolitics, that space evaporated. The local oligarchs rushed to hand over control to the United States, in the hopes that this new colonial metropole would be able to unlock the peasant economy.

The foundation for the political ethic of the working population, in contrast, was satisfying the needs of local communities. They created their own existence, one that the public authorities didn't promote or even really bother with at all. They didn't have the resources they would have needed to seize or manage the realm of international politics, the source of their original dispossession and enslavement. But from the beginning of their revolutionary activity, the population emerged and evolved in total autonomy, outside the parameters and spheres of action of the public authorities. As we will see in the final three chapters, they converted the colony into a land of settlement, using limited technological means to do so. The path taken by the oligarchs followed no compass except their Eurocentrism. Though they were surrounded on all sides by racist imperialism, the captives, in contrast, marched forward in complete autonomy. Their world flourished without too much difficulty for most of the nineteenth century, thanks to the economic disinterest of the great empires for the Caribbean region.

Polvérel's approach had represented the only republican project for compromise with the laborers. Once it was rejected, the local oligarchs lost all the advantages they might have used to rebuild the plantations one by one. For two decades, Christophe's kingdom managed to slow down the flight of capital and brains that accompanied the deepening of the crisis. Once it fell, and despite the stubborn resistance expressed by agricultural regulations and rural police codes, economic life was invaded from all sides by an aggressive peasant production that responded to the rapid growth of the local population. The only thing left for the oligarchs to do was to take refuge in a modest, urban ivory tower that was itself gradually penetrated by the agricultural and social services emerging from the counter-plantation.

National integration took place from below. The peasant populations invaded all spheres of community life, even those articulated in the hearts of the towns. In this way, the two memories born of colonial life and its crisis, which began their trajectories separately, moved toward each other because of the increasing dynamism of the peasant society. In response, the oligarchs reiterated the principles of segregation in order to enclose and defend the space they occupied. The concordat with the Catholic, Apostolic, Roman Church, for example, brought them a certain amount of support. But it didn't change their total lack of influence over rural life.

The two divergent social orientations—the governance of a public administration founded on an unrealizable reconstruction of the plantation system and that of the labor force that multiplied and administered their own lives in the midst of autonomous communities indifferent to government policies—evolved separately. The most modest sectors of the urban centers were absorbed into the ways of life that were flourishing in the countryside. The local oligarchs survived by allying themselves with expatriate groups protected by the foreign consulates, until the U.S. Marines disembarked and took over political power and the state bureaucracy.

The rural codes responded to the demands of the intermediary classes—employees of the police forces, low-level functionaries, and merchants with modest resources—who were victims of the revolution of 1804 but couldn't retreat with the metropole when it was defeated. The laws sought to furnish them with the free labor necessary for the exploitation of the large properties they granted themselves. But the government they monopolized still needed to resolve the problems of acquiring capital as well as the technical and managerial knowledge needed to rebuild a successful plantation system. They also had to address the lack of outlets for the potential agricultural output. By accepting the payment of the debt of independence in 1825, the Boyer regime was hoping to open up new opportunities for trade in order to deal with this problem. But the major concessions they made to France made a dialogue and rapprochement between the labor force and capital even more difficult.

In recognizing that there was a debt to be paid for independence, they accepted all the premises of colonialism: the legitimacy of the conquest of the territory, the integration of the lands of Saint-Domingue into the domains of the king, his right to distribute portions of it to his favorites, and the rights of their inheritors to keep enjoying the property they had received in this way. They accepted the legitimacy of slavery itself. By the same token, the recognition of a debt of independence denied the captives who had been implanted in the colony against their will their right to existence and to the autonomous exercise of their liberty. It denied this right to their descendants as well. The recognition of the debt of independence, then, reproduced the colonial impossibility of promoting a social contract between landowners and potential agricultural laborers.

Despite the desperate and useless attempts of the oligarchs to invest themselves in modern/colonial relationships, meanwhile, the rural population organized a welcoming society in which customary law managed a collection of relationships of reciprocal solidarity. This provided for the daily needs of the peasantry and made the country a magnet for Caribbean populations who spontaneously came to share in Haiti's productive happiness (Manigat 2001, 2:93).

Chapter 6

The Citizen Property Owner

> Bodin affirms that the sovereign power is not imperial because it is not
> based on violence. The sovereign's weapon is the law, not the lance. By this
> we should understand the power's fundamental attribute is not to lead the
> army, but to control legislation. . . . Bodin argues that that the nature of
> sovereign power is essentially civil. The highest dimension of Bodin's
> republic is not the military but the civil. The privileged relationship is not
> that of violence, but that of the law. War is not a continuation of politics by
> other means, but its pronounced opposite.
>
> —Kriegel, *Etat de droit ou empire?*, 2002, 88–89.

Introduction: Sovereignty

The European conquest of America is, without a doubt, the necessary starting
point for any study of the contemporary Caribbean. For this very reason, I take
care not to allow the horror of the conquest as a right enjoyed by the strongest to
steal into my reflections on the formation of the social structures of the region.
From the start, I reject the majesty of this right. I am seeking to describe and
understand the behavior of those who chose death and collective suicide
rather than bowing before such a massive imposture. Haitian society in particular was born loudly questioning the rights colonial empires granted themselves. The conquest is an empirical fact, but it doesn't follow that it was or has
to be accepted, and even less that it controlled the behavior of the ancestors.
On the contrary, everything seems to indicate that to the present day, Haitians
have constructed their lives by ceaselessly questioning this conquest.

The methodology that guides my reflections is driven by respect for the
founders of the nation and, above all, for all those who died on fields of battle
but never received the posthumous veneration they deserve. Conceiving of
the lands of Haiti as properties of the state in 1804, and granting them to the
inheritors of the émigré colonists or putting them in the control of public authorities because of the perceived needs of a march toward superior civilization, has the same effect on the excluded populations as the colonial exercise
of the right of conquest. In both cases, the legitimacy granted to the right of
conquest leads to the negation of the rights of the conquered nations and of
the free will of those who composed them.

Considering the construction of the Haitian state without questioning the right to conquest of the great powers, furthermore, goes against the bases of both the French Revolution in its European context and the thought of Jean-Jacques Dessalines. The French Revolution conceived of all people as sovereign. Its maxims could not be applied in a colonial context that for two centuries had imposed the impossibility of internal sovereignty. For his part, Dessalines expressed his radical opposition to French predominance in all domains. Among the most recent studies on the topic, Deborah Jenson's (2010) shows in detail the scope of his political philosophy.

The classic history textbook by J. C. Dorsainville consecrated a phrase that all Haitians who have attended school know by heart. It is relevant to my argument here, since it directly questions the monopoly over land on the part of the oligarchs: "And the poor blacks whose fathers are in Africa, Dessalines asked, will they therefore have nothing!?" (Dorsainvil 1934, 147). The father of the nation, in other words, found it inconceivable that the public authorities would oversee the dispossession of the majority of the population. This is an extremely important ethical point for the study of the state. It is linked to the thought of Robespierre, cited in the previous chapter, regarding monopoly of material resources and the rights of people.

As early as 1500, John Mair argued that the spoliation of the American territories was justified only by the conviction that their inhabitants were essentially inferior to the conquerors and their descendants (Wynter 2003, 283). If we ignore the central role the racialization of human relations played in the establishment of the modern West, then willingly or unwillingly, we risk taking on the racism of the colonial powers and turning it into the axis of social relations. The conquered, whether the Taínos or "the poor blacks whose fathers are in Africa," were condemned to misery along with all their descendants through a process that decreed them to be inferiors and therefore justified the right to appropriate their belongings and even their bodies.

From the moment Haiti was founded, the acceptance of the French imperial state's right of conquest poisoned perceptions of what limits could be placed on the actions of the public authorities. This, in turn, limited the ideas about what kind of liberty could be exercised by the population. Robespierre's reflections suggest that the immoral and illicit character of the monopolization of landed property was due to the fact that it necessarily implicated the subjection of the human beings who, in order to survive, had to hand themselves over, with their feet and hands tied, to the whims of the lords who were the masters of the principle resource of the country. A power built on the sacred character of private property, and on its monopolization, created property owners as well as chained slaves and freed slaves. It might emancipate people, as it did in 1793 in Saint-Domingue, or reduce people to slavery once again, as it did in Guadeloupe in 1802. But these decisions always flowed from the reason of state. This was the same power that refused land to the "poor blacks whose fathers are in Africa."

There is, then, no logical link that can connect the 1789 revolution to the feats of arms of the *recognized* heroes of Haitian independence. In his January 1, 1804, proclamation, Dessalines decried the "ghost of liberty France exposed to our eyes" and contrasted it to a liberty based on the natural rights inherent to human beings. I call the latter a *liberty without borders*. It requires the use of a sovereign imagination that works to resolve the problems confronting it. It cannot be governed by the attempt to fit its survival strategies to the principles approved by the conquering state.

The historians Madiou and Ardouin accepted the metropole's right to conquest, which led them to a foundational rejection of any *Guinean* approach to social life as being contrary to civilization. For them, there was only one civilization! Vastey similarly considered it acceptable for King Henry to use his absolute power to withhold certain rights from his subjects. He had substituted himself for the Europeans, and was working on behalf of generous, humanistic sentiments that required the civilization of the Africans (Vastey [1814] 2013, 54). The French Revolution was founded on popular sovereignty, but that form of sovereignty was not recognized either in the northern Kingdom of Haiti or in the southern Republic of Haiti.

The 1789 revolution was conceived of and achieved in France. But by attacking the privileges of nobility and adopting dispositions that guaranteed the submission of the aristocrats to the new order, this revolution also attacked and countered the interests of Saint-Domingue's wealthy planters. By instrumentalizing and using the political force of the sufferers and the barefoot of France, the revolution seemed to invite the poor whites of the colony to expand their presence on the political chessboard. They made demands, but there was no way for them to imagine any equality or alliance with the workers reduced to slavery. For their part, the struggle of the freed (slaves) and the colonists of color was to penetrate into the emerging constellation of revolutionary forces in the metropole. In doing so, they hoped to significantly influence colonial society and economy. At the same time, they participated in this society's foundational racism. Both the poor whites and the group made up of freed (slaves) and colonists of color could have potentially played the role of the Third Estate of the colony. But their hopes for significant change in their status ran up against the implications of the French right of conquest over the territory. These hopes were, therefore, not receivable: "Saint-Domingue is the domain of the Crown; the colonists are its vassals" (Lattre 1805, 224).

In other words, a colony, by definition, could not be home to a sovereign people. The colonists of color and the freed (slaves) wanted to consolidate their influence in order to counteract the intensification of the racial discrimination that had been directed against them after the Seven Years' War, when metropolitan settlers fleeing the conditions created by this war and the eighteenth-century crisis in French agriculture arrived in the colony. Their demands for racial equality preceded the commotion of the revolution and were focused on the application of the provisions of the Code Noir. The starting point for the protestors in Saint-Domingue, then, was very different from those of the Third Estate in France. It had more in common with seventeenth-century mercantilism than with the thinking of the philosophes of the Enlightenment.

The political behavior of the triad made up of the white wealthy planters, the colonists of color and the freed (slaves), and the poor whites had little to do with the tenor of the processes institutionalized in the wake of the 1789 revolution. The concept of popular sovereignty couldn't be transplanted, even among the privileged of the colony, in the way that it was applied in revolutionary France. The absentee property owners made sure to prevent such a development.[1]

Neither the French Revolution nor its sworn opponents were capable of attacking the right of conquest or advocating for the right of nations within the colony. They could not move past the thinking of the Société des Amis des Noirs: "It is therefore to these islanders, these Creoles, most of whom are oppressed because of their color, that Raynal asks us to give the right to govern themselves, but in a way subordinated to the demands of the metropole, a bit like a lifeboat follows all the directions of the boat that is towing it" (Clavière 1791, 68).

When we speak of sovereignty, we are usually referring to the rights of nations. In the context of Saint-Domingue, there was in fact agreement between the royalists and the revolutionaries, as well as between the anti-abolitionists and the abolitionists: France would not negotiate over its right to the territory and would not submit to a local popular will. In the colony, France faced not a nation but a heap of individuals that it might in time absorb, in its own way and following its own rhythm, into the nation. The colonial state was understood as the sovereign manager of a conquered territory. In this context, the Haitian nation could not express its will to live freely. It could not define itself as a sovereign people while still respecting the modern, colonial right to property. The metropole and the capitalist West therefore had tailored a "ghost of liberty" (as Dessalines put it) that satisfied the oligarchs. The captives were supposed to accept this perspective. They were seen as having no father (or mother) in Africa, for they had been born into civil life with their act of emancipation (Code Noir).

The urban sectors had forgotten certain key facts that other contemporary actors remembered, including the colonialists themselves. Popular sovereignty was always present in the midst of colonialism. On September 21, 1793, Polvérel issued his Proclamation Relative to the Emancipation of Slaves Belonging to the State in the Western Province, to the Voluntary Emancipation of Slaves by Their Masters, and to the Promise of General Liberty. It clearly states the position of the brigands, which always created an incontrollable terror within official historiography:

> The Brigands of the North were armed. Ennery was under their control. Everything was in place for them to take Gonaïves, la Petite Rivière, les Vèrettes, le Mirebalais and Croix-des-Bouquets. General liberty was the foundation of this plan developed together by Biassou, Jean-François, the two Guiambois, Carreau, Despinville, Jean-Pineau and Jacinthe.
>
> But what liberty, by God! It was the brigands who granted it. They wanted to make more brigands just like them, take over all your properties and divide them amongst themselves. The plan for this distribution had been put forth by Guiambois and Biassou and adopted by Biassou. Jean-François, Biassou, and Guiambois were to be the three great regulators of the colony of Saint-Domingue. This plan was welcomed enthusiastically by the entire commune of la Petite Rivière. Guiambois was pressed to execute it immediately. This plan, and the communal decree that approved it, are both in the archives of the military tribunal. (Debien 1949, 364)

Carolyn Fick pursues this same argument, but her analysis has not yet retained the attention of our thinkers (1990, 161). The historian goes further in her presentation of the struggles for independence in the South of the country:

> Independence thus became a political imperative and it was the former slaves who provided the very foundation of that goal and the driving force that led to its achievement. As we have seen, there was no single or exceptional leader to direct and coordinate opposition to the French army during the early stages of that struggle. Rather, individuals serving in various capacities, both civil and military, had taken the initiative of organizing themselves clandestinely, in the face of overwhelming odds, to build a network of resistance. . . . All this took place in the South independently of, in spite of, and in opposition to, the black jacobin leadership, notwithstanding the difficult situation in which the black generals found themselves. The masses did not follow their leadership

into submission or accommodation with the French occupying forces, but, in their own ways, organized and prepared their resistance because they knew the alternative was a return to slavery. Absurdly, they would now have to be fighting each other in order to fight the French. (1990, 248)

The post-1804 Haitian state was structured by this context. It was shaped by a self-confident popular force, conscious of its differences and its own objectives of freedom, and with no intention of submitting to those urban leaders C. L. R. James called the *Black Jacobins*. The urban sectors followed the dictates of the (recognized) heroes of independence and sought to reproduce colonial society while putting into place only the most anodyne reforms possible. On the other hand, the population of the plantation workshops invested the countryside and organized themselves. Neither group could influence the other or make them diverge from their path. Over the course of the nineteenth century, their positions and particular logics got closer to each other without ever fusing. The behavior of the actors in each group was oriented by its particular logic.

The Right of Conquest and Executive Power

In Europe, the sovereign state institutionalized and consolidated itself thanks to the flow of resources from the colonies on the other side of the Atlantic. It was able to more firmly establish its power over competing suzerains within its territory thanks to its control over foreign territories and peoples. There, the sovereign state implanted the law of the arbitrary and nourished itself through theft and pillage. The myth that Europe existed prior to the establishment of the colonial matrix of power (Quijano 2000, 343) distorts our observation of social phenomena. The modern state developed in parallel to the imperial and colonial expansions that fed and consolidated internal sovereignty against the pretensions of the warlords who had emerged during the medieval period. On this point, Anibal Quijano's reflections parallel those of Blandine Kriegel, who describes the overseas colonial administration as a prince, "the lord of property and people gained through the right of violence and just war" (Kriegel 2003 56).

In the European context, official thought gives the impression that its institutional choices flowed naturally from the succession of historical phenomena. In the colonial space, in contrast, the presence of the conquistador suzerain was experienced as a hiatus, a deep wound—the *pachakuti*: "Thus, the 'foundation' that allowed European entrepreneurs, monarchs, and bourgeois to fulfill their supposed destiny was, for people of Tawantinsuyu and Anáhuac, a Pachakuti: violent destruction, relentless invasion, and disregard for their way of life—a convulsion of all levels of existence and the moment of the founding colonial wound of the modern/colonial world. Indigenous peoples in the Americas have not stopped struggling with that initial wound and are making their presence felt today" (Mignolo 2005, 53). The will and abusive decisions of the strongest reflected a flagrant lack of common sense, and their actions deepened this incurable wound every day. But the project of the vanquisher shattered against what the vanquished considered the normal and ordinary course of things. The vanquished continued to live in conformity with their own values and judgements.

This hiatus took different forms depending on the local histories of the conquered populations. In the case of Haiti, the colonialists did not erupt into the life of a people structured around a national or ethnic formation. Instead, a new formation was born in the midst of an unexpected arrival in the colony. And it set in motion a crisis that defied the entire colonial project. To put it another way, the Haitian nation was structured within the colonial wound provoked by the colonialists, in a place situated between colonialism and its immediate negation, a place the colonialists could not comprehend.

In this chapter I undertake an analysis of the crisis that stretched from 1791 to 1804 by showing how the oligarchs sought to take up the reigns of the plantation system focused on export commodities, and in the process to substitute themselves for the colonists. From there, I reconstruct the efforts of the captives to escape the plantation entirely, and not in order to better integrate themselves into it. Paraphrasing Walter Mignolo (2009, 4), I will argue that the captives became a specific nation by changing the terms of the conversation—from plantation to counter-plantation. The oligarchies of freed slaves and people of color, meanwhile, worked hard to modify the content of the conversation by constructing a form of plantation agriculture that better served their interests, which they presented as those of the population as a whole.

The search for a solution to the crisis varied according to whether the actors sought to achieve their objectives through the support of a despotic state, on the one hand, or the guarantee offered by an autonomous communal organization, on the other. The misery of a former slave like Dessalines, integrated into the plantation system, was different from that of a maroon wandering around with weapons in hand, opposed to captivity as much as to slavery. But there was less of a distance between a freed slave like Toussaint Louverture and a person of color like Ogé, both wronged beneficiaries of the colonial project. For them, the rigors of captivity and slavery could be negotiated. The distance was even smaller between a rich planter of color like Julien Raimond and a royalist functionary like Moreau de Saint-Méry, as we can see from their speeches in front of the Parisian legislative assemblies.

Within this range of socioeconomic interests, only those of the captives—that is to say, of 90 percent or more of the population—didn't involve a structural dependence on one or another metropole. The internal sovereignty of the state—that is, the sovereign participation in political decision making by the captives and their descendants—was not the result of a rupture with the metropole. There was no cause-and-effect relationship between external sovereignty and internal sovereignty. To the extent that popular participation in decision making showed itself to be impossible, the administrative apparatus of the state could eventually conform itself to the empire of law, but it would always be in opposition to the empire of rights. In other words, the state administration would be despotic and could not transform itself into either a state based on rights or a sovereign state.

In 1804, a sovereign state would have been one in which the former captives took their interests into their own hands. It is obvious that such an outcome was impossible during this period, since the nation was just barely beginning to structure itself. But that is not the key question. What we need to understand is whether the negotiations that were being carried out among the social forces present at the time were heading in the direction of building a state based on rights. I have already underlined the potentialities of Polvérel's agricultural regulations and its promise of popular participation. But when it opened the doors wide to reconciliation with France, the republican administration in the South demonstrated the impossibility of evolving toward the establishment of this kind of essentially civil political structure. The kingdom in the North, on the other hand, slammed the door in the face of the emissaries from the metropole. If it had been attacked, the kingdom would have had to accommodate a greater participation of the subordinated groups in decision making. This in turn could have led to the implantation of a state based on rights.

By affirming that the population living in captivity was the only social group in a position to negotiate its interests without making them those of the metropole, I do not mean to suggest that a state based on rights in Haiti could only have been a "peasant state" that turned its back on the plantation system. A state based on rights is not defined by the social and economic system that organizes the population, but rather by the participation of the population in defining that system. The choice between a peasant way of life, that of the counter-plantation, and an economy focused on the export of agricultural commodities depended on concrete circumstances and not on the prerequisites of economic theories. What counts is knowing whether this choice was the result of the desires of some autocrat, or the reflection of internal negotiation.

The public administration in Haiti was born under the control of military men exercising their functions who, in taking over the management of the power of the state and the power in the state, did not have to answer to a single community or a single group of traditions. Their subordinates shared two contrasting memories. Events beyond the control of either group brought these two memories together and forced them to coexist. The regime of the intermediary classes of the North was upended, and the administrative form that was universalized was based on the model from the South. It could not free itself from colonial despotism, or dress itself in either internal or external sovereignty.

The traditional Haitian oligarchs, the American colonists and the urban public functionaries, accepted the French right of conquest and the racist conception of the human race that went with it. They shared this with the white colonists. "So the secret and horrifying plan became known: The Colonial System is the Domination of the Whites, the Massacre or the Slavery of the Blacks" (Vastey [1814] 2013).

Far from questioning the control of Saint-Domingue by the French, the local oligarchs took it as their starting point and sought to consolidate the advantages they gained from it. That changed when the conflicts of the 1790s began, but the general insurrection had no impact on their prerevolutionary mentality. Their main concern was to pull themselves up, as quickly as possible, to the position of the metropolitans. "In the wake of the assassination of Dessalines there was a 'rush on the properties,' that was pursued until a distribution policy was set up, granting the most beautiful and profitable houses and plantations to the dignitaries of the Republic" (Moïse 2009, 75).

Starting in 1804, the public authorities fell into the hands of those who were in a position to grant themselves the right to conquest the French had enjoyed over the island of Haiti. On the basis of this inheritance, their political society hatched an immediate relationship with the claimed legitimacy of these rights, and not with the goal of negotiating the conflicts they provoked among the subaltern social forces. The traditional oligarchs formulated a state project that was not about finding solutions to the conflicts that pitted them against other national forces. Instead, they put themselves in a position of imposing their will on the latter, founding their existence on executive power rather than judicial power. Law and reason of state, and not rights, were the foundation for their political behavior. By tying themselves to this despotic model of government, they chose to destroy political society (Kriegel 2003, 63) and to follow a path that in all ways was similar to that of the slave colony founded on codes of law and not codes of rights (266).

By inscribing themselves into the lineage of actions taken in the wake of the Treat of Ryswick, the republican sectors of Haiti accepted the legitimacy of the slave trade and the rights of the French to reduce captives into slavery. They did so long before independence. They proudly proclaimed that they were embarking on a sacred crusade for the civilization of the Africans. They demanded the enjoyment of the corresponding privileges from the French revolutionary assemblies. Their participation in the conflicts that led to 1789, to the wars of independence, and then to their own control of the country all validated the racism that guided their behavior from the eighteenth century and was not dented at all over the course of the nineteenth century. The only things that bothered these *gens de couleur* and freed slaves were the injustices and infractions of the government toward them. Once they were at the top of things in 1806, they elaborated legal codes inspired by the behavior of the mother country and worked hard to apply to the new nation the vision modern Europe had of the world outside its borders. These Haitians of French allegiance (Casimir 2010, 69) distinguished themselves from Toussaint's high command mainly by the color of their skin and only secondarily through ideological nuances that had little impact on the institutionalization of the emerging administration.

The former colonists and colonial public functionary Moreau de Saint-Méry, one of the pillars of our national historiography, along with the ministers of the regime in the South, Thomas Madiou and Beaubrun Ardouin, never questioned the legitimacy of colonialism. They didn't defend the right or the duty of Haitians to rise up against the iniquity and injustice of the slave trade and the enslavement of millions and millions of innocent victims. The governments of the South found this state of things to be regrettable, but didn't go any further.

The oligarchs who accompanied Christophe were more respectful of the suffering of the oppressed classes. But they are not exempt from these same critiques. And in any case, they vanished as a significant group after the king's suicide. Their spokesman, Vastey, virulently attacked the abomination of colonialism and the racialization of social relations put in place by slavery. He documented the inconsistencies in the racist posture of the colonists and provided luxurious details about their atrocities, taking stock of the all the repulsion produced by the spectacle of their savagery in the face of the virtues of the Africans, as reported by European travelers themselves. The government team that he was a part of did offer civil services—that is to say, taking charge of populations condemned to precarity by colonialism—as one of the main axes of royal policy. This was put in the hands of a nobility selected from among varied social groups, in order to modify the disequilibrium in the distribution of races and skin colors promoted by colonial France (Dubois 2012, 62).

Starting in 1814, Vastey's historical research began circulating. It was based on the principle that Haitians were, without exception, full human beings with the same aptitudes as all people. The racist divisions and subdivisions of human groups in Saint-Domingue, according to Vastey (1819, 3, 4), had no logic and couldn't explain anything about colonial life. He refused to enter into the labyrinth of the self-interested classifications invented by Moreau de Saint-Méry, whose only goal was to strengthen white supremacy ([1814] 2013, 14). The foundations of his condemnation of the colonial regime are well known. Colombel, Pétion's secretary and spokesman, attacked them virulently. Vastey denounced Bourbon France which, in a climax of hypocrisy, negotiated a moratorium on the United Kingdom's ban on the slave trade so that they could repopulate the island of Haiti, after they had devastated it: "It is in the nineteenth century that men enlightened by the teachings of Christianity dared to propose the idea of totally exterminating a nation! Ah! And the voices of their compatriots did not unanimously rise up to silence these impious people! Let civilized France now pride itself on its enlightenment" (1816, 3).

But Madiou seems to have thought that these allegations were false, or wasn't aware of the re-establishment of slavery in Guadeloupe or the colonization wars in Algeria. As a spokesman for the oligarchy of the South, he began his monumental history of Haiti by thanking God for the civilizing dimensions of the cruelties committed by France in Haiti. The conquest of the island, the extermination of the indigenous people, the slave trade, slavery, the genocide of populations of African origin, the rape of indigenous and African women, all became just a step on the path toward civilization, the first stage in a story for which Haitians should be grateful. Here is what he wrote in his introduction to his history of Haiti, which describes the way of thinking of those he was addressing: "The possession of the territory by Europe gave birth to unspeakable crimes, and our reprisals also made humanity shudder. But let us admit that even the greatest of evils always leads to providence, even if it takes some time: civilization was introduced into the heart of Haiti despite the almost insurmountable obstacles that it encountered within the criminal system of servitude" (Madiou 1847, 1:i).

Ardouin participated in this same discourse. Nearly forty years after the publication of Vastey's works, he argued that it was French principles and ideas that called Haitians to liberty:

> France, indeed, nobly repaired all these injustices. . . . France understood that this young people whom its own principles and ideas had

called to liberty also deserved the respect they showed to all nationalities. France understand that this country, where it had deposited the germ of advanced civilization, deserved help so that it could deserve its own, still infant, civilization. It recognized Haiti's right to independence and political sovereignty. In acting differently, France would have gone against its mission in the world. Since 1789, hasn't it been a kind of lighthouse of liberty for all peoples? France, in fact, nobly repaired all these injustices. (Ardouin 1853, 1:17)

Without a doubt, the Haitian oligarchy wasn't writing these praises for the benefit of the French, who were much better informed in any case about their own role in the world. This exaltation about the good deeds of this "lighthouse of liberty for all peoples" was meant rather as a testament of the good feelings France's daughter felt toward Europeans. It was a way of transmitting a felicitous absolution, justified by France's apparent recognition of Haitian independence.

A potential debate about the role of France in the conquest of national independence should not distract us from analysis of this process. The divergence between Vastey's vision and that of Pétion's and Boyer's oligarchies does not obscure the fact that in both cases, political sovereignty was ably avoided. The fracture between the two oligarchies of the country was nourished by the same paternalism. Vastey and Christophe's bureaucracy both believed that it was impossible to speak about the rights of Haitians while ignoring that of Africans: "I started by defending the cause of my African ancestors, before discussing the rights of my Haitian compatriots" (Vastey 1816, 81).

The free people of color and the formerly emancipated based their demands for civil and political rights on the Code Noir because they couldn't have predicted the outcome of the French Revolution. The southern oligarchs didn't demand rights for Africans (or for Martinicans and Guadeloupeans still reduced to slavery at the time), given that they were planning on trampling those of the Haitian masses in a similar way. By taking the side of Africans, Vastey was led to attack the right to conquest of the French, along with the slave trade. And he sought a way to redirect society toward the construction of a state based on rights. Still, he authoritatively and in advance identified the goal of the nation as achieving the heights of Western civilization.

There was no divergence between the two branches of the oligarchy with regard to the role of property owners on the island of Haiti as the axis of the political system. More than a decade before 1804, Polvérel had enunciated the key position of the property owners in defining his Proclamation Relative to the Distribution of Revenues from the Confiscated Properties of Émigrés to the Warriors and Cultivators: "The right to property cannot exist without a protecting power: this power can exist only through the unity of the individual power of all property owners; for those who have nothing will not sacrifice themselves to defend other people's property" (Debien 1949, 43).

Starting in 1804, the executive power and the oligarchies saw the country as an aggregation of families led by the planters or renters, overseeing the plantations distributed by the state, which was the original and main property owner. Workers—slaves, cultivators, and the newly freed—disappeared as a social group endowed with differentiated interests when it came to the exploitation of the territory. Toussaint Louverture defined this familial economy in the 1801 Constitution: "Every plantation is a factory that requires a gathering of cultivators and workers; it is a tranquil refuge for an active and loyal family, where the owner of the land is necessarily the father" (Art. 15).

The colonial state during Toussaint's time showered this good father, the great landowner, with solicitude, so that he would take care of the cultivator, as was the case before general emancipation. The axis of the political system, the active citizen, was defined by his de facto ownership, which a magic trick transformed into a right to property. In this conception, as beneficiary of this right, he also gained the right to define the contours of life in the territory. The most liberal of the constitutions of the country, that of 1843, stipulated in its Article 164 that the only people who could exercise the right to vote were property owners, renters who had received a bail of least nine years from the administration, and professionals or business owners.

There was, then, from the beginning a consubstantial imbrication between the right to property and the state's right to conquest. The Indigenous Army defied the imperial state, but then took on its foundational orientation, imprinting it on the society by purging the labor leaders who contested the unity and tranquility of the familial plantation! The military apparatus inherited the empire's right to property by brandishing its own right of conquest. The foundation of this right remained the civilization mission of the Christian West. And adopting this mission ineluctably meant adopting the foundational racism of modern capitalist hegemony.

As a result, the divergences between the oligarchy of Christophe and that of Pétion with regard to popular sovereignty were limited to nearly imperceptible nuances. A state of law could not germinate in this compost without a total—and, in Haitian circumstances, impossible—assimilation of the population into their new state as people living in captivity on plantations that disposed of their labor and the fruits extracted from it.

In both the kingdom in the North and the republic in the West, the executives created a citizen property owner (Moïse 2009, 133) and imposed the possession of wealth as the demarcation line between social classes that they created from their all-powerful positions. The cultivators, as well as women—the other suppressed group in the population—were banished from the world of active citizens (1806 Constitution, Art. 18). The privileged position of the traditional oligarchies was born from the dispositions of the Code Noir, and that of the oligarchies of agricultural inspectors emerged on the field of battle in the wake of the 1791 insurrection. These two positions explain their political behavior.

The Itinerary of Colonial Property

When we overlook the historical circumstances that led to the implantation or the insertion of a national state in an exploitation colony, we constrain our ability to find a logic in the structures of power and the actions of this state. In Haiti, the normative principles and ideological orientation of governing institutions and public administration were an extension of those of the French state. But in Saint-Domingue, the metropolitan state installed only a colonial administration, which obviously was incapable of endowing a state of law with key principles. The relationship that united France and its colony was shaped by the racialization of human relationships, and that constant in the history of Haiti blocks all progress toward the establishment of a state of law—that is to say, a state where the law reflects rights. In consequence, in its administrative aspects of governance the national state in Haiti was an extension of the French colonial administration and not the state of law in France.

The colonial administration's starting point was the same, as P. Petit perceived in his 1771 treatise *Droit public ou gouvernement des colonies françaises*: "In the beginning the authority, the law, and the defense in the colony were confided in the property owners. In 1664, Colbert put them in the hands of the Company of the West Indies, still the owner of the islands. The councilors chose a few from among the property owners who acted in fact as lords of the islands" (Petit 1771, 66).

So the islands were put in the power of suzerains: France appropriated a territory with the goal of producing valuable agricultural goods with a labor force that was, primordially, destined to satisfy the needs of the metropolitan state and only superficially, local needs. Later, with the transformation of Saint-Domingue into Haiti, the signatories of the Declaration of Independence didn't question the implications of the right to conquest for the control of landed property, the management of the labor force, or the choice of leaders. That which was negotiated in metropolitan France through a voting system based on tax qualifications was, in the colony, a demarcation line between those who governed and those who were governed. Popular sovereignty was distanced in this way from the political structure of Haiti.

The nineteenth-century oligarchs began this period with the prideful satisfaction of having defeated Napoléon's army, the most powerful of the day, and therefore of having conquered the ownership and the management of the richest of colonies. From then on, they seemed satisfied to define sovereignty through their relationship with external powers and not in relation to the totality of the nation, on which they always turned their back. In doing so, they failed to realize that they were situated at the margins of the essential global transformations and were becoming incapable of participating in them as autonomous actors. In effect, their refusal of any limitations that might have been placed on the way landowners managed their labor force and chose the country's leaders was particularly disastrous because they were not equipped to predict the developments that European imperialism was promoting, which excluded them from the transformations of the world economy.

Their sense of self-satisfaction and complacency vis-à-vis the global and national population is probably what led to the casual way they offered up the island of Haiti for sale to France, just as France offered Louisiana to the United States. They couldn't have predicted that soon after their recognition by France, the few square kilometers under their control would become insignificant in the international order. In effect, fewer than seven years after the signing of Charles X's edict, the former metropole launched its African adventures by intervening in the affairs of Algeria. France's loss of influence in the Americas was amply compensated for by the establishment of its African empire, with its expansion into the Maghreb and into sub-Saharan territories, as well as into Indochine, Oceania, and Polynesia.

In the same way, the rivalries between Great Britain and France took a turn at the end of the eighteenth century that went beyond the predictions of Haiti's leaders. The hegemony of Great Britain and the transformation in economic structures it stimulated rendered the economies of the Caribbean marginal. These territories were left only with their geopolitical importance. And the United States, having established its borders, began applying the Monroe Doctrine and inaugurated the twentieth century, their "big stick" in hand.

In the context of the meteoric rise of the imperial West, the Haitian oligarchs remembered the privileged role they had had at the beginning of the nineteenth century, but had to negotiate their survival in a world in which they had lost all their advantages. They were born, had lived, and conquered their prestige and their livelihoods in service of the metropoles, depending on the oppressed classes only occasionally, when it was extremely urgent to do so. Orphaned during the nineteenth century, they maintained the same orientation. The large properties they granted themselves lost all their significance to the international economy, and the services they could potentially offer this world became useless. In this context, with minimal chance of success, they managed the Haitian nineteenth century.

In his classic work *Les Constitutions d'Haïti (1801–1885)*, Louis-Joseph Janvier included a declaration from an officer that confided the power of a suzerain in Dessalines: "In the name of Liberty, in the name of Independence, in the name of the People that he has made happy, we proclaim him the Governor-General for life of Haiti. We vow to blindly obey the laws that emanated from his authority, the only we will recognize. We grant him the right to make peace and war, and to name his successor" (1886, 29). Before the end of the year he was crowned emperor, justly: he was a lord who did not have to submit to any agreement on the part of his subjects. In his relationships with them he was not the leader of a sovereign state, since he created the law himself and placed himself above it.

In *L'État et ses esclaves*, Blandine Kriegel calls this power the *imperium*. "The imperium is the collection of civil and military powers that mark the fullness of power, such as the right to command the army, the right to war and peace (*jus belli ac pacis*), the right to life and death (*jus vitae necisque*). In Rome, this power was first invested in kings, then consuls, and then dictators during the time they were in power in the republic, before the emperors appropriated it" (Kriegel 2003, 53). In its Articles 19 to 36, the chapter of the Imperial Constitution of 1805 titled "On Government" details the characteristics of this state born of the conquest of the national territory by the Indigenous Army. It defined itself vis-à-vis the exterior rather than its own citizens. In virtue of its right to conquest, it appropriated the domains that previously belonged to the French. The law emanated from its right to administer this in the way it wished. Article 12 of the "General Dispositions" of the same Constitution stipulated: "All property that previously was owed by a French white is uncontestably and by law confiscated for the profit of the state."

But France had possessed all of Saint-Domingue. As a result, the new Haitian state authorized two types of owners of private property: those who owned land before 1804—a minority of free people of color and free blacks—and those to whom it was distributed. The public administration managed the meeting between these few landowners, both old and new, with the immense majority that found themselves thrown into a conquered territory without any means of legally accessing property. Given their total dispossession, the latter were supposed to submit to the landowners to survive. The public administration was not the expression of the will of the citizens or the guarantor of their patrimony. On the contrary, the citizens were the expression of the will of the public administration, and the small fraction of the domain that they were willing to get rid of was the foundation for their property: the active among the citizens had as their only patrimony that which the all-powerful executive was willing to approve through the intervention of its spokesmen.

The public administration therefore instituted citizens and defined them as it wished. It decided who could have control over their bodies and who could not—that is, who was an active and a passive citizen. They did so without authorization, and as they wished. The law that governed access to property was elaborated by the very property owners who were created or validated by the state administration. The colonial order was the inspiration for the executive and the property owners. They did not act according to the values and norms that would have allowed them to implant the law within rights. They could not act on the basis of a collective of principles accepted by all. The taking of the territory of Ayiti, and then Saint-Domingue, were two acts of piracy carried out by the Spanish and later the French. The distribution of the land in the conquered territory by the Haitian army was nothing more than the distribution of pirate's booty.

Those who were dispossessed before 1804 submitted to these dictates because they faced violence. From the point of view of the cultivators, the Indigenous Army had defeated a group of criminals, but then it installed itself in their place and acted in the same way. It adopted the procedures of the enemy and, far from becoming the protector of the victims of slavery, instead operated in the same vein as a dispenser of the same war booty. Once Dessalines's intention to distribute the land, which was never realized, was set aside, the declaration of independence in 1804 did not change the nature of political power.

The problem is that after that date, this war booty no longer had the same use that it had conferred to the capitalist economy of the eighteenth century. The political situation of the nineteenth century is easier to understand if we come to understand the behavior of the masses as that of normal social forces focused on their own objectives and indifferent to the wriggling of a public administration incapable of modifying the path these forces had chosen in full sovereignty. The idea that the population was ignoring, apathetic, and uneducated, with no class consciousness, brings us back to the fable of the fox and the grapes.

The decisions taken by the public administration in 1804 replicated the despotism of the colonial authorities and could not be appealed: the law was nothing more than the expression of the will of the executive. Nevertheless, starting in 1804, the power of the command of the public administration could no longer isolate itself from its entourage. The victory of the Indigenous Army took shape in the context of policies opposed to the sentiments of the workforce, and these forces then installed themselves as the government and monopolized the administrative structures of the state. This army/government carried its contradictions within, and that led to the development of the rupture between the military oligarchs and the popular masses. The first were no longer equipped to durably influence the local forces, all the more because the international community turned its gaze from the Caribbean.

I schematically distinguished between two types of military oligarchy, both the prisoners of a despotic conception of the administrative power of the state. The result was an unstable equilibrium between political forces, one that was not arbitrated by any larger force. During the nineteenth century the government was formed on the basis of regional powers who stopped warring with one another only when one of them was in a position to negotiate or impose a cease-fire or armistice on the others. The centers of regional power negotiated among themselves on the basis of forces, generally armed, that the notables of the provinces could mobilize.

The administrations of Dessalines and Christophe were predisposed to adapt European traditions to the new situation. The few months Dessalines spent in power after the rupture of 1804 suggest that there was an interventionist conception of the executive at work, similar to that of the group that succeeded him in the North with Henry Christophe. Both administrations carried out structural changes in land tenure and the administration of domains. In Christophe's case, social stratification, education, plantation management, foreign trade, infrastructure for science, and artistic production were all part of a rearrangement meant to drastically modify the habits acquired during colonization.

Colonial France, in contrast, served as the model of governmental administration for Pétion's party when it came to power in the West and the South. It jealously preserved its despotic power even as it made people call it republican. Its innovations were the result of the impossibility of putting even its most basic commands into practice. The criticisms made by Schoelcher about the carelessness of Boyer's presidency only confirmed those made by Vastey. The republic in the South had no impact on the daily life of the popular masses: it led to the laissez-faire model of Boisrond-Canal. His government operated in isolation both from the international community and the popular classes.

Almost the entire population carried the memory of how the slave trade promoted by the state had produced their dispossession and made their poverty necessary by proclaiming the sacred character of property granted by its right of conquest. Logically enough, the population never formulated any demands addressed to the political authorities, who felt no responsibility toward the population and never asked them their opinion. The history of the public administration unfolded without a hitch on the basis of the southern vision of the republic (Moïse 2009, 83). The people were divided into active citizens (the landowners) and passive citizens—the potential cultivators who, in the wake of the insurrections of Goman and Acaau, nibbled away with impunity at the lands of the landowners and organized agricultural production as they wished.

The operators of executive power moved along with perfect impunity. Popular pressure could overthrow their authority but not force them to introduce reforms. Despotism reproduced itself with no difficulty, day after day, to a large extent because its laissez-faire policy was nothing but a response to the sovereign actions of the rural population. Observers took note of the sentiment of satisfaction and well-being inspired by life in the countryside, but social science was unable to produce a holistic explanation of the divergent orientations of public and private life (Audain, in Vincent [1904] 1939, 182).

The truth is that the intermediary classes governed by forfeit, and that their control of land was completely nominal. The impression that the Haitian state is a failed state comes from those who confuse the state with the public administration, following the model established by French colonial policy. This administration did not prioritize or fulfill—and never fulfilled—any function demanded by daily life, even that of the collective of active citizens in the colony or the independent country. The passive citizens, meanwhile, watched what they were doing without much interest.

Land Ownership and Citizenship

In its beginnings, the national population was about a quarter to a half million inhabitants. There was plenty of land. In fact, for twenty-five years the island was unified from sea to sea, under the control of the administration of Jean-Pierre Boyer. It is hard not to take note of the parsimony with which land was distributed to the cultivators despite the abundance of available acreage. The only explanation is the need to maintain an underprivileged mass among the population. This was indispensable for enabling one form or another of servitude in the context of a hypothetical relaunching of the plantation system. The legislators, starting with Toussaint in his Règlement de Culture (Agricultural regulations) of October 12, 1800, stuck with the colonial definition of the cultivator—that is, the former slave—and condemned this worker to a permanent precarity.

Blancpain draws on the critiques of General Bonnet, Pétion's former secretary of state. Bonnet, who oversaw questions of land and agriculture for the government, highlighted the relationship between the need to control the process of land acquisition and the neglect of the need for a cadastral survey or the organization of a system of mortgages that could guarantee the security of real estate transactions (Blancpain 2003, 135). Emphasizing the apparently anarchic distribution of the overabundant surface of land, Blancpain notes that "from 1804 to 1864, nothing was done by the administration to gain perfect knowledge of the goods that were part of the private domain of the state" (2003, 166). Near the end of the century, on October 11, 1880, a law on the creation of a central administration of state property clearly illustrated the uselessness of prior efforts, though it didn't produce any better results.

While governments essentially abandoned the management of land ownership, they worried a great deal about controlling the process of land acquisition. The correlation between the rank of certain privileged individuals and the size of the grants they received is striking. Before 1814, only members of the military were beneficiaries of land concessions (Blancpain 2003, 133). In that year, the government added civil functionaries, medical officers, and judges to the list of those who could receive them. There were 10,000 beneficiaries over a surface area of up to 170,000 hectares (Moral 1961, 135).

European thought has traditionally conceived of the Caribbean as Europe's property, created by its hands, and unable to separate from it. In his reflection on the West Indies, John Stuart Mill established that these territories were locations where England sought to carry out economic activities in its own interest. They cannot therefore be considered countries that imported or exported merchandise (1852, 243–244). In France, during the debates that led to the decree of April 4, 1791, that granted civil and political rights to the emancipated, the parliament presented the same idea: "A colony formed at our expense and by us was created only for our use; we wish to reserve all its fruits for us. . . . You will always be considered a colony, that is to say, as the renters from a corporation that sees itself as the true owner of your property" (*Débats*, 1795, 181).

In 1805, Lattre reiterated that the lands of Saint-Domingue belonged to the state (Lattre 1805, 182). This insertion, or perhaps more accurately, this absorption into the domains of the state was what defined the difference between the metropolitan government and that of the colonies. The former emanated from a state of law that was the result of an agreement between those who had access to land, including the king. In the colony, in contrast, property owners were created and had only the rights accorded to them. As a consequence, the power to command in the exploitation colony was not something delegated to those who submitted themselves to the authority of the king. Its origin was outside these subjects or citizens: it was born in the metropole and in its appropriation of the resources necessary for survival. The state power monopolized all means of subsistence.

The state owned all land, whether through the intervention of the Company of the Indies or the intermediary of the colonial administration. By distributing portions of land, this authority guaranteed the personal dependence and subordination of the individuals who received the grants. The differentiated access to land defined the degree and form of allegiance demanded by power. Any social mechanism capable of limiting governmental despotism inevitably attacked this primary relationship between citizen and government, and therefore put into question the monopoly of the latter over private property. There were different forms of defiance to the appropriation of the territory, depending on the paths and means available to the protesting group. I have showed that the free people of color and Julien Raimond followed a different path from that of the working population. But in both cases, the parties positioned themselves, in their own way, against the goals of the despotic, imperial state.

The granting and taking back of large properties by successive administrations started with the concessions made by Louis XIV to the nobles and wealthy bourgeois of his regime. Later, the French Revolution didn't hesitate to sequester these properties because of the political choices made by those who had received them. That tradition has been repeated throughout Haitian history. Toussaint treated the property of Rigaud and his supporters with great casualness, Pétion's republic disposed of Dessalines's property, Boyer made himself the inheritor of all of Christophe's property, as well as that of his family and partisans, and so on, until the twenty-first century. Alain Turnier describes this constant in stupefying detail in his essential study *Quand la nation demades des contes* (When the nation demands answers, 1989). It follows that the uncontested power that the state administration enjoyed created insecurity around private property. But we have to admit there was a certain logic to this. In a regime where law derived not from rights but from the power of the colonial empire, the executive power remained the only entity that could give official sanction to the right to property. Governments, therefore, could use property at their discretion to reward their partisans and punish their opponents.

Above all, the recurrent granting and taking back of property was a normal mechanism for the management of political power. The apparent negligence surrounding the overseeing of state property, rather than being a sign of disorder or incompetence, indicates the existence of a market for favors negotiated among those who held power in the land regime. This was characteristic of the despotic states of both Saint-Domingue and Haiti. Land grants were one of the levers of accession to power and its preservation, whose particular use varied according to the context.

The French citizen who invested in Saint-Domingue was strongly sanctioned by the market if he abandoned his business or went bankrupt. The colonial entrepreneur acted within a right defined by the law, despite the obstacles that the colonists of color complained about. In 1807, after independence, in Law No. 106, Law Ordering the Payment of the Price of Rents Owed to the State, Article 9 stipulated that a renter of a sugar plantation could terminate his lease and that the president of Haiti could order the abandonment of a plantation and the transport of its cultivators to another plantation that was in a position to produce revenue (Linstant 1851, 1:286). From the beginning, the (recognized) fathers of the nation eliminated the market from the play of social relations they envisioned in their project for the country.

The management of the property of the great beneficiaries of the nineteenth century therefore depended on the good luck of those who were favorites of the regimes in place.[2] As a result, they couldn't negotiate over their loyalty without suffering major sanctions. The absence of security around real estate transactions guaranteed their loyalty and kept them safe from the market forces of a liberal economy. From the perspective of the Haitian population, land was not yet emancipated from its attachment to the primitive accumulation of capital. It remained a form of war loot.

The difficulties for the large landowners were not limited to their relationship to their benefactors. To understand how delicate the situation was, it is useful to remember that the citizen property owner was not exactly dealing with the state. Their behavior was not guided by a framing law through which the community as a whole fixed the prerogatives of the property owner. The agreement that created the state of law, which allowed Europeans at one point to cry, "The King is dead, long live the King," never emigrated to the colonies. Only its administrators undertook the journey.

The great beneficiary, then, was dealing with a government or public administration that constructed itself as a state after a victory over the French colonial empire. He had access to land (or the means of subsistence) because he benefited from the favors of a public administration that had usurped and appropriated the prerogatives of the state, while boasting of the fact that it was ignoring the mass of the dispossessed. The large property owner's interest and obligation was to maintain his links with political authority. This relationship to the state became more important than the outcome of his exploitation of the land, since he could lose the property at the slightest indiscretion.

But it was also necessary for this landowner to get along with a labor force that had just demonstrated its power to Leclerc's expeditionary army. The great beneficiary of the beginning of the nineteenth century had experienced the popular participation in the War of Independence. The fears expressed by Madiou and Ardouin, which I have already mentioned, testify to this. When the imperial state activated the political power of the captives by making them French citizens, and in so doing saved its external sovereignty over the colony, it destroyed the plantation system. This mode of production could be rebuilt only by making sure there was labor available on the market, which required taking the measures necessary for the nullification of internal sovereignty.

But even before the victory over the French was consummated, the Haitian oligarchs had arranged things so that the insurgent captives could not carry the country in the direction of *Guinean* habits and traditions. In the previous chapter, I showed how the two branches of the oligarchy agreed on this point. But unfortunately—from their perspective—decapitating the general insurrection and assassinating its leaders didn't destroy the strike force of those whom they, like the colonial empire before them, wanted to transform into cultivators. To wish, as Boyer did, to "convert them into citizens attached to the land" was nothing more than a pious hope, for the intentions of the executive power conflicted with daily reality.

Madiou recognized (1847, 6:455) that Africans had played a primordial role in the defeat of the French. This meant they remained a serious threat to the survival of the oligarchs who sought to replicate the model of an export-oriented plantation system. And despite the grandiose pronouncements in the Rural Codes of Boyer and Geffrard, it was the tenant-farmer model inaugurated by Pétion that ultimate took root, destroying the managerial unity of the colonial plantation. Agro-industry was fragmented into a multitude of small, autonomous enterprises, some agricultural, others limiting themselves to low-level artisanal transformations.

As a result, the executive power in 1804 imposed itself as a very particular kind of landowner, one very different from the large commercial companies of the seventeenth century or the colonial administration of the eighteenth. In the metropole, the rules that constrained landowners also constrained the king. The public administration of the colony, in contrast, operated as a kind of guardian of privileges, which it distributed following the rules established from the time of the famous discovery of the Americas. That was not the case in independent Haiti, where the list of established duties for the landowners as a whole did not constrain the state/government. It had no obligation to cultivate its own lands, to mark their boundaries, to enclose them and exploit them, or to guarantee that someone cultivated them, fenced them off, made them worth something, or even knew exactly how far they stretched. All these tasks were assigned to those who received concessions and especially to large landowners and those they hired to oversee their lands.

Access to land determined the degree of loyalty and allegiance expected from the beneficiary. Those who received land owned their loyalty to the government in power at the time, the head of the system. The state was not the product of links between warlords who gained access to land and who arbitrated conflicts, as was the case in the classic processes of the development of the nation-state in the West. The opposite took place in Haiti: the lords had access to the lands because they owed the executive a favor. They were vassals (Lattre 1805) obliged to maintain this link. They had to help ensure the survival of the executive that took itself for a state if they wanted to enjoy the essential component of the life of the citizen that was land ownership.

In distributing properties to their favorites, the public administration divided the national population into active and passive citizens. But the first were its servants and not its constituents. The latter, meanwhile, were strong and well organized enough outside the control of the state administrative that they could easily and autonomously pursue their path toward the establishment of the counter-plantation, their specific type of peasantry. Protected from the influence of the public administration, their sovereign behavior altered the political reality that the administration wished to implant. Contrary to the definitions offered by the constituted authorities, these citizens were far from passive. The majority of the national population was in a position to realize their life projects outside the spheres controlled by the executive. They imposed a bicephalous structure on the state, one that only the blindness of the state could deny.

Color Prejudice

The examples of the policies pursued by Toussaint and Christophe make clear that the reconstruction of the plantation economy could have been achieved only through militarized agricultural labor. But the practical context of politics in the nineteenth century made this impossible. The fact that there was a considerably reduced demand on the international market for the traditional tropical commodities produced in the Caribbean region helped the counter-plantation peasantry keep plantation projects in check. The gradual universalizing of peasant ways of life seems to have provoked a need among those in power to clarify for themselves how they conceived of the agricultural worker. This was all the more pressing because they were failing to achieve the intended results of their social project.

The monopolization of land was essentially limited to the levying of increasingly mediocre land rents, especially given the limited quantity of currency in circulation. Since the funding for the administrative machinery and services came from levies on peasant production, it is hard to imagine there could have been any kind of spectacular and cumulative enrichment in the broader area of services to the population. Several observers took note of the acute precarity of the Haitian oligarchs. So, if I limit my analysis to economic activities and their profitability, it is difficult to explain the preeminence the Haitian oligarchs enjoyed as the nineteenth century went on. In fact, if the relationship between the supposed landowners and the laboring masses had been untenable, the latter would have emigrated to the Spanish side (the eastern side of the island) or revolted. Taking stock of the relations of production does not allow us to determine the basis for the ladder of social stratification or to explain how the power of absentee landowners was perpetuated.

With each day, the counter-plantation rooted itself more deeply in the Haitian landscape. A malaise set in among the urban sectors, one that the commonly accepted vocabulary describes as *color prejudice*—a tendency to reinforce the significance of shades of skin in determining interpersonal relations. The urban sectors felt hounded and threatened by the increasing presence—real or perceived—of the provincial elites in the highest levels of the administration and civil services. This presence signaled a modification of the hierarchies of prestige inherited from the colony. The so-called descendants of the eighteenth-century people of color—the famous mulattoes of Haitian history—consoled themselves by inventing what they called the *politics of doubling*—that is, a supposed manipulation, from the wings, of leaders of rural background. Within this process of revalorizing the colonial indicators of social stratification, the ability to use the dominant language became one of the lines of demarcation between the urban and the rural, and especially between the civilized and the backward.

The supposed influence exercised through the politics of doubling is difficult to confirm. It did not depend on any kind of cultural superiority that the elites of the urban areas imposed on the rest of the population. It was reproduced, instead, essentially within social relations on a material basis. With the proclamation of independence, popular forces accelerated the erosion of interethnic boundaries and, at first glance, seemed to fragment them. The poor whites and the *métis* of the provinces fused into reds, the African disappeared from the local stage, and there was no more talk of the animosity between the Creoles and the *bossales*.[3] The oligarchs harvested the racialization of human relations for their official, urban language and subtly installed it within the management of society by maintaining a bureaucracy that served only the public functionaries. Their power was founded exclusively on the maintenance of relations of subordination to the international community—that is, to the coloniality of power. It didn't penetrate into the local structures that organized the exchanges of almost the entire population.

The slippage of the term *slave* into *cultivator*, which I analyzed in chapter 3, enabled the urban world to maintain the racialization of social relations that had defined the colony. At the end of the wars of independence, this was accompanied by a perversion of the meanings of indigenous vocabulary. A short footnote in Madiou reveals the word games that the oligarchs and urban intermediaries used to maintain the racialization of human relations and superimpose it onto a social hierarchy built around the new distribution of roles and functions. There was no direct referencing of the fissure between diametrically opposed ways of conceiving of life and social relations that separated the groups in the country. Writing of the events of 1802, Madiou noted: "Until now, we used the term *indigenous* to describe not just the blacks and men of color born in Saint-Domingue, but also the transplanted Africans" (Madiou 1847, 2:162).

Racial discrimination continued to subtend the fractures between public administrators at the higher levels, on the one hand, and both the lower levels of the administration and the collective of the governed on the other. Discrimination according to color defined the parameters for negotiation between the privileged and the disenfranchised, which was summed up in the entirely urban motto "Unity makes strength." The creation of all kinds of hierarchies of virtual skin shades made it possible to avoid confronting the true impasses and dichotomies of the society. The inaccurate use of the term *indigenous* shuffled the deck of social interaction, and obscured the prerogatives the powerful granted to themselves as a continuation of the colonial right of conquest. The governing classes justified their control over capital and labor by eliding the actual rupture between the colonizers and the colonized, between oligarchs and cultivators, between metropolitans and the national population. *Indigenous* was no longer a synonym for *native*. It denoted the perfectly colonized person, undifferentiated, without history, memory, or any particular civilization—as naked as a hand, to use the expression used by Toussaint Louverture as he described his situation at the Fort de Joux. It identified the starting point of a journey toward a civilization that was to be achieved by trading in the sword of the conquistador for the cross the missionary had touched to the shoulders of the conquered captives before they were put on the road to Calvary.

Obviously, and with good reason, the concept of the *indigenous* has no corollary in local vernacular. This was, after all, a language that the oppressed and particularly the cultivators appropriated to communicate among themselves, to express who they were, what they were, and what they did. The Kreyòl language didn't express what they were not, because it didn't grant any permanence to the conquest. The oligarchic lens used by Francophones on both sides of the Atlantic was limited to urban society. It rendered invisible, or else disdained, everything that was characteristic of and specific to the new society under construction. It sought to be a gloss for *conquest*. The indigenous were no longer born from their memory, from their experiences and the knowledge that accompanied it. They were created by Europeans, by the outside world, by colonial empire. The *indigenous* became what was not *white*, a beings denuded of their own existence, vanquished by the conquistador.

Visible social life—or at least that which people could or wanted to show—was inscribed within the legality and legitimacy of conquest and the enslavement of all that was not European. The whites and their knowledge were promoted to the role of fulfilling the ideal of humanity. They were what should be reproduced. The aboriginal people who had lived on the island for more than five thousand years before the arrival of Columbus were confused with the Africans brought there by the slave trade just a few years before independence. This mosaic of the oppressed was transfigured into a lot of identical individuals, defined by their lack of Europeanness. This enabled race to continue to serve surreptitiously as the axis of social organization. The quest for a more visible whiteness, free from all history before the discovery and the conquest, was transformed into an encounter—depicted as peaceful and harmonious—between civilizations.

The transformation of the colonized into the indigenous was not anodyne. Nor was the name chosen by the (recognized) heroes of independence to designate their most indispensable institution: the Indigenous Army. Among these newly minted natives, the black was recognized as the manual laborer, the oppressed person par excellence. The furthest from the European and the white, especially if he was a *bossale*, the black was essentially or naturally a cultivator.

There is an abundance of texts that deliberately used racial discrimination and recuperated it for the construction of national citizenship. Madiou reported that "three black men, cultivators and former soldiers, Acaau, Dugué Zamor, and Jean-Claude, had planned to meet at the Camp-Perrin and had declared a revolution against Rivière-Hérard, by starting an uprising in the plain and a part of the hills of the arrondissement of Les Cayes. . . . Acaau was a former police lieutenant, who knew how to read and write; Dugué Zamor, a former drum major from the 43rd regiment; and Jean Claude, a former sergeant major of the National Guard at Camp-Perrin" (Madiou 1847, 8:147).

Note that the historian could have described General Pétion, who was neither black nor a cultivator, in the same terms. Madiou was the former private secretary of Pétion's minister, Balthazar Inginac, as well as a former secretary of the republic under Boyer. But in this passage he categorized literate, urban soldiers as *cultivators*. From the time of general emancipation and in all the rural police codes, the cultivators had a very specific status that included assignment to a particular domicile. Acaau and his companions were not actually cultivators. They were, simply, blacks. Ardouin, whose writings about the events of 1800 I cited in the previous chapter, admitted that every time a law or code mentioned *cultivators*, it was understood that they were talking about blacks (Ardouin 1853, 4:360).

We know that Boyer's Rural Code, like that of Geffrard, was not put into practice. But in my reflections here I want to dwell on the vocabulary used by these thinkers and the leaders at the highest levels of the republic. Why were urban soldiers called *cultivators*? Further corroboration for the use of this key word in the context of racial stratification comes from the work of Claude Moïse, who in his *Constitutions et luttes de pouvoir en Haïti* (Constitutions and power struggles in Haiti) describes the period during which the authors I have mentioned were writing: "In January 1843, during the first moments of the insurrection, the leader in charge, Riviére-Hérard, recommended in a letter written to Honoré Féry, the president of the center of Jérémie, and the lieutenant Larocque, to make sure above all that no cultivator entered the ranks of the National Guard, which should be composed exclusively of property owners, sons of property owners and renters, subrenters, etc." (Moïse 2009, 124).

What is going on with these cultivators who under Toussaint didn't cultivate the land? Who were Madiou's urban, military, literate, functionary cultivators, the adversaries of the property owners? Why did Rivière-Hérard think cultivators weren't worthy of being part of the National Guard? In 1843, the year when Rivière-Hérard made the remark mentioned by Claude Moïse, Victor Schoelcher identified an irrepressible evil: "People of color, good and sincere, have sworn to us that they consciously consider themselves fundamentally and organically superior to blacks, though through an inconsistency that pride explains perfectly, they don't consider yourselves inferior to whites" (Schoelcher [1843a] 1973, 235–236).

The examples I have cited refer primarily to the first part of the nineteenth century. But as the century progressed, the officials and privileged members of the urban sector confronted a more and more irrepressible response on the part of the rural workers. This forced them to update their ideal, but inoperative, model. The external characteristics they considered to define the cultivator—the color of his skin—had the advantage of targeting what was superficial about him while avoiding an engagement with his way of life and thinking, which defied the image the oligarchs wished to project of the country. This obfuscation, and mutilation, of the true characteristics of the majority of the population made it possible to maintain and manage the role it was given within the dominant society. That was especially the case when individuals from that population were called on to occupy certain higher-level positions through the "politics of doubling," though it too lost its luster in the wake of the administration of the emperor Soulouque, which didn't work out the way that the oligarchs had hoped.

The colonial racial hierarchy was transposed to postindependence Haitian society, where it tended to maintain the plantation society at the level of form without creating conflicts with the real movement of ideas and goods in daily life. Subtly, the color hierarchy was replaced by a differentiated mastery of French culture and more particularly by virtuosity in speaking the language of the Île-de-France. This was similar to a phenomenon observed by Fanon in the French Antilles (1952). National urban society covered itself with a varnish meant for the consumption of the outside imperial community, without disturbing the normal course of things in the country. There were social roles visible to foreigners that it was best not to confide to cultivators and their descendants. This was necessary in order to protect the ceremonial social order that could satisfy the ideologies that dominated on the international level. Under this cover, it was impossible to know whether, in their intimate lives, a person behaved as indigenous or as European! The main thing was to keep up appearances, not necessarily as an expression of true bovarism, but maybe only because the (imperialist) fashion of the period demanded it!

Conclusion: Ill-Gotten Property Rights

Trapped in the world built by the Christian West during the nineteenth century, Haiti organized itself as a modern state, for better or worse. In principle, it was sovereign. The character of this sovereignty, and the way it was exercised, had been determined by the large-scale popular mobilization that had followed general emancipation and then independence. The political power that the workers accumulated during the unfolding of these foundational events enabled them to set and accomplish their own objectives. The fact that the army had obtained independence was a double-edged sword. Once the crucial independence was won, the army put itself in charge of the powers of the state. From then on, it worked to satisfy its own needs without answering to anyone, and certainly not to the people. Its will, however, had no significant effect on the structuring and formalizing of popular political objectives either before or after 1804, because the population was split into two structurally distinct formations.

The Haitian state was the daughter of modernity, but it organized itself in its own way. It followed a course very different than that of those metropolitan, modern, capitalist, racist states served by a centralized public administration capable of carrying out projects developed through consensus. The administration that sought to govern Haitian society was inherited from French colonialism. For a century, it was held in check by the sovereign people and their communal organization. It was just as modern, capitalist, and racist as the rest. But that government was distinct from the state it actually served, and which imposed the rules of the political game based on an opposing orientation.

To understand this duality, it is important to return to classic texts and observe the evolution of the political structures of nineteenth-century Haiti. For the country cannot say, "In the beginning was the state of law!" (Lagarde, in Kriegel 1998, 130).

> "What is a state?" There is a troubling fact: the statutes through which the juridical condition of a collectivity, an association, and generally a town are defined go against the old contracts of the fiefdom. The latter was founded on the situation of the land, which put requirements on individuals, linked the living together, and stipulated a personal and transitory dependency. The former was established based on the condition of people, and it organized a collectivity, enlisted multiple generations, and organized the functioning of an institution within the constraints of durable knots. The coercive rules "fixed the whole of the juridical status of a community." This status defined the state of a group, the totality of its rights, which were primitive franchises and privileges in the medieval sense, but also communal rules and collective principles in the modern sense. The state is a state of collective and juridical rights. (Kriegel 1998, 131)

The circumstances that led to the creation of the public authorities that were taken over by the Indigenous Army defined the juridical status of the nation that was being born, but it did so within an international community comprised of colonial empires. As a distinct and active collectivity—as a people—Haitians existed thanks to the significant presence of the military. Their decisive defeat of the French enabled Haiti to construct an internal coherence beyond the interethnic fragmentation of the eighteenth century.

These positive consequences were not linked to the intentions of the generals who led the army. And they didn't change the fact that the public authorities in question founded their administrative governance on brute force and not on the right of the national population to live freely and according to their own will. The rights of the national collectivity had no existence in the face of the prerogatives of the army. Following the example of the international community, the administrative authorities didn't recognize that this collectivity had a distinct and distinctive political will. The public authorities they exercised claimed to be a substitute for the state (Boyer's Proclamation No. 1440 1838, 381). The nation, on the other hand, became embodied as a political actor endowed with a sovereignty that forced the leaders to put their antinational projects in the archives, even as they lamented the powerlessness (disguised as incompetence) of their own bureaucracy. The specificity of the process of national construction came from the fact that it was accompanied by the structuring of two dissimilar civil societies, each endowed with their own culture and institutional organization. I will expand on this aspect of the question in the three final chapters.

The national community that was structuring itself existed in a parallel dimension to that of the public authorities, protected from its harmful effects. For the leaders of the victorious army, these soldiers in rags and their communities remained the same savages that they had been forced to try and civilize and discipline in colonial times. They treated them with the same rigor, the same casualness, and the same lack of respect as the French authorities: the terror inspired by their swords stood in as the source of public order. But while a unified colonial army had faced a multiplicity of ethnic groups who were in the midst of evaluating their new situation, the Haitian generals commanded a fragmented army that was demobilizing itself. The rank-and-file soldiers joined in the process that was reshaping the culture, as the subordinated groups merged into a unified ethnicity. That new ethnicity consolidated itself with the passage of time and the natural reproduction of successive generations.

For the administrative authorities of the nineteenth century, internal politics—what Louis XIV called his solicitude for his subjects in the Code Noir—was limited to assuring that property-owning citizens had access to the services of laborers. The external sovereignty that justified, supported, and sustained the governmental bureaucracy operated beyond the daily experience of the sovereign people and its field of vision. The political nation could not germinate and bloom, because the civil dimension of the public authorities—a relationship based on rights—never overtook the military dimension. The reason of state always took precedence, and however justified it might have been, it always remained arbitrary. There was no logic shared by the national collective that could support it. The transformation from Saint-Domingue into Haiti resulted in the installation of an executive power that was despotic by nature. It was a power that was reasonable, but could not transform itself into a state of law.

In its constitutional affirmation that bracketed its own prehistory, the nation uses its presentation of the demand for the rights of people to present itself as a reaction and corrective to the classic formulations of the doctrine of state. This was a democratic reaction to the right of the state, initially defined in the context of monarchical republics. It declared that sovereignty was henceforth national, in other words, that the origin of sovereignty necessarily could be found only within the people. It was clearly enunciated in Article 3 of the Declaration of 1789: "The principle of all sovereignty essentially resides within the nation, and no body or individual can exercise any authority that does not expressly emanated from it." But the Declaration of 1793 went even further.

It transferred all the attributes of sovereign power to the people. It tipped the entire principle of the right of the state toward the nation. It even abolished the right of the state to the profit of the right of peoples. The people were the sovereign, but were only the sovereign. (Kriegel 2002, 169)

The reigning oligarchies sought out international support, particularly in France. The idea that the cultivators might gain access to a level of social participation of the kind suggested by Polvérel seemed totally aberrant and ludicrous to them. They were happy to mime metropolitan ways of life and accept the imperial language, the Christian religion, ethnocide, the organization of executive, legislative, and judicial power—in short, a framework that didn't fit with the nation that was coming into being and was appropriate to the interests of only 5 to 10 percent of the urban dwellers, a minority of the total population. The national identity envisaged by the oligarchs excluded cultural production inspired by local experience and, at the same time, never considered anything that might aim at a viable integration of these experiences into the vision of the world of the governing classes. The bit of French culture over which the traditional oligarchs preserved a monopoly had to reproduce itself through spontaneous generation among the tiny minority that tried to pass itself off as an elite.

Normally, the public authorities of a national state tend toward cultural homogenization by trying to harmonize the social practices within its borders. In Haiti, because of a lack of control over material production, from 1806 on they instead sought to maintain the differentiation between composite parts, and to vivify the disjunction between them in order to assure the subalternity of the majority inferior classes they considered backward. As long as the primary wealth in the country was limited to land, its hoarding could be justified only by the inferiority of the population and the civilizing mission the oligarchs took on for themselves. The public authorities in Haiti were incapable of promoting a reintroduction of capitalism into the country and supporting the development of a local bourgeoisie that was capable of serving as its communication channel for its relations with the international community.

For its part, the sovereign people could not create a functional space for themselves within the government system as long as the right of conquest, the right to appropriate the property of another with impunity, remained the sacrosanct basis for private property. By seizing the lands of the country, both colonial France and the Indigenous Army installed their deep profession of faith in racism—attenuated, by political necessity, through the language of color prejudice—as the backdrop for their concept of public power.

Blancpain's analyses (2003, 28) document the installation of a republic of large-scale planters to whom the government leased land. But starting in 1806, these planters disappeared and those who leased the properties tended not to pay their rent. In 1807, Law No. 106 showed that the executive power was incapable of forcing them to pay or to cultivate their domains according to the terms of their contracts. They were incapable of staying dressed up as planters or producers, and had to content themselves with wearing the clothes of property owners who leased out their land.

The labor force saved the oligarchs threatened with extermination by the enemies of republican France. This increased their political power to the point that the public administration could not impose the role of indentured laborers on them any longer. The regulations prescribed by the agricultural regulations and rural police codes were impossible to enforce. From the first days of its establishment, the republican administration was reduced to playing the role of managing the disjuncture between the property owners and the dispossessed who occupied the territory. For better or worse, the two groups had to live together.

Gérard Barthélémy argues that capitalism was *almost* defeated by the 1804 revolution (1989,19). If we accept that conclusion, it becomes clear that the formula of the modern Western state wasn't appropriate for the Haitian nation. The oligarchs who governed it during the nineteenth century didn't have the political, economic, or ideological resources necessary to satisfy the sovereign people's most basic needs. Their social and economic projects were never achieved. They survived by gathering together various mechanisms to preserve their distance from the popular sovereign masses and avoid being absorbed by them.

But, starting during the 1790s, there was also interpenetration between the two civil societies. This accelerated on both sides of the class divide during the first half of the next century. There was an increasing homogenization of practices in the private lives of all social groups, either because of the indifference of the colonial and postcolonial authorities or through the deliberate efforts of those involved. Throughout the entire nineteenth century, property owners and the dispossessed moved closer to one another, and by the end of that period the socioeconomic landscape offered a standard of living that was superior to that of the rest of the Caribbean region. The country entered the twentieth century experimenting with forms of equilibrium that were abruptly interrupted by the foreign intervention of 1915.

The independence that followed the defeat of the French expeditionary army cut the economic and social system in two. The relationship between the two sides was limited to forms of negotiation that the state administration and Eurocentric intellectuals were unable to formalize, because they were completely new. In the nineteenth-century laws of the country, the Haitian countryside was defined the same way it had been during the colonial period. It was made up of a collection of plantations populated by cultivators. The public administration never called them peasants, just as they had refused to do during the colonial period. They didn't imagine them as autonomous individuals who were responsible for themselves and their families. For the oligarchs, there could be no rural life that was independent from that of the plantations. The status of a sharecropper, or a *de-moitié* (a tenant farmer who kept half of what they produced), seems to have been the highest level that the official geography could allow in the career of a cultivator. There was no possibility that they would ever have access to property that wasn't marginal.

For the public authorities, the countryside wasn't a place where the population was born and lived and might need social services. The landscape as they saw it was one where the cultivators worked on other people's lands, or lands where others took charge of them. They had no existence of their own. This official rhetoric excluded them from state sovereignty. But it clashed with people's everyday life, where land ownership was defined in a very different way. The population itself created and lived within a form of sovereign power that was civil in nature, based on customary law and communal institutions. Order and public well-being flourished without the support or participation of the public authorities.

The stable disjuncture between the governments and rural communities constituted the state in Haiti during the period under study. Blandine Kriegel concludes, "The state is a status of juridical and collective rights" (Kriegel 2003, 131). I paraphrase this by saying that the state in Haiti is a status of customary juridical and collective rights. Sovereign communities operated within this stable normative structure, indifferent to public authorities subordinated to the colonial empires.

Chapter 7

Public Order and Communal Order

Introduction: State, Administration, and Community

In his March 1, 1794, proclamation, Sonthonax affirmed that "property is the foundation for all societies; it is the representative sign of civil existence" (Ardouin 1853, 2:370). Life in such a society was structured in relation to the capacity to possess. The right to use and abuse of property was a straight-jacket forced onto those owned by the colonists. Within their prison, they were given permission to tailor a space to live in as long as it respected the public order that flowed from this enunciated principle. The Haitian constitutions that followed later similarly endorsed the connection between rights and property as an axiom. But in practice, the order guided by this principle had to accommodate the changes produced by the revolution that unfolded from 1791 to 1804, in particular the end of the open exercise of power by an external imperial force.

The few people who were not owned by the colonists of Saint-Domingue, a little more than 2.5 percent of the population, owed them a liberty conceded as a favor. Among them, about two hundred *gens de couleur* who had been born free and therefore never emancipated contested this pretension and defended their rights as Frenchmen. But the majority population appropriated by the colonists, those reduced into slavery, liberated themselves collectively in the wake of the upheavals that exploded during the last decade of the eighteenth century. In the wake of the general insurrection, the first group of emancipated (slaves) had to thwart the French plan to deport them or exterminate them along with their rebel servants. The two groups joined together and founded an independent nation. But it was the emancipated (slaves) who took control of its governance.

To study the history of Haiti on the basis of the premises and objectives of the colonial empire is to lock our analysis within the itinerary it laid out and allow ourselves to be governed by its concepts. This makes it easier to close our eyes to the fundamental illegitimacy of the property in captives and territory. As a result, the knowledge we gain becomes a corollary to the history of France and the very ideals that justified the creation of its colonial hell. Obviously, the people who were owned could not follow this path, and they necessarily transmitted their deep objections to the blatant injustices they had experienced to their descendants. The empire and its inheritors, therefore, invariably had to operate outside the application of rights, and could not achieve any kind of consensus.

When we follow colonial assumptions, we end up writing the history of Haiti as the sequel to that of Hispaniola, and then that of Saint-Domingue. We become simple witnesses to the successive spoliations of the island and its inhabitants. In fact, however, during the nineteenth century the supposed property owners failed to satisfy their material needs in the ways they wished. Instead, they were forced to rent out their properties and extract what they could from the independent village economies that, despite them, flourished without any major obstacles. In this chapter, I describe the articulation between the order created by the colony and then inherited by the oligarchs and the autonomous structures put into place by the laboring population.

In Article 6 of the 1807 Constitution, the authorities conflated the state and the government, or public administration. I return to this below. In this study, I use the term *state* to name the institutionalized complex of rules governing the political process in a particular national territory. What I call the *public administrative machinery*, or *government*, is the institution that seeks to orient the state to the benefit of the hegemonic classes. The latter institution is the articulation of all the social forces in the territory, and is characterized by the forms of negotiation over their interests. During the period under observation, these forces were made up fundamentally of two social classes in conflict: the oligarchs, accompanied by urban intermediaries, and the mass of rural laborers.

From the Treaty of Ryswick to Haitian independence, Saint-Domingue was organized by an imperial, despotic, secular, modern, and racist state. From 1804 to 1915, the public administration in Haiti inherited all these traits, though they deployed them in new ways. It governed the two groups I have already described: the oligarchs, who won a Pyrrhic victory at the end of the wars of independence (Casimir 2009), and the mass of former captives. Those who controlled executive, legislative, and judicial power were chosen from among the large-scale property owners. They installed themselves at the head of the administrative machinery of the state and worked to orient the actions of the popular masses so that they would satisfy the needs of those in power. But, meanwhile, the social and economic process unfolding in the country went largely against the interests of the oligarchs. They responded during the nineteenth century by inventing a mythology meant to explain away their failures, one that was also put to good use by those in the international community with whom they collaborated.

The actual order of the state in Haiti wasn't the visible order that the public functionaries presented as their project. In this chapter, I show how the arrangement they sought to impose actually had no impact on the unfolding and rhythm of daily life in the country, which flowed on freely during this period. What is urgent for us today, however, is to describe and understand the content of this daily life in nineteenth century Haiti. Though I don't have the space to go as deeply into the details of the internal structure of the communal order as I might wish, I aim at least to establish clearly how it triumphed over the public order.

The French Language, Vehicle of Local Despotism

From the moment of their insertion into the plantation society, the oppressed groups who made up the majority of the population created their own communities. These flourished and grew thanks to the general insurrection of 1791, the first major breach in the system of oppression. Soon after the declaration of independence, these groups rapidly focused on consolidating the communal collectives that protected them. Their primary goal was to ensure the survival and reproduction of the population and consequently to counteract the noxious effects of the slave trade and the personal dependency it had instituted.

The high-level officers of the Indigenous Army—with the exception of the close advisors of Dessalines and Christophe, who deserve a more nuanced judgment—seized the reins of local government and the public administration with the avowed goal of reproducing the structure of the colonial administration without too many modifications. They claimed to be copying the model of the French republican state. But they didn't make an interpretive distinction between the organization of the French metropolitan territory and that of the colonial empire. This allowed them to avoid confronting the fact that the imperial government had always used the local public administration as its primary tool for its colonial project. The state created in 1804 inherited the machinery of colonial governance and absorbed the principal tools of oppression used against the majority population of agricultural laborers. But its leaders elided this fact.

This erasure allowed the very people who had helped enforce the public colonial order to transform themselves into the heroes of independence, and to re-enforce their pre-existing social role. They turned adherence to colonial principles into a civilizational project that served to legitimize their authoritarian control of daily life. In the nineteenth century, however, the only way to preserve a modicum of peace was to accept a different kind of conviviality, based on the consenting participation of the laboring population in the construction of the society's future. The former members of the colonial police forces were unable to really comprehend the new order being created by the population. But their blindness to it did not affect this new order at all.

I am struck by the level of detail and the minutiae contained in the nineteenth-century rural codes and laws relating to agricultural production. The first instructions administering the rural order just after the general insurrection and emancipation were made up of just a few dozen articles. Over time, their successive formulations became more and more explicit and detailed. Eventually, the Haitian administrations produced a river of regulations of a kind that the planters of the slave colony would have considered totally superfluous. Boyer's Rural Code, for instance, includes strikingly precocious efforts at central planning, which the oligarchy's thinkers themselves admitted had no significant impact on daily life. My goal here is to understand the economy of the agricultural regulations and rural police codes. The very fact that they had to be issued over and over again makes clear the extent to which agricultural labor had liberated itself from the vise in which private property had sought to imprison it. The fact that labor had the power to decide freely when and where to work, without going through a labor market, made capitalist development impossible.

After the general insurrection, no authority—with the exception of Polvérel—ever considered that the newly freed might have anything useful to say with regard to how their labor should be used. It is important to recall that two-thirds of the captives who set the wars of independence in motion were born in Africa. As some contemporary observers recognized, most of the population hadn't experienced four centuries of spoliation. They disembarked in Saint-Domingue and were introduced into slavery as adults. They had already been educated and culturally formed in their communities in Africa. Any reflection on the plantation economy of the nineteenth century has to begin from an understanding that the cultivators would never have bowed to plantation discipline of their own accord, after a relatively short period spent in chains.

The Haitian republican system was inspired by that of France. So there is no reason to expect that within a short time the administrative authorities would have allowed the newly freed to escape the misery into which they had been deliberately buried *by* France. They did not really consider offering them a political role as powerful as that seized by the sovereign people in the metropole. At times, they pretended to do so, but the population was perfectly aware that this was a form of imposture and deception. It would have made no sense at all to place one's hope for the future in the hands of the public administration, awaiting its benevolence.

When we look at things from the perspective of the agricultural workers, we end up with a more nuanced set of observations about the privileged strata of the population who had just gained hegemony. The planters among the oligarchy, of whatever color, didn't really survive the loss of Saint-Domingue. Those people of color and formerly freed individuals who didn't leave the country during the crisis shared some characteristics with the more experienced planter capitalists, but not the most important one: they were not capitalists, and had almost no knowledge and ability when it came to managing agricultural enterprises. Those who rushed to take over lands left vacant by the departure of the planters were the veterans of the police forces and the members of the tiny tertiary sector (Moïse 2009).

In the nineteenth century, the agro-industrial complex fell into a flagrant anemia. Given the complexity of the production in a plantation system and its unavoidable external costs, there really was no way that the traditional oligarchy could have successfully managed the economic model that it claimed it was adopting. And they very likely understood they were committing themselves to an impasse. That said, the oligarchy that emerged after the general insurrection—whose core group brought together former slave drivers and the agricultural inspectors of Toussaint's regime—had acquired a modicum of experience in the management of plantations. Christophe's regime was able to profit from that experience, and it breathed life back into large-scale agriculture, which had been in decline for almost two decades. But aside from the leaders of this period, I find it hard to imagine precisely who, outside a few bureaucrats, ever imagined that they could actually rebuild plantation agriculture, and how they could have done so given the resources at their disposal.

My goal is to understand the perspective of the social actors excluded from participation by both the colonial administration and the oligarchs who replaced them. They were largely uncompromising. There was a moment in the process of their enslavement when they must have realized that, without any justification, they were being turned into private property, owned by another person. This must have been so disconcerting that it created a panic on the edge of madness. Whatever these unfortunates might have thought about private property in the abstract, the fact of one's own self—of one's being, defined by free will—being converted into a possessed object must have symbolized the ultimate annihilation. It was a state to be avoided at all costs. As they creolized themselves, however, the so-called *bossales* also had to learn how to survive in the new reality. This required understanding that the self-proclaimed masters considered any resistance to the idea of private property an unacceptable breach of conduct.

After emancipation, there was no way that the formerly enslaved were going to express any propensity for reintegrating themselves into the plantation economy. Reconstructing an agrarian policy based on export commodities would have required the creation of a differentiated social class, and therefore the successful repression and indoctrination of the labor force. This would have required the application of an ideological tool—the racialization of human relations—and the budgetary means to satisfy the material needs of the repressive force needed to control the labor force. The reigning oligarchs had at their disposal neither the immaterial nor material resources necessary to carry out this project, and they must have understood that.

The physical and spiritual subjection of the captives was conceived of, justified, and expressed in French. This language denied any past and any future they might imagine or create. But their lived experience as commodities who were considered merely tools of material production didn't modify their behavior as prisoners. The concepts and institutions that surrounded their labor and specified their tasks belonged to the French language. All the justifications for the existence of slaves and cultivators, and the limits placed on what they did or could do, were contained and transmitted in French. That language described as the dregs of humanity, deserving of total disdain, and even more repugnant if they contested the state to which they were condemned. The sociogenesis of the slave was invented and forged in French. None of those who spoke this language, in France, Saint-Domingue, or Haiti, could imagine that former slaves could construct a life worth living on their own, precisely because these people were former slaves.

In his study of the formation of the Kreyòl language, Lambert-Félix Prudent (1980, 24) notes that it was marginalized during the period when the French bureaucracy invested itself in the promotion of export agriculture. At the time, the wealthy planters adopted the prestigious dialect of the Crown and let the subordinated classes speak in the language of the provincial sailors. The influx of captives led to an appropriation of the nascent Creole by the sectors of agricultural laborers, who standardized the vernacular language, probably during the end of the eighteenth century. That gave birth to an insurmountable gap between the exploiters and the exploited. It is worth noting in passing that the rupture between the two linguistic groups happened at the same time as the establishment of the powerful police forces and militias.

Everything the Haitian population remembers of its past, everything it makes of its present, everything it believes it is and believes it might become on its own terms, is all expressed in its own language, Creole. It appropriates and reconstructs this language in service of its own needs. It elaborated its means of survival and ways of pursuing them in Creole, outside of French. To inscribe their goals in reality, the people used their own knowledge system, not that of the master. To dream and move forward, they built a field of ideas and thoughts that was not dependent in any way on the categories of the colonial language. Creole certainly borrowed some of its vocabulary from the latter, but the population redefined these words according to their own circumstances, in a discourse formulated and enriched through each new experience generated by changes in imperial policy. The oligarchs of the colonial system were kept at bay, so that they couldn't harm, dominate, or subjugate this divergent thinking, which hatched through the negation and surpassing of oppression.

In French, in the language of the masters and their interpreters, 95 percent of the population in Saint-Domingue existed as an empty collection of human beings. Sonthonax subsumed them into the term *the natural born of the country* (Ardouin 1853, 2:179; Madiou 1847, 2:162). As we saw in chapter 2, the intermediaries of the country preferred gathering them under the label of *natives*. In order to successfully exist as a distinct entity, the population expressed itself and contradicted dominant thought, overturning the process of their annihilation. Despite the fragmentation of the society of Saint-Domingue into a multitude of self-sufficient units of production (Anglade 1982), the emergence of the Kreyòl language demonstrates that at the end of the eighteenth century the mass of agricultural laborers was constructing itself as a collective, and inventing a proletarian nation to which they belonged.

This collective never spoke the imperial language. At first they used multiple languages, often within the same plantation, and in time developed their own language. Though there were clearly observable variations, it is clear there was increasing intercomprehension. We can assume that the language was definitively standardized after independence. The Haitian nation was born by changing the terms and vehicles for communication between social groups. Haitians became a people by collectively expressing their will to live by weaving together, in one connected process, a different social order, an impenetrable and impregnable citadel, the true citadel!

The metropole successfully organized the plantation economy to produce tropical commodities, considering laborers as merchandise reproduced on the market. The public administration executed its instructions and made sure the profits from these activities filled its coffers. An entire armature of philosophy, ideology, projects of social engineering, instructions, investments, and management all made Saint-Domingue the Pearl of the Antilles. The French state gave itself a goal, and it fulfilled it. It used its institutions to achieve a result that it made sure to record and boast about.

When France withdrew in 1804, it left behind an administrative carcass along with a set of norms, principles, and ideologies inherited by the Haitian public authorities. Despite the best intentions of the reigning oligarchies, the plantation—imperial France's marquee institution—followed it in its retreat.

Despite the patient and sophisticated reformulations attempted by the new administrators, the set of tools devoted to the installation and maintenance of this economy became obsolete. The French language transmitted these sterile, powerless principles and instructions. But the oligrachies faced a new reality. Economic productivity was nil. It would make sense to assume that the oligarchs would have understood this, and set aside this now completely unproductive system.

In 1804, the main potential allies of the military caste that seized power were the formerly freed of the towns. In the old colonial regime, they had operated the repressive machine. They did so thanks to the decisive support of metropolitan norms and institutions. If we believe Madiou's observations regarding the predominance of *Guinean* traditions, it seems very unlikely that these allies mastered the imperial language. Starting in 1806 they became a class of owners, but they lacked a class of overseers with the material and spiritual resources needed to carry out the social repression necessary for the maintenance of the plantation economy.

Without the hegemony of the French language or another imperial language that could secure exchange on the international market, and without the support of a professional police force that could coerce laborers to succumb to the discipline required, the plantation system collapsed. The cultivation of commodities for export, supported by a philosophy that gave it a congruence and dynamism, was not managed—and could not be managed—in Kreyòl. The loss of control over the production of commodities for the external market by the carriers of the imperial language was accompanied by the decomposition of the modern colonial order. Their influence over the mechanisms that governed private life progressively vanished.

As they lost their mastery over the local economy, these carriers of the imperial language inscribed their monopoly over social prestige outside of the daily life of the majority, within the modern colonial sphere. These oligarchs kept control over the relationships with the great empires, waiting for the moment when they would have the capacity to reactivate their old prerogatives as intermediaries. In the interregnum, they ruled over those economic activities that fit with colonialism. It seems reasonable to conclude that very early during the nineteenth century, the development of the plantation system, while remaining the declared priority of the oligarchs, actually gave way to the project of preserving their social preeminence through means other than the pursuit of impossible material wealth. Their despotic administration functioned within what Michel Hector (2006, 7) calls an antislavery, anticolonial, antiracist, and antiplantation state. The local population, on the other hand, evolved within a decolonial matrix that empowered them to articulate the dimensions through which they could reproduce, day to day, their will to live and their independent and sovereign nature.

Landed Property and Clientelism

Saint-Domingue was built from above. A state authority transmitted and instituted century-old rules and orientations and controlled settlement and economic activities in the territory. It was meant to welcome Christian subjects and the privileged who had received donations or leases of land from the king. Indentured laborers from France, and later slaves who were to be baptized on arrival, were to work this land. The imperial state invented social categories and racial stratification. It executed its project with an iron hand in the context of a monopoly system that assured the supply of laborers into the colony and of tropical commodities to the metropole. The imperial state controlled what happened in its overseas territories. It dictated the rules, constraints, and rights and privileges that framed social exchange. It determined the condition of the individuals who lived in these territories. Their existence and future was based on the normative principles that emanated from the imperial state. By emancipating the slaves, Sonthonax reasserted the importance of this despotic imperial state as the pivot for the colonial system, even as he created the beacons of a new kind of citizenship for those who inhabited the territory.

With its sovereignty threatened, the state used its authority in order to take back the rights it had conceded: it decreed general emancipation and seized the property of the émigrés. Toussaint made war against Rigaud as both of them accused each other of insubordination. Sonthonax and Polvérel were put on trial for having overstepped their authority by liberating the slaves, and they defended themselves by arguing this was the only way to save the threatened territory for France. Toussaint departed for France with all the documents he thought necessary to successfully confound those who accused him of treason. Even if they had accidentally broken the law, they all declared, it was only with the goal of preserving the sovereignty of France over the territory and preserving its right of conquest and its control over Saint-Domingue.

In the context of this struggle over the imperial state's control over the colony and the harmful uses of human resources this state claimed to possess, the independence of Haiti budded and grew with unexpected speed, in parallel with the secession of the colonial administration. The new administration constituted itself as the direct inheritors of the territory, using the same reasoning that France did when it signed the Treaty of Ryswick: the

Indigenous Army was the most powerful force among those claiming power over the island. After 1804, it seized the territory that the French state had seized before it, and Boyer concluded in his June 15, 1818, Proclamation to Encourage Agriculture: "When we expelled our enemies, the territory became our property. We own weapons, and we own the land. The laws have made a wise distribution of the land conquered by our valor, and we will conserve it" (Recueil general des Lois et Actes du Gouvernement d'Haïti, No. 542, 42).

A series of accidents prevented the colonial project from surviving the crises created by the French Revolution, and the territory separated from the empire. The structural transformations that led to the independence of the newborn country coincided with these accidents, which ensured the feasibility of that independence. But there was no cause-and-effect relationship between them. On the one hand, the mass of laborers reduced to slavery pursued their own autonomy; on the other, the dust of the intermediaries who had used the metropole to administer the colony seized the reins of public power. They did so in context shaped by two distinct, though concomitant, projects. The irrepressible need for a borderless liberty on the part of those oppressed in captivity guided the first project. The modern Western obsession with taking and possessing everything guided the second.

The recognized leaders of independent Haiti based their conception of the state on the experience they had during the colonial period. They identified the state with the colonial administration. As they sought to gain their civil and political rights during the French Revolution, they did so while maintaining the idea that state of law and the cohesion of its necessary elements were not meant to cross the ocean to implant themselves in Saint-Domingue. Like their French contemporaries, they accepted the fact that republican France's imposition of its sovereignty overseas preserved the absolutism of royal power and wore the purple garb of imperialism. It remained tainted with despotism, arbitrariness, and blood. The Republic of Haiti inherited this concept of external sovereignty. The idea that the sovereign people were the pivot of the republic was foreign to it.

In the minds of the oligarchs, the government was the state, and it was all-powerful. Sonthonax's August 1793 proclamation determined the limits of the liberty of the newly freed. Dessalines's Imperial Constitution decreed the Haitians were all blacks, and that the Poles of the Indigenous Army were Haitians. Boyer signed the recognition of the Act of Independence on his authority alone, and his Rural Code decreed the fate of nearly the entire population by making them *citizens attached to the land*. Geffrard's Rural Code, for its part, apologized for violating the rights of citizens, but shut its eyes on abuses and offered no recourse. When Article 6 of Pétion's 1807 Constitution stipulated that the "government of Haiti takes on the title and will be known as the Haitian State," there was no sense that this confusion of the two posed a problem.

The relationship between the government and the supposed citizens was one of subordination. The government did not answer to them. Still, there was an important nuance that differentiated the colonial context and the national one. The public administration of the first depended on a pre-existing, structured state of civil law. In nineteenth-century Haiti, by contrast, the political authorities didn't have to defer to higher-ranking civil authorities that had been put in place as part of a broader social contract. They never experienced the control of institutions capable of confronting their military power and forcing them to obey. The only reference points these authorities had were those they had observed in the functioning of the colonial administration.

During the crisis that ended in the colony's secession it became necessary to free the slaves while keeping them on the plantations. So the authorities led by Toussaint Louverture inaugurated a system of militarized labor. In 1804 they decided that they possessed the lands of the new country, and they distributed them to the active citizens. But except in the kingdom in the North, they didn't have the laborers necessary for agricultural exploitation or the means required for the production and circulation of plantation commodities. Unsurprisingly, the labor force continued to set its own course according to its own philosophy of the world, gradually disregarding the directives of an executive power that had no roots in reality.

There are striking similarities between the land concessions granted by the state after 1804 and the distributions of plantations by mercantile commercial companies of the late seventeenth and early eighteenth centuries. Ultimately, it was the high-ranking officers of the army who controlled land distribution. But Article 4 of the General Dispositions of the 1805 Constitution declared that the "army is essentially obedient, and no armed force can deliberate." There was, therefore, no formal political body during the nineteenth century, since theoretically, all citizens were part of the active or reserve armed forces (Midy 1972, 33). The omnipotence of the public administration shattered any collective action on the part of the oligarchs.

In the eighteenth century land ownership was managed by an administration that followed strict and standardized procedures. The concessions, leasing, and sequestering of the rights of émigrés, the management of the domains granted to agricultural inspectors, the taxes owed and sums to be paid to absentee owners, the return of the émigrés, and the cases surrounding properties that had been granted to a third party in error, all signal this clearly. By 1807, however, Pétion was already complaining about the disorder that was being introduced into the land sector.

By maintaining the public administration's right to dispose of the lands of the republic and grant property to individuals according to its chosen criteria, the oligarchs accepted the colonial idea that these lands legitimately belonged to the domains of the king, as French laws had claimed since 1674 (Blancpain 2003, 28). When they got rid of the foreign sovereign, they didn't exchange him for any effective substitute. They no longer had a state—a civil and juridical institution that tied together the social forces—to refer to. So the government became the state, or at least thought it could substitute for the state.

The supposed rights that executive power had over the lands and people of Haiti were echoed by the Indigenous Army, whose power was not based on the relationships between people tied together within a collective, or on any kind of collective at all. The army usurped the role of the sovereign, but didn't administer power in its name. Combined with the executive, it determined which collectivities the administration considered legitimate and which voices could be expressed when it came to public affairs. According to its own logic, it became the midwife of the nation, of society and all its constitutive parts. It didn't represent Africans, the vast majority of the population. It represented the West, and, as an inheritor of colonialism, it fell to it to transform and civilize the people for their own good, following the definitions of the modern colonial world.

In dethroning sovereign France, the national public administration took care to prevent the emergence of a political class: "Remember that I [Dessalines] sacrificed everything to rally to your defense; family, children, fortune, and now I am rich only with your liberty. . . . If ever you refused or grumbled while receiving those laws that the spirit guarding your fate dictates to me for your own good, you would deserve the fate of an ungrateful people" (Dubois and Garrigus 2006, 190–91). In place of what he called the ghost of liberty that France was using to deceive the powerful people, Dessalines substituted a ghostly genius that was to watch over their destiny. Those who occupied land were "usufructuaries, concession holders, tenants whose rights were more or less assured" (Blancpain 2003, 28), and whose privileges depended on the good will of the administrative authorities. This property was not secured by a collection of laws that the authorities obeyed. Rather, the beneficiaries owed their good fortune to the *great men* in power. They could therefore not negotiate their loyalty to them without suffering severe sanctions and ultimately destitution, which the *ungrateful* deserved. The absence of security in real estate transactions guaranteed the loyalty of the privileged.

The absence of a cadastral survey and the apparently insurmountable difficulties involved in carrying one out (for two centuries!) maintained political clientelism. The state/government didn't know the extent or the contours of its domains and had no control over them. But it jealously guarded the key. This control over land, crafted out of an alliance of arbitrariness and reason of state, enabled the renewal of the despotic character of the public authorities. The state/government transformed the favorites to whom it granted the privilege of land ownership into sworn enemies of the state of law. A lack of property, meanwhile, was taken as the primary indicator of the status of *cultivator*—that is, an indentured servant or a virtual slave.

The public authorities didn't emerge from a web of relationships validated by the citizens. They drew a border, inside of which they promoted a rationality that assured the obedience and support of those social forces they authorized. They invented nationals to whom they granted privileges, instead of and in place of rights. These were the active citizens, created by the state's monopoly over the available resources, and separated from the passive citizens, those left to their own devices. The appropriation of the means of existence enabled them to typify the citizen attached to the land, the cultivator, as someone who had to be controlled through regulations applied by the rural police force. By definition, the police codes and agricultural regulations didn't depend on the consent of the agricultural workers. The public bureaucracy made sure they were executed, no matter what.

This personalistic relationship with the government meant that the assembly of potential citizens lost its characteristic as the source of a national sovereignty of the kind articulated in the Declaration of the Rights of Man and Citizen. The political system did not respond to a sovereign (Kriegel 2003). In the metropoles, it was the property owners themselves who allowed the administration to differentiate between the active citizens and the dispossessed or passive citizens. In the former colony of Saint-Domingue, it was the administration that differentiated between the two. The property owner was a vassal, not a citizen. In the nineteenth century, Haiti could have become a republic of property owners, if they had been able to claim to have created it. But it was the republic that invented them, and held them on a leash.

As a consequence, clientelism, far from being an anomaly, actually assured the functioning of the public authorities in Haiti. It was constitutive of them. It maintained, on the level of personal relationships, the dependency that had united the colony to its metropole. The political apparatus conceived of itself as a set of relationships uniting the state to its favored notables, rather than as a set of rights and privileges inherent to those notables which were negotiated among themselves in order to create the peculiar institution called the nation-state. The state administration of 1804 had been created from outside the territory, and it remained subordinated to the colonial empire that had created it. Barely emancipated from guardianship of the imperial entity, it worked to renew the dependency that its despotism could not live without.

Militarized Labor and Autonomous Civil Service

The landowners didn't have the political power necessary to direct the state and successfully pursue their social project. So what path did they follow as clients at the heart of the military government? Arbitrary ownership of land was necessarily accompanied by a specific way of treating those who were deprived of it. In chapter 5, I approached this question from the perspective of the laborers by analyzing marronage as a refusal of militarized labor. Before the revolution, landowners who were free people of color claimed to own a third of the slaves of the colony, and treated them like any other slave-owners. It could, of course, have been possible for these landowners to constitute, or think they were constituting, the richest social group living in Saint-Domingue without necessarily behaving or wanting to behave like the other rich people in the colony did toward the labor force. But after independence it was not possible, in principle, to inherit the properties of the colonists without embracing the reasons they had used to justify their monopoly over them. The new landowners, then, inherited the spirit of the colonists they replaced. It wasn't possible to falsify property titles in order to appropriate them without dreaming of becoming a colonist, at least in principle. To think like the colonists was to think with the mentality of the colonists and the battery of concepts that guided their actions. It meant (again, at least in principle) speaking and thinking in French like a colonist. But given that the repressive apparatus that defined the colonist no longer existed, how could the landowners be considered colonists?

The transformation of a group of eighteenth-century emancipated slaves of modest condition into the all-powerful landowners and politicians of the nineteenth century can be explained by their role in the Indigenous Army. From the beginning of the eighteenth century, the royal administration granted to certain privileged individuals the lands it had obtained as loot through conquest. Other entrepreneurs leased land. Land obtained through royal grants cost nothing to the private owner. It became a form of capital that the owner had to make profitable so that he could pay the debts he took on to launch his agricultural enterprise and profit from it. This landowner either possessed or could procure the resources necessary for the purchase of slaves and the hiring of administrative staff. In his ordinance of February 6, 1801, Toussaint sought to assure that those who sought land to acquire would have "the means to create and sustain an establishment" (Ardouin 1853, 4:319). This preoccupation didn't cross the minds of the political authorities of the nineteenth century. But the problem it raises was still there.

It wasn't simple to manage a plantation. Malenfant created a hierarchy of plantation personnel based on their levels of prestige. He described six levels: the attorney-manager, the manager, the treasurer of salaries, the first or second overseer, the overseer of specific tasks, and finally the cultivators organized into larger or smaller work gangs. The cultivators had different specializations: sugar makers, field laborers, wagonmakers, livestock guards, carpenters, barrel makers, hospital staff, and so forth (Malenfant 1814, 305). In his police regulations, Pétion also distinguished between six classes of cultivators (Law 110, Art. 7). The plantation economy, particularly on sugar plantations, was a sophisticated system of production based on technical knowledge and the division of labor. It demanded attention to detail, control, and regularity.

The governments seeking to reconstruct the plantation during the nineteenth century wanted to keep the country on a path of scientific and technological development and reinstitute this meticulous division of labor. It made the arrangements needed to endow the larger properties with the managerial knowledge and means to satisfy the exigencies that were the basis for productive activity. Julien Raimond was certainly not a typical planter, but the breadth of his knowledge and the scale of his connections give us an idea of what was required for the successful management of plantations during the second half of the eighteenth century (Fick 1990; Geggus 2002).

After 1789, the properties of royalists who went into exile were sequestered, seized, and leased to planters and high-level civil servants. The government put in place a more extreme militarization of agricultural inspection in order to make sure industry functioned well. It granted itself the internal management of some plantations. Many émigré properties were taken over by the state and put at the disposal of individuals, serving as political loot taken by the most enterprising: politicians, merchants, or simple adventurers.

From the general emancipation of 1793 to Christophe's suicide, the sequestration of the property of the émigrés didn't decapitate the administration of private enterprises. The authorities made sure that the newly freed didn't assert their rights to the point that they abandoned the plantations. Before the death of Christophe, colonial administrators walked a tightrope between the large-scale leasers of state-owned land, whose commitment to a vocation as agro-industrial entrepreneurs was often dubious, and the recalcitrant cultivators. The agricultural regulations and other laws referring to agriculture make this clear. Militarized labor, and the broader militarization of agriculture, was meant to push this equilibrium in the right direction. Leaning on the Indigenous Army, Toussaint and Christophe channeled their political power into a latifundia system, and their administrations directly organized a plantation economy aimed at the production of export commodities.

The southern republican state acted as the protector for inheritors of uncertain ancestry and the dispenser of land to the favorites of the regime (Moïse

2009, 83). It started down an economically risky path, because it couldn't impose itself within the political structure with the same strength and confidence as the colonial administration or Christophe's regime. Absenteeism became the rule, and the direct management of commodity-production plantations the exception. This was the opposite of what had been the case during slavery. Land remained the foundation for the political system, but it lost its character as capital, preserving only that of war loot. Sibylle Fischer (2004, 270) notes the similarities between the different leaders of the country. But I would argue they had no real choice but to base their political power on land ownership, and that there was something specific to the republic in the South. There are definitely nuances when it comes to the kingdom in the North, given the rigor surrounding the maintenance of accounts and the way the regime dealt with absenteeism: "Still, all Haitian leaders since 1802 seemed to agree on two basic principles: first, that slavery was never to be allowed on Haitian soil; and second, that the large-scale export-oriented plantations be maintained and that land was to be distributed only for political advantage" (Fischer 2004, 270).

One of the key problems of the nineteenth-century economy had to do with the entrepreneurial competencies of the new landowners and the technical resources they mastered. There were definitely many planters who had been free people of color or emancipated before 1789 who could define themselves as *colonists of color* or *American colonists*. It is reasonable to assume that Pétion was thinking of them when he criticized the treatment of cultivators in the South. He referred to those colonists who had made the regions of Les Cayes, Aquin, and Jérémie wealthy, many of whom fled into exile during the conflicts that preceded independence. Descourtilz put it bluntly: "Emigration increased prodigiously. It wasn't only the whites who were terrorized. The mulattoes began fearing danger to themselves, and fleeing with their families, following the example of the whites. As long as they fulfilled the formalities and paid the established tax, Sonthonax let them leave. He was secretly glad, and well convinced that the more slave owners who left, whatever their color, the fewer enemies he would have" (Descourtilz 1795 315).

Most of the formerly free or emancipated who survived the passage from colony to independent nation were urban dwellers. The studies of King and Rogers show they were largely involved in smaller professions and the service sector (King 2001; Rogers 1999). Pétion himself was a jeweler. After 1806 the administrative authorities allowed a subsector of this group, generally of mixed ancestry, to take control of lands they didn't know how to exploit. They lacked knowledge regarding agricultural production. Pétion and his party couldn't easily pass themselves off as American colonists, since they were much closer to Blanchelande's *pompons blancs*.[1] The reality is that not just anyone could improvise and be a planter, especially not a planter in charge of a large plantation.

The high-ranking officers of the southern army were in no position to become respected overseers capable of enlisting new property owners and converting them into planters. This explains the strange combination we find in the rural codes: they are full of detailed instructions, multiple authorizations, related to all levels of the social structure. There are sanctions threatening both landowners and cultivators, as well as those who supervised the latter. The South organized itself as a republic of landowners that the public authorities dreamed they could transform into planters.

The military bureaucracy sought to hand these virtual entrepreneurs of the nineteenth century the most important capital they needed: land and labor. Before 1793, the workers were slaves. But they did cost the colonists something. Pétion had discretely promoted a sharecropping system. But under Boyer, the state sought to put into place a process of free distribution of the *citizens attached to agriculture* to the landowners. This makes clear what they truly thought of those who lacked resources. The proposed economic system carried no risk for the landowners, and protected social relations from the characteristics capitalism brought to the global economy. The detailed 1826 Rural Code seems mainly to offer instructions on how to take care of resources that had effectively been granted free of charge. It sought to create an economy without a market. It died in the egg, before it could even hatch.

Given the lack of agricultural entrepreneurs and plantation managers in the society, the landowners who were suddenly granted this status were as just as confused as the cultivators, who were in any case eager to cut their ties with the commodity-producing plantation. Dealing with the combination of novice entrepreneurs and laborers acting in bad faith, the governmental administration found itself forced from the beginning to suggest what types of crops to plant, how much land should be devoted to each, the changes necessary from year to year, and how to move goods from one place to another. It substituted itself for market mechanisms in a mad, precocious attempt at central planning. But the administration had no mastery of the knowledge necessary to effectively distribute the labor force according to the types and tendencies of different plantations, or to distribute capital and transform it into profit.

The regulations commanded cultivators to remain fixed on a particular plantation. It was the rebirth of the initial Spanish system of *repartimiento*. There was no negotiation between the workers and their employers, or between the class of cultivators and the recipients of large land grants. The fact that the auction blocks and the sale of slaves was so present in recent memory presumably made the promulgation of this kind of policy easier to imagine. The administrators considered that to be productive, a given amount of land required a certain minimum labor force, and they wished to satisfy an intense demand for workers. They sought to fulfill this demand in other ways as well, through immigration schemes that lay behind the supposedly humanitarian welcome extended to captives seized on vessels that were boarded and searched off the coast of Haiti, as well as the efforts to open the doors to emancipated people from the United States.

But Haitian administrators had no plan for a potential decrease in the international demand for tropical commodities. An economic crisis spread through the region, making it even more difficult to rebuild the plantation economy as they hoped. In the wake of the changes in the world economy incited by Great Britain, the old economies of the plantation islands collapsed. Throughout the region, the plantation had a difficult time recovering, and an altered form of a peasant economy implanted itself in order to confront the economic difficulties of the affected territories (Marshall 1963, 1968).

It was increasingly difficult to find local labor to fulfill the needs of the plantation economy. Its cost was prohibitive. The specter of famine threatened the rural populations of certain islands where the monopoly over private property was still effective. In the 1830s, the contraction in the availability of local labor was dealt with in the British Caribbean through the massive importation of indentured laborers from South Asia destined for the more productive plantation economies in the virgin lands of Guiana, Trinidad, and Suriname (Rodney 1981).

Given that the plantations of the French and British colonies of the Caribbean were facing such difficulties, it seems odd the Haitian governments obstinately pursued the reconstruction of their own plantation economy. But while that was indeed the official policy, it was never really put into practice. Negotiation between different social actors was impossible, given the profound divergence in visions of what was at stake. Employed workers had to think about their own subsistence and that of their families. If there had been more respect for private property, they might have found themselves forced to bend to the conditions laid down by the administration. But most of those who might have been employed on the plantations instead established polyvalent cells of agricultural production that offered support to communal life. These community systems ultimately won out over the need for salaried labor. The landowners saw the plantation and its provision grounds as the model to follow. But the potential workers were thinking in terms of family, lineage, *lakou*, and the local market for agricultural products. Their plan for the territory and for establishing themselves within it represented a new social geography, one unknown on the island until then.

The administrative machinery of the state, anchored in the world of landed property, attempted to overcome its lack of knowledge about the international environment by trying to impose its own view of agricultural exploitation on the population. But it consistently failed. From Pétion's Agricultural Regulations to Geffrard's Rural Code, the bureaucracy's claims were always the same. They tried to instill respect for work hours and to control the presence, absence, and movement of workers. Misunderstanding the mechanisms of the market, they granted themselves the right to determine how many workers should be on a particular plantation. They could also reassign them to new ones in cases of closures because of war or bankruptcy. "When there are more cultivators on a plantation than are necessary to cultivate it, the commander of the arrondissement, on the basis of a report from the officers of the gendarmerie, will be able to determine, based on the terrain and the number of cultivators that need to remain on the first plantation, how much surplus can be placed on another plantation in the same commune that is ready to be cultivated" (Code de Police de Pétion, Art. 5).

While the workers dodged arbitrary orders, the public administration reinforced its presence in labor relations. When workers were hired and paid, officers and magistrates, assisted by rural police and local guards, oversaw the process. This supposedly granted more legitimacy to the transactions that were carried out, but it didn't necessarily add any expertise to the situation. Everything suggests that these observers shared essentially the same feelings about the plantation as the rest of the population, though it is difficult to see how their views could have modified the way things unfolded.

In its pretension to replace market mechanisms, the civil service took on a role doomed to failure. It was incapable of operating with transparency and through consensus. A law from 1828 aiming to make labor available, for instance, placed the government in charge of deciding how many cultivators should be assigned to a particular plantation, based on land acreage. The aim was to make sure they didn't abandon work on the major plantations. It was impossible for the landowners or the cultivators to determine whether these regulations were abusive or appropriate, since the structure of the plantation was not regulated by the market. The logic of these decisions even escaped the favored landowners, who were poseurs rather than planters, as well as the agricultural inspectors, who were soldiers rather than managers. The laborers, meanwhile, were more peasants than salaried workers. There was no way they could understand the logic of such regulations. The public authorities issued instructions inspired by the bygone era of colonialism. They didn't fit with the new reality.

The public authorities issued instructions that, even in the most favorable conditions, couldn't be applied to daily life. The actors they were meant to serve weren't asking for their presence, and indeed would have preferred living without it. In fact, the civil service itself never really had a vocation to serve the population. It had no one to report to. They were asked to apply the instructions of the executive, but the civil servants carried out this role without worrying too much about the objectives set by the central authorities. They gradually liberated themselves from the economic armature promoted by colonialism. The demands of the international market for tropical commodities were no longer connected to their daily life. The civil servants and the population developed a new routine.

But Boyer wouldn't have been able to govern as long as he did over a quarter century of failures. The agricultural economy didn't absorb all of social life. His regime created the conditions for the omnipresent civil service to permanently establish its autonomy. Administrative sinecure became a way of life for the former emancipated of the colonial period.

From the Police Force to the Bureaucracy

The generals who supported the stampede of the urban intermediaries onto the properties of the émigrés were guilty of a double imposture. They justified the inequalities in the distribution of land by declaring it was necessary to reactivate the plantation economy. But those who benefited from their land tenure policies were not planters. They didn't even express any specific intention of investing in agricultural development. Following Hénock Trouillot, historian Leslie Manigat (1962, 70) underlines the importance of an observation by the nineteenth-century writer Céligny Ardouin. "As agriculture increasingly ceased being profitable to those who couldn't cultivate or personally manage their properties," Ardouin noted, "commerce became the refuge from all industrial production." The import-export trade become the most important part of this "refuge." Among those unable to manage their properties were the more modest sectors that emerged from the colonial police forces and the small professions. They were oriented toward the tertiary sector rather than a direct participation in material production.

The administrative machinery drew from those involved in this tertiary sector, who were simply not equipped to manage the transformation of dubiously qualified landowners into planters, and even less to convert nonlandowners into cultivators. But the ideologues and bureaucrats of the republican system, lacking experience in productive activity and little inclined to devote themselves to it, were incapable of imagining anything beyond the classic plantation. They certainly couldn't imagine openly promoting the counterplantation, since that would have stimulated the development of African traditions. The result was that sharecropping became the only reasonable productive mechanism available to the new landowners, and agricultural food production for local markets became generalized. But these productive practices were never the object of legal codes or any specific set of regulations aimed at rationalizing their development. There was never any plan for how to increase the profitability of local resources. Despite the lack of any official policy, an inevitable consensus emerged around these arrangements, which had been unknown in the colonial period. The intermediary urban classes simply didn't see a need to regulate their functioning. The emerging bureaucrats, meanwhile, distanced themselves at once from the landowners and from the supposed cultivators, stubbornly but pointlessly promoting agriculture aimed at the production of export commodities.

Boyer's Rural Code provides an excellent window into the ideological breeding ground out of which the bureaucracy emerged. It envisioned a trio formed by the main landowner or renter, the cultivator, and the civil servant. These characters were to meet each other on several occasions, including when a notarized work contract was signed between the first two parties. This key component of labor relations was meant to outline the role the bureaucracy wished to promote for the worker within the agricultural enterprise, which it confided to the management of the landowner.

Contracts are based on language and writing. The only written language in the context we are examining was one that the potential workers did not speak and which the new large-scale landowners themselves had difficulty writing. So from the beginning, the ownership or leasing of a plantation, along with the mastery and ability to write and read French, separated the majority of the landless from a minority of landowners/agro-industrial entrepreneurs, who themselves were at the mercy of their associates and protectors, the bureaucrats.[2] There was ample opportunity for the resentments between the governed and the governing to multiply, and no one was predisposed to follow laws whose spirit might be partly comprehended, but whose content and details were rarely understood.

Furthermore, since an unknown but probably significant number of landowners were ignorant of the machinery of the state bureaucracy and its instructions, land fell from its hegemonic position in the eighteenth century to become a necessary but insufficient condition for access to the new political power structure and participation in its decision-making process. In parallel, the bureaucracy organized itself as a service rendered to landowners who were not in a position of sufficient importance to ask for a rendering of accounts.

The civil service made every effort to enable the functioning of an improvised and artificial economy and society. Their policies went against popular aspirations and thought, and could be carried out only through constantly reiterated instructions and pressure from the police or military. The policy of development depended on interventions by the government, agricultural inspectors, magistrates, officers of the rural police force, and local guards, who had to guide those who executed the policy and force them to follow the dictated path. Every page of the laws demanded applications for permits, authorizations, certificates, declarations, and reports—a whole collection of documents produced by civil servants in a society in which the military rulers thought they could decide from above how to produce material life. The tasks required of the actors concerned would not have occurred to them as important if they were evolving freely. But the bureaucracy didn't have the capacity to force them to execute what was mandated.

The rural codes navigated against the current as they sought to orient social relations in directions that were undesired by most social actors. But the collection of laws and directives they created was useful to the bureaucrats whose livelihood depended on drawing them up and on their apparent enforcement. Peasant agriculture didn't seem to need any instruction, orientation, or help from any bureaucrat. The public administration never thought about regulating it because it didn't help them maintain the vicious circle that provided the reason for their existence.

The instructions surrounding agriculture were addressed primarily to the landowners and not the workers who, following the established colonial tradition, were supposed to obey the orders they received from the former. They were written and circulated in French, even though it would have been possible to produce them in the vernacular language. Colonial officials had proven this by issuing proclamations in Kreyòl, although they had done so during a period of crisis, perhaps even panic, when it was essential to address the agricultural workers. During this conjuncture, furthermore, the authorities had control over a fairly imposing repressive force. The national administration found itself in different circumstances, but that was not the problem. Either they had no wish to provide information to the agricultural workers or they saw no use in doing so because it wouldn't profit them.

Faced with the urgent need to protect metropolitan sovereignty over the colonial territory, Polvérel had to confront the problem of the equality of all citizens of the republic. He conceived of a solution and took the measures necessary to circulate the instructions contained in the *Code rural pour les nègres emancipés* (Rural Code for Emancipated Blacks). He opted for a simple formula that could have been replicated and improved on over time: "One of his first measures was to write up a code of rules to observe on the plantations. These rules were printed and published, and orders also given that at fixed times and with short intervals they would be read to the blacks, in their language, on all the plantations" (Clarkson and Macaulay 1835, 9).

It is clear that the objective of the colonial administrators during Polvé-rel's time was to ally themselves with the laboring classes. This was quite different from the goal of the oligarchs after 1806. And by this date, the literacy skills of the Francophone landowners, including their aptitude for interpreting written instructions, had probably diminished considerably. Given the state of public education in the colony and its likely decline during the wars of independence, it is doubtful that a majority of those who grabbed the lands left vacant after the departure of the colonists distinguished themselves in their mastery of reading and writing. It is difficult to imagine how the public authorities imagined they would organize a national economy, based on the commodity-producing plantation, depending on amateurs who were incapable of overcoming their lack of experience as planters by comprehending and applying the detailed instructions in French contained in the rural codes. Whatever help they got from magistrates, officers of the rural police, local guards, and acting military officers, none of whom were better versed in reading and writing or in the arts and professions of agricultural enterprises, would not have been sufficient to sustain an agrarian policy based on the reactivation of large-scale agriculture.

During the eighteenth century, the government granted or rented out land, and the beneficiaries procured the workforce and the technology indispensable for agricultural production, at their own risk and peril. During the nineteenth century, the administration put land at the disposal of the regime's favorites, who didn't know how to exploit it on their own, couldn't hire the managers they lacked, and seem to have been incapable of following the instructions they received. If we add to this incompetence on the part of the capitalists the fact that the laborers resisted the work of the commodity-producing plantation, we can conclude that this approach to agricultural development was clearly doomed, with or without the support of the civil service.

Until the fall of Soulouque in 1859, almost all of those who led the country had been educated during the colonial period (Casimir and Hector 2003) and had experienced the complexity of the plantation economy. In light of the obstacles that had to be faced in order to rebuild it, the vague desire to plan seems as naïve as the idea of applying the kind of system of self-management imagined by Polvérel. Rather than the reactivation of the economy, this policy actually aimed at the conservation and reconstitution of colonial subordination, and of the social hierarchy that implied. Vastey's *Essai sur les causes de la révolution et des guerres civiles d'Hayti* (Essay on the causes of the revolution and the civil wars of Haiti, 1819) is an indictment of the republic built by Pétion that illustrates this fundamental orientation in luxurious detail.

The civil servants ended up refereeing the impossible relationship between amateur agricultural entrepreneurs and laborers who were little disposed to negotiate the forms of their personal dependence. They profited from it, accumulating the experience needed for their transformation into unproductive bureaucrats. The agricultural regulations and rural codes fed a bureaucracy that reproduced the urban middle classes without really worrying about agricultural development.

This was an omission not only on the part of Pétion and Boyer, but of the entire Haitian political system. Throughout the entire period, this system was never able to either recall the solution used by Polvérel or to imagine another way of stimulating the primary agricultural sector. The approach taken earlier by the civil commissioner, or any other approach that might realistically encourage agricultural development, risked encouraging a renewal of rural life. And this would have destroyed the social preeminence of the intermediaries of the police forces converted into military bureaucrats. The warnings issued by Rivière-Hérard during the unrest that led to overthrow of Boyer emphasized this point (Moïse 2009, 124).

The production of the written word, detached from daily life, presented itself as an attempt to standardize the activities to be undertaken and supervised. In fact, it was itself a substantial activity. It emanated from the highest spheres of the bureaucracy and came back to it in the form of reports. In Boyer's Rural Code, everything unfolded as if the government hoped each Sunday to receive a detailed chart outlining agricultural activity, allowing it to manage agricultural production on the national level. But this production never even got started. From the top of the pyramid, the head of state could in principle, on paper, manipulate the zones of production and the agricultural products that were to be cultivated, and make necessary dispositions and decisions to optimize the results. He behaved like the aristocratic absentee owners who, in colonial times, managed their plantations from afar. But everything unfolded in a vicious circle with no link to the reality of rural economic life. The absentee owner was protected from reality by the bureaucracy.

In the meantime, the apparent mastery of the imperial language reinforced a monopoly over the bureaucratic machinery and political know-how. This presumed knowledge created an opacity around the government and consolidated the autonomy of the state's administrative machinery. From within its impregnable fortress, the bureaucracy trapped the landowners in clientelist networks in which it pulled the strings. The promotion of the cultivation of export commodities as a specialized economic activity served as a pretext for the presence of the civil service in rural areas. Negotiations between landowners and cultivators energized the bureaucracy, but not the economy.

The rural codes, then, promoted the development of a class of civil servants cut off from the agricultural workers and landowners. Once the French colonists from the metropole who had established themselves in the colony had been eliminated from the political theater, the people of color and free blacks of the towns imposed themselves as the titled agents of the imperial language. They instructed the low-level functionaries about the demands they should make on the excluded and how to treat them. In this way, the monopoly over writing and the dominant language consolidated the existing monopoly over the police force. This vastly multiplied the distance between the functionaries on one hand and the landowners and agricultural laborers on the other. Furthermore, it protected the civil servants from any accounting and therefore from any subordination to the population itself. The apparent incompetence of the public administration of the nineteenth century cannot obscure the consummate artistry with which it promoted the interests of the urban sectors who placed themselves at the top of society during the regimes of Pétion and Boyer.

Two Interlaced Orders

In the wake of the signing of the Treaty of Ryswick, the imperial state imposed itself on a geography emptied of any form of organization legitimated by the population itself. The same was true of the Haitian state after the eviction of the French. In both cases, these were regimes of acquisition, and not of institutions. Both were systems of despotic government.

It is worth remembering, however, that in 1697 the French state was a state based on law, and that it expressed its sovereignty through laws imposed on all those who lived within its borders. In the tradition inaugurated by Christopher Columbus in 1492, it implanted itself in Saint-Domingue through the cross and the sword as a suzerain, master of lives and property. In Europe, the political system was evolving toward the structuring of a sovereign, republican state. In Saint-Domingue, meanwhile, the arbitrary and piratical nature of the public administration was increasingly accentuated, to the point that after a century implanted in the colony it was able to plan for the genocide of the population, before being driven out. Its primary objective from 1697 to 1804 was to secure its ownership of the island—that is, its external sovereignty. In the European case, the protection and conservation of the lives of those who lived in the territory was central. In Saint-Domingue, it invited questioning, and a serene analysis.

Like any suzerain, the French state implanted on the island of Haiti did not think, and could not think, about transforming itself into a state based on rights. Moving deeper and deeper into the realm of arbitrary rule (Kriegel 2002, 110) and criminality, it extracted resources that enabled it to consolidate the empire of law and of rights in the metropole (Quijano 2007 and Mignolo 2000).

In 1697, the authorities that signed the Treaty of Ryswick concentrated their absolute power on the inhabitants who lived in the part of the island they took control over. The same was true in 1803 when the French expeditionary army capitulated. In Saint-Domingue, however, in contrast to the situation in Haiti, there was a civil authority overseeing the armed forces. During the first years of independence on the island, the government claimed to absorb the state, as Article 6 of the 1806 Constitution stipulated: "The Government of Haiti will take on this title and will be known under the denomination of the State of Haiti" (Janvier 1886, 83). Despite appearances, the country was governed from its beginnings by an elective monarchy (Madiou 1847, 7:17), which in fact was an imperial elective monarchy. No civil wing of the government emerged above the military hierarchy to impose itself in the face of its despotism. Colonial slavery and the ferocity of the struggles for independence seem to have institutionalized the disdain professed by the public authorities—both colonial and independent—for human life. This devalorization of citizens matched the untrammelled investment on the part of the administrations in the defense of the property of the dominant or governing classes.

Toward the end of the eighteenth century, the territory was shaken by a game that pitted everyone against one another. The laboring population took up arms, and emerged victorious. And it was precisely the maintenance of what the authorities understood as public peace that endangered the values and goals of the popular majority, not to mention their very existence. In the wake of emancipation, the highest authorities expressed this: "Toussaint's November 15, 1798, ordinance reinforced the rigor in the treatment of cultivators, who from then on were placed under the regime of the military administration. . . . The military leaders who commanded districts and neighborhoods had the duty to put all cultivators to work and punish vagabonds, thieves, or those who disturbed public order. They became personally responsible for public tranquility and the good order of the plantations" (Blancpain 2003, 88).

The public order thus conceived by the state/government, both before and after 1804, did not maintain any immediate connection with the well-being and protection of the population. The installation of the armed forces as the pivot of political life, and the choice of the reason of state as the mechanism of the government, made it possible to define a social organization that was dedicated exclusively to the promotion of the oligarchies and the dominant classes. This notion of an order imposed from the outside maintained the experience of centuries of French and Spanish colonization.

We must assume that for the insurgents, the very idea of a social order emerged from communal life, from the need to protect and maintain it in those spaces they were able to remove from colonial influence and govern with complete autonomy. Starting in 1791, they expressed more and more forcefully their will to live according to the order they were inventing for themselves. The militarized bureaucracy, backed up by the rural police, no longer fulfilled the need for social tranquility and public order in the territory, which it had more and more difficulty controlling. From that moment, it makes sense to distinguish the order of the public authorities from the public order—that is, the communal order. During the nineteenth century, the self-governance of communities escaped positive law. That is made clear by the insistence, and even fierceness, with which the legal order fought what it perceived as flagrant disobedience, or else the survival of embarrassing atavisms. The laziness and vagabondage that this parallel order seemed to encourage, or at least to tolerate without too many restrictions, as well as the organization of settlements, language, religion, music and song, and customs—this whole collection of aspects of social life didn't correspond to Western norms.

There was no time for a process based on lived experience to sediment during the lightning passage—about fifteen years long—from merchant slavery to national independence, and from colonial subjection to political autonomy. The governing classes were knocked down by the insurgents of the popular sector; they had to innovate. The result was that at the beginning of the nineteenth century the Haitian state attempted to synchronize two orders, two traditions, and two contradictory exigencies, one colonial and one *Guinean*. That state was not the expression of a national ethos or a negotiated project for the common good.

The Act of Independence was a kind of birth certificate for the nation. It established the necessity of living together. But it was not the expression of a single national entity or a collective way of life that had already been constituted. The Indigenous Army guided the birth of this new formation even as it preserved the public colonial order. But it didn't produce a vision of the nation that channeled and expressed its internal sovereignty. On the contrary, 1804 froze the existence of two opposed social projects: the colonial administrative order carried on by the (recognized) heroes of independence and the autonomous communities organized by the revolutionary insurgent masses.

Madiou, along with the broader group of Haitians of French allegiance, didn't perceive the asymmetrical but complementary relationship between the two poles that composed the state. They had a particular idea of what constituted the public order, one guided by the existence of the public authorities they controlled. They envisioned the peaceful organization of a social order that was to be as close as possible to the colonial form of organization, and anchored in so-called European civilization. They made themselves the champions of the eradication of African traditions, which they believed had to be civilized through a modified form of merchant slavery. Their order was based on the invisibility, or more precisely the erasure, of the population and its traditions and experience. The oligarchs dreamed of molding the amorphous clay that they unrestrainedly dubbed the *newly freed*, seeing them as people with no past or future.

This order was inspired by colonial France. It disdained any form of ethics and enshrined instrumental reason at the heart of political life, justifying the legitimacy of torture, brutal violence, and the slow-burning massacre of the sovereign people. It revered the existence of the formerly freed as a political class, without understanding that the continued use of the very concepts distinguishing the *formerly freed* and *newly freed* ratified the slave trade and slavery, and even offered disguised praise for them.

The two poles, colonial and *Guinean*, each remained indestructible in this form of organization, because each maintained the other. Colonial traditions were legitimized based on the need to take the place of the colonists and civilize the people of *Guinean* background. And the upholders of *Guinean* traditions increasingly dug in their heels as they armed themselves to resist the European project of annihilation and move beyond the mode of production of material life that subtended it. Starting in 1791, France became incapable of governing Saint-Domingue in the way a colonial empire should. It lost its Pearl of the Antilles; the *Guinean* traditions won out. In 1804 two social forces were born, moving in opposite directions. Neither could conquer the other, and neither could defeat the metropole without the other. "We made up a muddled mosaic of contrary forces" (Madiou 1847, 5:111). The foundational order of the state was the result of the artistry with which the two poles avoided each other. The state of 1804 was a tacit agreement that allowed the two poles, with their contradictory directions, to exist alongside each other without creating uncontrollable fires of conflict. It enabled the coexistence of secession and revolution.

The capitulation of the French in 1803 represented the end of only one skirmish in a long war that pitted the new political entity against the modern, capitalist, and racist West. Louis XVIII's minister Malouet put it bluntly: "If we can defend ourselves only by re-establishing the power of our color and of property, aren't Europeans called to create a confederation of their interests against their natural enemies?" (Vastey [1814] 2013, 8).

Despite the ceremonial declarations made by the founders of the new nation, in fact, neither of the two core social groups could claim the laurels for this particular skirmish. Madiou and Ardouin agreed on the primacy of the Africans in the general insurrection as well as the absolute impossibility of leaving the leadership of the new political entity in their hands. The administrative machineries of the state and the army were indispensable institutions, precisely because the victory of the French was not a victory over the West: the international community was committed to the idea that the existence of what it called a black state (or the first black republic) in its midst represented a threat to the Atlantic public order. The amphictyonic meeting of Latin American nations in Panama in 1826 demonstrated that Haiti had no friends ready to invite it to sit at the negotiating table with the great empire and its allies.

The independence of Haiti, then, was an unexpected phenomenon. It created such a commotion on the shores of the Atlantic that Haitians, despite the irreducible antagonisms, couldn't tear each other apart. There were too many birds of prey surrounding Haiti, and as was the case in 1802, they didn't differentiate—at least not in the way that the privileged would have liked—between the emancipated and the captives. And they didn't make an equivalent distinction between the emancipated who had long been free, whose ancestry was more mixed, and those of the recent floods, who were blacker.

The much-celebrated union between the leaders of the Indigenous Army hid the gap between them and the victorious troops, both the professional soldiers and the maroon soldiers. The fairly ephemeral alliance among the military leaders themselves coexisted with the general distance between all of them and the popular masses. The new political formation was defined by this fracture and not by the union among the powerful oligarchs. There was a separation between the Haitians of French allegiance connected to the former members of the police force and militias and those who were emancipated after the general insurrection of 1791 and emerged from Toussaint's troops, who were closer to the oppressed classes. After Christophe's suicide, however, this interest group no longer had an autonomous existence.

Louverture, Dessalines, and Christophe sought to guard against external aggression by flirting with the masses of agricultural laborers, and therefore with internal sovereignty. Pétion and Boyer, in contrast, preferred installing the potential aggressors right in the heart of the republic. This policy allowed them to protect themselves from the constant strengthening of the *Guinean* traditions. By agreeing to pay France an indemnity, accepting the debt of independence, this sector of the oligarchy mortgaged any possibility of creating a state based on rights in the country. Their obsession with creating roadblocks for the Africans led them to promote a segregation of worldviews, and excluded any option for negotiation and participation over how they might fulfill the needs that flowed from the worldview of the rural majority.

The oligarchies of the South had Goman at their heels, and later confronted the defiant turbulence of the Piquets and the Cacos. These conditions left the governments defenseless in the face of the imperial powers and the consulates. The elites were more panicked by the idea of negotiating with the *Guinean* traditions than by the notion of joining the colonialist camp. But their reintegration into the bosom of the modern West was accompanied by humiliations and exactions that only got worse with time, incurring deeper and deeper wounds against the tradition of national pride that had emerged from the wars of independence. This malaise and suffering became even more painful after 1915.

So, despite the struggles and conflicts that followed 1804, the hostility of a racist and proslavery international community forced the coexistence of the contradictory poles that characterized the Haitian state. The society could move from one short circuit to the next without ever ending up in a complete conflagration. A system of uncomfortable negotiation tied the poles together. In its dealings with the international community, the state had to consolidate the conquest of the territory, which was the major step gained in November 1803. More important than all the internal dissensions was the imperative to live together. This uncomfortable situation grew worse when the social forces of the early nineteenth century belatedly discovered that the production of agricultural commodities in their territory didn't particularly interest the former colonizer or the other powers. The intellectual and political elites evolved in three directions that were not necessarily compatible with one another: an intense effort to integrate into Western culture, a renewed rejection of the racialization of human relations, and an increasing permeability to the influences of the popular masses.

The obstacle to the decisive endorsement of national sovereignty was the fact that the *obligation* to live together—made unavoidable by the increasing disdain and contempt of the international community—could not substitute for the *desire* to live together (Kriegel 2003, 186) on the part of groups who had very little affection for one another. This obligation wasn't a sufficient motivation to inspire choices and sacrifices that might have energized the collective and, in the process, moved beyond the constitutive dichotomy of the state. Under the increasing pressures of an imperialism that was in full expansion, the governments responsible for the maintenance of public order during the second half of the nineteenth century didn't have the strength to penetrate the communal order or to protect themselves from international developments. Powerless, they watched over what Cary Hector has called a "systematic collapse" (Hector 2014).

The Archives of the Communal Order

Fanon's argument in *Black Skin, White Masks* fits the oligarchs and the modest urban sectors like a glove:

It becomes evident that we were not mistaken in believing that a study of the language of the Antilles Negro would be able to show us some characteristics of his world. . . . There is a retaining-wall relation between language and group. To speak a language is to take on a world, a culture. The Antilles Negro who wants to be white will be the whiter as he gains greater mastery of the cultural tool that language is. Historically, it must be understood that the Negro wants to speak French because it is the key that can open doors which were still barred to him fifty years ago. In the Antilles Negro who comes within this study we find a quest for subtleties, for refinements of language—so many further means of proving to himself that he has measured up to the culture. (Fanon 1986, 25)

In Haiti, however, French is spoken by a minority of the population and remains at the margins of national society. As a result, the supportive relationship between language and the collectivity does not play out in the same way as in the French Antilles, and certainly not in favor of the French language. As Mignolo points out, when Nebrija presented the first grammar of the imperial language to Queen Isabella of Castile, he recalled the words of the Bishop of Ávila: "'Soon Your Majesty will have placed her yoke upon many barbarians who speak outlandish tongues. By this, your victory, these people shall stand in a new need; the need for the laws the victor owes to the vanquished, and the need for the language we shall bring with us. My grammar shall serve to impart them the Castilian tongue, as we have used grammar to teach Latin to our young" (Mignolo 1992, 307).

But we have to explore the opposite question as well: what happened to the colonized who disembarked, beginning more than the two centuries before the battles of 1791, without speaking the language of the colonizer, and without a common language of their own? And who appropriated the popular forms of speech, transforming them into a tool of expression that completely escaped the comprehension of a supposedly all-powerful political power? These colonized people instituted principles of conviviality that counteracted the public order constructed by the forms of memory rooted in the imperial project. The fact that the French language could not impose itself in the daily life of the emerging Haitian people, and systematically retreated starting in 1791, suggests that there was a gradual reversal in the class relationships that supposedly dominated the dynamic of the evolving society. The universal implantation of a language of contestation consecrated an epistemological rupture whose significance has not been fully explored. It shattered the colonial matrix of power. I argue that this rupture imposed itself as a constitutive element of the state in Haiti. And I insist on the centrality of the question posed by Madiou in the introduction to his reflections (1847, 1:v): "For his part, did the African—even though enslaved—ever completely cease to be free?" In other words, was he even colonized?

The communal order and the colonial public order emerged from contrasting forms of memory and knowledge. The latter rooted itself in an international community that lost its influence during the Haitian nineteenth century. The former emerged from the revolution of 1791 to 1804. It is impossible to account for the coexistence of two orders through some kind of logic, or a conceptual combination of the different norms and values that organized social life. In daily practice, however, within the borders of the republic, this distance ended up being eroded. The daily conviviality obtained near the end of the century allowed the antagonistic classes to clear a common path, opened up slowly but surely by compromises developed in order to find solutions to problems they confronted together. Footbridges were built through daily activities that were woven together through trial and error, as people accommodated themselves to a communal existence that straddled the necessarily dualism. The conditions that made possible a consensual, dual vision of the world supported the period of agricultural well-being described by Leslie Manigat, which corresponded to the thirty-five years of political stability that preceded the major global economic crises of the end of the nineteenth century (Hector and Casimir 2004). The intellectual elites trumpeted the supposedly Latin nature of local culture, but that fact only proves that most observers didn't see Haitian culture in this way.

The two processes, chaperoned respectively by the public authorities and the community, became interlaced. But neither ever absorbed the other. The ethical stance declared at the time of the Bois Caïman ceremony by the insurgent laborers demanded negotiation with the sovereign people. But this was something that—except in the case of Polvérel's proposals—the colonial empires and the emancipated who served them could not tolerate. That was the reason for the purge of the maroon leaders on the eve of the declaration of independence. In time, however, the focus shifted to creating and protecting a space in which the generalized communal order could reign. And nineteenth-century life conditions managed to check the implementation of despotic policies and gradually forced those in power to take popular interests into account. The assassination of Dessalines incited a peasant movement that, in truth, the armies of the republic were never able to control or to absorb. But above all, as the signal article by Michel Hector (1998) describes, Goman and Acaau didn't share the fate of earlier figures like Halaou and Lamour Dérance. And although his time in power was brief, Sylvain Salnave sat in the president's chair as an enemy of the oligarchs and the foreign consulates who sponsored them.

A mesh of not-yet-codified relationships wove together reciprocal connections. These were deepened by the cultivators' revolts, which facilitated the political ascension of several leaders from among the ranks of the dispossessed. One of the most famous examples of this penetration into the urban world is that of Mérisier Jeannis, the focus of the classic work by Alain Turnier (1982). But beyond the individual cases we might inventory and analyze, I want to emphasize the deep waves that moved the national population as a whole and transformed the society's foundations. This slow construction of a consensus and unity followed endogenous parameters that we can identify.

Paradoxically, it was the social services that the public authorities didn't offer or support—physical and mental health services, religion, leisure, the establishment and maintenance of urban and rural markets, public education, the maintenance of travel infrastructure—that ended up as spaces of sharing and connection between antagonistic social sectors. The regional oligarchies reconstituted themselves by *blackening* themselves. Even as they tried to retain the core markers of social distinction, they carefully adopted the traits of the subordinated populations. All of this was constructed in the context of a vaguely administrative public authority that didn't create too many problems of consensus, given its extreme, if unavoidable, tolerance of the violations of its directives and regulations.

The population moved steadily on the path toward the satisfaction of what was needed for them to live together. They pursued the goal, present from 1791 on, of achieving an acceptable degree of food security. The failures in the implementation of official policy are sometimes interpreted as a string of defeats. But that is because, during this period of hegemonic European imperialism, neither the ideals of the counter-plantation system that defied those of the government nor the successes achieved by the triumphant peasantry were institutionalized. The reiteration of official projects confirms that these alternative solutions ultimately dominated because they were more practical and sustained the pursuit for well-being. The public administration could not contain, replace, or appropriate them. Whether the administration wanted to or not, it ended up accommodating itself to these local traditions, and conforming to them.

To the extent that law and legislation remain the essential characteristics of sovereignty (Kriegel 2002, 98), the never-ending repetition of governmental instructions makes clear that the public administration had no control over the governed. This was emphasized in the announcement of the publication of the Code Rural d'Haïti in 1863 (Saint-Amand 1872). These repetitions exposed the lack of internal sovereignty on the part of the regime, as well as its marginality in relation to the increasing cohesion of social life in the Haitian countryside. Throughout the country, communal forms of life gradually took control. But the intellectual elites were too busy trying to pass themselves off as Africa's eldest daughter to take notice.

All of this teeming change took place in Kreyòl. The elaboration and universalization of the national language is evidence of the irrepressible rise of popular sovereignty. The population of the nineteenth century thought in the national language, spoke to each other in the national language, remembered the past and imagined the future in the national language. Only the dust of the urban oligarchs remained resolutely Francophone and practiced a European version of Christianity. The Kreyòl language and the national collective sustained each other and defined the coherence of the Haitian nineteenth century.

Practices Straddling Two Cultures

The concrete social practices that were put in place by the free blacks long before the Haitian Revolution were a striking tangle of two cultures: the colonial/modern culture and the resistant culture of the dominated. The fact that to this day they remain intertwined shows that the revolution is unfinished. The popular culture developed during the struggles for independence was never able to fully flourish and satisfy the needs of those who created it, particularly the need for security and autonomy. They perpetually had to negotiate with imperial thinking.

Stewart King (2001) describes the social practices the free blacks, who were a tiny part of the population. Using the notarial archives of the period, he analyzes how the forms of solidarity developed in captivity enabled the emancipation of certain captives, despite the fact that they had no material resources. Once free, these individuals maintained and reconstituted the communal connections they had woven during their imprisonment, using them to support and consolidate their fragile achievements. These free blacks made their way through the colonial universe by elaborating respectful rules of social exchange, to the extent possible. They had interpersonal relationships and common interests that continued to connect them with those still in captivity.

King highlights the itineraries of what he calls the "military leadership," who were members of the militia and employees of the police forces. He shows how they reinforced their integration into the urban intermediary sector by manipulating relationships of kinship, or pseudo-kinship, woven together through private life. These connections of family and friendship between captives and the emancipated seem to have existed outside the relations of domination that defined the relationship between master and slave, or at least to have muffled them. The networks King describes juggled two different normative systems. One governed forms of human solidarity that aimed to protect the oppressed, whether they were emancipated or still in captivity. The other institutionalized the lack of rights of the captives and the statutory discrimination against the emancipated, shaping the class conflicts that constrained their public life.

The privileged minority, whether free blacks or American colonists, shared complimentary interests that were opposed to those of the captives as a whole. But different values oriented their public and private lives. Publicly, the American colonists tended to reinforce their relationships to the wealthy white planters from the colonial metropole. The intermediary urban classes, in contrast, stood out by the closeness they maintained with those still living in captivity, and even with the recently disembarked *bossales* (King 2001, 228, 248). Communal solidarity, which became the axis of the nation under construction, could be found at all levels. But it tended not to operate as openly in the spaces where the relationship with the metropole and metropolitans was being negotiated. There, expressions of solidarity with the captives could be counterproductive.

Colonial laws and regulations codified the norms and values that were the foundation for the claims that the oppressed were inferior. The norms and values governing communal solidarity, however, emerged from a consensus orchestrated through practice of the most widely shared habits and customs. When they gained their freedom, the emancipated slaves started out with extremely limited resources. They sought to compensate for this by taking advantage of kinship or pseudo-kinship relations through participation in weddings and funerals, and by drawing up notarial acts, being good neighbors, and becoming godparents. In this way, the free blacks equipped themselves so that they could maneuver better within the dominant system. In the process, they used the categories defined by colonial thinking, the only ones modern racism could tolerate. They were cautious about allowing the communal relationships and ethnic solidarities of the antislavery resistance to filter into the dominant universe. They did not directly question the superiority in which the masters and their institutions had enrobed themselves. The free blacks sought to rid themselves of their African ethnic identities, and they took on the attributes that colonial modernity had chosen for them. This enabled them to move within the public sphere, seeking out the resources necessary for survival. Whether they wanted to or not, they became the perfect colonial blacks.

Having escaped the difficulties and torments of slavery, the urban sectors absorbed the colonial/modern approaches to managing life. They diluted their differences to become part of a black race as defined by the West. At the same time, and in often hidden ways, they negotiated their allegiance to the forms of solidarity emerging from the struggle of the oppressed classes. In this way, they juggled their roles as civil servants with their ethnic affiliation. In their roles in the administrative centers, they carried out the task of maintaining the supposed hegemony of the white race. To do this, they had to turn their backs on forms of class resistance that defied the public order. They invested themselves in the forms of individual advancement and interpersonal competition that characterized the pursuit of the privileges that might be granted by the dominant modern system. It became indispensable for them to identify with the black race, itself the fruit of a modern colonial sociogenesis. That was part of the strategies for survival they pursued through civil service and the management of the commodity-producing plantations. In urban contexts, the color question replaced national or tribal diversity and superimposed itself over the ways of knowing, thinking, and acting characteristic among the captives. The manipulation of the chromatic universe, along with debates about color distinctions and the advantages that could be drawn from them, became more important than the functioning of the communal relations that had emerged from the soldering together of the ethnicities imprisoned in the labor camps.

We can see, then, the emergence of a social division. On the one side, the interethnic relationships developed by people reduced to slavery became the pivot for communal cohesion and social life. The worker who had been kidnapped, bought, and recently disembarked was remodeled into a new person, forged through the creation of the oppressed community in which he lived, and militated. Interethnic relationships developed in a space of struggle against enslavement. The black person described in Dessalines's constitution was a product of the idea that *tout moun se moun*, every person is a person. That person was born out of struggle. The Ashanti, Ibo, Wolof, Kongo, and others became Haitians as they defended themselves from the tortures of slavery. Their perspective included a clear identification and understanding of the workings of colonial domination.

But within the world defined by colonial emancipation, such relationships of solidarity were renegotiated. The modern black, personified by the emancipated slave, had been created through the imposition of the kinds of competitive individual relationships that characterized the modern world and produced the colonial worker. The behavior of the tiny strata of free blacks was profoundly changed by their integration into the dominant society. Still, given the precariousness of their existence, they could not disregard interethnic relations of solidarity. These reappeared openly in the form of Western-style kinship or pseudo-kinship relationships. But their deep roots were nourished through participation in the popular practices of Vodou, even though that was generally hidden and denied. The notarial archives consulted by King wouldn't reveal these practices, but based on an analogy to contemporary practices in Haiti, I would posit they were already in place.

In colonial society, individuals distributed along a hierarchy based on race and a continuum of skin color competed for the privileges enjoyed by the hegemonic classes and those who served them. For those kidnapped from Africa, meanwhile, social privilege derived from relationships within the culture of the nation in formation, which opposed the colonial empire. In order to better take advantage of the privileges they gained through color prejudice, the free blacks revived interethnic relationships of solidarity. The American colonists, on the other hand, jealously maintained the relationship with the metropole that guaranteed their privileges. Blacks, emancipated mulattoes, and American colonists all met in the contested arena of color prejudice, and they all jealously protected their shared preeminence by trying hard not to raise the question of class. But properly interethnic class relations unified nearly all the population against the dictates of the colonial empire. The result, however, was that a sanitized French and European culture—one that had become somewhat unrecognizable when it came to the management of the institutions responsible for public order—was venerated by these privileged groups, in place of the national culture born of the uncompromising refusal of colonial, capitalist, and racist modernity.

The nineteenth-century Haitian authorities who embraced metropolitan thought and carried out the politics of doubling tried to justify their arrogant pretensions by promulgating flashy and highly trumpeted instructions meant to operationalize the maintenance of the modern/colonial public order. But among the majority of the population, the universality of the customary norms encouraged those who professed them to remain in a state of isolated self-sufficiency and turn their backs on any forms of negotiation that might link them to imperial institutions. This dichotomous situation dated to the eighteenth century, when, as King's study shows, there was a stable set of behaviors among the free blacks, recognized by the largely urban administrative community.

The two cultural collectives, one oppressed and the other dominant, crossed paths in the administrative centers. But the concrete social behaviors that developed there were shrouded in an ambiguity that can make it difficult to see exactly how these two collectives became imbricated with one another. The difficulty of interpretation is compounded by the fact that social institutions are embedded within cultural groups, while behaviors are the result of daily activities or practices. A Christian marriage (an institution) celebrated with great fervor (a practice) was an indicator of a certain status within the social hierarchy. But it wasn't necessarily proof of cultural integration, or evidence of allegiance or adherence to the Christian faith. The management of the patriarchal nuclear family promised by marriage expanded the prestige of the couple and served as a trampoline to their social mobility, especially when the wedding was carried out with great ostentation. But this didn't mean that the same couple didn't also operate within communal collectives defined by other kinds of familial and gender relations.

The open combination of Christian and Vodou marriages is simply unthinkable. These institutions consecrate diametrically opposed kinds of family relations. In the dominant Christian society, as the notarial documents consulted by historians show, both parties tended to bring to a marriage material goods consigned according to the relevant contracts. But it was precisely the lack of any possessions that defined the majority of the population reduced to slavery. In nine-tenths of the universe under consideration—whether we are talking about slaves or free people—it was impossible for a matrimonial union and the constitution of a family to replicate the form of the Judeo-Christian institution. The latter was anchored in the ownership and exchange of private property and material goods, managed by a patriarchal figure.

Interpersonal behavior in urban or urbanizing contexts unfolded at the border between the two cultural collectives. This confused many foreign observers, who were incapable of explaining how those who officiated over and participated in a Vodou ceremony on Saturday night made sure not to miss mass on Sunday morning. But the visible actions and behaviors that announced belonging to the colonial society can be interpreted as simple expressions of rank on the part of colonial social actors. They did not modify the less visible observance, where appropriate, of the norms and values of communities defined by solidarity.[3] Marriage, public education, and use of the French language operated as simple survival strategies used to camouflage the cohesion expressed through relationships governed by the oppressed culture of popular origin. The struggles over color prejudice were grounded in the struggle to gain access to property and the pursuit of a modern ideal of status. But that didn't remove any of the vitality from the exercise of another culture, whose motors of development escaped the urban mechanisms of political control.

Conclusion: Private Life, the Common Denominator

The agricultural regulations decreed after the declaration of general emancipation had the impossible task of ending slavery while guaranteeing the equality of all citizens, including the laborers destined to work on the plantations. The idea of organizing a labor market was unthinkable among the workers, as Polvérel noted judiciously in his 1793 Proclamation (Debien 1949), and even more so among the presumed landowners, who were used to disciplining slaves. It seemed inevitable that the police would be used to force the necessary workforce to put itself in the service of capitalism. But militarized agriculture disappeared after Christophe's death. And the cultivators and the police came from the same social group; the government didn't have the material or spiritual resources to extract some of them from the larger population in order to create a privileged group distinct from the masses of laborers.

Both the colonial state and the public administration that emerged after 1804 guaranteed themselves the monopoly over land. But they didn't count on the shrewdness with which the cultivator would move toward seizing and making use of this property (Ardouin 1853, 4:359). The workers fought to preserve their own monopoly over the labor force, and negotiated over what products to cultivate and what benefits should be drawn from the conquest of the territory. They forced the supposed landowners to try and figure out either how to weaken the workers' control over their own labor or how to get around that control. Political leaders, unable to control the laborers, couldn't control material production. They had to content themselves with managing the distribution and sale of the circulating merchandise on the market, preferably outside the country.

The argument I have presented in this chapter is based on the analysis of the agricultural regulations and the rural codes that came after them. I probably would have come to the same conclusion if I had decided to study the constitutions and other laws of Haiti. It was totally impossible for the population to penetrate the domain of the judicial system, where public authorities were systematizing their forms of management. That was especially true once that population took on the attributes of a sovereign people.

The protection of private property across the islands of the Caribbean is the origin and the source of our suffering. It was the spine of the judicial system inherited in the colony, which of course functioned in the imperial language. A tiny minority of the population, originally landowners, used this language. The relationship to the global economy was administered in French. It didn't derive itself from existing domestic and communal life, which was administered in Kreyòl. Instead, it represented a continuation of the system that had created the trade in blacks.

Both before and after independence, the plantation economy existed in direct opposition to the flourishing of the domestic or familial economy. In the same way, the imperial language sought to annul or destroy the popular sovereignty born of the functioning of private life and local institutions. The plantation economy and the imperial language supported each other to make sure that the decisions taken at the level of the family economy, spoken in Kreyòl, didn't affect public life, which was seen as the foundation for a socio-economic system focused on the international market.

But, unsurprisingly, the conjoined structuring of private life and the vernacular language progressed to a level of such universality that it served as a marker for national identity. Only a small coterie of about 5 percent of the population was linked to the outside world through French. They felt as if they were floating above the country's daily reality, foreigners to its material production and manual labor. Above all, they considered themselves irredeemably soldered to the outside world. But many of the landowners of the nineteenth century were illiterate, and many of those who were Francophone were probably unable to write.

Given the direction of the global economy in the nineteenth century, knowing French didn't really help in the development of a plantation economy. Instead, it served primarily to control where the merchandise produced by economic activities the literate couldn't control ended up. An emerging class of scribes and interpreters served as the hinge between the public authorities and the oligarchy, on the one hand, and those who worked in agricultural production, on the other. The public administration had discovered a function for itself: creating an inescapable mechanism for levying taxes on family agricultural production in order to benefit the relatively idle urban oligarchs. The illiteracy of rural residents, whether they were landowners or cultivators, turned out to be useful for the reproduction of the civil service that busied itself with supporting the distribution of the fruits of economic activity but not promoting this activity. The more self-sufficient agriculture blossomed, the more the public administration and its bureaucrats worked to assure the survival of the urban oligarchy.

Once the landowners of color of Julian Raimond's kind—the American colonists—were gone, modern capitalist enterprise no longer penetrated the primary sector of the economy. Agricultural activity in rural Haiti protected itself from the financial extraction put in place by urban commerce and the public administration. The mastery of the imperial language, meanwhile, served to protect the urban oligarchy from any local attempts to control the government and force it to adapt to local realities. Language itself became an instrument of government. Those who spoke French were assured a minimum degree of well-being and a superior social status.

The public authorities claimed to be carrying out a civilizing mission. But in truth, they had neither the intention nor the means of doing so. The only purpose in making this claim was to justify the maintenance of a colonial-style administration and of the ideas that had accompanied its establishment. But all these ideas did was to provide comfort to the powerless minority who controlled the state/government during this period, but couldn't get anyone to obey them. The 95 percent of passive citizens held the reigning oligarchs in check. The conceptions promoted by the state/government, therefore, didn't at all translate into lived reality.

Nineteenth-century international economic development, accentuated by imperialism, forced the oligarchs to move closer to the rural masses in two very clear ways. The first was the structuring of the national language. All social groups spoke this language of contestation and used it universally in their private lives. Paraphrasing Nebrija, I would say that the community used Kreyòl to *teach the young how to resist*.

The oligarchies comprised of the emancipated and descendants of emancipated, along with the class of agricultural laborers, acted as one linguistic community. As this community organized its daily life, it struggled to free itself from imperial thought. There was a conviviality at that level that suggests a unified consensus. That is why it is often difficult to apprehend the duality of the Haitian situation. The oligarchies had been born from a colonial tradition founded on the destruction of communal relationships, and so of course they sought to detach themselves from the oppressed classes. But their own struggle for survival made it impossible for them to cut the ropes that tied them to the popular masses. During the late nineteenth-century apogee of imperial capitalism, the oligarchs were besieged by an inescapable precarity. Their daily lives were, in fact, dictated by the rhythms of the popular classes.

That gave rise to the other domain in which the oligarchs fused with the masses. They participated in the establishment of a national culture with regard to the structuring of autonomous private life. Already during the eighteenth century, as Madiou noted, both the large landowners of the rural areas and urban families contributed to forms of conviviality of *Guinean* origin. The people exercised their autonomy not just in plain view of the administrative authorities, but with their complicity. Every day, the exercise of popular sovereignty was strengthened by relationships governed by customary law. The civil service didn't participate directly in the negotiated order that developed. But the rural communities produced and governed the social peace of the nineteenth century, without the intervention of the political authorities, and often despite their intervention.[4]

There is no doubt that the oligarchies jealously guarded their power when it came to the visible control of the state apparatus. Since they played no role in production, their daily bread came from civil service. But, unsurprisingly, they also sought to keep their private life safe from imperial interference. Their reticence to cut ties with the oppressed classes was logical, given how inconstant and inconsistent the colonial empires had been in providing support for the colonial population. Napoléon's policies were a clear example of this. In Haiti, the most Catholic bourgeois of the city had to maintain courteous exchanges with the *manbo*, the *houngan*, and the others who served the *lwa*. He had to protect himself from their thunder, which wasn't limited to the spiritual domain. In his interior life, this bourgeois had to accommodate a certain presence of popular spirituality, natural medicine, forms of collective indivisible property, and the reciprocal relationships that wove together daily conviviality. The oppressed culture and the counter-plantation controlled all these aspects of private life. I will expand on their importance in the next chapters.

The complexity of this imbrication of private and public life shaped the specific form taken by the Haitian state. Its role became managing the disjunction between these two spheres, as well as that between the oligarchic and popular classes. The Western powers maintained a stranglehold over the management of the entrances and exits to and from the territory. The formal civil services of the colonial and national administrations handled the negotiations and trade with these powers. But particularly after August 1791, the Haitian people created themselves by seizing and monopolizing the management of activities related to local material and spiritual production, as well as the production and management of their private lives. They took control of their own reproduction, and therefore that of the nation and its people. And the postindependence conquest and apparent appropriation of the territory by the propertied class wasn't operationalized in a way that enabled it to break or hold in check the complex knowledge system developed through the solidarity of communal and familiar relationships. Foreign powers and their intermediaries didn't govern the public order of the national community. The sovereign people invented it and administered it as they constituted and reproduced themselves.

From the beginning of colonization, it was difficult to separate the order imposed by imperialism from the structures of conviviality built by the national community as a way of fulfilling their need to operationalize their will. When the *bossales* disembarked, they couldn't survive without learning the rules of the dominant system into which they had been unwillingly projected. They needed to understand colonialism. But the space into which they entered had been created to consume and destroy them. Only by opposing their assimilation into this system could the new arrivals escape the parameters set up to crush them. They took their lives into their own hands by opposing it with a qualitatively different system. It was based on the boundless liberty of their oppressed culture, which synchronized the contributions of all those actors called to operate under the empire of colonial despotism. Their world and their sovereign order was besieged by much more powerful forces, resolutely antagonistic toward any form of autonomy. But it responded to the existence and the specificity of the nation and its people. The Haitian nineteenth century unfolded to the doubled rhythm of a communal order and a public order. They existed together without any major conflicts. The oligarchs participated in the communal order, if only because they couldn't depend on their allies in the international sphere. They had no other option.

Chapter 8

The Power and Beauty of the Sovereign People

Introduction: The Contrast

The dominant way of thinking takes care never to veer too far from the colonial vision of the world. It observes Saint-Domingue from above—from France toward its colony and from the oligarchs toward the masses. It takes as self-evident that French rights to the territory were legitimate, and that the preeminence accorded to the oligarchs from the beginnings of colonization was justified. This perspective inevitably renders banal the efforts the sufferers made to survive against the winds and currents—that is to say, with or without the metropole. This posture emerges from the Discovery and the Conquest. It doesn't take them as facts caused by and accomplished through lived experience, but rather as a necessary, ineluctable, and even desirable history.

This choice is sneakily, profoundly political. If I start there, and try to explain how the French and their descendants established themselves on the island, I introduce into my interpretation the self-importance of those who granted themselves the right to civilize the Indians and the Africans. I take on the disdain with which they see the population. And I help them poison Haitian life. Until the end of the nineteenth century, the Liberal Party and its sympathizers gathered around a newspaper called *The Civilizer*. The National Party and its affiliates threw down the gauntlet in response not because the people didn't need to be civilized, but because they considered they would be better at saving the population from themselves (Moïse 2009, 257, 289). The chicanery of the civilizers turns the sovereign people into a collection of marionettes waiting for their puppet master.

Hispaniola, Saint-Domingue, and Haiti have all been governed by despotic powers. The militarization of all these regimes responded to an unchanging need: protecting the land seized by the metropole so that it could benefit the king, his subjects, and their descendants, and furnishing the owners of this land with a labor force that was cheap, preferably free. During the nineteenth century, the public authorities lost all control over the labor force, but the state administration preserved its despotic and military style. As a political structure at the pinnacle of the entirety of the population, it limited its action to making sure the conflicts between regional groups or antagonistic social classes didn't get so bad that they would endanger national independence.

The existence of this endemic war between the dust of the oligarchy and the rest of the population might lead us to see the sufferers as wallowing in a kind of inertia. But their vigorous resistance and power of obstruction refutes that. A people resists only actions they see as nefarious. And as far as I can tell, as they faced a people they claimed they would civilize, the oligarchs didn't actually make any effort to attain any particular goal at all. Given the inaction of this self-proclaimed elite, I am not sure what the popular masses had to oppose. The administrative institutions and local oligarchs frequently sought help from foreign institutions, including the Catholic Church, foreign banks, and the consulates. But, powerless, they watched the steady rise of the rural population. All they did in response was to formulate one policy after another that they never methodically put into practice. They were never able to either orient or counteract the advance of the popular sectors. Colonialism invented and maintained a precarious situation for the popular masses, but when that was successfully countered in Haiti during the last years of the nineteenth century, the local privileged classes couldn't escape their increasing lethargy or try and figure out new ways of practicing politics.

I interpret the retreat of the sufferers from the political realm (Moïse 2009, 387) as a project of isolating the internal sovereignty they had invented for themselves so that they could defend it against incessant attacks from the international community. Those attacks began long before this community began pressuring the Haitian state through its local consulates, as it did during the second half of the nineteenth century. Facing the passivity and lack of imagination on the part of the reigning classes, the subordinated sectors demonstrated initiative, while the governmental bureaucracy repeated itself monotonously and with discouraging irrelevance.

When I change my perspective, I can see how from 1697 to 1804 the population had no way of reproducing itself. It increased only through the acquisition, year after year, of unfortunates kidnapped from Africa through the most villainous means. "The slave trade! These words contain so many crimes! How many horrors and abominations can be found in this simple expression!" (Vastey [1814] 2013, 17)

These deportees were incorporated against their will into colonial life. They lived in conditions that until then had never been experienced by human beings, in a territory that modern colonialism is unashamed to celebrate as the richest possession in the world. Then, from 1804 to 1915, this same population—that the West wishes to see as made up of former slaves rather than former captives—multiplied fourfold through its own means. They attained a standard of living that was previously unknown to them, and better than that of the neighboring territories that were still possessed and governed by this same modern, civilized West. It is worth noting that we are talking about a Western civilization whose populations were, during this same nineteenth century, fleeing their life conditions en masse to establish themselves on new shores!

I feel called to recognize the power of this mass of descendants of deportees, and to observe how on their own they were able to move beyond the conditions of captivity and successfully establish themselves in a land and in conditions not of their own choosing. In place of a population distributed by France to various concentration camps along the plains and hills of the country, and an economic life carried out to the rhythm of cracking whips and the unstable needs of the metropolitan market, I contemplate the flourishing of garden-villages (Anglade 1982) everywhere in Haiti, and a daily life cadenced by the calendar of rural markets that functioned to fulfill the needs of the consumers and the market-women who circulated between them. I contemplate the beauty of the incontestable victory of the sovereign people.

The Misery of Colonial Empire

During the seventeenth and eighteenth centuries, the labor force of the slave made possible the movement of merchandise along the sinews of the triangular trade. The state managed this movement either through the intermediary of mercantilist commercial companies or directly through its bureaucratic functionaries. The goal of empire was to control the artificial economy of the colonial society it had produced. It had to acquire the labor energy needed for the smooth functioning of the economic activities without spending money on the production and biological reproduction of this labor.

In Africa, slave traders pursued and hunted people who, with rare exceptions, were living there peacefully. Their capture and transport to the colonies involved unspeakable humiliations. The authorities in the colony took measures to make sure that, on arrival, these prisoners were tamed so that they would be docile servants. The slave trade flourished and enriched French ports.

To force the captives into submission and convert them into something they weren't—slaves—they had to be taught to be ignorant. Both they and the host society had to be convinced that they were boundlessly stupid. This ignorance did not exist.[1] It was an image that was systematically and carefully produced through the destruction of the captives' past and their immersion in a new world that was supposed to be the only one that exists, or at least the only one that deserved to exist. The Eurocentric modern state placed the newly arrived Africans in a universe that had nothing in common with their communities of origin. It carried out a campaign of distortion and occultation against the knowledge these Africans carried with them. By removing them from their history and their world and inserting them into the plantation society, the French state forced them to visit the apocalypse. They had to get used to the absence of any logical structure or reference point.

All behavior implies knowledge. The disorientation of the captive was always sudden and destabilizing. They discovered an incomprehensible way of life and progressively realized that they were being asked to live and act like animals deprived of all reason. They had no landmarks. The fact that they seemed lost was interpreted as congenital stupidity. But it was the French state and modern colonial society that had created this chaos and submerged the captives in it. The captives had only one path to survival: an apprenticeship into the unreasonable rules of life in a plantation society. Traditionally, sociology has described this process as creolization or acculturation. Following Santos (2009, 67), we can elaborate this definition by adding that it was an apprenticeship in the knowledge and rules that operationalized the logical of modern colonialism. The functioning of slavery depended on the results of this systematic production of ignorant people.

The only way for captives to reduce the amount of torture and physical abuse they received in order to make slavery function was to understand and conform to the rules of the plantation society (Casimir 1981, 91). Above all, the development of servile reflexes became the condition of possibility for emancipation and the reduction of visible servitude (Vastey [1814] 2013, 74). Emancipation was a gift from the master and, according to the Code Noir, it served as the birth certificate of the freed slave. In this way, he gained access to French nationality. A favor granted by the colonial state and the planters was dressed up as liberty. This pretension eliminated its character as a natural right. Pirates and criminals dressed themselves up in the right to property, which included the extravagant right to possess other humans.

By granting emancipation as a gift to the slave for his good behavior, the modern colonial empire was able to control the labor force by using a submissive and docile minority as the apostles and guardians of the system. A fringe group of zealous servants installed themselves within the slave society, and in the process slavery was legitimized by its victims. The sons and daughters of slaves accepted the right of the French state and the planters to own human beings, along with its right to include lands taken from other people in its domain, to distribute and sell them, and to manage them or have them managed for its profit. The emancipated slaves invented by the property owners were in no position to question the right of the state and the planters to use and abuse their property.

There was a conflict between two incompatible knowledge systems: that which represented the interests of the imperial state, the property owners, and other free people on the one hand, and that of the captives reduced to slavery on the other. The property owners, whether white, mulatto, or black, didn't share a common universe with their human property. There was not a single origin for the social inequality shared between them. The opposition between material interests was doubled by an opposition between the basic principles that subtended knowledge itself. The property owners and their thinking property conceived of and observed the world from antagonistic perspectives.

The slave owners gained fleeting control over the Africans who were hunted and captured. But it lasted only as long as the surprise and panic created by the unbelievable experience of becoming merchandise to be trafficked. The proof is that once this initial surprise and fright had passed, the slave traders could never for a moment stop using torture or the threat of torture to terrorize their prey. The modern colonial state and its protégés took charge of making the control over the captured person permanent, and of making its conversion of a human being into merchandise seem normal and natural. By terrorizing the sufferers it had kidnapped, the French colonial empire imposed its society, way of life, language, religion, customs, history, and laws. It presented them as the only legitimate and rational forms of life, the only ones worthy of being adopted by human beings. It demanded these be embraced by those who wanted to escape the bestial condition in which its own social engineering had imprisoned them with consummate artistry.

In order to control the slaves during the time they were useful to it, the modern French state created and reproduced the invisibility of the captive person as a rights-bearing individual capable of a respectful exchange of ideas and opinions. The state didn't recognize captives, only slaves. In order to perpetuate slavery, it constantly gave birth to those who didn't exist as legal subjects or objects of solicitude. There was no question of offering them services, which would have meant interfering in the management of the colonist's private property. On the contrary, the slaves were one part of the "promptness of our help" the king and the state offered the colonists toward the "needs" of those it considered its subjects (Code Noir, Preamble).

Saint-Domingue was the Pearl of the Antilles because the slaves, who made up the vast majority of the population, were invisible, or at least not part of the modern, colonial society. The Pearl of the Antilles existed thanks to their energy and work, which was extracted by the master who was their legitimate owner, and without whom the island would have been a place of shocking poverty for the metropole. France, or more specifically the French state, didn't have and could never have the objective of guaranteeing the well-being of the slaves and their descendants. It is only thanks to this crime against humanity that France obtained and maintained its pearl.

The Master of Misery

Slave owners were the centerpiece of the colony. They were responsible for its proper functioning and the wealth it produced. The Code Noir declared the "promptness" on the part of the king in fulfilling "their needs" by regulating "the condition and quality of the slaves in said islands" in the Americas. The king's subjects experienced this royal solicitude in their daily life.

That said, the metropolitan state was part of a network that connected it to other European states. And in a century of constant rivalries with Great Britain, royal solicitude often left a lot to be desired. During certain periods of varying duration, the colonists had to organize themselves to guarantee the development of their plantations without significant support from the mother country. Among the colonists were several families of mixed blood who contributed to the territory's startling economic expansion. A number of them reached the summits of colonial society, to the extent that life in Saint-Domingue before the 1780s resembled that of Brazil or Jamaica, where wealthy people of mixed race enjoyed the same prestige and preeminence as white colonists (Garrigus 2006, 7).

After the defeat in the Seven Years' War, however, France's administrators and metropolitan colonists took action to alter this situation and forced the society to adopt a configuration that was closer to that of the U.S. South and Louisiana. Families that between 1770 and 1780 were part of the colonial elite found themselves discriminated against and subjected to severe humiliations. This elite was integrated into both the local bourgeoisie and the financial and commercial bourgeoisie of European port towns. They took advantage of the social changes that led to the 1789 revolution to demand their rights. The members of this group called themselves the *American colonists* and proudly declared their belonging to the cream of Saint-Domingue's colonial society.

These facts are well known. No one doubts that the oligarchy made of these free people born of free parents included some of the most successful operators in the Pearl of the Antilles. And it is well recognized that the regrettable episode during which Ogé, Chavannes, and their companions lost their lives was the spark that set off the powder keg of colonial society. What is less often discussed is that at the same time the oligarchy of planters of color and emancipated slaves proudly circulated among the most prosperous levels of colonial society, they also earned the reputation as the local group that was the most ferocious in its exploitation of the slaves. The master-slave relationship was not just a characteristic of the connection between the former metropole and colony or between whites and blacks. It was at the heart of the exchanges between the traditional oligarchies and the mass labeled *newly freed*.

It was the duty of every slave owner—black, mixed-race, or white—to extract the labor energy of the captives, control their existence, and deny their knowledge. They removed them from their own history to introduce them into a universe that refused to accept them as people and therefore had to make sure they had no way of retaking control over their bodies, their time, and their spirits. Whether black, mixed-race, or white, the property owners profited from the misery of the enslaved. What defined them as social actors was their irrepressible superiority complex and the deep disdain they professed for the unfortunate sufferers. These attitudes were not inscribed in skin color, and they weren't extinguished with the proclamation of Haitian independence.

The union that gave power to the 1804 revolution, then, has implications that are difficult to erase. The morgue created by the former slave owners didn't disappear after this date. It was not replaced by a sense of guilt. In fact, it is more reasonable to conclude that the resentment of former members of the police forces and militia was sharpened by the fact that the former captives used their increased power to silence the voices of the self-proclaimed landowners, or at least to prevent them from turning the distance that separated them from the collective of the sufferers into an economic advantage.

The Unfortunate Sufferers

The word *malere* (unfortunate sufferers) is the generic term used in Kreyòl to name persons who live a precarious existence. These include the slave and cultivator, but also the worker and artisan, as well as the widow, orphan, and sick. It was the first history of Haiti written by a Haitian, Baron de Vastey's *Le système colonial dévoilé* (1814), which suggested the centrality of this concept to me. Vastey uses the term nearly ninety times in the one hundred pages of the work. But two hundred years later, the expression still identifies the majority of the population and remains a key concept in popular knowledge.

As is the case in French, the word evokes the absence of a connection between the state or status of the person (their free will, history, desires, courage) and the reality of their daily life. It suggests that a deplorable accident has created a situation in which the victim is powerless. Misery doesn't affect the victim's essence or the definition of who they are. It certainly doesn't imply an attitude of resignation. The term suggests taking stock of an inconvenient situation, and the will to suffer through it with autonomy, dignity, and pride. The victim maintains his or her right to respect and earn admiration for showing imperturbability in the face of adversity.[2] While personal effort is indispensable, it isn't determinant in the reversal of fortune. The end of suffering is awaited as a different and happy possibility, but it is just as unexpected and unpredictable as suffering itself. Only constant vigilance makes it possible to seize relief from suffering. This attitude in the face of misery is so profoundly anchored that a person who is complimented for some significant achievement might respond, with false modesty, "Malè pas mal"— "Misery is always possible." In other words: I was lucky.

This concept of misery and the unfortunate sufferer opens up onto a universe situated outside of time. One doesn't escape misery gradually. The understanding of this condition implies a stable way of life maintained by conviviality among the collective of the unfortunate. Harmonious interpersonal relationships sustain this way of being. And it is very unlikely anyone will escape it in the foreseeable future. After all, material success and its passing effects have all the same fortuitous and fleeting characteristics as misery. Like bad luck, good fortune shouldn't impact the interface with other people. A person's way of life can always be modified suddenly, with no apparent reason. It is a good idea not to depend too much on individual performance. Given the fragility of the unfortunate sufferer, a little bit of luck is essential for any happy outcome.

In my opinion, this concept preserves the memory of enslavement even as it protects the unfortunate from the trap of emancipation. The granting of liberty by the master shouldn't modify the relationships of solidarity that united the recipient of the benevolence and their comrades in misfortune. These relationships offered protection from potential reversals in a context where those who were promoted had no control over public institutions. But protecting oneself from the trap of emancipation did not mean refusing it. That would have been absurd. The point is not to internalize its premises, which aim to modify the relationships of solidarity and reciprocity with all the other unfortunate sufferers. In a word, it is important to understand that at base, the objective of individual emancipation contradicts the collective interests of the community of sufferers. There were therefore two definitions of emancipation in colonial society: that of the colonists, who used it as a reward for zealous servants, and that of the captives, who conceived of it as a form of good luck that didn't modify the fundamentally perverse nature of the regime.

The *bossale* captives were on the bottom rung of the ladder that potentially led to freedom. They were the prototype for the unfortunate sufferer. Nothing they had done previously, nothing about their lineages, could justify their misery.[3] It is not surprising that their state as slaves remained inexplicable, because it was constructed on the basis of a supposed absence of history. The authors of the Code Noir could construct this status only by silencing their individual histories. Those who produced this code "threw the black slave on the docks, at the end of the ports of Saint-Domingue. . . . A black person in the Caribbean came from elsewhere and was a slave, that was all" (Sala-Molins 1987, 7). The captives' resistance refused the West's image of the slave that modernity had invented so that it could admire itself and its own development. While the West took pleasure in its self-adoration, the prisoners reconstructed their liberty, rooted in their own history, and refused the dominant attempt to empty that history. The prisoners celebrated their own beauty, which they renewed by surpassing their misery.

The captive persons the Code Noir wished to transform into slaves could not be imprisoned or placed in chains, because they were invisible to the dominant system. More specifically, the *bossale* person—in contrast to the black person, the opposite of the white—could not be named in French legislation, because that legislation could not imagine that anyone could not be Christian and Western. The legislation's victims, meanwhile, also could not understand or conceive of the institutionalized cruelty put in place by the Code Noir, the code of their misery. In rejecting this collection of supposed laws and the principles they were derived from, the captive vomited up the modern, colonial state. Newly disembarked, the *bossale* appeared as a condensed form of the unfortunate sufferer: an innocent sufferer. After a period of creolization, she acquired an understanding of the signal and revolting cruelty of those who claimed to possess her.

The modern, colonial state and the national public administration clothed the sufferers they created in a variety of castoffs. The woke captive understood this: she was first a *slave* or a *deserter*, then an *African* or *cultivator*, then a *citizen attached to the land*, an *outlaw*, a *vagabond*. The public order created these denominations, which enameled legislation and official discourse. But the political system could not seize and manage these characters they invented, precisely because these definitions had no impact on the people dressed up in this way. The names didn't influence them to modify their behavior in any permanent way. They spent their lives dodging the consequences of the images projected onto them.

The victim of misfortune didn't produce her condition, and she saw a change in her situation as an act of chance. The objective of rational behavior was less to modify what was beyond reach than it was to defend and protect oneself from imponderables. From this angle, the goal of the education or creolization of the *bossale* and the unfortunate sufferers was not to teach them the norms, principles, and rules of the dominant system. Instead, the point was to teach peers to manage their relationships within the constraints placed on them by this collection of external directives that victimized them. The militant actions of the sufferers did not aim to change a situation that was outside their control, but rather to reinforce solidarity in the face of this situation of persistent misfortune, and to create stable life conditions for themselves.

From this perspective, the captive and the contemporary sufferer both define themselves as those who can *use* the dominant system—manipulate it—but without altering their deepest being. Above all, they perceive themselves as those who avoid *serving* the system, or allowing themselves to be manipulated by the system, at all costs. The emancipated and intermediary classes tended to reject this attitude of distancing (*delinking*, in Walter Mignolo's term), and transformed themselves into servants of slavery. This road ended with them allowing themselves to be possessed, converted into prisoners of the white public (Vastey [1814] 2013, 14). They could choose to invest themselves deeper and deeper into the cruelty incarnated by the public authorities. But they could never guarantee that they wouldn't, at some point, end up its victims. The popular wisdom, meanwhile, encouraged the building of a door to escape through in case things got tough.

The Public Authorities in Plantation Societies

What is power in the plantation Caribbean? The attitude of the majority of the population in the face of this external, unreasonable violence forces us to ask the question. The plantation, after all, is not Caribbean. It is, as John Stuart Mill noted in the eighteenth century, a European institution implanted in the region. This point was made in the 1795 debates on the Law of April 4, cited earlier.

I distinguish between three types of plantation societies, according to the circumstances of their implantation. The first comprise classic, or total, plantation societies (Beckles 1984). Barbados and Martinique were the prototypes of these kind of societies. They were founded during the seventeenth-century period of mercantilist piracy. The second type is the hybrid plantation society, represented by Saint-Domingue, which transformed the typical plantation during the first half of the eighteenth century. The third type includes the late plantation societies, such as Guyana, Trinidad, Cuba, Puerto Rico, and the Dominican Republic, which emerged in the eighteenth century and flourished at the apogee of capitalist imperialism.

In all plantation societies, the captives lived at the mercy of the colonial power structure. The efforts they made on their own behalf aimed to expand their opportunities and profit from them as much as possible. The vulnerability and the cohesion of empire came together to create a dynamic that Walter Rodney described in this way in 1981:

> Each day in the life of a member of the working population was a day in which there was both struggle and accommodation. Struggle was implicit in the application of labor power to earn wage and grow crops, while accommodation was a necessary aspect of survival within a system in which power was so comprehensively monopolized by the planter class. Some persons resisted more tenaciously and consistently than others; but there was no simple distinction between those who resisted and those who accommodated. Moments of struggle and moments of compromise appeared within the same historical conjuncture, but ultimately, resistance rather than accommodation asserted itself as the principal aspect of this contradiction. (Rodney 1981, 151)

In 1984 Hilary Beckles (1984, 53) began his analysis of the seventeenth and eighteenth centuries in Barbados by citing this reflection by Walter Rodney about nineteenth-century Guyana. But unlike in Barbados, Guyanese society was governed by an empire at the height of monopolist capitalism, with two centuries of experience managing agro-industrial slavery. The Guyanese population after the emancipation of the slaves included workers from the villages of the country, immigrants from Barbados, indentured laborers freshly disembarked from India and those who had decided not to return home at the end of their contracts, as well as indentured laborers from Portugal. But the dynamic of accommodation and resistance remained unchanged from the beginning of the seventeenth century to the end of the nineteenth. Barbados was home to the first of the modern plantation colonies. Its population, almost completely Creole, contrasted with that of the plural society in Guyana, the jewel of imperialism.

Historians often privilege the observation of concrete actions on the part of the social groups in a given place and time. But in his *Una espitemología del Sur* (2009), Santos pulls out two broader processes that explain the contradiction between the forms of accommodation and resistance demanded by the context of slavery. He distinguishes between the process of learning about the rules of the plantation system and that of elaborating freedom-knowledge that makes it possible to surpass this system (2009, 63). During the first process, the captives moved toward the integration and assimilation that allowed them to accommodate themselves to the plantation society through creolization or acculturation. They learned to live as slaves. The second process was one of transculturation, during which an inventory was taken of the knowledge of other workers, so that a collective search for the ways and means of satisfying the needs of all the exploited could be undertaken. To survive, the oppressed had to know the system's rules. But forms of freedom-knowledge, the *reinvention of knowledge*, were indispensable for any practice of resistance based on the support of social groups formed through solidarity. Facing a system whose tentacles were global, the oppressed developed a coexistence between compromise with the rules, or at least respect for them, and a process of resistance and struggle for self-emancipation.

This duality is particularly visible when we examine the last decades of the history of Saint-Domingue. An unprecedented crisis within the imperial power's internal structure and its relationships with rival metropoles created deep fissures that resulted in upheaval in the colony. Saint-Domingue's geography was more like that of Guyana than the traditional plantation islands, and it was home to territories that were contiguous but distinct in their organization. Maroon, or *doko*, societies neighbored the plantations, and captives and maroons exchanged information, weapons, and people. *Bossales* were the majority in both spaces, imposing their approach on the Creoles. To make matters worse, the masters, mirroring the metropole, divided themselves into factions and coteries—republicans and royalists; wealthy whites, poor whites, and people of color; residents and absentee owners. Fighting each other, they turned to their slaves to try and earn the respect of their enemies of the moment.

Two decades of upheaval in the colonial empire and an inability to create order in the slave society created a context where processes of accommodation and resistance on the part of the captives materialized with increasing acuteness and visibility. That is why, in 1981, I argued that there existed two distinct knowledge systems that *typically* were carried by Creole captives and *bossale* captives, respectively. I called one of these knowledge systems an *oppressed culture*, because it was the prisoner of a local dominant culture (Casimir 1981b).

The Hobbesian situation in colonial Saint-Domingue during the last decades of the eighteenth century made clear the limitations of a colonial administration that believed itself to be, and wished to be perceived as, all-powerful. The situation was different in the British plantation colonies, where, as Walter Rodney has shown, power was fully monopolized by the planters. Still, Ciro Cardoso highlights a key fact that historians of these colonies have sometimes overlooked, though it was evoked in Eric Williams's classic *Capitalism and Slavery*. "The most productive idea in Eric Williams's *Capitalism and Slavery* is that which the author develops the least. It is in the chapter called "The Slaves and Slavery." Contrary to what the population, and even well-informed people, thought, at the time when the political crisis was deepening in Great Britain, it was the slaves themselves who constituted the most dynamic and powerful social force in the colonies" (Cardoso 1974, 203).

On December 25, 1799, Napoléon issued a proclamation requiring Toussaint to write on his flags that only the French people recognized the liberty and the rights of the blacks. Toussaint responded: "We are free today only because we are the strongest. The Consul has maintained slavery in Martinique and Bourbon island; we would therefore be slaves if he were strongest" (Moïse 2001, 35).

The contexts analyzed by Eric Williams, Hilary Beckles, and Walter Rodney highlight the necessity for slaves and indentured laborers to adapt themselves to plantation life. But in Saint-Domingue it was clear that the French metropole and the planters—particularly the people of color—unsuccessfully consented to major financial sacrifices in order to try and save their sinking ship. In other words, their monopoly over the public administration, far from erasing the power of the oppressed, was itself checked because the oppressed were powerful and, from day to day, defied them more and more boldly.

In Saint-Domingue and throughout the Caribbean, the oppressed confronted brute force, and the power of weapons, with resistance nourished by their intelligence and their knowledge of the context—their freedom-knowledge. This allowed them to constrain the colonial empire, at least in certain spaces. They exercised their limited sovereignty in their daily life. For this very reason, resistance was inseparable from compromise. In the case of Saint-Domingue, a series of favorable circumstances temporarily made the power of resistance greater than the forces put in place by the metropole. This enabled the captives to erupt into public life.

This process was similar everywhere, but varied according to circumstances that didn't depend on the Caribbean itself. Plantation Barbados emerged at the dawn of mercantilism, Saint-Domingue was initiated into modernity during the transition to liberal capitalism, and Guyana confronted nineteenth-century imperialism. So we cannot analyze the forms of public administration in the Caribbean without paying attention to the specificities of the exploited class. These two social forces defined the political structure that we call the state, whatever the public administration and its bureaucrats thought about their own monopoly over power. The monopoly of power on the part of the imperial forces was more normative than it was actualized or real. That made the Haitian Revolution possible. The British Empire, on the other hand, had the means to enforce their norms. Its colonies didn't experience a revolution like that which unfolded in Haiti.

The plantation societies of the Caribbean are the creation of modern Europe. Whether they are colonies or independent countries, the international order that surrounds them determines their material well-being. Using one mechanism or another, this international order extracts what we produce through our efforts, and leaves us with only what it determines corresponds to our needs. In the eighteenth century Great Britain and France decided that the territories in the Caribbean were of capital importance. In the nineteenth century, however, their insignificance was incontestable (Williams 1970, 409).

Political behavior in the Caribbean comes down to being ready to profit from opportunities when, and if, they present themselves. In the midst of the confusion that characterized the end of the eighteenth century, Haiti replaced Saint-Domingue, and its plantation economy vanished once and for all. In the neighboring colonies, between 1815 and 1894, exports from the plantation colonies increased. But the general emancipation of the slaves took place between these dates. In Barbados, without any migration into the colony, sugar production doubled in 1861 (Williams 1970, 367). In 1894, exports were six times greater, and comparable to that produced by the industrial progress of Cuba, Trinidad, and British Guyana (Williams 1970, 367), despite the fact that Barbados had not absorbed the technological changes that characterized these late plantation societies. In the absence of acute productivity, it was the working population, whether enslaved or not, that paid the cost of development alone.

Stanley Engerman and B. W. Higman take note of the considerable increase in migration after the end of slavery in the British colonies in 1834. Late plantation societies, which were much more productive, attracted laborers from the classic plantation societies. The authors estimate that between 1861 and 1901, thirty-one thousand people left Barbados, about a quarter of the population of the island in 1861. They add that after 1901 "migration in Barbados further accelerated, and the annual level of the first two decades of the twentieth century was over three times that of the last four decades of the nineteenth century" (1997, 68).

Whether Saint-Domingue was the Pearl of the Antilles or not had nothing to do with the life conditions of 99 percent of the population. Haitians were the poorest people in the Americas at the very moment when France exhibited its pearl as the model for modern development.

The Order of the Public Administration in the Haitian Nineteenth Century

From the moment it was installed in Saint-Domingue with the Treaty of Ryswick in 1697, the modern/colonial public administration had only one period where it deviated slightly from its itinerary: the twenty years from 1801, when Toussaint's Constitution was promulgated, until the suicide of King

Henry in 1820. With the exception of these two decades, this administration conserved a despotic structure and political composition of deep consistency. Toussaint's government drove Napoléon crazy by juggling with independence. Christophe's government distinguished itself from that of the republic in the South through its policies of reparation for the harms caused by slavery and its attempt to create means of communication between the two sectors of the population. But all three regimes, of Toussaint, Christophe, and Pétion/Boyer, took on the prerequisites of a despotic public administration, first enunciated in the preamble of the Code Noir—namely, that in the colony the king had subjects and their slaves. We can translate this into contemporary vocabulary by arguing that from its implantation to the present day, the modern/colonial state has absorbed two groups into the institutionalized political system: French citizens and their descendants and foreigners, the *gens du dehors*, or outsiders (Barthélémy 1989).

The plantation economy depended on the existence of a canyon between these two groups in order to function. After independence the model remained unchanged, and the improvised social structure that was imposed from the heights of its externally inspired hegemony preserved its immutable character. Starting with the Treaty of Ryswick, the French inaugurated a despotic administration in which the victory of the sword and the cross were presented as the source of all law and all justice. The order of the public authorities, or the reason of state, guided the management of the population. In this kind of formation there were no citizens, no political rights, no rights of man (Kriegel 2003 65).

The order of the public authorities defined itself without taking into account the opinions or feelings of the masses of the slaves or the cultivators who replaced them. After general emancipation, economic life demanded a form of slavery based on militarized agriculture, dependent on one form or another form of open and permanent coercion. But this militarization had functional demands and could not do without an army or a professional police force. Since the state administration couldn't fund these during the nineteenth century, it accommodated itself to handing over fractions of its central power to provincial caudillos, with all the hazards this kind of regionalization entailed. During this era of the apogee of European imperialism, the public authorities found themselves incapable of relaunching a modern economic expansion. They had to negotiate with the counter-plantation economy as they awaited the arrival of the twentieth century. Only outside assistance enabled them, in 1915, to maintain and arm a professional military that functioned on a national level, and therefore to stabilize the political system by pointing it in the direction desired by the colonial empires.

The particularities of the development of the public authorities in Saint-Domingue were the result of well-known and codified historical accidents. The citizens of the colony were besieged by the armies of rival European powers and by their slaves who had risen up. This upended the political and social structure as a whole.

Theoretically, the general emancipation of 1793 meant that all the foreigners living in captivity—that is, almost the entire population—became as French as their former masters. But the compromises of the 1801 Constitution and of Toussaint's regime couldn't secure the development of the plantation economy without leaving a door open to some version of the slave trade. The governments of Henry Christophe and Jean-Pierre Boyer confronted the same problem, and complained about the lack of laborers. These impasses reinforced the despotic character of the state apparatus, independently of its ideological directions. To make matters worse, the political choices of these accomodationist regimes were constrained and shaped by the conflicts between the imperial sea powers of the era.

This explains the policy of Napoléon Bonaparte, who, as he was about to impose himself on much of Europe, decided to end all prevarication with Saint-Domingue by abrogating the decree of the abolition of slavery, decreeing the deportation of all property-owning citizens who were not white, and ordering extermination of the newly freed so that the island could be repopulated.[4] In the wake of the general insurrection, the re-establishment and success of a plantation economy demanded the renewal of the labor force, either by the sword, by forcing assent through torture, or by preventing access to land.

Haiti's rural police codes make clear that there was a single public administration in the national territory, along with two parallel societies. There was no professional army to overcome the canyon between these societies and to force one to submit to the other. So the plantation economy died from exhaustion. But there remain unanswered questions: Why, throughout the nineteenth century, were those in control of the public authorities incapable of understanding the foundational characteristics of the disjointed system they were trying to control? How could they not see that another economy was flourishing around them, despite the foundational division, and that it had emerged as an alternative to the modern capitalist system? This recognition of reality would have been all the more logical given that their social group, which wasn't actually dominant, didn't make up even a tenth of the population.

Compared to other plantation societies of the region, Saint-Domingue stood out for its absence of social services and the lack of efforts with regard to the cultural homogenization of the population. The indifference of the public authorities to the well-being of the population never changed throughout the nineteenth century. It wasn't linked to the poverty of the country, for the feast of resources that had made it the Pearl of the Antilles during the nineteenth century had increased rather than reduced this poverty.

How should we think about poverty in Haiti in the nineteenth century? We can't do so through a comparison to the other islands in the region. They didn't experience independence, the payment of debts, or a blockade; nevertheless, they found it impossible to feed their populations and prevent them from migrating. Caribbean poverty is the result of a mode of human exploitation through the plantation economy. And we also need to ask why so many Europeans left their continent during the same period, flooding into the rest of the world. Where did all these destitute people come from, the tens of millions escaping the opulent societies of the West?

Only a rare few, such as Victor Schoelcher (1843a), alluded to the modest quality of life of the Haitian oligarchy. They found themselves incapable of relaunching the modern enterprises of the previous century and doing what those whom they imitated proudly had done in the eighteenth century. They weren't able to follow in the footsteps of the important role played by Julien Raimond alongside Toussaint Louverture. The Haitian oligarchies ended the nineteenth century by resigning as significant economic actors. Unable to recognize the failure of their policy, they preferred closing their eyes to the power relations that subtended the local structures of power.

The founder of the republic and the oligarchs who joined his camp after the death of Christophe seemed satisfied with the way land was distributed among different groups in Haiti. They never had to make any pronouncements on the subject. And, from the Treaty of Ryswick to the U.S. occupation, the Haitian people they faced never demanded landed property or spectacularly invaded the large properties. They only nibbled at them, little plot by little plot.

From my angle of interpretation, I cannot peremptorily affirm that the former captives had a conception of land owning that differed from that of the planters. I do take note, nevertheless, of the fact that during the crisis that preceded independence, the oligarchs and colonial authorities sacrificed their slaves to save their rights to land ownership. As the crisis moved toward its denouement, the captive population took measures to protect their labor force without entering into a conflict with the property owners, on a terrain where the latter were particularly sensitive. G. Paul (1836) underlined this fact emphatically, and I will come back to this topic to analyze its implications later. For the moment, I take note of the fact that with regards to land ownership, the collective will was not set in motion, but that the same people who passively accepted the apparent monopoly over landed property rose up as one to protect personal liberty.

Madiou (1847 2:322) and Ardouin (1853, 2:361) wrote that it was impossible to allow the *Guinean* forces (i.e., the African system) to take control over the insurrection. But there is a big distance between that and not even trying to negotiate with them or institutionalize their participation in the process of production. Pétion's letters to Generals Marion and Beauvais reveal the superiority complex on the part of the large landowners of the South, and Gérin and Rivière-Hérard's declarations expose, without reservation, what Pétion argued cautiously. The oligarchs preferred negotiating control of their country with the former metropole over sitting down with the flock of unfortunate sufferers who surrounded them to talk about the labor regime or liberty.

Pétion's eagerness to throw himself into the arms of the French can logically be explained by his fear in the face of the rise of the *Guinean* traditions. In the colony of Saint-Domingue, starting in 1789, the public authorities no longer had the means to impose the ways of life described in their instructions, or to take the necessary measures for the reproduction of the labor force either through the slave trade or locally. Their own way of life, therefore, was in danger. The cultural homogenization Madiou observed long before independence became the norm, which explains the dilemma the oligarchy of people of color faced because of the universal ascendancy of an African vision of social life. As the historian notes, during the crisis that led to independence, "many of the mixed-bloods, who as a group made up a tenth of the population, were nearly identical to the blacks with regards to customs, habits and aspirations" (Madiou 1847, 5:107).

Writing about the end of the period I am analyzing here, Jean-Price Mars echoed Madiou in a long and beautiful paragraph. Here, in my opinion, he synthesized the concept of the unfortunate sufferer:

> If the same belief leads the bourgeois little by little to communion with his servant in the same fear of the unknown, because unusual things such as grilled corn, blighted leaves, and other ingredients have been gathered in his courtyard whilst someone in his entourage is stricken by illness or death; if the same imperturbable optimism galvanizes the energy of everyone in the gloomy moments of discouragement because with each of us, in the elite as in the plebian, confidence in the correction of things here below by some providential intervention forms the potential for action; finally if this miracular thinking which is at the base of Haitian life and confers upon it its own identity—the mystical

tonality—if all of that is drawn from the common reservoir of ideas, sentiments, acts, gestures which constitute the moral patrimony of Haitian society, then it will be in vain for the arrogant among the elite and plebian to jibe at the joint responsibility for faults and transgressions, for dilettantist bovarism to dictate to both acts of cowardice and falsehood, for imbecilic class egotisms to trigger attitudes of antipathy and measures of ostracism—nothing will know how to prevent tales, legends, songs received from the past or created and transformed by us from being a part of ourselves, released as an exteriorization of our collective ego, no one can hinder latent or formal beliefs from the past that have been transformed, recreated by us from having been the driving elements of our conduct and having conditioned the irresistible heroism of the throng which was slaughtered in the days of glory and sacrifices for the sake of implanting Negro freedom and independence on our soil. (Price-Mars 1983, 173–174)

This observation directs our attention to the distinction between public and private life as these two spheres developed through daily life. The colonial state governed public life, but in their private life the population—both formerly emancipated and former captives—developed a response to colonialism and worked to overcome a disastrous, unpredictable, and uncontrollable imperial policy. Following Madiou and Price-Mars, I emphasize that cultural homogenization—of customs, habits, and aspirations—was not pursued by the racist and Eurocentric public authorities. It was, rather, a production carried out by the sufferers long before independence in all the corners of private life and in the services it required day to day. The despotic and segregationist political structure required the population to create for themselves the services that were lacking. The collective of the sufferers gradually absorbed those who operated the public forces—the mixed-bloods who formed a tenth of the population. This was an awkward situation for the latter, but it was one that they experienced primarily in their intimate lives, protected from the embarrassment that might have come from the gaze of outside observers.

The order put in place by the public authorities couldn't cross the thresholds into private life. The simple mercantile production of the counter-plantation monopolized agricultural economy and offered no foothold for structural dependency. The majority of the labor force was involved in this sector and the activities connected to it. The doors of the public realm were, to be sure, closed to them, but this labor force had no desire to change this world oriented toward the outside.

The oligarchs of the nineteenth century controlled the public administration. But they didn't control the country's economy. The few Francophones among them monopolized the representation of the republic on the international stage, but this did not guarantee them the influence required to transform the apparatus of production. In the meantime, the counter-plantation and local culture confronted the great economic crises of the late nineteenth century alone, and without much success. That is where the feeling that the Haitian state totally failed comes from. It is the result of a set of observations made from above, looking down, from the outside looking in. The oligarchs did not serve as an effective channel of communication between imperialism and the population.

The Power of the Sovereign

In the colony of Saint-Domingue, and in a general sense, in any exploitation colony, the captives, the emancipated, and the colonists did not struggle against the abuses of the metropole together, in pursuit of common goals. That makes it difficult to gain a clear idea of the behavior and feelings shared by the oppressed population on the basis of the observations of the oligarchs and their intellectuals. The slaves of the plantation societies adapted, for better or worse, to the power that dominated them. The path traced by the Christian West was their only avenue to survival. But we pay less attention to the fact that this path was judged and shaped by the captives, and we often consider them stripped of critical sensibility. But it was on the basis of an evaluation of their experiences that they developed a local culture, properly Caribbean.

In the first pages of *Le système colonial dévoilé* (1814), the Baron de Vastey recounts the well-known episode reported by Garcilaso de la Vega involving the indigenous leader Hatuey, who declared he didn't want to go to heaven because he might encounter Spanish people. Haiti's contemporary thinkers have all read Jean Fouchard's infuriating descriptions of the introduction of Africans into the plantation society and the range of tortures used to guarantee the success of their tragic initiation, their *seasoning period*. Torture assured the good functioning of this "total institution" (Smith 1967, 229). The captives had no way to protect themselves from the norms and principles of this Gehenna they had been shipwrecked in, and we often forget to ask what they thought of those who presumed to be their masters, and of their culture. It doesn't cross our minds to think about what our ancestors did when faced with even the smallest opportunity to detach themselves from the social relationships of this kind of madness. But if we do explore this, then the fate of the deserter (of the fugitive, the maroon) becomes the center of reflection, for every captive carried one deep inside themselves.

In 1814 the Baron de Vastey provided a meticulous description of the feelings of repulsion and indignation incited among the Africans by the colonial way of life. The interpersonal relationships imposed by the colonists on their victims nauseated the *bossales*, for whom it was unimaginable that their pigmentation had created a set of essential differences between them and other people. Based on this initial aversion, the new arrivals developed their own idea of Western culture and of those who carried and promoted it. Vastey laid out all the erudition he had to call on to avoid being unjust toward Westerners as a whole, given the sampling of whites he had before his eyes in Saint-Domingue:

> Can I paint all the horrors of slavery for the eyes of my readers? Shall I
> go and exhume the corpses of my unfortunate compatriots, those the
> colonists buried alive, to interrogate their ashes and shock all human
> beings with the horrible tales of the crimes of these monsters? . . . Often
> I have asked myself, what rights did these ex-colonists have to torture
> the unfortunate slaves? What? Is there, in this world as there is in the
> next, a race of executioners destined to torture human beings? Are
> the ex-colonists on earth what demons are in hell? . . . This height of
> audacity and cruelty fills my soul with indignation! . . . Let me stop.
> I was going to curse Europe and the authors of this terrible invention,
> even generous Sismonde de Sismondi, Wilberforce, Clarkson, and all
> you sensitive and virtuous Europeans. ([1814] 2013, 91–92, 48)

Unfortunately, the collective of the captives didn't share the erudition of the man who tutored Henry Christophe's children. So it is hard to imagine what the mass of the workers in the colonies thought of the colonists and of modern, enslaving Europe.[5] Among all the laborers and especially among new arrivals, the unavoidable need to know and master the culture of the plantation society in order to survive coexisted with a profound desire to distance themselves as much as possible from the values and principles that inspired the Christian West to create this bizarre society into which they had been brought. From the moment one was introduced into the plantation system, the urgency of protecting oneself from the notions that inspired the Europeans depended on the ability to express oneself freely, at least in one's deep interior world. But the preservation of the mental health of the captive also depended on the unavoidable necessity of discovering some collective means of expression that differed from the reigning savagery. Forced to survive and to live at the same time, the captive had only one possible exit: going in the opposite direction, delinking themselves from the plantation system by inventing a way of re-existing (Mignolo 2012).

The Response to Suffering

According to the Code Noir, the centerpiece of the architecture of Saint-Domingue, the colonial laborer was not a person within the state, the only political structure the metropole considered legitimate. He began to exist, but as a minor partner, only on the day he was emancipated, which Article 57 of the code considered his date of birth. Before this birth into French law, he had no civil status and was not part of society. When the 1793 decree of general emancipation rendered the Code Noir moot, the colonial administration issued agricultural regulations that specifically operationalized his inferiority as an active citizen. Haitian governments developed these regulations into rural police codes, and an entire chapter of the juridical history of the country consecrated his status as a second-class citizen. J. Saint-Amand underlines the fact that Law No. 3 of the Rural Code of 1823 "violated common law, and placed those who made contracts (the cultivators or agricultural workers) under a kind of legal tutelage" (1872, 12).

Of course, the observer isn't required to consider the Code Noir and the regulations that emanated from it to actually be the basis for a society, or a state. When I carry out my own research within the confines created by the social categories invented by the agents of the colonial and national socio-economic dynamic, I imprison myself within the philosophy that guides them. On the other hand, I can rediscover the true contours of society by moving closer to the categories excluded by the legal apparatus invented by the conquerors. In doing so, I grab hold of interpretive tools that allow me to identify the reasons for the norms developed in these other spaces. This enables me to situate the power to create human groups within the social actors themselves, and the ways they operated through daily exchange with one another. I focus on the very practices the legal codes sought to destroy. As a researcher, I cannot confuse the objectives of the colonists with reality, and I certainly cannot endorse those objectives.

With this new focus, I take away the power empire grants itself to invent new life on its own terms. Instead, I grant that power to the autonomous social actors who did what they could to survive from day to day despite the predispositions and dispositions of the constituted powers. With this gesture, my research arms itself with the tools necessary to perceive the structuring of the universe that gradually emerged in response to the inhuman exploitation validated by the laws in force. Beyond the creation of the normative categories that flowed from the Code Noir, I discover the counterpower of the sufferers, the difficult path of their negotiations, as well as the nimbleness with which they seized the opportunities that all too rarely were offered them.

This reading treats the foundational social categories the colonial system sought to implant as projects that failed because of the stubborn perseverance of the oppressed. The colonial categories were not palpable, obvious, indisputable realities, capable of creating a large-scale direction to society simply because they existed. They were the result of a particular reading of society. The economic success of the Pearl of the Antilles certainly proves the extent to which France profited from the implementation of these categories. But this success should not obfuscate the rise of contestation and the promotion of currents that opposed the system, which required the colonial administration to deploy a colossal military force to stabilize this artificial society under construction, without success. The social groups that burgeoned through spontaneous generation grew quickly, and the expansion of a structure of interdependent classes endowed with a basic reproductive dynamic was definitely not the result of common denominators put in place by the dominant system. The categories promoted by Louis XIV didn't encompass the entire society of Saint-Domingue. And this society was not abnormal simply because it took a different path than that imagined by the Sun King.

While it lasted, the confinement of the captives established an insurmountable inequality between them and their owners. This forced disequilibrium neither erased nor reduced the resistance on the part of the victims. The fact that the repressive machine was on constant alert proves this. But there was no way to predict that during the conflicts, generals from the established colonial army—a proslavery army—would end up uniting with rebellious captives, setting in motion the final phase of the struggle for independence. This union and opposition did not emanate from the logical economic and social interests of the social categories of the plantation society. They had foundations that were imperceptible from the perspective of the empire's angle of vision.

The *bossale* was a witness to, and privileged carrier of, what the indigenous people of South America called the catastrophe, or *Pachakuti*. He lived the apocalypse in his flesh. The notions used by the Christian West to control the captives, and to control the entire universe—authority, natural resources, economy, knowledge, gender (Mignolo 2005)—besieged the niche they built to guarantee themselves a bit of mental health. Every day, they had to expose the lies used to enslave them.

The *bossales* disembarked in Saint-Domingue, and more generally in the Americas, literally naked and isolated, individuals who were absolutely vulnerable. They had no connections to draw on. They were stalked, terrorized, trembling with fear and with no institutional recourse. They had to experiment and invent for themselves everything that might help them survive, including the possibility of solidarity with the companions in misfortune they had just encountered and discovered. Nothing—especially not the whip—united them with their masters.

The indigenous peoples of the continent and the Jews during the Exodus suffered in groups, and as a result could depend on and comfort one another. The *bossales*, in contrast, were inserted into a structured society as powerless witnesses who even had to reinvent their tools of observation. Their advantage, and probably their only one, was that they didn't live through the defeat and destruction of the universe they had come from. They didn't experience the unspeakable sufferings and humiliations of watching the spectacle of the installation of foreigners in their lands, with all the arrogance and haughtiness of the all-powerful.

Ripped from their world, the *bossales* could still imagine, at least in their phantasms, those they had left behind developing normally or possibly recovering from a lost battle. They carried, in their baggage, the memory that somewhere a family survived, that there was a lineage and a nation that they could dream was proud, strong, and even prosperous: the *lwa* of *Ginen*. These were precisely the *lwa* of *Ginen* that the social sciences don't yet dare think about—following the path indicated by Kate Ramsey (2011)—as the laws of *Ginen*, laws where merchant slavery and its promised apocalypse have no place. The social groups these *bossales* created in America did not share the experience of the collapse of a way of thinking, a way of seeing the world and the lifestyle that sustained this knowledge (Rey 1998).

This set of memories, though fragmented, formed the backdrop for all the ordeals experienced by the *bossales*, which to them seemed a series of accidents, events that were painful but random and didn't derive from any rational principle: misfortunes. Their innovations opened up onto a future, however precarious it might be, that was not superimposed on mourning for nation and culture that had been degraded beyond anything the human spirit could imagine. The cultures of Haiti and the Caribbean were born of American experiences, and they didn't carry the burden of communal defeat and irreparable apocalypse.

The *bossales* survived by creolizing themselves. They carried a consciousness of the scope of their suffering. They hid the horror they felt in the face of their misfortune, which was always experienced suddenly because it was empty of all logic, behind their creolized knowledge so that they could operationalize their potential for captive rebellion. Their forms of mutiny shaped the experiences of those who were subjugated and educating themselves to survive. In the end, they reproduced themselves as Creole captives, a merchandise to be sold, but one with a double function. They became double-edged swords.

Among these astutely creolized individuals, the masters chose some to be drivers who were put in charge of distributing and overseeing the rhythm of plantation labor (Rey 1998, 359). In order to fulfill this task, these drivers were given certain privileges, and masters tolerated a certain flexibility in the way they managed their own time and movement. But it was precisely these characters, the cornerstones of the system of exploitation—among those responsible for the splendor of the Pearl of the Antilles—who organized the conspiracy that set fire to the powder keg of the Northern Plain and enabled the forms of contestation developed in the context of isolated and dispersed rural plantations to ignite. It makes sense to read the history of Haiti while keeping in mind that the Bois Caïman ceremony was developed and planned by creolized individuals, by Creoles.

The image of this ceremony communicates the absence of mourning for vanquished civilizations and cultures, instead demonstrating an optimistic will in the face of what the future has to offer. The oath takers of Boïs Caïman compare their God advantageously to the God of the whites. Their God protects them, so they can throw themselves into struggle confidently: "Our God listens to us from high in the clouds and sees the injustices the whites commit against us. The God of the whites pushes them to crime." It makes it easier to understand the meaning of the oath if we replace God with *law* or *lwa*. The argument it presented was not derived from the contents of the metropolitan discourse (Cugoano 1787), and it was not directed to the colonists, but rather to the captives. It presented their operational cultural values: their gods (their *laws* or *lwa*) are alive, and victory is possible. The viability of the insurrection that the Creole leaders derived from these values was based on a mastery of the dominant culture that was sufficient to keep the power of the colonists in check long enough to negotiate on the basis of the demands of the oppressed community.

The collective of the captives moved ahead in full autonomy, without thinking about independence within the schema of modern and colonial social organization, that of the nation-state. Their experience led to them to distance themselves as much as possible from this structure, which had been the key to their oppression and exploitation, and to try to avoid its oversight over their communal life. In 1791 they still identified with their ethnic origins, but they gradually fused into the Haitian nation as they reabsorbed the differences that separated them during the period of the insurrection.

One of the specific characteristics of the Haitian nation emerged from the fact that during these struggles, individuals, foreign to one another, were forced to move closer together in order to guarantee their survival. This led them to articulate themselves into a previously nonexistent national unit. Their struggle was inseparable from the invention of a new nation and an uncompromising defense of their right to have a nation, which structured itself definitively during the nineteenth century.

That was the foundation for the radical aspect of their opposition to the oligarchs who had emerged from the colonial social structures. Their initial position made them incapable of negotiating an agreement with the representatives of the imperial state. There is ample evidence that it was the popular and intransigent spirit of the insurrection that required Toussaint Louverture's high-ranking generals and the other leaders linked to the conspiracy launched at Bois Caïman to jealously retain the threat of a scorched-earth campaign as the ultimate recourse in case of defeat.

The drivers who became the organizers of the August 1791 general insurrection all emerged as leaders of the Haitian Revolution. They served as Toussaint Louverture's high-ranking officers and represented a group of emancipated during the storms produced by the insurrection. As the crisis deepened, they were joined by the veterans of the colonial militia and police forces who at first had been part of the expeditionary army under the orders of General Leclerc. These were the traditional emancipated who respected the colonial order and came back from France with the goal of following Napoléon's orders to put an end Toussaint Louverture's autonomist tendencies. After the initial successes of this mission, Napoléon made clear his intention of re-establishing slavery and eliminating this interest group as one that could significantly influence policies. They ended up on their own, without support or resources, and in order to save their own lives they quickly had to make an opportunistic alliance with those who had served as Toussaint Louverture's high-ranking officers. Last-minute mutineers, who just a few months earlier had happily thrown themselves into the assault on Crête-à-Pierrot, they had no plan of their own separate from service to the metropole.

These veterans of the colonial militia and police forces had gained privileges based on the zeal with which they served colonialism and slavery. Once their lives had been saved after 1804, they had to invent a reason for existing and a place for themselves far from the society based on *Guinean* roots, which they repressed with a holy fervor and the vocation of Christian missionaries. But it was the power of the insurgent captives that had undergirded the negotiations that sustained the privileges gained by the members of Toussaint Louverture's high-ranking staff. Issuing directly from the society based on *Guinean* roots, these officers always remained ready to use the scorched-earth strategy that was central to the 1791 general insurrection.

The Haitian oligarchy of 1804 was bicephalous. It included the French Haitians, the emancipated of colonial mentality, and the *Ginen* Haitians, those who had created the institutional crisis (Casimir 2010, 69). The distinction between these two groups was based more on the roles they played during colonization than on the color of their skin. The newly emancipated tended to manipulate the popular classes they were closer to in order to defend their own interests, while the French Haitians tended to depend on the metropolitan authorities in pursuing the same goal. Both sectors pretended to cultivate a healthy distance from the popular classes, but the precariousness of their private lives always forced them to compromise on this.

When we reconstruct the behavior of the captives, we need to remember that individual emancipation was an exception in colonial society (Debien 1974, 369). It is therefore clear that the processes of upward social mobility offered by the plantation society couldn't have significantly influenced the behavior of captives. They saw clearly that an improvement in their situation in the midst of the slave system could emerge only from collectives of the oppressed and from the experience they had gained on the plantation, supplemented by the contributions made by recently arrived ethnicities. Their survival strategies on the plantation and the forms of defiance and contestation at their disposal did not predispose them to follow the models of power relations used during the Enlightenment to govern interpersonal relations. The conception and logic of power that they could imagine and to which they could submit themselves on their own terms could only be based on a foundational equality between the members of the communities they created and on solidarity between these communities.

The plantation and its promoters were part of the vision of the world held by Toussaint, his officers, and the mutineers from the Leclerc expedition. They had been born in this world. Especially after the British invasion, the oppressed ethnicities were conscious of the fact that the chains of slavery were forged by the international community. A victory over the French was one clash in a bigger and more complicated war. Pamphile de Lacroix reported that Toussaint offered a principle that posed a dilemma for both the attackers and the defenders of Crête-à-Pierrot. "The liberty of the blacks can be consolidated only through the prosperity of agriculture" (Lacroix 1819, 1:324).

The modern/colonial nation racialized human relations and invented blacks. It emancipated a few of them, and they gave birth to the mixed-bloods and people of color. The public authorities built in 1804 had a modern, liberal vision of the world, and they conceived of their role in a way that was incompatible with the social relations that the former captives developed. These guaranteed their well-being and offered a victory over their original misfortune.

From the perspective of those brought in captivity to Saint-Domingue, slaves and planters disappeared from the local geography and, along with them, laborers and capitalist entrepreneurs vanished, too. They conceived of themselves as a collective of inhabitants who were transforming themselves into a unique ethnicity or nation. The public administration and the major landowners were excluded from their world and had no control over the activities they carried out there. So the monopoly of power that the modern executive supposedly kept for itself was exercised over a potential, and perpetually renewed, void. The public authorities had no real power over the population, which took note of their own apparent omnipresence and got to work eluding these powers and following a parallel path of development.

The power of the rural population was such that it kept the objectives of both oligarchies in check. That is clear when we look at things from their perspective. Through the movements of Goman, Acaau, and later the Cacos, they evaded the rural codes and police regulations and directly defied the plantation economy. At the same time, they anchored the conditions for social negotiation and forced the intermediary oligarchs to stop representing metropolitan interests and, like Vastey, to choose the camp of the *Ginen* Haitians.

Experience and Knowledge

Mercantile slavery created an opposition between the subjects or citizens of a metropole and foreigners (Meillassoux 1998; Rey 1998; Benot 2003). This fracture had a deeper impact in Saint-Domingue, where the encounter between the majority of the foreigners and the French went back only a few decades at most. Their relationships had not sedimented by the time of the revolutionary conflagrations that followed 1789. But a significant minority of emancipated slaves—which Madiou estimated at 10 percent of the total population—had been linked with the French for nearly a century. The Creole identity of this group cannot be compared to that founded on four centuries of relations between the Spanish and the indigenous nations of "Latin" America. While they kept their distance from the captives who had just disembarked, the mass of Creoles was too fragile as a group to allow themselves even the smallest autonomy in their relationship to France. The complexity and fluidity of the Haitian context was the result of the coexistence and interactions between these poles that were distinct rather than separate, and in fact complementary.

The privileged groups, particularly in urban areas, had the habit of judging the survival strategies of the captives on the basis of the parameters set by the colonial empire. This helped justify the civil nonexistence of the remaining 90 percent of the population. This social nonexistence is so deeply ingrained in French-language Haitian thought that there are few written reflections on the political and economic impact of this group, and particularly of their contributions to local thought. They rarely garnered attention, and were seen negatively during the period under study, and long after it.

These prejudices at the heart of the plantation society made it impossible to recognize and respect the behaviors occasioned by the knowledge carried by the suffering captives. European disdain for the contributions of the African continent compounded this, and it got more pernicious and calumnious as colonialism appropriated more and more of the continent's riches. So the French-influenced social groups couldn't conceive of any positive contribution coming from Africa. This was true of most of the late nineteenth-century intellectuals. Rosalvo Bobo, whose nationalism cannot be questioned, wrote this phrase, which is heartrending precisely because it was written by one of our most valiant revolutionaries: "Our little habitat is an insult to the New World, because it is the only one that still offers a refuge to Africa, that is to say, to crime, barbarism, and life in the shadows" (Hoffmann 1990, 11).

The reality was that Haitians of African origin were in fact the first on the American continent to stop receiving deportees from their motherland. After 1793, no more *bossales* came to Haiti. And yet it remains one of the lands in America most influenced by African traditions. This particularly bothers those Haitians ashamed of their links to Africa and slavery. Everything indicates that those acquired by Saint-Domingue's colonists had effectively surrounded themselves with a protective wall that enabled them to victoriously resist the impact of a modern colonial society that was supposedly dominant but actually included only a tiny minority of the population. In order to do this, they had to possess enough political power to neutralize the patronage of the French-influenced oligarchs and defy the basic principles of racist colonial thought.

Arriving in Saint-Domingue, the young *bossale* had to learn to behave like a piece of merchandise, something that was owned. Her transposition of her natal Africa to the New World was experienced as a kind of immersion into chaos, since the society into which she arrived could only seem immoral and absent of all reason. Incapable of comprehending the justifications for her state, she ipso facto became an ignorant person, unable to orient herself effectively. Her self-preservation demanded an apprenticeship in the regulations of the dominant system. She was supposed to discover some order in the disorder that welcomed her on arrival, where one could survive only through calculated obedience. Any initiative on her part was unthinkable. Any solidarity with her companions was subversive. The colonial order absorbed her only by refusing her liberty to use her own reason, intelligence, and conscience as she wished.

She was constantly subjected to physical violence, both latent and manifest. There was no recourse from it. So she learned to adroitly manipulate the instructions she received from her master, simulating complete assent. Gradually, she discovered that there was a hidden door through which to escape. The monopoly on knowledge the owner of slaves granted himself created a kind of invisibility for the captive, woven together with the calumnies and misinterpretations used to interpret her deviant behavior. She was seen as a pariah, ignorant of the impulses that drove the master's behavior. But the master didn't understand the logic behind her behavior, either. The master's prejudices protected her initiatives, because the logic and normative content that inspired them escaped him. The all-powerful authority constantly boxed with shadows. In this narrow universe, safe from her captors, the sufferer sustained the feeling of her captivity, producing and reproducing a knowledge of how to live. She protected that knowledge for discovery and persecution. She furnished herself with a spirit infused with values, norms, principles, and knowledge that went against the system and were adapted to her painful circumstances.

Caught up in this infernal dynamic, the reflex for self-defense encouraged the captive person to create solidarity in autonomous units by gathering with her companions in misfortune. This made it possible for her to overcome her attitude of suicidal revolt and instead transform herself into a sufferer—that is, someone who could weigh the amplitude of her suffering and find an escape from it. Popular wisdom advised her not to add a departure from this life to these already infinite calamities. It was not up to her to overthrow the suffering—that could only happen if God willed it!—but she could impose herself in the face of her bad luck. Only a person with bad luck ended up caught in the nets of the slave trader and the colonial state. But only a naïve person would allow herself to be killed pointlessly.

It was during this time that the autogenesis of the Creoles began. They were in a position to adequately evaluate the historical juncture and the nefarious accident that had projected them into this insane world. In relation to these new experiences and unexpected challenges, the knowledge that the captives had carried deep inside them was reconverted as they journeyed far from Africa and the communities from which they had come. The knowledge system inaugurated in America was not a mestizo culture or a mix of African and French knowledge. It was a form of consciousness, along with representations, feelings, and knowledge, extracted from the local conditions of the lives of companions who found themselves, through random misfortune, in abominable situations. This knowledge came to them through experiences accumulated in their daily lives in Saint-Domingue. There was no mixing of ideas, values, and norms, but rather the creation, on the basis of a new social reality, of principles that were to guide actors caught up in unexpected situations. The only, fragile lifeline for the captives lay in discerning these new circumstances and finding a way to order and master this unexpected world, to situate themselves in such a way as to annul its negative impact as much as possible.

The slave trade didn't introduce structured groups of captives into the territory. So the knowledge produced by the victims of slavery enjoyed a certain kind of autonomy in relation to the traditions inherited from their ancestors. They arrived isolated and without connections. Their preservation of the traditions that identified them as a nation and the sustenance of the structured institutions that survived the odyssey of the crossing depended strictly on the ultimate contribution these cultural traits could make to their survival. What made the creation that sprouted in the new context so original was the way that chose what was needed from among so many memories coming from diverse peoples.

In this way, the captive pulled herself back from the chaos-order that welcomed her, and built a new world, a space for managing resources that were conserved or gathered along the way. From the experience of surviving thanks to practical understanding of the knowledge-rules, she extracted a form of knowing that liberated her, making it possible to construct a universe where she could realize herself as she envisioned. This knowledge began with solidarity with her companions in misfortune. Like her, they were creating knowledge that surpassed the conditions of survival and opened the doors of the prison of the chaos-order of colonialism (Santos 2009, 86). They initiated a new tradition, a new memory.

We know that during the decade that preceded the revolutionary conflagrations of Saint-Domingue, the slave trade poured forty thousand Africans a year into the colony. The young adults brought to the Saint-Domingue plantations had fresh memories of their experiences in the land of their birth, and of their traumatic experiences of sequestration, desocialization, branding, and acclimation to the workshops and forced labor. They overcame their misery by reconquering their mental health thanks to a "miracle of human creativity" (Nesbitt 2008, 127).

These individuals contributed to the apogee of the plantation society, which was closely followed by its destruction starting in 1791. Over the course of the next fourteen years, these recently arrived Africans focused on carrying out activities inspired by their will to live and outdoing the conditions of existence imposed on them. In Saint-Domingue, they found a society where the colonial administration was caught up in a spiral of crises, culminating in its agony in 1803. From 1804 on they gave free reign to their imagination, inventing and constructing a new world for themselves.

As time passed, the rural world was increasingly shaped by these ongoing innovations, which flourished and had a widening range of action and influence. Their success was all the more striking because of the decline of the urban centers and their service activities. The oligarchs, meanwhile, were unable to articulate the new political system, which was powerless. So the countryside remained wide open as a space for the former captives and their children. The oligarchs announced their intention to patch up their status and power, but it was the project of small-scale rural farming on the part of the popular masses that advanced inexorably. The military bureaucracy of the kingdom of Christophe put the masses of agricultural laborers there back to work on the plantations for two decades. But that was the exception. Everywhere else in the country, any opposition to the new way of life was forced to retreat.

Gradually, the accumulation of freshly disembarked Africans converted themselves into groups or networks of people linked together by common expectations and habits. They shared a complicity and solidarity as they pursued a better life, and a knowledge of how to live, from within their abominable situation. The very activation of African ways of life and traditions so feared by Ardouin and Madiou materialized, but with a difference: while this collection of practices was certainly influenced by the memories of a distant *Ginen*, it remained essentially Haitian and Caribbean. Haiti witnessed the edification of a right to invent human relationships that went beyond the known world until then, and the construction of an institutional citadel to protect those relationships.[6]

The imprisoned were not familiar with the larger context built by the modern state. But they responded to their experience of it through the elaboration of specific forms of knowledge that escaped the dominant institutions because they were focused on social values, norms, and interests (economic, political, and cultural) of the imprisoned themselves. In this context, the captives' knowledge of the regulations promulgated by the modern, capitalist, and racist state to maintain public order became a tool they used to invent a universe that escaped oppression. Boaventura de Sousa Santos identifies this as the collection of liberation knowledges (Santos 2009, 63). What emerged was a constellation of norms, values, and foundational principles that gave a powerful libertarian flavor to emancipation and the process of liberation from the control of the public authorities.

The division between the unchanging aspects of each of these knowledge systems—regulation-knowledge and liberation-knowledge—converted the misfortune of the oppressed into an ethnic question, sustaining the birth of a nation and people distinct from the metropolitan formation. The Haitian nation had its own way of seeing and managing the environment shaped by social actors. The barriers that separated the two ethnicities present—the metropolitans and the Haitians (as defined by Vastey)[7]—were constructed based on the centrality of one or another knowledge system for the preservation of the implicated social actors. The interface between the two social formations that were linked in this way was taken care of by an opportunist sector of intermediaries who were good at manipulating both systems at the same time.

The itinerary of the captive *bossales* began with individual isolation in a chaotic, incomprehensible situation. They carried knowledge inherited from their African parents and created solidarity with one another as unfortunate sufferers. On this basis, they constructed an alternative order, the counter-plantation system. They learned to submit to the regulations imposed by the colonial public order, even as they sought out ways to escape this order by inventing a collection of forms of knowledge. This liberation developed in the interstices of the modern colonial state without defying it directly. The captives found it difficult to understand the sources of the dominant political structure, because these were situated beyond their daily experience. But their knowledge helped them invent a new life and elude slavery, without offering the tools necessary for a complete escape from it.

The unfortunate sufferer was, in the end, a victim of circumstances that exceeded what he could possibly predict. So he tried to protect himself from a hostile external world using his capacity for response and transformation and ability to envision an existence beyond slavery. He protected his internal sovereignty and the communal world he built with his companions.

The public authorities—first metropolitan and then national—constructed their order to control those caught up in this net. It was an oppressive political structure nourished from the outside, and those subjected to it protected themselves by limiting the structure's ability to manage the circumstances of their own daily lives. The public authorities were perceived as a threat that could dissolve links of solidarity and conviviality. The nation invented by the oppressed never really converged with the constituted authorities. The nation just did its best to protect itself, while the authorities remained committed to pursuing their initiatives and interventions, which aimed to marginalize that nation and force it to integrate itself into the modern/colonial economy.

Private Life

The market reproduced the slaves of Saint-Domingue. Like all merchandise, these slaves who were created by others had no control over their production and reproduction. Inanimate objects generated by the modern/colonial state, they had no independent will or social behavior. Or, more precisely, their will had no public effect (Sala-Molins 1987, 77). Within the public sphere, they were things. The imperial state extracted them from the realm of judicial power.

The public authorities couldn't actually convert the slave into a thing. That was beyond their capacity. Instead, they sought to bring the slave to the point where he behaved like one. To do so, they needed to grant themselves the attributes necessary for the management of a power relation capable of annulling the contrary will of the person who was being transformed into an animal deprived of reason. The modern colonial administration could not prevent the captives from reproducing biologically. But it could prevent them from doing so within an institution and within a properly human environment. The administration sought to occupy the space where the prisoners who needed to be converted into slaves lived, and to prevent the appearance of any stable and structured connection that would break up the animality that defined the operations of the modern/colonial plantation.

The family was the antithesis of the slave trade, so it became the privileged target of the imperial administration. Colonialism could imagine only a patriarchal nuclear family, so it took the measures necessary to prevent it from emerging. The slave couldn't own anything and had to follow the master, and therefore found it impossible to behave like a father or to exercise paternal authority. He couldn't choose a spouse or get married without the master's consent. Children inherited the status of their mother. They were merchandise, just like her, and could be sold to the highest bidder according to the whims of the supposed owner. Potential spouses could, of course, also be separated from each other. In fact, men and women could be forced to couple against their will, according to the need for slaves on a particular plantation.

The public administration carried out a constant, sneaky war against the development of the family. It made sure the family could not establish itself within a private, distinct perimeter. The situation in Saint-Domingue was all the more precarious because the metropolitan struggles against the influence of the clergy closed the door on the systematic diffusion of Christian norms and principles. Vodou, the institution invented by those reduced to slavery in order to practice their spirituality, became, along with the family, a target of calumnies and persecutions, to the point that these two institutions—the most commonly shared in the country—are also the least studied by social science and the least understood by urban dwellers.

But as an economic enterprise, the commodity-producing plantation was the most complex and advanced of modern times. That created an environment where these things and potential animals nevertheless had to live alongside one another, and as a result, the family and other social groups abundantly multiplied the opportunities for creating and standardizing social connections.

The colonial administration couldn't prevent the multiplication of these groups and couldn't guarantee that the labor force, as fragmented as it was, behaved like merchandise. The institutionalization of new social connections was inevitable.

As long as the merchandise-person could associate with his peers, the captive person was reborn like the phoenix. The modern/colonial executive power ended up in constant opposition to all the relationships between the social groups that it sought to point toward slavery. There was an inevitable gap between what the public authorities said about the *slave* and ordered her to do, on the one hand, and what they were able to make the *captive person* do, on the other. The powers saw the goal of forcing the captive into a certain kind of mold as a conquest that had to be carried out. The captives were an active totality that had to be bullied relentlessly. But between the *slave* and the *captive* there stood autonomous groups constantly reproduced by their own will to survive.

The effectiveness of the captives' will to contestation, and the possibility for them to inscribe their institutions within daily reality, depended on external circumstances, especially the power of the colonial empire over the slave system and its success at inserting it into the global economy. It proceeded from the articulation of a civil society that was unique and articulated through solidarity, and collectively produced new forms of knowledge.

The dominant system's need to convert the captives into slaves remained inseparable from the production and reproduction of a system of emancipation-knowledge by the dominated. What developed was a perennial conflict between two sovereignties: the external sovereignty of the colonial administration and the internal, personal, and communal sovereignty of the captives who structured a distinct civil society in their efforts to grant themselves a modicum of control over their own well-being. This conflict was always latent, but it is harder to perceive in moments when captive individuals didn't have the space necessary to block their conversion into people reduced to slavery, into the structured fragments they were expected to be within the broader modern/colonial assemblage. When the system of domination entered into crises and those who were imprisoned gained latitude to defend themselves against the aggressions of external powers, however, the intensity of this contradiction becomes much easier to see.

The effectiveness of the agency of the captive, in any case, reveals its visible manifestation rather than its actual existence. Because the colonial administration's power to dominate varied between empires and from one period to another, the journey from captive to slave didn't follow a simple, linear path. The prisoners captured in Africa and brought to Saint-Domingue or elsewhere in the Antilles were uprooted from their home territories and stripped of the social relations that connected them to those like them. They appeared on the auction block of the slave market as individuals, as potential human beings. They realized their potentiality in two ways, and in two different contexts, even as the colonial powers who conceived of and imposed slavery offered only one exit: emancipation, an individual liberty granted by the master.

In principle, emancipation always remained accessible as an outlet. It was negotiated in terms of the conflict between social classes. It depended on the mastery of the dominant system's regulations, which led to a contradictory connection to the slave owner. A set of common interests, based on the same formula of the production of material life, became the basis of negotiation. This approach can typically be seen in the trajectory of the insular, total plantation societies that were established starting in the seventeenth century. Pieces of it can also be found in the urban agglomerations of Saint-Domingue, where most of the freed people of the colony lived.

But the hope for individual emancipation gained significance in shaping the behavior of those reduced to slavery if, and only if, the imperial power had the means to gag and master any subversive impact resulting from the social links the prisoners always created. When this wasn't the case, the captive reproduced himself as such by deliberately acting like a slave, and then as a freed slave, in the hope—often illusory—of a deeper ultimate rupture with the dominant system.

When the oppressive situation offered no exit for the captive, the only thing left for her was to reconquer her autonomy in the heart of the slaving empire. Thanks to this autonomy, she conserved and maintained the consciousness of the injustice of her imprisonment, and delayed her internalization of the coloniality of power. Her links of solidarity with her companions in misfortune nourished a feeling of contemporaneousness between modern, colonial oppression and her suffering, her struggle for survival, and the solution to her imprisonment—even temporary—found through communal solidarity. The result was a quest for liberty that was the opposite of individual emancipation. It accelerated the struggle for national liberation, making it logically and chronologically anterior to the class struggle. This search for cohesion was oriented toward the establishment of a new ethnicity or nation. When, on the other hand, the colonial empire was able to master the conditions of the oppression of the laboring population, class struggle preceded and guided the construction of the nation, or at least was inseparable from it.

Individual emancipation depended on the comprehension of and submission to the logic of the exploitation colony. There was a risk of being imprisoned in this logic, and a rejection of the possibility of a collective rupture between the captives and the owners of slaves. In Saint-Domingue these two approaches coexisted, but were not of equal importance. The number of those among the freed people who had shown a strong tendency to choose the route of individual emancipation was relatively small: no more than 30,000 among 500,000 captives, so less then 6 percent of the population. And even among the imprisoned population, Creoles were a minority, no more than a third of the total. Finally, and above all, the international crisis made it impossible for the colonial administration to adequately structure and master the slave milieu. So a gaping door was left open for radical opposition.

Facing a failing colonial power, the captives structured themselves into welcoming groups defined by their contestation. They created spaces that escaped the control of both those who had acquired them and, definitively, the failing modern/colonial administration. Given the absence of common characteristics between the dominant and the dominated, the ethnic relationship between metropolitans and foreigners was not transformed into a class conflict. There was no guarantee that the colonial empire could master the environment of slavery and so circumscribe the maneuvering of the oppressed. The laborers in question, captives who had to be turned into slaves, were constantly renegotiating their relationship to the public authorities on the basis of their own life system. They created a space where they, rather than the plantation system, controlled the reproduction of their labor force.

The reproduction of the slave followed the rhythm of arrivals into the modern, agro-industrial enterprise, fulfilling the necessity of transforming captives into merchandise. The transatlantic market was the center of the colonial landscape. But even while the empire exerted mastery over the environment in which the plantation system developed, another context structured itself through the interpersonal relationships developed in the workshops. Among the groups of workers there developed a contradictory space in which the captive person learned to manage her captivity. The first context defined the public life of the colonial worker, her conversion into a slave. But her private life developed in the second context, where she invented herself as a person, as a human being, outside the modern/colonial world. When production within the capitalist, plantation slave system couldn't impose itself fully, the ways of thinking of institutions responsible for private life ended up taking control.

The worker reproduced herself through her own means naturally, as a sovereign, in the midst of a network of local relationships that aimed to satisfy her own needs in complete independence. She took advantage of the tiniest failures of the system of domination. The structuring of private life accelerated during the last two decades of the eighteenth century in Saint-Domingue, to the point that the natural reproduction of the population became possible. At the end of this period an interior market emerged, in the midst of a territory that was no longer simply an island of treasures or a sugar island. In opposition to the plantation system there emerged an exchange system whose goal was to resolve the difficulties surrounding the local management of the lives of the captives, who had snatched their freedom from unwilling powers. This new system of social relationships obviously took into consideration the satisfaction of material and spiritual needs, along with other necessities that sustained group solidarity. There was a potential overflowing of private life into other spheres. What emerged was a whole civil society whose aim was to serve the workers and strengthen their power to negotiate.

When the public authorities exercised control over individuals who were chained, humiliated, dehumanized, desocialized, and decivilized (Meillassoux 1998, 101), their job was easy. It consisted largely in keeping these people vulnerable within their state of isolation and encouraging them to articulate themselves as part of humanity through the means and paths offered by the authorities of the modern/colonial world—that is, within the contradictory dimensions of class conflict. But within all the spaces that escaped the powers in place, and particularly within the private sphere, there was a structuring of a site for the renewal of the very social power these authorities needed to control to assure the conversion of captives into slaves. The colonial landscape, then, was conceived as a place where the captives and those reduced to slavery occupied the same location. The transformation of captives into slaves was never complete. And the victims of the system of exploitation always had the alternative of choosing one or another character.

The captives of Saint-Domingue created and sustained, deep inside them, representations that protected them from the attacks of modern/colonial slavery. This universe was inaccessible to the masters. It was a miniscule bubble of fresh air, one that expressed the embryo of power (Zavaleta 1977, 59). From the heart of the plantation system, it launched the structuring of their private life, a life where one was free to evaluate Western propositions and reject or escape them, fully sovereign. These spaces of intimacy slipped into the interstices of plantation life. They developed and bloomed first within family units and then in the first elements of communal life, nourishing and enriching themselves at the antipodes of the social and political organization of the modern/colonial regime. The captives invented a universe that evolved within the geographical space of the plantation, but outside its spiritual and normative space, outside of modern/colonial, racist, and Eurocentric thought.

This seemingly cramped universe of the captive's private life defied the plantation head on. By counteracting the commercial reproduction of the slave, it imposed itself, by definition, as a subversive milieu. It was the cradle of the Haitian family, which converted itself into the antithesis of the slave trade. This new universe structured itself as a space of resocialization, repersonalization, and recivilization. A sphere of minimal power flourished there, one whose political, economic, and cultural interests were incompatible with those of the operators of the emerging world economy and their representatives in Saint-Domingue. Its fragile presence was nonnegotiable. But its relationship with the global institutions necessarily involved escape, flight, and fake loyalty, everything that characterized marronage.

The workers recruited through the slave trade and subjected to processes of individuation that worsened their vulnerability and exploitation sought to elude the excessive toll of that exploitation as best they could. They did so by organizing relationships of solidarity at the heart of their private lives. The full potential of the communal networks that developed in this way is most visible in specific institutional complexes, notably the *lakou* and the maroon villages (*doko* or *manieles*). These institutions perpetuated and developed the initial opposition to slavery hidden away in the private lives at the center of the plantation workshops, carrying it to its full conclusion.

> With the end of the trade in 1793, the half-liberation of the slaves, and the slowing down of production even in those areas occupied by the English, there was a serious decrease in work. Despite the fact that some colonists stayed or returned and that managers sought to oversee plantations for absentee owners, despite all the agricultural regulations, the slaves and the new cultivators devoted much more time than before to cultivating their own food. At the same time, as if spontaneously, there developed an equilibrium between the two sexes among adults, a predominance of Creoles, and the multiplication of children and the elderly. There were even many plantations where there were more women than men. This erasure of men was the result of the death of combatants during the unrest, the drafting of the best subjects for colonial regiments, but above all the slave trade that brought in so many men. We still haven't determined whether the relationship between men and women during this time was similar among free people of color, free blacks, and the slaves. But there is no doubt that while the upheavals led to the deaths of many people, in the end they also encouraged births. Nothing demonstrates more clearly how fragile and artificial the groups that had made up the plantation workshops were. (Debien 1974, 360)

Along with the maroon villages, the cells that made up private life, so hidden during the colonial period, expanded their potential during the interlude that stretched from 1793 to 1804. And, after 1804, once the modern/colonial plantation had been shattered, these cells flourished in all their splendor.

Conclusion: The Rebirth of the *Moun*

The beauty of the sovereign people is clear. Despite the determination of an external universe that, from the time of the Discovery, endeavored to implant the sources of Western thought and their vehicle in its midst, this sovereign people managed to reign over their local circumstances. After 1804, they didn't move away from the self-proclaimed centers of power to establish themselves elsewhere on the island. That is certainly not because the state/government monopolized landed property and the resources connected to it, for it was incapable of making its monopoly effective or of putting an end to flight to the Spanish side of the island, the traditional response to the rigors of life on the colonial plantations. We have to conclude that the orientations and interests of the popular classes, as well as their conception of how land and power should be used, did not involve a need to accumulate large tracts of land as individuals or families, or to project themselves to the front of society as an obviously hegemonic force.

The sovereignty of the French state over Saint-Domingue began with the seizing of the territory and the distribution of land to the king's subjects. The workers reduced to slavery avoided a direct confrontation with those who had benefited from this supposed right to property. Instead, they emphasized the usufructuary rights over land that was owned or might be owned. Their economic system and autonomous reproduction, furthermore, was based on arrangements of reciprocity. It is true that the limited circulation of money during the nineteenth century made the commodification of human resources nearly impossible. But commodification was also bypassed by methods that fixed prices and distributed products, fluctuating depending on the availability of buyers and producers. The Haitian people—that is, the nation in its will to live (Dussel 2006)—created for itself a path focused on satisfying its needs as they were defined within a particular geography. They optimized the social mechanisms accessible to a civil society that brought together producers and consumers.

Colonial modernity invented a plantation landscape that was fragmented, disjointed, and dependent. Rural Haitian life, in contrast, was produced by the population itself. It flourished and reached its full potential after independence was achieved. The chosen path opened up onto a fabric of exchange that strengthened the original institutional cells: extended families, *lakou*, homogenous villages and regions. It was held together by rural markets, which had not existed in the plantation society. These sustained the reproduction of garden-towns (Anglade 1982) linked to them and ultimately to the entire nation. The transatlantic market was reduced to a complementary role, satisfying needs that the national community could not immediately fulfill. During the end of the period under study, the rural population ended up supplying the external market as effectively as had been the case during the most productive periods of colonization. The major exception was the supply of sugar, because the forms of labor servitude required for its production were seen as unacceptable by the population, and the technology and capital necessary were inaccessible.

The rearrangement of national life was established steadily after the end of the slave trade. As soon as the first indications of the collapse of the plantation system were visible, the majority of the population set about building a society of villages by chiseling the fragments of clans and lineage systems into an approach to life I call the *counter-plantation system* (Casimir 1981b). The government made no contribution to this system, which did not tolerate any interference on the part of the colonial authorities in its own endogenous development.

As soon as the 1791 insurrection began, the inhabitants of the land refused to be treated as things and merchandise. The Haitian Revolution created institutions that operated for the satisfaction of the need to live and those who promoted this need. It replaced the primacy of exchanges with the outside world with service to those who lived within the country, through a nonnegotiable quest for the well-being of the local population in all domains of human life. The popular revolution defined itself as the conversion of the merchandise-being into a person who could reproduce herself within family and communal institutions she invented, a person who deserved to be served in her unstoppable quest for sovereignty and self-expression.

The local family, community, and internal markets, along with other stable institutions and arrangements that developed across the nation, successfully escaped the public authorities and their legal system both before 1804 and after. Indivisible family property, the Kreyòl language, the forms of spirituality encapsulated in Vodou, the calendar and rhythm of communal life, leisure, dance, music . . . all these were dimensions of national life controlled by the decisions of the sovereign people. The public administration was incapable of regulating, planning, or obstructing this cadence. Legal texts only rarely allude to these institutions and structural arrangements, and only to criticize them, to seek to turn them to ash, or at best to transform them into something that the sovereign people didn't want.

The hundreds of thousands of people who were enslaved didn't get any benefit, of any kind, from the institution. There was nothing beautiful or attractive about their misery and precarity, which was the result of the monopoly on available resources the oligarchs and public authorities grabbed onto with a sick tenacity. The way the people surpassed this colonial/modern misery and precarity reveals the full, sublime splendor of these victims, who rose up on their own with no other resources than their intelligence and will to build a better tomorrow (Vastey 1816, 4).

Before 1804, when the captives sought to escape the influence of these adverse forces seeking to annihilate them, they were called *runaways*, *deserters*, and especially *maroons*, a word which is often used as a synonym for savages. Those who refused to be branded became barbarians, while those who treated them like animals were canonized as the bearers of human progress. These propositions did not flow from a realistic vision of the local situation. Vastey, a contemporary of these events, exposed this approach as early as 1814. The deliberate refusal to understand the universe only through the lens of colonialism was already apparent at the end of the eighteenth century, even among the privileged. If even they were conscious of the prejudices that served to persecute and marginalize them, I cannot imagine that the unfortunate sufferers of the time were not aware of the enormity of the falsehoods and lies that undergirded the colonial/modern ideology and its pretensions.

It is worth remembering Sonthonax's words to the National Convention: "The Blacks are the true sans-culottes of the colonies, they are the people, and only they are capable of defending the nation" (Dubois 2003, 294). But the civil commissioner could not have imagined that our sans-culottes would impose their sovereignty despite, and even without, the modern, colonial state.

Chapter 9

An Independent State without a Sovereign People

Introduction: Two Exclusions from the Slave Plantation

From the French point of view, the slaves were the fuel—the input—for the plantations. To survive and transcend this transformation, those who were bullied by this system had to overcome privations, humiliations, and unspeakable tortures (Vastey [1814] 2013; Fouchard 1972). Toward the end of the eighteenth century, the political conflicts within the metropole and between it and its rivals offered the enslaved the opportunity to liberate themselves, and they conquered the territory they had been shipwrecked on.

The former captives were inspired by a locally developed vision of the world, and they collaborated with the minority of former slave owners in the construction of a state that presented itself as national. But it was the former slave owners, who before 1804 had considered themselves to be French (Raimond 1791a, 68, 1793), ended up monopolizing the positions in the public administration. They refused to accept that the *people outside*, the descendants of the African foreigners reduced to slavery, might formalize their own social project within the territory, on their own terms. The former slave owners considered this territory to be their hunting grounds, and preserved the illusory colonial goal of transforming the newly freed into workers whose status was as close as possible as that of indentured laborers.

The formal, visible structure of the public administration of the nineteenth century was built on the basis of the conceptual primacy of the colonial plantation. The administration preserved the plantation's principles of land tenure and land use. From the time of the promulgation of Code Noir in 1685 to the general insurrection of 1791, the constant increase in demand for tropical commodities drove an expanding demand for imported labor. Modern/colonial society functioned on the basis of a disaggregated workforce made up of isolated individuals, the only kind that could sustain a flourishing plantation system within the geopolitical space of empire.

The sovereignty of the state born in 1804 was the result of the accidental and temporary victories of the coalition made up of oligarchs and workers. But as it sought a place among the exclusive club of modern empires, the governmental administration used the commercialization of export commodities as its calling card. The constituted authorities thought they could relaunch the plantation enterprises that specialized in producing tropical commodities. In order to do so, they sought to institute measures to force the working population to continue to behave like a collection of human merchandise. They wished, in other words, to create an internal colony with the same contours as the slave system. They did everything they could to prevent agricultural workers from getting access to landed property, and to limit their will to live as they pleased.

But the governmental administrations confronted a dilemma. In order to exercise their monopoly over the police forces they now supposedly controlled and hoped to use to orient the sovereign will, they had to enlist the very barefoot people they hoped to contain. Given their chronic lack of resources and the absence of a coherent ideology tying together the two principal social groups, however, the administration couldn't realize this goal. The key questions raised by this period are: How did the majority population successfully use its political power to prevent the sector that claimed to govern the country from fulfilling its goals? How did it impose its own popular sovereignty, and refuse the plans of the oligarchs? It was, after all, the majority population that determined the approach to daily life that defined the economic landscape of the nineteenth century: a village society centered on itself.

My analysis foregrounds the relationship between the sovereign people and independence. Before 1804, the slave trade remained essential to the development of the plantations, and the colonial/modern empire had no interest in the natural reproduction of the labor force. The laboring population was acquired on the international market. The existence of family groups and the presence of women were superfluous in a society that supplied itself with labor from beyond its borders. In Saint-Domingue, the public authorities made sure that the family wasn't part of the reproduction of the economic system. The administration never served the family. The Code Noir sang an old tune that was widely adopted: the plantation owners were to treat their slaves as if they were good fathers to them (Code Noir 1685, Art. 54)! Toussaint took up the same refrain in his foundational law of 1801, in Articles 15 and 16 on the cultivators; the same old tune reappeared in Article 14 of Pétion's Agricultural Regulations, and then in the first article of the first chapter of the Law regarding Agriculture in the Code Henry, and finally in Article 61 of Boyer's Rural Code. Geffrard's Rural Code dropped it.

There were two telling, and foundational, absences in the colonial plantation, inscribed in official thought from beginning of French colonization in Saint-Domingue. The family and its pivot, the woman, were seen as unnecessary. They were ignored by the public authorities. The population was reproduced on the market, and its only reason for being was to sustain the international market with tropical commodities. As a corollary to this, the spiritual and material bases for communal life—its way of thinking or its culture—were condemned, because by definition, they worked against the satisfaction of the needs of the plantation, the imperial metropole, and international commerce.

The workers reduced to slavery or condemned to servitude lived at the opposite end of this journey forced on them by colonial modernity. Their primary goal was to survive, to save themselves. The creation of social links was unavoidably necessary, along with the creation of groups tied together by solidarity and the establishment of human community. In the modern Caribbean, the family and its axis, the woman, who are the primary creators of human existence, are situated at the antipodes of the slave trade, the great furnisher of beasts of burden destined to make the agro-industrial prison camps work. The regeneration of the population fell to African societies, while the reproduction of the workforce—the beasts of burden—was carried out by colonial society. Human existence could flourish and expand on the plantation only by opposing the needs of the modern, capitalist market.

The reflection that follows does not focus on the fate of women and the family. But it shows that the survival of the captives depended on an irreparable rupture between their private lives and objectives and the principles that undergirded the functioning of their workplace as conceived by the colonial/modern state and the public authorities. The captives were called to create their own specific, independent space where they could manage their lives and reproduction as a human population. Their existence as a collection of human beings aspiring to a little bit of respect and dignity depended on distancing themselves from the colonial/modern state and its activities. I want to show how and why they had to turn their back on the modern/colonial state.

After 1789, internal conflicts pitted the owners of slaves against each other. The general insurrection of the captives in the North followed in 1791, and then the invasion of rival powers. Local production prioritizing external demands was therefore put on hold, because its outlets were blocked. The workforce of agricultural laborers therefore no longer served the original objectives of enslavement. The political and economic crisis made the continuing cost of disaggregating this workforce, of maintaining it as a collection of isolated individuals serving only as inputs for agro-industrial production, prohibitive. As a result, from the point of view of the public and private powers focused on the outside world, there was a temporary overabundance of labor. The idleness, or rather the nonemployment, of this workforce required that it invest in its own preservation and from there, in its own regeneration. This conjuncture made the family, women, and the community the center of the daily life of the laboring classes. The structuring of this autonomous space imposed itself, unstoppable, on the public authorities. It developed in the very heart of the plantation, but outside the norms and systems of the plantation system.

Starting with Toussaint Louverture's 1801 Constitution, local political power erected itself against the popular will to live, and against its capacity to do so outside the norms of the modern, colonial, slaving economy. Starting in 1804, the exploitation colony of Saint-Domingue made way for a society capable of welcoming the oppressed and healing their wounds. But for all of Haiti's independent governments, the community and the family remained embarrassing institutions. They were seen primarily as the source of a population that the governments might sacrifice, following the policies of Napoléon Bonaparte and Louis XVIII, in pursuit of the goal of guaranteeing the full development and flourishing of an healthy, extroverted, competitive economy.

The political structure of the country depended on the solution found by the majority of the population to guarantee the best life possible for themselves. The executive, legislative, and judicial powers operated on the margins of this majority, which depended exclusively on its own resources. The political and economic measures adopted by the governments prevented the mass of the people from openly proclaiming that they had settled the territory in complete autonomy and effectively controlled it. But these measures didn't take away the actual control the population had, and the fact that they behaved like settlers, what they called *abitan*, or *inhabitants*. The governmental powers were incapable of modifying or reorienting the daily life of the masses. More precisely, over the course of the nineteenth century, their failure became more and more obvious. The population didn't develop entirely according to their own wishes, but they certainly did not follow the instructions issued by the established authorities.

In this chapter, I discuss popular sovereignty. I describe how it germinated in the very midst of the slave plantation, and how the workers distanced themselves from the propositions of the modern, colonial, and postcolonial oligarchies. The awakening of the sovereign people represented the worst nightmare of the governing classes of Saint-Domingue and Haiti, because it imposed the terms of the interface with the outside world and defied imperial orientations. But given the international developments of the nineteenth century, they had no choice but to be absorbed by the *Guinean* customs and traditions. This provoked the disconcerting, but understandable, contradictions in their discourse.

France's Sovereignty over Saint-Domingue

During the old regime the population of Saint-Domingue was made up of two groups: the subjects of the king, those people that "Divine Providence" had placed under the authority of Louis XIV, and the slaves on the island that belonged to him (Code Noir, Preamble). The first group was made up of whites and people of color. Some were born free, and others were emancipated—that is, freed slaves. The slaves themselves were almost all blacks. During the period from the French Revolution to independence the term *slave* was no longer appropriate, and the oligarchs used polite substitute terms like *black*, *African*, and *cultivator*. Independent Haiti inherited this last term, which bears witness to the fact that from the perspective of the political authorities, the function of the laborer remained the same before and after 1804.

A colony is created when a metropole and its subjects take possession of a territory and of those who live there. The privileged classes in Saint-Domingue were, clearly, French. But in the racist context of the period, the mixed-race individuals who were part of this class suffered from degrading discrimination, and the richest among them riposted by identifying themselves as *American colonists* or *colonists of color*. They perceived themselves as Frenchmen of the Americas. "Here are the great advantages France will find in the Decree (of the 4th of April) that will make the people of color what they are, and what it is impossible to contest: MEN, and FRENCH" (Raimond 1791a, 68; emphasis in the original).

This branch of the oligarchy didn't conceive of themselves as a conquered collectivity, and they took every opportunity to emphasize the infinite distance that separated them from the servile masses. French by birth, they didn't willfully cut themselves off from their motherland. But Napoleonic France threatened them with deportation or extermination, which forced them to momentarily cut the umbilical cord. Vastey, himself part of this group, qualified Alexandre Pétion, one of the most important leaders of color, as a "Haitian by accident" or a "Haitian despite himself." He did so as he described Pétion's efforts to repair the damage caused by this involuntary secession (Vastey 1819, 186).

At the other end of the spectrum, those without rights in the colony were not indigenous people. Furthermore, they hadn't all come from one nation within which, or against which, they could easily define themselves. They were recruited and socialized one by one, without ever having been subjected as a structured, complete entity. They were initiated and implanted into America as a cluster of individual prisoners captured by rival empires that wished to keep them as a homogenous aggregate at the bottom of the hierarchy of the races. They were brought into the process of colonization on the basis of the categories defined in the Code Noir, which instituted the modern racialization of human relations as the fundamental law of French colonialism.

There is a still a common perception that the populations of the Caribbean are black, and the rupture between Saint-Domingue and France is often conceived of as the establishment of the "first black republic in the world." But this naming avoids the question of the nation and erases the cultural and institutional content that inspired the class struggle in Saint-Domingue and Haiti. As a result, colonialism becomes just a step in the historical development of each collection of blacks, whose political behavior can be assimilated into a general contestation on the part of all labor forces who are the victims of real or imagined injustice. Haiti and Saint-Domingue, independent or colonized, black, white, or mixed-race, belongs to French culture, and its demands are identical to those of the oppressed of the metropole or anywhere else in the world!

If we follow this line of thinking, the independence of 1804 exhausts itself as a secession like that of the United States of America, which institutionalized a republic in which independence reinforced the demons of modern slavery. Haiti, the first black republic, can joyously construct itself on the shoulders of the "citizens attached to the land," because its leaders are black . . . and just as in this other (white) American republic, it is perfectly normal that the inequalities that preceded the secession should be reproduced! Such inequalities are accompanied by their justification, which is all the more effective for its insidiousness.

In other words, this interpretation of independence defers to the premises of the ideologies of a racist empire—an empire that invented the *colonial black* (Casimir 2004b). This vision of independence is based on the idea of the capitulation of the captive, compounded by his incapacity to contribute in any specific way to the history of humanity, since he identifies essentially as a freed slave who can congratulate himself for achieving the condition of a formerly or newly freed person. His exploit is limited to surpassing the status of those who, from the beginning and by definition, are slaves. All other possibilities for life—those that contest the liberating formula of the imperial, modern, and colonial state, those that emerge from the autonomous, interpersonal lives of those exploited by the plantation system—are set aside. The new universe carried by those who refuse slavery is destroyed, like everything that goes beyond the imagination of the hegemonic political formations.

Imperial ascendancy over a colony is not only defined by the relationship to the colonized. It begins with a scathing rivalry with formations of the same kind. The French colonial state had trouble imposing itself in competition with the United Kingdom and was unable to fully assert its supremacy over the territories it claimed. During the second half of the eighteenth century, the effects of the Seven Years' War (1756–1763) and then the 1789 revolution generated the proliferation of projects meant to compensate for French losses and fill the cracks in the imperial enterprise.

During this half century, colonial interest groups and lobbies often verged on dissidence and even insurrection, supporting projects opposing those of the metropole. The rebellion of planters impacted by the events of the late eighteenth century is usually interpreted as a continuation of the transformations underway in the metropole. Their attempts to create colonial assemblies foresaw the possibility of secession and defied royal authority over the colony (Lattre 1805, 182). They all failed miserably, but that didn't lead to a real examination on their part of the possible alternative that ultimately imposed itself: that rebel captives of insurgents would pursue plans of a similar nature.

The tendency in the historiography of this period is to note the multiplication of what are commonly called *maroon bands*, without paying attention to the hierarchization this choice of words implies, and even less to the historical conditions that gave rise to the use of this term. It seems important to me to emphasize two conclusions foregrounded by Carolyn Fick. She notes first of all that in contrast to other slave societies in which marronage developed, in Saint-Domingue the maroons didn't constitute separate and easily identifiable entities within the plantation society (Fick 1990, 236). Second, she points out that during the revolutionary conflagrations, the colonists rarely used this expression to refer to the armed captives. They spoke instead of *brigands, insurgents,* or *rebels* (242). This suggests that the term *maroon bands* was the invention of certain sectors of the military oligarchy, and not of the actors who were more directly impacted by the uprisings.[1]

In 1793 the imperial state entered into a conflict that it couldn't resolve in the context of the legal system in place at the time. It sought to preserve French sovereignty over the island by depending on a collective of slaves it emancipated in the process. It therefore attacked the interests of the property owners who had acquired land concessions in good faith and then equipped them with the property known as slaves, using the legal system in place. The state, however, couldn't protect these concessions without indefinitely appropriating slaves. By liberating the slaves and transforming them into citizens, the modern state deprived the plantations of one of the tools indispensable for their exploitation. General emancipation contradicted the goals of the journey the colonists had embarked on.

Forty years later, Great Britain, having ended the slave trade, transformed former slave owners into purchasers of labor while offering them significant compensation: they manipulated the relationship between supply and demand by injecting massive numbers of indentured laborers imported from South and Southeast Asia, and also instituted other favorable policies that protected the colonial economy from free trade. At the end of the eighteenth century, however, France was besieged from all sides by its enemies and was not in a position to consider such correctives. And so it overthrew, for reasons of state, the very juridical principles that supported colonialism.

Once the power relations in the Estates General had been modified, with profound repercussions on the European political scene, the interests of the republican colonial administration diverged from those of the royalist planters, the original pivot of Saint-Domingue's society. The most important thing for the administration was to protect the sovereignty of the national state, even if that meant freeing the slaves. The most important thing for the wealthy planters, meanwhile, was to protect their right to own slaves, even if that meant setting aside their loyalty to the motherland.

The captive labor force, meanwhile, couldn't have perceived the difference between a colonial empire that was moving toward a republican government and the potential transfer of the colony to an English or Spanish empire. These changes in the dominant society didn't have repercussions for their status as slaves and their lack of freedom and citizenship. The antiabolitionists clearly weren't promoting any improvement in their lives. And the abolitionists came around to the idea of improving their lives only because of the presence of the enemy at the gates. Proclaimed under such conditions, general emancipation could produce durable effects only if this menace remained a reality. For better or worse, the captive workforce had to stick to its own agenda (Fick 1990, 248; Dubois 2004b 160) whether they were facing French or English domination.

Great Britain occupied parts of Saint-Domingue and returned emancipated captives to slavery, which clearly and concretely indicated that the relationship between laborers and their self-proclaimed owners was anchored in the colonial/modern system as a whole. When it dominated the fragments of African nations it implanted in its territory, France acted as a cell within the broader Western colonial power structure. It was not alone in inventing the concept of race, the foundation of the slave trade. Any opposition on the part of the workers reduced to slavery represented defiance against the European power structure as a whole. In this global conflict, the November 1803 victory over the French expeditionary army represented just a skirmish in a titanic conflict with the architects of the racialization of the human race. The options available for the construction of the state in nineteenth-century Haiti couldn't escape the determination of colonial modernity to impose itself. The hegemony of the European, colonialist, capitalist, racist state established the parameters for the exercise of sovereignty on the part of the Haitian people and the management of this sovereignty.

Neither the colonial authorities dispatched by the republican government nor the Haitian oligarchs who took over from them in the nineteenth century could conceive of popular sovereignty and promote its institutionalization within the particular power structure of one country without taking into consideration the colonial global context. These authorities and oligarchs were stakeholders in the global system. Even Vastey ([1814] 2013), the most advanced of the ideologues of the Haitian Revolution, didn't take his starting propositions to their logical conclusion. He believed in the equality of individuals before the law, but accepted that there was inequality between civilizations. To me, the supposed superiority of Western civilization seems like just a euphemism for consenting to its hegemony. What can this concession mean other than accepting that the knowledge of the popular masses cannot impose itself on that of the colonial empires? For the oligarchs who were trying to convert themselves into an elite, it was necessary to join in the colonial matrix of power that was in the process of globalizing itself. Otherwise, they had to fuse with the resistant community and lose the favors granted by the patronage of the all-powerful outsiders.

Since the material conditions of production remained intact, the economy couldn't do without people without rights. And as long as it preserved its indispensable character, the slave trade had to recycle its foundational racist principles. Toussaint's 1801 Constitution declared that "all men are born, live, and die free and French" (Art. 3), even as it announced in the same law that "the introduction of cultivators is indispensable to the re-establishment and the growth of crops" (Art. 17). It would be useful to us if this Constitution had defined the nature and amplitude of the freedom of these nonslaves, or if the subsequent police codes that religiously followed its model had filled in this lacunae. We must examine the tenor of the liberty of the blacks for which Toussaint and the heroes of independence claimed they were fighting!

In short, the modern French state in crisis on the European stage was unable to assert its sovereignty over the colonial territory without attacking the interests of the colonists, and undermining its sustaining foundation by upending the anthill of exploited people in their service. The state, furthermore, could not reasonably indefinitely count on the Africans or cultivators to save a system that was incapable of offering them the kind of liberty they conceived of for themselves. Colonialism, therefore, had to hold one form or another of a re-enslavement of the labor force in reserve, even if it was more or less camouflaged.

Napoléon's dazzling victories cut the Gordian knot: by vanquishing the resistance of the royalist European states, he guaranteed French sovereignty over its colony. So he decided to exterminate the colonized workers who had been contaminated by liberty's bad habits and replace them with new recruits. A few years later, now with the assent of the royalist states at the time of the Restoration and the re-establishment of peace in Europe, the same genocidal project resurfaced, though luckily with far less success.

Whether under the republic, the Napoleonic Empire, or the Bourbon Crown, the colony and its plantation system had a choice between administrative autonomy and secession, but always within the context of one form or another of slavery. Both before and after 1804, the inheritors of the colony's planters couldn't conceive of the abolition of slavery and its corollaries—the exercise of citizenship by all in the nation and the elimination of all restrictions on their freedom. For the oppressed, who were called *slaves, blacks, Africans, cultivators, newly freed,* or *citizens attached to the land*, autonomy, secession, and independence all came down to the same thing: the annihilation of their civil and political rights (Blérald 1988).

The slave trade and the monopoly system were the motors of the eighteenth-century colonial economy. The fate of the actors in this economy, when observed in the context of its basic premises, led to the impasse I have described here. But if we liberate ourselves from the grip of the slave trade and the monopoly system and question their legitimacy, we come to other conclusions. A decade after independence, Vastey's work put on trial the right to conquest and its exercise, drawing on the older reasoning of Vitoria, Las Casas, and Veracruz. The right to conquest was justified on the basis of the postulate that the conquered were racially inferior. No decision on the equality of citizens could erase this postulate without redistributing the illegitimately conquered lands or renegotiating their use from top to bottom. As early as the end of the seventeenth century, Francisco de Jaca and Épiphane de Moirans had raised the question of what kind of reparations might be made for the wrongs done to the captives, arguing that such repair had to be preamble to any conversation on the respect for rights in the Caribbean. Their writings reached the highest levels of the Catholic Church and the Spanish royalty, but fell on deaf ears (Sala-Molins 2014).

Vastey placed women, and in particular his own mother, at the center of his reflection. He openly cursed the role of the slave trade in the peopling of the territory and declared it the source of all the misery of the Haitians. He highlighted and condemned the traditional oligarchy's preoccupation with finding an accommodation with the former metropole even as they silenced the problem of how the labor force had been supplied. The author couldn't believe that Pétion's government, following the Code Noir, could fail to question the legitimacy of the imprisonment of the captives, at a time when Louis XVIII was successfully negotiating a moratorium on the abolition of the slave trade with the goal of repopulating Haiti after carrying out a genocide on the model of what they had done in Guadeloupe. Vastey cites the abolitionist Sismondi, with whom he corresponded: "We have to recognize that we will only be able to re-establish the slave trade to Saint-Domingue after a war of extermination has eliminated all of the inhabitants of this vast country" (Sismondi 1814, 18).

By refusing to question France's right to conquest, Pétion and his team made racism and its by-product, color prejudice, perennial axes of the country's sociopolitical organization. They introduced a permanent inequality into the Haitian legal system based on whether persons were Africans or descendants of Africans who had been reduced to slavery versus descendants of owners of property originally granted by the conquerors. The nonlandowners of the republic retained the role granted them by the 1793 emancipation, as passive citizens incapable of expressing their will in the public sphere and with no opportunity to participate in political or economic leadership. For Vastey, the inhabitants of Christophe's kingdom, in contrast, were all subjects of the king and not divided into active and passive citizens. They enjoyed the same rights, but their equality did not mean a mixing up of rank and wealth (1819, 154). Land ownership remained a privilege granted by the king, who handed out concessions as he wished, as had been the case under the Old Regime (Lattre 1805, 182).

Accepting the idea of inequality between civilizations and cultures means codifying the stratification of the international order. The West dominates Africa. Is it therefore in advance of it? Understanding the larger context, King Henry Christophe sought to carry out a form of social engineering that would allow him to authoratively construct a more just society, one better equipped to defend its external sovereignty. His approach constrained the political will of both the nobles and the masses, but it was above all sure to displease the population of agricultural workers, who were deprived of all protection once the edifice constructed by Christophe collapsed.

The French Revolution clearly enshrined popular sovereignty at the heart of the governance of modern metropolitan states. But it placed it beyond the reach of the colonial political formations, which had served as the trampoline for the construction of its own modernity (Quijano 2000). So it is difficult to discern the real relationship between the ideas of the revolutionary French state and the general emancipation of 1793, which failed to codify the liberty and equality of all potential citizens. The French colony was besieged by English and Spanish imperial forces as well as the rebel armies of brigands and insurgents (Fick 1990, 242). Its authorities attempted to stave off a debacle by negotiating the support of the insurgents, the natural allies of the captive laborers and agricultural masses. For all the states involved in these conflicts—modern, colonialist, and racist states—and particularly for the state of Haiti that resulted from these military conflicts, the sovereign people were a threat to be managed.

In other words, in the context of global capitalism's sovereignty *over* a colonial territory or a former colony, external sovereignty necessarily implied gagging internal sovereignty. It was the funeral of the sovereign people. So what path were they to take? How could the plurality of individuals scattered by the slave trade in Saint-Domingue in greater and greater numbers during the end of the eighteenth century be articulated into a collective capable of acting for itself? How were the sovereign people of Haiti born, and how did they act within a context hostile to their self-fulfillment? How did they establish their sovereignty *within* the territory?

The fierce opponents of the *Guinean* traditions were unable to imagine that it was that form that would ultimately impose itself. But in practice, the issue was not choosing between hegemonic Western culture at the global level and the *Guinean* traditions that were solidly implanted at the local level. The real question was whether the hegemonic culture had the capacity to enforce its power in Haiti. Unable to impose the colonial matrix of power, the state in Haiti instead gradually institutionalized the joint management of the two concurrent forms of thinking.

While the privileged maintained the idea that the West was superior as a way of conserving their status, those previously been reduced to slavery were resolutely in an opposite space. They didn't have to carry a European history that was just barely beginning to universalize itself. Their own experience taught them that it was not guaranteed to succeed in this project. The captive populations fighting for their liberty did so on the basis of their own ideas about themselves and the society in which they had arrived. From their point of view, the equality and sovereignty they were building were nonnegotiable. They thought through their situation and did so autonomously, fully sovereign, from the place where they were situated. It is profoundly illogical to imagine they should have taken into account the global capitalism in the process of formation, which insisted on turning them into nothing more than merchandise that could talk—that is, to annihilate them.

The feeling of Western superiority could bud in the hearts of the intermediary classes only as a way of justifying their pivotal role. The superiority of a civilization capable of committing the crimes that had victimized the workers was far from obvious. They had, after all, just defeated that civilization's most avid defenders. The idea of this superiority certainly couldn't influence the choices of the laboring class or chip away at their aspiration for a borderless liberty.

It was an insolvable equation. There was no middle ground between the goals of the slave masters and those of the workforce. So we have to analyze how race operated in a colonial society in the process of mutating into independent Haiti. In this social formation, given the limits of the modern commodity-production plantation economy, the majority of the population had experienced an incomplete, if not failed, process of creolization/acculturation. So the idea of racial inferiority affected only very limited sectors of colonial society, perhaps even only a minority of the Creoles.

The Plantation and Colonial Society: A Dead End

The slave plantation was the basic building block that enabled the construction of the oldest French colonies of the Caribbean, and it was also used to build Saint-Domingue. But there were particularities to its history there, including the swiftness of the rhythm of exploitation and the fact that the geography of the colony didn't allow for the implantation of a *total institution*, because it was a noninsular and large, mountainous territory with fluid and porous borders. In Saint-Domingue, France sought to get rich faster, and therefore pitilessly, while using ineffective means of political goverance.

The colonial agricultural complex was the knot of the system. It operated as a military prison, a kind of penal colony, whose central actors were meeting for the first time and didn't share any common ideas and had few means of communication other than brute force. The first task of the detained was to understand the principles and values of the institution, which had been produced through a kind of social engineering whose goal was to exploit their labor force in every possible way. The slave plantation was a typical institution during the period of primitive accumulation of capital. It was anchored in piracy, plunder, and pillage.

The prisoners had not been condemned for any legitimate reason. They were required to submit to demands that would have been unimaginable and unacceptable in the societies they came from. Their alterity was recognized, as we can see from the pejorative characterizations and unthinkable slanders directed at them, and confirmed by the fact that the master-jailer had to carry out a training process in which they were taught to be servile and submissive. Their difference created obstacles that the authorities had to destroy in order to transform them into useful slaves. These authorities, of course, faced serious difficulties in overcoming the monsters they had invented, because they confused their own phantasms with the realities of the captives with whom they were dealing.

The colonial system of modern times manufactured labor reduced to slavery to satisfy its own needs. The plantation extracted profits from the slaves without offering them anything. "We declare that the slaves cannot own anything that does not belong to their master" (Code Noir, Art. 28). The instructions to the plantation residents had to be followed to the letter; there was no plan to educate them or integrate them into its structure, only to compel their blind obedience as long as they had a bit of strength and life left in them.

To survive and escape the all-powerful master and his correlative refusal to treat them as beings endowed with intelligence, the captives maintained their self-respect even as they submitted to the slave order and the culture of the plantation society. Their servile behavior, paradoxically, gave them some space or opportunity to improve their life chances through their own initiative. Their submission and performance of the most obsequious behavior might last their entire lives, but they never lost an underlying and irrepressible desire to free themselves, if they could, from those fetid and unbearable shackles (Fanon 1961, 54).

The right of the colonists to possess slaves/merchandise, and the values and norms that explain the behavior derived from this extravagant right, were inscribed in metropolitan culture. The individuals who had to be trained to play the role of inert merchandise came from a variety of different ethnicities. They didn't behave according to a collection of already configured points of reference. They had to invent standardized responses. The end point of the apprenticeship process that taught the rules of the plantation and its environment was the transition from tension between master and slave to an indecipherable submission to the indisputable and unquestioned omnipotence of the master-owner. But the tension was not necessarily defused.

Some of those reduced to slavery even earned their freedom as a recompense for their servility. The freedom they earned was called *emancipation*, a term that underlines the fact that this act belonged to the social geography of the modern colony (Vastey [1814] 2013). The colonized became a character familiar with the useful knowledge of the dominant system and experienced in the paths and means that could be used to protect themselves from its ravages. They adroitly managed conflicts.

As long as they stuck to the norms and principles of the plantation, the colonized conformed to mode of life the dominant society expected of them. Their futures depended on the desires of the master, and were transformed into successions of passing moments, chains of experiences deployed and given meaning exclusively within the history and future of their jailers. Nothing depended on their will or choices. The slaves, whether emancipated or not, were stripped of any future they might map out for themselves: they fulfilled themselves by copying the image of their masters.

The dexterity with which a slave followed the plantation's rules depended on a transition from ignorance—the realization that chaos surrounded him everywhere—to the gradual discovery of the rules of his concentration camp (Santos 2009). His enslavement started with his capture in an African village (Meillassoux 1986) or on the battlefield (Thornton 1993), continued with being *devoured* as a colonial worker (Hurbon 1987), and ended only with his death, or the improbable victory of a power stronger than that which had chained him.

The slave, by definition, could not escape the universe where she was imprisoned. Even the simple thought of leaving this universe proved that she didn't belong there, and that only an external force could maintain her as a captive. She was subjected to techniques of social engineering that were constantly enslaving her and confining her within a supposedly universal way of thinking that was not meant to be questioned, and therefore to the gradual destruction of her individuality and autonomous initiative. Within an expanding plantation society, the need for a constant supply of replacement labor meant that the planter had to carry out the intensive, serial manufacture of slaves. This required a regular supply of captives. As soon as the tamed captive could no longer offer productive labor, the system discarded her without a second thought and replaced her with a new acquisition to be transformed into a useful slave through the same crushing process.

Plantation labor itself created an inevitable apprenticeship process that compounded the impact of concrete interests in distinguishing between two parts of the same prisoner: the captive, who was legally or potentially a slave; and the functional slave, who was useful to the master, and the only one capable of enriching the plantation economy. The slaves and the emancipated survived thanks to the constant maintenance and improvement of their services to the masters. Their submission was their salvation. Questioning was a mortal sin, subject to the most severe punishment.

The contradiction and complementarity of these two types of social actors were contained within one person: the captive who was ready to rebel and the slave who was seeking emancipation. The two actors were conjugated through a daily practice comprised of precarity and instability, the consequences of the impunity with which the master distributed or cancelled punishments and rewards. Dispossession and poverty lay in wait all along the path that the potential escapees from the system of exploitation might take. So they had to cultivate the elements and markers of solidarity with one another to make sure that they would find refuge among the dispossessed in case of possible misfortunes or even just a bad mood on the part of their master.

In contrast, as the emancipated slave consolidated his social status he distanced himself more and more from the unfortunate captives, sometimes by performatively exaggerating what a zealous servant he was and intensifying his search for favors from the system in order to transform them into habits and rights that were recognized and sanctioned at the highest levels. As I have already mentioned, the colonists of color carried out a relentless struggle to reintroduce the provisions of the Code Noir into legislation that would insti-tutionalize the hopes incited by the French Revolution among the oppressed of the metropole. During the fleeting moments when their interests coincided with those of the barefoot and the sans-culottes of France, the colonists of color never missed the opportunity to point out the salutary distance that sep-arated them from the captives reduced to slavery

When Napoléon's racist policies reminded them of the blindness of the modern/colonial empire toward all its servants, even the most zealous, the camouflage of this infinite, necessary, and embarrassing distance was sud-denly translated into the motto written on the flag of the Republic of Haiti—"Union is strength!"—as opposed to the motto originally chosen—"Liberty or death!" The most devoted servants overcame their misery through nego-tiation with the plantation masters and not in a confrontation that promised to become a form of collective suicide.

In a plantation society, emancipation was within the reach of only a tiny minority. The metropole's need to rapidly accumulate wealth required it to strictly limit the number of slaves who were freed (Debien 1974, 369), and it demanded of the colonists that they radically eliminate any behavior that might interfere with the transformation of captives into effective and useful slaves. Under these circumstances, the plantation accelerated the standard-ization of enslavement—that is, the transformation of people into robots de-prived of free will, individuality, and their own objectives to pursue. The slave was an automaton; perhaps specialized, but above all, servile in every corner of his soul. A cursed zombie: that was the profile of the character modern Eu-rope sought to create from the sons of Ham whom God had placed at their service.

Emancipation was limited to individual liberation and cannot be compared to a conquest of liberty (Fanon 1952, 199).[2] In the world of buccaneering mercantilism, the slave couldn't fulfill himself and enjoy his autonomy in the same way as the master par excellence, the white master. The latter couldn't be emancipated or liberated, and didn't experience the discrimination that littered the path of the free people of color. The modern white was defined as a free person by his very nature! The *libre de couleur*, a newcomer born in Saint-Domingue, carried in his memory the experiences of liberty charac-teristic of slave societies, where unwarranted discrimination disturbed and wounded people despite it's clear illegitimacy.

The case of the slave, even the Creole, differed from this profoundly. She lived specific experiences of a form of coercion that was established in refer-ence to African cultural traits—that is to say, the knowledge, behavior, and emotions that defined her as a prisoner. She carried these traits, but the col-lection of measures taken to gag her reflected them too. As long as the system of oppression was unable to eradicate the experience of a boundless liberty from her memory, her behavior as a slave remained a mask, an unavoidable demand placed on her by norms external to her own will and freedom to act. The captive remained invisible until the point where the blindness of the colonial state institutionalized the normal and natural character of this normative demand—that is, until the free will of the captive no longer had any place to express itself outside the normative prescriptions that had become daily habits. The collection of captives became a herd of slaves, and the march toward emancipation became the only possible path.

As Frantz Fanon and others have established, this process was never completed anywhere. In fact, it is itself proof of the perennial reproduction of the search for a boundless liberty. And in any case, this evolution wasn't completed in Saint-Domingue during the period that comprised the enslavement of the contingent of captives who rose up in 1791. I can't say the same of the free people educated in urban areas from the beginning of the eighteenth century. The judgmental comments of Julien Raimond, which I have cited repeatedly, illustrate this clearly.

In this context, any resistance on the part of the captives to their appropriation by the colonial plantation provoked a necessary response on the part of the planters, who had to get rid of the deviant behavior or the pariahs in the group. They unhesitatingly purified the labor force through the massacre of all the prisoners who refused to behave like slaves. Genocide, or simply the threat of it, served to create the optimal conditions for the welcome of the new *bossales* the colonists brought in to replace troublemakers. The extermination of the insurgents was never completed in Saint-Domingue, but it was carried out in Guadeloupe sufficiently to shatter the will of those who resisted.

It is important to keep in mind that the collection of new arrivals did not comprise a cohesive mass. The revolution in Saint-Domingue began with a crisis of the dominant system, rather than because of a clash of contradictory interests among opposed classes (Fick 1990, 239). Starting in 1789, France was threatened by dangers much more menacing than the latent opposition of the imprisoned laborers, who at the time were still disaggregated into disarticulated ethnic entities. But these threats forced the planters to displace the slaves from their ordinary productive activities and involve them in properly political ventures. While the masters fought each other in an internecine war (Lattre 1805, 41), the French imperial power's rivals contested its sovereignty over the territory. It was incapable of simultaneously maintaining order and defending its possession using its local police and metropolitan armies. It therefore rushed to negotiate the temporary participation of the captives in exchange for partial liberation. In the process, it primed and awakened the very political force it meant to destroy. France's fragility in the face of British and Spanish rivals forced it to negotiate with the contestation that was flourishing and consolidating itself among the imprisoned workers, and to attempt to channel their insurrection in a way that could help defend the colony from foreign enemies.

Inviting the apparently obsequious servant to participate in the conflicts between masters was a double-edged sword. It instrumentalized the servant's self-transformation, attempting to make him into a zealous domestic. The process of destroying his autonomous will in the isolated laboratory of the prison camp was put aside and replaced by direct participation in the spheres where the broader colonial society functioned and was supported. This maneuver offered him, simultaneously, a window onto the deep structure of the oppressive structure, a sharper consciousness of the conditions of his captivity, and a broader vision of his group's political power within the colony. As different interest groups in the colony openly negotiated their conflicts with the metropole, they exposed the nature and orientation of their power. The colonial empire was in free fall, and it grabbed at whatever opportunity it could to catch its breath, including the most dangerous one—emancipation. Its panic accelerated its own degradation and accentuated the visibility and vulnerability of its mechanisms of domination.

The slave was deprived of a future that she could build with her own hands. But the slave-owning planters were also prisoners of the circumstances created by their metropole. The plantation, and more broadly the plantation society, didn't rest on strong institutional foundations. It couldn't possess its own future. Or, rather, its future was completely defined by that of the metropole. The plantation system either disappeared in the wake of an uprising, as in Saint-Domingue, or else fell victim to productive forces that developed in the metropoles where plantation profits accumulated, propelling the global economic system toward industrial development and the free market. This evolution has been studied in Barbados (Beckles 1984) and can be observed in Martinique and Guadeloupe (Blérald 1988). In Saint-Domingue, it took the form of the autonomist movements of the wealthy whites and of Toussaint Louverture. After independence, the oligarchs sought to institutionalize the militarized agricultural labor that Louverture had put into place through the agricultural regulations promulgated by Pétion and Christophe and the Rural Codes of Boyer and Geffrard. But they couldn't guarantee the secure circulation and flow of money and merchandise.

This awkward situation within the international market was worsened by the fact that at the dawn of the nineteenth century, at the very moment when the free market was sending a new wind into the global capitalist system, the entire Caribbean began to barely scrape by. The region lost its competitiveness and was maintained essentially through subventions and favorable trade policies. French planters in the region sought to rebuild the monopoly system while others, subjects of the British Empire, similarly requested the destruction of the "fetish of the free market" and protectionist policies that would shield them from the hazards of global competition (Casimir [1991] 2007, 213). To protect themselves from the early stage of liberal capitalism, the planters took refuge in an increased administrative autonomy that allowed them to preserve relations of production that were out of step with those of the economic centers. In the process, they freely increased the forms of exploitation used with the slaves, the newly freed (Casimir [1991] 2007, 81), the cultivators, and indentured laborers.

The oligarchs who inherited metropolitan political power in 1804 differed from those who had been in control in the colony. But they remained the product of the racialized system that had created them. They had neither the means nor the intention of modifying the fate of the agricultural workers in any way. All progress in this direction was the result of the efforts of the subordinated classes rather than any economic projects supported by the oligarchs. They maintained the principle of the equality of the races, or more accurately of the epidermis, while validating race as a significant indicator of social stratification. They constructed the history of the country as one of a struggle between mulattoes and blacks, and emphasized the pursuit of equal opportunity among individuals of different skin colors. But this was limited to the spheres the oligarchs governed, the civil service and tertiary sector.

This interpretation of Haitian society accepted the justifications for colonialism and the slave trade, which emphasized the military power of European societies, and accepted the discourse about a hierarchy of civilizations. The history of the colonized country was therefore situated within the path set by the great powers. This interpretation was stripped of all moral or ethical considerations. The game of skin colors was installed at the heart of official policy, and claims about the superiority of imperial civilizations were used to whitewash the foundational crimes that had created America.

There was an advantage to deliberately deploying race as an explanatory category. The curse of Ham was refused, but his brother's right to conquest was preserved, and his lack of respect for conquered nations accepted. The superiority of Western civilization was accepted, and its vocation for softening the customs of the barbarians through violence legitimized. The first Haitian Declaration of Independence was pronounced "in the name of black people and people of color of Saint-Domingue" on November 30, 1803 (Malo 1819, 274). We can see the French white hidden in the shadows of this declaration, which was elaborated with the conceptual material he had furnished the rebels. The declaration discreetly formulated the wish of the people described as *black* and *of color* to become *white*. It issued a call to émigré colonists asking them to return and take up their former place in the colony.

Just as imperial France was incapable of effectively administering the components of the planation society while fighting other colonial empires, the Haitian oligarchs who followed them couldn't firm up their supremacy while juggling their relationship to the great powers and their management of the available workforce. Like France at the end of the eighteenth century, they had no choice but to deal with the power of those they tended to perceive and treat as newly freed or cultivators. This was all the more inevitable because France and the other colonial empires were launching the conquest of the entire globe, supported by the prestige of scientific racism. The Caribbean became the least of their worries, and the protectionism offered to the plantation system was a nuisance to the development of the global economy. Haiti and the region as a whole were structured by the West as an appendage to their own economies, and never as one that could be self-sufficient.

The True Haitian

The passage from freedom into merchant slavery, and even that from African slavery to American slavery, exceeded the imagination of the unfortunate *bossales*: village dwellers, agriculturalists, merchants from the Sahel, or Kongo soldiers captured by slave traders or their agents. The commodification and mass use of human beings—as disposable, nonrecyclable inputs for enormous agro-industrial complexes—marks the difference between American and African slavery. The treatment of the human being in the two cases was shaped by different systems of thought.

As they preserved or recuperated their mental health, the victims of American slavery embarked on a project of self re-education that gradually led them to protect themselves from the abuses and humiliations of the colonial plantation. The desocialization and absolute isolation at the heart of this Gehenna were overcome through the weaving of relationships of solidarity with their companions in misfortune. In this way, the solitary individual the slave trader sold became a member of a new social network, a grouping of peers that she had to discover beyond the ethnic fragmentation inherited from her birthplace, and had to construct thanks to fortuitous encounters with potential companions. Within these new social relations, any form of cumulative, self-propelled well-being had to emerge from the deployment of these links. They became primary, superimposing themselves over identities received from Africa, and tended to replace them. The golden rule of survival consisted in making sure not to weaken these improvements in the life conditions of this embryonic community, no matter how small they were. These gains were always necessarily precarious and provisional, constantly threatened by the arbitrary, unpredictable, and irrational decisions of the slave traders and their supporters.

The captives were now linked to one another. In order not to collapse mentally and physically within the corset imposed on them by European modernity, they worked to categorize the demands placed on them by their imprisoners. They identified those that weren't negotiable, and couldn't be openly skirted, versus those they could possibly delay or avoid responding to. They had to learn to distinguish between what they were and what the plantation and colonial society demanded of them.

In order to create norms that could guide their behavior and increase their chances of survival, this cluster of newly arrived individuals had to discover the logic of the milieu and gradually elaborate a coherent collection of references they could use to upend it. Once they had recognized the central role of torture in their socialization, they realized they had an unquestionable interest in comprehending and mastering those elements of the dominant culture that were indispensable for their survival. The apprenticeship encouraged by the master connected with their need to allow themselves to be trained. The colonists similarly chose the elements of their cultural background they wanted to inculcate so that the captives would behave along lines that were foreign to them. The captives, meanwhile, used the forms of knowledge they carried and the experiences they shared with their peers to select those traits of the dominant culture that were most useful to survival as they conceived of it.

The imprisoned individual began her journey in profound solitude. There was nothing logical about the arbitrary nature of her kidnapping, deportation, and exploitation. It was impossible to comprehend it spontaneously. Each of the myths and other justifications for racism that had led to her fate seemed more stupid than the last. The colonized built a new foundation for thinking on their own terms, through a daily practice that was judged on the basis of their particular cultural inheritance and the experiences they accumulated on site. The ongoing introduction of foreigners of diverse ethnic origins into the agro-industrial enterprise made their adaption more tortuous: different degrees of acculturation separated the successive waves of new arrivals, which created misunderstandings between creolized workers who had been broken in and had a knowledge of the context and prisoners who were closer to an ancestral heritage incompatible with the treatment meted out to them.

The survival of the agricultural workers in the midst of the plantations was the result of their irreducible will. There was incomprehensible and insurmountable opposition between the privileges enjoyed by the king's subjects and the total lack of rights experienced by the captives. But this contrast served to constantly rekindle the captives' determination. Though it began as an individual experience, this process of confronting and overcoming the situation also implied the gradual erosion of primary ethnic identities. The accumulation of daily experiences shared among comrades in misfortunate inspired new forms of solidarity. As they got to know one another, the suffering workers multiplied the cultural markers that linked them to each other. Together, they were able to better understand, interpret, and resist the imperatives derived from the racialization of human relations that dictated their daily lives.

Daily life became the soil in which the imprisoned cultivated and harmonized their counterinterpretations of the plantation and colonial society. Collectively, they learned how to survive within it. We can conceive of the conviviality in the workshops along with the conflicts between ethnic groups as a laboratory in which the captives discovered principles and rules of solidarity through contestation and the pursuit of liberty. They worked together in a little piece of hell on earth. But there, all day long, they defied the pivot of the plantation economy: the natural and social death to which they were supposedly condemned. And they also came to understand what methods for emancipation were the most viable. In the very heart of the plantation, they converted private life into an elemental building block for liberty, a place where they ingeniously built a space whose vocation was to embrace their entire existence. Commenting on Hegel's response to the Haitian Revolution, Nick Nesbitt emphasizes that the private life of the captive remained the only place where it was possible to establish an order that was, in principle, not built on any presupposition. This private life excluded all that preceded it, all that was historical or traditional. It was an order that represented a radical, unprecedented reinvention (Nesbitt 2009, 119).

The survival mechanisms that resulted from the patient construction and reconstruction of relations of solidarity and the production of communal knowledge reproduced the feeling that captivity and imprisonment were unacceptable. These processes contradicted the production and arrival of the slave as the substantive being that the master, armed with what he thought was his all-powerful nature, sought to manufacture. The interpersonal connections through which the prisoners depended on one another had two aims: managing the relationships to the dominant institution, and the relationships among peers. Combined, these gave birth to what I call family education, an education received from elders and older siblings in the community. This was distinct from the public education dispensed by official institutions, the schools and the churches, and which were pillars of the dominant system centered on cultivating the ideal functioning of the workplace.

The captive was educated and protected within the cocoon of private life. Her personhood was her only property. It was something neither the colonist nor the state could seize. Taking care of it became the only way she had to try and prolong her life. In this crucible, the captive reproduced herself day after day. She condensed her patrimony and history, a collection that necessarily excluded and refused the exploitation and domination orchestrated in the space of labor and the public sphere. Madiou made reference to this inaccessible, uncaptured, being when he asked pointedly: "Though the African was enslaved, did he ever stop being free?" (Madiou 1847, 1:v).

With sparse resources, the foreigner in chains reconstituted her individuality by working to create meaning and a reason to live within the world she saw around her. She tried to find the logic in the way she was received and trained on the plantation. She necessarily had to combine a knowledge of the rules of the plantation with the development of a parallel system of knowledge that enabled her to take care of herself. This system had to oppose, and substitute for, that of the modern, colonial state and the institutions whose task was extracting a maximum of labor energy from her. This parallel system became the foundation for the world she built. Its primary function was to delay or even potentially prevent her absorption into the plantation society. It represented a tenacious effort to sterilize the gestation process of the substantive slave. The interpersonal relationships woven by the captive aimed to delay her transformation into a disposable piece of merchandise to be used and discarded. Her intimate world was born through a daily, relentless struggle against the public life organized for her by the state and the plantation society with the goal of absorbing everything she produced.

The prisoners of the plantation arrived ignorant of the rules and principles of colonial society. On arrival, they began a period of apprenticeship that enabled them to understand and interpret the insane order of colonialism. They did so thanks to the development of their own system of emancipation-knowledge (Santos 2009). The mastery of the new environment went hand in hand with the deepening of solidarity among the comrades in misfortune. In a context defined by solidarity, the prisoners came to manage certain parameters of the host society through common agreement and to the profit of their new community. Their emancipation-knowledge moved them beyond the absolute disorder into which they had arrived, carrying them toward a response to slavery: the counter-plantation order.

The fact that the Africans surrounded themselves with what their bosses considered superstition signalled that they refused to negotiate the consciousness of their alterity, or the foundations for their dignity and right to freedom. As a group, they unflinchingly expressed their refusal to accept the proposals of the colonial/modern state as truths. They refused to lock themselves inside the unintelligible dogmas transmitted by the dominant institutions. They obeyed values they had given themselves, through practices defined by tradition and experience and carried and validated by their peers.

The key to understanding the social exchanges of the period doesn't lie in the content of the embryo of the oppressed culture in formation. It does not lie in the collection of *wangas*—or fetishes—and their virtues. The *wangas* probably didn't offer any more protection than a crucifix. But as a marker of identity, they did change the terms of the conversation (Mignolo 2000).

The garden plots the captives cultivated on plantations were the foundation for the development of the entire structure of the peasantry after independence. But even more essential was the way they challenged the foundations of plantation society. Originally set up simply to decrease the costs of the planter, the gardens had the unexpected function of enabling the reconstruction of the private lives of the workers and the creation of a set of social links that lay outside the dominant system. The space of the garden plots, seemingly integrated into the system of exploitation, became a foyer of subversion. The simple fact of coming up with a solution that deviated from the behavior and performance expected of plantation workers, the simple fact of not wanting to be rapidly consumed in order to enrich the planter, implied dreaming of a different life, a valid and plausible one. It signified the development of a response outside the norms of the plantation society. At the very heart of a plantation world built on colonial principles and objectives, the captives invented a practice of distinctive autonomy. This was the beginning of the development of collective, sovereign will, which imposed itself within narrow, furtive spaces, invisible to the dominant system.

By re-educating themselves in order to survive the slave system, the captives used a critical analysis of the plantation to build on and enrich the knowledge they had inherited and carried from their African homelands. Their cultural inheritance shaped their survival strategies. But as they increasingly adapted to their new context, they moved beyond this original inheritance and created tools for life tailored specifically to their new circumstances. As they negotiated the implementation of these strategies, they came to know and discover the inheritances of the companions in misfortune who shared the concentration camps in which they lived. At the same time, they codified the signs that separated this collective of colonized agricultural workers from the establishment's prison guards. People trapped in the same condition built networks structured by common behaviors and experiences. A border was drawn between the French on the plantations and the foreign prisoners—the people from outside—even as the different ethnicities that comprised the oppressed classes came together in a kind of watershed.

As they integrated themselves into the plantation society, the captives explored aspects of the new dominant system they were encountering. But they also discovered the resources their companions in misfortunate had to offer. They reorganized their universe, inventing a new totality situated outside the cruel, narrow landscape in which the master sought to trap them. It incorporated but also went beyond the African environment they had come from. In this way, they subtracted themselves from the plantation society, escaping its negative effects as best they could. Without having to leave the physical environment in which they lived, they transformed the landscape by creating spiritual institutions. They created a new space based on their own way of understanding the world.

The human beings living in captivity were deprived of any future in their lives as slaves. So they made sure not to dilute themselves into this category, which guaranteed they would have no tomorrow built on their own terms. The masters, meanwhile, understood neither the worlds the captives came from nor the worlds they were creating and moving within on the plantations. Within those worlds lived ideas, significations, beliefs, forms of social relations, memories, and even beings, all totally unknown to the masters. Armed with an arsenal the dominant couldn't see, the captives set about reinventing and redefining their present (Vázquez-Melken 2014). They did so by systematically reactivating the absences the plantation deliberately produced and reproduced. They exploited all the available avenues to decouple their daily life from the plantation (Santos 2009). They learned to move within a dimension outside the system.

The masters didn't understand how important these worlds were. Presumptuously arrogant, they used the diagnostic of savagery to interpret these emergent forms. Their obsession with controlling and exploiting the captives led them to disdain the multiform universe of experience and knowledge being built by the new ethnicities introduced into the system. The swarm of experiences that led these arriving groups to connect with one another, and the logic of the responses they offered to the plantation order through their self-education, eluded the vision of the authorities. The architects of the modern/colonial system couldn't perceive the gradual development of the consciousness of their class enemies. This only gave the oppressed more room to maneuver.

The culture of Mother France was the foundation for the thinking of the oligarchs. The self-management of the oppressed culture, meanwhile, was based on shared daily experiences and the gradual mastery of the ambient context. This made possible the synchronization of the captives' resistant behavior. Their thinking was verified and validated through innovations in daily practice. The plantation oligarchs didn't have any knowledge of the virtues of their prisoners. They compensated for their ignorance with an increasingly brutal imposition of the dominant culture and its whims. In order to defend themselves, the captives had to depend on managing the knowledge validated and universally shared within their community.

Even a profound understanding of the norms and regulations governing the plantation and colonial society shows us only one piece of life in the New World, the part governed by the piratical project of the metropole and all that flowed from it. The dominant culture understood the plantation system in a way that prevented it from envisioning the potential birth of a peasantry from the foundations of slavery. It couldn't imagine the conversion of the slave into a peasant, especially since it reserved the monopoly of land for itself. Underneath the relationships created by the dominant system, the captives' experience moved them toward the invention of the reverse of the plantation. They wove a new social fabric on based on an appreciation for the daily behavior of all actors, without exception. We can therefore see why the Haitian legal system could only ever see cultivators in the countryside. Over more than a century, not a single peasant crossed its line of vision!

When France's imperial rivals besieged the colony, the captives saw their opportunity. The collective management of these new and unexpected forms of social life and solidarity expanded and fully realized itself through a revolutionary movement that institutionalized practices that contested the established order on a larger scale. The historical sedimentation of these practices transformed the military victory of 1804 into a full-scale social transformation. The exploitation colony of Saint-Domingue became a settler society completely different from that originally imagined by modern colonial France. This new reality was not contained within the forms of knowledge available to the planters and colonial officials (Casimir [1991] 2007, 30). What the planters and their entourage considered unexpected and unthinkable appropriated the real and reconstructed daily life (Trouillot 1995). The architects of this new social structure built it with the goal of recognizing one another and fully realizing their own projects.

A new world was built in Haiti after 1804. The cultures of origin had passed through the screen of the concrete experiences of the plantation and the wars of independence. They converged toward an oppressed culture that was shared by the insurgent cultivators and offered the norms and principles necessary for the unfolding of the social life characteristic of independent Haiti. From then on, the population was no longer recruited on the slave market, and the women of the country could procreate in complete peace. The conditions of existence were modest, but the slave trade and the repugnance it provoked became an unpleasant memory buried in the dungeon of collective memory.

The colonial/modern state had produced the plantation by appropriating the universes of African societies carried by those living in captivity. Its goal was to silence and destroy them. It worked hard to invent their lack of history and tradition and, on this basis, to assert the incapacity of those assigned to this infra-world to produce their own autonomous knowledge, or to be sovereign in any way. The colonial society demanded that the captive let go of the free will that structured their world, to renounce the use of that will, without compensation for that loss. It demanded that they disappear.

The interlacing of links of complicity and solidarity between companions in misfortune allowed for the rebirth, like the phoenix, of another universe better adapted to struggle. The imperial West condemned this universe. But gradually, the prisoners of the slave traders built their own social order, their own world in the Americas. They began doing so on the ships that carried them from Africa, then continued in the workshops within the community of captives on a given plantation or in the *lakou* of the *doko* or maroon villages. In time, their initial will to live fully transformed itself into the sovereignty of a community of equals (Beaubrun 2010, 200). They cultivated new identities and new reasons to respect themselves. At the same time, they built new weapons with which to face their kidnappers. People who started out merely sharing the same condition, the same social class, ultimately molded themselves into people of the same birth, of the same nation. It makes sense here to follow Kriegel and keep in mind the original definition of sovereignty: "What is sovereignty? The emergence of the concept dates from Jean Bodin's proclamation, in the first lines of his major work: 'The Commonweale is a lawfull government of many families, and of that which until them in common belongeth, with a puissant sovereigntie'" (Kriegel 2002, 86).

The birth of the Haitian nation was not distinct from the Haitian Revolution. One produced the other. The oppressed class and the dominated nation emerged from the same process. The nation appeared in opposition to the colonial/modern state. It was the conversion of a cluster of individuals into an organic totality through the generation of a cohesive group essential to the survival of each individual within it. Each day, in response to the misdeeds and meanness of the colonial/modern state and its successor, a culture developed in response, elaborated from the experiences of the oppressed and the invention of new institutions ranging from groups of peers and families to *lakou* and village communities. The nation is the expression of sovereignty in all the domains of social life. It is the sovereign people in all its grandiose beauty.

The colonial executive had a monolithic view of the reality of Saint-Domingue as made up of a network of slave plantations functioning by respecting the racialization of human relations. Each plantation was linked to a given metropolitan entity and independent from the others (Anglade 1982). But in the interstices of the social fabric constructed by colonial domination, those in captivity patiently established institutions resistant to the external order and essential to the reproduction of their own consciousness of the coloniality in which they were submerged. The master claimed to possess the body, the time, and the space of the slave. But he still had to conquer, invade, occupy, and furnish it. He could make progress in this only during the periods of colonial peace, which Saint-Domingue no longer experienced after 1789. Without realizing it, the owner of a cluster of isolated individuals contributed unwillingly (and from his point of view, tragically) to the birth of the new nation. The only way to rebuild the plantation was to envisage the extermination of this newborn nation.

National sovereignty in Haiti, as elsewhere, emerged from knowledge that was oriented toward the taking charge of oneself, and in this way, toward the autonomy of the oppressed group's community and family. National sovereignty could not emerge from the apprenticeship process through which the colony's regulations were internalized. It didn't fall from the sky, like manna, for the state to use. It was experienced by the nation's residents as internal sovereignty, and from there was translated into political institutions capable of founding, negotiating, and defending external sovereignty. There was no way to protect this sovereignty against foreign power or friendly nations without depending on the popular will.

The ineffable beauty of the sovereign people emerged against the winds and the tides, in the very heart of a modern empire that did not hesitate for a second to try and exterminate them. It flourished as the result of a process through which diverse, isolated, degraded, desocialized, disoriented ethnic groups who were tortured, humiliated, and disdained by the entire Western world succeeded in gradually weaving together a sovereign nation. They did so under astonishing conditions of oppression, and the only resources at their disposal were their will, their determination to live, and their knowledge.

> Se gran chimen m te ye, kolobri,
> tout moun pase y ap ri mwen,
> Se gran chimen m te ye,
> lapli tonbe, mwen pa mouye.[3]

The Weakness of Collective Memory

There is a profound division between the two parts of our national memory. This division goes without saying for the oligarchs who detached themselves from the captive masses and wanted to believe they dominated it thanks to the institutions the colonial state put at their disposal. Long before the secession from France, the so-called superior classes were well aware of this foundational rupture in colonial society. They used the political progress of the republic to ensure the exercise of their civil and political rights as Frenchmen. Without batting an eye, they conceived of a plan for the modern state to arrange a sort of liberty for the newly freed that was essentially a form of house arrest. The development of the colony and the metropole, and the oligarchs' own well-being, depended on this feat of social engineering. All the nineteenth-century laws relating to vagabondage and idleness reflected the oligarch's sense of superiority, anchored exclusively in the approval of the conqueror.

On July 10, 1793, Sonthonax spoke to the National Convention on behalf of the civil commissioners and explained how this new concept of liberty would preserve the colony: *"It is with the natives of the country, it is with the Africans,* that we will save the ownership of Saint-Domingue for France" (Ardouin 1853, 2:179; emphasis in the original).

General liberty was perceived as a favor granted by the French metropole. It functioned within the ideological terrain established by the right to conquest and the racism from which it derived. It limited itself to a general emancipation that took care not to interfere with the political primacy of the conqueror, with his right to use and abuse his property, including the former slaves, who were now known as the newly freed. Through general emancipation, the supreme will of the state pretended to break the chains of the slaves. They presented this act as a gift. But the state didn't undermine its original right to property over its victims. And it didn't hesitate to retract this favor when it wished, and according to its own needs. The inhabitants of Guadeloupe and Guiana paid dearly for this retreat. The traumas of the reestablishment of slavery have never been forgotten there.

Aside from the pomp of its preamble—"Men are born and live free and equal in rights. This is the French gospel"—the 1793 general emancipation remained a favor granted by the sovereignty of the modern/colonial state to a cluster of individuals. Its gospel turned a blind eye to the rights of nations and of people. The newly freed didn't have the complete use of their free will, and were not allowed to think of themselves and construct themselves as a distinct political presence defined by their community's experiences. The general emancipation of 1793 was only a pause in the history inaugurated by the Code Noir, which created the process through which isolated individuals were reduced to slavery. The French authorities fixed a horizon for the newly freed that constrained them to ongoing submission to the sovereign people of the metropole or, preferably, a complete dilution into the colonial universe.

The decree of general emancipation only disguised the colonial matrix of power.

On November 18, 1803, the Haitian oligarchs inherited France's right to conquest. Caught in this straightjacket and the racism inherent to it, they acquiesced to the abolition of slavery but retained the house arrest of the workers, a form of captivity indispensable for the cultivation of export commodities. Toussaint's administration, based on militarized agricultural labor, confirmed this when it declared, "The liberty of the blacks can be consolidated only through the prosperity of agriculture" (Lacroix 1819, 1:324). By going in this direction, the oligarchs conserved the most formidable of barriers to human self-realization: they granted themselves the right, despite the absence of the colonial/modern state, to distribute land concessions according to their own policy and to impose this on the national population. It was the same key used by Louis XIV: the sovereignty of the state over everything that might emerge from the colonized society served to lock the Haitian political system in coloniality.

That was the basis of the coloniality of the public administration and its bureaucracy, but not that of the state created in 1804. The nineteenth-century oligarchs had only nominal control over the land and natural resources. They certainly exercised their political authority effectively over individuals, but not over any structured, stable group, any community, or any institution other than the army and the governmental administration. They didn't dictate gender relations or family organization. The basic knowledge needed for the successful functioning of national society escaped them. They were not equipped to produce any kind of new knowledge that would increase their empire over local society. That was what forced them to detach and clearly distinguish the state from its administrative framework, and to redefine it as an institution whose aim was to reorganize Haitian society after the defeat of the colonial, modern state in November 1803.

In the wake of the crisis of the last decade of the eighteenth century, the captives who made up almost the entire population set in motion their own liberation by defining themselves within another world that they built for themselves in America. Once they were liberated by the colonial/modern state—which had no other choice, we should remember—there was no way they would be satisfied by the offer of such a limited use of their capacities. Once France had called on them to defend its right to conquest, the colonial matrix of power shattered. It couldn't be reconstituted without a completely new process of conquest and a reconstruction of how it was managed. The oligarchs claimed a monopoly over natural resources, but they couldn't translate this claim into reality. They declared war on vagabondage, which was simply the refusal of the conditions of hiring imposed by the landowners, just as sharecropping was a refusal of the intensive monoculture of tropical commodities for export. By refusing to behave like a citizen attached to the land and imposing the breaking up of the plantations into small plots, the sharecroppers and vagabonds destroyed the relationship between capital and labor, and brought all the dimensions of the colonial matrix of power tumbling down.

After 1804 the only thing left of the colonial, modern state was a colonial, modern administration. It had no socioeconomic reality to administer except its own structuring. The descendants of the conquerors faced a monumental task: to destroy the universe created by the captives their ancestors thought they had vanquished. The oligarchs built a public administration based on the principles of the coloniality of power, and in this sense they were the real victims of 1804 (Casimir 2009, 205). But the oligarchs couldn't ultimately impose their vision on the anticapitalist, anticolonialist, antiplantation, and antiracist state that emerged after 1804 (Hector 2006, 7).

Writing a decade after independence, Vastey identified the power of slavery as the expression of the total control the conqueror had to institute over a conquered population ([1814] 2013, 74). If the conqueror managed to make captivity the accepted way of life for its subordinates, emancipation became a substitute for liberty, since it was better than nothing. But it obscured the fundamental role played by the state's whims in the process of liberation. Liberty, in such circumstances, lost its character as a natural right, or at least became something that had to be recognized through a favor granted by a friendly sovereign. The captive's perennial power to express his or her will to live could be materialized only within the context defined by the conqueror.

But from the moment it had to knock on the captives' door, the French colonial administration could no longer reproduce itself by transforming its preeminence into a normal and natural fact of life. It could no longer turn captives into slaves. That is why Leclerc turned to the strategy of a war of extermination. If the French colonial empire under Napoléon Bonaparte faced this dilemma in this way, what are we to say of the Haitian public administration, which, having taken on the continuation of colonialism, still dreamed of rebuilding the plantation?

Sonthonax's July 10, 1793, proclamation boasting of saving French sovereignty over Saint-Domingue thanks to the Africans (Ardouin 1853, 2:179) was certainly pretentious. But it represented a concession that outside all-powerful colonialism there was another power at work, and that the task for modern colonialism was to prevent this alternative power from finding expression within the state. But it was a challenge to seek help from this other sovereignty while simultaneously recognizing that the social organization at its core had to be defeated in order to insure the continuing control of the territory. This other power, after all, focused on and enabled the autonomous development of a sense of the universe's meaning and the free determination of what the future would look like.

As long as the captive didn't confuse or identify herself with the character of the slave or the newly freed, she maintained the right to decide for herself, and on the basis of a different value structure, what she would do. She could therefore make decisions freely and exercise her will—that is, her individual sovereignty. She consolidated this sovereignty within the plantation workshops, in the midst of concrete groups of accomplices who were captives like her. Together, they built a communal sovereignty. By preserving the memory of being free and autonomous, she channeled a shared demand on the part of the population as a whole, one the ineffable Madiou once again captured in a sweeping passage that juxtaposes the beliefs of Vodou with the establishment of a national vision of the world: "During the wars of liberty from 1791 to 1794, Vodou contributed crucially to the success of the insurgent slaves by overexciting their fanaticism to the highest decree. . . . The masses, black and having acquired all civil and political rights, gained ground everywhere. Their customs, which were fundamentally African, took root. Many of the mixed-bloods who made up a tenth of the population in all were almost identical to the blacks in terms of their customs, habits, and aspirations" (Madiou 1847, 5:107).

Twenty years after independence, Boyer gathered civil and military authorities who trembled in the face of the threats issued by the Baron de Mackau to force him to sign the ordinance of France's Charles X recognizing the independence of his colony. Madiou narrates this while noting the path that had been taken to achieve national sovereignty:

> They [the civil and military authories] mostly arrived influenced by the worries of the urban families who feared a bombardment and the consequent destruction of their interests. These worries existed primarily among the wealthy classes of the population who were afraid of the rude, painful, and nearly homeless existence of those who lived in the plains and the mountains. Here it is worth remembering that the cruel and heroic war of independence had been supported only by the inhabitants of the mountains and plains, that they alone had furnished the battalions among whom there were only few rare men from the elite who had been educated and raised in the towns. (Madiou 1847, 6:455)

The public authorities linked to the imperial community were part of a different history from that of the captives, who, in expressing their grievances, did not seek to conquer the colonial/modern administration. These two histories are of a fundamentally different nature. The public administration adapted the Code Noir to the political powers that emerged through the upheavals caused by the French Revolution. The captives attacked the Code Noir itself, along with the very foundations of the imperial community.

The oppressed necessarily sought to construct a society that took their needs into account, a society that reproduced and nourished itself. They couldn't have imagined that freedom depended on the reason of state, or have been satisfied with handing over the defense of their interests to the supposedly literate former owners of slaves. Haitian collective memory has two ears. One listens to the anxieties of the classes "afraid of the rude, painful, and nearly homeless existence of those who lived in the plains and the mountains" and seeks only to guarantee the high patronage of a metropole. The other nourishes itself from the experiences and needs of the civil society that it built and, against tremendous odds, managed to satisfy—modestly, but in full sovereignty.

Sovereignty and Independence in Haiti

When the threat of losing their slaves became imminent, the colonists of Saint-Domingue developed the idea of seceding from France. They considered their slaves property acquired entirely legitimately (according to the Western, modern, colonial norms!) and in good faith. The attack by metropolitan legislators on this property in slaves differed from the seizures of the properties of nobles and clergy by revolutionary France. The slaves represented labor as it existed in the colonies. This strategic position granted these unfortunates a power to resist that the nobles and clergy couldn't exercise. In the colony, the state suddenly invited foreigners that it had put to work against their will to become involved in its conflicts. But it needed to plan some way of controlling the defiance this involvement encouraged, and some means of protecting the weakened relationship between capital and labor.

The jurists and legislators moved between two different worlds—that of the metropole and that of the colony—but with a collection of knowledge that belonged to the former. Given the fundamental role the colonial link played in the construction of modern Europe, the effort to transpose the progress of their philosophy to the slave colonies endangered the sovereignty of the imperial state and the territories it possessed, as well as the structural dependency of the overseas enterprises it supported. Their inopportune intrusion into the universe of the captive individuals revealed the Achilles heel of the modern/colonial state, destabilized the economic structure in its possessions, and retroactively fueled the crisis of the imperial political system.

The abolition of slavery by France was an expedient taken for reasons of state. Soon afterwards, French merchants were outlawed from participating in the slave trade. In addition to defending its colonies with armies of the newly freed, France also sought to weaken the British Empire by encouraging slave revolts in its territories (Dubois 2003, 293). In other words, the metropolitan authorities felt they had so much power over the slaves that they could use them against the international economic system. Enlightenment philosophers certainly attacked slavery to protest against its abuses, but also and above all to "install a colonial condition that was more durable, effective, and profitable" (Hurbon 1987, 79). And we should add that they also hoped to promote the hegemony of the French Republic. The fate of the slaves was entirely secondary in the unfolding of the events during which the captives briefly saw their chains shattered.

So the causes and consequences of this measure taken by the French state were very different from those that surrounded British abolition a few decades later. The latter seems to have been connected to changes in the global imperial economic structure. The British ended the slave trade in 1807 and then, a quarter of a century later—that is, a generation later—set the process of the abolition of slavery in motion. The French general emancipation of 1793 belonged to a world in which brute force imagined itself capable of molding reality according to its will. The empire maintained the right of slave traders to import imprisoned cultivators. It sought to motivate the victims of this foul trade to change their behavior and express gratitude to a benefactor disposed to import new workers whenever convenient. The events that led to the execution of General Moïse, Toussaint's adopted nephew, expose the contradictions and the arrogance of the presuppositions that underlay this decision. Article 17 of the 1801 Constitution, on the introduction of cultivators into the colony, leaves many questions unanswered, for no one can explain how to reconcile liberty and the slave trade.

As for the emancipated of Saint-Domingue, their struggles for civil and political rights had been going on for almost a century before the incendiary demands of the Third Estate. At the beginning of the French Revolution, these colonists tenaciously and vehemently demanded privileges from a regime that was in the midst of being destroyed by the very revolutionary wave they wished to ride. In doing so, they placed themselves at odds with the economic transformations being set in motion by the implantation of the laws of free trade, just as the colonists later chased from the island did: "This revolution [caused by free trade] is not yet finished, but it is unavoidable, though unexpected and not perceived by the planters who wish to re-establish Saint-Domingue. They are asking for us to give them back not just their island, but the ancient times, as if someone was still holding onto the past" (Simondi 1814, 49).

The *cahiers de doléances* (registers of grievances) of the American colonists and the emancipated, then, were essentially a breviary for the slave-owning planters of the late eighteenth century. They wrapped themselves in the milieu of the Old Regime and didn't adopt any specific aspirations from the French Revolution, much less those of the captives reduced to slavery. Julien Raimond attested to this in numerous publications, including in this telling line from his polemic with Moreau de Saint-Méry: "I start by declaring that I will take care to distinguish the cause of the citizen property owners of color from that of the cause of the slaves. . . . They are as distinct from one another as light is from darkness" (1791b, 2).

Furthermore, it is important to remember that the general insurrection organized by Boukman didn't ignite the entire territory. And, following the abolitionist Thomas Clarkson, it is not even correct to attribute the destruction of the riches of Saint-Domingue to the march toward general emancipation, for at that time, the question of emancipation was not being raised either among the planters or in the metropole.

> It was during that period, namely in 1791 and 1792, before there was any discussion of the emancipation of the slaves, that the greatest part of the horrible massacres and fires that have marked the history of the island took place. These deplorable events were not caused by the liberty granted to the slaves (no one was thinking of that) but by the quarrels between white planters and people of color, and between royalists and revolutionaries who, to quench their desire for vengeance against one another, in effect called on their respective slaves for help, but without any intention of granting freedom to them. (Clarkson and Macaulay 1835, 3)

The center of the civil war imported from France remained the treatment and management of property—both slaves and land concessions—and its implications for the civil and political rights of the property owners. The problem of emancipation or of general liberty was not discussed at the highest levels of society. At the very moment when revolutionary France was raising the standard of the sovereign people and seizing the property of the nobles and the clergy, the planters in the colony were seized with panic and fighting to ensure the primacy of the conquering, modern, racist state. It was, after all, the source of local political power and the key foundation for colonial property. The intermediary groups, whose roots were as mercantilist as those of the colonists, brandished the sovereignty of the state—and not that of the people—as their political objective. The question of determining whether the French or the English state would best secure the property rights of the privileged in the colony became secondary for the oligarchs of metropolitan background. But the majority of the colonists of color preferred allying with the French, given the situation of their peers in the British colonies. Before August 1791, the wind of liberty for the slaves never blew in either camp.

From the time when the pirates and corsairs laid down the law in the Caribbean, there emerged a conception of sovereignty as the seizure or conquest of a territory by the state. Its domination over the local population went without saying. Starting in 1789, the eruption of popular sovereignty into politics led to a new institutional structure where the European political structures came to derive their power from this new force. But in the colonies, the authorities and oligarchs brandished the supremacy of the power of the modern state, in its dimension as a form of governmental organization, as the axis of their contribution to the life of the republic. They did so just as this dimension was being diminished in the metropole. We can already see the profile of this republic, a kind of operetta that never intended to bow to the sovereign people of the colony.

It wasn't that the people of color and the emancipated remained feudal and distinguished themselves significantly from the republicans of the Age of Enlightenment. The distinction between them and their metropolitan interlocutors came from the fact that their ideas were applied in two different, though inseparable, contexts—metropole and colony. Created as subjects of the king by the Code Noir, the emancipated fought on the chessboard of 1789 to obtain their rights as French citizens. But as the Greek city-states and the United States of America clearly prove, there is no relationship between citizenship rights for some and slavery for others. It is important to recall, following Blandine Kriegel, that "after it was promulgated in 1789, it took a century for the Declaration of the Rights of Man and Citizen to reappear in the texts of positive law of the French Constitution, from which it was purely extirpated, banished, and ostracized through the entire nineteenth and early twentieth centuries. Can we really believe that this disappearance was just the result of a lack of attention?" (Kriegel 1998, 130).

If there was a revolution in Haiti, it was because there were other forces in play beyond those inspired by Enlightenment philosophy. The noncreolization of the *bossales,* and their creation of a distinct culture, indisputably founded the Haitian *tout moun, se moun* (every person is a person). While those emancipated from the life of a slave fought for their rights as citizens, the *bossales* and the true Haitians who joined them went to war for the pure and simple rights of a human being. In the modern, liberal world of French tradition, in contrast, it was only citizens who had rights, not foreigners who could be reduced to slavery.

The colonial authorities and oligarchs of Saint-Domingue, particularly the colonists of color, were not fighting nobles alongside the popular classes the way the metropolitan bourgeoisie did. They did not make the popular demands into their own. Only belatedly, and for opportunistic reasons, did they grant some legitimacy to the grievances of the wretched and the sansculottes of the colony. The civil commissioners admitted this directly in their testimony defending themselves against accusations of treason. The people of color didn't offer their material support to achieve popular sovereignty, but rather to defend the French, republican, imperial, colonialist, and racist state. Indeed, far from resisting the antirepublican rise of Bonaparte and the lobby of the wealthy planters, a number of them enlisted in the expeditionary army to support the policies of the autonomist colonists. In doing so, they showed that their interests coincided with those of the colonial/modern state, which spared them having to choose between the consulate and the republic. It is worth emphasizing that, in contrast to the choices made by many other heroes of independence, it was precisely to oppose Napoleonic policy that Vastey returned to his birthplace.

The formerly freed appropriated the demand for the abolition of slavery only after the civil commissioners found themselves forced to abolish slavery as an expedient to prevent the collapse of the colony and its surrender to the nation's enemies—that is, after the struggle between slave owners had reached its paroxysm (Clarkson and Macaulay 1835, 3). Madiou and Ardouin constructed their histories of Haiti on the basis of the Haitian oligarchy's opposition to any form of equality with those emancipated after 1793. They shared a profound conviction that the formerly freed were superior to the newly freed. Ardouin wrote: "The maroons had initiated resistance to European oppression, and so it was natural that they had this ambitious pretension [to organize the insurrection]. But it is obvious that since each of them wished to organize it according to the stubborn ideas they carried from the African tribe to which they belonged in their birthplace, they could never have managed to work together: *they therefore had to submit to the yoke that intelligence always has to impose on ignorance, for its own best interests*" (Ardouin 1853, 5:275; emphasis in the original). And Madiou: "The people had been a savage bull that ended up bringing down its masters, and now it had to be humanized and socialized" (Madiou 1847 7:111).

The French and Haitian Revolutions were not part of the same family of events. To conceive of the first as having inspired the second does not do justice to France's contribution to human history: the enthroning of popular sovereignty within the political. The modern nation did not construct the Haitian nation. Nation building is just an imperialist illusion that camouflages administration building. The Haitian nation invented itself alone in the context of a European, modern, colonial state that was at war with its very conception, from the moment the first embryo of sovereignty hatched. "As they waited, they [Dessalines and Pétion] resolved to continue fighting the leaders of the bands who, by emphasizing their priority in the struggle, would become a major obstacle for the realization of the projects [for independence]. As we'll see, it was necessary to control them through violence, and get rid of a few, because each of them in some way represented *an African tribe*, and could envision organizing the insurrection only through this barbaric approach" (Ardouin 1853, 5:261; emphasis in the original).

The problem of defining governance as being either civilized or barbaric is different from the question of popular sovereignty and the structure of the state. Starting with the struggle of the Creole generals against the leaders of the insurgents whom they called *maroons*, the people's sovereignty was perceived, recognized, and refused by the authorities. Polvérel noted this, as Debien (1949, 364) shows, and it was confirmed in the first Declaration of Independence of November 29, 1803 (Malo 1819, 274). The political forces active in the country came together around a common desire for independence (Plummer 1988, 94; Mathon and Turnier 1985, 6), but they brushed aside any possibility for popular participation in government. In other words, the popular forces who "initiated the resistance to European oppression" were not a political force! In fact, the marginalization of the popular forces in the final stages of the struggle for independence echoed the plans for independence that had earlier seduced the royalist planters, who also had no intention of transforming the colonial, modern state of Saint-Domingue. Madiou was perfectly conscious of the difference between the orientation of the state in Haiti and that imprinted by the French Revolution in the metropole. "Few men, even among the elite, profoundly felt the principles of 1789, even though they had produced liberty and independence. The traditions of the old regime had been only slightly weakened in people's customs" (Madiou 1847 5:103).

The only filiation between the French and Haitian Revolutions is that both involved the scission between an old and a new regime. In both cases, the structures that were the result of the old regime were attacked, and official versions of the new regime worked desperately to expunge them. The oligarchs conceived of the Haitian Revolution as the achievement of national independence, and a symbolic rupture with France. Any resemblance between the republic of 1806 and the French Revolution—which at the time was well and truly defunct—was limited to the verbal framing of legal texts. In fact the public administration of Haiti, to paraphrase Madiou, still hasn't gotten back up on its feet after the fall it took at the hands of the savage bull!

The formal structure of the administration the public authorities sought to institutionalize was not the product of the revolution of 1791 to 1804. Particularly after 1806, it was in fact counterrevolutionary. From Toussaint

Louverture to today, these powers govern a virtual nation, a nation that still has to be invented or built, with no connection to daily reality. They seem to believe the Haitian nation is Christian, French or French-speaking, Latin, and civilized. "A few Haitians who are partisans of a 'closed' or 'autarchic' community," lamented Dantès Bellegarde in 1938, mistakenly believed that "because Haitians are of African origin," they should "pursue the ideal of creating, in the center of the Americas, a Dahomean kingdom with a Bantu culture and a Dahomean or Arada religion" (Bellegarde [1938] 2004, 346–348).

It does not do justice to the 1804 revolution to lock it into a construct incapable of acknowledging the centrality of the political projects of the laboring masses who carried it out. I emphasize the absence of a filiation between the French and Haitain Revolutions to highlight the fact that in the first case, the pursuit of well-being was defined by the collective of all citizens, while in the second, those who appropriated the leadership of the revolutionary movement constituted themselves into a group that relayed colonial, modern power. They granted themselves the right to define the well-being of the population and to evaluate the desiderata expressed by the sovereign people, selecting only those aspirations that met the approval of the imperial powers.

Throughout the nineteenth century, the national oligarchs claimed that the Haitian people had a basic incapacity. For Edmond Paul, the Haitian people were "barely born into intellectual life," and therefore needed a mentor before they could reach sovereignty: "The sooner we enlighten the masses, the sooner and more certainly we can restrain political bad faith" (Paul 1882, 48, 63).

My conclusions will always be richer and more promising if I follow not the empire's gaze on Haitian society, but rather Haitian society's gaze on empire. When it comes to popular sovereignty and individual rights, the path taken by the Haitian oligarchs—like that of the French bourgeoisie during the entire nineteenth century—deviated from the path traced by the 1789 revolution. It would be unjust to see a family resemblance between this and the 1804 secession, just as it is inaccurate to link the deep changes incited by the Haitian Revolution to a West African or West Central African vision of the world. The recent work of historians studying the origin societies of the *bossales* document a notable social stratification there, but there is nothing similar in Haitian society.

Christina Mobley (2015) has analyzed the characteristics of the African societies where many of the last captives disembarked in Saint-Domingue had come from. They were from the regions surrounding the Loango coast and had been raised in complex, differentiated societies whose political and economic organization clashed with the simplicity of plantation society. The different military conflicts carried out by the kingdoms into which they had been born, the mechanisms used by the royal houses and the merchants to amass wealth, and the port facilities that these formations offered, along with their alliances with European powers, shaped the varied and relatively broad contexts of social stratification. There were glaring inequalities in these mother societies, and the slave trade reinforced them.

There were five main causes for the loss of freedom in this coastal region: wars, legal punishments, witchcraft accusations, debts, and sequestration. The result was that the victims of the foul slave trade were taken from all social strata. When they disembarked in Saint-Domingue, the *bossales* were carrying their societies' ideas of ethnic variation and the distribution of individuals along pronounced hierarchies of social inequality. They had been exposed to the idea of the possibility of personal dependence, but it was dependence for reasons and according to values that were shared between masters and slaves.

When we observe the transposition of captives destined for servitude in Africa to the context of Saint-Domingue, it is important not to lose sight of the essential difference between domestic and merchant slavery, emphasized by Meillassoux. Captivity certainly existed on both sides of the Atlantic, but the institution fulfilled different functions. In Africa, it was ancillary to the ways of life of majorities who were differentiated but shared one culture and related languages. In Saint-Domingue, it was the spine of a self-propelled system of production of merchandise that profited a tiny minority who were isolated in their culture and their language.

The inequalities between captives and their kidnappers, and within each group, were not comparable in the two contexts. Mobley's study confirms that, in Central Africa, inequalities were reproduced within a complex and stable way of life. Saint-Domingue's monoculture and the simplicity of its social structure were based on a dichotomy between captives and slave traders as well as on relationships that didn't tolerate a significant differentiation among the oppressed on the basis of norms they generated for themselves. The captives didn't all fulfill the same tasks or enjoy the same levels of prestige on the plantation. But the differences established by the masters didn't incorporate the differentiations born from the interactions within the oppressed group itself, which had different objectives and criteria.

An attentive reading of the historiography on the societies of West and West Central Africa where the captives of Saint-Domingue came from allows us to conclude that in all probability, the invariant of Haitian culture, the *tout moun se moun*, was a local creation that didn't come from African ethnicities or societies. This pivotal value remained the central weapon used by the agricultural workers reduced to slavery to resist the pressures of the imperial power and, ultimately, to defeat it. Haitian cultural production was situated outside the nature of slave systems, whether African or modern and colonial. The social inequalities it considers acceptable do not center individual achievements as the criteria for stratification and the distribution of privileges.

Conclusion: Escaping the Coloniality of Power

European colonialism inscribed new categories of human beings into social reality. Along with the whites and the blacks, it invented free people and slaves. In doing so, it succeeded in converting a plural world (Mignolo 2011, 28) into a dualistic one in which the free and the whites were fused together by opposing them to blacks, who became slaves by definition. Through the same process it produced the reasons for the existence of the emancipated, who were seen as second-class people, and for the mulatto, a black of the first class.

As they emerged after independence, the Haitian oligarchs appropriated this reading of the hierarchy of humanity and made it their own. The incorporation of foreigners, the black slaves, into colonial society is generally perceived and studied as an inevitable process of absorption into the modern world, a process that began with creolization and led to integration and assimilation. But in his 1814 masterpiece *Le système colonial dévoilé*, Vastey had already vividly described the repugnance and disgust felt by the captives who were introduced into the Gehenna of the plantation and had to adapt themselves to it. Neither those who managed the colony, and later independent Haiti, nor their intellectual guides, however, ever took note of the irrepressible need on the part of the majority to depart from the paths laid out by their exploiters.

Vastey's testimony dwells powerfully on the commitment of the oppressed to clear a path toward another world. As the slave system collapsed, their determination was propelled by the intensity of the suffering provoked by their experiences of captivity, by the consciousness of having had to live, powerless, in infinite disgrace over the course of sometimes two or three decades of their lives, and by the bitterness of having had to get used to this disrespect. Despite all this, with brazen will, they emerged from their tomb of dispossession. They stood up. This explains the use of the motto "Liberty or death" during the struggle for independence, which Jacques Pierre translates into Kreyòl as *Swa nou viv, swa nou mouri* (2011, 169). This conviction gave them the energy to confront and defy the unavoidable difficulties they faced as they sought to create a life that surmounted the profound limitations placed on them by the lack of material means at their disposal, and educated their families and communities in a situation of constant penury and the inevitable threat of ever-deepening indigence.

They had to build this new order on the foundations created by the initial dispossession of the colonial worker, a fragile and isolated person, the deliberate product of the trade in blacks and the institutions that promoted and benefited from it. The slave trade gave birth to workers on the marketplace, far from their mothers and their entire family. They couldn't share their lives with a chosen companion. In 1791, therefore, the nascent society was made up of a culturally and socially fragmented society. As it gradually gained autonomy, it took responsibility for its own destiny, for its reproduction and continuity. Haitians faced a nineteenth-century Western world in the midst of expanding and consolidating its totalizing vision of the universe. In response, they built themselves. They were desperately vulnerable in their singularity. They were creating something never before seen. And they were insignificant. They had only one refuge in the hostile world they were liberating themselves from, only one space for intelligibility, for a reasoned negotiation of conflicts, for envisioning the future. That was the community of peers they built outside of the dominant political structures created by the modern, colonial, Christian, and racist order, which remained inexorable and uncontrollable. Trapped within an expanding global capitalism, the world of the Haitian peasantry sought to hatch and grow. It defied the spokesmen of the West within Haiti, the oligarchs of colonial origin who remained immured in complete ignorance of the conditions of life of the majority population, and completely incapable of addressing even its most pressing needs.

The 1789 revolution established the popular sovereignty of the French people in opposition to a royalty of divine origin. The Haitian War of Independence was not carried out by a pre-existing sovereign people, united through traditional connections. Instead, it was the process through which the Haitian people were born, and invented themselves. It was the primary expression of the people's own sovereignty, as it was being constructed. If the Haitian nation had been several centuries old, the 1804 declaration of independence would have represented an end point, and the rupture with the colonial empire would likely have become the moment of the creation of a truly national state. Independence and the sovereignty of the nation-state would have been the same thing. But that was not the way things were. It is vital, therefore, that we avoid celebrating 1804 at the expense of the sovereign people and the specific form of civil society whose formation accelerated once independence was proclaimed.

The concrete conditions surrounding the formation of the Haitian people made the independent state of Haiti unique. Caught within a broader concert of nations dominated by colonial empires, Haiti's state did not emerge through the institutionalization of the rights of Haitians within locally produced political structures. The independence proclamation did not coincide with the promulgation and inauguration of popular sovereignty at the heart of national life, and it didn't reflect an expanded respect for the rights of the nation that was in the midst of rooting itself in its new environment. An alliance of oligarchs had successfully removed the territory from the direct influence of the imperial metropoles. But despite their grandiloquent speeches, they were stuffed with as many racist prejudices as good intentions, and they acted to prevent the power of the people's sovereignty over the territory.

The independence of Haiti accommodated the project of defending the rights of citizens that had been at the center of the French Revolution. But the oath at Boïs Caïman went further, putting into practice a decolonial project in which the rights of man were truly made central in a way that the French metropolitan state would only institutionalize starting in 1946. While the authorities who declared Haitian independence satisfied themselves with a minority of active citizens, the revolution of 1804 defined a decolonial project of the defense of the rights of man that didn't distinguish between those who were citizens and those who were not. The revolution embraced the sovereignty of the entire nation.

Searching for the sources of popular sovereignty, in this book I have returned to the colonial plantation. I have shown the difficulties surrounding the functioning of this institution within the historical circumstances of the eighteenth century. The captives retained many spaces of autonomy, and the metropole only reinforced them as it tried to deal with its urgent crises. The way the metropole navigated the political chessboard of the revolutionary period created an opening for the captives, and this accelerated their mutation into a unique ethnicity struggling to operationalize their will to live.

During the nineteenth century, the popular forces made themselves the masters of daily life in Haiti. The oligarchs, meanwhile, had tremendous difficulty gaining admittance into a Western community busy appropriating much of the space of the planet. The opaque curtain of their discourse, couched in the official French language, couldn't prevent their gradual absorption into local, popular thinking. They preserved the Eurocentric façade they had worked so hard to develop, but were molded by the *Guinean* customs and traditions that had, as Madiou suggested, surrounded them since the eighteenth century. Still, when they wrote about Haitian daily life, set as it was to the rhythms of local norms, they did so with a gaze that strove to be Parisian, painting a quirky portrait dedicated to Parisians and the other foreigners who never understood what was in front of them.

Their interpretation of Haitian society was based on external perspectives and produced for the benefit of foreigners. They looked at their country through Christopher Columbus's opera glasses, those he used to take in the island from the bow of the *Santa María*, producing a collection of interpretations that obscure the reality and beauty of the phenomenon that is Haiti. The earliest versions of these interpretations were those that attributed the revolution to the union of the blacks and the mulattoes, which is a way of subordinating its success to the behavior of the social categories invented by the West. These were the very categories long used to quietly justify the West's right to conquer and reduce the sons of Ham to slavery, turning them into merchandise for its insane traffic.

The motto "In union there is strength," superimposed on the arms of the Haitian Republic, represents the sacralization of this colonial classification of humanity. Since 1806, there have been efforts to replace the motto consecrated in Dessalines's flag—"Liberty or death!"—whose trenchant character was attenuated in previous constitutions by the call for "Liberty, equality, fraternity." The promulgation of the idea of unity has obfuscated the true distance between the class of colonists of color and that of the slaves, a distance that Vincent Ogé, the hero of the colonists, and Julian Raimond, their thinker, were willing to die to protect. This distance was supposedly overcome with a strike of the pen, for the greater good of a republic that existed only on paper.

The interpretations that describe 1804 as the "first successful slave revolution" are no better. Naming the process in this way validates the preceding sociogenesis of the slave. Revolutionary slaves can exist only in the nightmares of slave traders and colonists. Wandering there, these figures establish for all who have eyes to see that they refuse to live as slaves, and even less to consider themsevles slaves. When an observer opts for a perspective that goes against the victims, they take on the position of the aggressor. In the Haitian case, this makes it impossible to comprehend the content of revolutionary thought. The experiences, knowledge, feelings, and religious practices and beliefs of the classes in struggle are overlooked. Conceiving of something called a slave revolution perpetuates an oxymoron by seeking the causes of this revolution in the philosophy of the slave owners and slave traders, far away from the actual thoughts of their victims. This approach renews the convictions of those who desperately sought to recuperate or recreate their slaves in the wake of the unleashing of this glorious revolution, whose precise point was to prove that authors of the revolution didn't consider themselves inferior despite all the laws and definitions proffered by the modern, colonial West.

The same is true of the veneration of the first black republic. It shares with the celebration of the first slave revolution the virtue of synchronizing these events with the 1492 discovery of *Indians* born of Columbus's bad calculations, inhabiting an *America* that didn't yet exist. It drives the modern classification of humanity into *whites*, *blacks*, and *Indians*, the racialization of social relations and the need to justify this racialization.

This misapprehension has a second advantage, which is that it avoids grappling with the relationship between races and political organizations. The race of Haitians doesn't define their republic. In 1791, the general insurrection put an end to France's capacity to convert Ashanti, Mandingo, Ibo, Nago, and Kongo captives into *blacks*, into homogenous colonial workers. Understanding this can help us explain the intense conflicts between *bossales* and Creoles during the revolution, though it does not justify the assassination of the leaders of the insurgent soldiers (the maroons) throughout the colony. Haiti was a black republic only in the minds of oligarchs and foreigners who never perceived significant differences between the ethnicities that made up the working class. They didn't understand why Haitians might be different from other blacks.

If we decide to limit our analysis of the change produced in 1804 to the simple arrival of an independent state and a republic, we validate the pre-eminence of the king's colonial subjects and later the active citizens, privileging the prerogatives of private property that served to define their status, prerogatives rooted in contempt for the rights of nations. Contempt for the rights of man, and therefore for the pivot of the revolution, becomes the foundation for a biased set of interpretations. We end up searching for the stench of the capitalist, modern, colonialist, and racist system within the observed transformation, and avoid taking note of the structural upheavals and the revolutionary content that defined the historical rupture.

The beauty of the Haitian Revolution comes from its invention of a people. In nearly impossible conditions, that revolution established a context for life that was more just, one in which the population gave itself the means to flourish and grow. This put them on a path to natural and autonomous self-realization, and above all to the expression of a will to live unfettered. We must give the Haitian people credit for this victory, for having annulled the impact of official institutions derived from the colonialist, racist, and Eurocentric model of governance, and having focused instead on embodying the definition of the citizen formulated by the Enlightenment, through the creation of a robust, internal civil society.

The Haitian Revolution has traditionally been examined without taking into account the exercise of popular sovereignty in the establishment of Haitian society. This ends up propping up an apartheid-like schema. We imagine the revolution without taking into account the primacy of internal sovereignty. In considering independence without revolution, we refuse to see how the sovereign people emerged exclusively from the social relations they controlled and managed themselves. We overlook the fact that these relations were the only guarantee for national independence. But any formulation of independence that does not follow the lead of the sovereign people remains stuck in the coloniality of power. This leaves the administration seeking to take charge of independence to be buffeted by the winds of the international community, like a weather vane. "The pre-eminence of internal politics over external politics, the supremacy of the civil dimension over the political dimension, the basic concern for good administration and effective justice, all open the way for the refusal of the seigneurial model" (Kriegel 2002, 93).

The people anchored their sovereignty by exercising it locally. Haitian thought didn't come from France, or from elsewhere. It was produced through local social relations that were sufficiently cohesive to impose themselves on the external world and absorb the increasingly large sectors of the urban groups of the nineteenth century.

The Haitian peasantry—and those of the entire Caribbean—constituted themselves in opposition to the processes of integration and assimilation to the commodity-producing plantation. Their culture was and remains a response to slavery, a form of self-defense responding to the abuses inflicted by modern, colonial society. From the moment the captives took control of their gardens and provision grounds and demanded more free days in the wake of the general insurrection, the counter-plantation system and the institutions through which it was articulated were put into place. These included gender relations, family, the *lakou*, indivisible collective property, Vodou temples, rural markets, garden-towns, leisure, crafts, the arts. They were reproduced within and thanks to the local language the counter-plantation system appropriated. Taken together, all of these became specific tools for the class struggles of the Haitian peasantry. All the attempted attacks from the modern/colonial world represented by the oligarchs of the country shattered against these ramparts. Those who imagined they could fight on another terrain were not conscious of the characteristics of their social class. They could not comprehend the collection of structured institutions that make the Haitian a Haitian.

The words of Aunt Tansia recorded by Mimerose Beaubrun in *Nan dòmi* (2010, 200) define the local community as the cradle of national sovereignty: "The *lakou*, aunt Tansia told me, is a well-defined geographical space. But the civil authorities have no authority over this space."

Chapter 10

The State in the Nineteenth Century

Introduction: The State

Imperial societies were shaped by centuries of common life among the diverse social forces that composed them. Today, reflection on the state in these societies tends to focus on the functioning of the public administration, on the legitimacy of the institution, its formation, its norms, the principles that guide its management, and how well it performs. The social groups that emerged from these imperial societies perceive and experience the foundations of this public administration as being obvious. Their structure and the antagonisms they produce have come to seem natural and necessary, and it seems nearly impossible to question their reason for being, since their existence and that of the total institution they are part of define one another reciprocally.

When the authorities in imperial societies appropriated overseas territories, they determined that the colonies they had created from whole cloth had to be commanded by managers they implanted there. The legitimacy of these installed bosses was obvious only to them. But imperial powers had enough power to destroy all intentions that opposed their own. In fact, they did not even concede that any of these alternatives had a good reason to exist. What they, in concert with the oligarchies they created to manage the colonies, perceived as the state was nothing more than a hat they placed on the heads of colonized people. In their vision of their world, this one-eyed state was comprised entirely of the public administration to which they granted the monopoly on force. Its mission was to eliminate or at least neutralize all resistance to the colonial project. They did not comprehend that the fact that they had to constantly try and get rid of the obstacles they encountered represented an admission that the opposition's resistance was stubborn, and represented an inveterate rejection of their imperial principles.

When the conquerors of America established colonial public authorities, they wanted to believe that their conquest had been completed once and for all, that the powers they had created were eternal. The fact that they felt all-powerful led them to operationalize a model of public governance that privileged the effectiveness of the public administration, rather than emphasizing the negotiation of conflicts between social forces on the ground in the colony. The colonists didn't consider that the lack of equity in their decisions, which they compensated for through brutality, negatively impacted their effectiveness. Colonial political formations in which majorities allowed themselves to be guided by ancient demands for justice were described as *failed states*, or else *weak* or *maroon*. The colonists and their spokesmen pretended not to understand that these qualifiers described governments rather than the state itself. And the governments deserved it. In their arrogance, they thought they could do without any attempt at obtaining the submission of the governed.

The few indigenous people of the Caribbean didn't tear each other apart. So why did the modern state depend on such large armed forces, or later, on the constant threat of intervention by foreign powers, in order to manage the population? Why didn't the administration and public authorities negotiate a social order in a civil way with the miniscule regional populations? Why did they need to use such force to impose control over the territories with their imperial or mercenary armies?

In observing the history of the state in Haiti, I postulate the existence of a social force there that, since the formal beginning of the colony in 1697, has developed its own norms, institutions, and modes of functioning. The aim of this social force has been to limit the profit making that the supposedly all-powerful West granted to the colonial public authorities. I cannot lock my conception of the state within the imperial perspective tailored for the colonies. And I cannot conceive of administration in the colony as being limited to the public realm and its government. When I examine the history of the country, I certainly do not observe a uniform, clear effectiveness on the part of the political structure that was supposedly dominant, either before or after independence.

My argument is that the state in Haiti was ultimately forced to embrace the very social forces that had held the colonial administrations and their technocrats in check. These forces shaped the efforts the state actors put in place in seeking to fulfill their objectives. The particular modernity of this state, then, was not organized along the lines of a classic Western state. That was because, from the beginning, the public power faced another form of power, one that didn't seek compromise with the institutions defined by colonialism and was not at all interested in integrating itself into this oppressive structure. The state in Haiti included both the Western model, supported by the international community, and the political power of the oppressed who habitually and openly contested it and ignored governmental regulations.

The history textbook I grew up with taught me that when Desssalines proclaimed himself emperor on September 22, 1804, he was emulating Napoléon Bonaparte, who had given himself the same title on May 18 of the same year (Dorsainvil 1934, 144). Whatever the motivations of the emperor and his entourage—or of the historian who suggests this connection—the fact is that the state Dessalines controlled, like France during the same period, was an empire, a despotic state. The political powers in France and in Haiti were based on military force. They instituted a relationship of subjection that imitated that of the suzerain and his vassals or the master and his slaves (Kriegel 2003, 52–53). In both cases, right and law were absent from the relationship between the emperor and the subordinates.

The foundational act of state that inaugurated independence was the conquest of the national territory by the Indigenous Army. The government defined itself through a confrontation with its enemies, and by appropriating the domain that previously had belonged to the French colonial state. That is where it derived its right to govern this domain and its inhabitants. This was recorded in the act that proclaimed Jean-Jacques Dessalines governor on January 1, 1804 (Janvier 1886, 29). This oath defined liberty in terms of the rupture between the former colony and the metropole, and not with regard to the potential rights of the subjects or citizens to govern themselves freely. There was no discussion of the population's right to dictate their will through an expression of sovereignty directed at the governor-general and his successors. On the contrary, the January 1, 1804, Proclamation of the General-in-Chief reminded the people: "If ever you refused or grumbled while receiving those laws that the spirit guarding your fate dictates to me for your own good, you would deserve the fate of an ungrateful people" (Dubois and Garrigus 2006, 191).

The same was true for the regimes that followed Dessalines. They copied the formula inaugurated by Pétion and reinforced by Boyer (Moïse 2009): "We have seen that with the 1816 Constitution Pétion had in reality founded an elected monarchy. In this he had strongly moved toward the instincts of the nation. Boyer did more in 1819. He concentrated almost all power in his hands by retracting the law of August 7, 1817, on the attributions of the Secretary of State, the Great Judge, and the General Secretary and replacing it with that of March 22, 1819" (Madiou 1847, 6:17).

These historical observations, however, raise more questions about the functioning of this ceremonial sovereignty than they answer. The absolute power of the governors was exercised on individuals who were initially perceived as individual soldiers. It didn't govern the political, economic, social, or cultural life of the community these individuals formed. It didn't govern its subjects. It didn't even institutionalize a means of communication to address them as a structured entity, to instruct them or hear their grievances. It used a language its subordinates didn't even speak. It didn't govern the nation, only its detached, scattered particles. So we have to ask ourselves: what is a sovereign who commands but doesn't reign, who neither directs or listens to the structured nation he claims to govern?

My research shows that despite the illusions they maintained for themselves, Haitian governments were not sovereigns. Their absolute power could have been obeyed only by a herd of isolated individuals. But the population they faced was structured as a nation and, through this voice, expressed that will to live that makes a people a people (Dussel 2006). They didn't need the government's policies, and openly manipulated them to reinforce and protect the institutions they created and which protected them. Sovereignty belongs to the people. It cannot be delegated. It cannot be represented. The state in Haiti is the articulation between the governments and oligarchs issued from the modern, colonial state and the Haitian people, a sovereign people who created themselves.

A Sterile, Despotic Administration

At the end of Saint-Domingue's golden period, the majority of the population was made up of a mass of exiled workers, most of who had arrived directly from Africa. The colonial administration, weakened by the conflicts that destabilized the metropolitan environment, retreated when faced with the more and more forceful advances by rebel groups who imposed new rules. These groups experienced the increasing effectiveness of their actions, which incited them to move more directly from sly acts of marronage to open defiance by armed agricultural workers. They were recognized as insurgents or rebels.

These atoms of suffering, disdained, and humiliated humanity had been scattered across the auction blocks of slave markets, then bullied and terrorized on the plantations. At first, their efforts focused on simply overcoming their initial isolation. They worked on connecting with one another. They structured themselves into cohesive units and operationalized their will to live so that they could control their survival and reproduction, with weapons in hand if necessary. I focus on this journey and refer to the activities of the privileged only in order to better illuminate it. I observe two processes:

(1) How the Haitian nation was born under the iron rule of an imperial administration that used all its might to transform a multitude of adult foreigners into disposable merchandise to be used and discarded. My goal is to explain how this heteroclite heap was transformed into a structured ethnic totality.

(2) How this qualitatively new totality became a people by institutionalizing the procedures through which a nation in the process of being born translated its will to live into a reality distinct from official projects.

In reflecting on the conversion of a cluster of adults into a nation, and then a people who comprised an active unit, I observe their opposition to the despotic, imperial state. I construct a concept of the state that emerged from the particular history of the people I am studying. For, as far as I understand it, each people has its own history, and its own state.

This nation and people emerged from a collective of survivors made up of the multitude of captives reduced to slavery. These captives didn't waste their time taking stock of the riches of their environment and had no idea they had been invited to life in the "Pearl of the Antilles." The very means for measuring and admiring this pearl escaped them, and they were incapable of imagining that there was anything splendid or marvelous about it. They didn't size up the world surrounding them, and didn't evaluate themselves based on a hierarchy of well-being, since their own well-being didn't depend on their actions. They didn't evaluate themselves on the basis of how much merchandise they produced, or how much profit their oppressors amassed. Their fundamental desire was to end their captivity and slavery, to reappropriate their bodies and spirits. That necessarily propelled them into a war against the entire scaffolding of the institutions that conceived of and reproduced their ownership. They couldn't revere merchandise and put it on a throne. The main goal of their actions was to destroy the malefic colonial state, a state cursed by its very nature.

The colonial system granted itself an abusive power over workers living in captivity. This power was based entirely on brute force, and it deliberately produced their destitution and dispossession. Nothing could justify these government procedures or the destruction of their victims. The products of the despotic state didn't belong to it. The procedures this global institution used in generating these products had no logic the captives could comprehend. The state and conditions in which they were imprisoned had no relationship to their own achievements and successes. There was no way they could imagine rationalizing or restoring the authority of the imperial state. Their ideal goal, though one beyond their power, was the destruction of this authority. A state without authority, therefore, was a route to satisfying their most profound aspirations. They were driven by an unstoppable and permanent determination to escape the colonial public administration as well as the private administration of the plantation where they were imprisoned.

The captives reduced to slavery lacked everything. They didn't know why, and they didn't understand why they weren't allowed to acquire anything. To dream of liberty is to dream of escaping a hellish, vicious circle. To be free is to endow oneself with a natural capacity for action, for new creation, without regard for what has come before (Nesbitt 2008, 127), without regard for random and illogical accidents like state administrative structures, or for the historical particulars of the empire of evil. To be free is to invent one's world, a world made viable despite the presence of public authorities that can't be shaken off or transformed, but which there is no reason to reform or modify. To be free is to build a world safe from the harmful powers that live off your captivity and commodification.

In contrast to the classic European state, which reinforces its sovereignty by strengthening the links with the sovereign people, the despotic colonial administration clearly fortified itself by depending on its relationships with an external world hostile to the sovereign people in question. Any move closer to this oppressed people, any exercise of political rights by them, the smallest expression of their will to live on their own terms, all augured the end of local colonialism.

The colonists of color, a subordinated sector of the landowners, sought to strengthen their civil and political rights by profiting from the social movements that led to the passage of the Declaration of the Rights of Man and Citizen. But as they pursued their profoundly proslavery initiatives, they destabilized the system of oppression. Without meaning to, they made demands for the respect of the captives' rights of man viable. Between 1789 and 1793, their actions rapidly cracked open the colonial political structure and made the continuation of slavery impossible. Yet this opening also facilitated the installation of a despotic government that took over from the colonial administration in 1804, after the leaders of the masses of the insurgent laborers had been assassinated and their armed bands were forced to retreat. The national independence of 1804 was not the successful realization of the militancy of the *bossale* labor leaders or the deserters of the plantation system. That militancy continued with Goman. To speak of vagabonds and the lawless within the juridical system in place was just a politically correct way of referring to the deserters and rebel fugitives who had also existed before the 1793 emancipation.

This secession altered the links between the new administration and the racist international powers under whose patronage it had been used to operating. For better or worse, the budding political formation had to accommodate itself to the novel relationships with the agricultural workers, despite the feelings of repulsion that this rapprochement provoked among those in power. For their part, given the international proslavery environment, the collective of agricultural workers couldn't get rid of even a relatively powerless despot. They got used to parrying and escaping in order to annul the effectiveness of the application of governmental decisions. They purposefully made it hard for the administration, born out of this new relationship between the sovereign people and the public administration, to perceive them. At the beginning of the nineteenth century, the end of colonialism on a global scale was still far away. The West, in fact, was getting ready to conquer the world. There was a danger that the international community might set aside its differences and make sure Haiti was put out of commission, so that it couldn't export its revolution. The agricultural workers and political leaders had to find some sort of compromise. The only option for the new political formation consisted in trying not to be noticed and calming its own revolutionary ardors.

These ambiguous relationships between the Haitian population, the national government, and their international political entourage shaped the nature of the civil service in Haiti. It was caught between hammer and anvil. It couldn't devote itself to executing government decisions in harmony with the orientations of the hegemonic powers that were turning their backs on Haiti. And it couldn't measure up effectively to the sovereign people. It ended up burdened by the management of unending parries and escapes, the very expressions of the behaviors and orientations it sought to reduce. The despotic government and the sovereign people imprisoned each other in a vicious circle, and the system they produced turned around and around when it came to Haiti's insertion into the international community. The government displayed the superficial characteristics imposed by this community, even as it rubbed shoulders with a sovereign people who jealously guarded their decision-making power over their community life.

There were two worlds in Haiti that endlessly escaped each other: the world the captive workers developed by liberating themselves, and that of the public authorities. But they both needed the other. There was no way slavery and captivity could have evolved toward an institutionalized reign of a borderless liberty. Haiti was imprisoned by a then flourishing imperial logic of oppression. The two worlds present were born of antithetical values: the radical equality of human beings versus the modern racialization of human relations. They entered into contact only in order to reciprocally manipulate each other. Their imbrication defined the Haitian state, a concrete social reality that brought together two systems of thought. One of these systems, however, was repugnant to the modern international powers that sponsored the other.

I do not claim to offer a definition of the state applicable to the majority of circumstances, but simply to explain how I have used the word in this book. It is impossible to assimilate the history of Haiti to that of European countries, and it does not make sense to think it must follow the path of the colonial metropole that had assembled its components. I have sought to deduce how conviviality was structured in the daily life of the territory it controlled. I have not sought to describe its history as such. Paying attention to its evolution from the Treaty of Ryswick to the U.S. occupation, I have drawn a picture of the structure that resulted from the choice of its components (Heller

1961, 223). The fact is that despite the conflicts and contradictions dividing the social classes, they lived with one another. And those who take the time to compare their relationships with those of the metropoles and neighboring countries will see that they lived with an exemplary harmony during the century I have analyzed.

The state I observe in Haiti is not distinct from the situation of Haiti, the state of the country. I have emphasized that the pretension that the leaders had to act as leaders, as central actors in local social relations, did not correspond to the daily reality they lived. That is not their fault. In the specific circumstances of the Haitian nineteenth century, governments didn't modify economic and social life, and exercised no influence on the production and the management of the surplus of economic production. Whether emperors, kings, or presidents, whether dictatorial or sympathetic, they didn't significantly impact the goods produced in the country or the distribution of those goods, despite the taxes levied to finance the public administration and the lifestyles of the rather idle oligarchs. The actions of different governments did have some impact on daily life, of course, but they didn't modify or even significantly influence it. Neither the colonial state nor the nineteenth-century state governed the community of Haitians as an organic entity linked together by the institutions that characterized its civil society. Both states addressed a sum of isolated individuals who were not seen as being tied together in a social network.

In this study I have taken inspiration from Herman Heller to argue that a study of the state as a political and administrative structure has to take into account the "state of things"—that is, the environment upon which the actions of the institutions are exercised, and which in turn puts these actions in motion. The definition of the state that I offer includes all the social actors participating in the situation. The study also explores the projects state institutions put into place, or attempted to, in the context in which they acted, as well as the origins of these projects. I argue that this context (this state of things) was made up of two large, disjointed structural formations, and that the state (the acting structure of power relations) traditionally took care of managing and reproducing this disjunction, making sure that conflicts that might lead to the destruction of one or another of its foundational components did not get out of control.

The Haitian people germinated within the colonial, racist state of modern times. It excluded all popular participation. It possessed a metropolitan machinery for governance that allowed it to act in some ways, but not with the success it wished for. The civil service that took over in 1804 demonstrated an identical disdain for the knowledge and practices of the people, but it couldn't bully, influence, or change them. It was even less capable of getting rid of them, despite the plethora of agricultural regulations, rural police codes, and legal dispositions it issued through concordats or conventions.

The public authorities had no understanding or control over what the sovereign people were achieving. The population, meanwhile, was largely indifferent to the path taken by the national political authorities. The observer who compares this state administrative machinery to models issued from different histories and operating in different contexts cannot get a clear picture of the evolution of the population from 1804 to 1915. This approach remains caught in the normative, colonial, modern model without taking into account the unequivocal changes the Haitian Revolution imposed on it.

My goal has been to understand the radius of action in which the social forces of the colonial or national territory evolved. I therefore speak of the colonial state with terms similar to those I use to describe the arrangement put in place in 1915. There was no reason for the Haitians to want to reform the colonial administration installed by the U.S. occupation. They were deliberately excluded from modern-day colonial formations. But since the people's situation didn't change, or changed very little, they certainly took note of the failures of these formations, or of the relatively short-lived nature of their apparent successes. In Saint-Domingue as well as Haiti, these modern colonial institutions didn't have the success they were haloed with in Europe and the United States, because in Haiti the sovereign people were muzzled. I am trying to detect the logic underlying this stable, immutable form of existing and re-existing.

The insurgents of Bois Caïman and the Cacos at the end of the period I analyze here were socially significant groups who represented much greater majorities than those who operated the public administration—namely, Leclerc's expeditionary army and the expeditionary army of the U.S. Marine riflemen. The performances of the colonial state, whether before 1804 or after 1915, could never satisfy those who gathered at Bois Caïman and the other captives reduced to slavery, or the Cacos and the Haitian rural populations. The fathers of the nation prevented Napoléon's France and that of the Bourbons from exterminating the rebel population. In 1915, the U.S. expeditionary army and the collaborationists who accompanied them defeated the Cacos. The policies of the two invasions, like those of the administrations they left behind in the country, didn't force the populations to deviate from the establishment of their own civil societies situated at the antipodes of these supposedly civilizing projects. It wasn't that the international community was incapable of overcoming Haitian resistance. It was just that the cost of this subjugation was too great, and the potential benefit too small, to justify it.

The popular social classes and the oligarchs encountered one another from within separate civil societies, each searching for solutions to their specific needs in their own, autonomous way. The historical development of the state testifies to the existence of a particular constellation of institutions and norms articulated in the wake of the standardization of the relationships these distinct civil societies maintained. I postulate that these institutions and norms existed, though they were not yet codified, and served to manage the relations between the oligarchic minority and the popular majority. They arbitrated the conflicts between these two antagonistic groups, which tended to standardize and perpetuate themselves, and made sure that the interventions of one or the other didn't endanger internal equilibrium and coexistence.

The state in Haiti is comprised of this collection of institutions and norms managing and regulating the relationships between antagonistic entities. This state articulated the national population, the majority of whom were indifferent to the efforts of the despotic governments and their international allies. The majority saw this minority for what it was, a group opposed to life and thought focused on Haiti itself. Separately, each group remained powerless in the face of the local and international dimensions of Haitian reality. The invisibility of this system results from the fact that the constituted authorities—who were only so in appearance—refused to recognize that the behavior of the popular sectors had a rationality of its own. Meanwhile, during the period of study, the population didn't follow the authorities or endorse even their most well-intentioned projects. Their obstinacy was all the more flagrant given that these authorities not only participated, like all Haitians, in this oppressed culture that kept their civil service in check, but also actually contributed to the sterility of this civil service, or at least to its functioning along the lines the colonial, modern world expected.

The Birth of the Indigenous Haitian

The population that became Haitian during the nineteenth century disembarked from slave ships as a cluster of detached pieces, samples of humanity with no structured belonging to a significant social group. For the modern colonial state and its operators, the population destined to slavery was made up of perishable merchandise to be reproduced on the international market to fulfill the needs of the economic enterprises. Human life, the raw material of the system of production, became disposable (Mignolo 2015, 31), something to be immolated on the altar of capitalist accumulation.

Through their own initiative, these stocks of slave-commodities transformed themselves into people who created the web of relationships that define what it is to be human. Despite the colonial state and its operators, these workers converted themselves into communities capable of thinking for themselves, of protecting their members and offering them comfort in their distress. From the moment they arrived on the plantations, the market's impact on their lives was counteracted by the establishment of social connections. These networks worked directly against their conversion into things that could be bought and sold, and they sustained their sense that their captivity was unjustified. They overcame their absolute dispossession, defying the trade in blacks and appropriating the "right to the state of law" (Sala-Molins 1987, 24). They imposed themselves on the emptiness offered them by modern colonialism. The inexistence that the Code Noir sought to force on them was destroyed by the creation of the paths and means of their re-existence.

If the colonial empire had managed to gain the upper hand in the conflicts that began in 1791, the development of their private lives, the cradle for their larger social achievement, might have remained circumscribed to the plantation gardens and provision grounds and the *doko* and never have impacted the global sociopolitical structure. It is important to separate the genesis of this private universe from the external circumstances that enabled its viability and permanence. The modern, colonial state took the measures it deemed necessary to attempt to sterilize a new world that rose up anyway. It made the children of the captive-slave a possession that could be bought and sold by their master like livestock. The reproductive power of these arrivals fed the market for plantation products. Rather than offer an alternative to slavery or undo the effects of the slave trade, the colonial state used the fullness of its power to make use of the private life of the slave-workers to reduce the cost of the merchandise obtained on the slave market. It took measures to channel private life into the reproduction of public life, and reinforced these measures in every way possible.

The role of the slave trade in furnishing labor to Saint-Domingue was reduced significantly because of the circumstances that led to the issuance of the 1793 decree of general emancipation by the proslavery metropole. The captive population used the spaces available to them in the midst of the moribund plantation enterprises to invent themselves and put in place the means—material and institutional—of subsistence and re-existence. They organized themselves in order to insert the central institution in the reproduction of the human species, the family and its pivot, the woman, into this precarious and fragmented space. Private life flourished in the midst of the modern, colonial plantation, in opposition to the orientations of the public and private powers, to the powers of the state and the landowners.

The Haitian family, therefore, defeated the most important contribution capitalism made to the formation of the labor market. It defeated the slave trade not by producing the laborers demanded by the market, but by taking the steps necessary to eliminate the very offer of merchandise that animated this market. The offer of labor was literally removed from the market. Capitalism wasn't able to structure a labor market in the places where the rural community, the primary social cell, took root and imposed itself in response to the commodification of human beings. Initially, the Haitian family constituted itself specifically in order to systematically refuse placing its members on the slave market. Then, during the period that followed, it structured itself in order to prevent the generations to come from ever having to offer their energy to the labor market. The education it offered its members wasn't about preparing them to become the robots of agricultural industry. The community organized itself in open struggle against the alienation of human labor.

The working class, in other words, responded to the way the plantation demanded heaps of naked agricultural laborers. They did so as soon as they were able to. This was the collective response of a community that wove its social networks together outside the norms and principles of the reigning economic system. This community changed the terms of the conversation (Mignolo 2009) and in the process, reduced the negotiation power of the agro-industrial enterprises, whose arguments could influence only isolated individuals and which was unable to take control over the immaterial principles of communal solidarity.

In Saint-Domingue, capital and labor were not articulated so that they reproduced each other. The family, and the Haitian community that housed it, built a kind of autonomy for themselves that destroyed the pre-existing traffic in labor energy focused on tasks that escaped their control and responsibility. Even if some of its members had to sometimes transit through this market as aggregates of individuals, this incursion was seen as marginal to the life of the community. Those who participated in the labor market did so with resolution to skip out on the hiring contract as soon as possible. Individuals alienated their labor in obvious bad faith. And members of the labor force could count on the complicity of their companions as they extracted, as much as possible and with impunity, all kinds of advantages the contract didn't provide for.

As soon as there was a need for the captive population to reproduce itself outside of the slave trade, the colonial state insisted—starting with Toussaint Louverture's regime—that a normal family is mononuclear, patriarchal, and Catholic. This seemed to go without saying in a context where private property was sacred, although fathers among the agricultural laborers didn't have access to it. The imposition of this formula ensured a congruity between two institutions—the family and the labor market—and the harmony of their constitutive relationships responded to the capitalist economy's needs for its own reproduction. Refusing this obvious trap, the Haitian family accentuated its communal character and deployed its robustness and variety in the pro-vision grounds and gardens, in the *lakou*, in the *doko*, and in the villages. It invented of a rural landscape that had been unknown and unsuspected dur-ing the flourishing of the commodity-producing plantation. The working population eluded private property and the nuclear family at the same time. To cement and perfect the new life they invented for themselves, they en-dowed themselves with their own language, spirituality, and memory.

The result of this process was that the first generation issued from the end of the slave trade hatched a collective of people of the same birth, of the same nation. It was a nation built in America—an indigenous nation. This indige-nous nation emerged from a past of suffering and struggle, and sought to im-pose its cultural centerpiece, the idea that *tout moun se moun.* The speeches of Dessalines and the texts of Vastey expressed it in its full glory at the very moment when it was being born.

This True Haitian had nothing in common with Madiou's indigenous fig-ure, emptied of all content (1847, 2:162), the fruit of a deficiency in whiteness and the inequalities that flowed from it. If the social engineering put in place by the colonial, modern French state had possessed a modicum of effective-ness during the second half of the eighteenth century, it would have prevented the transformation of the budding nation into a people endowed with the means of overseeing their own reproduction in full sovereignty. But in re-sponse to the rising power of the local labor force, the metropole decided that the only solution was the genocide of the population and the deporta-tion of the officers of the colonial army. This poor decision led the nation that was germinating to operationalize its will to live in a radical way. They ac-cepted the challenge, and the possibility of collective suicide, and converted themselves into a state entity capable of defending its internal sovereignty de-spite the contradictions that weakened it from the inside.

Over the course of the last quarter of the eighteenth century, the majority of the working population was still being initiated into colonial life. They did not model their political behavior on that of the leaders guiding the French Revolution. It seems reasonable to conclude that the difference between the subject of a king and the subject of a republic escaped them. The foundation for their behavior was a conception of the rights of man situated at the an-tipodes of the modern racialization of human relations. They were foreign-ers to the colonial political system because they were new to a life of captivity. They were incapable of distinguishing between the rights of the citizen and those of man. Their daily experience certainly taught them that in either case, they had no rights, and in the best case, they were beneficiaries of the master's favors, even the favor of being allowed to exist. The conversion of the mass of workers into merchandise, the sale of both their physical being and their labor energy, could only seem irrational and abominable to them.

The political behavior of the Haitian people in formation was forcefully condensed in their opposition to the slave-owning planters who desperately tried to exercise a right to property this possessed population could only find vile, illegitimate, irrational, and immoral. The owner of slaves claimed that the individual he allowed himself to acquire, and didn't know, should function like a member of his family. Even worse, in his delirious fantasy, he imagined the slave as a minor with an empty mind. In this way, he dared to convert an exploitation based on uncontrolled use of brute force and the vile law of the strongest into a benevolent, civilizing favor. A reading of the history of Haitians from this point of view becomes a new verse in the history of France, a gloss on its illusory vocation as the "lighthouse of liberty" (Ardouin 1853, 1:17).

But I refuse to grant the metropole the right to define the itinerary of these new arrivals. Instead, I repatriate the power to create a society and its institutions to those autonomous adults who struggled to impose themselves within and upon their daily lives. This shift in perspective makes it possible to offer a reading of the advent of the Haitian nation, of the invention and exercise of its sovereignty.

The Haitian nation built itself as a response to the excessive labor exploitation promoted by the Code Noir and the laws and categories derived from it. Beyond the categories exported by the modern colonial empire lay the counterpower of these "wretched of the earth" (Fanon 1961) and the path their negotiations took. The Haitians were a people of agricultural workers born in the heart of colonialism who flourished by turning their backs on the harmful principles that lacerated their skin without mercy, and with complete impunity. Rebel groups seized the opportunities offered to them at the end of the eighteenth century and the beginning of the nineteenth, in order to re-exist. And they refused to invest themselves as an aggregate of individuals in the utopian project of an independent state that was the child, and double, of the imperial, modern, colonialist and racist state.

The Haitian Revolution was the conversion of an exploitation colony into a welcoming host society. It brought together the human groups woven together by the oppressed on the plantations, in the urban centers, and in the *doko*, first to escape colonial exploitation and then to fight it head on. This transformation required the negation of the racialization of human relations and the creation of the Haitian, an indigenous person who emerged beyond the colonial barriers of color. As Laurent Dubois proclaims in the title of his book, *Avengers of the New World: The Story of the Haitian Revolution* (2004), this child of the American continent took pride in having avenged the indigenous nations of the continent. She contributed to the reconstruction of new social categories without respecting the racial stratification invented by modern colonialism. The new indigenous person hatched as the response of a structured collectivity to the efforts of individuation characteristic of the modern, colonial labor market.

A New Identity

In an exploitation colony, the relationship between the town and the colonial countryside was defined by the dependency of the territory on the metropole. To achieve its objectives, the colonial, modern state sought to eliminate all reciprocal exchange between the countryside and the urban zones. In Saint-Domingue, as in other exploitation colonies of the Caribbean, the countryside was a creation of the town, particularly of the metropolitan port town (Mill 1852, 314). The case of Saint-Domingue was perhaps worse than those of colonies of the British Crown. As we have seen, Lattre noted the visceral dependence of the colonists of this island, who had no opportunity to develop their own autonomy. At the same time, colonists sometimes seemed to forget that the modern state's right to property over the territory itself was what had given birth to the colony (Lattre 1805, 182).

The inhabitants of the port towns interpreted the gesture of independence in a way that gave themselves a heroic role in the history of the Haitian nation. But they were holding up stolen trophies. Madiou denounced this usurpation: "The cruel and heroic war of independence had been supported only by the inhabitants of the mountains and plains . . . they alone had furnished the battalions among whom there were only few rare men from the elite who had been educated and raised in the towns" (Madiou 1847, 6:455). It is easy to understand the justification behind this sentence in the general dispositions of the first constitution of Haiti, the Imperial Constitution of 1805: "When the cannon sounds the alarm, the towns disappear and the nation stands up."

When we add to this a consideration of Christophe's policies promoting the production of food crops, everything seems to indicate that the nation budded, rooted, flourished, and protected itself essentially *outside* of the towns, among the agricultural workers. The port towns were and remained the weak link in the changes set in motion by the August 1791 ceremony. After 1804, the rural workers who invested most strongly in the struggle for independence chose to identify themselves as the *true inhabitants* of the country. This was similar to the way the planters of color had defined themselves as the true inhabitants of Saint-Domingue based on their struggles against the local colonial administration, and in contrast to the absentee planters. Those who *truly* inhabited the country were those residents ready to negotiate greater freedom of action and potentially cast off the ropes that tied them to the imperial metropoles. In both cases, the economic activities of the true inhabitants, the *True Haitians,* whether the American colonists or the captive workers, took place outside the walls of the towns.

The opposition between the colonial towns and their rural zones of influence reproduced the antagonism between metropole and colony. And the urban residents of independent Haiti desperately tried to maintain the administrative role the urban areas had played in colonial times, as a site for services and fundamentally for services required by the metropole. This role was, by definition, an obstacle to anticolonial change.

The colonial public administration was assigned to metropolitan functionaries. They used the trading posts of the port towns to implant colonialism, and enlisted the emancipated slaves they gathered in the towns into the police force and militia. The port towns became a communication channel for the resources that were gathered and transmitted to the metropole. The public administration took pains to sprinkle a few crumbs around to the members of the rachitic urban community who served it—its merchants, functionaries, and emancipated slaves. This cramped urban machinery didn't emerge from the productive work of the plantations, and didn't offer any significant services to the rural areas. The plantation tended to be self-sufficient. The public administration nevertheless claimed it had created the countryside. The town was conceived of as French, the seat of the representatives of colonial power, including the army and the police. It was the nursery of the emancipated slaves who were responsible for maintaining the colonial order and offering personal services to the colonists. The town's role was to install and to preserve the exploitation colony, feigning the execution of an unending civilizing mission. This was the base justification for its parasitic nature, and that of the colonial empire more broadly.

That is why the local definitions of the *inhabitant* are so important. They represent a break with and surpassing of the metropole based on a distinction between the interests of the central power and those of the colonized entity. Through his work, Julien Raimond (1791a, 1791b, 1792) persistently denounced the errors and racist bad faith of Moreau de Saint-Méry, who collapsed the free people of color born into families a few generations away from slavery and the emancipated slaves (people who were emancipated themselves or were the children of emancipated slaves). Raimond's pamphlets and his correspondence with his companions living in Saint-Domingue, the American colonists, make clear that this group made their living from the management of their plantations and not from being civil servants. The American colonists doubtless shared common interests with the metropole, but they also had interests that were specific and distinct from those of the emancipated slaves, who served the metropole without reservation. I haven't found a case yet in which the term *inhabitant*, in the sense of colonist or settler, was used to describe urban dwellers, whether emancipated slaves or poor whites.

The evidence we have at our disposal regarding the conflicts between the colony and the metropole shows the American colonists as being closer to Toussaint Louverture than to Lerclerc's expeditionary army. The emancipated slaves, in contrast, were more zealous servants of France. Like Toussaint and his high-ranking officers, American colonists who were agricultural entrepreneurs focused on the need to modify the state political structure in order to ensure the reconstruction of large-scale agriculture, the basis of their social status. Their relationship with the labor force was certainly racialized, but this was nuanced by degrees of creolization and of the mastery of the dominant culture.

The arrival of workers reduced to slavery in Saint-Domingue happened at such an accelerated pace that the upheavals that led to independence were incited by a population at the other pole of society, made up of a majority of *bossales* or first-generation Creoles. The authorities did their best to contain them in the role of passive citizens. The intention was to make clear that they wouldn't have access to all civil and political rights. Boyer, as I have noted, went so far as to imprison them in the incredible concept of *citizens attached to the land*.

But from the moment of the conquest of general liberty, these popular forces never envisioned a reformation or a restructuring of the organization of the plantation and the existing colonial state. That was in part because of the experiences they had carried from Africa, but especially because they clearly perceived the role the public and private powers played in their enslavement and merciless exploitation. Their political exclusion from this system probably didn't cause them any malaise, either before or after independence. They defended their rights, and therefore engaged in political activity, but did so without engaging with the institutions of the modern, colonial state. All evidence suggests that these newly freed didn't perceive the modifications in the public sector in 1801 or 1804 as significant changes in the structure of colonial power (Magloire 1909, 46, 288; Carpentier 1949), though that didn't prevent them from incorporating a response to the administrative structures into their activities and supporting these changes.

The population—less than four hundred thousand people who survived the passage from Saint-Domingue to Haiti—would not have uniformly been able to identify themselves with this land to which they had been deported. It is worth comparing the historical processes that subtended the diverse identities and experiences we observe in Haiti and Saint-Domingue with those formed in the other plantation islands populated largely by Creoles.

The work of Hilary Beckles enables us to see how, in a classic plantation society like Barbados, successive generations of captives in the same lineage lived on plantations owned by one family of masters over a century and a half before emancipation. By the end of the eighteenth century, nearly all the whites and all the blacks on the island were Creoles. It was possible for families of slaves to belong to the same family of masters over periods stretching six successive generations, which gives us a sense of the density and cohesion of Barbadian society. This was totally unthinkable in Saint-Domingue. There, masters were generally absentee owners, or returned to their birthplace in France as soon as they could. They never had the opportunity to impose on those kidnapped from Africa—two-thirds of the population—the spectacle of a lifestyle which, from generation to generation, ended up seeming natural and normal to everyone, both the dominators and the dominated.

To make matters worse, after the capital flight provoked by the wars of independence, the country lost its local, self-made entrepreneurs. The country was born with a residue of Haitians of French allegiance confined to the port towns and working in service activities. They didn't know how to manage productive work, particularly the work relations characteristic of the large-scale agriculture of commodity-producing plantations. As a result, Haitian society was put in place by a population composed of a majority of foreigners, educated outside the Western vision of the world. But it was led by the dust of public functionaries or those who sought places within the administration, novices in both the management of state bureaucracy and of agro-industry.

It follows that the sequestered laborers from Africa and their descendants had free reign to organize their own society. They didn't allow the initial circumstances of their establishment in the country to determine where they went from there. From the beginning of the upheavals of the 1790s, the agricultural laborers connected with one another through specific relations of solidarity and gradually became Haitians. They had never had the time to convince themselves of how powerful the economic and military forces of colonial society were, or to discover any kind of excellence in European ways of thinking and living. Their history, furthermore, saved them from the misfortune of experiencing the all-powerful military might of the West. After 1804 they didn't have to negotiate with any economic institutions, or any functional project producing and reproducing daily life, of European origin. There was no model of excellence to copy.

To understand the specificity of Saint-Domingue and Haiti, we need to keep in mind that the accumulated experience of the oppressed—almost the entire population—over the two decades spent on the plantations, along with the system of thought they extracted from that experience to organize their daily life, were at least as constitutive of this society as the metropolitan projects of social organization. The social project of the French hadn't mastered the workers they sought to reduce to slavery. It certainly hadn't satisfied their daily needs. During the conjuncture of the last decades of the eighteenth century, plantation regulations didn't lead to the reproduction of the workforce, and the capital invested in them, that the colonial administration hoped for. The planters of the colonial state didn't possess sufficient power to reproduce labor and capital and to force the captives to seek out only their own prospects for individual survival within the plantation regulations rather than other forms of contestation.

In Barbados the omnipotence of Great Britain was such that at the end of the seventeenth century the workforce was largely produced locally and from within the imposed structure of production. A hundred years later, Saint-Domingue's society was torn apart by the worst political crisis in its history at the same time as it welcomed the two dozen different ethnicities who disembarked in large numbers from Africa. The social relationships these new arrivals set in motion were not boxed in by the colonial offer of sociability.

Daily life necessarily led the labor forces in Saint-Domingue to invent a set of cultural tools distinct from the collection of rules and values of the plantation. Kidnapped from Africa, they, and their descendants, couldn't help but to produce an autonomous and sovereign world. Administrators sought to minimize the results these laborers achieved, presenting them as extremely limited. But even if this was the case, the captives and their descendants remained committed to managing their relationship with the outside world themselves, despite the pretensions and intrusions of the oligarchs and imperial powers.

The captive workers obviously didn't enjoy being slaves and couldn't have been satisfied by their illusory promotion to the rank of cultivators. The term *peasant*, which intellectuals used to describe them, was refused them by colonial society and the public administration of the nineteenth century. But nothing indicates that they conceived of themselves as simple cultivators or peasants, in the sense of being members of a layer of society subordinated to higher classes. It seems highly unlikely to me that the workers of Saint-Domingue broke their chains just so that they could find themselves at the lowest level of a social pyramid of a European type, with former members of the militia and police forces at its top. The colonial workers placed by history in Saint-Domingue found it impossible to comprehend their subjection to the West or to formations of a Western kind, and couldn't incorporate this form of obedience into the schema of the culture they were putting into place. Their thinking was articulated on the basis of the nonnegotiable equality of human beings. They reconstructed this equality in the heart of communities in struggle against the capitalist agro-industrial enterprises.

I am inclined to believe that the concept of the peasant served as an alibi that fit with broader perceptions. It was a way of responding to the challenge posed by the Haitian Revolution, and the entrance of this country into the concert of modern states on terms that Haiti itself had chosen. The concept of the peasant served to manage and obscure the disjunction between the two components issued from colonial society, and to overlook the complexity of the conflicts maintained between them as well as the fundamental reasons for their antagonism.

By designating rural people as peasants, intellectuals justified the primacy of the towns. But, along with urban dwellers, they were the only ones who perceived this primacy. Making the transition from slave to peasant the connecting thread of analysis served to validate the property rights of the colonists and to undermine the project of the internal sovereignty of the nation and all efforts at self-determination and self-reliance on the part of the population. The concept of the peasant assumed a rural life that didn't exist before 1804. Its application to postindependence society subtly consecrated the idea that the strata of emancipated slaves were the avant-garde, and at the same time validated slavery.

A Nazi concentration camp or a penal colony situated in the countryside isn't considered a rural community. Similarly, a plantation cannot be understood as a rural institution, unless the slavery and the destitution of the rural worker that were at the heart of this productive system are accepted as normal, legitimate, and even necessary. In that case, the only path forward for the potential peasant would be to cultivate provision grounds in the hope of eventually transforming himself into a small, independent producer. And the system would guarantee he could never move toward the higher levels occupied by the strata of large-scale plantation owners or the urban emancipated slaves placed in the saddle by France from the beginning. To aspire to this particular path as a peasant, those condemned to live in a penal colony would have had to start by accepting their foundational dispossession and annihilation. Those observers who saw a transition from slavery to a peasantry accepted the idea that the French and their descendants had legitimately monopolized the right to the land in the colony. And they took this as the necessary point of departure for Haitian society. We should remember that Dessalines paid with his life for questioning this right.

All immigrants, I would argue, lay out their paths in their new society in relation to the particular cultural baggage they carry with them, rather than by donning a straightjacket that the new society tailors for them. Based on this, I would distinguish between the *Ginen* Haitians or the True Haitians and the

French Haitians, or those of French allegiance (Casimir 2010, 69).[1] This is a way of recognizing that while France sought to impose particular conditions for existence, the victims of colonialist policies chose other options. The plantation society of Saint-Domingue wasn't a classic plantation society like Barbados, and the colonial regime could not impose its principles on the flock of *bossales* it received. As time passed in Saint-Domingue, there were fewer and fewer reasons for the exploited to draw on the variety of institutional models offered by France, especially given that the colonial power failed to put them into practice despite the unspeakable crimes committed by the colonists and the French expeditionary army (Vastey [1814] 2013).

The distinctive features of Haitian society come from the True Haitians, characteristic figures whose way of life became increasingly dominant in the country during the course of the nineteenth century, much more than from the few Haitians of French allegiance. In their interpersonal relationships and within the perimeters of their private lives, even the latter group took on a Haitian version of African cultures re-elaborated over the course of two decades of life in the colonial, modern plantation. The idea that Western culture was diffused among Haitians during their first century of independent life is a blatant falsehood, developed for foreign export purely as a way of maintaining a distinct identity for the oligarchs.

The Haitian version of French culture certainly offered access to the prestigious positions in urban areas, particularly in the civil service, that were linked to the outside world. But the point of departure of the construction of the nation was not situated within French culture, which was carried only by a tiny urban group drawn from the class of colonial intermediaries. Rather, the roots of the nation lay in the local culture produced by the population as a whole. The development of these local forms of thought animated the private and communal lives of all Haitians. The mastery of the oppressed culture served as a supplement for those seeking to penetrate the dominant social structure. It offered a safety net to families who sought upward social mobility, one that enabled them to avoid the possibility of falling from the heights of prestigious social roles. But the most prominent personalities of the nineteenth century, such as the presidents Alexandre Pétion, Lysius Salomon, Nord Alexis, as well as the emperor Faustin Soulouque, organized their private lives following the precepts and habits of the local culture, and this surprised no one.

Managing the disjunction between the oligarchs and the popular sector was complicated. The Eurocentric intellectual elite was besieged by the deployment of imperialist capitalism and the hegemony of racist scientific thought in the broader world. They sought temporary refuge from these aggressions through the bovarism Jean Price-Mars found irritating (1959, 76).

That is how, at the end of the nineteenth century, this elite developed the concept of the peasant, which offered the state a way of thinking about the colonial worker and their descendants that kept them imprisoned in their relative dispossession and precarity. The concept also made it possible to avoid foregrounding the actual primacy of rural customs and habits in national life, or having to directly deal with the question of the right to property. This right was, after all, denied to foreign whites, but above all, to almost all Haitians. In this way, the apparent hegemony of the Francophone oligarchs was preserved, and the founding inequality that separated the former captive from the "French" emancipated was maintained.

The popular sector in Haiti, in contrast, defined itself as a collective of *inhabitants*, and thus as colonists or settlers who had replaced the American colonists. The urban sector got used to referring to the peasant in a way that assumed that the two terms—*peasant* and *inhabitant*—were synonyms, or that the word *peasant* in French was translated as *abitan* in Kreyòl. This, however, was contradicted by the juridical literature of the eighteenth century, which opted for the term *cultivator* to describe them.

The idea that there was an equivalence between the inhabitant and the peasant, furthermore, is challenged by the fact that during the debates surrounding general emancipation, the French elites of the eighteenth century—whites and people of color—distinguished peasants from slaves. They did so to argue that one or another group was better off. But they also always insisted that there was no place for peasants in the colony. They used the term *peasant* to describe a figure within the imperial world, and reserved the concept of *inhabitant* for the European colonists. The juridical apparatus of the nineteenth century (as well as the twentieth) maintained this modern, colonial vocabulary, modeled on the Western concept of society and economy. It didn't perceive any social actors called peasants or inhabitants, in the sense of the colonist or settler, within the national territory. Only at the end of the nineteenth century did the latter term start to insinuate itself into the writings within the country. The strata that saw themselves as superior and cultivated saw the term *inhabitant* as a consequence of what they considered to be the characteristic ignorance of Creolophones, rather than considering it a term that was carefully chosen and imposed by the social group that determined the ways of life of the rural context.

The fact is that, in legal texts, the concept of the cultivator supplanted that of peasant. No provision was made to imagine, or even manage, the potential upward social mobility—and therefore integration—of this figure who was at once the majority and marginal. On the contrary, the cultivator was treated like his predecessor, the colonial worker, as a foreigner to the modern world and the formal political system.

The term *inhabitant*, on the other hand, did not imply any fixed social position. It could encompass a multiplicity of professional activities. A fisherman or carpenter might conceive of himself as an inhabitant, depending on whether he lived in the administrative center or town and whether he served the intermediary class or resided in the countryside serving the rural population. Above all, the term signaled the separation between the rural world and the urban world. Acknowledging this highlights the need for more research on the function of the towns, which remained prisoners to the role granted them by the colony. Everything seems to indicate that once he passed through the walls surrounding the city, the migrant gradually lost the attributes of an inhabitant.

Starting with Geffrard's government, but especially toward the end of the nineteenth century, Haitian society stabilized itself. This period that began with Salnave's execution and ended with the departure of Nord Alexis saw the emergence of the web of relationships between the provincial towns and their zones of influence, described in the work of Georges Anglade (1982), Leslie Manigat (2001, 107), and Roger Gaillard (2003). Citing the remarkable description by Candelon Rigaud, Roger Gaillard offers a panorama of the complex relationships that connected the landowning bourgeoisie to the inhabitants and to a bourgeoisie that was urban, industrial, commercial, and bureaucratic. The observer noted that land ownership helped those seeking to climb the echelons of political world and, from there, opened onto more lucrative economic activities. In order to exploit their patrimony, the landowners had to possess tools and other instruments of production, draft and livestock animals, and technical knowledge. But they also tended to manage small shops in the towns and, if possible, to receive regular salaries as civil servants. They grew sugar cane to produce rum, syrup, and raw sugar, and managed the institutions surrounding this production.

Then the rural world suffered the repercussions of the major global economic crises. The era of migration toward regional labor markets, and then toward the cities of the country, began. The nineteenth century reproduction of cultural duality had not cultivated ways of thinking that went against the propositions of capitalist modernity. Rather, it translated simply into the absence of these propositions. Haitian modernity developed its own version of thinking that corresponded to the history of its working class. The reigning racism made it impossible for this to be translated into an adequate agricultural policy. The failures of Toussaint and Christophe, combined with the departure of the American colonists, left the country in the hands of a class of low-level public bureaucrats, urban intermediaries with no concrete experience of the plantation economy and its implications. The offers of modernity made to the working population over the course of the second half of the nineteenth century were carried by skillful, but ultimately obsolete, pirates—capitalist adventurers, low-level consuls, bourgeois merchants—with whom there was no point in negotiating versions of self-reliant life within the global context. The civil service reigned without guard rails, except for budgetary limitations, and as a result, it fulfilled a task that most of the population didn't find particularly necessary.

The Exercise of Sovereignty

The crises provoked by the sovereign people of France when they imposed themselves on the pre-existing public authorities created disequilibrium among the landowning classes of Saint-Domingue. This led to civil war (Lattre 1805, 41). Taking advantage of this situation, the groups created by people recently incorporated into the labor force set themselves on a path that led to the invention of a new nation endowed with forms of life and customs better adapted to their interests and life conditions. The response of the workers defied colonial violence. It didn't seek to adapt to life within the plantation system offered by colonialism.

The structural changes of the French Revolution placed the established public authorities in opposition to a constituted nation expressing its will to live and a desire to organize itself differently. French philosophers of this nation sought to define and situate this expression of popular will within the collection of power relations in transformation. In Saint-Domingue and Haiti, meanwhile, there emerged a new nation and a people who germinated from a different past, with no affinity with the itinerary mapped out and followed by the French, whether revolutionary or not.

Europeans thought they monopolized all the property in their society, including those they called slaves. That didn't prevent the workers they had placed in chains from strongly rejecting this absurd pretension. For the conquering state and the oligarchs it created, the social order was founded on respect for the property they secured by invoking the law of the strongest, which they were the only ones to respect. The captives' efforts to move beyond their life conditions exacerbated the broadening fissures in the structure of colonial society. The hopes and achievements of these sufferers prospered in the interstices created by the political crisis. The incomplete character of territorial domination and the subordination of the unfortunate workers explain the expanding effectiveness of their rebellious behavior.

My research moves against the processes of oppression I observe. It seeks to exhume the unflinching conquest of liberty, and to accompany it. It examines what the sovereign people fashioned for themselves, and the visions their behavior institutionalized, despite the winds and tides, to save them from the hell in which the colonists wished to bury them. It navigates against the currents of the ambitions of the oligarchs and their intermediary classes, who were incapable of identifying with the sovereignty giving birth to itself all around them. These oligarchs and their intermediary classes were more interested in imagining themselves as products of the metropole, and as self-proclaimed deputies for its civilizing mission. They were not attracted by the risk the sovereign people were taking of being exterminated, of committing collective suicide. But their acceptance of the metropolitan mission was not the only option available to them. There were always other possibilities, and there still are.

Over the course of this study, I have considered how people who were bought one by one and placed in captivity in Saint-Domingue ended up, for their own salvation, rejecting individual submission to the colonial, modern metropole. They developed a relationship to rights that they negotiated with one another. Within their community, they wove together a sovereign power that accords with the classic definition of sovereignty (Kriegel 2002, 87). Facing despotism in Saint-Domingue, this community of companions living in chains fulfilled the role Jean Bodin had confided in the state. The emergence of this community enabled a move toward the demilitarization of society. A new space was opened up for a self-regulated life whose internal sovereignty took primacy over the dominium of outside powers, at least in the spheres of private life. In this way and in this autonomous space, the nature of sovereign power became civil, for it was nourished simply by the decisions of community members.

In Haiti, this primacy of internal sovereignty flourished in the nineteenth century and translated its de facto monopoly—which positive law pretended not to notice—over the management of available resources. Exercised by popular forces, this monopoly held in check the oligarch's projects of domination, including the dream of genocide they concocted in collaboration with the Catholic Church and the Christian West. During this period, the population produced and managed the economic surplus they acquired on their own, along with the entire matrix of social relations tied to the reproduction of material life.

The urban tools used for political domination excluded the sovereign people from decisions taken in the public sphere. But the people constructed themselves as they constructed their own civil society, organizing their specific forms of existence and guaranteeing their own reproduction. The Indigenous Army and the institutions it created to govern the country sought to act as the lords of lives and property and to exercise power it had gained at the ends of its bayonets. But these pretentions to power were countered effectively by forms of parrying that grew more sophisticated with each passing day.

It is urgent to more deeply analyze, and codify, these forms of parrying that contributed to the shaping of the state in Haiti. The reason it is difficult to understand the political structure of the country is that its self-appointed spokesmen refused to accept that from 1791 on, there was a significant distance between the two factions of the Indigenous Army and a third entity that formed the core of the nation.

The inheritors of the colonial system found it insufferable that the proposals of the (recognized) fathers of independence were defeated by a counter-plantation society structured by workers previously reduced to slavery and deserters from the plantations. But from the moment of the Bois Caïman ceremony on, the future inhabitants made do without external authorities to co-ordinate them and guide their decision making. Their way of life gradually absorbed the oligarchic sectors of the society—including the civil servants—who were incapable of living by following the European sponsors they claimed to venerate and imitate.

It is worth dwelling on this process through which the thought of the appointed workers absorbed the intermediary sectors. The apparent monopoly of violence seized by the Indigenous Army in 1804 situated itself within the terrain and boundaries established by the colonial administration. There was no transformation in this tool of governance, and it couldn't evolve into a structured civil service that offered services from the state to the population as a whole. Given its origin and the conditions of its formation, the national government couldn't mutate into a structure guided by a relationship with the population founded on the law and dependent on a demand for obedience that was effectively internalized by the citizens. During the period under study, and long afterwards, the budding citizens—the insurgents of 1791—didn't feel as if they were obeying laws that were fruit of a shared legal system that benefited everyone. Haitians could not impose their rights on the constituted authorities, or limit their power. Like the colonial government, the national government constantly operated on the basis of the reason of state, in opposition to the reason of the citizens.

Respect for private property as it was defined by colonialism therefore continued to serve as the cornerstone of the public order and the compass for the administrative apparatus. It did without the consensus or assent of the subordinated, who just yesterday had been merchandise to be traded. But in response to this order that was imposed to support new agro-industrial economic enterprises, those who had always been excluded structured their daily lives on the basis of consensual norms called customary. They reserved sovereign decision making surrounding property rights for the community itself, and took care to support the practices that undergirded life and the survival of communities. The new function given landed property displaced the center of the management of daily life from the institutionalized public authority—the state-organism—to a diffuse community. Public administration during the nineteenth century, suspended in emptiness, had no control over the major economic enterprises and couldn't nourish itself. It couldn't even assure the private lives of its functionaries and the urban residents, who in general fell back on the norms of the solidarity practiced by the popular sectors.

Before and after 1804, communal life worked to escape and manipulate this supposedly supreme power. But it did so without confronting it or trying to modify its modes of functioning. A consciousness of the fact that this kind of administrative power remained essentially an enemy power structured the community. It was impossible to get rid of this administrative structure, but it was also stupid to accept the violence it exercised without even attempting to cover itself in a varnish of legitimacy.

During the late nineteenth century in Haiti, the state administration didn't reflect service to the *res publica*, the republic. It saw itself as imposing a public order imported from France (Price-Mars 1967, 39). As a result, its goal was to institutionalize the dual composition of society and reproduce the two human groups inherited from colonialism. The majority group, both before and after 1804, focused on their self-centered objectives and flourished without competition, while the small coterie that had taken over the management of state power attempted to impose its Eurocentric vision. It failed because it couldn't put economic coloniality into practice. But the extraversion of this miniscule group did enable it to negotiate Haiti's interface with the Western powers.

It is true that the country was organized by a single state and had only one public administration. But the state was essentially a normative institution, while the administration defined itself as an organism-institution. The first was an order of things, an arrangement, an interplay of stable and standardized relationships. The second operated by issuing a collection of directives and regulations that could either reinforce the arrangements in place or modify them. The responses and behaviors of the population as a whole focused on the foundational arrangement, systematically resisting and disobeying the injunctions of the public authorities that aimed to transform them. While the public authorities and the local operators they deputized to carry out their injunctions considered it their right to correct, reform, or potentially destroy the contributions offered by the majority of the population, in their daily lives these same operators joined the governed in order to sap and ultimately hold these incongruous norms in check.

Emerging from a relatively short colonial period, Haitian political actors— of all colors and ideologies—began their journey carrying two systems of thought, built from very different life experiences. The American colonists and emancipated slaves had never experienced a society that wasn't founded on slavery. They carried an outwardly centered knowledge system and tended to adapt the ideal of the modern, colonial, racist, proslavery, Western state to the defense of their interests. The other system was based on memories and practices carried by foreigners to this modern, proslavery tradition, and it oriented habits without needing to refer to outside guides for behavior. It didn't seek validation outside the community of peers. This knowledge system was built in parallel with the construction of an egalitarian society based on an embryonic division of labor that made it possible to move away from any form of personal dependency.

There is nothing to suggest that the passing of time dulled the conflict between these two orientations, one focused on the defense of modern, individual rights, particularly property rights, and the other, more widely shared, tending toward the defense of the rights of man, people, and communities. Despite their divergences, these two orientations coexisted during the nineteenth century. But it doesn't make sense to compare the social climate in Haiti to the life of emancipated workers elsewhere in the Caribbean or those of the indentured servants from South and Southeast Asia. There is more. The Haitians had no reason to envy the hellish life the West imposed on the natives its empires colonized in Africa, Asia, Australia, and America, or the life conditions that during the same period compelled the exodus of myriad Europeans away from their original homes.

So why didn't the operators of the public authorities, witnesses to the universality of European imperial violence, simply reject the norms and experiences that had been applied in their territory during the preceding century? And if they did subscribe to these values, why didn't they put the orders and regulations they issued, which reflected modern, colonial Western thought, into practice in their own daily lives? The behavior of all the representatives of the Haitian oligarchy, from Toussaint Louverture to Vilbrun Guillaume Sam, make clear that they avoided applying these values in their private lives and, over time, therefore sabotaged the very norms they promulgated.

In comparing the public order and the communal order, I observe that the wars of independence of our first black republic(!) were just a skirmish in a long-term national liberation struggle. Our bicephalous oligarchs took on the traditional role of the hinge between the Haitian community and the modern, colonial world. The privileges that flowed from this role were of the same nature as those enjoyed by the militias and police forces of the eighteenth century, but they were accompanied by the same instability and insecurity. The splendors of the Pearl of the Antilles they had experienced before 1804 clothed metropolitan France and not the palaces of the colonists of

Saint-Domingue, and even less the homes of the employees of the militias and the urban artisans.

After independence, the only stability they gleaned in their lives as operators for the public authorities came from the solidarity they managed in their relations with the counter-plantation. Despite their illusions, the Haitian oligarchs didn't actually belong to the dominant European, colonial, and racist society. They simply lived in the service of this world whose dynamics they could not control. They couldn't cut themselves off from the Haitian nation, the only reliable and predictable structure they knew, and the only place in which they could hope to negotiate a bit of control. Haiti didn't have a dominant class capable of identifying and achieving its own objectives. The nation as a whole was itself dominated, and its superior strata couldn't divorce themselves from the rest of it.

I therefore propose that we consider the state in Haiti during this period as the limping, disjointed coupling of two distinct social groups, both prisoners of imperial dispositions from the outside world. Neither group sought to manage the split between these two social formations as if it was a conflict between two antagonistic classes. They didn't carry out any collaborative activities from which they could negotiate the sharing of profits. The oligarchic groups inherited a feeling of superiority with regard to the cultivators from the colony, and they formulated measures to operationalize that superiority. But they couldn't put these measures into practice. The cultivators experienced this pretension as one aspect of the situation to which they adapted themselves. But they didn't have to obey when it didn't suit them.

At the end of the period, the evolution of the local economic system prompted the establishment of some footbridges that united the two segments of the population, and a certain form of national unity and coherence began to emerge on the basis of the principles of the popular, sovereign components of society. I define the state as the collection of these rules for living together, the processes developed by two formations that began as strangers to one another but cohabited throughout the nineteenth century so that they could know one another, and develop a form of mutual recognition.

The Limits of Sovereignty

This work examines how and with what tools Saint-Domingue became Haiti, and describes the emergence of social forces that in various ways defied the colonial system. I have sought to illuminate how these forces distinguished themselves from one another, and how they were imbricated with one another in producing a new state of things, a new society. The events that set in motion the French Revolution influenced the colony like a catalyst in a chemical reaction. They led to a crisis that provoked the transformations we observe there. Without wanting to, the colonists set in motion a process of rapprochement among the local social forces. This process led to the construction of the national Haitian state during the nineteenth century.

The particularities of the colony gave birth to a series of significant, characteristic social groups. The captive agricultural laborers became the preponderant social force by creating links to protect and recreate their human existence despite the commodification promoted in their new context. This was the foundation for the birth of the Haitian nation and allowed it to grow. Groups of captives and other sufferers fused with one another by weaving together forms of solidarity that gradually appropriated a hope for life and for the mastery of their own reproduction as human beings. It goes without saying that the Haitian nation budded in the midst of colonial society. But the majority didn't identify itself with this exterminating structure. From the beginning, there was an antagonism between the nation and colonial society. I describe the path that was taken toward their rapprochement.

The specific weight of the captive workers, far more numerous than the free, granted them a major significance within the configuration of the slave society. In effect, the advancement of the colonial system depended to a large extent on the effectiveness of its management of the oppressed who were being converted into commodities, as well of the other unfortunates used to guarantee the smooth functioning of this process. For better or worse, the troops made up of people of color and the emancipated, both mulattoes and free blacks, had to clear a path for themselves in the colony. They seized upon the republican values introduced by 1789 and sought to improve their life conditions within the colonial context, though not at the expense of the values that shaped their private lives. They used colonial ideals to revive privileges granted in the seventeenth century, but not in order to apply them to the barefoot of the colony. They demonstrated no intention of overturning the public order or of modifying their daily routine. Compared to the captive workers they were a small minority, and were too weak to impose themselves on the metropole. So they were indissolubly dependent on the colony for their existence and social status. Their survival depended on their attachment to France, and they knew it.

And that survival, like that of all the subordinated groups in the colonial urban milieu, depended on their involvement in the space of public life. Since their approach of alliance with the colonial system was not guaranteed success, the emancipated slaves always kept a door open to solidarity with those who, like them, lived in precarity, though a much more serious one. It was in these other circles that the budding nation flowered, growing from the forms of solidarity developed in private life. Only the luckiest among the free could attempt to cut themselves off from the dispossessed, in the hope that their good fortune would last.

Before it detached itself from France, the island's society was composed of the wealthy white planters along with two other major entities with divergent interests as well as economic and political orientations that were based on what was most likely to enable them to survive. The urban sector lived off the services they offered to the representatives of the metropole and for the maintenance of the colonial order, while the captive workers primarily worked to produce agricultural commodities for export. Given the severity of colonial exploitation, the urban sector, though privileged, couldn't escape precarity. The colonial government offered no social services. So when it came to the principles that shaped their daily lives the urban servants, the mulatto and black emancipated slaves, had something in common with the captive manual laborers. They all had to manage a poverty whose acuteness was the result of the different aspects of the colonial policy responsible for private life. In this regard it is worth keeping in mind Madiou's observation, cited earlier, that "*the customs, habits, and aspirations* of the mixed-bloods, who made up barely 10 percent of the population, were *identical* to those of the *blacks*" (Madiou 1847, 5:107; emphases added).

From the beginning of their process of formation, the two sectors shared the same national language, the same reservoirs of know-how and knowledge, the same health services, the same leisure activities, and the same spirituality.[2] Their juxtaposition was reinforced during the second half of the nineteenth century because they were competing for access to the same traditional services, the supply of which was constantly decreasing due to the declining economic significance of the Caribbean plantation for the Western powers. It is worth adding, though, that the creeds that determined which tools and methods for survival each sector used were based on their roles in public life, and didn't impact the relationships and practices in their private lives.

The U.S. occupation of 1915 revived the distinctions seperating the oligarchs from the popular masses. By transforming the public sector, particularly the parameters surrounding international relations, and creating a mirage of great economic development, the occupation convinced some of the virtues of a more effective management of the government and public life. The intrusion of the United States strengthened the barriers built during the first period of colonization.

As it operationalized its will to life, the Haitian nation had to manage its fragile status within the concert of modern imperial nations and the foundational dependence of its oligarchs and its urban sectors, who were closer to these imperial metropoles than to the sovereign people. Haitians were prisoners of a global, colonial society, but had to take their future into their own hands. They refused, as a people, to surrender. They couldn't avoid the dependency of their urban sectors and oligarchs on the Western world. They had experienced the beginnings of the genocide ordered by Napoléon Bonaparte, and its leaders caught wind of the intentions of the Bourbon kings to take up the same Napoleonic project. Powerless, they watched the massacre of Cacos by the U.S. occupation forces. There was no choice but to develop a conception of the world that accommodated the fact that they had to deal with the modern, colonial, and racist West in order to survive. But the goal was to protect, as much as possible, the principles that gave the nation its existence and made it live.

The oligarchic social forces never tired of proposing a formula for economic organization that would allow them to live like Europeans and conserve their privileges in relation to the lower classes. Their insistence never resulted in any convincing results. It didn't change their precarious situation, and it didn't impact the lives of the population as a whole. The policies they put into place leave the impression of an age-old stagnation in Haitian society and economy. Unsurprisingly, the imperial modernity they breathlessly pursued reproduced their marginalization within the international community. In fact, it even accelerated it.

The dilemmas surrounding their autonomous insertion into the concert of Western states had been present since the divergences between Toussaint and Napoléon. Toussaint systematically sought to institutionalize a way of life that could move the governance of the territory from that of an exploitation colony to that of a colonial state, as defined by the Surinamese sociologist Maren Schalkwijk (1994): a subordinated state confided to actors equipped to negotiate and defend their specific interests.[3] The alliance of Toussaint and Julien Raimond boded well for the viability of this strategy. Napoléon's position, however, was to reactivate pre-1789 society, just as the Caribbean planters including Moreau de St. Méry and the Club Massiac wanted, with the support of the intermediate colonial classes made up of veterans of the militia and the police forces.

The Napoleonic instructions were inspired by pre-1789 policy, which made it so the colonial population could fulfill their specific needs only within the circle of private life. The best that population could do within the public sphere was to survive according to the needs of the metropole. As an organized system of power, the colonial public bureaucracy could not pursue any distinct objectives. It was meant only to facilitate the reproduction of as many captive laborers as possible, through the slave trade or a labor market as similar to it as possible. The determination of these laboring populations to live rather than just survive had to be contained, so colonial administration put in place a battery of measures aimed at reducing the laborer's power and increasing the qualitative importance of the oligarchies and urban residents.

In independent Haiti, in contrast, these two sectors inevitably lived side by side within the territory. All the state could do was to manage their relationship by intervening as little as possible in their internal organization. The inescapable need for mutual support ("In union there is strength")—if not actual solidarity—defined the approach and the path imposed by the international community on the public authorities. The precarity of the constituted society could only be overcome by accentuating the links between its components—that is, by reinforcing the nation, its spheres of private life, and the civil society founded on local norms. In this way, the oppressed culture of the counter-plantation generalized itself, as long as the colonial empires had their backs turned and didn't think about intervening in a significant way in the affairs of the country.

There is no need to reproach the state for not resembling the other states of the entire world. There is no need to reproach it for being weak, or strong: it was born as a political system during a siege, where all those besieged were on the verge of being killed. They didn't plan to promote a new way of life, but simply and modestly to assure their most elemental existence in a context whose confines were set by modern, racist imperialism.

In 1804 and throughout the nineteenth century, the public authorities operated and could only operate by doing their best to survive in the given context. They saw and wanted to promote the country as a Catholic, Francophone land disposed to attract the good graces of the colonial empires. National independence—external sovereignty—was brandished with great pride. But it had to juggle independence with forms of opportunistic servility required by the demands for survival in a world that imprisoned the weakest.

In 1804, the majority of Haitians—the True Haitians or *Ginen* Haitians— constituted a group of new arrivals within the American universe. The country was the only one of its kind to emerge from a non-Creole population, accompanied by first-generation Creoles. Haiti emerged from an aggregate of foreigners who, in solidarity with one another, converted themselves into a sovereign indigenous nation under the protection of a military bureaucracy. This bureaucracy was the inheritor of the colonialist aims that defined the international environment of the time, but didn't have the means to put them into practice. A wise analysis suggests that in the midst of an excessively proslavery world context, these 300,000 to 400,000 people were not in a position to quarrel with neighboring powers who were conquering territories as vast as the Belgian Congo and the South African Union. So these few hundreds of thousands of people followed their path, without fanfare, and ended up a population of nearly two million at the end of the century, keeping themselves out of the way of the imperial powers as best they could.

For their part, the minority of French Haitians remained committed to the concept of a modern, colonial state. They claimed to have taken on the role of forcing the foreigners within their country to adapt themselves to the normative corset tailored for them by the West. They sketched out a path for survival based on minimizing conflicts between them and the Western world. But they tried to keep up in the race to progress, investing all the effort their meager resources would allow into promoting themselves and trying to get the sovereign people to participate in the civilization offered by the late nineteenth-century West. But it was never clear that this Western, imperial nineteenth century was actually interested in welcoming them!

The economic decline of the Caribbean region as a whole diminished external pressures on Haiti. The natural reaction of the majority was to further escape the injunctions that limited their way of live. They flourished, and confronted the oligarchs and the urban groups only when necessary to make sure they didn't interfere with village society. The sovereign people imposed their system without much effort, and they further developed their self-sufficiency by continuing to absorb ample parts of the urban sectors. These advances and this coexistence—which wasn't always peaceful, we should add—came to an end with the 1915 occupation when the United States decided to include the country in its geopolitical strategy.

Living Independence

Access to land ownership, and to the ability to conserve and reproduce that ownership, was the dividing line between the two important social classes in colonial and national society. The subjects of the king and later the citizens of the republic had access to land; the captive strangers didn't, and neither in the end did the cultivators. It is useful to recall that during the nineteenth century, particularly in the zone of influence of Goman and Acaau, the relationship between the oligarchs and the cultivators developed (M. Hector 1998, 2006) in such a way that the agricultural regulations, particularly those of 1826, remained a dead letter.

Respect for private property was the cornerstone of the modern, colonial order. The new actors—those who were not recognized by the Haitian political structure—enshrined respect for the dignity and equality of human beings as the necessary axis of the social order they put into place. In the foundational texts issued by the descendants of the emancipated slaves, private property unsurprisingly was presented as the pedestal of social life and public order. For the former captives, meanwhile, personal independence managed within a community of peers was the connecting thread of social relations. Personal autonomy was conceived as the pivot of adult human existence, best embodied in those who in the vernacular were called the *granmoun*, or *grandes personnes*, the older people. This alliance or superimposition of two relationships—one to the property over land, the other to property of oneself as a human being—produced a particular form of governance. Everyone in Haiti is familiar with it and recognizes its particularities, but no one has yet codified it.

Rather than establishing themselves outside the control of the landowners on land that, at the time, was widely available, the masses of the landless focused on their deliverance from the dependency that tied them to those who owned land. The fact that they didn't consider colonizing new lands seems to indicate that, to them, the subjection of another person had become out of the question. They could now enforce this refusal in their daily reality. So the question of who used the land, of who worked on it, became more important than the question of who owned it. In other words, the population held themselves outside the control of the owners of private property without having to move around the landscape. But the usufruct of land does require a minimum of land tenure, or tenure over a minimum of land. The working population ingeniously appropriated or at least gained control of small plots of land. Once they had fulfilled this need (either through customary practices, or through the market), they obstinately strove to remove this land, now family land, from circulation on the market.

If this is true, it is logical to postulate that those who worked the land before 1804 considered that the public authorities at their service should have pursued the task of satisfying their demand for personal independence. Once that was accomplished, they would take care of their material well-being themselves. In other words, in shattering their chains the population that had been implanted in Saint-Domingue as an undifferentiated mass of workers had as their primary objective reversing the alienation of the labor force. So the task required of the legitimate authorities should have been to facilitate their expression of the need for personal sovereignty, and the sovereignty of their community, starting with their family. Liberated from the control of the slave traders (of all colors), the foreigners or the *bossales* considered themselves fully capable of dealing with the penury of their daily life. But they considered insane the idea that this life might be defined completely by other people, without the mediation of the institutions that they or their community controlled.

The relationship between the urban oligarchies and the inhabitants developed into a dialectic of living and survival, private life and public life, property and usufruct, personal dependency and the mastery of communal life.

The formal structures of the public authorities barely allowed the population to survive, while this population transformed survival into life as their communities appropriated the everyday control of social relations. The struggle against slavery—seen as the worst form of personal dependency—was crowned with success without any intervention on the part of the public authorities.

The former captives invented Haitian rural life, the garden-towns, the rural market (Anglade 1982), and all the institutions of productive happiness (Manigat 2007). Despite the availability of unused cultivable land, the populations who were the artisans of this achievement accepted being cramped on tiny plots of land. Or, perhaps, they didn't perceive themselves as being cramped on these small plots. The key thing for them was their independence. That was more important than individual or family property (Paul 1836, 35). Acquired land was left to inheritors through an institutional structure organized around kinship. Everything seems to have unfolded as if land was acquired in the name of a current family or a family to come, and not to serve just the person who acquired it considered as a person with no attachments. That person's inheritors had to be in a position to enjoy the land, to transmit it as an inheritance to successive generations. The land would guarantee them the possibility of emancipating themselves from the yoke and the subordination of the daily wage laborer. The pursuit of independence depended on the strengthening of the links within the *lakou* and with neighboring *lakou*.

Collectively and unflinchingly, the rural population opposed any kind of enslavement, whether open or surreptitious. But it didn't directly and collectively attack the property of the oligarchs, who claimed to own land but were incapable of exploiting it. The rural population's main goal was not trying access to a means of production that would enable it to pursue an ever-increasing standard of living. What was critical to them seems to have been the establishment of an institutionalized mastery of social relations that would eliminate the insufferable and uncontrollable commodification of their labor in a relation of dependency to capital and the market.

The institutional and communal control that enabled the 1804 revolution put an end to individual powerlessness and insecurity in the face of the economic ups and downs of the external market. Given the precariousness of the life conditions inherited from colonialism, the seat of internal sovereignty resided in the communal collectives whose articulation through rural market networks created a mesh of social relations that the population controlled and understood. This structure satisfied what they considered their daily needs. The apparent modesty of the results obtained doesn't diminish the importance of the fact that they had gained autonomy over the management of the relationship between needs and their satisfaction.

As they searched for an approach to life different from that offered by colonialism, without any help from the civil service, the fragmented space of the plantation world was transformed into a regionalized geographical structure, articulated by a network of rural markets. These were created by the inhabitants with the help of notables of peasant origin or people tightly linked to the small, independent producers. During the nineteenth century, the reproduction of daily life was satisfied through a new economic and social fabric, diametrically opposed to the atomization provoked by the extroverted economy of the previous period. The social life of social actors was shaped by locally dictated norms, on the basis of principles of conviviality born of a relatively peaceful coexistence. There was no guilt complex or inferiority complex in relation to what the Western world was promoting. The development of institutions meant to assure the natural reproduction of the population—the extended family, the *lakou*, forms of spirituality, the rural markets—enabled this system to flourish.

To the great displeasure of the inheritors of colonialism, private and communal life gradually became homogenized around principles emanating from the village societies that shared a foundation of autonomy, solidarity, and respect for family units. The values carried by the laboring classes profoundly shaped these principles. The cultural and ethnic nation, the collective of people of the same birth origin, structured itself in time without allowing itself to be influenced by a public power monopolized and administered by the minority of urban oligarchs.

What I call the state was the rules or institutionalized relationships between a popular sector reticent to invest itself in politics and the oligarchic, urban minorities who monopolized public positions and the country's international relations. I note that the tendency of the state to maintain a separation between the evolution of each of these sectors has declined since the 1915 occupation, which undermined the gradual imposition of the norms of respect for the dignity of the human being that animated social exchanges during the nineteenth century.

The imposition between 1804 and 1915 of a new territorial arrangement by previously subordinated classes invites us to recall, with Blandine Kriegel, that "the origin of sovereignty necessarily resides with the people. This was enunciated explicitly in Article 3 of the 1789 Declaration: 'The principle of all sovereignty resides in the Nation. No body or individual may exercise any power other than that expressly emanating from the Nation'" (Kriegel 2002, 169).

The sovereign people of Haiti expressed the will of a nation that constructed itself under specific circumstances. In moving beyond the humiliations and vexations they had experienced, and giving birth to themselves, this nation learned that *tout moun se moun*—that is, that we are all equal before the law. It converted itself into a people and expressed its will to live, so that none of its children would experience the personal dependency that typified modern colonial relations.

Conclusion: Empire and Republic

Colonialism centered its political power and administration, its central nervous system, in towns built around ports and fortresses. This complex served the empire and was not implanted overseas to serve the needs of the inhabitants or guarantee riches to the colonized. With independence and the secession consummated in 1804, the patrimony of Haitians included the sum of goods inherited from this situation. The new administration distributed them to a few favorites of the political power structure and the public administration. This was just a fraction of the state-owned domains, and the government was willing to part with them as a concession to this minority and not because they had a right to its riches.

The power to legislate and govern derived from the appropriation of the victory over the French metropole, and not from the consensus of the insurgents or a delegation of authority granted by them. The axis of the state constructed in 1804 was the will and power of the Indigenous Army, its natural right to use force to protect itself and exercise its authority. The right to security and life, the right to property, well-being and happiness, were eclipsed by the natural right to self-defense in the face of the exterminating army of General Leclerc. The law issued by those who held power reflected not the rights of individuals, but the right of the state and the homeland—as it was perceived by the generals—to exist.

Situated in the Caribbean basin in the middle of the Western Hemisphere, the state administration constituted in this way stuck to the terms dictated by the modern, colonial West. To secure the victory they had obtained, these leaders and governments installed themselves by massacring the leaders of the insurgent laborers and rebel workers, including Goman. Disdaining the most elementary rights of man, they institutionalized the marginalization of the popular radical thought that had been born at Bois Caïman in 1791.

The point is not to deny the importance of the creation of the modern state in Haiti. Rather, it is to understand that the very essence of the modern state, in its production of public policy, is colonial and authoritarian (Fick 1990, 250). The will of the citizens in Saint-Domingue and in Haiti did not create the public authorities. On the contrary, these powers invented their own citizens and defined them as they wished. The public administrators created a group they called *active citizens*, the only ones with the right to express their will. Both before and after 1804, the law therefore became the simple expression of the will of those in power. The situation was similar in France and elsewhere during the period. But our goal should be to analyze the concrete path that the oppressed classes in Haiti, and elsewhere, took in response.

The imperial power of commandment (here and elsewhere) does not operate in a vacuum. Popular political forces with opposed tendencies presided over the victory of the Indigenous Army. It then metamorphosized into a government and then, having declared its claims to power, into a state.[4] The result of this latent confrontation was an unstable equilibrium of regional military forces. The government exercised its power through regional factions of the army who constantly fought one another, even after armistices were negotiated between them. The centers of power represented regional bases controlled by provincial notables (Anglade 1982; Gaillard 2003; Manigat 2001).

Political science analyses tend to limit themselves to the study of the structured, visible interest groups or lobbies that engaged with executive power: figures like Goman, Acaau, Rivière-Hérard, and their partisans; and Salnave and the Cacos and other caudillos of the nineteenth century, leading up to the U.S. occupation that claimed to stabilize what it thought was the structure of the national state. From the 1791 general insurrection to the 1915 occupation, there was an endemic dissatisfaction that converted the sovereign people into a nursery that sustained palace revolutions. These, in turn, obscured the ongoing negotiations over social structure.

If the cultivators and inhabitants are seen as overgrown children manipulated by malevolent leaders, then the traditional explanations hold up. But if I realize that I am dealing with adults who were conscious of their life conditions, and I pay attention to the continuity of this discontent, I can see how these revolutions that emerged from provincial agitation were forms of sociopolitical negotiation. I can therefore understand their evolution after 1804, and take note of the period of stability that stretched from the 1870 execution of President Sylvain Salnave to the fall of President Nord Alexis in 1908.

The second half of the nineteenth century saw the gradual institutionalization of a stable political structure thanks to the establishment of bridges of communication that linked the port cities to the smaller regional centers, towns, and the countryside. This mesh of relationships created a balance between the provinces and the port cities. This helps us see, at least partially, why it was the Cacos and the wealthy landowners of the interior who resisted the occupation, rather than the urban dwellers and intellectuals who were more likely to collaborate. Everything unfolded the way it did during the wars of independence (Madiou 1847, 6:455), when those who imagined themselves to be the country's intelligentsia sensibly distanced themselves from the danger of death, safely in the hearts of the port cities that had traditionally served external forces (and the occupation), and didn't pay attention to the deep countryside.

The occupation in 1915 brought the country back to where it started. The idea of a colonial or supposedly Haitian government obligated to listen to the sovereign people became ludicrous, since the occupiers and the governments they chose and imposed were convinced that they knew what the nation really needed. Administrative decisions became infallible, and the interests of the imperial power were henceforth considered coterminous with those of the occupied country. As was the case before 1804, reason of state reclaimed its right to command, and didn't have to answer to any local authority. It seems ridiculous to have to repeat that it is impossible to have a state of law in Haiti as long as the sovereign people, with its actual characteristics, cannot impose itself on the governments of the republic and on the assistance offered by "friendly countries" and their international organizations, which are impossible to control.

The sovereign people have always frightened the intermediary classes who lead the country in the name of the international community. The private life of the citizen, his actual daily life, was definitively removed from the Civil Code and was of no interest to the administration of the law. The *lakou*, *plaçage*, the relationship between husband and wife, gender relations, godparent relations, familial and community education, hierarchies based on age, inheritance rights, collective individual property, the *konbit*, the *sols*, reciprocal relationships in general, the rural markets, religious traditions, secret societies, and so many other institutions of so-called customary law—none of these were the subject of any concern or attention. There was no effort to convert any of them into positive law. These institutions once again became invisible, as had been the case during the colonial period. The military conquest of the country by the expeditionary army of the U.S. Marines placed national sovereignty under its tutelage . . . and later that of its contemporary successors. The productive citizen (the inhabitant), the male citizen who headed a household (*le placé*), the commercial citizen (*la madan sara*), the working citizen (the farmer or livestock breeder, the fisherman, the artisan) were nowhere to be found in the legal codes. They had to be transformed in order to force them into the law, so they could be married, hired, educated, and educated through one form or another of colonization.

The intentions of the public authorities and the oligarchs were articulated in their legal codes. But, as had been the case before, they faced huge obstacles in their efforts to actually apply and enforce them. The public authorities were incapable of imposing the social order they had imported from outside: "As they juggled their own appetites our 'elites' effectively had to recognize their incapacity to create order in our financial chaos by elaborating and applying a program meant to save the poor peasantry and disarm the Caco. To maintain their supremacy, they therefore necessarily supported a convention [with the U.S.], a negotiated form of assistance in which their economic and political desiderata would be respected" (Gaillard 1981, 137).

The Haitian oligarchs and their friends abroad could not accept that *tout moun se moun*. But whether they liked it or not, the sovereign people remained, despite appearances, the largest and most powerful component within the state. The management of its force of inertia, presented as the weight of its ignorance, dominated the daily political reality of the population the oligarchs dreamed of leading about by the nose. Popular sentiment and the conviction of equality among all people led to the constant manipulation of external powers and the tireless outmaneuvering of their commands.

Starting in 1915, the powers and public functionaries of Haiti recuperated the suzerainty they had before 1804, which the nineteenth century had slowly eaten away. The sovereign people continued to get the better of them, though the struggle was a costly one. The technocrats among the oligarchs popularized their desire to restore the authority of the state. But the question was how to create the authority of a real state. For their state—which since Pétion's 1807 Constitution had been synonymous with the government—had never been obeyed because despite its pretensions, there was no way to confuse it with an institution that embraced all the citizens of the country. The laws issued by the operators of the government couldn't create obedience, because they were not connected to the feeling of obligation that are born in the citizen when the law is the expression of his rights. To the great despair of the technocrats and international aid, there was even a widespread will and intention to ridicule the government and its laws. The people simply considered it absurd to submit to powers that couldn't clearly assert the justification for their orders and show that they emanated from the rights of the sovereign people. They understood these powers did not consider themselves accountable to the sovereign people.

The population obeyed the administrative machinery of the state only because of the punishments meted out for insubordination. The governments and their sponsors were essentially illegitimate. The laws never left the drawers of the bureaucracy. The country would always be a bicephalous state, a state where the powers and the civil service commanded and the sovereign people acted as they wished, following the path they had chosen themselves.

My reading of the history of Haitians suggests that we should define the Haitian state as a structured field where the forces or poles present either agreed to cancel each other out or were forced to do so. In its daily functioning, the state, here as elsewhere, was certainly a government, administration, and form of management of political power. But above all, the sovereignty that ultimately validated it and made it effective came from its unconditional subordination to the rights, privileges, and obligations that the international community conceded to it, and the extent to which it operated by and for the promotion of the rights, obligations, and privileges of that external community. So the state was more than an acting structure (government and administration). The sovereign state was the armature of rights, privileges, and obligations of a sovereign community that dictated to the governmental and administrative apparatus the behavior and actions it should take. The acting structure of the sovereign state, its administration and civil service, couldn't violate the rights and privileges of the sovereign. Otherwise, it would immediately set in motion the development of a set of rules that undermined its irresponsible action. The sovereign people, the collective of Haitians, understood their powerlessness in the face of the external powers promoting the irresponsibility of the Haitian administration. So they exercised their sovereignty through an endemic escape from government regulations, even those that seemed favorable to them. They did so simply because the regulations came from a government they considered illegitimate.

The moral of this story is expressed well in a traditional dictum about how to behave in the face of a potentially harmful force: "Fe chimen w, m ap fè pa m. M pa detounen w, pa detounen m."[5] This divergence of approaches doesn't prevent the existence of good neighborly relations and coexistence prescribed by another dictum that is part of popular wisdom: "Chat konnen, sourit konnen!"[6]

There is no need to escape from this: the sovereign people are the nation in its will to live as it pleases: "What distinguishes nations is neither race nor language. Humans feel in their hearts that they are the same people when they have a community of ideas, interests, memories, affections, and hopes. That is what makes a nation. That is why humans want to walk together, work together, fight together, live and die one after another. The nation is what we love" (Kriegel 1998, 276).

Notes

Foreword

1. *Online Etymology Dictionary*, s.v. "Indigenous (adj.)," accessed April 4, 2020, https://www.etymonline.com/search?q=indigenous&source=ds_search.

2. *Encyclopaedia Britannica Online*, s.v. "Creole (people)," accessed April 7, 2020, https://www.britannica.com/topic/Creole.

3. I am intentionally playing here with Lloyd Best's well-known call for "independent thought and Caribbean freedom" (Best 1997).

4. In the same spirit, on the state form becoming unsustainable, the decolonial politics of the National Indigenous Congress, and the role of the speaker María de Jesús Patricio Martínez, see Mignolo and Vazquez (2017).

Preface and Acknowledgments

1. "Dessalines, meanwhile, was starting to pronounce himself openly against the expeditionary army. He avoided and hated even their language. That is why he harshly attacked the son of a property owner in Gonaïves, a Creole of Saint-Domingue, who advised him to speak [good] French. 'Use your own language,' Dessalines replied disdainfully, 'Why use someone else's?' ['Tiembé langue à vous, . . . pourquoi chercher tienn' les autr'?]" (Descourtilz 1809, 281). Note that he was talking to the son of a colonist—that is, a *white Creole*.

Chapter One

1. The qualification "modern" refers to that which is contemporary, and it has a positive connotation. But in my analysis the term does not carry this implication conferred by imperial languages. Instead, I use it to name the institutions that emerged in modern times in colonialism's zones of influence. The slave trade and the slave plantation are modern institutions, even if they no longer characterize our contemporary moment.

2. "Remarkably, the word 'slave' does not appear anywhere in this document [*Lapriyè Ginen*], more than 75 pages long, which celebrates the heroes of our country's independence. . . . It is therefore, consequently, reasonable to affirm that the understanding of our ancestors was that the grand-parents of today's Haitians were never slaves, but simply people who were abused, tricked, deceived, mystified and too often even sacrificed without anyone taking what they wanted into account" (Beauvoir 2008, 23–24).

3. It is impossible, in the Caribbean, to write a text similar to Miguel Leon-Portilla's *El Reverso de la Conquista* (1964) or *Visión de los Vencidos: Relaciones Indígenas de la Conquista* (1971), because the nations that today inhabit the region did not exist before

the arrival of Europeans, whose presence and victory was accompanied by efforts to destroy these nations.

4. Julien Raimond varied the spelling of his name in different publications. It was sometimes spelled with a *y*, as "Raymond."

5. "The category of 'Indian' designates the colonized group and necessarily refers to the colonial relation. The Indian emerges with the establishment of the European colonial order in America. Before then, there is no Indian, only peoples with their particular identities. The European creates the Indian, because in all colonial situations there must be a global definition of the colonized as a different, inferior being (in their totality: racially, culturally, intellectually, religiously, etc.). On the basis of this categorization of the Indian, the colonizer rationalizes and justifies their domination and their position of privilege (conquest is transformed, ideologically, into a redemptive and civilizing enterprise)" (Bonfil Batalla 1981, 19).

Chapter Two

1. The state and the French settlers claimed to own *slaves*. As observers, we see *captives*. In this kind of society, the captive who was liberated by the person who claimed to be their master was an *affranchi*, or emancipated person. If they liberated themselves without asking for the authorization of the established authorities, they were considered a *deserter*, *fugitive*, or *maroon*. I use italics here to emphasize that the meanings of the common terms vary according to who uses them, whether the masters and their assistants (willing or not) or the captives themselves.

2. Francisco José de Jaca, *Conclusions sur la liberté des Noirs et de leurs ascendants autrefois païens et désormais chrétiens, Mémoire adressé l'an 1681 au roi d'Espagne, Charles II*; and Épiphane de Moirans, *Esclaves libres ou Défense juridique de la liberté naturelle des esclaves*, cited and analyzed by Louis Sala-Molins (2014).

3. After 1804, the former slaves that the oligarchs designated as *cultivateurs* (field-workers) or *nouveaux libres* (newly freed people) decided to call themselves *inhabitants* (settlers), and in doing so they appropriated the name that the European colonists, and subsequently the free people of color, had given themselves.

4. On the two sections of the Haitian oligarchy, Claude Moïse distinguishes between "the new Haitian oligarchs produced by Saint-Domingue revolution," which he also describes as "the small numbers of new property owners that emerged from the upending of colonial society (1791–1804)" (Moïse 2009, 66) and "the oligarchy of the former *affranchis* [emancipated]" (87). In my own recent texts I have called the latter "the American colonists" or "the long-standing *affranchis*" or "the *affranchis* of colonial stability," who can be usefully contrasted with "the newly emerging *affranchis*" or "*affranchis* born of the crisis of 1791." (Casimir 2009, 208).

5. It is important to add that the European military powers, turned toward other skies during the nineteenth century, were of no significant help to the Haitian leaders in obstructing the development of greater autonomy on the part of the laborers. In 1860, Haitian authorities sought out support by signing a concordat with the Vatican that gave the Catholic Church the opportunity to control the production of knowledge among the rural population. They carried out religious persecution, but without success. Unable to either conquer or suffocate a flourishing rural society, the authori-

ties opened up the country to foreign capitalists, who were not all that interested. When the United States arrived on the continental scene at the end of the nineteenth century, the urban oligarchs were ready to greet them with open arms.

6. In Spanish, *doko* is translated as *palenque*, in Portuguese as *quilombo*, and in English as "bush society" or "free village."

Chapter Three

1. Two decades later, Vastey, also a child of free parents, and having experienced the racism inherent in metropolitan hegemony, used the same argument very differently to emphasize that people of color should identify with the captives in order to defeat slavery: "We will allow for no distinction on the part of this so-called free people, because while they didn't have distinct masters, the white public was their master. . . . Under the colonial regime as under the era of liberty, we will designate the population of Hayti under the generic denomination of Haytiens" (Vastey [1814] 2013, 14).

2. "The implication of everything you have just said is that the majority of the class of people of color was born free, of free parents, legitimately married, and those who are illegitimate are born of free mothers. Out of this entire group, there are not even 200 who were truly slaves and were emancipated. As for the free blacks who are included in the group of free people of color, there are not even 1,500 in all, and more than two-thirds were born free, the others emancipated. These facts and calculations can easily be verified by looking at the militia rolls and parish registers" (Raimond 1791a, 13).

3. My reflections on the insertion of families of color into colonial and metropolitan society are based on the analyses of Florence Gauthier, *L'aristocratie de l'épiderme: Le combat des Citoyens de couleur, 1789/1791* (2007), and John D. Garrigus, *Before Haiti: Race and Citizenship in French Saint-Domingue* (2006).

4. My reflections on the free blacks are inspired by the work of Stewart R. King, *Blue Coat and Powdered Wig: Free People of Color in Pre-revolutionary Saint-Domingue* (2001).

Chapter Four

1. These villages developed in the Lesser Antilles when the system entered irrecoverably into crisis during the nineteenth century. Export agriculture flourished in the late plantations of this period only thanks to the introduction of massive numbers of indentured laborers within a barely disguised system of slavery. In plantation colonies established since the seventeenth and eighteenth centuries, meanwhile, export agriculture collapsed despite the fact that living conditions were sometimes worse than during slavery. Nowhere did the classic plantation system feed its agricultural workers, and the societies adjusted through forms of emigration verging on depopulation and exodus. That was notable particularly during the nineteenth century, as Colin Clarke remarks (2011, 269).

2. "The serf is of a different essence than the knight, but it is necessary to refer to divine right to legitimate this difference in status. In the colonies, the foreigner come from elsewhere imposed himself thanks to his cannons and his machines. Although

domestication was achieved, despite appropriation, the colonist always remains a foreigner" (Fanon 1961, 43).

3. When the word was used elsewhere, it did not identify a particular way of life. Madiou indicates, for instance, that during the siege of Les Cayes by the Army of Independence in 1803 the soldiers "disguised themselves" as "peasants"—that is, as rural residents—to sneak into town and clandestinely buy ammunition (1847, 3:20), and that Schoelcher admired the "peasants" who rode their horses bareback (1847, 8:61), and he shares a sensible comment by a "peasant" regarding the governments of the *mulâtres* (1847, 8:172).

4. To my knowledge, the first mention of the peasant in Haitian law was the result of Élie Lescot's invention of a special birth certificate for peasants. Duvalier's 1963 Rural Code used this vocabulary in its preamble, but not in the resolutions that translated the social project of the public administration.

Chapter Five

1. "The name Ayiti (normalized as Haiti) marks the historical and epistemic shift that the revolution introduced, and it breaks away from both the slavery period and French imperial domination. Language and the power of naming, as these movements show, contain radical potential for 'epistemic revolution'" (Mignolo 2005, 112).

2. After World War II, in the context of an increasingly positive attitude toward the Haitian Revolution on the part of the members of the Indigéniste school and the thinkers of Negritude, the governmental authorities and urban public opinion exhibited the *unknown maroon* as the symbol of the irreducible refusal of slavery and a struggle to death against its atrocities. The famous statue commissioned by François Duvalier served as a prestigious symbol of national identity and the city dweller's representation of the social ethos. This sacralization obscured daily reality by selecting traits that superficially linked it to France. The unknown soldier in France is celebrated after the known soldiers have been placed on the shield. In Haiti, it would be impossible to venerate the known maroons without questioning the purges carried out by the heroes of independence, unless the Eurocentric justifications of Madiou (1847, 2:322) and Ardouin (1853, 2:262) are accepted unequivocally.

3. The policy of seeking to rebuild a semi–slave plantation turned out to be no less naïve, and no more viable.

4. In the introduction of this study, I underlined that the two pillars of national historiography excused the killings of the labor leaders, and considered the approaches and methods they had used to defend themselves against slavery to be repugnant (Ardouin 1853, 2:361; Madiou 1847, 2:322).

5. "It was likely during a relatively fleeting historical period, during which the greatest social differences were felt in the heart of the city and had to do with one predominant trait, that of work, which wasn't obfuscated by any other real or ideological differences—between the city and the country, the civilized and the barbaric, nobles and plebeians. The entrepreneur was a bourgeois without any noble titles and the proletarian an Englishman without a drop of barbarian blood. This concrete situation, this bare form through which the structure of exploitation was expressed, helped

considerably to clarify a substantive problem in social evolution. The attempt to solve it was carried out through the application of the most precise tools of philosophy and social science. The genius and intellectual merit of Marx enabled him to construct a system that was also classic, coherent and influential in the interpretation and transformation of social reality" (González Casanova 1969, 197).

6. "By the fundamental laws of the empire, Saint-Domingue has been subjected from the time it was established to the needs of the metropole. It was because of this, and in order to not alter this servitude, that the lands were not sold to the colonists. The king granted concessions, and those who received them were his vassals; their lands were held in vassalage. What was grown and produced could be only what the state demanded according to its interests. This servitude was not exactly feudal, but rather one of national interest" (Lattre 1805, 182).

7. Article 15 mentioned the existence of land concessions made by the state, but did not define the beneficiaries.

Chapter Six

1. "Fully 15 percent of the Constituent Assembly of 1789 actually owned property in the French colonies (Blackburn 1988, 167). The colonial policy of the National Assembly between 1789 and 1791 was systematically designed to protect the interests of metropolitan property owners" (Nesbitt 2008, 16).

2. At first, this group was comprised of those who benefited from the large land grants made by the state to those who considered deserving by the authorities based on their service to the nation. Later, the term identified large landholders in general.

3. It is useful to remind readers that *mulatto* is a social category that was strictly urban, and that according to Haitian vocabulary, unions between Polish soldiers and black women, for instance, created *reds*, not *mulattoes*.

Chapter Seven

1. The *pompons blancs* were groups of militias organized by Governor Blanchelande to suppress an insurrection in the early 1790s. According to Vastey, Pétion had fought as a *pompon blanc* under the orders of Colonel Mauduit and under the banners of the wealthy planters (Vastey 1819, 225).

2. This maneuver, which we might call the linguistic trap, is so common that it seems essential to the good functioning of the government. Vastey complained bitterly about it, referring to Pétion's use of it during the negotiations for recognition of the country's independence by the French.

3. Stewart King offers an example of one marriage that straddled communal and colonial realities, which would surprise no one in Haiti today. In his marriage contract, "Malic took the even more unusual step of recognizing an illegitimate child by another relationship. . . . He reserved enough for a mutual donation that established the community of property in the marriage contract to purchase and free the little girl, currently the slave of a fellow militiaman. . . . He purchased and freed the girl the next year" (2005, 257).

4. In chapter 3 of *La culture opprimée* (2001, 124), I cite numerous accounts of observers during the period, particularly Sténio Vincent, Frédéric Marcelin, and Georges Sylvain.

Chapter Eight

1. "There is no ignorance in general, nor knowledge in general. All ignorance is ignorant of a certain knowledge and all knowledge is the surpassing of a specific ignorance" (Santos 2009, 114).

2. A Creole proverb describes the situation in this way: "God gives the dog a wound behind the head so that he can't lick it."

3. It is true that many *bossales*, particularly from the Kongo, arrived in Saint-Domingue after having been defeated on the battlefield. In the eyes of their fellow sufferers, they were seen as responsible for the enslavement of others. But this failing was not retained in popular memory as a marker of social stratification or differentiation, for it was inscribed in another system of signification specific to African societies where enslavement operated according to rules different from those of merchant slavery.

4. It is worth noting that the abolition of slavery in the French Antilles was obtained only after the conquest of Algeria, at a time when these island economies, like all those in the Caribbean, were losing their importance within the global economy.

5. We do need to introduce a caveat regarding the minority of urban workers who had a more diversified experience of the modern European world, through contacts at the beginning of colonization with the collection of sailors who were part of a semi-enslaved, proletarian community of sailors in the ports of the Atlantic (Nesbitt 2008, 72).

6. "In Saint-Domingue this struggle for freedom took the form not of the defense of personal choice, thought, or an inner freedom in an unfree world but specifically what Arendt would describe as 'the freedom to call something into being which did not exist before, which was not given, not even as an object of cognition or imagination, and which therefore, strictly speaking, could not be known,' in other words, a freedom of active creation" (Nesbitt 2008, 2).

7. "Under the colonial regime as during the era of liberty, I describe the population of Hayti using the generic term Haytiens" (Vastey [1814] 2013, 74).

Chapter Nine

1. It is worth remembering that in the common language of Haitian urban areas, the term *maroon*, a synonym for *savage*, carries the connotation of something improper and unacceptable.

2. The vast majority of Guadeloupeans and Haitians do not deserve Fanon's diagnosis, which applies only to the tiny minority of free people of color, mostly living in the urban centers. I have cited Madiou's comments about the refusal of Haiti's urban population to participate in the struggles for independence in several instances above.

3. This traditional Haitian song can be translated thus: "I was on the main road, hummingbird / all the people going by laughed at me / I was on the main road / it rained, but I didn't get wet."

Chapter Ten

1. The term *Afro-Haitian*, used by Kate Ramsey, 2011 and its corresponding term *Franco-Haitian*, both correspond to another local history. The use of the term *African* or *Afro* in Saint-Domingue during the Haitian nineteenth century responded to certain particularities identified by Vertus Saint-Louis that do not coincide with the conditions of its use in the United States.

2. "The Vaudoux religion was that of both good and bad passions, and it bled into the entire society. The Haitians who weren't part of it were still impregnated, without even realizing it" (Madiou 1847, 5:105).

3. Schalkwijk (1994) suggests we emphasize the historical trajectory of the state in the Caribbean. He identifies the existence of a colonial state that developed into a national state, appearing at the moment when a local elite was in a position to seize control of the colonial administration and defy the imperial power.

4. "The Government of Haiti takes on the title and shall be known under the denomination of the State of Haiti" (1807 Constitution, Art. 6).

5. "Go your way, I'll go mine. I won't turn you from yours, you don't turn me from mine."

6. "Neither the cat or the mouse have been fooled!"

Bibliography

Adam, André-Georges. 1982. *Une crise haïtienne 1867–1869: Sylvain Salnave.* Port-au-Prince: Éditions Henri Deschamps.

Anglade, Georges. 1982. *Atlas critique d'Haïti.* Montréal: Groupe d'Études et de Recherches Critiques d'Espace et Centre de Recherches Caraïbes de l'Université de Montréal.

Ardouin, Beaubrun. 1853–1860. Études sur l'histoire d'Haïti. 8 vols. Paris : Dezobry et E. Magdeleine.

Barbé-Marbois, François. 1789. *Mémoire laissé à M. l'ordonnateur, en conformité des ordres du roi.* Port-au-Prince: Imprimé par Mozart.

———. 1796. *Réflexions sur la colonie de Saint-Domingue: ou, Examen approfondi des causes de sa ruine, et des mesures adoptées pour la rétablir; terminées par l'exposé rapide d'un plan d'organisation propre à lui rendre son ancienne splendeur; adressées au Commerce et aux Amis de la prospérité nationale.* Vols. 1–2. Paris: Garnery, Libraire.

———. 1826. *Opinion de M. le marquis de Barbé-Marbois, sur le projet de loi relatif à la répartition de l'indemnité stipulée en faveur des colons de Saint-Domingue.* Séance du 19 avril. Paris: Chambre des Pairs.

Barnet, Miguel. 1968. *Biografía de un cimarrón.* Mexico City:, Siglo XXI.

Barthélémy, Gérard. 1989. *Le pays en dehors: Essai sur l'univers rural haïtien.* Port-au-Prince: Éditions Henri Deschamps and CIDIHCA.

Beaubrun, Mimerose P. 2010. *Nan dòmi, le récit d'une initiation vodou.* La Roque d'Anthéron, France: Vents d'ailleurs.

Beauvoir, Max D. 2008. *Lapriyè Ginen.* Port-au-Prince: Éditions Près Nasyonal d'Ayiti.

Beckles, Hilary. 1984. *Black Rebellion in Barbados: The Struggle against Slavery, 1627–1838.* Bridgetown, Barbados: Antilles Publications.

Bellegarde, Dantès. 1938. *La nation haïtienne.* Paris: J. de Gigord.

Bellegarde-Smith, Patrick. 1985. *In the Shadow of Powers: Dantès Bellegarde in Haitian Social Thought.* Atlantic Highlands, NJ: Humanities Press International.

Benot, Yves. 2003. *La Modernité de l'esclavage. Essai sur l'esclavage au cœur du capitalism.* Paris, La Découverte.

Best, Lloyd. 1997. "Independent Thought and Caribbean Freedom." *Caribbean Quarterly* 43 (1–2): 16–24.

Blancpain, François. 2003. *La condition des paysans haïtiens: Du Code Noir aux codes ruraux.* Paris: Karthala.

Blérald, Alain Philippe. 1988. *La question nationale en Guadeloupe et en Martinique: essai sur l'histoire politique.* Paris: Harmattan.

Bonfil Batalla, Guillermo. 1981. "Utopía y revolución: El pensamiento politico de los indios de América Latina." In *Utopía y Revolución: El pensamiento político*

contemporáneo de los indios en América Latina, edited by Guillermo Bonfil
Batalla, 11–59. Mexico City: Editorial Nueva Imagen.

Brutus, Edner. 1948. *Instruction publique en Haïti, 1492–1945*. Port-au-Prince:
Imprimerie de l'État.

———. 1968. *Révolution dans Saint-Domingue*. Vols. 1–2. Brussels: Éditions du
Panthéon.

Bulletin des lois de la République d'Haïti. 1862. Aux Cayes: Imprimerie Nationale.

Bulletin des lois et actes de la République d'Haïti. 1838. Port-au-Prince: Imprimerie du
Gouvernement.

Cardoso, Ciro F. S. 1974. "Sobre los modos de producción coloniales de América." In
Modos de producción en América Latina, edited by Carlos Sempat Assadourian
et al., 193–242. 2nd ed. Cordoba, Spain: Pasado y Presente.

Carpentier, Alejo. 1949. *El reino de este mundo (Relato)*. Mexico: Edición y
Distribution Ibero Americana de Publicaciones, S.A.

Carteau, Félix J. 1802. *Histoire des désastres de Saint-Domingue: Ouvrage où l'on
expose les causes de ces événemens; les moyens employés pour renverser cette colonie;
les reproches faits à ses habitans, et les calomnies dont on les a couverts; enfin, des
faits et des vérités, qui, justifiant ces colons, sont encore propres à fixer le
gouvernement sur les moyens de faire refleurir la culture dans cette isle infortune*.
Bordeaux: Chez Pellier-Lawalle, Imprimeur-Libraire.

Casimir, Jean. 1973. "Los 'bosales' y el surgimiento de una cultura oprimida en Haití."
Problemas dominico-haitianos y del Caribe, edited by Gérard Pierre-Charles et al.
31–82. México, UNAM, Facultad Nacional de Ciencias Políticas y Sociales.

———. 1981. *La cultura oprimida*. Mexico City: Nueva Imagen.

———. 1984. "La Caraïbe et sa structure sociale incomplète." *Pensamiento
Iberoamericano, Revista de Economía Política: Cambios en la Estructura Social* 6
(July–December): 171–186.

———. (1991) 2007. *La Caraïbe, une et divisible*. Port-au-Prince: Imprimerie
Média-Texte.

———. 2001. *La culture opprimée*. Port-au-Prince: Imprimerie Lakay.

———. 2004a. "Le planteur avait une esclave, ma grand-mère était une captive:
Peuplement et latinité en Haïti." In *La latinité en question: Colloque international,
Paris, 16–19 March 2004*. Paris: L'Institut des Hautes Études de l'Amérique Latine
et L'Union Latine.

———. 2004b. *Pa bliye 1804, Souviens-toi de 1804*. Port-au-Prince, Imprimerie
Lakay. Spanish edition: *Acuérdate de 1804*. Mexico City: Siglo XXI.

———. 2009. *Haïti et ses élites: L'Interminable dialogue de sourds*. Port-au-Prince:
Éditions de l'Université d'État d'Haïti.

———. 2010. "De marasa Ayisyen-yo, de mòn ki pou kontre." In *Refonder Haïti?*,
edited by Pierre Buteau, Rodney Saint-Éloi, and Lyonel Trouillot, 69–84.
Montreal: Mémoire d'Encrier.

Casimir, Jean, and Michel Hector. 2003. "Le long 19e siècle haïtien." *Revue de la
Société Haïtienne d'Histoire, de Géographie et de Géologie* 78 (216): 35–64.

———. 2011. "Caribbean Social Structure in the Nineteenth Century." In *General
History of the Caribbean*. Vol. 4, *The Long Nineteenth Century*, edited by K. O.
Lawrence, 283–333. Pari: UNESCO.

Chambon, M. 1783. *Traité général du commerce de l'Amérique.* Vol. 1. Amsterdam: Marc-Miche Rey.

Christophe, Henry. 1812. *Code Henry.* Au Cap-Henry, Chez P. Roux, Imprimeur du Roi.

Clarke, Colin. 2011. "Demographic Change and Population Movement." In *General History of the Caribbean.* Vol. 4, *The Long Nineteenth Century,* edited by K. O. Laurence, 259–281. Paris: UNESCO.

Clarkson, Thomas, and Z. Macaulay. 1835. *Haïti ou renseignemens authentiques sur l'abolition de l'esclavage et ses résultats à Saint-Domingue et à la Guadeloupe avec des détails sur l'état actuel d'Haïti et des noirs émancipés qui forment sa population, traduit de l'anglais.* Paris: Hachette.

Clavière, E. 1791. Adresse de la Société des Amis des Noirs, à l'Assemblé Nationale. Paris: Imprimerie du Patriote Français.

Cugoano, Ottabah. 1787. *Thoughts and Sentiments on the Evil and Wicked Traffic of the Slavery and Commerce of the Human Species.* London.

Dard, M. 1821. *Observations sur le droit de souveraineté de la France sur Saint-Domingue et sur les droits des colons propriétaires de cette île.* Paris: Imprimerie de Dondey-Dupré.

Débats entre les accusateurs et les accusés dans l'affaire des colonies, imprimés en exécution de la Loi du 4 pluviôse. 1795. Vol 2. Paris: Imprimerie Nationale, Pluviôse.

Debien, Gabriel. 1949. "Aux origines de l'abolition de l'esclavage." *Revue d'Histoire des Colonies* 36 (127–128): 348–423.

———. 1974. *Les esclaves aux Antilles françaises (XVIe–XVIIIe siècles).* Basse-Terre, Fort de France: Société d'Histoire de la Guadeloupe, Société d'Histoire de la Martinique.

Delacroix, Jacques-Vincent. 1771. *Mémoires d'un Américain: Avec une description de la Prusse et de l'isle de Saint-Domingue, première partie.* Lausanne: V. Regnard et Demonville.

Delaporte, Abbé. 1775. *Le voyageur françois ou la connoissance de l'ancien et du Nouveau Monde.* New ed. Vol. 11. Paris: Chez L. Cellot.

Descourtilz, Michel Étienne. 1795. *Histoire des désastres de Saint-Domingue: Précédé d'un tableau du régime et des progrès de cette colonie depuis sa fondation, jusqu'à l'époque de la révolution française.* Paris: Chez Garnery, Libraire.

———. 1809. *Voyages d'un naturaliste, et ses observations.* Vol. 3. Paris: Dufart.

Dorsainvil, Justin Chrysostome. 1934. *Manuel d'histoire d'Haïti.* Port-au-Prince : Procure des Frères de l'instruction chrétienne.

Dubois, Laurent. 2003. "'Citoyens et amis!' Esclavage, citoyenneté et République dans les Antilles françaises à l'époque révolutionnaire." *Annales: Histoire, Sciences Sociales* 58 (2): 281–303.

———. 2004a. *A Colony of Citizens: Revolution and Slave Emancipation in the French Caribbean 1787–1804.* Chapel Hill: University of North Carolina Press.

———. 2004b. *Avengers of the New World: The Story of the Haitian Revolution.* Cambridge, MA: Harvard University Press.

———. 2005. *Les vengeurs du Nouveau Monde: Histoire de la révolution haïtienne.* Translated by Thomas Van Ruymbeke. Rennes, France: Les Perséides, 2005. Haitian edition: Port-au-Prince: Éditions de l'Université d'État d'Haïti, 2009.

————. 2012. *Haiti: The Aftershocks of History*. New York: Metropolitan Books.

Dubois, Laurent, and John D. Garrigus. 2006. *Slave Revolution in the Caribbean, 1789–1804: A Brief History with Documents*. New York: Bedford Press.

Dubuisson, Pierre Ulric. 1780. *Nouvelles considérations sur Saint-Domingue: En réponse à celle de M. H. Dl. par M. D. B***: Première partie*. Paris: Chez Cellot and Jombert fils jeune.

Dussel, Enrique. 2006. *20 Tésis de Política*. Mexico City: Siglo XXI.

Engerman, Stanley, and Barry Higman. 1997. "The Demographic Structure of the Caribbean Slave Societies." In *General History of the Caribbean: The Slave Societies of the Caribbean*, ed. Franklin Knight, 45–104. London: UNESCO.

Fanon, Frantz. 1952. *Peau noir, masques blancs*. Paris: Éditions du Seuil.

————. 1961. *Les damnés de la terre*. Paris: François Maspero.

————. 1986. *Black Skin, White Masks*. Translated by Charles Lam Markmann. Forewords by Ziauddin Sardar and Homi K. Bhabha. London: Pluto Press.

Fick, Carolyn E. 1990. *The Making of Haiti, The Saint-Domingue Revolution from Below*. Knoxville: University of Tennessee Press.

————. 2014. *Haïti, naissance d'une nation: La révolution de Saint-Domingue vue d'en bas*. Montreal: Les Éditions du CIDIHCA.

Fischer, Sibylle. 2004. *Modernity Disavowed: Haiti and the Cultures of Slavery in the Age of Revolution*. Durham, NC: Duke University Press.

Fouchard, Jean. 1972. *Les marrons de la liberté*. Paris: Editions de l'Ecole.

Gaillard, Roger. 1981. *Les Blancs débarquent, 1915: Premier écrasement du cacoïsme*. Port-au-Prince: Imprimerie Le Natal.

————. 2003. *Le cacoïsme bourgeois contre Salnave (1867–1870)*. Port-au-Prince: Éditions Fondation Roger Gaillard.

Garran, Jean-Phillippe. 1797. *Rapport sur les troubles de Saint-Domingue, fait au nom de la Commission des colonies, des Comités du salut public, de législation et de marine, imprimé par ordre de la Convention nationale, et distribué au Corps législatif en ventôse, an V*. 4 vols. Paris: Imprimerie Nationale.

Garrigus, John D. 2006. *Before Haiti: Race and Citizenship in French Saint-Domingue*. New York: Palgrave Macmillan.

————. 2011. "Vincent Ogé Jeune (1757–91): Social Class and Free Colored Mobilization on the Eve of the Haitian Revolution." *The Americas* 68 (1): 33–62.

Gastine, Civique de. 1819. *Histoire de la Republique d'Haiti ou Saint-Domingue, l'esclavage et les colons*. Paris: Plancher.

Gauthier, Florence. 2007. *L'aristocratie de l'épiderme: Le combat de la Société des Citoyens de Couleur, 1789/1791*. Paris: CNRS Éditions.

Geggus, David Patrick. 2002. *Haitian Revolutionary Studies*. Bloomington: Indiana University Press.

Glissant, Édouard. 1997. *Le discours antillais*. Paris: Gallimard.

González Casanova, Pablo. 1969. *Sociología de la explotación*. Mexico City: Siglo XXI Editores.

Gouy d'Arsy, Louis Marthe de. 1792. *Idées sommaires sur la restauration de Saint-Domingue, présentées à la nation, au roi et à la colonie*. Paris: Imprimerie de Boulard.

Hector, Cary. 2012. "Quelques perspectives des rapports 'paradiplomatiques' entre la Prusse de Friedrich Wilhelm III et le Royaume d'Henry Christophe (1811–1820)."

In "L'historiographie allemande et la révolution haïtienne: Approches récentes," edited by Cary Hector and Oliver Gliech. Special issue, *Revue de la Société Haïtienne d'Histoire, de Géographie et de Géologie* 245–248 (January–December): 182–202.

———. 2014. "Aux origines endogènes de l'occupation américaine d'Haïti (1915–1934)." *Conjonction* 227:8–24.

Hector, Michel. 1998. "Mouvements populaires et sortie de crise (XIXe–XXe siècles)." *Pouvoirs dans la Caraïbe* 10:71–95.

———. 2006a. *Crises et Mouvement populaires en Haïti.* 2nd Edition. Port-au-Prince, Presses Nationales d'Haïti.

———. 2006b. "Réflexion sur les particularités de la révolution haïtienne." In "La révolution et l'indépendance haïtiennes: Autour du bicentenaire de 1804, histoire et mémoire, actes du 36e colloque de l'Association des historiens de la Caraïbe, Barbade, mai 2004." Special issue, *Bulletin de la Société d'Histoire de la Guadeloupe* (November): 7–13.

———. forthcoming. "Marronnage." In *Dictionnaire historique de la révolution haïtienne,* edited by Claude Moïse, new edition. Montreal: CIDIHCA.

Hector, Michel, and Jean Casimir. 2004. "Le long 19e siècle haïtien." *Revue de la Société Haïtienne d'Histoire et de Géographie* 216:35–64.

Heller, Hermann. 1961. *Teoría del Estado.* 4th ed. Mexico City: Fondo de Cultura Económica.

Hilliard d'Auberteuil, Michel René. 1777. *Considérations sur l'état présent de la colonie française de Saint-Domingue.* Vol 2. Paris: Grangé.

Hoffmann, Léon-François. 1990. *Haïti: Couleurs, croyances, créole.* Port-au-Prince: Éditions Henri Deschamps et Les Éditions du CIDIHCA.

Hormoys, Paul D'. 1862. *L'Empire de Soulouque.* Paris: Écrivain et Toubon, Libraires.

Hurbon, Laënnec. 1987. *Le barbare imaginaire.* Port-au-Prince: Éditions Henri Deschamps.

Inginac, Joseph Balthazar. 1843. *Mémoires.* Kingston, Jamaica: J. R. de Cordova.

Janvier, Louis-Joseph. 1886. *Les Constitutions d'Haïti (1801–1885).* Paris: C. Marpon et E. Flammarion.

Jenson, Deborah. 2010. *Beyond the Slave Narrative: Politics, Sex, and Manuscripts in the Haitian Revolution.* Liverpool, UK: Liverpool University Press.

King, Stewart R. 2001. *Blue Coat or Powdered Wig: Free People of Color in Pre-revolutionary Saint Domingue.* Athens: University of Georgia Press.

Kriegel, Blandine. 1998. *Philosophie de la république.* Paris: Plon.

———. 2002. *État de droit ou empire?* Paris: Bayard Éditions.

———. 2003. *L'État et les esclaves, Réflexions pour l'histoire des États.* Paris, Éditions Payot & Rivages.

Labat, Jean Baptiste. 1742. Nouveau voyages aux isles de l'Amerique: Contenant l'histoire naturelle de ces pays, l'origine, les mœurs, la religion & le gouvernement . . . Nouv. ed. augm. considérablement. Paris: Chez Théodore Le Gras.

Lacroix, Pamphile de. 1819. *Mémoires pour servir à l'histoire de la révolution de Saint-Domingue, avec une carte nouvelle de l'île et un plan topographique de la Crête-à-Pierrot.* Vol. 1. Paris: Chez Pillet aîné, Imprimeur-Libraire.

Lattre, Ph.-Albert de. 1805. *Campagnes des Français à Saint-Domingue et refutation des reproches faits au capitaine général Rochambeau.* Paris: Locard Libraire, Arthus-Bertrand, Amand Koenig.

Laujon, Alexandre P. M. n.d. *Précis historique de la dernière expédition de Saint-Domingue, depuis le départ de l'armée des côtes de France, jusqu'à l'évacuation de la colonie; suivi des moyens de rétablissement de cette colonie: En deux parties.* Paris: Chez de La Folie, Le Norman, Imprimeurs-Libraires.

Lecointe-Marsillac. 1789. *Le More-Lack, ou Essai sur les moyens les plus doux et plus équitables d'abolir la traite et l'esclavage des nègres d'Afrique, en conservant aux colonies tous les avantages d'une population agricole.* London.

Lemonnier-Delafosse, M. 1846. *Seconde campagne de Saint-Domingue, du 1er décembre 1803 au 15 juillet 1805; précédée de Souvenirs historiques et succincts de la première campagne, expédition du général en chef Leclerc, du 14 décembre 1801 au 1er décembre 1805.* Le Havre, France.

Leon-Portilla, Miguel. 1964. *El Reverso de la Conquista.* Mexico City: Editorial Joaquín Mortiz.

———. 1971. *Visión de los vencidos: Relaciones indígenas de la Conquista.* Mexico City: Universidad Nacional Autónoma de México.

Lepkowski, Tadeusz. 1969. *Haití.* Havana: Casa de las Américas.

Lewkowicz, Ignacio. 2012. *Pensar sin estado: La subjetividad en la era de la fluidez.* Buenos Aires: Paidos.

Liébart, Deborah. 2008. "Un Groupe de pression contre-révolutionnaire: Le Club Massiac sous la Constituante." *Annales historiques de la révolution française* 354: 29–50.

Linstant, S. 1841. *Essai sur les moyens d'enrayer les préjugés des blancs contre des Africains et des sang-mêlé.* Paris: Pagnerre, Éditeur.

———. 1851. *Recueil général des lois et actes, gouvernement d'Haïti depuis la proclamation de son Indépendance jusqu'à nos jours.* Paris: Auguste Durand.Louis XIV. *Le Code Noir: Édit du Roi sur les esclaves des îles de l'Amérique (mars 1680), suivi de Código Negro (1789).* Digital version. 2005. Saguenay, Quebec: Jean-Marie Tremblay, at http://classiques.uqac.ca/collection_documents/louis_XIV_roi_de _France/code_noir/code_noir.html.

Lugones, María. 2003. *Pilgrimages/Peregrinajes: Theorizing Coalition against Multiple Oppressions.* New York: Rowman and Littlefield.

Madiou, Thomas. 1847–1848. *Histoire d'Haïti.* 8 vols. Port-au-Prince: Imprimerie de Jh. Courtois.

Magloire, Auguste. 1909. *Histoire d'Haïti. 2e partie, Les insurrections.* Vol. 1. Port-au-Prince: Imprimerie-Librairie du Matin.

Malenfant, Le colonel. 1814. *Des colonies, et particulièrement de celle de Saint-Domingue: Mémoire historique et politique.* Paris: Chez Audibert.

Malo, Charles. 1819. *Histoire de l'île de Saint-Domingue: Depuis sa découverte jusqu'à ce jour, suivie de pièces justificatives.* 2nd ed. Paris: Chez Louis Janet et Chez Delaunay.

Malouet, M. 1788. *Mémoires sur l'esclavage des nègres.* Neufchâtel.

———. 1797. *Examen de cette question: Quel sera, pour les colonies de l'Amérique, le résultat de la Révolution française, de la guerre qui en est la suite, et de la paix qui doit la terminer?* Paris: Pougin, Imprimeur-Libraire.

Manigat, Leslie F. 1962. *La politique agraire du gouvernement d'Alexandre Pétion (1807–1818)*. Port-au-Prince: Imprimerie La Phalange.

———. 2001–07. *Éventail d'histoire vivante d'Haïti: Des préludes à la révolution de Saint-Domingue jusqu'à nos jours (1789–1999), une contribution à "la nouvelle histoire" haïtienne*. 5 vols. Port-au-Prince: Collection du CHUDAC.

———. 2007. *Évolution et revolution: Marronnage et révoltes puis révolution à Saint-Domingue-Haïti et les idées politiques de la révolution haïtienne d'indépendance Nationale*. Port-au-Prince: Média-Texte.

Marshall, Woodville K. 1963. "The Social Development of the Windward Islands, 1738–1865." PhD diss., Cambridge University.

———. 1968. "Notes on Peasant Development in the West Indies since 1863." *Social and Economic Studies* 17 (3): 252–263.

Mathon, Alix, and Alain Turnier. 1985. *Haïti, un cas: La Société des Baïonnettes, un regard nouveau*. Port-au-Prince, Imprimerie Le Natal.

Meillassoux, Claude. 1986. *Anthropologie de l'esclavage*. Paris: Presses Universitaires de France.

Midy, Franklin. 1972. "L'armée dans les sociétés dépendantes: Haïti." *Nouvelle Optique* 6–7 (April–September): 31–51.

Mignolo, Walter D. 1992. "On the Colonization of Amerindian Languages and Memories: Renaissance Theories of Writing and the Discontinuity of the Classical Tradition." *Comparative Studies in Society and History* 34 (2): 301–330.

———. 2000. *Local Histories/Global Designs: Coloniality, Subaltern Knowledges, and Border Thinking*. Princeton, NJ: Princeton University Press.

———. 2005. *The Idea of Latin America*. Malden, MA: Blackwell.

———. 2006. "El pensamiento descolonial." *América Latina en movimiento*, September 14. https://www.alainet.org/es/active/13357.

———. 2007. "El pensamiento descolonial: Reflexiones finales." *Comentario Internacional* 7:186–192.

———. 2009. "Epistemic Disobedience, Independent Thought and De-colonial Freedom." *Theory, Culture and Society* 26 (7–8): 1–23.

———. 2011. *The Darker Side of Western Modernity: Global Futures, Decolonial Options*. Durham, NC: Duke University Press.

———. 2012. "Delinking, Decoloniality and Dewesternization." Interview with Christopher Mattison. *Critical Legal Thinking*, 2 May. http://criticallegalthinking.com/2012/05/02/delinking-decoloniality-dewesternization-interview-with-walter-mignolo-part-ii/.

———. 2014. "No se trata ya de resistir sino de re-exisitir." Interview with Ángel Ricardo. *La Prensa de Panama*, November 17. https://www.prensa.com/blog_periscopio/resistir-re-existir-Entrevista-Walter-Mignolo_7_4075162454.html.

———. 2015. *Habitar la frontera: Sentir y pensar la descolonialidad (Antología, 1999–2014)*. Barcelona: Center International Affairs (CIBoD) and Universidad Autónoma de Ciudad Juarez.

Mignolo, Walter D., and Pedro Pablo Gómez. 2015. *Trayectorias de re-existencia: Ensayos en torno a la colonialidad/decolonialidad del saber, el sentir y el creer*. Bogota: Universidad Distrital Francisco José de Caldas.

Mignolo, Walter D., and Rolando Vazquez. 2017. "Mexico Indigenous Congress: Decolonizing Politics." *Al-Jazeera,* September 27. http://www.aljazeera.com /indepth/opinion/mexico-indigenous-congress-decolonising-politics -170926093051780.html.

Mill, John Stuart. 1852. *Principles of Political Economy, with Some of Their Applications to Social Philosophy.* 5th ed. Vol. 2. London: Parker, Son, and Bourn.

Mobley, Christina Frances. 2015. "The Kongolese Atlantic: Central African Slavery and Culture from Mayombe to Haiti." PhD diss., Duke University.

Moïse, Claude. 2001. *Le projet national de Toussaint Louverture et la Constitution de 1801.* Port-au-Prince: Éditions Mémoire.

———. 2009. *Constitution et luttes de pouvoir en Haïti: La faillite des classes dirigeantes, 1804–1915.* Port-au-Prince: Éditions de l'Université d'État d'Haïti.

Moral, Paul. 1961. *Le Paysan haïtien: Etude sur la vie rurale en Haïti.* Paris: Fardin.

Moscoso, Francisco. 2003. "Chiefdoms in the Islands and the Mainland: A Comparison." In *UNESCO General History of the Caribbean.* Vol. 1, *Autochthonous Societies,* edited by Jalil Sued-Badillo, 295–315. Paris: UNESCO.

Nesbitt, Nick. 2008. *Universal Emancipation: The Haitian Revolution and the Radical Enlightenment.* Charlottesville: University of Virginia Press.

Pagès, Pierre Marie François de. 1782. *Voyages autour du monde et vers les deux pôles, par terre et par mer, pendant les années 1767 à 1776.* Paris: Chez Moutard.

Paul, Edmond. 1882. *Les causes de nos malheurs.* Kingston: Geo. Henderson and Company.

Paul, G. 1836. *Les affaires d'Haïti.* Paris: Chez Renard and Chez Delaunay.

Pétion, J. 1790. *Discours sur les troubles de Saint-Domingue.* Paris: Chez Desennes, Libraire au Palais-Royal.

Petit, M. 1771. *Droit public ou gouvernement des colonies françaises, d'après les loix faites pour ces pays.* Vol. 2. Paris: Chez Delalain, Libraire.

Petit-Frère, Roger. 1992. "Le Code rural de Boyer vu par un professeur d'histoire." In *Code rural de Boyer de 1826,* edited by Petit-Frère, Roger, Jean Vandal, and Georges E. Werleigh, 61–69. Port-au-Prince: Coédition Archives Nationales d'Haïti and Maison H. Deschamps.

Petit-Frère, Roger, Jean Vandal, and Georges E. Werleigh, eds. 1992. *Code rural de Boyer de 1826.* Port-au-Prince: Coédition Archives Nationales d'Haïti and Maison H. Deschamps.

Pierre, Jacques. 2011. "L'Acte de l'Indépendance d'Haïti en créole Haïtien." *Journal of Haitian Studies* 17, 2 (Fall), 168–180.

Pluchon, Pierre. 1979. *Un négociant juif et des esclaves nègres à Paris.* Port-au-Prince: Institut Français d'Haïti and Imprimerie Henri Deschamps.

Price-Mars, Jean. (1919) 2001. *La vocation de l'élite.* Port-au-Prince: Éditions des Presses Nationales d'Haïti.

———. (1928) 1954. *Ainsi parla l'Oncle: Essai d'ethnographie.* New York: Parapsychology Foundation. Reprint, Saguenay, Quebec: Jean-Marie Tremblay.

———. (1959) 2010. *De Saint-Domingue à Haïti, Essai sur la culture, les arts et la literature.* Paris: Présence Africaine. Reprint, Saguenay, Quebec: Jean-Marie Tremblay.

———. 1967. *Lettre ouverte au Dr. René Piquion sur son "Manuel de la négritude": Le préjugé de couleur est-il la question sociale?* 2nd ed. Port-au-Prince: Les Éditions des Antilles.

———. 1983. *So Spoke the Uncle: Ainsi Parla L'Oncle.* Translated by Magdaline Shannon. Washington, DC: Three Continents Press.

Prudent, Lambert-Félix. 1980. *Des baragouins à la langue antillaise: Analyse historique et sociolinguistique du discours sur le creole.* Paris: Éditions Caraïbéennes.

Quijano, Aníbal. 2000. "Colonialidad del Poder y Clasificación Social." In "Festchrift for Immanuel Wallerstein, Part I." Special issue, *Journal of World-Systems Research* 11 (2): 342–386.

———. 2007. "Coloniality and Modernity/Rationality." *Cultural Studies* 21 (2–3): 155–167.

———. 2008. "Coloniality of Power, Eurocentrism, and Social Classification." In *Coloniality at Large, Latin America and the Postcolonial Debate,* edited by Mabel Moraña, Enrique Dussel and Carlos A. Jáuregui, 181–224. Durham, NC: Duke University Press.

Raimond, Julien. 1791a. *Observations sur l'origine et les progrès du préjugé des colons blancs contre les hommes de couleur; sur les inconvénients de le perpétuer; la nécessité, la facilité de le détruire; sur le projet du Comité colonial, etc.* Paris: Chez Berlin, Desenne, Bailly.

———. 1791b. *Réponse aux considérations de M. Moreau, dit Saint-Méry, député à l'Assemblée nationale, sur les colonies.* Paris: Imprimerie du Patriote Français.

———. 1793. *Réflexions sur les véritables causes des troubles et des désastres de nos colonies, notamment sur ceux de Saint-Domingue; avec les moyens à employer pour préserver cette colonie de la ruine totale, adressées à la Convention nationale.* Paris: Imprimerie des Patriotes.

Ramsey, Kate. 2011. *The Spirits and the Law: Vodou and Power in Haiti.* Chicago: University of Chicago Press.

Raynal, Guillaume Thomas de. 1785. *Essai sur l'administration de St. Domingue.* Paris.

Recueil général des lois et actes du gouvernement d'Haïti. 1814. Port-au-Prince: Imprimerie de l'État.

Rey, Terry. 1998. "The Virgin Mary and Revolution in Saint-Domingue: The Charisma of Romaine-la-Prophétesse." *Journal of Historical Sociology* 11 (3): 341–369.

Rigaud, André. 1797. *Mémoire du général de brigade, en réfutation des écrits calomnieux contre les citoyens de couleur de Saint-Domingue.* 18 Thermidor, an V (August 5). Aux Cayes, Haiti: Imprimerie de Lemery.

Rodney, Walter. 1972. *How Europe Underdeveloped Africa.* London: Bogle-L'Ouverture Publications.

———. 1981. *A History of the Guyanese Working People, 1881–1905.* London: Heinemann Educational Books.

Rogers, Dominique. 1999. *Les libres de couleur dans les capitales de Saint-Domingue: Fortune, mentalités et intégration à la fin de l'Ancien Régime (1776–1789).* PhD. Dissertation, University Michel de Montaigne, Bordeaux III.

Saint-Amand, J. 1872. *Le Code rural d'Haïti, publié avec commentaires et formulaire, notes et annexes, à l'usage des fonctionnaires, officiers et agents de la police rurale.* 2nd ed. Port-au-Prince: A. Guiyot.

Saint-Louis, Vertus. 2000. "Les termes de citoyen et Africain pendant la révolution de Saint-Domingue." In *L'insurrection des esclaves de Saint-Domingue (22–23 août 1791),* edited by Laennec Hurbon, 75–96. Paris: Karthala.

———. 2006. "Le surgissement du terme 'Africain' pendant la révolution de Saint-Domingue." *Ethnologies* 28 (1): 147–171.

Sala-Molins, Louis. 1987. *Le Code Noir ou le calvaire de Canaan.* Paris: Presses Universitaires de France.

———. 2014. *Esclavage réparation: Les lumières des capucins et les lueurs des pharisiens.* Paris: Lignes.

Sannon, Pauléus. 1905. *Essai historique sur la révolution de 1843.* Cayes, Haiti: Imprimerie Bonnefil.

Santos, Boaventura de Sousa. 2009. *Una epistemología del Sur: la reinvención del conocimiento y la emancipación social.* Mexico City: CLACSO y Siglo XXI.

Schalkwijk, Marten. 1994. "Colonial State Formation in Caribbean Plantation Societies, Structural Analysis and Changing Elite Networks in Suriname, 1650–1920." PhD diss., Cornell University.

Schoelcher, Victor. (1843a) 1973. *Colonies étrangères et Haïti.* Vol. 2. Pointe-à-Pitre, Guadeloupe: Émile Désormeaux, 1973.

———. 1843b. *Colonies étrangères et Haïti: Résultats de l'émancipation anglaise.* Paris: Pagnerre.

———. 1847. *Histoire de l'Esclavage pendant les deux dernières années (deuxième partie).* Paris: Pagnerre.

Sibire, Abbé. 1789. *L'Aristocracie négrière, ou refléxions philosophiques et historiques sur l'esclavage et l'affranchissement des Noirs.* Paris.

Sismondi, Jean Charles Léonard (Simonde) de. 1814. *De l'intérêt de la France à l'égard de la traite des nègres.* Paris: J. J. Paschoud.

Smith, R. T. 1967. "Social Stratification, Cultural Pluralism and Integration in the West Indies Societies." In *Caribbean Integration,* edited by Sybil Lewis and Thomas Matthews, 226–258. Rio Pedras, PR: Institute of Caribbean Studies, University of Puerto Rico.

Thornton, John K. 1993. "I Am the Subject of the King of Congo: African Political Ideology and the Haitian Revolution." *Journal of World History* 4 (2): 181–214.

Trouillot, Michel-Rolph. 1990. *Haiti, State against Nation: The Origins and Legacy of Duvalierism.* New York: Monthly Review Press.

———. 1995. *Silencing the Past: Power and the Production of History.* Boston: Beacon Press.

Turnier, Alain. 1982. *Avec Mérisier Jeannis: Une tranche de vie jacmélienne et nationale.* Port-au-Prince: Imprimerie Le Natal.

———. 1989. *Quand la nation demande des comptes.* 2nd ed. Port-au-Prince: Éditions La Natal.

Tussac, F. Richard de. 1810. *Cri des Colons contre un ouvrage de M. L'Evêque et Senateur Grégoire.* Paris: Les Marchands de Nouveautés.

Vandal, Jean. 1992. "Le Code rural de Boyer vu par un juriste." In *Code rural de Boyer de 1826*, edited by Roger Petit-Frère, Jean Vandal, and Georges E. Werleigh, 70–81. Port-au-Prince: Coédition Archives Nationales d'Haïti and Maison H. Deschamps.

Vastey, Pompée-Valentin, Baron de. (1814a) 2013. *Le système colonial dévoilé*. Port-au-Prince: Société Haïtienne d'Histoire, de Géographie et de Géologie.

———. 1814b. *Notes à M. Le baron de V.P. Malouet, Ministre de la Marine et des Colonies, de sa Majesté Louis XVIII, et ancien Administrateur des Colonies et de la Marine, ex-colon de Saint-Domingue, etc. en Réfutation du 4ème Volume de son Ouvrage, intitulé : Collection des Mémoires sur les colonies et particulièrement sur Saint-Domingue, etc.*. Cap-Haïtien: Chez P. Roux.

———. 1816. *Réflexions sur une lettre de Mazères, ex-colon français, adressée à M. J. C. L. Sismonde de Sismondi: Réflexions sur les noirs et les blancs, la civilisation de l'Afrique, le Royaume d'Hayti, etc.* Cap-Henry, Haiti: Chez Roux.

———. 1819. *Essai sur les causes de la révolution et des guerres civiles d'Hayiti: Faisant suite aux réflexions politiques sur quelques ouvrages et journaux français, concernant Hayti*. Souci, Haiti: Imprimerie Royale.

———. 2014. *The Colonial System Unveiled*. Translated and edited by Christopher Bongie. Liverpool: Liverpool University Press.

Vázquez, Rolando. 2011. "Modernity, Coloniality and Visibility: The Politics of Time." In *Asking We Walk*, edited by Corinne Kumar. Bangalore: Streelekha Publications.

Vázquez-Melken, Rolando. 2014. "Colonialidad y Relacionalidad." In *Los desafíos decoloniales de nuestros días: Pensar en colectivo*, edited by María Eugenia Borsani and Pablo Quintero,173–196. Neuquén, Argentina: EDUCO, Universidad Nacional del Comahue.

Vienot-Vaublanc. 1797. *Rapport fait au nom de la commission des colonies, compose des représentants Tarbé, Helot, Villaret-Joyeuse, Bourdon (de l'Oise), & Vienot-Vaublanc, sur l'organisation intérieure de la colonie de Saint Domingue*. Corps législatif, Conseil des Cinq-Cents, Séance, du 11 Thermidor, an V (July 29).

Vincent, Sténio. (1904) 1939. "Réponse au discours de réception du Dr Léon Audain à la Société de Législation de Port-au-Prince." In *En posant les jalons*, by Sténio Vincent, 54–55. Port-au-Prince: Imprimerie de l'État.

Wilder, Gary. 2005. *The French Imperial Nation-State: Negritude and Colonial Humanism between the Two World Wars*. Chicago: University of Chicago Press.

———. 2009a. "Untimely Vision: Aimé Césaire, Decolonization, Utopia." *Public Culture* 21 (1): 101–140.

———. 2009b. "Visions intempestives: Aimé Césaire, la décolonisation et l'utopie." *Revue de la Société Haïtienne d'Histoire et de Géographie* 87 (238): 2–39.

Williams, Eric. 1970. *From Columbus to Castro: The History of the Caribbean*. New York: Harper and Row.

Wimpffen, Baron de. 1797. *Voyage à Saint-Domingue, pendant les années 1788, 1789 et 1790*. Vol. 1. Paris: Chez Cocheris, Imprimeur.

Würtz, Docteur. 1822. *Second Mémoire relatif aux anciens colons de Saint-Domingue: Servant de suite à celui qui à pour titre Mémoire sur le moyen de réparer les torts faits au commerce de la France, par l'insurrection de l'isle de Saint-Domingue; et prouvant la facilité de l'exécution du projet, qui y est propose.* Paris: Treuttel et Würtz.

Wynter, Sylvia. 2003. "Unsettling the Coloniality of Being/Power/Truth/Freedom: Towards the Human, after Man, Its Overrepresentation—an Argument." *New Centennial Review* 3 (3): 257–337.

Zavaleta Mercado, René. 1977. *El Poder Dual, problemas de la teoría del estado en América Latina.* México: Siglo XXI Editores.

Index

Code Noir, 26, 68, 71, 91, 95, 106, 178, 268–269, 217; application of in Saint-Domingue, 9, 28–32, 54–55, 61, 69, 72, 80, 139, 306–307, 310; and family, 81; and free people of color, 59, 151–152, 154, 183, 190, 267, 321, 341; and Haitian oligarchy, 67, 172, 176; impact on historical interpretation, 15, 42, 51; legacies in Haiti, 44, 67, 198, 200, 278, 285–286, 315, 334; and property, 102, 145–146, 160, 164, 318; responses of the enslaved to, 20, 35, 43, 59, 272, 338, 362, 365

coffee, 65, 86, 136, 164, 338, 340

Columbus, Christopher, xi, xxv, 2, 4, 15, 98, 213, 245, 349

Constitution of 1801, 37, 199, 277, 279, 309, 314, 339

Constitution of 1805, 17, 44, 48, 202, 230, 231, 256, 366

Constitution of 1806, 146, 200, 246

Constitution of 1807, 94, 95, 156, 171, 221, 230, 392

Constitution of 1816, 354

Constitution of 1843, 199

cotton, 164, 166

Counter-Plantation System, xii, xx, xxviii, 120, 137–138, 262; definition of, xxvi, 304; emergence of, 142, 193–194, 210–211, 296, 328, 351, 384; and the Haitian state, 157, 177–178, 184, 240, 253, 278, 282–283, 377, 380

Creole, definition of, 72

Creole culture, 92, 293–294

Creole language. See Kreyòl language

Creole population, 92, 318, 321, 368–369, 384; in Barbados, 274; conflicts with the African born, 60, 140, 142, 153–155, 211, 275, 350; and family structure, 81–84, 302; and Haitian Revolution, 40, 287–288, 291, 343; in independent Haiti, 17–18, 117, 135, 137, 183; as plantation owners, 36, 69, 75, 85–86, 190; as slaves, 29, 71, 300; in urban areas, 14–15, 151–152

Crête-à-Pierrot, Battle of, 158, 289, 290

Cugoano, Ottabah, 29

Delgrès, Louis, 111

Délorme, Demesvar, 65

Depas-Medine, Michel, 158, 167

Depestre, René, 54, 104, 116

Derance, Lamour, 19, 252

Descourtilz, Michel Étienne, 104, 116, 236

Dessalines, Jean-Jacques, viii, xi, xxiii, 47, 60, 65, 136, 140, 193; and Africans, 161, 343; assassination of, 36, 38, 46, 158, 195, 207; attitude towards plantation laborers, 141, 249, 252; Constitution of, 256; and distribution of land, 203, 371; as Emperor of Haiti, 204, 223, 230; flag of, 349; and Haitian Declaration of Independence, 16–19, 117, 162, 232, 354; political thought of, 188–190, 364

doko, 12, 59, 62, 142, 275, 302, 332, 362, 364–365, 397n6

Dubois, Laurent, xxi–xxii, 12, 84, 120, 365–366

Duvalier, François, 398n4, 398n6

Enlightenment, 96, 154, 190, 290, 339, 341, 350

Family, xii, 50, 116, 129, 143, 254, 333, 335; and counter-plantation system, xiv, xxviii, 4, 238, 260, 301, 304, 309, 351, 388; and Creole population, 82, 83, 258; and education, 327; and European peasantry, 109, 113; and land, 131, 167, 386, 387; and plantation life, 18, 38, 107, 164, 168, 199, 301–302, 365, 369; and slavery, 52, 53, 106, 110, 113, 114, 287, 297, 307, 347, 362–364; and Vodou, 258

Fanon, Frantz, xxii–xxiii, 215, 250–251, 322, 365

Fick, Carolyn, 63, 116, 191, 312

Firmin, Anténor, 41–42, 63, 67, 143, 152, 191

Fischer, Sibylle, 236

Gaillard, Roger, 65, 131, 374

Gardens: and counter-plantation system, 68, 132, 387; on plantations, xxi, 174, 329, 351, 362, 364

Gastine, Civique de, 108

CPSIA information can be obtained
at www.ICGtesting.com
Printed in the USA
LVHW050915020523
745784LV00005B/670